GENERAL MANAGERS IN ACTION

GENERAL MANAGERS IN ACTION
Policies and Strategies

SECOND EDITION

FRANCIS JOSEPH AGUILAR

New York   Oxford
OXFORD UNIVERSITY PRESS
1992

Oxford University Press

Oxford   New York   Toronto
Delhi   Bombay   Calcutta   Madras   Karachi
Petaling Jaya   Singapore   Hong Kong   Tokyo
Nairobi   Dar es Salaam   Cape Town
Melbourne   Auckland

and associated companies in
Berlin   Ibadan

Library of Congress Cataloging-in-Publication Data
Aguilar, Francis J. (Francis Joseph)
General managers in action : policies and strategies—2nd ed. /
Francis Joseph Aguilar.
p. cm.   Includes bibliographical references and index.
ISBN 0-19-507367-3
1. Chief executive officers—Case studies.
2. Management—Case studies.   I. Title.
HD38.2.A39   1992
658.4—dc20   91-25992

2 4 6 8 9 7 5 3 1

Printed in the United States of America
on acid-free paper

To
Gillian, Bruce, John, Kim,
and Anne-Marie

PREFACE

This book is about things general managers know and do. My objective in preparing *General Managers in Action* has been to provide a means for learning about the job of the general manager with an appreciation for its complex and dynamic character and for its rich human dimension. The book combines introductory chapters that discuss the general manager and issues of general management with cases that explore real situations where concepts can be tested and shaped and where the discovery of new ideas can take place.

Just in the four years since the book was first published, the world of business has witnessed and experienced important changes. To name a few: the drive to global business operations has accelerated among leading North American, Western European, and Pacific Rim firms; in all of Europe—East and West—a state of economic flux has been set into motion; strategic alliances as a way of extending operations have proliferated; the aura of junk bonds subsided; information and communications technologies continue to revolutionize organizational capabilities; and less traditional managerial considerations having to do with business ethics and corporate governance have been gaining attention in executive offices and boardrooms as well as in public and legal forums. The need to acknowledge these changes coupled with the need to update case materials were compelling reasons for revising *General Managers in Action*. A new edition also provided an opportunity to add materials focusing on industry and competitive analysis in response to the needs of business policy courses and general management programs.

Three new chapters were added to the text. Chapter 6 discusses the evolving scene in global business activities and the growing need for general managers to strive for world-class competitive advantage. Chapter 7 addresses the major concerns general managers face in deciding how to ensure sound financial policies and structure in the context of the firm's overall corporate strategy. Chapter 8 explores the often conflicting interests and responsibilities of general managers and boards of directors for U.S. publicly-owned corporations as they face major and sometimes unexpected changes in public expectations, in the laws that regulate such matters, and in accepted business practice. The original chapters have also been expanded to treat more extensively such topics as multibusiness corporate strategy, strategic alliances, company capabilities and value chain analysis, and the management of change. Ten new cases reposition the classroom discussion material in line with the revised text.

Videotapes. On many occasions, teachers can find themselves frustrated in straining to give their students a feeling for the people in the case—their character and their demeanor. Without this insight, the classroom analysis lacks a vital dimension, for any course or program about general management is really a study about general managers, individual men and women.

To bring to life the general managers involved in the cases, many were videotaped in the classroom as they discussed their thinking and their actions either with M.B.A. students or executives. Though the book can certainly be used alone, the videotapes can bring an immediacy into any classroom, providing the students with information about the general manager which would be difficult or impossible to convey in words on paper. It would be difficult to exaggerate the added dimension to teaching that these tapes provide. The general managers I have come to know over the years as a casewriter, management consultant, and director were invariably interesting people. Many were quite impressive. Some were genuinely extraordinary individuals.

A final word. This book represents a tribute to the general manager. The American businessman and public official David E. Lilienthal observed in his book, *Management: A Humanist Art,*

> This I believe, and this my whole life's experience has taught me: the managerial life is the broadest, the most demanding, by all odds the most comprehensive and most subtle of all human activities. And the most crucial.

I also believe this to be true, especially for the general manager.

Boston, Massachusetts   F.J.A.
May 1991

ACKNOWLEDGMENTS

My greatest debt of gratitude is owed to the general managers who made this book possible. They were gracious with their time and almost without exception desirous of contributing to management education. They were also very busy people, which made their involvement so much more appreciated.

I am also indebted to a large number of people who have contributed to making this book possible: to Jay W. Lorsch and James Sailer for CEO Evaluation at Dayton Hudson, to Michael E. Porter for Coca-Cola versus Pepsi-Cola and the Soft Drink Industry, to Malcolm S. Salter and Jiro Kokuryo for the Asahi Breweries case, to Elizabeth O. Teisburg and Sarah Collins for McCaw Cellular Communications Inc. in 1990, and to Michael Y. Yoshino and Thomas Malnight for Eli Lilly and Company: European Pharmaceutical Operations; to Arvind Bhambri, Carolyn Brainard, Dong Sung Cho, Richard Hamermesh, and Paul Lawrence for their part in co-authoring some of the other cases included in this volume; to Joseph Auerbach, Dennis J. Encarnation, Samuel L. Hayes, III, Timothy A. Luehrman, Scott P. Mason, and Louis T. Wells, Jr. for their comments on the new text on global business, finance, and corporate governance; and to Betsy Barker for her skill and forbearance in preparing countless drafts of the manuscript. To this list I must add the teachers of business administration in the United States and abroad who have encouraged me to produce this revised edition by reporting favorably on their experiences with the original book and by providing good ideas on how it might be made even better.

CONTENTS

I

THE GENERAL MANAGER

1

The General Manager's Job

Imagine that you are attending a business conference dinner and are seated at a table with five strangers. At someone's suggestion, everyone in turn introduces himself or herself.

The woman on your left says that she is the vice president of marketing for a consumer product company. You would have a good idea of what she does for the most part. The job would typically involve decisions about pricing, channels of distribution, sales, advertising, and perhaps customer service and even product design. The man next to her describes himself as a vice president of manufacturing, and you conjure up an image of someone involved with plants, equipment, materials, and workers. Job titles of chief financial officer and vice president of personnel evoke equally descriptive mental images. But when the fifth person at the table says, "I'm a general manager," your understanding of what that meant might not be nearly so clear.

In real life, of course, no one uses the title *general manager* unadorned. Rather, your table companion would be more likely to specify a title such as division general manager, country manager, group vice president, president, or chief executive officer, and all at the table would nod their heads in acknowledgment. But even so, most people's understanding of the general manager's job would still be fairly limited, seldom going much beyond the vague notion of being the boss.

The General Manager Defined

Kenneth R. Andrews' seminal book on corporate strategy opens with the following definition of general management:

> Management may be defined as the direction of informed, efficient, planned and purposeful conduct of complex organized activity. General management is in its simplest form the management of a total enterprise or of an autonomous subunit. Its diverse forms in all kinds of businesses al-

3

ways include the integration of the work of functional managers or specialists.[1]

The notions of "total" and "integration" in this definition are essential characteristics of this job. John P. Kotter defines general managers as "individuals
who hold positions with some multifunctional responsibility for a business (or
businesses)."[2] And Peter F. Drucker observes, "There are a number of tasks
which are top-management tasks . . . because they are tasks that can be discharged only by people who are capable of seeing the whole business and of
making decisions with respect to the whole business."[3]

Since our view of the general manager emphasizes action, the following
definition might serve us better as a starting point: "The general manager is
the person in charge of an enterprise (a relatively autonomous operating organization) with responsibility for the timely and correct execution of those
actions promoting the successful performance and well-being of the unit."

The chief executive officer of a corporation, the president of the League of
Women Voters, and the mayor of Boston are all general managers of relatively
autonomous entities for whose overall health and development they are directly responsible. All three share a significant opportunity for deciding what
needs to be done and for ensuring that it gets done.

To develop a fuller understanding of what the general manager's job entails, we turn to a brief case history. Although the tasks each general manager
must do differ significantly in detail and emphasis, the following account is
representative of a chief executive officer's position and applies in large part to
other, more restricted general management positions as well.

A General Manager in Action

In April 1982, fifty-five-year-old C. Robert Powell, executive vice president in
charge of chemical operations at Diamond Shamrock, accepted an offer to head
Reichhold Chemicals. This manufacturer of industrial chemicals, with sales approaching $1 billion, was experiencing a seriously declining profit perfor-
mance, and Powell was recruited to take corrective actions.

The first thing Powell did as Reichhold's new chief executive officer was to
take stock of the situation. He had already concluded from his initial assessment of the company that it had parted from its specialty-chemicals origin to
become a volume-driven commodity-chemicals producer. A review of the product
lines uncovered a "hodgepodge, with some pretty decent technology in the
portfolio and some duds."

"I thought that I knew Reichhold Chemicals pretty well when I joined it,"
Powell later remarked. "It had been one of my important customers for years,
and the board gave me access to all information during our negotiations. However, I found out one thing in a hurry—you never really knew what's going
on in a company until you work there." A cover story in *Chemical Week* (July
10, 1985,) noted that

> he was "appalled" at the lack of organization structure and personnel man-
> agement. From what Powell could determine when he came on board, there

wasn't any. There were four executive vice-presidents, but no organization chart. Everybody reported to the founder-chairman, and he was the only one with profit-loss responsibilities.

Powell soon concluded that Reichhold was in need not just of a fine tuning, but of a major overhaul. First, though, he would have to convince the board of the necessity for the company to change its strategy, its structure, and its people. Complicating this task was the membership of the board; a majority comprised incumbent senior managers, including the firm's founder and sole previous CEO for over fifty years, and his protégé and former heir apparent, the company's president.

Powell moved quickly on three fronts. He took various steps to gain greater independence from his predecessor's pervasive influence. He decided to focus the company's efforts on building its good-technology products and to divest its other lines. And he lured an up-and-coming personnel manager from Diamond Shamrock to launch and direct human-resource development for Reichhold.

The tailspin Reichhold had been experiencing played itself out in 1982. Sales declined as a result of depressed economic conditions, and divestiture of several unprofitable operations produced nonoperating losses. The financial results for the year, as shown in Table 1.1, were poor; but Powell pointed to the strengthening of the company as the measure to watch. The investing community appeared to agree: The common-stock share value rose from the $10 to $12 range at the time Powell joined Reichhold to an all-time high of $19⅝ by the end of the year.

Progress occurred on many fronts in 1983. Several unattractive facilities were sold or shut down, and several small operations were acquired to strengthen the company's principal product lines. To support the growing emphasis on asset redeployment, Powell seized the opportunity to attract GAF's former chief financial officer and recently appointed president when he fell victim to an unfriendly takeover action.

Recognizing the need for people who could formulate Reichhold's business strategies as well as carry them out, Powell gave high priority to strengthening the management team. He carefully assessed the quality of his people as he worked with them on operating and planning problems. Managers showing promise were given additional responsibilities; others were encouraged to leave. A new participatory style of management was introduced to stimulate management initiative and teamwork. As Powell was later to remark, "In the past, managers were rewarded for loyalty and punished for mistakes. In contrast, we reward achievement. We do not punish mistakes, only people not doing anything."

With two audiences in mind—the financial community as well as his management team—Powell announced ambitious financial goals for 1987. The principal objective was to achieve a 20 percent return on shareholder's equity. This figure was compared in the annual report with a 14 percent average ROE for all U.S. manufacturing companies in 1982 and with Reichhold's historical return of 6 percent to 7 percent.

Table 1.1 Reichhold Chemicals' financial results, 1979–82 ($ millions).

	1979	1980	1981	1982
Sales	844	854	916	786
Net income	12.2	16.1	14.7	4.7
Return on sales	1.4%	1.9%	1.6%	0.6%
Return on equity	5.7%	2.8%	6.8%	1.0%
Share price: high	$16\frac{1}{2}$	15	16	$19\frac{5}{8}$
low	$10\frac{7}{8}$	$9\frac{5}{8}$	$11\frac{1}{8}$	10

New Directions. Financial goals were only one vehicle by which Powell sought to set new standards for performance. As the year opened, he also made a formal declaration as to the kind of company he wanted Reichhold to be. As can be seen from the new statement of corporate philosophy contained in Box 1.1, emphasis was to be placed on creativity, reasonable risk taking, delegation, and teamwork. This proposed management style stood in marked contrast to the centralized decision making and relatively static atmosphere that had come to characterize Reichhold's management.

Leading the company in new directions occupied Powell's attention, but he was not unmindful of the need to consolidate his own position. To this end, three departing "inside" directors on the board were replaced by three outsiders friendly to Powell's aims.

The financial results for 1983 also helped Powell to consolidate his position. Earnings were up almost fivefold to $21.7 million, and return on equity climbed from 1 percent to 10.8 percent. The financial community took note, and the stock price rose from around $20 to over $38 per share.

With favorable results confirming the validity of his approach, Powell turned his attention to developing the organization. His letter in the 1984 *Annual Report* noted:

> We also instituted team-building and participative management activities that are reaching virtually all levels of the organization.
>
> Of course, a reward system is one of the best personal motivators available. Reichhold now has in effect programs whereby virtually every salaried employee is eligible for some form of incentive bonus to reward outstanding individual effort, including a sales incentive compensation plan—a rarity in the industry.

Powell also set out to strengthen the company's financial structure and to engage his managers in developing the corporate strategy. Common stock was issued to retire bank debt, and a decision to enter the adhesives business launched a search for a suitable acquisition. Financial results for 1984 again showed marked improvement over the preceding year. But even while the good news was being celebrated, telltale signs of a weakening market were evident as Reichhold sailed into 1985.

The year began on a high note as Reichhold consummated two major ex-

Box 1.1 The Reichhold philosophy.

The pursuit of excellence in all phases of our corporation—our goals, our products and services, our people and our life styles.

Our corporate goal is to become a high-technology, specialty chemical company with a 20 percent return on equity.

Quality is essential—in our products, our working environment and our people. Economy comes from high value not from low cost.

Professional management will be practiced throughout our organization—people act and are treated as professionals. Trust is implicit: creativity and reasonable risk taking are encouraged.

Decisions should be made at the lowest possible level with responsibility and authority clearly defined.

Dedication to the principle of honesty and openness is expected. Attainment of goals requires the action of a team. The free flow of information and ideas is essential to the team effort.

We want people to be able to say that Reichhold is a fun place to work and that it supports and recognizes individual achievement.

To this end:

- Pursue your own standards of excellence
- Share responsibility well and be a good team player
- Plan and work to make things better
- Enjoy the difficult tasks
- Learn from mistakes
- Believe your efforts can make a difference

January 1983

pansion moves: purchase of the majority holdings of its Canadian subsidiary for $55 million; and acquisition of Eschem, a worldwide adhesives and coatings business, for $54 million. These purchases were to be financed in part with funds made available from several major divestitures. Delays in selling off these properties forced the company to incure more temporary debt than anticipated and to carry money-losing operations on its books for most of the second quarter. That predicament, along with a general business slump, raised a red flag as second-quarter earnings fell below the year-earlier period. By midyear, it had become clear that Reichhold was facing a difficult period.

While pressure was put on the operating divisions to improve current performance, Powell continued to invest in long-term development. Product- and management-development programs were maintained. Strategic planning efforts were also continued, resulting in a statement of corporate strategy. This statement, contained in Box 1.2, indicated the company's emerging focus on supplying specialty polymers to the adhesives, paper chemicals, coatings, and plastics markets.

During the course of the year, two additional outside members were added to replace the founder and another long-standing member of the board. In January 1986, the former president resigned from the company and board. His place was filled by another outsider, leaving Powell as the only inside director.

Setback and Turnaround. By the end of 1985, Reichhold had disposed of eighteen businesses, with total yearly sales of about $300 million, and acquired five businesses with roughly equivalent total sales. While the newly acquired properties performed better than expected, Reichhold's core businesses continued to slide. As a result, the fourth quarter produced operating losses. A $50 million provision for losses associated with the disposition of unwanted assets resulted in a net loss for the year of $27.8 million. The share price dropped from a midyear high of $43⅛ to the low 30s.

Powell commented to the board on the poor showing as follows:

> The market was tough this year, but I've got to say that we could have done a better job than we did. As a result, I've decided to award no bonuses, including my own, except for a few lower-level individuals who did outstanding work.
>
> It would have been easy to avoid the low operating results by cutting back on R&D and management development. But I refuse to mortgage the future in this way. It's important to show our people and Reichhold watchers that management is truly committed to long-term improvement and to excellence.
>
> In some ways I regret the easy accomplishments in 1983 and 1984. They lulled us into a false sense of security. As a result, we tried to do more than we had the talent to do. As business got tough, we still have too many people sit back and wait for instructions, just like they used to do.
>
> If I've learned anything over the past three-and-a-half years, it's this: It is much easier to change strategy than culture.

Powell's outlook for the future was generally optimistic, as reflected in his remarks on January 11, 1986, to the Conference Board:

> I've got to admit that I feel a little like the general and his troops who find themselves surrounded. The troops ask, "What should we do?" There's only one answer. "Attack!"
>
> One of our primary objectives this year is to instill in our people a sense of urgency, a bias for action. The only way we can fail is for our people to lose faith and give up. My main job is to see that that doesn't happen.

The benefits from restructuring and plant modernization were first felt during the latter part of the year, and Reichhold reported significant progress in 1986 toward achieving its long-term goals of 5 percent return on sales and 20 percent return on equity (see Table 1.2). A deflationary economy, however,

Box 1.2 The Reichhold strategy.

Reichhold Chemicals has developed a broad range of specialty polymers serving a multitude of industries. The focus of our business is
on customer responsiveness and flexibility of design based on technology and the economics of changing raw material bases. Our mission is to perpetuate this specialty nature by:

1. Increased penetration of adhesives, paper chemicals, coatings
   and plastics markets through new product development and
   through niche acquisition of companies, product lines or technology.

2. Providing applications research and customer service to preserve the specialty nature of the business.

3. Continued infusion of capital for plant modernization to
   maintain cost efficient production.

4. Adjusting the technology of the business by exiting stagnat-
   ing product lines.

5. Expansion into niche markets of the world where Reichhold's
   technology can be exploited.

6. Targeting a financial strategy that creates a single A debt rating but allows flexibility to take advantage of special business
   opportunities.

7. Completing investment in a participative management philosophy which develops achievement-oriented, agile people.

November 1985

---

continued to depress the company's markets in 1987 and consequently to delay
the gains that Powell anticipated. On June 9, before the turnaround could be
completed, Powell received a letter that would put to a halt all of his other
efforts.

Change in Control. In this letter, Shigekuni Kawamura, president of Dainippon Ink & Chemicals, revealed his interest in acquiring Reichhold's entire
equity at $50 per share. This price was said to represent a 37 percent premium
over the most recent closing market value and a multiple of twenty-one times
Reichhold's latest twelve-month earnings per share. Powell's reactions were
first to inform the board of directors and then to retain First Boston as investment banking advisers and Sullivan & Cromwell for legal counsel. Both firms
were prominent in the merger and acquisition field.

Table 1.2 Reichhold Chemicals' financial results, 1982–86 ($ millions).

	1982	1983	1984	1985	1986
Sales	786	747	801	822	766
Operating income	14.5	34.5	43.6	8.2	39.4
Net income	4.7	21.7	25.7	(27.8)	15.9
Return on sales	0.6%	2.9%	3.2%	negative	2.1%
Return on equity	1.0%	10.8%	13.3%	negative	8.5%
Share price: high	$19\frac{5}{8}$	$38\frac{7}{8}$	$35\frac{5}{8}$	$43\frac{1}{2}$	$38\frac{1}{4}$
low	10	$18\frac{1}{4}$	23	$31\frac{7}{8}$	$28\frac{3}{8}$

On June 25 Dainippon Ink & Chemicals made a public tender offer for all shares of Reichhold at $52.50 per share. The board rejected the offer as inadequate and instructed First Boston to examine possibilities for financial restructuring and to search for alternative acquirers. With a variety of takeover measures in place to help forestall the Dainippon attack, Powell and the board parried and negotiated for better terms. On August 25 the board unanimously approved an amended all-cash offer of $60 per share.

The strength of Reichhold's management and strategy was affirmed by Dainippon's decision to allow the company to continue as before. Powell retired for personal reasons in April 1988, and was succeeded by his able second-in-command, Tom Mitchell. Powell's influence, however, continued after his departure, as Mitchell pursued the legacy of strategic focus and participative management. By 1991 Reichhold Chemicals, with recent annual sales in excess of $1 billion and operating income of $60 million,[4] had achieved financial results and a positioning for future growth that appeared to justify Dainippon's initial confidence in its corporate strategy and, according to Mitchell, probably explained the autonomy Reichhold management has enjoyed in running the company.

Characteristics of the General Manager's Job

This account of Robert Powell at Reichhold Chemicals reveals several characteristics that distinguish the job of the general manager. One is its *importance*. In this case, as chief executive officer, Powell was rescuing a troubled corporation and positioning it for long-term growth and prosperity. His decisions and his actions had important financial, human, and business consequences. They put to greater productive use the hundreds of millions of dollars invested in the corporation. They had a significant impact on the lives of the many people working for or otherwise connected to Reichhold Chemicals. And they conceivably even altered business practices in the industry sectors in which the company competed. While the scale of consequences is likely to be reduced for general managers in lesser positions, the scope remains much the same. Group, division, department, and project general managers generally are in a position to affect significantly the operating and financial performance of their units and to improve or worsen the lives of their subordinates and other people. By their example, they too, on occasion, might advance or retard business practice in their fields of operation.

The job of the general manager is also *demanding* and *complex*. As evident in the portrayal of Powell's activities, there were always more tasks requiring his attention than he could handle at any one time. As he dealt with some issues, others waited for his attention and new ones arose. The backlog of pressing matters can become inexhaustible to the conscientious and ambitious general manager. The complexity of many of the issues the general manager encounters contributes to the demanding nature of the job. They are typically multifaceted and multifunctional as illustrated by Powell's concern with the price of Reichhold's common shares. To improve this vital number, he had to deal with corporate and business strategies, organizational capabilities, cash flows, investor relations, and board support in a coherent and timely manner.

Unpredictability and *disorderliness* are other common attributes of the general manager's job. In practice, as demonstrated by Powell's experience, a general manager seldom has the luxury of addressing key tasks in an orderly and leisurely manner. Problems requiring the attention of general management intrude from any and all quarters, and at any and all times, with the result that the general manager's day is usually fragmented, as he or she shifts attention from one pressing issue to another—taking positive steps on this one now, studying that one next, regrouping on another one after that, all the while trying to make sure that everything gets done correctly and on time. In these encounters, problems are rarely solved. Rather than a sense of completing, one has a sense of work in progress.[5]

Moreover, general managers often face challenges that are important, demanding, complex, unpredictable, and disorderly at the same time. The unexpected bid by Dainippon Ink & Chemicals to take control of Reichhold is a good case in point. Once the firm was put into play, Powell and Reichhold's board of directors were forced to engage in difficult and highly charged negotiations and to consider costly maneuvers under enormous time pressures. In such untoward circumstances, they faced the formidable task of finding a path that neither lost control under terms unfavorable to shareholders or employees nor inflicted crippling self-damage in fending off attackers.

Key Tasks for the General Manager

In examining Powell's actions, we see him dealing on many fronts as he strives to consolidate his position, to set a strategic direction for the firm, to build its capabilities in line with this direction, and to carry out day-to-day operations. The specific tasks he performed can be classified in various ways, but the fol-

lowing list provides a comprehensive basis for describing the general manager's job:[6]

1. Creating and maintaining organizational values and norms;
2. Setting strategic objectives and direction;
3. Negotiating with stakeholders;
4. Marshaling, developing, and allocating people and other resources;
5. Organizing the work;
6. Attending to ongoing operations.

A word of caution is in order as we examine these key tasks. This list and
the following discussion might suggest an orderliness of process. But, as was
noted earlier, the general manager's job is characterized by fragmentation and
disorder. One moment Powell is discussing with subordinates the business
strategy of the Canadian adhesives group, the next talking on the phone with
customers, followed by a brief meeting with a potential management hire, and
so on. We should also keep in mind that these six tasks, as part of a whole
cloth, interrelate and overlap in many ways. For example, setting strategic objectives cannot be separated from negotiating with important stakeholders, if
only to set practical limits to what is feasible. Likewise, the way the general
manager attends to ongoing operations has a direct bearing on how organizational values and norms are maintained. And the general manager's concerns
with establishing and raising standards of performance, as we shall see, pertain to all six tasks.

Creating and Maintaining Organizational Values and Norms

The basic belief system or philosophy of a firm, encompassing the values and
norms important to it, serves as a unifying force to define the kind of business
a company is in, the kind of people it wants associated with it, and how these
people operate. According to Terrence E. Deal and Allan A. Kennedy, "Managers and others throughout the organization give extraordinary attention to
whatever matters are stressed in the corporate value system."[7] Referring to the
pattern of beliefs and expectations shared by the organization's members as
culture, Howard Schwartz and Stanley Davis consider the resulting norms as
socially created standards that help people to interpret and evaluate events and
to distinguish between appropriate and inappropriate attitudes and behaviors.[8]
Edgar H. Schein goes further to conclude that culture "influences *everything*
that the manager does, even his own thinking and feeling."[9] In discussing
IBM, former chairman Thomas J. Watson, Jr., stresses the critical role values
and beliefs play in achieving success over time:

> Consider any great organization—one that has lasted over the years—
> and I think you will find that it owes its resiliency, not to its form of orga-
> nization or administrative skills, but to the power of what we call beliefs
> and the appeal these beliefs have for its people.

This, then, is my thesis: I firmly believe that any organization, in order to survive and achieve success, must have a sound set of beliefs on which it premises all its policies and actions.

Next, I believe that the most important single factor in corporate success is faithful adherence to those beliefs.

And finally, I believe that, if an organization is to meet the challenges of a changing world, it must be prepared to change everything about itself except those beliefs as it moves through corporate life.[10]

There are two reasons why a strong culture can be valuable. One is to motivate behavior that is supportive of the corporation's strategy. The other is to generate organizational commitment, thereby enhancing people's dedication and enthusiasm for their work and for the mission of the corporation. These benefits of culture provide a firm with a competitive edge.[11]

In practice, the top executive or executives set the basic tone and character of the firm. This essential spirit reveals itself in various ways. For example, a company's basic approach to doing business might be characterized as one of being lean and mean, classy or prestigious, innovative, bureaucratic, or professional. Or as a place to work, a company can be known for steady and secure employment, for personal challenge and development, or for high pressure, high rewards, and survival of the fittest. Style of operation can be formal or informal, hierarchical or participative. And ethical considerations can serve as the overriding decision criteria or be subordinated to pragmatism. Although these labels are not precise, they can portray the essence of the underlying spirit of the firm, reflecting the values of its leaders.

Although it was nine months before Powell articulated Reichhold's philosophy, his views on what kind of company he wanted to run were undoubtedly firmly in place when he took the job. His basic beliefs and values shaped every major decision and action from the moment he took charge.

Setting Strategic Objectives and Direction

In long-range planning, there is a saying, "If you don't know where you're going, any road will do." Obviously, what needs to be done depends on what one wants to accomplish. Knowing what an enterprise is to be and is to do— its strategy—serves as a prerequisite for taking purposive actions.

Rarely does a general manager have the luxury of setting objectives and direction from scratch. As we saw with Reichhold, firms or divisions are normally engaged in ongoing business activities with many attending personal and organizational commitments. The economic costs associated with change, comfort with the familiar, and vested interests are all inertial forces favoring the status quo.

As the principal agent of change for an enterprise, the general manager has to ensure that (1) developments that threaten to undermine the effectiveness of the organization's strategy and opportunities to improve it are perceived; (2) the necessary economic and competitive analyses are well done; and (3) a strategy suitable to the company and to the circumstances is selected. (A "suitable" strategy reflects the spirit and philosophy of the firm, the resources and skills the firm has or can obtain or develop, and the opportunities and threats the firm does, might, and will face over time.)

For most complex business situations, the general manager must involve others to help formulate strategy. For example, Powell could not possibly know each of Reichhold's major businesses well enough to conceive and evaluate alternative strategies for them. He had to rely on other people capable of assisting him in these efforts. The need to involve others in strategic planning introduces many difficult administrative decisions, such as who should be involved and in what manner. Powell decided to rely on Reichhold managers rather than on outside consultants. But not all of his key people were capable of undertaking strategic analysis. He had to decide whom to involve, how to help them to do the best job, and what outside people to bring in for business operations not otherwise covered.

Once strategy making is under way, the general manager must juggle the counterpressures implicit in a process that is creative, practical, timely, and thorough. At the same time the process should respond adequately to the interests of various key parties (stakeholders).

Negotiating with Stakeholders

The task most often associated with general management is that of ensuring that the interests of the various important stakeholders are met. Stakeholders here are defined as parties with a claim on benefits arising from the firm's operations and the value of its assets and as parties with power—operational or latent—to affect the firm's abilities to function. Even the self-employed professional or artisan must balance his or her personal interests with those of client or customer and with societal expectations as reflected in laws and norms. For the general manager of a large publicly owned corporation, stakeholders include customers, suppliers, creditors, shareholders, employees, communities, and even the nation in matters of military security or international relations.

To a considerable degree, top management's negotiations with stakeholders is driven by its desire to remain free from their power and to preserve its leadership position. This commitment to survival requires senior management to balance the demands made on them by three competing constituencies where cooperation is vital for their firm's success. The first of these is the capital market, which includes both the shareholders and the major suppliers of the firm's debt capital. This constituency expects corporate managers to preserve and enhance the money it has placed, at risk, in the corporation. The second is the product market, comprising the firm's customers, suppliers, and its host communities. This constituency's claim on corporate wealth takes on various forms: customers want low prices and reliable products, suppliers want high prices and long-term commitments, and host communities want stable employment and tax revenues with minimal demands for public services and minimal environmental damage. Third is the organizational constituency, which consists of all career employees including top management. Their principal goal is to have a secure, stimulating, and rewarding career experience.[12] Each of these constituencies is capable of undermining a firm's survival if its expectations are ignored. The capital market can raise the cost for additional funds and, at the extreme, bring about a change in the control of the corporation or force bankruptcy. Failure to compete effectively in a given business can lead to lower revenues and higher costs as volumes decline. Failure to provide psychic and material rewards to the organization can undermine morale and the company's ability to attract and keep talented people.[13]

In practice, balancing stakeholders' interests involves constant adjustments as changes in circumstances and performance alter the assumptions and expectations of the various constituencies involved. Negotiating with stakeholders should be interpreted in its broadest sense, involving positioning as well as discourse. Changes in Reichhold's board membership was as much a part of Powell's negotiations with that body as were the many discussions he undoubtedly held with board members concerning specific decisions.

Marshaling, Developing, and Allocating People and Other Resources

A firm needs human, information, material, and financial resources to carry out its strategy. The general manager has to ensure that these resources are available when and where they are needed in an organization.

The keystone resource for most enterprises is human. There is a need for people who can discover specific business opportunities, who can figure out how to exploit the opportunities, and who can carry out the job successfully. As a result, most general managers are called on to devote considerable attention to the various tasks associated with building and utilizing human resources: recruiting, training, evaluation, compensation, job assignments, and terminations. When Jack Welch, soon after becoming CEO of GE, was asked what he considered to be his most important activity, he responded:

> The people process! I am the ultimate believer . . . [in] people first, strategy second. I spend my time managing the people equation. I am involved in the selection, the compensation of some 125 in detail and 500 with a pass-off. Everyone knows when they put their slate of five together for job X, Y, and Z, that I will review it.[14]

Information is another important resource to be marshaled and allocated. There is an obvious connection between information and human resources. But not all important information resides, or needs to reside, in an organization's knowledge bank. Organizations might have to rely on outside parties for information about dynamic developments outside the firm (such as shifts in defense procurement priorities or political developments in South Korea) and about specialized considerations (such as the arcane case law connected with takeover practices). Concern with marshaling critical information extends beyond the information itself to include the enterprise's ability to obtain such information when needed or when useful information first comes into being. Reliable information sources are another important resource.

Plant, equipment, and money are obvious supporting resources. Other resources—such as brand recognition, trade relations, or raw material access—can also be critical for conducting certain businesses and need to be developed or acquired.

The call for resources in an enterprise usually exceeds its availability, and the general manager must devote considerable attention to allocating what is available. Scarcity is not the only reason for allocating resources within an organization. Sensitive information might have to be disseminated selectively to preserve its confidentiality. Whatever the reason, since resources translate into power within an organization, this process requires considerable sensitivity to internal politics as well as to economics. Various organizational mechanisms—such as long-range plans, staffing plans, operating budgets, and capital budgets—are typically employed to carry out the resource-allocation process.

Organizing the Work

Where success depends on the energy and initiative of more than one person, the general manager must assign work and motivate employees to act in the best interests of the company. Questions of organizational structure and work assignments typically occupy a great deal of a general manager's time as he or she tries to marry the work to be done with the capabilities and interests of the available people. This job can become particularly difficult as the organization is changing its strategy, growing rapidly in size, adding many new employees, or, as is often the case, is experiencing some combination of the three.

Planning, budgeting, control, compensation, communications, and other management systems serve as important organizing mechanisms. Staff specialists are often heavily involved in designing and implementing such systems. Nonetheless, since the purpose of these systems is to enable line managers to develop organizational capabilities and to manage ongoing operations, the general manager plays a special role in ensuring their appropriateness to the specific needs of the organization as well as overseeing their proper use. Taken together, these systems are the machinery that keeps a business operating effectively.

Attending to Ongoing Operations

Good thinking and planning are important elements of a general manager's job, but they are not enough. As Peter Drucker has noted so aptly, "If objectives are only good intentions, they are worthless. They must degenerate into work."[15] Ultimately, changes in strategy have to translate into ongoing operations, and the general manager bears responsibility for that conversion.

The general manager is also responsible for the improvement and the continued success of ongoing operations. This task might be less glamorous or exciting than those of changing strategy and structure, but it is no less important. It is where operating profits are finally realized.

In managing operations, general managers typically get involved in such activities as staffing, coordinating, controlling, enforcing standards, troubleshooting, arbitrating, and giving commands. There are few rules to how they should go about these activities. Involvement can be direct and explicit or suggestive, continuous or on an as-needed basis, decisive or flexible. Whatever the approach, general managers must be committed and sufficiently knowledgeable about operations to make the right things happen at the right time and in the right way.

Since ongoing operations involve the most people and the most resources for most established enterprises, their direction typically places heavy demands on the general manager. For this reason, in many large corporations this task is separated from the others so that it can receive the attention it requires. The chief operating office carries this burden for the chief executive officer.

Key Roles for the General Manager

In dealing with the six key tasks, the general manager must play several important roles. He or she must ensure that decisions are made and actions taken when called for, that important items take precedence, that the myriad initiatives undertaken form a cohesive whole, and that the organization continually strives for superior performance. In effect, the general manager has to be an instigator, a priority setter, an integrator, and a taskmaster.[16]

Implicit in the following discussion of these key roles is a recognition that general managers accomplish much of their work through other people. While responsible for the performance and well-being of their organization, they themselves do not have to do—indeed, could not possibly do—everything that has to be done. What they do have to do is to make sure that tasks are completed in a timely, efficient, and effective manner. General managers delegate assignments to others for a variety of reasons. One is simply to spread out the workload. Another is to give subordinates an opportunity to develop important knowledge and skills. A third is to involve people who are better qualified to perform the job. The advantage another person might have over the general manager for a particular duty could rest on special expertise (such as legal or engineering), on knowledge about specific circumstances (such as how a critical market behaves), on ancillary abilities (such as negotiating skills or command of one or more languages), or on other personal attributes (such as age, gender, race, or health).

The General Manager as Instigator

However valid a program of change might be, it is bound to encounter moments of apathy, pockets of resistance, or a loss of interest because of fatigue or distraction. As a result, vital deliberations and actions are not initiated or lose momentum, and progress falters or comes to a standstill. It is up to the general manager to ensure that there is enough push behind each vital element in the program to carry it through these obstacles in timely fashion.

As instigator, the general manager has to goad thinking and action wherever needed in the organization. This can be done in various ways—for example, by direct involvement or by involving others—once the need is recognized. But recognizing the need for initiative or push can pose problems. For a general manager attempting change on many fronts, the difficulty of keeping track of the numerous efforts under way or still to be undertaken poses serious practical limits to timely intervention. The difficulty in recognizing a need for added push can be exacerbated if the general manager receives feedback that is unwarrantedly favorable, either because of mistaken optimism or by subordinates' reluctance to admit failure.

Providing sufficient impetus to each move at the outset, before resistance or apathy can build up, has obvious benefits. Doing it right the first time can spell the difference between success and failure, especially in those cases where the general manager is operating at the limits of his or her resources. But it is in just such circumstances that the general manager will find it most difficult to follow this approach. Although preventing fires is better than fighting fires, it would be foolhardy to disperse all firefighters to inspecting facilities and instructing the public about fire prevention and not to have a force available to fight the inevitable fire. For the same reason, general managers with limited resources have to choose carefully where to invest their time and how much to invest in specific activities and how much to keep in reserve. They must set priorities.

The General Manager as Priority Setter

Although general managers must concern themselves with all of the key tasks described above, they need not, and indeed normally should not, devote equal attention to each. The importance of being selective and of setting priorities is underscored in the following comment by Andrall E. Pearson, former president of Pepsico:

> [A] primary skill of general managers is to pick the specific areas where their involvement will have the greatest impact on business results. As we have seen, the scope of the job is such that a GM nearly always faces many more problems and opportunities than he or she can possibly deal with personally. So at one time the GM may decide to put greater emphasis on strategy and superior execution; at another time the focus will be on people development or the working environment. Knowing what to emphasize, when to emphasize it, what and when to delegate and to whom to delegate are crucial decisions.[17]

At Reichhold, Powell emphasized different tasks at different times, sometimes moving on several fronts, other times focusing heavily on one (see Figure 1.1). His decisions regarding his priorities and the emphasis he placed on them were no doubt influenced in part by the particular course of events at Reich-

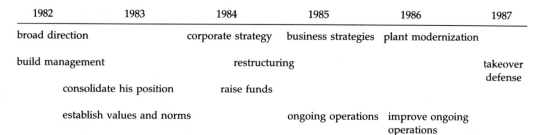

1982	1983	1984	1985	1986	1987

Figure 1.1 Tasks Emphasized by Powell at Reichhold Over Time.

hold as well as by his own personal style and preferences. But a major consideration for making these decisions was the basic nature of the situation in which he found himself. Another person in Powell's place probably would have acted similarly, and Powell in another situation probably would have acted differently.

Reichhold was a mature, multibusiness corporation with a well-entrenched management experiencing operating difficulties and under shareholders' pressure (through declining stock price) to change. Powell's initial attention to setting broad direction, building management capabilities, and dealing with the board (negotiating with stakeholders) would seem correct for that situation. His subsequent decisions to emphasize building a new culture, formulating business strategies, and restructuring (buying and selling businesses) in sequence over the ensuing three years would also seem in keeping with the situation.

Had Powell been called on to take charge of a company experiencing rapid growth, he would have followed a quite different course of action. Marshaling resources—people and skills as well as funds and other assets—would have been prominent among the tasks receiving his emphasis and priority. Such a situation might also have called for increased attention to changes in organizational structure and management support systems.

In effect, we can identify a number of prototyical situations calling for certain responses. For example, start-up situations typically have many problems in common and tend to have a similar profile with respect to which tasks need to be emphasized and in what order. The same is true of troubled enterprises requiring turnaround actions. (A general manager, naturally, stresses different tasks in dealing with a start-up compared to a turnaround.) Rapid growth of an established firm and a plateauing mature business each impose their own requirements for action. With respect to complexity, a company with many related businesses poses different challenges to a general manager from one predominantly in a single business or one in many unrelated businesses (conglomerate). The general manager of a subsidiary unit (a division or a strategic business unit, SBU) must approach problems and act differently from a chief executive officer. And a general manager trying to make major changes where strong external pressures are in play faces a different challenge from one where such pressures are absent.

In reality, any situation must involve a combination of the above proto-types: An enterprise can be start-up, rapid growth, mature, or failing; it can be single-business, related multibusiness, or conglomerate; the general manager can be at the top or in the middle of a firm; and clear pressures for change might or might not be present. This simple list of governing characteristics would result in forty-eight prototypical combinations, and the list can easily be enlarged. What we must conclude is that any attempt to provide comprehensive guidelines for general managers is likely to meet with failure. We and they can gain some insight about how to deal with a situation from an understanding of similar situations, but most circumstances are sufficiently complex to resist simple solutions. In setting priorities, the general manager must discern what is distinctive and what is typical about his or her situation, and respond accordingly.

The General Manager as Integrator

The general manager by definition has multifunctional responsibilities, and often multibusiness responsibilities as well. As such, he or she bears a special responsibility for meshing the many organizational activities into a cohesive whole. This responsibility has both horizontal and vertical dimensions, requiring an integration of efforts across the organization and over time.

In a single business enterprise, the general manager must ensure the consonance of different functional policies. To leave marketing, manufacturing, engineering, finance, and the other functional areas on their own, however competent the department managers might be, is a little like a woman asking a milliner, a dressmaker, and a leather stylist to furnish her with their greatest creations. The individual hat, dress, bag, and shoes might be extraordinarily beautiful, but as an ensemble they might draw attention for the wrong reasons, with clashing colors, textures, and designs. The most effective marketing plan probably will clash with the best manufacturing plan, and both might be at odds with the most advantageous engineering approach or with optimal financial maneuvering. The need for functional policies to relate to each other as well as to competitive and market forces is discussed in the next chapter, as are the ways in which a general manager with multibusiness responsibilities can consider the relationships between and among business units.

The general manager also has to be concerned with the pattern of efforts over time. Attention must be given to the order (first things first), consistency, and continuity (no key steps missing) of sequential actions. As author or sponsor of an organization's game plan, the general manager must monitor the plan's implementation to ensure that it makes as much sense in action over time as it did in concept. This is not to say that modifications should not be made as events change or as the organization learns how to respond better. But the general manager must assure everyone concerned, outside stakeholders as well as employees, that the enterprise knows what it is doing and that its efforts make good business sense. A general manager can undermine support very quickly by projecting an image of confused and erratic actions.

The General Manager as Taskmaster

Several studies of America's best-run companies thrust the word *excellence* into some prominence in the business jargon of the 1980s. One important conclusion, not surprisingly, is that the person in charge (the general manager) has to care about the quality of accomplishment and has to promote it constantly for excellence in performance to occur.

Caring about excellence has its origins in a person's basic beliefs and values. On the foundations of such values, challenges and standards of performance must be defined and enforced. But in striving for excellence, it is the underlying values that provide the energy, the tenacity of purpose, and the inspiration needed to achieve superior performance. As Thomas J. Watson, Jr., argues in his discussion of IBM's success:

> Men who have accomplished great deeds in large organizations might have done less if they had been challenged with less, and they would have realized less of their potential and their individuality. . . .
>
> *We believe that an organization should pursue all tasks with an idea that they can be accomplished in a superior fashion.* . . . An environment which calls for perfection is not likely to be easy. But aiming for it is always a goad to progress.
>
> In addition to this persistent striving for perfection, we believe an organization will stand out only if it is willing to take on seemingly impossible tasks. . . . T. J. Watson used to tell our people, "It is better to aim at perfection and miss than it is to aim at imperfection and hit it." [18]

Specific challenges and standards of performance are defined in various ways: the mission statement, the strategic plan, the budget, departmental plans, and in setting the individual's objectives. These challenges and standards are in turn interpreted and enforced in the feedback of reviews (approval and disapproval) and through the reinforcement of rewards and punishments. The kind of people advanced and supported in an organization is a vital element in raising standards of performance and in upholding high standards. In his biographical sketch of Jean Riboud, the late CEO of Schlumberger, Ken Auletta touched on this connection:

> On several occasions, he has said that the company's goals should be "to strive for perfection." To this end, he searches for fighters, for independent-minded people who don't, in his words, "float like a cork." In 1974, when he appointed Carl Buchholz his vice president of personnel, it was largely because Buchholz was not afraid to speak out. Riboud recalled first seeing Buchholz at a Schlumberger management conference in Geneva. "All the people were reciting the Mass, and suddenly Buchholz said, 'You're full of it!' I said, 'This is a fellow who speaks his mind.' " [19]

Expediency is to excellence as friction is to motion. Without constant pressure, momentum will be lost. The danger for a struggling-to-succeed organization to cut corners and to go for the sure and easy payoff is easy to understand. Lacking confidence in its abilities to achieve superior performance, the organization is conditioned to accept less. Indeed, in such cases, the general manager may have to start with modest challenges and standards, raising them over time in line with improved results and increased confidence.

The force of expediency is also a menace for organizations that dominate their field. The general managers of enterprises enjoying monopolistic powers must constantly fight apathy and disregard. But so too must those responsible for enterprises that have succeeded through excellent performance. Thomas J. Watson, Jr., expressed concern about this peril:

> Unless management remains alert, it can be stricken with complacency—one of the most insidious dangers we face in business. In most cases it's hard to tell that you've even caught the disease until it's almost too late. It is frequently most infectious among companies that have already reached the top. They get to believing in the infallibility of their own judgments.[20]

The quest for superior performance is a never-ending battle. The general manager must constantly set the high standards for excellence and goad performance to meet them.

Evaluating the General Manager

Boards of directors have a responsibility for evaluating the performance of the CEO. Investors have good reason for so doing as well. Senior-level general managers must evaluate lower-level general managers. Even subordinates will evaluate their general manager in deciding their level of commitment to the enterprise.

Where an organization's performance improves or deteriorates markedly over time, evaluating the general manager may be a relatively simple and straightforward matter. But for those critical occasions where a general manager is just starting out, or where unforeseen events suddenly invalidate an established strategy or render proven practices obsolete, such evaluation is far more difficult. In situations such as these, an evaluation of the general manager must rest on an assessment of what he or she is doing or not doing. But these situations are usually sufficiently complex and the relationships between cause and effect sufficiently obscure to frustrate any definitive evaluation. There will remain considerable room for doubt and opposing opinions. It is something like judging a pudding while it is still cooking. The only proof is in the eating. Still, the cook cannot suspend judgment until that moment, at least if the pudding is not to be burned.

Difficult or not, senior managers of publicly owned corporations are, in effect, constantly being evaluated by their shareholders through the price of the common shares of equity. If shareholders' satisfaction with management's performance and confidence in its abilities are low, the corporation becomes vulnerable to a change in control. The threat and reality of takeover impose a discipline on performance with the haunting message to senior managers and

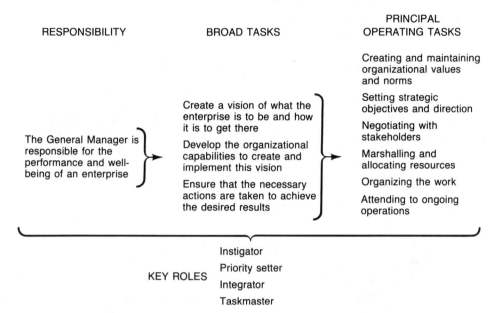

RESPONSIBILITY   BROAD TASKS   PRINCIPAL OPERATING TASKS

Creating and maintaining organizational values and norms

Create a vision of what the enterprise is to be and how it is to get there

Setting strategic objectives and direction

The General Manager is responsible for the performance and well-being of an enterprise

Negotiating with stakeholders

Develop the organizational capabilities to create and implement this vision

Marshalling and allocating resources

Organizing the work

Ensure that the necessary actions are taken to achieve the desired results

Attending to ongoing operations

KEY ROLES

Instigator
Priority setter
Integrator
Taskmaster

Figure 1.2   The job of the general manager.

corporate directors to do their job well or else to face the prospect of being replaced.

Figure 1.2 attempts to summarize the description of the general manager's job. It can be a helpful reference for evaluating the general managers described in the cases to follow and for thinking about the job in practice. But as was cautioned earlier, any suggestion of conceptual completeness or orderliness of process should be rejected. A difficulty in using such a framework, as we saw earlier in the discussion on setting priorities, is in taking situational considerations into account. Just what general managers do and how they do it depends on a variety of factors, some having to do with the business setting, some with the job, some with the personal attributes of the man or woman holding the position, and some with specific events and conditions of the moment.[21] It should come as little surprise that the job of the general manager is likely to differ in a rapidly changing business environment as compared to a stable one, or during an economic upswing as compared to a decline. Similarly, the job of a CEO differs significantly from that of a division manager, and the job of a general manager with global responsibilities differs from that for someone with just a domestic purview. The style and personality of the general manager also modifies the way in which the job does and should get performed. Finally, specific events and circumstances can introduce uncommon opportunities and constraints that also have to be taken into account.

To complicate the task even more, any proper evaluation of a general manager must include consideration of what is not acted upon as well as what is. This chapter has stressed the action side of the general manager's job—doing something, directing action, making decisions. But there is also an important realm of positive inaction, where the general manager consciously or instinctively decides not to act. In discussing executive decision making, Chester Barnard stresses the importance of decisions not to decide, concluding:

> *The fine art of executive decision consists in not deciding questions that are not now pertinent, in not deciding prematurely, in not making decisions that cannot be made effective, and in not making decisions that others should make.* Not to decide questions that are not pertinent at the time is uncommon good sense. . . . Not to make decisions that cannot be made effective is to refrain from destroying authority. Not to make decisions that others should make is to preserve morale, to develop competence, to fix responsibility, and to preserve authority.[22]

By now it should be apparent just how complex and challenging the general manager's job can be. It is not a job everyone can do or would want to do. The job calls for personal qualities such as intelligence, high energy, self-assurance, a willingness to take big risks, adaptability, and good character. Above all, it calls for insightfulness and good judgment. For there is still a great deal of art and spontaneity in the general manager's job.

Notes

1. Kenneth R. Andrews, *The Concept of Corporate Strategy*, rev. ed. (Homewood, Il., 1980), p. 2.
2. John P. Kotter, *The General Managers* (New York, 1982), p. 2.
3. Peter F. Drucker, *Management* (New York, 1973), p. 609.
4. The net income, return on sales, and return on equity measures were no longer comparable to earlier years because of Reichhold's highly leveraged capital structure under Dainippon's ownership arrangement. In effect, net income was eliminated by the interest payments on the debt used to acquire Reichhold.
5. In his early study of managerial work, Mintzberg identified the following six distinguishing characteristics: (1) much work at an unrelenting pace; (2) activity characterized by brevity, variety, and fragmentation; (3) a preference for current, specific, and vital activities (as opposed to routine, general, and comprehensive issues); (4) dominance of verbal communication; (5) serving as link between the organization and outside parties; and (6) a balance between controlling affairs and being driven by issues and events. See Henry Mintzberg, *The Nature of Managerial Work* (New York, 1973), pp. 29–51.
6. The listing of managerial tasks has a long and illustrious history. Henri Fayol identified five basic managerial functions: planning, organizing, coordinating, commanding, and controlling; see *Administration Industrielle et Générale* (Paris, 1916). His concept was elaborated twenty years later with the articulation of POSDCORB—Planning, Organizing, Staffing, Directing, Coordinating, Reporting, and Budgeting—as defining the work of the chief executive. See Luther H. Gulick, "Notes on the Theory of Organization," in L. H. Gulick and L. F. Urwick, eds., *Papers on the Science of Administration* (New York, 1937), pp. 1–45. Variations of POSDCORB have been devised ever since, such as the alliterative 7-S framework of management—Superordinate Goals, Strategy, Structure, Skills, Style, Staff, and Systems—popularized by McKinsey & Company and by Richard Tanner Pascale and Anthony G. Athos in their book *The Art of Japanese Management* (New York, 1981), p. 202.
7. Terrence E. Deal and Allan A. Kennedy, *Corporate Cultures* (Reading, Mass., 1982), p. 33.
8. Howard Schwartz and Stanley M. Davis, "Matching Corporate Culture and Business Strategy," *Organizational Dynamics* 1 (Summer 1981), pp. 30–48.

9. Edgar H. Schein, *Organizational Culture and Leadership* (San Francisco, 1985), p. 314. For further discussion of the influence that organizational values have on individual members, see Amitai Etzioni's *The Moral Dimension: Toward a New Economics* (New York, 1988). He writes as follows: "In effect, numerous studies have established, beyond reasonable doubt, that the sources of communication that people choose to expose themselves to and the message they hear, and the way they interpret what they have heard after they hear it, and the conclusion they draw, are all highly subjective, and, to a significant extent, socially shaped. . . . Even what is perceived to be *self*-interest is group shaped" (p. 189).

10. Thomas J. Watson, Jr., *A Business and Its Beliefs* (New York, 1963), p. 5.

11. Charles O'Reilly, "Corporations, Culture, and Commitment: Motivation and Social Control in Organization," *California Management Review* 31 no. 4 (Summer 1989), 16.

12. Gordon Donaldson and Jay W. Lorsch, *Decision Making at the Top* (New York, 1983), pp. 38–39. To these could be added a fourth constituency having to do with governmental regulations. EPA, ERISA, and the various laws defining fair competition pose constraints and impose costs for the corporation. Senior management has some choice in deciding how close to the line it wants the company to be in complying with the regulations and how much effort to devote to influencing the political process governing regulations.

13. For a full discussion of these ideas, see Donaldson and Lorsch, *Decision Making at the Top*, and Gordon Donaldson, *Managing Corporate Wealth* (New York, 1984).

14. "General Electric Company: Dr. John F. Welch, Jr.," Harvard Business School videotape 882–024, 1982.

15. Drucker, *Management*, p. 101.

16. For an alternative listing of managerial roles, see Mintzberg, *Nature of Managerial Work*, pp. 58–93. He identifies ten roles in three groupings: interpersonal, informational, and decisional. The interpersonal roles include the manager as figurehead (representing the firm to outsiders and to employees), as leader (providing guidance and motivation), and as liaison (creating and maintaining a network of outside contacts). The informational roles include the manager as monitor (seeing and interpreting relevant information), as disseminator (passing on information to others in the organization with a need to know), and as spokesman (transmitting information to outside parties). The decisional roles include the manager as entrepreneur (initiating and designing controlled change in the organization), as disturbance handler, as resource allocator, and as negotiator. Relatedly, Leonard R. Sayles in *Leadership*, 2nd ed. (New York, 1989) identifies management's ability to assert influence and power as a necessary condition to carrying out its various roles. This ability depends on its skills in obtaining compliance, gaining credibility, and coping with resistance (pp. 37–63).

17. "Role of the General Manager," Harvard Business School publication 386–041, 1985, p. 11.

18. Watson, *A Business*, pp. 27 and 34.

19. Ken Auletta, "A Certain Poetry," *The New Yorker*, June 6, 1983, p. 89.

20. Watson, *A Business*, pp. 63, 64.

21. For a discussion of a contingency theory of managerial work, see Mintzberg, *Nature of Managerial Work*, pp. 101–31.

22. Chester I. Barnard, *The Functions of the Executive* (Cambridge, Mass., 1960), p. 194.

2

Strategy and
the General Manager

Setting strategic direction ranks among the more dramatic and visible acts of the general manager. The importance attached to strategic direction can be more fully appreciated if we are mindful of the central role strategy plays among the general manager's tasks. As a vision of what the enterprise is to be and how it is to get there, strategy represents a practical embodiment and articulation of an organization's basic values and norms. It serves to steer the development of organizational capabilities and to guide day-to-day operations. It is the nexus for negotiating with stakeholders.

The Concept of Strategy

The word *strategy* has its origins in military science. It is defined in the dictionary as the "science and art of employing the armed strength of a belligerent to secure the objects of war, especially the large-scale planning and directing of operations in adjustment to combat area, possible enemy action, political alignments, etc." As used in business, the meaning of strategy includes the character and purpose of an enterprise. According to Andrews:

> Corporate strategy is the pattern of decisions in a company that determines and reveals its objectives, purposes, or goals, produces the principal policies and plans for achieving those goals, and defines the range of business the company is to pursue, the kind of economic and human organization it is or intends to be, and the nature of the economic and non-economic contribution it intends to make to its shareholders, employees, customers, and communities.[1]

Corporate strategy, as defined above, applies to the whole enterprise. How a firm intends to compete in a particular business is called a business strategy. For a single business corporation, corporate strategy is essentially equivalent to business strategy. For a multibusiness firm, the distinction between corporate and business strategy takes on practical importance, because each of these activities typically involves different people, different managerial processes, and different conceptual tools. Corporate strategy is usually the responsibility of the chief executive officer, and business strategies of the divisional general managers. The focus of corporate strategy is on managing a business mix to achieve corporate goals. Attention is given to such matters as selecting which businesses to enter or exit, allocating resources among businesses, and deciding how the operating units should relate to each other. Central to this analysis are cash flow, earnings, and other financial matters associated with differing business strategies. For business strategy, the conceptual tools generally focus on the structure of an industry and on the dynamics of doing business in that industry. This chapter first examines strategy as it applies to a single-business enterprise and then discusses multibusiness corporate strategy.

Strategic Analysis

To prepare for battle, the commanding and staff officers must take into account the strength and readiness of the enemy, the skill of its officer corps, its position and deployment, its weapons and supplies, its will to fight, and the possibilities of reinforcements. The same officers must examine their own forces in similar fashion. Weather, terrain, and other local conditions also have to be considered. Only when these factors have been carefully analyzed can the command devise a strategy of battle—whether, where, when, and how to fight. Rightly or wrongly, the commanding officer's decision can be strongly influenced by such personal considerations as his willingness to risk death and his desire for power and glory.

Business has its counterparts to the military situation. The general manager is the commanding officer. Competitors are the enemy forces. The enterprise represents the general manager's forces. The economy, laws and regulations, and technology correspond to weather, terrain, and other ambient conditions. The military analogy begins to break down when we consider customers and products, but it is sufficiently close and vivid to suggest a basis for business strategy analysis.

For our purposes, we focus on the battle environment (enemy and local conditions), one's own forces, and the commanding officer's will. For business, these three cornerstones of strategic analysis translate into competitive environment, company capabilities, and management values.

Competitive Environment

The evaluation of the competitive environment of a business should begin with an analysis of the dynamics and structure of its industry context. Michael Porter, in his work on competitive strategy, notes:

The first fundamental determinant of a firm's profitability is industry attractiveness. . . . Industry profitability is not a function of what the product looks like or whether it embodies high or low technology, but of industry structure. Some very mundane industries such as postage meters and grain trading are extremely profitable, while some more glamorous, high-technology industries such as personal computers and cable television are not profitable for many participants.[2]

To analyze the inherent attractiveness of an industry, Porter devised a simple and powerful construct (see Figure 2.1) with five driving forces: competitors, buyers, suppliers, potential entrants, and substitutes for the product or service. In industries where these forces are strong, he argues, profitability is likely to be low; in industries where the forces are weak, a firm could reasonably expect high profitability.

In assessing the forces associated with competitors and potential entrants, consideration needs to be given to entry and exit barriers. High barriers to entry—such as might result from high required investments, proprietary technology, and established brands—clearly diminishes the threat that potential entrants will further crowd the field of competitors. Low barriers to exit for firms already in the industry also adds to an industry's attractiveness. If troubled firms can exit easily, fewer survivors remain to divide the pie. If exit is difficult, troubled firms can disrupt the market in their struggles to avoid collapse. Not unlike the new breathable waterpoof fabrics that allow body moisture to pass out and block rain water from coming in, "easy out" and "difficult in" contribute to industry attractiveness.

The metal-can and pharmaceutical industries provide two examples to illustrate this concept. Metal-can suppliers face: (1) large and powerful customers, such as Anheuser Busch and Campbell Soup, who self-manufacture cans as a way of applying pressure on the merchant suppliers; (2) large and powerful raw-material suppliers, such as U.S. Steel, who can set and hold raw-material prices high; (3) an increasing number of substitute products as packaging and food technology change; and (4) struggling competitors who are unable to exit because of large investments in plant and large unfunded pension liabilities. Not surprisingly, corporate financial results are generally poor in this industry, and those can companies that can afford to diversify into other fields do so.

The pharmaceutical industry stands in marked contrast to the can industry. The long-standing record of high industry profitability is largely attributable to several favorable industry features. First, pharmaceuticals really comprise many different and distinctive medication groupings, such as cardiovascular, analgesics, respiratory, antiinfective, and internal medicine. Pharmaceutical firms tend to specialize in one of these groupings, thereby reducing direct competition among themselves. This specialization is carried to the point where many pharmaceutical firms generate most of their profits from one or two individual drugs. Second, raw materials represent an almost insignificant cost for most drug companies, giving suppliers little bargaining power. Third, buyers also have limited leverage. That doctors prescribe and patients pay certainly weakens the buyers' position. The threat of generics is blunted by the feeling of

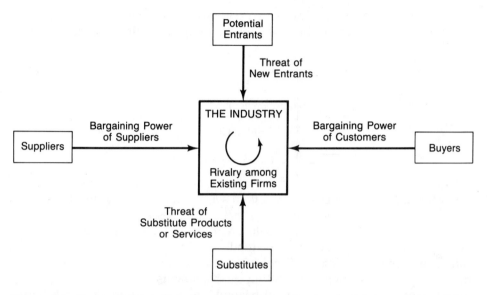

Figure 2.1 Forces Driving Industry Competition. Reprinted with permission of The Free Press, a division of Macmillan, Inc., from *Competitive Advantage: Creating and Sustaining Superior Performance* by Michael E. Porter. Copyright © 1985 by Michael E. Porter.

well-being that established brand names give to both doctors and patients. Fourth, high R&D costs and long delays in drug approval discourage entry. Fifth, there are few substitutes for conventional medicines. Genetic engineering is more an integral part of pharmaceutical technology than a substitute. With all five industry forces greatly attenuated, there is little wonder as to why successful pharmaceutical companies are content to stick to their knitting.

Most industries fall somewhere between these two examples with respect to industry attractiveness. Obviously, in selecting an industry—such as Peter Grace did for W. R. Grace in picking chemicals as a replacement for the moribund South American shipping business, or as more commonly happens in decisions concerning the relative emphasis to be given to different businesses in a firm—the general manager usually does well to favor the more attractive industry. That freedom of choice, however, may be limited or unavailable for many general managers. They are obliged to do the best they can in their industries.

Whatever the level of attractiveness an industry might hold, some firms will do better than average, and some might even do better than firms in more attractive industries. Identifying and assessing opportunities and risks in a business environment calls for a wide-ranging view and considerable ingenuity. At the center of this analysis is an understanding of who the customers are and what they want or might want, and who the competitors are and what they provide. Strategic analysis seeks gaps between what is wanted and what is provided. These gaps represent potential business opportunities for the firm. Gaps always exist, since customers will always welcome lower prices, higher quality, and better service. Moreover, compromises usually have to be made, as the following notice on the customer's counter in a print shop so well illustrates:

> PRICE
>
> QUALITY
>
> SERVICE
>
> Pick any two

In this instance, the customer gets to select what he or she has to give up. In most cases, it is the supplier who makes that selection, not the customer. McDonald's is organized to compete on price and delivery, with acceptable quality. But its limited selection of foods and its informal ambiance will not satisfy the person seeking haute cuisine or a romantic setting. These limitations provide opportunities for other eating establishments.

Strategic analysis has to extend beyond customers, suppliers, and the immediate competitive arena. Changes in technology, laws and regulations, international affairs, and any of a multitude of other factors can lead to new opportunities and risks. For example, when deregulation of air travel fractured a long-standing, entrenched oligopoly, Continental, TWA, Pan Am, and Eastern soon fell victims to the onslaught of the new low-cost carriers that seemed to sprout from the turbulence. Conversely, firms that anticipated the power of the computer were able to create new, profitable businesses, such as Mead Corporation did in developing Lexis to facilitate legal research and Reuters did with its financial information network. These experiences, both negative and positive, point to the need for general managers to look beyond near-term and familiar business activities to longer-term and less familiar considerations when analyzing the competitive environment.

Company Capabilities

The second cornerstone of strategic analysis concerns the company's ability to devise and carry out a program of action. If an assessment of the competitive environment addresses the question of what is possible, an assessment of a company's capabilities addresses the question of what it can do. These capabilities involve skills and competencies, physical assets, business relationships, and proprietary rights and knowledge.

Skills and competencies have to do with human resources. A firm needs people capable of setting strategic direction, of making the products or performing the services, of selling, of organizing people and activities, and of marshaling the other resources needed. The specific skills and competence needed will, of course, depend on a company's business, its strategy, and its particular makeup.

Physical assets include money, plant and equipment, office space, and the like. Although money can resolve many physical asset problems, it has its limits. A paper manufacturing firm that decides to expand its coated paper operations with state-of-the-art equipment in order to take advantage of high market demand will require about two years to build the plant and another several years to bring it up to full speed. Throwing money at the problem will not accelerate this timetable very much.

A firm's capabilities also depend on the relationships it enjoys with suppliers, customers, and the investment community. Good relationships with unions, government regulatory bodies, the leadership of communities in which it operates, and with the general public can also be of critical importance to successful performance, as is access to reliable information sources. Many of these relationships can require years of careful nurturing. Since important business relationships typically are not cost free, the general manager has to give careful thought to the priority and emphasis each should receive, just as if he or she were developing a firm's other capabilities.

Patents, copyrights, brands, confidential proprietary information, and customer lists also represent important resources for a firm. We have only to observe the zealousness with which Johnson & Johnson (J&J) protects it Band-Aid registered mark and Polaroid its patents to appreciate the concern a general manager must devote to such matters.

Defining Resources. A company's resources—human, physical, relational, intellectual—in and of themselves are of value in a strategic sense only insofar as they contribute to the firm's competitive advantage. Managers can lose sight of this simple truth. They sometimes acquire resources because other companies are doing so without considering just how their company's needs are served. A clear example of this is how many companies uncritically acquired each generation of computer offerings. Without management having a clear idea of how the added computing power could be used, the equipment often remained grossly underutilized. This inclination to follow fashion can also involve human resources. For example, in the 1980s, issues management became a popular concept and company after company created staff units to perform this function without fully understanding what it was or how it could be made to contribute. A related problem is management's failure to divest resources that have lost their competitive relevance. For evidence of this failing, we have only to look at the plethora of redundant assets that were divested in connection with takeover activities over the past decade.

General managers are responsible for ensuring that the company or business unit has correct resources to provide the capabilities needed for competing successfully.[3] The principal questions they must ask are:

- What resources do we need to achieve our goals in light of the competitive environment we face?
- What resources will we need in light of future competitive needs?

An explicit evaluation of the resources on hand is a good place to start this analysis: How do they help the company to compete? Are there ways to improve the effectiveness of each? In elaborating the *value chain* concept, Porter provides a powerful analytical construct for answering these questions.[4]

The value chain defines the collection of interdependent activities that are performed to design, produce, market, deliver, and support its product offerings. These are laid out as shown in Figure 2.2 and defined as follows:

Primary Activities

- *Inbound Logistics.* Activities associated with receiving, storing, and disseminating inputs to the product, such as material handling, warehousing, inventory control, vehicle scheduling, and returns to suppliers.
- *Operations.* Activities associated with transforming inputs into the final product form, such as machining, packaging, assembly, equipment maintenance, testing, printing, and facility operations.
- *Outbound Logistics.* Activities associated with collecting, storing, and physically distributing the product to buyers, such as finished goods warehousing, material handling, delivery vehicle operation, order processing, and scheduling.
- *Marketing and Sales.* Activities associated with providing a means by which buyers can purchase the product and inducing them to do so, such as advertising, promotion, sales force, quoting, channel selection, channel relations, and pricing.
- *Service.* Activities associated with providing service to enhance or maintain the value of the product, such as installation, repair, training, parts supply, and product adjustment.

Support Activities

- *Procurement.* Activities referring to the function of purchasing inputs used in the firm's value chain (e.g., procedures for dealing with vendors), not to the purchased inputs themselves.
- *Technology Development.* Activities that can be broadly grouped into efforts to improve the product and the process.
- *Human Resource Management.* Activities involved in the recruiting, hiring, training, development, and compensation of all types of personnel.
- *Firm Infrastructure.* Activities including general management, planning, finance, accounting, legal, government affairs, and quality management.
- *Margin.* Margin is the difference between the collective cost of performing the value activities and the total value gained.[5]

By disaggregating the important business functions, this model of the firm's activities helps managers consider a company's capabilities in two important ways. One is to call attention to the full range of relevant specific capabilities. A common failing is for managers to focus on certain ones, overlooking important opportunities in other activity areas. For example, Johnson & Johnson

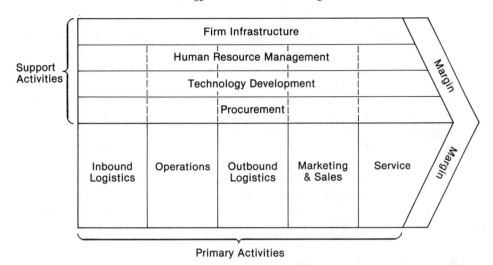

Figure 2.2 The generic value chain. Reprinted with permission of The Free Press, a division of Macmillan, Inc., from *Competitive Strategy: Techniques for Analyzing Industries and Competitors* by Michael E. Porter. Copyright © 1980 by The Free Press.

managers have had a long-deserved reputation for excellence in operations, marketing, and service. Around 1980, American Hospital Supply (AHS) was making serious inroads into J&J's competitive position by attacking with respect to outbound logistics. Taking advantage of emerging computer network technology, AHS was able to offer hospitals significant benefits in processing orders and controlling inventories for the multitude of drugs and supplies involved. Value-chain analysis might have helped J&J managers to uncover these opportunities before AHS forced the issue. General managers need to examine each activity and ask if there is some way to add value. An effort must be made to think imaginatively about possible alternatives and not to be constrained by present concepts.

The second way in which such disaggregation can help managers to enhance capabilities is in facilitating the consideration of linkages. First are the ways one value activity in the chain can alter the cost or performance of another. For example, field service can be improved enormously in both cost and performance by incorporating self-diagnostic features or by designing complex equipment with modular subunits that can be easily replaced. Or human resource management can generate improved performance by identifying the need for expertise in areas such as logistics. Second are the possible constructive relationships between a company's value activities and those of suppliers, distributors, and customers. For example, working with suppliers to improve their outbound logistics can benefit a company's inbound logistics with respect to administrative and inventory control and carrying costs. Similarly, as AHS demonstrated, working with customers to improve their inbound logistics can benefit a company's selling, outbound logistics, and service activities.

The second question concerning future resource needs involves the same kind of analysis as that described above. In this case, however, managers have to try to anticipate likely changes with respect to customers' expectations, competitors' moves, public services and infrastructure, technology, governmental regulations, and other relevant factors. Managers can start by considering the kinds of changes that could take place in connection with the most critical functions for their industry. For a steel manufacturer, process technology and pollution control would be among the high-priority activities to focus on in this manner; a fast-food chain might look at human resource management (hiring, training) and procurement (including site selection). Another approach is to consider the possible implications of major transformations in the business environment. For example, information technology is more than likely to have a profound impact on how almost every facet of a business will be conducted in the future. Managers should try to anticipate the likely effects on manufacturing operations, geographical coordination, linkages with suppliers, linkages with customers, and so on. Once the possible requirements for different resources are identified, a company should prepare to adapt as its industry changes. Far more rewarding are the opportunities for a company to gain competitive advantage by redefining industry practice, as did American Hospital Supply with its innovative computerized automatic ordering system. The capacity to improve existing skills and learn new ones is arguably the most important resource an organization can acquire.

Selecting Resources. Even after frivolous and nonproductive assets and capabilities are discarded on the basis of value-chain analysis, a company might be unable to fund and otherwise support its remaining list of desirable resources. Choices have to be made. Inherent in the selection process is the decision of how much to invest in specific assets and capabilities. What complicates this analysis is that the support or investment can be multidimensional. The investment usually involves money. It also involves management's time and attention. Marshaling skills and competencies provide the clearest examples of the choices that have to be made. Monetary compensation in different forms (base, incentive, deferred) is one way to attract and motivate the people who can provide specific capabilities. Attractive work conditions and policies and practices that offer career opportunities and employment security are other forms of compensation. Senior managers' commitment of time and attention to their people's welfare is critical to this endeavor.

More support might be better for a particular asset or activity, but when dealing with constrained resources (money, time, and human energy), choices have to be made on the basis of where a given input can result in the greatest incremental benefit to the company. The decision on how much to compensate people and how much time and attention senior management should devote to the company's human resources depends on the need for the company to invest in other assets and to deal with other problems.[6] Such choices are subject in some degree to senior management's values.

Management Values

Even while addressing questions of what is possible (the competitive environment) and of what the enterprise can do (company capabilities), general managers must consider what they and other key managers would like it to do. Here we encounter the values the leader brings to the situation. The critical role such values can play in shaping a general manager's expectations and demands is well illustrated in the following account by Thomas J. Watson, Jr., of IBM:

> My father was the son of an upstate New York farmer. He grew up in an ordinary but happy home where the means, and perhaps the wants, were modest and moral environment strict. The important values, as he learned them, were to do every job well, to treat all people with dignity and respect, to appear neatly dressed, to be clean and forthright, to be eternally optimistic, and above all, loyal.
>
> There was nothing very unusual about this. It was a normal upbringing in rural nineteenth-century America. Whereas most men took the lessons of childhood for granted, however, and either lived by them or quietly forgot them, my father had the compulsion to work hard at them all his life. As far as he was concerned, those values were the rules of life—to be preserved at all costs, to be commended to others, and to be followed conscientiously in one's business life.[7]

The general manager's attitudes toward work, taking risks, public attention, prestige, social responsibility, ethical behavior, social interaction, and other similar considerations bear on strategy in important ways. Most crucial in this regard is how senior management interprets its principal role. There are those who argue that senior managers, as agents of the firm's owners, should strive to maximize shareholders' value. In practice, however, the dominant view appears to be quite different. An in-depth study of twelve major U.S. corporations gives strong evidence that their primary goal is the survival of the corporation in which they have invested so much of themselves.[8]

As noted in chapter 1 in the discussion on negotiating with shareholders, a firm's survival depends on the cooperation of the capital market, the firm's product/market (including customers, suppliers, and host communities), and its career employees (including management). The study shows how corporate management strives to minimize the potential for dominance by these constituencies, to relax the constraints imposed on them, and to increase the opportunities for managerial discretion. Gordon Donaldson and Jay Lorsch point to the uncertainties that concern senior managers:

> Self-sufficiency enables these managers to deal successfully with the often conflicting objective constraints imposed by their constituencies. Experience teaches them that no company, however large and mature, can afford to take for granted the continued cooperation and support of its constituencies. An unexpected change in circumstances may turn a mutual interest into a conflict in which the vital interests of each party are at stake; and these challenges can come from any quarter: from the many external orga-

nizations and institutions upon which the firm depends or from within, from the organization itself. In either case, at such times top management's only protection comes from the capacity to act independently of its constituencies.[9]

Closely connected to survival in these managers' minds is their desire to succeed and to be seen by others as successful.

To avoid dependence on the capital markets, corporate management relies primarily on internally generated funds and a conservative amount of debt to finance corporate growth.[10] Concerns with improving job security and with providing opportunities for expanding professional responsibility favor a policy that combines continued growth with human resource policies and programs. Exposure to product market risks is countered in two principal ways: (1) divisional or business unit general managers seek to reduce vulnerability by gaining competitive advantage via high market share, product innovation, and efficient operations; and (2) senior managers can reduce corporate dependence on a given product market by diversifying business operations.

These responses are largely in conflict with each other. The efforts to contain corporate exposure to capital markets restrict the supply of funds. Meeting the needs for growth to enhance organizational loyalty and for product and/or pricing leadership to secure the firm's competitive position in turn can stimulate heavy demands for funds. When the availability of funds is limited, the actions for satisfying the organization compete with those for securing product market positions. And within the product market realm of considerations, efforts to diversify can compete for funds and attention with efforts to strengthen existing business operations.

The trade-offs to be made in satisfying these conflicting demands are decided in part by management's perception of the firm's relative vulnerability on each front. They are also decided to a large extent by the vision senior managers share with respect to objectives and the organization's distinctive competence, by their willingness to take risks, by the degree of autonomy they desire, and by other personal values and preferences they might have.

It is wrong to protest that personal preferences are extraneous to professional management. Business is fundamentally a human endeavor, and as such it can never be divorced from the human spirit. When the stakes are high and success is in question, a person has to believe in what he or she is doing. For a general manager to promote a strategy that goes counter to his or her values and beliefs can lead only to frustration and discomfort. Either the strategy or the person will have to be changed.

The Corporation's Strategy

A sound analysis of the competitive environment, company capabilities, and management values will suggest directions to follow and to avoid. General experience certainly plays a role in this analysis. Consideration should be given to practices and tactics that are widely recognized as effective. For example, in going up against an entrenched competitor, a firm can make inroads by changing the terms of engagement so as to favor its strengths while playing down the strengths of the incumbent. But even when clear lessons are pertinent to a corporation's situation, the distinctive elements of the particular circumstances still require the general manager to make difficult judgments in defining the objectives, policies, and plans that make up a corporation's strategy (see Figure 2.3).

Objectives

An enterprise's objectives define what management intends it to achieve. Objectives can be specific and results-oriented, or they can be broad and inspirational. In all cases, their role is to provide impetus and guidance for action.

Publicly owned corporations invariably use financial performance objectives, such as return on equity, return on net assets, profit growth, debt rating, and shareholders' value. Industry ranking along various dimensions is also common. For example, Jack Welch demands that each of GE's businesses be among the top two profit-makers in its industry. Specific objectives can also be used to disaggregate a strategy into manageable components, prescribing the results to be accomplished and the timing for each. Such objectives enable subordinates to concentrate on specific actions with the knowledge that their efforts are in line with the efforts of others, thereby contributing to the broad strategic direction of the enterprise. For the general manager, such objectives are a means for dividing the total undertaking into smaller and simpler assignments, for tracking progress with measures appropriate to each task, for setting standards of performance, and for targeting intervention when performance appears inadequate.

Business is sufficiently complex and dynamic to defy precise planning. Unanticipated events can invalidate specific targets or can call for new actions not covered by established targets. To deal intelligently with the unexpected, an organization needs to understand the spirit and broad thrust of the basic intentions underlying specific objectives. Only then can an organization avoid a slavish adherence to specific objectives that are or have become unsuitable. The important validating reference is provided in broadly stated objectives that stress the principle of the matter rather than the details of execution. For example, Cray Research has an explicit commitment to offer the most powerful commercially available supercomputer. This central objective serves as a litmus test for all of the company's specific decisions and targets.

Even more broadly encompassing are those objectives that articulate the core organizational values driving strategy. These objective provide the most fundamental and enduring guidelines for action. Their potential to inspire derives from their readily identifiable association with important human values and aspirations.

In effect, the general manager employs a hierarchy of objectives—ranging from specific targets to broader guidelines and finally to fundamental imperatives—in order to guide and motivate the organization in sufficiently diverse

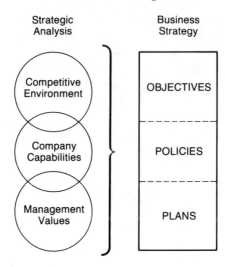

Figure 2.3 Strategic considerations.

ways so as to be as comprehensively relevant as possible with respect to situations and audience.[11] In general, specific objectives guide and motivate actions, and broad objectives validate the continuing suitability of the specific targets. Jointly, they set standards of performance, providing a reference by which the general manager signals to subordinates as well as to investors and other outsiders what is acceptable and what is not. The difficulty for the general manager in setting standards is in finding that point where the objective is ambitious enough to be challenging and is still realistically achievable. If objectives fail to be taken seriously—because they are too easily achievable, unrealistically difficult, or for any other reason—they lose their effectiveness in motivating performance.

Policies

Individual policies serve as guidelines for action. Business policies collectively define the way in which an enterprise has chosen to compete. To promote a consistent and coordinated program of action, specific policies should be articulated for each important aspect of doing business. The resulting list of important policies can be long, covering various aspects of the products offered (selection, quality), research and engineering, manufacturing, marketing, finance, relations with important external parties (unions, government, the public), personnel, organization, and administration. In the absence of specific policy guidelines, immediate operating pressures can more easily lead to decisions that undermine the integrity of a firm's efforts and that put into question management's strategic concepts and its command of the situation.

To be effective, individual policies must meet three tests. First, they should make sense in the competitive environment. Second, they should be consistent with each other. Third, they should reflect management's objectives and underlying values. Understanding how each policy fits within the total scheme is essential in formulating strategy. Of course, not all policies are of equal importance. Usually, one, two, or at most a handful of policies play a dominant role in a business strategy. For these policies, good fit with the key requirements of the competitive environment, with the general manager's objectives and values, and with each other should be stressed. Other policies play a supporting role, and care should be taken to ensure their fit with the dominant policy or policies.

For many organizations, the passage of time or the immediacy of pressures from ongoing events can obscure which policies are critical to success and which are only of secondary importance. General managers must not only keep this distinction in mind, they should ensure that everyone concerned also knows the difference.

Plans

To make strategic concepts and business policies actionable, a general manager has to make decision with respect to priorities, timing, individual assignments, responsibilities, and other important administrative considerations. These decisions as to who does what, when, where, and how provide the grist for strategic plans.

Since plans, as compared to objectives and policies, tend to be more vulnerable to circumstances, they are more susceptible to change. If a key person gets sick, if a competitor makes a surprise move, or if a new relevant bill is enacted in Congress, plans may need to be revised, even when objectives and policies remain unchanged.

Circumstances can change at any time. Judgments and assumptions can be mistaken. For these reasons, plans should not be applied rigidly or followed blindly. Managers should have room for maneuver and be encouraged to do so. Jack Welch remarked on this world of action soon after he took over leadership of General Electric, "In business, you don't get from here to there in a straight line. The good manager has to be a broken field runner, weaving and bobbing in response to the independent forces of competition, technology and customers."[12]

Corporate Strategy for Multibusiness Firms

A vast majority of larger U.S. industrial corporations are engaged in more than one business. In a multibusiness firm, corporate strategy focuses on the selection of businesses and on the relationships among business units. These relationships depend on senior management's principal reasons for engaging in multibusiness operations and consequently vary widely among corporations. At one end of the spectrum, businesses are viewed as a portfolio in independent units, to be acquired, built, pared, or divested as circumstances change. In this setting, cash flow and earnings performance become the key considerations. With respect to cash flow, the general manager seeks a mix in which the more mature business units can throw off sufficient excess cash to nourish the growth businesses. At the same time, these businesses collectively should generate steadily growing earnings. Corporations following this strategy are characterized by lean corporate staffs and freestanding business units.

At the other end of the spectrum is the related multibusiness corporation where management seeks synergistic relationships between and among businesses. In this setting, corporate strategic planning seeks to strengthen businesses by recombining organizational units, by acquiring operations to fill gaps, and by divesting operations that do not fit. Corporations following this strategy—General Electric, for one—are characterized by large corporate staffs and by frequent organizational reshuffling to accommodate new business concepts.

The diversification strategy followed by individual corporations was often a reflection of the time period in which it was carried out. For much of this century, U.S. companies generally emphasized diversifying into business activities that were closely related to their existing operations by virtue of a link in technology, product function, or customers. Firms like General Foods, Minnesota Mining and Manufacturing (3M), and Johnson & Johnson diversified their business operations over the years in this manner. By 1960, as the post–World War II growth began to slow in the United States, many corporations sought to take advantage of the opportunity to push up earnings through acquisitions. Tax and accounting rules at the time enabled firms with high price/earnings ratios to leverage the market value of their shares by acquiring companies with lower P/E ratios. The rapid earnings growth that could be generated in this manner and the resulting positive effect on share price encouraged managers to look further and further afield in their search for potential acquisitions. Any reluctance managers might have had to take on unrelated business activities with which they were unfamiliar was eased by the growing number, prestige, and influence of MBA graduates who came on board with a readiness and a professed expertise to manage any business.

Intellectual support for conglomerate business combinations was supplied by Bruce Henderson and the Boston Consulting Group (BCG) in their successful promotion of the *experience curve* and *growth-share matrix* concepts. Studies purportedly showed that costs of value added decline approximately 20 to 30 percent in real terms each time accumulated experience is doubled.[13] This premise led to an important strategic implication: For a specific product, the firm with the largest volume output should have important cost advantages over its competitors. The growth-share matrix, in turn, focuses on corporate cash flows as a critical dimension for strategic planning.[14] Cost reductions associated with the experience curve represent a source or generator of cash for a firm. In contrast, investments associated with growth and expansion represent a use of cash. These two major factors influencing net cash flows are put together in the form of a matrix to highlight the characteristic cash flows for each combination of growth and market share, as shown in Figure 2.4. Each business is labeled as either a *cash cow, star, dog,* or *question mark.* Cash is supposed to flow from cash cow businesses to star and promising question market businesses. Dog and less promising question mark businesses are subject to divestment.

The portfolio concept of independent businesses has lost much favor with

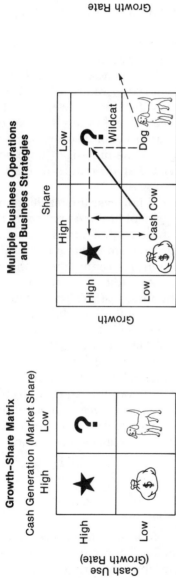

Growth–Share Matrix

Cash Generation (Market Share)

High   Low

Cash Use (Growth Rate): High / Low

Multiple Business Operations and Business Strategies

Share: High / Low

Growth

Cash Cow — Wildcat — Dog — ?

→ Cash Flow
- - → Change in Business Status

Stars both generate cash as market leaders and use cash to support growth. Normally, such products are about in balance in net cash flow. Over time, as growth slows, stars eventually become cash cows if they hold their market share and dogs if they fail to so do.

Cash cows are net cash generators because of their large market share and slow growth.

Question Marks are net cash users because of their high growth and low market share.

Dogs, low in growth and market share, are essentially worthless and should be divested.

Figure 2.4 Cash flow strategic management.

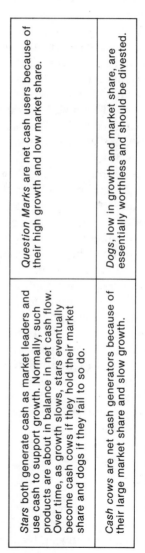

A Typical, Successful Diversified Company

Growth Rate: 20% / 10%

Ratio to Market Share of Largest Competitor: 4.0 2.0 1.0 .5 .25

Note: The size of each balloon is proportional to the sales volume of the product.

the overall poor performance by conglomerate corporations since the 1960s.[15] The idea that good managers could manage any and all businesses proved untenable in practice. And the idea that a corporation should diversify for the benefit of its shareholders was rejected by sophisticated investors who preferred to diversify their own portfolio of investments rather than have companies do it for them. The notion of synergy between businesses—often expressed as "two plus two equals five"—that had gained such popularity in the 1970s also proved elusive in practice. Even when the potential benefits from integration or some other form of coexistence appeared clear-cut, firms were commonly frustrated in bringing them to fruition. In time, synergy lost favor as a comprehensive rationale for all mergers and acquisitions and was increasingly restricted to related business combinations.

Through the 1970s and into the 1980s, diversification was increasingly driven by yet another consideration, the need to defend against takeover threats. The objective of the merger or acquisition was to make the corporation less attractive as a target by increasing its size, adding complexity, and reducing its cash reserves. Since timing was often critical, availability often outweighed other criteria—such as whether a business was related in some way—for selecting acquisitions. The rush to acquire businesses as a means of discouraging takeovers abated considerably following the collapse of the high-risk (junk) bond market in the late 1980s and the somewhat related credit crunch of the U.S. banking industry.

Whatever the motivation for diversification and however the resulting multibusiness operations are handled, senior management has to demonstrate that value is added as a result of the combination if the corporation is to gain the approval of the capital markets.[16] The root of the problem is that multibusiness operations inherently incur costs. Most obvious in this connection is the corporate overhead burden superimposed on business units. For large corporations, these costs can run into the tens and hundreds of millions of dollars. Even more costly, although less visible, are the loss of flexibility because of the need for business units to conform to corporate-wide rules, and the impairment of a business unit's ability to respond quickly because of the need for corporate approvals. As a result, the multibusiness structure is inherently at a disadvantage unless management can exploit potential benefits that the collection of businesses might have to offer. Investors know this and are likely to penalize the equity value unless they see a good business reason for the combination of businesses. That is why share price will typically rise when a corporation announces its intention to divest business operations that are not central to it strategic focus.

Synergy

The concept of synergy has taken on new significance as managers have become more experienced in identifying and exploiting opportunities for beneficial interactions between businesses. Such interactions arise from sharing activities, from transferring management and technical know-how, and from added flexibility in dealing with competitors.[17]

The opportunity to share activities can occur throughout the value chain. For example, with respect to marketing activities, two or more business units in a corporation can share a field sales force, advertising staff support, billing, delivery, or service. Similar opportunities can be found for production, technology, or procurement, or for support activities such as personnel, insurance, and legal. Coordinating activities between business units, however, invariably incurs costs. Management time and effort must be expended to make the necessary arrangements. Moreover, compromise and added complexity often accompany any attempt to have one activity serve two or more business units, each with its distinctive needs and priorities. Consequently, care has to be taken in selecting opportunities where the benefits outweigh the costs. This requirement favors interactions that involve activities accounting for a significant percentage of operating costs and that have potential for reducing these costs. Economics of scale, learning curve improvements, and complimentary utilization of capacity (such as when one business has a peak demand for assembly operations or warehouse space in winter and a second business requires extra capacity in summer) are common means for cutting expenditures.

Sharing management know-how is similar in many respects to sharing activities. As with sharing activities, there are costs associated with transferring knowledge or expertise from one business to another. Consequently, such interactions should be limited to opportunities for significant improvement in the recipient business unit. The third type of interaction applies to companies that face one or more competitors on more than one business front. In such situations, senior management can coordinate the competitive actions of the businesses concerned to signal, threaten, or retaliate in ways not possible with a single business. For example, a firm threatened in one industry might blunt the attack by threatening retaliation in another industry where the competitor is vulnerable or has a great deal at stake.

Senior managers are responsible for ensuring that the business units exploit the important opportunities they have for sharing activities and know-how and for acting in concert against a common major competitor. As discussed in chapter 4, for a variety of organizational reasons, such constructive interactions are rarely initiated by operating unit managers. For this reason, corporate management must actively promote this behavior through the infusion of supporting organizational structures, management systems, and human resource practices.

Important operating and strategic resources are not necessarily affordable or available within a corporation. Senior management might have to look outside the firm for critical resources or support. This search might be forced by changing industry standards, as when, for example, a company with a limited offering feels compelled to fill out its product line to meet competitors offerings and customer demands. The search might also be motivated by management's insight into pioneering opportunities that would give the firm a distinctive competitive advantage. Whatever the source of motivation, management has three principal ways to acquire the desired additional assets, know-how, relationships, or funding support. It can attempt to develop its requirements internally. It can acquire an ongoing business operation that has all or some of the needed input. Or it can enter into some kind of partnership agreement with another business organization to share the critical resources and activities.

Strategic Alliances

Senior management might find the best way to obtain resources, lower costs, or spread risks is to collaborate with another firm. Such efforts, commonly called *strategic alliances,* are normally based on mutual needs. For example, the European telecommunications partnership between Philips and AT&T was to give Philips access to AT&T's superior technology in the field and AT&T improved access to European markets. Neither company would have been able to fulfill its requirements so quickly or for so little cash outflow either by internal development or through acquisition.

The structures of such collaborative partnerships vary widely. AT&T and Philips created a joint venture that had its own management. In contrast, the business alliance agreement between United Technologies' Pratt & Whitney company and Daimler-Benz's Motoren—und Turbinen—Union (MTU), while motivated by similar reasons—sharing product development costs (approximately $1 billion for a new commercial aircraft engine) and developing a more powerful presence in Western Europe in preparation for its economic coalescence in 1992—applied selectively to new commercial aircraft projects of mutual interest. The news release of March 27, 1990, announced, "Both Pratt & Whitney and MTU will retain their own management. However, operations in programs of mutual interest will be conducted as if we were one organization." The choice of collaborative structure reflects the business strategies of the partners, the nature of the collaborative efforts, the relationships between management groups, and other factors.

Recourse to strategic alliances has multiplied in recent years. According to one study, the number of such partnerships between American, Western European, and Japanese firms grew thirtyfold between 1979 and 1985.[18] This rapid rise in cross-company collaboration is driven by several factors. One is the increasing importance and the escalating costs of technological change. Advances in electronics, materials, and the like are outstripping the abilities of most firms to remain at the leading edge on all technological fronts. Important economies can be gained when firms pool or exchange complimentary technologies.

Another factor driving the rapid rise of strategic alliances is the accelerating movement toward international and global competition (see chapter 6). This development can affect a firm's requirements in two ways: in raising competitive standards as world-class companies enter local markets, thereby requiring local firms to improve their technology; and in motivating local and regional firms to expand their operations into geographical areas where they lack presence.

Changes in national policies toward being less restrictive and more encouraging of interfirm collaboration represent a third force contributing to the rise of strategic alliances.[19] A closely coupled reason is the business community's growing familiarity and experience with such arrangements.

Strategic alliances normally involve firms that are not direct competitors. But even direct competitors will join forces when facing a common opponent or very difficult business conditions. For example, major pharmaceutical companies—such as Johnson & Johnson, Glaxo, Squibb, and SmithKline Beecham—use each other's sales forces to build market share for their products, and much of the exploration and development of difficult oil fields is performed jointly by competing firms.[20] Given that any firm might become a competitor of any other firm at some time in the future, a corporation should manage all strategic alliances with caution.[21] The risk is that one partner gains the core technology or skill of the other, thereby changing the balance of power between the two and putting an end to the need for collaboration to the disadvantage of one.

A Winning Strategy

Military strategy aims to engage in battle so that the outcome increases the likelihood of winning the war. So too, at the heart of business strategy, is the idea of achieving a sustainable competitive advantage. Basically a firm can gain such advantage in one of two ways. First, it can price lower than the competitors for a similar product or service. To do this over time, the firm must have a cost advantage. Second, it can offer the customer something not readily obtainable elsewhere. Special product features, delivery, and service are common ways of differentiating industrial products. Many consumer items gain advantage through brand recognition, where brand is perceived to ensure quality or to enhance a user's status. In his writings on competitive strategy, Michael Porter argues that a firm failing to achieve *cost leadership* or *differentiation* will compete at a disadvantage. He terms such firms as being "stuck in the middle."[22]

Along the same lines, Gary Hamel and C. K. Prahalad see an organization's capacity to improve existing skills and learn new ones as the essence of strategy.[23] For them, the strategist's goal is not to find a niche within an existing industry structure but to create new conditions (such as products or practices) that are uniquely suited to the company's own strengths. With reference to industrial companies, they argue that the real sources of advantage are to be found in management's ability to consolidate corporatewide technologies and production skills into competencies that enable the organization to adapt quickly to changing opportunities.[24] NEC's know-how in semiconductors, telecommunications, and computers, 3M's in substrata coatings and adhesives, and Philips' expertise in optical-media are examples of such core competencies. The goal is to gain leadership in a number of interrelated basic competencies that can make significant contributions to the perceived customer benefits of the end product. To sustain leadership in its chosen core competencies, a company has to actively promote the sale of core products (defined as the physical em-

bodiment of core competencies, such as engines for Honda) to generate revenue, gain vital market feedback, and influence the evolution of applications in
the end markets. The third and final requirement is to offer end products capable of gaining market share and profits because of superior features that flow
from the company's leadership in critical competencies. Along with being a
source of competitive advantage in ongoing business operations, core competencies are a wellspring of new business development and consequently provide a rationale for a corporation's pattern of diversification.

Beyond these sound but rather broad prescriptions, the general manager
still faces infinite possibilities. The purpose of strategic analysis is to uncover
opportunities and constraints, to define a firm's strengths and weaknesses,
and to indicate the risks and rewards associated with various courses of action.
There are limits to what any firm can accomplish, but these are ultimately
defined by the general manager's imagination, ingenuity, and daring.

The opportunity to redefine business practice is always present. Business is
a sufficiently complex undertaking, involving so many factors and so much
chance, that no body of experts can ever model a "best strategy" for a firm.
There is always room for insight and invention. The general manager might
well consider the words of Ogden Nash's shortest poem, "In the land of mules,
there are no rules." [25] Business might not reside in the land of mules, but it is
within walking distance.

Notes

1. Kenneth R. Andrews, *The Concept of Corporate Strategy*, rev. ed. (Homewood, Ill., 1980), p. 18.
2. Michael E. Porter, *Competitive Advantage* (New York, 1985), pp. 4, 5.
3. A fundamental paradigm of strategy states that a firm's distinctive competencies and resources
   need to match the key success factors for the industry (those tasks or attributes that are required) for it to perform well. This result was confirmed for selected mature industrial business
   sectors by Jorge Alberto Sousa de Vasconcellos e Sá and Donald C. Hambrick in "Key Success
   Factors: Test of a General Theory in the Mature Industrial-Product Sector," *Strategic Management Journal* 10, no. 4 (July–August 1989), 367–82.
4. Porter, *Competitive Advantage*, 33–61.
5. Ibid., pp. 38–43.
6. The notion of investing to obtain resources applies as well to the capital that a company needs
   for investing in other assets and capabilities. As discussed in chapter 7, the cost of funds
   depends on the perceived risks that investors have to bear. The kinds of "payments" a company must make to obtain funds on favorable terms include a conservative debt/equity ratio,
   the avoidance of unexpected profit setbacks, continuous dividend payouts (where applicable),
   and senior management's continuing efforts to keep investors informed about the firm's future
   prospects through press releases, regular reports, and road shows to important investment
   centers.
7. Thomas J. Watson, Jr., *A Business and Its Beliefs* (New York, 1963), p. 12.
8. Gordon Donaldson and Jay W. Lorsch, *Decision Making at the Top* (New York, 1983), p. 7. The
   remainder of this discussion draws on this work.
9. Ibid., p. 160.
10. For further comment on the practice of creating reserve borrowing capacity, see also Jeremy
    C. Stein, "Efficient Capital Markets, Inefficient Firms: A Model of Myopic Corporate Behav-
    ior," *Quarterly Journal of Economics* 104 (November 1989), 655–69.

11. See Charles H. Granger, "The Hierarchy of Objectives," *Harvard Business Review* 42, no. 3 (May–June 1964), 63–74.
12. "General Electric Company: Dr. John F. Welch, Jr.," Harvard Business School videotape 882–024, 1982.
13. Bruce D. Henderson, "The Experience Curve—Reviewed; I. The Concept" (Boston: The Boston Consulting Group, 1974).
14. Bruce D. Henderson, "The Experience Curve—Reviewed; IV. The Growth Share Matrix or the Product Portfolio" (Boston: The Boston Consulting Group, 1973).
15. Studies of diversification show that firms employing a strategy of unrelated diversification in general have been less successful than those employing a strategy of related diversification. See. R. P. Rumelt, *Strategy, Structure and Economic Performance* (Boston, 1974); H. O. Armour and D. J. Teece, "Organizational Structure and Economic Performance: A Test of the Multidivisional Hypothesis," *Bell Journal of Economics* 9 (Spring 1978), 106–122; M. S. Salter and W. S. Weinhold, *Diversification Through Acquisition* (New York, 1979).
16. For large and powerful firms, the ability to demonstrate that the aggregation of business operations adds value can be a vital defense against antitrust. This consideration was of vital concern to Reginald Jones for General Electric in the 1970s and was important to IBM in countering efforts to break it up.
17. This section draws on Michael E. Porter, *Competitive Advantage* (New York, 1985), pp. 317–442. He labels these three types of interactions *tangible, intangible,* and *competitor,* respectively.
18. Michael Hergert and Deigan Morris, "Trends in International Collaborative Agreements," in Farok J. Contractor and Peter Lorange, eds., *Cooperative Strategies in International Business* (Lexington, Mass., 1988), p. 101.
19. For a list of examples, see Jordan D. Lewis, *Partnerships for Profit* (New York, 1990), p. 13.
20. Ibid., p. 24.
21. See Gary Hamel, Yves L. Doz, and C. K. Prahalad, "Collaborate with Your Competitors—and Win," *Harvard Business Review* 67, no. 1 (January–February 1989): 133–39. They observe: "A strategic alliance can strengthen both companies against outsiders even as it weakens one partner vis-à-vis the other" (p. 133).
22. Michael E. Porter, *Competitive Strategy* (New York, 1980), pp. 41–44.
23. Gary Hamel and C. K. Prahalad, "Strategic Intent," *Harvard Business Review* 67, no. 3 (May–June 1989), 69.
24. C. K. Prahalad and Gary Hamel, "The Core Competence of the Corporation," *Harvard Business Review* 68, no. 3 (May–June 1990), 79–91.
25. Ogden Nash, *The Private Dining Room and Other Verses* (Boston, 1953), p. 60.

3

Formulating Strategy

In all too many companies, strategic planning efforts produce little more than window dressing for poor thinking. Even in cases where considerable management time and energy are devoted to the task, where a good strategic planning system is in place, and where the chief executive officer is an enthusiastic supporter, the output is often characterized by insipid ideas and flawed strategies. In time, the managers involved become disappointed, frustrated, and even scornful of strategy and strategic planning.

Some indication of the pervasiveness of this problem was given in an article reviewing the state of strategic planning in 1979: "The consultants share a somewhat dirty little secret: most believe that over 90 percent of American companies, their clients included, have so far proved incapable of developing and executing meaningful corporate strategies."[1]

In 1990 Tom Peters made much the same assessment: "Today's organizations, especially the giants, are not designed for innovation. They are the by-products of a more placid environment [when] doing yesterday's job just a little bit better—at the most—was *the* prescription for success."[2] Although these assessments may be exaggerated, the general manager still faces, and will always face, a difficult challenge in managing the quality of strategic thinking.

Strategy Making in Complex Settings

Setting strategic direction is an inherently difficult task. It can involve considerable organizational effort and typically requires making decisions with a limited understanding of the forces at work, challenging established views, and facing an uncertain chain of events and outcome. It can mean upsetting established relationships with suppliers and customers, established approaches to manufacturing and marketing products, and the power and influence of individual managers. In general, the intended benefits of a strategic move are far more uncertain than are the associated costs, so there are always strong reasons for maintaining the status quo or for making small adjustments at most.

48

The singular accomplishments of inspired leaders in conceiving and carrying out powerful strategies, such as William Gates for Microsoft and Sam Walton for Wal-Mart stores, are impressive. They are even more so when the major inputs come from the contributions of many people—often separated by age, experience, and rank.

To enact a strategic change involves both insight and commitment. Someone has to come up with an idea for change. Someone has to commit company resources. In complex corporate settings, these "someones" are not likely to be the same person. The someone generating new business strategies typically resides at the middle-level ranks of management, where the industry knowledge and operating responsibility are to be found. The someone committing corporate resources is likely to belong to senior general management at the corporate level.[3] The less connected they are in terms of trust and confidence, the more difficult will be the marriage of insight and commitment. This difficulty reflects the uncertainties and risks associated with most strategic changes. Conclusions rest on judgments and conjecture and are vulnerable to doubts and to contradiction. Under these circumstances, one person's considered opinion can easily be another's idea of nonsense.

Necessary Conditions for Developing Good Strategies

To develop a good strategy requires a person or persons with the ability to understand the underlying concepts of strategy, with strong diagnostic skills, and with good business judgment. A manager has to be able to generate new strategic ideas before he or she can propose or promote them, in the same way a senior manager has to be able to evaluate new strategic ideas before approving or rejecting them.

In view of the difficulties and uncertainities associated with strategy, coupled with its visibility and importance, it is understandable how a manager might perceive an element of personal risk in playing too active a role in this planning process. Apprehensions of this nature can dampen a manager's willingness to promote or to approve new ideas that depart from established practice or that run counter to entrenched commitments. Managers, able as they might be, also have to be *willing* to create and advocate new strategic ideas. And a senior-level manager has to be willing to commit resources to attractive but unproven, and usually unprovable, new strategic moves.

We now have two basic elements in the strategy-development process—conceiving good ideas and approving them—and two necessary human attributes—ability and willingness. When put together, as shown in Figure 3.1, we can identify four enabling conditions for effective strategy formulation: (1) an ability to conceive and to advocate new, effective strategic ideas; (2) a willingness to conceive and to advocate new, effective strategic ideas; (3) an ability to evaluate the new strategic ideas and to commit the necessary resources; and (4) a willingness to evaluate the new strategic ideas and to commit the necessary resources. These four elements might involve only one person, as is often

PERFORMER(S)' ATTRIBUTES

		Ability	Willingness
	Insight	able to conceive and advocate new concepts	willing to conceive and advocate new concepts
TASKS	Commitment	able to evaluate new concepts and to commit resources	willing to evaluate new concepts and to commit resources

Figure 3.1   Enabling conditions for developing strategy.

the case for a small enterprise, or they might involve many people at different levels of authority, as is typical for a large, complex enterprise.

The distinctions between ability and willingness and between insight and commitment have practical significance for the general manager. Little is gained in sending a divisional manager to a management course on strategy if that person is holding back new ideas because of an unwillingness to confront a perceived reactionary corporate review. Likewise, little is gained in eliciting business strategies from managers if the corporate reviewer is incapable of evaluating the resulting proposals. For each of the four conditions, the reasons for inaction and ineffectiveness are likely to differ, as are the corrective actions needed to deal with the problems.

The Problem of Inability

Not surprisingly, lack of ability is a widespread reason for poor strategic planning. According to an unpublished study on strategic planning, many of the general managers responsible for setting corporate or business direction do not understand the underlying concepts of strategy, and some do not possess the analytical skills needed to do this kind of work.[4] Just because a person is good at running an ongoing operation does not ensure that he or she is also good at conceptualizing new strategic approaches.

The reasons for limited abilities and the possible corrective actions are neither straightforward nor simple. The individual manager's intellectual capacity and his or her developed skills for dealing with strategic concepts are obviously relevant. But a manager's abilities to think about new strategic moves are also influenced by contextual considerations.

Experience and conventional wisdom are valuable assets for a manager, but they can also be liabilities, stifling innovative thinking. A general manager who has performed successfully in an industry for twenty years can find it very difficult to think along fresh lines. A cohesive and detailed concept of how things work, reinforced by the proof of long experience, is a powerful mental anchor. Moreover, the more strongly one's respected colleagues share these established views, the more inhibiting this conventional wisdom is likely to be to new ideas. The "repressive powers of corporate mythology" was the way one senior executive put it.

The kind of information that the general manager normally receives also affects his or her ability to conceive or to commit to new strategic ideas. The information most line managers receive tends to be heavily skewed toward operational considerations.[5] Information from conventional sources—such as industry publications, industry association meetings, an individual's network of industry-related personal contacts—can suffer from inbred myopia. Information from unconventional sources not related to the industry carries the extra burden of having to be proved relevant or urgent. The more distant in time or substance an issue is to current industry concerns, the more difficult it is for managers to establish that it applies to their business in some significant way (relevancy) and that it should be addressed now (urgency).

Ironically, a formal process of strategic planning often does more to inhibit than to enhance innovative conceptual thinking. The study on strategic planning referred to above uncovered several reasons for this outcome. For example, many managers became confused and distracted by the mechanics and terminology (jargon) of the elaborate planning systems increasingly in vogue. This was especially true in companies where the planning system was in a continual state of revision. More time went into trying to figure out what was wanted than into thinking about the business.

Also, managers often became enamored with specific planning concepts, employing them with a fervor that inhibited sensitivity to special considerations and that diverted attention from other important issues. In such cases, planning degenerated into mechanical routines or into exercises in sophistry as the focus of attention shifted from the underlying business issues to the conceptual constructs in use. In this connection, planning concepts created new corporate myths as repressive as the old. For example, in several large industrial firms where portfolio planning approaches had been firmly implanted, senior managers complained that operating managers had become so conditioned by their assigned "cash cow" business role that they were insensitive to possible growth opportunities in segments within the overall charter of their unit.

The most deleterious situations were those where general managers abdicated their responsibility for setting strategic direction to staff planners. The trappings of a well-packaged planning system, supported by consultants and an aggressive planning staff, would be taken as evidence that strategic planning was in good hands, leaving the general manager free to take on other tasks more to his or her liking. In the absence of lop-level involvement, subordinate managers would soon accord planning lower priority. In companies where the CEO failed to participate, divisional general managers typically considered the planning effort as just another instance of corporate staff intrusion and responded accordingly. For example, planning forms were viewed as a nuisance and were relegated to lower level divisional personnel for completion. Or the resistance was more overt, sometimes leading to heated confrontations between line and staff employees.

Even when a general manager engages in the planning effort, form can be mistaken for substance. A well-structured planning system and a detailed, comprehensive plan can give managers the illusion of having done good planning when no constructive imaginative thinking has actually taken place. This pitfall is well illustrated by the CEO who came to my office to inquire about his experience with strategic planning:

> I don't really know whether or not I have a problem. We used the [consulting firm] planning system, the division managers prepared strategic plans for each of our businesses, the corporate officers reviewed and approved these plans, and we now have a corporate strategic plan. Everything seems in order. The only thing that bothered me was that I felt no sense of excitement about the whole affair.

Little wonder. It was old wine in a new bottle. The strategic plans were little more than optimistic expansions of the company's ten existing businesses. A subsequent, more spirited and challenging rethinking of the strategy eventually led management to push two businesses more aggressively and to exit from six of the other businesses.

Based on a study of nine large companies, James Brian Quinn made the following assessment of formal planning as a tool for strategic decision making:

> Although the formal planing approach is excellent for some purposes, it tends to focus unduly on measurable quantitative forces and to underemphasize the vital qualitative, organizational, and power-behavioral factors that so often determine strategic success in one situation versus another. It can easily become a rigid, cumbersome routine, used primarily as a basis for financial control, rather than a creative direction-setting challenge.[6]

Senior-level general managers responsible for committing corporate resources face several problems with respect to their ability to assess the quality and appropriateness of new business strategies. First is their limited knowledge and understanding of the facts. A business general manager who moves up to corporate responsibilities can quickly lose touch with his or her former industry. The problems of limited knowledge is intensified in multibusiness companies for those businesses where the senior managers have not had direct experience. Fred Borch, while CEO of General Electric, gave a clear indication of just how severe this problem can be: "With hundreds of products ranging from electric pencil sharpeners to diesel engines and nuclear plants, it is difficult to do an effective job of planning. It is, in fact, impossible for management to have a direct, personal feeling and knowledge about so many business environments."[7]

Second is the extent to which a senior general manager is systematically or even deliberately excluded from the decision-making process. William Wommack, deputy chairman of the board of directors for the Mead Corporation, described this problem: "The idea that the organization will present strategic alternatives to top management is a fiction. If alternatives are ever generated, they get eliminated as they move up the organization. Top management is then faced with accepting or rejecting the one proposed plan that survives the organizational screening."[8] When senior managers feel the way Wommack did, they are likely to be cautious in their support of new and different strategic moves.

With limited ability to evaluate the business situation directly, a senior manager's decision to commit resources often rests heavily on his or her assessment of the person or persons making and carrying out the proposed strategy. A division president's record of successful accomplishments can be far more reassuring to a CEO than the logic of the strategy, especially if any of these accomplishments are related to the proposed course of action.

Although an assessment of the proposer can serve as a legitimate proxy for an assessment of the proposal, this substitution can also distort the evaluation. The senior general manager can be strongly influenced by the charm, guile, appearance, and other qualities of the proposor that might have little bearing on the merits of the proposal.

The problems just discussed have to do with a senior general manager's limited knowledge about an individual business. This person must also be able to assess how each business strategy fits into the total range of concerns for the corporation. How does each proposed move relate to the other known corporate business activities and concerns in terms of importance and possible interactions? How might a specific move enhance or constrain the corporation's overall future opportunities? Are there other issues of importance to the corporation being overlooked? These are questions not easily answered.

The Problem of Willingness

Some people are gamblers, and others feel comfortable only when dealing with givens and knowns. Some people want to stand out and lead the pack, others prefer to avoid conflict and are content to follow. In like manner, managers differ greatly with respect to their desire for recognition, their tolerance for ambiguity, and their willingness to bear personal risks. Although there is probably relatively little that can be done to alter an individual's innate proclivities in this regard, general managers can still influence employees' willingness to engage in strategic planning in several important ways.

The priority a general manager assigns to strategic redirection is probably the most important factor motivating people. In companies where strategic change was constructively under way, the general manager's clearly perceived determination to have strategies improved was most often singled out as the principal reason for its success.

Willingness to undertake the rigors and stresses associated with developing new strategies and practices also depends on other pressures. Evidence of poor financial results, loss in market share, or mounting customer dissatisfaction can help to overcome an organization's natural inertia in favor of the status quo. Threats to a company (and to a lesser extent, opportunities) can also provide strong incentives for strategic redirection.

Even a CEO bent on improving strategy-making can face an uphill battle in trying to obtain serious organizational involvement when not "blessed" with threats or crises. As one senior executive of the Coca-Cola Company once put it during its heady days of industry dominance: "The very ongoing success of this company works against its planning for change." The unwelcomed in-roads by Pepsi Cola probably did as much as anything else to help Coca-Cola to change its ways. Figure 3.2 shows how the general manager's commitment to improve strategies and the firm's ecnomic situation or prospects combine to set a climate for strategic planning.

The clarity of senior management's goals for change has a major effect on strategy making. The healthiest situations are those where the CEO and other senior managers have a clear idea of the desired direction and urgency of stra-tegic change, and where this thinking is clearly promulgated to the line and staff managers responsible for business strategies. In these situations, middle managers are able to calibrate the personal risks attached to strategic change and can feel some security in advocating changes that are in line with senior management's goals. Where top management is unclear and vacillating in its position with respect to strategic change, the risks of advocating new ideas escalates for operating managers.

New strategic ideas are often in need of modification and almost always vulnerable to second-guessing. The way senior managers react to strategic ideas greatly affects the way their subordinates perceive the risks of advocacy. No one cares to be embarrassed or punished. How ideas and proposals are cor-rected or rejected is a vital consideration with respect to encouraging or dis-couraging further participation, not only by the business managers directly af-fected, but by all his or her peers who are likely to experience the same treatment. In one company, the CEO had a habit of firing division managers when new strategies did not work out. It came as no surprise to find business managers throughout the company most reluctant to advocate any changes. Admittedly, how to deal with a manager who has advocated a strategic move that proves a flop is not a simple matter.

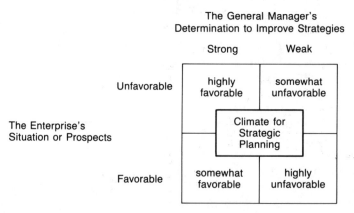

Figure 3.2 The influence of the general manager and circumstances on the climate for strategic change.

The formal measurement and reward systems also influence the climate for change. In most companies, great attention and effort go into budgeting. Managers are evaluated and often compensated by how well they do with respect to yearly profits. This stress on short-term results can act as a deterrent to good strategic thinking. Management's concern for "making budget" often leaves little time for thinking ahead. Moreover, this pressure for current performance tends to give disproportionate importance to moves that produce near-term profits.

To realign the measurement and reward systems so as to encourage the development of good strategies is not easy. These systems in large companies are ponderous and deeply rooted. To change them requires great effort and time and can be upsetting to an organization. Moreover, management still has to run the company's operations, and the requirements for this task do not necessarily coincide with the requirements for encouraging new strategic moves.

Improving on Enterprise's Strategy-Making Capabilities

For the CEO or division general manager intent on improving corporate or business strategy, a good place to start is with an assessment of the enterprise's strengths and weaknesses with respect to each of the four enabling conditions noted earlier in Figure 3.1. This analysis should take into account the following questions:

- Are the organizational missions clear and compelling?
- Does the organization have qualified people in the right positions to be sensitive to the needs for changes and to be effective in their responses?
- Does the organization have systems and practices that support innovative and well-reasoned stratetgic thinking?

The object is to have an organization that is sensitive to opportunities and threats, that is able to come up with sound ideas on how to respond to favorable or unfavorable events, and that encourages creative new thinking.

Core Mission and Strategic Intent

In discussing the many challenges Cray Research has faced over the years, John Rollwagen, chief executive officer and chairman, points out how the notion of building the most powerful supercomputer serves as a mainstay for the organization. He explains, "Whatever anyone is doing, he or she knows the one thing that Cray Research is all about . . . building the most powerful computer. It is what inspires our thinking and our actions. It is also the glue that keeps this loose, innovative organization together."

To be effective, a corporation's core mission must motivate efforts to achieve sustainable competitive advantage.[9] Cray Research's obsession with offering the world's most powerful supercomputer, Microsoft's passion for dominating

PC software, NEC's compulsion to lead in computing and communications, and Asea Brown Boveri's focus on electric power systems are clear expressions of strategic intent that provides each firm with a rallying point for developing competitive advantage. The power of such concepts lies in their ability to inspire organizational enthusiasm and commitment. For motivating people in an organization, the idea of creating shareholders' wealth or achieving record earnings per share is not so compelling as a mission to provide the nation's finest health care services, or a goal to advance new consumer or industrial products that satisfy pressing needs, or a determination to remain as an industry leader, or a quest to unseat an industry leader. The power of strategic intent also lies in its providing a valid reference point for ensuring a cohesiveness of action while leaving room for creative adaptations to changing circumstances. Not only does it provide criteria with which to evaluate ideas, but it also reveals vital areas by which to evaluate people's performance. By indicating what is ultimately to be accomplished, strategic intent helps senior managers to uncover omissions and failures to act as well as to consider those actions that are proposed.

Providing direction and an overarching goal is a vital prerequisite for motivating excellence in strategic thinking, but it might not be sufficient by itself. Creating dissatisfaction with the status quo is often also necessary. Without a strongly established sense of dissatisfaction with the status quo, the general manager will have difficulty in coping with the self-doubts that are bound to arise as the risks associated with specific strategic moves become apparent. In view of these difficulties, the strongest possible case for strategic change needs to be developed at the outset. Where the enterprise has been experiencing difficulties or is facing significant dangers, this task might be a relatively straightforward one of highlighting and emphasizing these problems at every opportunity. Where circumstances fail to provide obvious compelling grounds for strategic redirection, the general manager might have to search for less obvious, compelling reasons to serve this purpose.

A thoughtful examination of possible future developments for the industry can usually uncover such reasons. For example, through informal discussions and formal strategic-planning workshops, the CEO of a successful major newsprint company emphasized the emerging threats posed by the increasing concentration of newspaper chains (buyers) and by the impact of interactive electronic media on future newspaper usage to challenge his managers and board of directors to reconsider the firm's strategy.

To motivate strategic change, the general manager must in effect undermine management's confidence in the strategy already in place. Its inadequacy or vulnerability must be made clear. The more relevant and urgent the reasons for change can be made to appear, the more power they will have to motivate managers to search for and to adopt a new strategy.

People

The sine qua non for effective strategy making is to have people able and willing to generate and advocate new ideas and people able and willing to make good resource-allocation decisions with respect to these proposed changes. To populate an organization with such people requires attention to recruiting, to training and human resource development, and to the selection of candidates for positions of higher authority in the organization. The object of recruiting is to seek out and attract people who have strong potential for initiating and championing good strategic thinking and possibly some who have already proven themselves in this regard. Training, job assignments, and individual coaching have to be coordinated to develop people's talents and to broaden their skills and capabilities. Promotions to senior management positions play two important roles: the company's most gifted and accomplished people are placed in positions where they can most effectively contribute to the organization's leadership; and junior managers are sent strong signals as to the kinds of skills and behavior that are most valued.

Any effort to upgrade the quality of strategic thinking in an ongoing organization is likely to require that senior management choose between improving the requisite abilities and attitudes on the part of a manager who already holds a position with strategic responsibility or replacing this manager with another person who already has the desired abilities and attitude, or at least a greater potential for acquiring them. The choice between these two courses of action depends on the expected ease of retraining the manager in place, on the availability of a more qualified candidate, and on the administrative problems a change might entail. On this last point, even when a replacement is called for, violating precedence or a policy favoring internal development and job continuity might demoralize staff. In some cases a CEO might decide to leave in place a well-entrenched, powerful general manager who is near retirement to avoid disruptive infighting in the management ranks.

Concepts and Coaching. The ability to conceptualize strategies is neither inborn nor commonplace; most managers need to develop this skill sometime in their career. As with most skills, development typically depends on some mix of theory (analytical concepts), instruction, and hands-on experience.

Analytical concepts, such as those described in chapter 2, can help people to think about strategy. Even simple concepts can provide a helpful structure for analysis. For example, the management of a large company manufacturing industrial products employed a "test for winning strategies." The idea was that a strategic proposal must show a clear competitive advantage with respect to at least one of the following considerations: input factors (raw material/labor); process; product; selling/distribution; service; or special. "Trying harder" was explicitly ruled out as a basis for a winning strategy. With this simple checklist, management was able to shift some consideration from the content of a strategy to its merits.

Formal analytical decision-making techniques can also help a general manager in thinking about complex problems. They can provide two related but somewhat contradictory benefits. One is to discipline and structure thinking; the other is to free up and stimulate thinking. Faced with a complex problem and under pressure to act, managers risk making a decision with only a fuzzy and incomplete understanding of the situation. Key assumptions can be left unexamined, consequential interrelationships between various factors undefined, and attractive courses of action overlooked. In forcing a decision maker to define the elements of a problem explicitly and comprehensively, structured analysis calls attention to each of these vital considerations. Financial models, for example, can help the general manager to identify and keep track of factors that affect the outcome of a decision. Assumptions and relationships are made explicit. Another relatively simple analytical tool, the decision diagram or decision tree, focuses attention on defining and comparing alternative solutions and on taking uncertainty into account.[10]

Avoiding serious mistakes is only one benefit that carefully structured analysis helps to provide. In calling attention to less obvious courses of action, to a company's sensitivities to changes in the situation, and to uncertainties, such analysis also can provide the general manager with new insights. The use of simulation models to explore *what if* questions not only tests for risk exposure, but is also likely to stimulate thinking. The payoff for the general manager is to discover innovative solutions that surpass the obvious courses of action.

Providing analytical concepts is not enough for most managers. They also need help in using them. The planning memoranda and manuals on which many companies rely for instruction are grossly inadequate. In at least one respect, strategic thinking might be likened to tennis: Some people might be able to learn good tennis from a book, but most need coaching, and lots of it. The need for coaching seems to hold true for strategic thinking as well, for all levels of management.

Supportive Management Systems and Practices

All management systems, in one way or another, are likely to influence the strategy-making process—either by the information they provide or by the priorities and orientations they signal. For greatest effect, senior managers have to develop a cohesive ensemble of organizational processes and practices capable of encouraging and assisting adaptation and innovation. They do this by the way they use a corporation's regular planning and control systems, by adding activities that can contribute to innovation, and by constantly reinforcing these innovative efforts at every opportunity.

Use of Traditional Systems. Corporations customarily use a variety of planning and control systems to direct and monitor their people, funds, and other resources. Robert Simons shows how top managers can guide organizational learning and thereby influence the process of strategy making throughout the firm by involving themselves in the decisions of subordinates through one of the existing management control systems.[11] The choice of the control system to be used interactively in this manner (as opposed to the normal diagnostic use for reviewing past performance) depends on the nature of the uncertainties that could have the greatest strategic impact on the firm. For example, in firms competing on the basis of brand marketing of mature consumer products, senior managers are likely to interact with their subordinates through brand revenue systems that show the impact of price, promotion, and packaging on customer buying habits. Similarly, senior managers in firms that compete on the basis of product technology tends to become heavily involved in project management systems. Simons observes that senior managers do not involve themselves interactively in more than one control system at a time except possibly when faced with a crisis situation. He explains the reason for this selectivity and indicates one important result: "Since organization attention is limited, top managers must decide what to emphasize and what to de-emphasize. By using selected control systems interactively and others diagnostically, top managers can signal where organizational attention and learning should be focused; this systematic focusing allows top managers to guide the emergence of action plans and new strategic initiatives."[12]

Scanning Activities. The quality of strategic thinking depends on an organization's ability to sense both needs and opportunities for constructive adaptation. According to Donald Hambrick, environmental scanning—the managerial activity of learning about events and trends in the organization's environment—can be conceived of as the first step in the ongoing chain of perceptions and actions leading to an organization's adaptations to its environment.[13]

Most companies are able to provide ongoing business information. Where many fall short is in providing information to stimulate thinking about potentially important considerations that are further out in the future or that fall outside the normal purview. As shown in Figure 3.3, organizations should be encouraged to consider events beyond the near and familiar. Some companies do this by bringing in experts to address such issues with management. Industry associations and outside board membership are other possible sources for such stimulation. And because most people have difficulty ascertaining the relevance of information that is not currently applicable, efforts must be taken to make such information as urgent and germane as possible.[14]

One of the most effective ways of doing this is for managers at all levels to discuss future considerations with each other. For example, senior managers can encourage the constructive exchange of information by using task teams comprising members from different business units, different geographical regions, and different functional backgrounds for strategic analysis and decision making; or by holding planning conferences with participants broadly representing the entire organization.

The organizational process of people interacting to generate, interpret, and use business intelligence becomes more difficult when expert inputs are required. Part of the difficulty is integrating the expert input in the decision-making process (getting the expert to address the relevant business issues and to communicate these issues clearly to decision makers who are not expert in the subject).[15] Another part of the difficulty is in getting the experts to benefit from one another's skills and knowledge of the organization's environment. Without proper coordination, relevant issues can be overlooked and vital inputs that relate to each other left unconnected.[16]

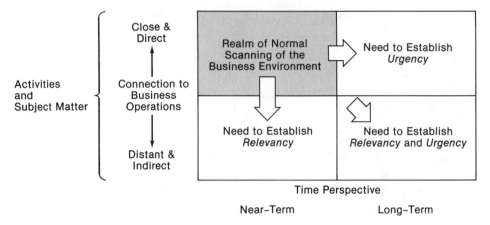

Figure 3.3   Environmental scanning beyond near-term and familiar issues.

Reinforcing Activities. Senior executives can reinforce good strategic thinking by encouraging constructive efforts at every opportunity and by removing obstacles. The use of rewards and punishments is likely to be critical in this regard. Rewards include access to senior management, public praise, approvals of proposals, increased budgets, and promotions to positions of higher authority. At the same time, senior management has to be careful in how it deals with failed results. A clear distinction must be made between failures resulting from legitimate business risks and those resulting from incompetence or lack of effort. To punish the former would inevitably escalate people's perceptions as to the level of personal risk they face in trying to be innovative.

Lowering Personal Risk

As we noted earlier, where managers perceive a great deal of personal risk associated with strategic planning, they are less likely to engage fully in the process. Clear concepts and good coaching can go a long way to give managers some reassurance that they are doing the right things and will not be made to look foolish. The general manager would be well advised to consider what else could be done to lessen anxiety about strategic planning.

An intermediary between corporate and divisional general management—such as a corporate staff planner or an outside consultant—can play a valuable role in reducing the perceived risks inhibiting innovation. A division manager in a large insurance company gave some idea why he valued such an arrangement.

> Having someone from the corporate planning staff work with us in depth is valuable. I appreciate the opportunity to try out new ideas on one of these people rather than to spring a full blown new idea on top management without this earlier testing. Not only can the staff coordinator help me to shape my ideas in a way that will be most convincing to senior managers,

he also can be very helpful in explaining to senior managers what we are doing.

In effect, such an intermediary can serve as an informed and nonthreatening sounding board for the divisional manager and as a "friend in court" in arguing the merits of the strategic plan with senior managers. In this liaison role, the corporate staff planner also can contribute to senior managers' confidence in the new ideas by having served as a corporate agent in the process.

Another way for the middle-level general manager to reduce the risk of having a proposal cut to pieces by or before his or her superiors is to be able to test the ideas early in their formation with senior managers. When this is possible, a manager can "try out a new idea for size," and can then drop it, modify it, or push it, depending on the nature of the feedback.

These early and repeated exchanges also serve to give senior managers confidence in a new idea. By being exposed to a new idea as it grows over time, the senior executive has an opportunity to shape it and to become comfortable with it. In practice, managers will make every effort to test ideas and to check for support as strategy is developed, whether or not explicit mechanisms have been created for this purpose. In his book on strategic decision making, Quinn gives an excellent account of how and why senior executives behave in this way:

> Even under extreme pressure, effective top executives often consciously delayed initial decisions, or kept such decisions vague, to encourage subordinates' participation, to gain more information from specialists, or to build commitment to solutions. They were extremely sensitive to organizational and power relationships and consciously managed decision processes to improve these dynamics. Even when a crisis tended to shorten time horizons and make decisions more goal-oriented than political, these executives consciously tried to keep their options open until they understood how the crisis would affect the power bases and needs of their key constituents.[17]

This description of top-management behavior would also apply for general managers at operational levels.

Time to Think

Developing good strategic ideas is a creative act. Sometimes it comes as the result of an explosive insight. More often, it is the result of careful thinking and rethinking of the business situation and of the many possible ways in which the enterprise might deal with it.

Such thinking requires time. As James March and Herbert Simon have warned, "Daily routine drives out planning."[18] Strategic thinking is certainly one of the most vulnerable aspects of planning; it needs to be constantly nurtured and protected. Otherwise, it risks being stunted or stillborn.

There are many ways in which the general manager can increase the time devoted to strategic thinking. One common practice is to have the managers involved set aside one or several days for discussing strategic issues. The purpose of such meetings can range from one of stimulating thinking and identifying relevant issues to one of analyzing specific developments or possible courses of action. While some structure is usually advisable for such deliberations, if only to provide a sense of discipline and purpose, there should also be ample opportunity for exploratory thinking and "noodling around."

As the following remarks by a CEO indicate, getting quality time devoted to strategic thinking depends on the general manager's ingenuity and persistence: "I give a lot of thought on how to keep my people thinking about strategy. I try to get together with each of them in an informal setting to kick around ideas. Sometimes we'll do this at lunch, or we may have an impromptu meeting at some other time of day when we have some free time. Traveling together, a round of golf, anyplace where we can have a little time to think and talk."

Another way to increase attention to strategic concepts is to schedule enough time for a thoughtful interchange between middle and senior managers in the review process. The all-too-common practice of scheduling an annual marathon of planning reviews tends to be self-defeating. Almost always, there is too much ground to cover in the time available.

In order to get thoughtful and thorough reviews in the Norton Company, business-strategy review sessions were spread throughout the year so that only one business would be reviewed at a time. In this way, senior managers had time to become deeply engrossed with a particular strategic proposal. If more time was needed for discussion, there was no "next planning item" to rush closure.

A newcomer to Norton's top management ranks gave his impression of this practice.

> I really like the idea of holding strategic review meetings for different businesses at different times during the year. By looking at one business at a time, we get a chance to focus our thoughts and to concentrate on the distinctive aspects of that business. The opportunity to go into depth in a given business has also helped us to gain new insights into some of our other businesses.[19]

Organization Shapes Strategy

There is a general premise that structure follows strategy, where structure is shorthand for organizational structure, managerial processes, and people's skills and attitudes. Simply put, the general manager should put into place the combination of structure, processes, and people that would be best for carrying out the strategy of an enterprise.

This prescription is sound, but the relationship between strategy and structure is not so simple. Consider the following three points: (1) organizational structure and processes strongly influence the way people think and act with respect to their jobs; (2) the kind of people an enterprise employs affects what gets considered and how; and (3) strategy is a product of what and how people think. If you agree with these assertions, then you would have to conclude that strategy is also an offshoot of structure.

The interplay between structure and strategy can often be subtle and unintentional. An account of what happened at the operating level when Monsanto introduced a zero-based budgeting system to contol and redirect its marketing, administrative, and technical expenditures is instructional in this regard. The following scene took place at a divisional meeting of business and staff managers to rank requests for resources in order of priority: [20]

> John Coulson, manager of Commodity Chemicals, defending his interest, threw up his hand like at traffic cop to confront Joe Roboh, R&D manager, on the ranking of R&D projects.
>
> "Wait a minute Joe, your next four increments all involve basic research aimed at consumer products."
>
> "Well that's where the future is, John."
>
> "But we're in the present and won't ever reach the future unless we pay our bills," Coulson said adamantly. "There's no support for my stuff!"
>
> "Calm down. If we want to get to the future, we have to start now. Besides, we have applications research and production service for Commodity Chemicals in the threshold."
>
> "But, that's just a tiny bit. Hell, my products pay the salaries around here, and we deserve a fair shake. I want those increments that have my stuff in them ranked now, before we spend all we've got on a future we're not sure exists."
>
> At this point Fred Ellis, manager of Consumer Chemicals, broke in. "John, demand in your markets isn't growing, and competition may soon start to drive your margins down. I know you are producing most of the cash generated by Queeny, but we ought to use that cash to support the best opportunities we've got, and right now those opportunities are in Consumer. Besides, when you consider . . ."
>
> Coulson interrupted, "That's bull! Our demand continues to grow and our competition won't change all that much. The fact of the matter is, Commodity Chemicals continues to be the mainstay of this division, and we would be crazy to weaken it. Process improvements, and that means R&D, and hard-driving marketing are what it will take to keep this cash cow producing."

Later in the same meeting, the following dispute occurred with respect to advertising:

> "Right now I've got 90 percent of current advertising expense in the budget," Brewster, manager of Oil Additive Chemicals, said. "Rates will go up at least 15 percent, and if we take my next increment, I'll be just short of my current level in advertising purchase power. If we take Consumer's increment, Fred will be at 160 percent of current. I don't even understand why we're wasting time talking about it."
>
> "Maybe it's time to start cutting your advertising," responded Chris Hubbard, division general manager. "You've been spending at high levels, but you dominate the market now and you keep telling me you get terrific

word-of-mouth. You haven't convinced me that this advertising increment will have much effect on either your share or profitability."

"I'm the one who needs the advertising," Fred Ellis interrupted. "Consumer is right where you were a few years ago. We are at 'take-off.' We have terrific products in a growth market, and we have to get out there and establish a dominant position. Right now, getting more awareness and supporting our distributors is critical." Brewster looked straight at Chris Hubbard, speaking in a slow, deliberate voice. "If our ad budget gets cut, I can't promise the profits we've delivered in the past. We've been damn successful, and our advertising has been an important part of our marketing program. It doesn't make sense to change a successful strategy."

These managers are ostensibly discussing budget allocations, but what they are really arguing about is strategy. These disputes reflect two areas of confusion about business strategies. First are the differences of opinion as to the prospects for each unit. Figure 3.4 indicates how the different managers seem to view the various business situations.

The second source of difficulty reflects the different judgments the managers have concerning the effects of specific moves in implementing the strategy. Conceivably, Coulson's arguments relate less to the issue of whether or not Commodity Chemicals should serve as a "cash cow" than to the issue of "how much fodder to feed the cow to keep it healthy for milking." Coulson is arguing that Hubbard is cutting back too fast and too far.

Brewster's resistance is of a similar nature. Hubbard wants to cut fat from a unit whose growth is beginning to slow down. Brewster argues that the cuts will sever muscle and not fat. The necessary judgments undoubtedly involve a great deal of conjecture, since the business appears to be entering a state of transition.

Someone can argue that the disputes reflect the need for more hard data and a clearer statement of strategy. While this argument has some merit, no amount of data or elaboration of strategy can remove the need for judgments with respect to specific actions. Since the information available in practice is far from perfect, differences of opinion are to be expected and encouraged, not rejected. The new budgeting system forced the conflicting judgments to be "placed on the table" where they could be weighed. As with case law, where specific court decisions interpret and give shape to the law, so the specific budget commitments at Monsanto interpreted and gave shape to strategies.

The events at Monsanto were driven in part by competitive considerations. They were also driven by the kind of people involved, their values, and the general approach being followed in introducing the new system to the company. In their comparative study of Japanese and American management practices, Richard Pascale and Anthony Athos point to the success of firms where management not only recognizes the importance of each of these considerations, but purposely shapes them in a coordinated and cohesive manner:

> Executives have only a limited number of "levers" to influence complex large organizations. We have explored seven—superordinate goals [including human values], strategy, structure, systems, skills, style, and staff. . . .

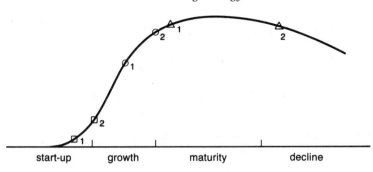

start-up	growth	maturity	decline

□₁ Consumer Chemicals as viewed by Coulson.
□₂ Consumer Chemicals as viewed by Ellis.
○₁ Oil Additive Chemicals as viewed by Brewster.
○₂ Oil Additive Chemicals as viewed by Hubbard and Ellis.
△₁ Commodity Chemicals as viewed by Coulson.
△₂ Commodity Chemicals as viewed by Ellis and Hubbard.

Figure 3.4 Managers' differing views of business situations.

> All of our outstanding companies are very advanced in their grasp of strategy, structure, and systems, but, unlike less successful firms which rely primarily on these S's, the best companies also have great sophistication on the four "soft" S's. Thus the best firms link their purposes and ways of realizing them to *human values* as well as to economic measures like profit and efficiency. . . . [I]t is probably the least publicized "secret weapon" of high-performing American firms.[21]

Every strategic change involves a step into the unknown. As a result, there are limits to just how far managers can plan innovative changes without taking actions to test their thinking. In many respects, *doing* is just as helpful to *thinking* as thinking is to doing.[22] While it can be useful for general managers to focus attention on how to manage the quality of strategic thinking or to focus on problems of implementation, neither can be done well without consideration of the other.

Notes

1. "Playing by the Rules of the Corporate Strategy Game," *Fortune*, September 24, 1979.
2. Tom Peters, "Get Innovative or Get Dead," *California Management Review* 33, no. 1 (Fall 1990), 19.
3. The different roles that managers at different levels play in connection with strategic change were clearly identified in a study on internal corporate venturing in a diversified, major firm. The initiation and championing of ideas occurred at the operational levels in the organization. Middle-level managers were key in reconciling new and different ideas with the accepted corporate concept of strategy. Senior corporate-level management's involvement was largely in setting a structural context that would influence the innovative process at lower levels in the organization. Robert A. Burgelman, "A Process Model of Internal Corporate Venturing in the Diversified Major Firm," *Administrative Science Quarterly* 28, no. 2 (June 1983), 223–44.

4. This unpublished study by the author, conducted in the late 1970s, focused on the problems of strategy making in complex, corporate settings where insight and commitment involved different people. The information was gathered primarily through unstructured interviews with general managers who were responsible for corporate or business strategies and with staff managers responsible for various aspects of the planning process. About 150 managers in twenty firms participated in the study.

5. Francis J. Aguilar, *Scanning the Business Environment* (New York, 1967), p. 43.

6. James Brian Quinn, *Strategies for Change: Logical Incrementalism*, (Homewood, Ill, 1980), pp. 14, 15.

7. "Norton Company: Strategic Planning for Diversified Business Operations," Harvard Business School case number 377–044, 1976, p. 2.

8. "The Mead Corporation," Harvard Business School case number 9–379–070, 1978, p. 7.

9. See Gary Hamel and C. K. Prahalad, "Strategic Intent," *Harvard Business Review* 67, no. 3 (May–June 1989), 63–76.

10. For an introduction to decision diagrams, see Paul A. Vatter et al., *Quantitative Methods in Management* (Homewood, Ill, 1978), pp. 3–19, 63–67.

11. Robert Simons, "Strategic Orientation and Top Management Attention to Control Systems," *Strategic Management Journal*, 12, no. 1 (Summer 1991), 49–62.

12. Ibid., p. 61.

13. Donald C. Hambrick, "Specialization of Environmental Scanning Activities Among Upper Level Executives," *Journal of Management Studies* 18, no. 3 (1981), 299–320.

14. For a discussion of the difficulties companies have in getting broad business intelligence used for decision making, see Sumantra Ghoshal and Seok Ki Kim, "Building Effective Intelligence Systems for Competitive Advantage," *Sloan Management Review* 28, no. 1 (Fall 1986), 49–58.

15. For a discussion of sharing knowledge in the process of environmental monitoring, see Gregg Elofson and Benn Konsynski, "Delegation Technologies: Environmental Scanning with Intelligent Agents," *Journal of Management Information Systems* 8, no. 1 (Summer 1991) 37–62. For a broader discussion of distributed problem solving—where an overall solution requires several agents to communicate with each other, to solve subproblems, and to integrate these subproblem solutions—see E. H. Durfee, V. R. Lesser, and D. Corkill, "Cooperation Through Communication in a Distributed Problem Solving Network," in M. N. Huhns, ed., *Distributed Artificial Intelligence* (Los Altos, Calif., 1987).

16. A. W. Reinhardt, "An Early Warning System for Strategic Planning," *Long Range Planning* 17, no. 5 (1984) 25-34, observes that 80 percent of scanning activities that are uncoordinated might focus on only 30 percent of important environmental indicators. Hambrick points to one source of this problem in showing that managers in different functional areas do not specialize in their scanning efforts (with the exception of those responsible for accounting and financial matters). This lack of inherent structure to information gathering and interpretation in an organization can result in what he terms "scanning voids." He concludes that an effort to structure "scanning responsibilities may result in more effective and efficient environmental scanning within an organization" ("Specialization of Environmental Scanning Activities," *Journal of Management Studies* 18, no. 3 [1981], p. 316).

17. Quinn, *Strategies for Change*, p. 21.

18. James March and Herbert Simon, *Organizations* (New York, 1958), p. 185. The authors go on to explain: "When an individual is faced both with highly programmed and highly unprogrammed tasks, the former tend to take precedence over the latter . . ."

19. "Norton Company," Harvard Business School case number 377–044, p. 13.

20. "Monsanto Company: The Queeny Division (A)," Harvard Business School case number 9–380–048, 1979, 6–7, 9–10.

21. Richard T. Pascale and Anthony G. Athos, *The Art of Japanese Management* (New York, 1981), pp. 202, 206.

22. For a spirited attack on those who would separate the two, see Henry Mintzberg, "The Design School: Reconsidering the Basic Premises of Strategic Management," *Strategic Management Journal* 11, no. 3 (March–April 1990), 171–95.

4

Implementing Strategy

Creating a vision of what the enterprise is to be and how it is to get there is only one of the general manager's broad tasks. He or she also has to develop the organizational capabilities needed to implement this vision. After all, a brilliant strategy is empty without people able and willing to carry it out. In considering the need to provide for an enterprise's readiness and capacity to act, the general manager might well heed the words of Edward Gibbon: "The winds and waves are always on the side of the ablest navigators."

Clearly, even Gibbon's navigators could not master wind and waves without the special instruments of that craft, sextant and chronometer. So, too, must the general manager ensure that his or her people have the "instruments" needed to perform their duties. Raising funds in the capital market (or securing corporate funds for a division) and marshaling other necessary assets are serious and challenging tasks. Even more complex and challenging are the tasks of ensuring that the navigational instruments get used to full advantage as the enterprise strives to follow its plotted course. It is to this second challenge of employing one's people effectively that we now turn our attention.

The General Manager's Means of Influence

General managers have a variety of means at their disposal to influence how well an enterprise carries out its strategy. These can be broadly grouped along the following lines:

> *Organizational structure:* The definition of responsibilities and reporting relationships for employees.
>
> *Planning and allocation of resource systems:* The mechanisms and processes for deciding in concept and in practice who will do what with what. Planning represents intended commitments of company resources for specific

purposes; the allocation of resources involves the actual commitments of money, assets, and people.

Information and control systems: The collection and dissemination of information for analysis and operations.

Reward systems: The various rewards and punishments that can be meted out to members of the organization to influence their behavior.

Staffing and people development: The various activities connected with the selection and recruitment of people, their placement and movement in the organization, and the development of their managerial and technical skills.

Leadership: The manner in which the general manager relates to his people to inspire their involvement and commitment to the enterprises and its purpose.[1]

Rarely will the general manager be expert in any one of these organization-related fields. He or she will have to rely on the expertise of specialists as well as on his or her general experience with the workings of an organization. But there is an important, even critical, perspective that the general manager must bring to the consideration of these organizational structures and processes: that of the strategy of the enterprise.

No single organizational structure, no particular compensation scheme, no specific planning system is intrinsically superior to all others, whatever their proponents might claim. The merits of each depend on what the general manager is trying to accomplsh and on the nature and complexity of the enterprise itself. The driving forces of strategy—competitive environment, strengths and weaknesses of the enterprise, and management's values—are also the driving forces for organizing the enterprise. On this point, Kenneth Andrews concludes:

> [T]he chief determinant of organizational structure and the processes by which tasks are assigned and performance motivated, rewarded, and controlled should be *the strategy of the firm,* not the history of the company, its position in its industry, the specialized background of its executives, the principles of organization as developed in textbooks, the recommendations of consultants, or the conviction that one form of organization is intrinsically better than another.[2]

Emphasis and Priorities

While general managers need to be concerned with each of the means to influence implementation and how they relate to the firm's strategy and to each other, they must also be sensitive to possible priorities of importance. Various circumstances can call for special attention to one or another of these elements. For example, when a firm is in need of people with special expertise who are in short supply, such as software designers or merger and acquisition deal makers, recruiting activities and compensation systems are likely to be of particular importance.

The stage of an organization's development also affects the relative importance of the various elements. Managers starting up an enterprise tend to experience many similar implementation problems. The same can be said for managers in firms experiencing rapid growth, relatively stable conditions, or serious decline.

A brief look at the special problems by rapidly growing companies can serve to illustrate this point. Marshaling and assimilating resources is typically of critical importance in such situations. Where this growth requires a rapid expansion in the number of employees, the general manager has to pay special attention to how good people can be identified and attracted and to how the newcomers can be assimilated as quickly as possible. What makes this difficult is that the people already on board are usually under pressure to deal with the expanding work load and have little time to help acclimate the new people. Moreover, the responsibilities of key people are often in flux as ad hoc arrangements are made to cover new tasks until new people can be added and as the support systems are quickly outgrown. In sharp contrast is the firm experiencing a severe business downturn, where survival is at stake. Here, cash flow is likely to be of critical importance, and attention is likely to be placed on controlling costs, allocating resources, and possibly reducing the work force.

Contextual Fit

We saw in chapter 2 how business policies, to be effective, had to fit with the firm's environment, with the firm's nature, with management's values, and with each other. In like manner, each organizing vehicle must fit with these strategic cornerstones and with each other.

The earlier discussion of Reichhold Chemicals can help to illustrate. Powell's decision to decentralize operations and decision making reflected the distinctive technical and marketing requirements associated with each of the several markets the company had chosen to serve and the importance of responding quickly to the ever-changing customer requirements for specialty chemicals. This decision also reflected Reichhold's new policy to enter and exit businesses as particular chemicals enjoyed increased specialty usage or degenerated into commodity items. In line with these requirements and with a decentralized structure was Powell's decision to encourage a participative style of management. This style also fit with his personal preference on how to relate with his key people.

The ideal overall situation toward which a general manager should strive is to have the strategy of the firm, its organizational structure and managerial processes, and the skills and values of its people all fit with each other and with the world in which the firm competes. With good management and reasonably stable conditions, firms can achieve this powerful alignment, where every element reinforces every other element in line with purpose.

AT&T in the 1960s and early 1970s provides a classical example of this achievement. In an environment somewhat frozen for some fifty years by regulation, the company achieved a remarkable degree of fit among its strategy, structure, processes, people, and the world in which it operated. Its strategy focused on providing superior telephone communications for people throughout the land (rural as well as urban). The successful accomplishment of this mission gained the popular and political support the company needed to deal with the regulatory authorities. A functional organizational structure ensured well-organized operations throughout the vast and complex system. An emphasis on engineering and field service aimed to maximize the quality and reliability of telephone service. Customer satisfaction, a key measure of performance, was tracked through monthly interviews. For most of AT&T's more than 1 million employees, the fond reference to Ma Bell reflected a sense of family and lifelong commitment. Pride lay behind the AT&T's employees' self-deprecating admission to having bell-shaped heads, an allusion to a corporate-wide mentality prizing competence and service. Their working world was indeed bell-shaped during those golden years.

In considering organizational fit with strategy and the environment, Raymond Miles and Charles Snow point to its effect on performance:

> Corporate excellence requires more than minimal fit. Truly outstanding performance, achieved by many companies, is associated with tight fit—both externally with the environment and internally among strategy, structure, and management process. In fact, tight fit is the causal force at work when organizational excellence is said to be caused by various managerial and organizational characteristics. . . .
>
> In short, the causal dynamic of tight fit tends to operate in four stages: First, the discovery of the basic structure and management processes necessary to support a chosen strategy create a *gestalt* that becomes so obvious and compelling that complex organizational and managerial demands appear to be simple.
>
> Second, *simplicity* leads to widespread understanding which reinforces and sustains fit. . . .
>
> Third, simplicity *reduces the need for elaborate coordinating mechanisms*. . . .
>
> Fourth, as outstanding performance is achieved and sustained, its *association* with the process by which it is attained is reinforced and this serves to further simplify the basic fit among strategy, structure and process.
>
> It should be emphasized that we do not specify "finding the right strategy" as an important element of this causal linkage. In fact, finding strategy-structure-process fit is usually far more important and problematic.[3]

Responding to Changes in Circumstances

An enterprise experiencing major change in its circumstances normally encounters new requirements for conducting its business successfully. Such changes in circumstance can occur in a firm's environment or in the firm itself. Where established strategy, organizational structure, administrative practices, and people were particularly well suited to the earlier conditions, the general manager likely has to make changes in some or all of these elements to have them conform to the new requirements.

External Causes

The travails of AT&T and the Bell system since 1980 provide a good example of how disruptions in the environment can set off a chain reaction of accommodative changes in strategy, structure, and people.

Successive waves of new technologies for transmitting electronic signals (microwave, satellites, and fiber optics), the convergence of communications and data processing, and a general move toward deregulation in the United States combined to undermine the erstwhile placid world of telephone service. As the forces battling to dismantle AT&T and its near-monopolistic hold on telephone communication approached victory, management turned its attention to how the surviving enterprises would compete once the restructuring came into effect.

New strategies changing the emphasis from engineering to marketing and aiming to provide new services were devised reasonably quickly. More slowly, management adopted new organizational structures, new planning processes, new information systems, new reward systems, and new leadership styles. But the people were still "bell-shaped," with bell-shaped mentalities and bell-shaped values. And the more senior the individual in rank, the stronger his or her commitment to this perspective was likely to be. After all, the legal reasons for the demerger notwithstanding, these values were responsible for one of the best-run enterprises in the world and for the successful careers of these managers.

This history is depicted in Figure 4.1. As the left column shows, the original Bell system was designed to fit its regulated bell-shaped world. The new arrangement defined by the courts exposed the newly formed seven regional companies and AT&T (retaining the long-line operations, Bell Labs research center, and Western Electric manufacturing facilities) to an openly competitive, market-driven world, represented by a square. As indicated in the right-hand column, the strategy could be "squared" to fit the new world and the organizational structure and processes "squared" to fit the new strategy, but the people's skills and attitudes could not be so radically transformed. While established managers and staff might "square" their appearances and while new "square" talent could be recruited, the dominant shape of skills and attitudes would remain bell-shaped.

Imposing such a radically different strategy and structure at the outset could prove unworkable, given the degree of misfit with the skills and attitudes in place. Figure 4.2 depicts how strategy and structure might be modified to bridge the gap between the new square world and the bell-shaped people. The modified strategy would still emphasize the introduction of new products and ser-

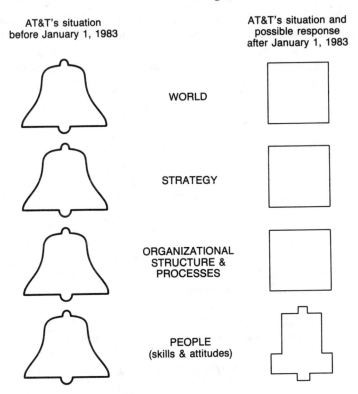

AT&T's situation
before January 1, 1983

AT&T's situation and
possible response
after January 1, 1983

WORLD

STRATEGY

ORGANIZATIONAL
STRUCTURE &
PROCESSES

PEOPLE
(skills & attitudes)

Figure 4.1   Fit and change for AT&T, radical response.

vices for existing and new markets, but might give priority to those moves where engineering and field services are most valued. In this way, management would avoid the dangers associated with a sudden status diminution for the powerful technical-functional units, as well as an excessive reliance on the newly enhanced and still-unproved marketing function. In like manner, management would position the organizational systems to serve as a bridge between the mostly square strategy and the largely bell-shaped people. For example, the marketing department might be put on a par with the engineering and operations units in the organizational hierarchy, marketing information might be given some prominence, market penetration might accompany service reliability as a key performance measure, and highly qualified marketing managers might be recruited at all levels.

The various compromises would reflect management's recognition of the need to make an orderly transition from one strategy to another and its desire to retain the best features of the firm's traditional bell-shaped approach to doing business. In time, training, new recruits, and retirements would transform the skills and attitudes of the people to fit the new requirements, and strategy and structure could be further squared. Of course, the world is also likely to change in the intervening years, further complicating the general manager's already formidable undertaking. Indeed, less than ten years after the demerger, *Busi-*

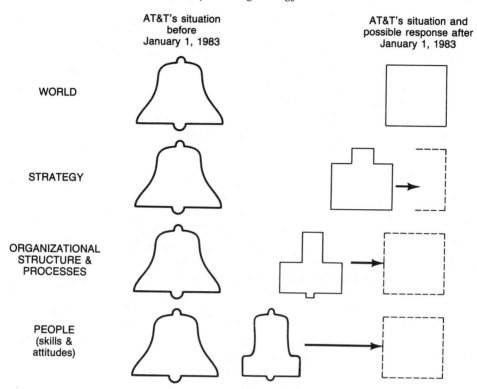

Figure 4.2 Fit and change for AT&T, transitional adaptation.

ness Week, in a major article entitled "The Baby Bells Learn a Nasty New Word: Competition" (March 15, 1991, pp. 96–101), refers to signficant developments in such technologies as microwaves, fiber optics, wireless phone systems, and the rapid growth of cable television networks as seriously threatening to erode the telephone companies' core business by providing opportunities for business firms and individuals to bypass the traditional telephone system.

Internal Causes

The stimulus for changing an enterprise's mode of operations can also arise from internal causes. For example, a general manager might need to introduce a more elaborate organizational structure, increasingly formalized management systems, and people with different administrative skills in a firm that has experienced considerable growth. All of these changes may be required, even when the strategy remains ideally suited to a relatively static environment.

Changes in internal conditions can also lead to new strategies, which in turn might require organizational changes. For example, as a successful single-business company serving the domestic market increases its human and financial resources, management might favor exploiting opportunities with moves the firm could not have afforded earlier, such as expanding operations abroad or into related products and services. To implement either of these moves, the general manager might have to replace a functional organization with a divisionalized structure and place more emphasis on formalized planning and resource allocation to deal with the increased complexity of doing business with the new strategy.

Earlier we discussed how each stage of organizational development (start-up, growth, maturity, decline) had its own characteristics and requirements. Moving from one organizational stage to another (which could result from internal or external causes) almost always involves considerable difficulties in adjustment.[4]

The well-publicized changes in Apple Computer provide a good case in point. Steve Jobs, Steve Wozniak, and a small coterie of other pioneers were extraordinarily successful as they shared the early heady experience of almost unfettered rapid growth. IBM's entry into the personal-computer field soon slowed Apple's growth. No longer could Apple simply do its own thing. The freedom it enjoyed with respect to technical design, product introductions, pricing, service, and almost every other activity would henceforth be severely constrained by the pressure of IBM's attack. In time the company came to recognize the need to introduce more structure and discipline into its operations. John Scully was recruited from Pepsico to help Apple to function in an environment of slower growth and tough competition. As anyone who has followed the news accounts since 1985 would know, the transition was not accomplished without considerable turmoil and pain.[5]

The Difficulty of Responding to Changes in Circumstances

Dramatic discontinuities of the kind AT&T encountered or the clear and undeniable pressures for change that Apple faced are exceptions rather than the rule. Most enterprises experience a gradual drift of circumstances. Customers' needs, technologies, relationships, and a host of other factors may change imperceptibly month by month, like a young child growing up. And just as this child will soon outgrow its clothing, the enterprise will find its strategy and practices increasingly ill-fitting over time.

The general manager dealing with unobtrusive change faces a difficult challenge. The unwelcomed initial signs of pending trouble are no match for the eagerly sought-after signs of accomplishment in competing for management's attention. And even when noticed, they are easily rebuffed. The attitude many managers are likely to adopt can be characterized by the saying, "If it ain't broke, don't fix it." In time, as evidence of trouble mounts, defenders of the status quo fall back on the reassuring argument, "This approach has a proven track record. All we have to do is work harder at it." And finally, as Peter Drucker observed, when the need for change can no longer be denied, "they often set up beautiful mechanics, 'decentralize' their organization chart, preach a 'new philosophy'—and go on acting just as before."[5]

One of the most difficult challenges a general manager faces is in sensing

when a successful approach to doing business is beginning to lose its appropriateness and power and needs to be changed. This challenge involves a difficult dilemma. On the one hand, there are serious risks associated with abandoning practices that have worked successfully in favor of an untried, new
approach. A premature or wrong move can be quite costly. On the other hand,
the best time to make such changes is when the enterprise is healthy and
strong. But the best time to make major changes is not necessarily the easiest
time. The evidence pointing to weakness is often tenuous and debatable; the
internal resistance to change is likely to be strong and entrenched. The general
manager must have genius and courage to recognize emerging problems and
to act while the firm is still doing well.

The Management of Change

Strategic changes can be incremental or bold. With reference to Japanese automotive manufacturers, Richard Pascale argues the virtues of responsive, incremental adapatations involving many people in the firm:

> Contrary to myth, the Japanese did not from the onset embark on a
> strategy to seize the high-quality small car market. They manufactured what
> they were accustomed to building in Japan and tried to sell it abroad. Their
> success, as any Japanese automotive executive will readily agree, did not
> result from a bold insight by a few big brains at the top. On the contrary,
> success was achieved by senior managers humble enough not to take their
> initial strategic positions too seriously. What saved Japan's near-failures was
> the cumulative impact of "little brains" in the form of salesmen and dealers
> and production workers, all contributing incrementally to the quality and
> market position these companies enjoy today. Middle and upper manage-
> ment saw their primary task as guiding and orchestrating this input from
> below rather than steering the organization from above along a predeter-
> mined strategic course.
> The Japanese don't use the term "strategy" to describe a crisp business
> definition or competitive master plan. They think more in terms of "stra-
> tegic accommodation," or "adaptive persistence," underscoring their belief
> that corporate direction evolves from an incremental adjustment to unfold-
> ing events. Rarely, in their view, does one leader (or a strategic planning
> group) produce a bold strategy that guides a firm unerringly. Far more fre-
> quently, the input is from below. It is this ability of an organization to move
> information and ideas from the bottom to the top and back again in contin-
> uous dialogue that the Japanese value above all things. As this dialogue is
> pursued, what in hindsight may be "strategy" evolves.[6]

But the need for a bold strategic move, however rare, cannot be ignored.
Such responses are in order when the firm encounters major opportunities or
life-threatening events. The adaptive approach to making strategic decisions
should not be equated with incremental strategies. With effective orchestration, as the above passage indicates, it can lead to radical changes over time.

But without such orchestration, it is more likely to lead to incremental strategic changes, even when conditions call for bold responses. Jack Welch, General Electric's chief executive officer, warns of this danger: "Most bureaucracies—and ours is no exception—unfortunately still think in incremental terms rather than in terms of fundamental change. . . . We've seen huge chunks of entire industries preside over their own orderly death, while making what could be called incremental progress."[7]

The challenge for the general manager is to create a strategy-making process that allows bold moves—when these are called for—to be conceived and implemented in ways that foster interactive learning and opportunities for adjustment and change.

The managerial requirements vary considerably for incremental and radical strategic and organizational changes. Incremental change typically can be managed by existing organizational structures and processes. Radical changes require special attention to the change process itself as well as to the strategy and organization that are the subjects of change. To help managers do this, Richard Beckhard and Reuben Harris identify the period between the current or starting state of the organization and the desired future state as the *transition state*.[8] They argue that the transition state is critical in that it greatly determines the quality of the future state and yet has characteristics that make it quite different from either the current or future state. For example, during this interim period, established ways of doing things are often altered, people are expected to acquire new knowledge and to develop new skills, new relationships have to be established, and outsiders (consultants) might play a major role in what goes on.

Bringing about major change in a large and complex organization is a difficult and challenging task.[9] One problem is a natural human resistance to change. People need a certain degree of stability and security, and change presents unknowns that can cause anxiety. Strengths developed over a lifelong career might not be as suitable for the new organizational requirements as for the old. Or new working relationships might undermine long-term loyalties. Moreover, people might truly believe that the way things are done is better than the proposed change. A second problem stems from the fact that the existing management systems and procedures are usually inappropriate for new and evolving information needs; designed for steady-state use, they are largely incapable of helping people to manage the transition. The result can be a breakdown in the coordination and control of the transition effort as well as of ongoing business operations. A third problem concerns possible shifts in the organization's balance of power. This can be either threatening or appealing to different individuals and groups and will motivate actions accordingly.

Each of these problems needs to be addressed for a major transition to succeed. To overcome resistance, management has to give the people concerned good reasons for the change. As long as people are satisfied with the current state, they will not be open to change. Managers can also reduce resistance by enabling the people affected to participate in making the changes and by rewarding cooperation and support. To avoid the second problem, the disruption of ongoing organizational processes, senior management must make special arrangements for managing the change. These arrangements might include the designation of a respected manager to be in charge of the transition, the allocation of adequate resources (money, people, and whatever else might be needed) for the transitional efforts, and the creation of management structures and systems (such as task forces, pilot projects, and experimental efforts) just for transitional needs. Finally, to eliminate power struggles, senior management needs to mobilize a critical mass of powerful individuals and groups to support the change. A classical example of this stratagem was when Fred Borch refused in 1971 to implement a McKinsey and Company consulting recommendation to do away with General Electric's senior management hierarchy and to put in its place a trimmed-down strategic business unit structure. He recognized the political impossibility of what was in effect demoting over 200 of his 250 most powerful and talented managers.

Once a transition is completed, senior management must make an effort to institutionalize, or "freeze," the new set of conditions.[10] New norms are always weaker than those they replace. Without follow-up actions to strengthen new attitudes and behavior, people are likely to backslide to the norms that previously prevailed.[11] To prevent such backsliding, management must act with an understanding of the underlying psychology of commitment. Charles O'Reilly describes the different stages of commitment:

> *Organizational Commitment*—What is meant by the term "organizational commitment"? It is typically conceived of as an individual's psychological bond to the organization, including a sense of job involvement, loyalty, and a belief in the values of the organization. There are three processes or stages of commitment: *compliance, identification,* and *internalization.* In the first stage, *compliance,* a person accepts the influence of others mainly to obtain something from others, such as pay. The second stage is *identification* in which the individual accepts influence in order to maintain a satisfying, self-defining relationship. People feel pride in belonging to the firm. The final stage of commitment is *internalization* in which the individual finds the values of the organization to be intrinsically rewarding and congruent with personal values.[12]

He goes on to list several mechanisms for institutionalizing the new attitudes and norms. One is to encourage people to involve themselves in the new organizational stage, to make incremental choices, and to develop a sense of responsibility for their actions. Another is for senior management to provide interpretations of events for the organization's members and generally to send clear, visible signals about its own commitment to the new order. A third is to reward desired behavior. It should be apparent by now that freezing the new corporate condition in effect calls for the same managerial actions that are required to bring about the change in the first place. The extension of these efforts simply recognizes that people need time and opportunity to disengage from their previous commitments and to replace them with new ones.

Multibusiness Corporations

Most large U.S. corporations have decentralized their operations into autonomous business units with profit responsibility. Among many reasons for this structure are the unit general manager's unambiguous responsibilities, the opportunity to focus on a particular strategy, and the clear measures of performance that can be rewarded or punished.[13]

For all its strengths, the business unit structure also has serious weaknesses. The resulting division of a corporation's mission and resources can lead to suboptimization in two important respects.[14] Since no single business unit may (1) feel responsible for maintaining a viable position in the corporation's core products or (2) be able to justify the investment required to build world leadership in some core competence, this structure can lead to underinvestment in the fundamentals for long-term competitive advantage. Since business unit managers are measured on their unit performance, they are likely to hold on to their best people and to any other assets of value to them, even if these resources are more valuable to another unit. This self-centered orientation runs counter to the notion of collaborating with other business units for the good of the corporation as a whole. Indeed, business units often view each other as rivals competing for limited resources and senior management's approval.

In addition to any reluctance business unit general managers have concerning a loss of autonomy and control, other factors are at play. For example, the benefits from interacting are more often than not asymmetric for the collaborating units. The business unit with the most to gain is likely to favor the interaction, whereas the unit with less to gain might prefer not to participate. Issues of fairness and equity arise when managers in one business unit feel put upon to "carry" another unit. This sense of imposition is often reinforced by incentive systems that fail to reward managers for being good corporate citizens. Moreover, major differences can exist with respect to procedures, location, management style, and other aspects of business management that can undermine effective collaboration. Two general managers not liking or respecting each other is all it would take to prevent earnest efforts by their business units to interact constructively.

Corporate managers might be equally reluctant to tamper with decentralized operations for fear of inhibiting business unit initiative. Joint efforts also increase the difficulty of measuring performance, giving business unit managers room for making excuses. To overcome these organizational impediments, corporate management needs to take actions that make clear to operating managers the value of business unit interactions. Managers must be made to understand that the well-being of the corporation as a whole takes precedence over the optimization of any business unit's performance. Clearly, individual operating units must be soundly managed for the corporation to succeed. But, as illustrated in Figure 4.3, a minor strategic accommodation by a small electric motors business unit might produce benefits in other units that surpass the modest losses incurred by the former. (This is shown by the move

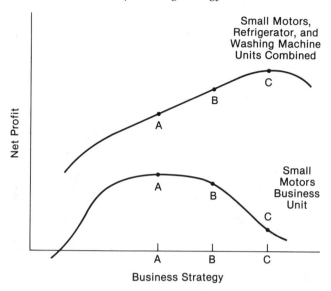

Figure 4.3 Optimizing corporate-wide performance versus business unit profits.

from point A to point B, which might involve sharing a field sales force or production facilities.) The net effect is to benefit the corporation as a whole (the upper curve). Conceivably, it might be in the corporation's best interest to alter the small motors business unit's strategy significantly from its optimal competitive perspective in order to benefit the other business units (point C). In this situation, the role of the small motors business unit changes from one of industry competitiveness to that of internal support. To help promote this kind of analysis and to motivate the necessary decision-making actions requires supporting organizational structures, management systems, and human resource practices.[15]

Horizontal Structure

One of the most powerful mechanisms for encouraging business unit interactions is to group them around interrelationships that are most significant for competitive advantage. The general manager in charge of such a group (commonly called the group executive) would have responsibility for identifying, developing, and managing the collaborations within the cluster and even with outside parties (other groups within the corporation or third parties). A related structural accommodation is partial centralization. For example, procurement, research, and special manufacturing operations can be centralized at the group level to serve the member business units. Research, finance, accounting, legal, and parts of human resource management in turn can be centralized at the corporate level. Such arrangements can be permanent or ad hoc for special conditions. Cross business unit standing committees and working groups are a third mechanism for encouraging interactions across organizational lines.

Standing committees can be made responsible for identifying opportunities for beneficial interactions in marketing, technology, manufacturing, procurement, and administrative services.

Horizontal Systems

The most obvious area for attention is with respect to the measurement and reward system. Managers' efforts to identify and implement beneficial interactions between business units should be readily recognized and clearly rewarded. There is no more effective means for senior managers to convince their people that they mean what they say in this regard. Another important mechanism for integrating business unit activities is the strategic planning effort. Responsibility for identifying needs and opportunities for constructive interactions can be given to the corporate planning department, to a group executive, or to the business unit managers themselves. The core strategic mission of the corporation provides a basic reference for this effort.

Horizontal Human Resource Practices

The rotation of responsible managers among business units permits managers to uncover opportunities for constructive interrelationships between units and to share knowledge across divisional boundaries. It enables them to create a wide network of valuable personal contacts throughout the organization, and it promotes a corporate identity in addition to a business unit identity. In companies that are geographically dispersed, such as Philips, these people serve as the glue that binds the organization together.

The Evolution of Common Practive

Business decisions can be viewed from the perspective of the business's requirements or from the perspective of the individual's needs. The needs of the business and those of its employees often differ and can even be in conflict. It is vital that the general manager be aware of these differences and consciously attempt to find a proper balance in satisfying the requirements of each.

In their book on managing human assets, Michael Beer and his coauthors stress this point in discussing human-resource flows. They argue that "human resource flow [comprising inflow (recruitment), internal flows (promotion, lateral transfers, demotions), and outflows (terminations and retirement)] must be managed strategically so as to match organizational needs with the career aspirations of employees."[16] Their ensuing discussion on managing outflows illustrates well the kind of issues the general manager must consider:

> A company may attempt to improve its mix of competencies rapidly by increasing the outflow of personnel through early retirement programs and/ or layoffs of the lowest performers. Early retirement increases the percent-

age of younger personnel who management often believes are more flexible in adjusting to a changing business future than older, more entrenched employees. At the same time, personnel reductions allow for a rapid lowering of payroll costs, which can improve profitability in the short term. In the United States, this scenario has been used by companies in many industries as a response to recession and competition. . . .

The central strategic dilemma for managers is how to balance the needs and rights of employees for employment security with the requirements of the corporation to use personnel outflow as a means of cost reductions and renewal. Research evidence and experience demonstrate that employees who become insecure because of work force reductions are less productive and less committed to the organization.[17]

The need to balance business-driven needs and those of individual employees applies to the other organizational processes as well. To the economic and the motivational considerations noted above, general managers must also add their own values concerning efficiency of operations and respect for the individual. They must contend with ethical considerations as well as with economic concerns.

As complicated as the equation might already be for the general manager in trying to balance the business-driven and people-driven requirements in line with his or her values, the calculus is further complicated by major undercurrents of change. There are forces at work that profoundly affect each of these variables (business requirements, employee's expectations, and the general manager's values) and that could redefine common and acceptable organizational practices. Some of these forces, according to a recent essay on the history of human resource management in American industry, are the impact of increasingly powerful microprocessors on the deployment of people, the pressure of intense international competition, and emerging new values and expectations of a better-educated populace.[18] A newspaper article on the U.S. economy pointed to an important demographic occurence as a force for changing accepted practices over the next decade: "Because of the earlier 'baby bust'—the sharp, twenty-year decline in the birth rate that started in 1957—today's labor force is increasing slowly. . . . Over the long term, personnel policies will be a greater factor in success or failure than in the past."[19] Rampant merger and takeover activities and the increasing pressure on boards of directors to play a more active governance role might also alter the equation by redefining management's hegemony.

Richard Walton speculates on some of the consequences of these forces on management practices. Identifying mutuality as the dominant theme for future policies, he anticipates radical changes in how managers will organize and motivate people.[20] Table 4.1 compares his predictions of emerging practices with traditional practices.

Whether this particular pattern of emerging practices is correct and imminent or just how these changes will play themselves out are open to question. Moreover, as with any management practices, the general manager must judge how they fit with the organization's strategy and the values of its people. But

Table 4.1 Human resource management models.

Policy Areas	Traditional Control Model	New Commitment Model
Job design principles	Individual attention limited to performing individual job Job design "deskills" and fragments work and separates doing and thinking Accountability focused on individual Fixed job definition	Individual responsibility extended to upgrading system performance Job design enhances content of work, emphasizes whole task, and combines doing and thinking Frequent use of teams as basic accountable unit Flexible definition of duties contingent on changing conditions
Performance expectations	Measured standards define minimum performance Stability seen as desirable	Emphasis placed on higher, "stretch objectives," which tend to be dynamic and oriented to the marketplace
Management organization: structure, systems, and style	Structure tends to be layered, with top-down controls Coordination and control rely on rules and procedures More emphasis on prerogatives and positional authority Status symbols distributed to reinforce hierarchy	Flat organization structured with mutual influence systems Coordination and control based more on shared goals, values, and traditions Management emphasis on problem solving and relevant information and expertise Minimum status differentials to deemphasize inherent hierarchy
Compensation policies	Variable pay where feasible to provide individual incentive Individual pay geared to job evaluation In downturn, cuts concentrated on hourly payroll	Variable rewards to create equity and to reinforce group achievements: gain sharing, profit sharing Individual pay linked to skills, mastery Equality of sacrifice

Policy Areas	Traditional Control Model	New Commitment Model
Employment assurance	Employees regarded as variable costs	Assurance that participation will not result in job loss. High commitment to avoid or assist in reemployment. Priority for training and retaining existing work force
Management philosophy	Management's philosophy emphasizes management prerogatives and obligations to shareowners	Management's philosophy acknowledges multiple stakeholders: owners, employees, customers, and public

Source: Adapted from Richard E. Walton, "Toward a Strategy of Eliciting Employee Commitment Based on Policies of Mutuality," in *HRM Trends & Challenges* (Boston, 1985), pp. 37–40.

the point is that, for the general manager, familiarity with established practices is not sufficient. He or she must also be on the lookout for, and open to, new thinking for new times and new circumstances and must learn to distinguish between catchy management fads and valid progress.

The Importance of People

Well-designed organizational structures and processes can bring out the best in an enterprise's people. But these administrative mechanisms can help only to shape the clay; the quality of the clay itself is a vital factor in achieving excellence. Developing people with superior skills and attitudes is of paramount importance for the general manager.

While most general managers would agree unreservedly with this counsel, its implementation is often disappointing. As a staunch and successful advocate of people development, Andrall Pearson, former president of Pepsico, noted, in an unpublished speech in 1986:

> Despite the importance attached to people development, and the effort expended, very few companies—a handful, at best—succeed in assembling a dynamic cadre of accomplished managers.
>
> In the many companies that fail to get high marks for people development, there are, of course, many reasons for their lack of success. To begin with, there is no short-term payoff to emphasizing people development. Progress comes slowly, in contrast to shorter-term levers like strategy, or promotions or new products. So it is tempting to allow current volume pressures to overwhelm people development activities. . . . Also, people development is a detail-driven function, with few "home runs." So busy CEOs too often decide they're too busy to get deeply involved. And in many companies, the key managers have never seen first-hand the impact talented managers can exert on a business.

To these reasons can be added an understandable reluctance on the part of less talented managers to recruit or develop people who might outperform them.

As with improving the quality of strategic thinking, general managers must clearly signal their commitment to improving the quality of the organization's human resources in order to get others to support this effort. And as with so many other human endeavors, actions speak louder than words. The amount of attention and support the general manager devotes to this quest will be a prime motivator for subordinates.

Some of the principal areas for attention include recruiting, setting standards, performance reviews, job assignments, and training. The common reference point for all of these activities should be the kinds and levels of abilities and the attitudes the organization needs to succeed.[21] These attitudes have to do with commitment to quality performance, willingness to take risks, and adherence to other basic organizational values and aspirations.

The question of who should play what role in people development poses operational issues for the general manager to consider. As with conceptualizing new strategies, not everyone is equally gifted in developing people. Although the general manager should attempt to raise everyone's awareness of this process, the major burden will invariably rest on the shoulders of some line and staff managers. The roles that the personnel or human-resources staff and individual line managers should play will depend on the skills and interests of the specific people involved.

Pearson pointed out in the same speech the importance of setting higher performance expectations across the organization, using challenging job assignments, adjusting the work environment to help motivate talented managers, establishing a process for infusing talent at each organizational level, getting key line managers deeply involved, and making the personnel department a key player:

> The system I've just described takes a full-court press, over an extended period of time—and it affects nearly every aspect of running the business—strategy, work environment, resource allocation, operations and organization. That's why it's so hard to do it well.
>
> Personally, I found this whole process of people development to be the single most exciting, rewarding and important part of my job. I saw firsthand how this approach makes a difference—a tremendous difference—in the bottom line; in the strategic success; and in the fun people have when they come to work in the morning.
>
> That's why I'm convinced that building a dynamic management is top management's biggest challenge—and its best guarantee that the company will continue to be a leader, no matter how the competitive climate changes.

Success in upgrading people's skills and attitudes depends on a clearly thought-out approach and a determined, even dogged, effort to overcome inevitable organizational resistance, discouragement, and relaxation over time. Success also depends on the general manager's abilities as a leader to inspire others in this difficult task.

Notes

1. Each of these considerations commands its own field of study and discourse. It is not feasible in this volume to cover any of these topics in depth. Nor is it necessary for our purposes. The case studies touch on all of these organizing elements, but always in the context of a broader set of general management issues rather than as a central focus.

2. Kenneth R. Andrews, *The Concept of Corporate Strategy* (Homewood, Ill., 1980), p. 109.

3. Raymond E. Miles and Charles C. Snow, "Fit, Failure and the Hall of Fame," *California Management Review* 26, no. 3 (Spring 1984), 14–15. See also Miles and Snow, *Organizational Strategy, Structure, and Process* (New York, 1978).

4. Larry E. Greiner, "Evolution and Revolution as Organizations Grow," *Harvard Business Review* 50, no. 4 (July–August 1972), 37–46. The author maintains that organizations, as they mature, move through various distinguishable phases of growth, each of which contains a relatively calm period that ends with a management crisis.

5. Peter F. Drucker, *The Practice of Management* (New York, 1954), p. 247.

6. Richard T. Pascale, "Perspectives on Strategy: The Real Story Behind Honda's Success," *California Management Review* 26, no. 3 (Spring 1984), 63, 64.

7. John F. Welch, Jr., "Competitiveness from Within—Beyond Incrementalism," Hatfield Fellow Lecture, Cornell University, April 12, 1984.

8. Richard Beckhard and Reuben T. Harris, *Organizational Transitions: Managing Complex Change* (Reading, Mass., 1977).

9. David A. Nadler, "Managing Organizational Change: An Integrative Perspective," *Journal of Applied Behavioral Science* 17, no. 2, (1981), 191, 211. For a comprehensive discussion of the corporate renewal process, see Michael Beer, Russell A. Eisenstat, and Bert Spector, *The Critical Path to Corporate Renewal* (Boston, 1990).

10. The notion of freezing the change is put forward by Kurt Lewin, *Field Theory in Social Sciences* (New York, 1951) and L. E. Schaller, *The Change Agent* (Nashville, Tenn., 1978), among others.

11. Robert Blake and Jane S. Mouton, *Productivity: The Human Side* (New York, 1982).

12. Charles O'Reilly, "Corporations, Culture, and Commitment: Motivation and Social Control in Organizations," *California Management Review* 31, no. 4 (Summer 1989), 9–25. See also Charles O'Reilly and Jennifer Chatman, "Organizational Commitment and Psychological Attachment: The Effects of Compliance, Identification and Internalization on Prosocial Behavior," *Journal of Applied Psychology* 71 (1986), 492–99. While the comment is about commitment to the firm in general, it also applies directly to the organization in its changed state.

13. Kenneth A. Merchant, *Rewarding Results* (Boston, 1989), pp. 9–10.

14. C. K. Prahalad and Gary Hamel, "The Core Competence of the Corporation," *Harvard Business Review* 68, no. 3 (May–June 1990), 79–91.

15. Michael E. Porter, *Competitive Advantage* (New York, 1985), pp. 395–407.

16. Michael Beer, Bert Spector, Paul R. Lawrence, D. Quinn Mills, and Richard E. Walton, *Managing Human Assets* (New York, 1984), p. 92.

17. Ibid., pp. 91, 92.

18. Paul R. Lawrence, "The History of Human Resource Management in American Industry," in *HRM Trends & Challenges* (Boston, 1985), p. 15.

19. *Wall Street Journal*, April 14, 1986, p. 1.

20. Richard E. Walton, "Toward a Strategy of Eliciting Employee Commitment Based on Policies of Mutuality," in *HRM Trends & Challenges*, pp. 35–65.

21. Donald C. Hambrick, "The Top Management Team: Key to Strategic Success," *California Management Review* 30, no. 1 (Fall 1987), 88–108. The author lays out a systematic approach for improving the top management team based on the following four questions: (1) What are the key external and internal contextual factors that define the senior-level managerial challenge? (2) What managerial qualities are needed (with respect to values, aptitudes, skills, knowledge, cognitive style, and demeanor)? (3) What managerial qualities now exist? and (4) How should the gaps be narrowed? Some measures for narrowing the gaps include replacing people, adding people, upgrading people through training and development, and using outsiders (e.g., consultants, experts). If critical gaps cannot be sufficiently reduced, then senior management might inquire if the contextual factors could be changed.

5

The General Manager as Leader

The general manager is responsible for the overall performance and well-being of an enterprise. Whether this enterprise is the whole firm, an operating division, or some lesser, relatively autonomous unit within it, the general manager must ensure that there are people in the organization able and willing to conceptualize a sound strategy and to carry it out in a timely and forceful fashion. These accomplishments, taken as a whole, constitute organizational leadership. They have to do with giving an organization its vision of the future and its impetus to translate that vision into reality.

Earlier chapters focused on *what* the general manager should consider and do. Still missing is a look at *how* the general manager breathes life and enthusiasm into the organization as its leader.

Leaders

"Managers are people who do things right; leaders are people who do the right things." This catchy definition make the important distinction between efficiency (doing things right) and effectiveness (doing the right things). But it is not wholly acceptable in light of this book's treatment of the general manager. First, the opposite of the leader in our sense is the bureaucrat, not the manager. In our view, the job of the general manager is to lead *and* to manage.[1] Second, the general manager is responsible for ensuring that the right things happen, not necessarily for doing them.

What sets general managers apart from many other kinds of leaders is the presence of authority and power. According to James MacGregor Burns:

> Executive leaders have effective power (rather than merely formal authority) to the degree that they can activate the need and motivational bases of other leaders and subordinates in the organization. This power in essence is the traditional power to reward and penalize—but what do the respondents or power recipients consider to be rewards and penalties? In a large

organization these motivations are likely to be as varied as human needs can be—not only for security, higher income, and better working conditions but for affection, recognition, deference, esteem, and for both autonomy toward and dependence on the executive leader, for both conformity and individuality—traits that can exist in the same person. Other things being equal, the stronger the motivational base the leader taps, the greater control over that person the leader can exercise.[2]

But even if leaders have authority and power, Burns views authentic executive leadership as a collective process, involving a mutuality of interests. In their study of organizational leadership, Louis Barnes and Mark Kriger also advise against equating leaders with formal authority. In their view, anyone taking initiative in defining and fostering change is a leader, be that anyone boss, subordinate, or one of several people interacting with each other: "Managers inevitably occupy *both* leadership and followership positions due to the very nature of organizational hierarchies. All bosses, including CEO's, are also subordinate to other people or pressures."[3] They go on to define organizational leadership as a multiperson phenomenon, "where leader roles overlapped, complemented each other and shifted from time to time and from person to person."

From this perspective, the general manager's role as leader could be seen as fostering leadership by others. This is not to say that general managers can simply sit back and wait for the right things to happen. In their leadership capacity, they must, at the very least, create conditions conducive to making the right things happen, be prepared and able to recognize when the right things are happening, and support these initiatives with the power and influence of their office. In effect, then, *general managers as leaders are people who ensure that the right things get done.*

Leadership

An important distinction can be made between a general manager who gets people to achieve specific goals and one who gets people to achieve specific goals *and* develops a self-actualizing belief system or culture. Both are exercising leadership. But, to borrow Burns' terms, the first is dealing with *transactions,* the second is *transforming* the character of the organization.[4] A political leader who forms an alliance of several nations to counter a military threat, a corporate executive who organizes a coalition of companies to partition a takeover target, or an individual who hires casual laborers to harvest a crop are all engaged in transactional leadership. When the task is completed, participation ceases. In contrast, senior executives in companies that enjoy long-term success—such as Hewlett-Packard, Unilever, and Honda—are largely engaged in transformational leadership. Although both forms of leadership are valid undertakings for the general manager, the remainder of this chapter will focus primarily on transformational leadership, since it is the more complex and comprehensive of the two, and ultimately the more important.

Philip Selznick argues that the most vital mission of the leader is to infuse an organization with values so that it becomes prized for its own sake. Distinguishing between an organization as a technical instrument for achieving specific goals and an organization as an institutional fulfillment of group integrity and aspiration, he defines the leader as an agent of institutionalization:

> [T]he task of building values and a distinctive competence into the organization is a prime function of leadership. . . . The task of leadership is not only to make policy but to build it into the organization's social structure. This, too, is a creative task. It means shaping the "character" of the organization, sensitizing it to ways of thinking and responding, so that increased reliability in the execution and elaboration of policy will be achieved according to its spirit as well as its letter.[5]

Burns echoes Selznick:

> Some define leadership as leaders making followers do what followers would not otherwise do, or as leaders making followers do what the leaders want them to do. I define leadership as leaders inducing followers to act for certain goals that represent the values and the motivations—the wants and needs, the aspirations and expectations—of both leaders and followers. And the genius of leadership lies in the manner in which leaders see and act on their own and their followers' values and motivations.[6]

And Edgar Schein makes the strongest case for transformational or institutional (Selznick's term) leadership: "[T]he *only thing of real importance that leaders do is to create and manage culture.*"[7] He goes on to describe mechanisms for institutionalizing values:

> The most powerful primary mechanisms for culture embedding and reinforcement are (1) what leaders pay attention to, measure, and control; (2) leader reactions to critical incidents and organizational crises; (3) deliberate role modeling, teaching, and coaching by leaders; (4) criteria for allocation of rewards and status; (5) criteria for recruitment, selection, promotion, retirement, and excommunication. . . .
>
> The most important secondary articulation and reinforcement mechanisms are (1) the organization's design and structure; (2) organizational systems and procedures; (3) design of physical space, facades, and buildings; (4) stories, legends, myths, and parables about important events and people; (5) formal statements of organizational philosophy, creeds, and charters.
>
> I have labeled these mechanisms "secondary" because they work only if they are consistent with the primary mechanisms discussed previously. When they are consistent, they begin to build organizational ideologies and thus to formalize much of what is informally learned at the outset. If they are inconsistent, they either will be ignored or will be a source of internal conflict. But the operating cultural assumptions will always be manifested first in what the leaders demonstrate, not in what is written down or inferred from designs and procedures.[8]

Indeed, almost any administrative procedure might have a bearing on the distinctive role and character of the enterprise. The institutional leader has to be sensitive to the possible impact any proposed changes might have on the maintenance or enhancement of desired values.

Leading

There are many different ways in which a general manager can lead, but they all seem to share certain common elements, including espousing a vision of purpose, gaining organizational commitment to this vision of purpose, and providing the wherewithall to carry it out.

Vision. In their book on leaders, Warren Bennis and Burt Nanus write: "[A] vision articulates a view of a realistic, credible, attractive future for the organization, a condition that is better in some important ways than what now exists. . . . With a vision, the leader provides the all-important bridge from the present to the future of the organization."[9] The power of such vision is in its ability to energize the emotional and spiritual resources of the organization. High rank and formal authority are not necessary or sufficient conditions. The enthusiasm leaders have for their vision probably does as much as anything to infect others with its message.

Sheer enthusiasm, of course, is not enough. A vision must be understandable, credible, and uplifting. The vision Thomas J. Watson, Sr., had for IBM to become a dominant force in the information-processing field certainly met these requirements, as the following account testifies: "Preachers know good sermons make at most three points, and the Watson philosophy was simple, too. One, give the best service of any company in the world. Two, strive for superior performance. Three—the one IBMers think is the most important—respect the individual."[10]

The message was clear and straightforward. Its credibility rested on the good business sense of the practices espoused. Its power to inspire derived from the appeal to basic human values favoring respect for each other and excellence of performance.

As Bennis and Nanus observed:

> Great leaders often inspire their followers to high levels of achievement by showing them how their work contributes to worthwhile ends. It is an emotional appeal to some of the most fundamental human needs—the need to be important, to make a difference, to feel useful, to be a part of a successful and worthwhile enterprise.[11]

Such inspiration may be directed upward to include superiors, sideways to peers, downward to the ranks of workers, and outward to members of the board of directors, to shareholders, and even to union, governmental, and other social leaders.

Vision is viewed as a basic building block in our examination of leadership, and if we increase the magnification of our analytical microscope and train it on vision itself, we can see that it too has its own stages of development. A vision that is valid, understandable, credible, and uplifting is an end product in its own right. Occasionally, such a vision may spring full blown from the mind of an individual in a flash of inspiration, as Eve from the rib of Adam. More often, it evolves over time, taking on substantive changes and polish with the growth of insight and eloquence. In its earliest stages, vision might be no more than a nagging feeling that something is wrong (a dissatisfaction with the status quo). Yet even a vision as fuzzy and vestigal as "We seem to be headed for trouble and need to do something different" can serve as a catalyst for change. This was essentially Borch's state of mind in the late 1960s as he viewed the General Electric Company. Fifteen years later the company's chief executive officer, Jack Welch, articulated the resultant vision:

> A decade from now I would like General Electric to be perceived as a unique, high-spirited, entrepreneurial enterprise . . . a company known around the world for its unmatched level of excellence. I want General Electric to be the most profitable highly diversified company on earth, with world-quality leadership in every one of its product lines.[12]

Commitment. A general manager must become an impassioned spokesman for his or her vision in order to get others in the organization to understand, agree with, and finally to identify with it. Of course, we chuckle at the wry inconsistency of an executive admonishing his subordinates, "I want you to adopt a participative management style, or else." But the CEO who unabashedly accepts a big bonus while preaching the need for others to cut costs and tighten belts deserves the cynical response he or she is likely to receive. More likely to succeed is the way John Connelly went about getting commitments to cost cutting and customer service as the means to save Crown Cork and Seal Company from bankruptcy in 1957. He not only preached this message, he lived it:

> At Crown, all customers' gripes go to John Connelly, who is still the company's best salesman. A visitor recalls being in his office when a complaint came through from the manager of a Florida citrus-packing plant. Connelly assured him the problem would be taken care of immediately, then casually remarked that he planned to be in Florida the next day. Would the plant manager join him for dinner? He would indeed. As Crown's president put the telephone down, his visitor said that he hadn't realized Connelly was planning to go to Florida. "Neither did I," confessed Connelly, "until I began talking."[13]

Consistency of word and deed on the leader's part is absolutely necessary if others are to commit themselves to the personal and business risks associated with new and unproven courses of action. The general manager who runs hot and cold on issues will fail to encourage confidence in others—superiors and peers as well as subordinates. Nobody wants to go out on a limb and risk being abandoned at the first sound of cracking wood.

Although the consistency and forcefulness of a leader's articulation of vision and its inherent soundness are of critical importance, they will not guarantee commitment. The audience also has to be receptive to its consideration if commitment is ever to occur. This receptivity is a function of an organization's belief system.

All organizations depend on the existence of shared beliefs and ways of interpreting ideas and events to cope with complexity and ambiguity. A well-developed belief system provides powerful guidelines and impetus for organizational action. But such beliefs, when no longer appropriate to changed conditions, can become just as harmful to an organization's functioning. The following observation about basic organizational beliefs by Gordon Donaldson and Jay W. Lorsch really applies to all the organization's members:

> These beliefs are often a major barrier to strategic change because top executives have become so emotionally committed to them that they are unwilling—or unable—to alter practices that have been successful in the past. Events that transform the conditions under which a particular industry or firm operates are therefore difficult to accommodate. . . . Consequently, we argue that the ability to manage these psychological constraints is an important key to the success of individual companies and to the economy as a whole.[14]

The importance of managing the belief system is also made by Bennis and Nanus, who define social architecture as the norms and values that shape behavior in any organized setting:

> Social architecture, as we have continually emphasized, provides *meaning*. The key point is that if an organization is to be transformed, the social architecture must be revamped. The effective leader needs to articulate new values and norms, offer new visions, and use a variety of tools in order to transform, support, and institutionalize new meanings and directions.[15]

The general manager, at the very least, has to discredit established beliefs inimical to the new vision. Better yet, of course, is to institutionalize supportive beliefs.

Empowerment. A person committed to a new vision can do little if he or she does not have the necessary wherewithal to carry it out. To enable an organization to convert vision into reality, the general manager must ensure that the change agents (the general manager and/or others) are provided with what Rosabeth Kanter describes as " 'three basic commodities' that can be invested in action: *information* (data, technical knowledge, political intelligence, expertise); *resources* (funds, materials, space, time); and *support* (endorsement, backing, approval, legitimacy)."[16]

With vision, commitment, information, resources, and support, the scene is set for things to happen. We look next at how the general manager can go about energizing these ingredients.

Leadership Styles

People can perform the vital functions of leadership in very different ways. The general managers in the case studies that follow went about "getting the right things done" in their own manner. Some appeared more leaderlike than others, but such appearances can be deceiving. It is important not to confuse form with substance in evaluating general managers as leaders. What good these individuals accomplish is the true measure, not the manner in which they go about the task.

The style of leadership a general manager adopts depends on the situation and on his or her personality traits. The interplay between these two factors is complex. Some situations may favor one style; other situations may be largely indifferent to style. Some individuals can vary their style to accord with the situation; others cannot.

Leadership styles are complex and varied, depending as they do on many behavioral details. One way to consider leadership style is to look at how an individual goes about influencing others. Leaders can rely on their charisma as the prime force for change, on their mission or goals, on organizational processes, or on negotiating with key participants (those who are to carry out the mission and those who must approve). This delineation of leadership approaches or styles, however, is a matter of emphasis only. Rarely, if ever, in complex situations will a leader not employ multiple avenues of influence, often concomitantly.

Leading Through Charisma. For many people, the word *leader* evokes a romantic picture of a towering figure on a white horse, pointing the way to victory and projecting strength and wisdom. In a more contemporary vein, Winston Churchill, Charles de Gaulle, Eleanor Roosevelt, Mahatma Ghandi, Mao Tse-tung, John F. Kennedy, Pope John XXIII, and Martin Luther King, Jr., might be mentioned as examples of great leaders. And in the world of business and commerce, the names Ford, Wallenberg, Olivetti, Honda, Morita, Hewlett, and Packard are synonymous with leadership.

Charismatic leadership can be associated with three types of behavior.[17] The first, *envisioning*, involves the articulation of a desired future state that is challenging, credible, and worthy of pursuit. By creating vision, the leader provides a psychological focal point for the energies, hopes, and aspirations of people in the organization. The second, *energizing*, involves motivating people to act. Typically, charismatic business leaders leverage their own personal excitement and energy through direct contact with large numbers of people in the organization. The third, *enabling*, involves helping people to accomplish their tasks. This help might be in the nature of advice and additional resources. Or it might be in showing empathy for people's feelings and in expressing confidence in their ability to succeed in meeting the challenge.

Charismatic leaders serve as powerful role models whose behavior and enthusiasm set standards to which others can aspire. Supporters can become disciples, motivated by a deep, at times blind, personal trust of the leader.

Leading Through Mission and Goals. What characterizes these leaders is the emphasis they place on their mission or on specific goals, to motivate others. The cause or target serves as the fulcrum for change and action. "Being num-

ber one or number two in your industry" and "Making the world's most powerful computers," compelling rally cries for Jack Welch of General Electric and
John Rollwagen of Cray Research, provide a basis for inspiring and guiding
action.

In his Pulitzer Prize-winning account of the development of a new computer, John Kidder provides an excellent illustration of the enormous motivational power a mission can have on people. The challenge of designing a computer that could outperform the successful model of the archrival Digital
Equipment Corporation as well as the in-house officially sanctioned Data General computer development project drove Tom West and his ad hoc engineering team to work day and night. Their goal-oriented behavior is captured in
the following comments. West recruited the team: "We had the best high-energy
story to tell a college graduate. They'd all heard about VAX. Well, we were
gonna build a thirty-two-bit machine less expensive, faster and so on. You can
sign up a guy to that any day of the year. And we got the best there was." For
months during the project, Rasala, one of the hardware engineers, would come
home and tell his wife he had had a terrible day.

> But as he went on describing the day's events, his wife noticed, he be-
> came increasingly excited.
>
> "Maybe it's masochism," Rasala said, "But I guess the reason I do it
> fundamentally is that there is a certain satisfaction in building a machine
> like this, which is important to the company, which is on its way to becom-
> ing a billion-dollar company. There aren't that many opportunities in this
> world to be where the action is, making an impact." It struck him as para-
> doxical, all this energy and passion, both his own and that of the engineers
> around him, being expended for a decidedly commercial purpose. But that
> purpose wasn't his own. . . .
>
> Rasala said, "I was looking for"—he ticked the items off on his fingers—
> "opportunity, responsibility, visibility."
>
> What did these words mean to him, though?
>
> Rasala shrugged his shoulders. "I wanted to see what I was worth," he
> explained.[18]

Leaders espousing a mission or goal tend to confront key issues directly
and openly. Within legal and ethical limits, anything that contributes to the
desired end is sanctioned; anything that impairs its accomplishment is repu-
diated. Since a sense of right versus wrong prevails, this approach can involve
organizational conflicts resulting in winners and losers.

Leading Through Process. In his penetrating analysis of the Cuban missile
crisis, Graham Allison identified organizational features and procedures as one
possible explanation for the behavior observed and the decisions taken. In support of this view, he argued that the "preeminent feature of organizational
activity is its programmed character: the extent to which behavior in any particular case is an enactment of preestablished routines."[19]

Organization structure and management systems are powerful instruments
for directing behavior. A general manager can promote and guide action by

orchestrating the organizational context. In describing his reasons for reorganizing General Electric's sector structure, Jack Welch gives a dramatic illustration of this approach to leadership:

> Why did we reorganize this time? G.E. Information Services with all their networking and G.E. Credit were in two different places, under two different sector executives. We were convinced there was synergy in tying networking to financial services. The best way to do it . . . crash them together. Let the new sector head figure it out.[20]

Goals, compensation schemes, information networks, and approval structures are other aspects of an organization that can be modified and orchestrated by a general manager to promote and guide action in desired directions. Decisions in such matters as who is to be involved in key activities, timing, and the openness of debate can influence thinking and swing support one way or another.

General managers who are effective in structuring and using organizational context as a primary means of motivating people are sensitive to the limits of this approach. While rules, structures, and systems guide actions in general, situations calling for exceptional treatment are bound to arise. In his sociological study of bureaucratic organizations, Michel Crozier argues that a manager imposing rules must retain some freedom of action:

> To achieve his aims, the manager has two sets of conflicting weapons: rationalization and rule-making on one side; and the power to make exceptions and to ignore the rules on the other. His own strategy will be to find the best combination of both weapons, according to the objectives of the unit of which he is in charge and to the degree to which members of the unit are interested in these objectives. Proliferation of the rules curtails his own power. Too many exceptions to the rules reduce his ability to check other people's power.[21]

Crozier's reference to other people's power and his reasoning that a manager be open to making exceptions to the rules in order to accommodate such power touches on another approach to leading.

Leading Through Negotiations. With this approach, a leader seeks to achieve accord by accommodating those people with power to affect the organization's ability and willingness to change. The vision, which might be explicit or vague, serves more to guide the leader than to inspire others..

In their writings on leadership, Joseph Badaracco and Richard Ellsworth give the following rationale for this leadership style:

> Companies are rarely harmonious communities of benign, cooperating individuals who pursue broad strategic goals determined by rational analysis. Much more commonly, they are political arenas in which individuals jockey and bargain to advance their own interests and those of the organizational units for which they are responsible. . . . Executives who can maneuver astutely within and gently nudge the complex, often intense politics of a company can gain leverage over the centrifugal forces of politics and

can focus company efforts on strategic objectives—without running rough-shod over the autonomy and decentralization that their capable subordinates demand.[22]

This comment relates to senior-level executives. Clearly, the need to maneuver astutely in such an environment becomes even greater for lower-level general managers who lack the power to force their ideas on others, let alone run roughshod.

The principal skill for this approach is in finding and exploiting commonalities of interest as a means of gaining support, or at least of reducing opposition. This can be a slow and fragmented process as the leader probes for such commonalities of interest or waits for opportune occasions. This approach is characterized by negotiations, compromise, opportunism, incremental advances, and hidden agendas.

Personal Qualities of a Successful General Manager

In examining the general-management function and the general manager as manager and leader, we covered a wide range of considerations concerning responsibilities and concepts. But what about the person? As the cases make clear, there is no optimal model to describe the successful practitioner. He or she can be outgoing or private, dynamic or reflective, conceptual or empirical, tough or compassionate. Successful general managers defy any precise specifications, but they do seem to share certain personal characteristics: knowledge and skills, commitment, integrity, concern for others, resiliency, presence, and judgment.

Knowledge and Skills. Successful general managers typically have bright and facile minds. Although intellectual brilliance is not necessary—and might even be a hindrance if not tempered with action-oriented qualities—a general manager must reason well, make decisions in uncertain circumstances, and adapt as circumstances change—all of which call for above-average general intelligence.

Being well-informed about one's industry—its technology, customer expectations, and competitive practices—and about one's company—its culture, practices, and key people—is also valuable for the general manager. Admittedly, there is some controversy as to whether a good general manager can be effective in any setting or must rely on industry- and company-specific experience. The transferability of the general manager's capabilities to manage and lead in different settings probably depends on the specific situation and on the nature of his or her experiences.

The broad responsibilities of the general manager's job call for a breadth and diversity of managerial experience. Reporting on a study comparing successful senior executives with promising managers who plateaued or failed at high levels, Morgan McCall and Michael Lombardo pointed to characteristic differences in their track records:

Derailed executives had a series of successes, but usually in similar situations: they had turned a business around more than once, or they had
managed progressively larger jobs, but in the same function. By contrast,
the arrivers had more diversity in their successes—they had turned a business around *and* successfully moved from line to staff and back; or they had
started a new business from scratch *and* completed a special assignment
with distinction. . . . They showed a breadth of perspective and interest
that resulted (over 20 to 30 years) in detailed knowledge of many parts of
the business, as well as first-hand experience with *different kinds* of challenges.[23]

Since the general manager must work through others, he or she also must
have command of important administrative skills—such as how to organize
work and people, how to assemble a strong staff, and how to delegate. For
most complex business situations, no individual, no matter how brilliant and
energetic, can achieve as much as a well-trained and well-organized group of
talented people under gifted leadership.

Commitment. Senior executives devote long hours to their work. The enormous challenges general managers face in directing large, complex organizations invariably require hard work and a strong commitment to purpose. Ambition and self-sacrifice are common traits contributing to success. Good physical
and mental health is another invaluable asset for the general manager working
under pressure over time and facing inevitable obstacles, inertia, and setbacks.

Integrity. Trust plays a greater role in organizational life as one moves up
the management hierarchy, reflecting the increasing complexity and impreci-
sion of the work and relationships. For this reason, integrity—a generally desirable human quality—takes on special importance for the general manager.
McCall and Lombardo stress this point:

> One senior executive . . . said that he thought only two things differ-
> entiated the successful from the derailed—total integrity and understanding
> other people.
>   Integrity seems to have a special meaning to executives that is vastly
> different from its mom-and-apple-pie image. The word does not refer to
> simple honesty, but embodies a consistency and predictability built over
> time that says, "I will do exactly what I say I will do when I say I will do it.
> If I change my mind, I will tell you well in advance so you will not be
> harmed by my actions." Such a statement is partly one of ethics, but more,
> it may be one of deadly practicality. This seems to be the core method of
> keeping a large, amorphous organization from collapsing in its own confu-
> sion.[24]

Concern for Others. The most frequent cause for derailment, according to the
McCall and Lombardo report, was insensitivity to others.[25] A general manager's genuine respect and concern for others—subordinates, peers, superiors,

customers, and suppliers—form the basis for the cooperative interaction so vital to his or her functioning. As common experience would suggest, when managers fail to treat some parties with respect, others are likely to become more cautious in their view of management's true intentions. In like manner, when business leaders show concern for people on some occasions and are insensitive to them on others, their integrity is called into question. In both cases, it might be that senior management simply fails to recognize the moral dimension of the actions in question because it tends to view business ethics as concerned with big issues. But the aggrieved parties and sympathetic onlookers will recognize the disrespect and injustice. Moreover, they are likely to attribute management's behavior more to arrogance and self-serving than to oversight, since management is supposed to know what it is doing.

Resiliency. Everyone makes mistakes, and successful general managers are no exception. What separates these people from others is their ability to learn from their mistakes, to work on correcting the problems rather than on fault-finding, and to move on. Lee Iococca rebuilding from his painful fall from grace at Ford was a recent exemplar of resiliency.

Setbacks and failures, distressing as they may be, have their benefits. They can often be more powerful learning experiences than successful endeavors. And they can help the successful manager gain humility—a trait far preferable to arrogance in dealing with others.

Presence. General managers must ask a lot of their staffs and of others. People respond because they have confidence in the general manager's ability to handle the situation and to achieve purpose. To gain and hold this confidence, a general manager has to project personal maturity and competence. This is true especially in times of adversity. Falling apart, lashing out, or withdrawing are examples of behavior bound to undermine the grounds for trust.

Judgment. If knowledge and skill are the foundation of essential qualities for a person to perform well as a general manager, good judgment is the capstone. It is this quality to which GE's Jack Welch referred in extolling "street smarts" as critical to a general manager's effectiveness.

The general manager typically has to deal with an overwhelming array of demands, including problems that are messy, confusing, and insolvable. As such, he or she must be able to distinguish between what is important and what is not, what to do and what not to do. The kinds of judgment called for suggest a foundation in native good sense coupled with intellectual qualities that enable one to discern facts or conditions that are not obvious, to comprehend the significance of those facts and conditions, and to draw correct unbiased conclusions from them. To paraphrase Samuel Taylor Coleridge, judgment is common sense to an uncommon degree.

Success for the General Manager

In the case studies, we shall see general managers in action, dealing with a wide variety of issues in a wide variety of situations. The one common concern of all these studies is how well the individual performed as general manager.

To answer this question, we must consider how well the general manager has discharged his or her responsibility for the performance and well-being of the enterprise. Has he or she created a vision of what the enterprise is to be and how it is to get there? Has he or she developed the organizational ability and willingness to carry out this vision? Has he or she ensured timely and proper actions?

In accomplishing these broad tasks, the general manager ensures the achievement of purpose. This is one measure of success for the general manager. But beyond the achievement of purpose is the creation of an organization valued for its own sake. Selznick notes the following measure of success: "Successful institutions are usually able to fill in the formula, "What we are proud of around here is . . .' "[26] What better accolade could the general manager want?

Notes

1. Abraham Zaleznik argues persuasively to the contrary in his popular article "Managers and Leaders: Are they Different?" *Harvard Business Review* 55, no. 3 (May–June 1977) 67–78, and in his book *The Managerial Mystique* (New York, 1989). John P. Kotter also elaborates the differences between management and leadership, but concludes that when it comes to preparing people for executive jobs, companies attempt to develop leader-managers, ignoring the literature that says people cannot manage *and* lead (*A Force for Change: How Leadership Differs from Management* [New York, 1990]).
2. James MacGregor Burns, *Leadership* (New York, 1978), p. 373. According to Leonard R. Sayles, even in business, managers must earn authority and deference, whatever their titles. He writes: "To exercise authority, leaders/managers must learn how to: (1) Arouse followers to accept orders and initiations; (2) Gain credibility as a legitimate source of initiations; [and] (3) Cope with confrontations in which orders are ignored or disputed." *Leadership*, 2nd ed. (New York, 1989), p. 37.
3. Louis B. Barnes and Mark P. Kriger, "The Hidden Side of Organizational Leadership," *Sloan Management Review* (Fall 1986), pp. 15–25.
4. Burns, *Leadership*, p. 4. Strictly speaking, Burns uses the concept of transformational leadership in connection with the effects on the individuals involved.
5. Philip Selznick, *Leadership in Administration* (New York, 1957), pp. 27, 62–63.
6. Burns, *Leadership*, p. 19.
7. Edgar H. Schein, *Organizational Culture and Leadership* (San Francisco, 1985), p. 2.
8. Ibid., pp. 224, 225, and 237.
9. Warren Bennis and Burt Nanus, *Leaders* (New York, 1985), pp. 89, 90.
10. "Behind the Monolith: A Look at IBM," *Wall Street Journal*, April 7, 1986, p. 25.
11. Bennis and Nanus, *Leaders*, p. 93.
12. "General Electric: 1984," Harvard Business School case number 9–385–315, 1985.
13. *Fortune*, October 1962, p. 164.
14. Gordon Donaldson and Jay W. Lorsch, *Decision Making at the Top* (New York, 1983), p. 8.

15. Bennis and Nanus, *Leaders*, p. 139.

16. Rosabeth Moss Kanter, *The Change Masters* (New York, 1983), p. 159.

17. David A. Nadler and Michael L. Tushman, "Beyond the Charismatic Leader: Leadership and Organizational Change," *California Management Review* 32, no. 2 (Winter 1990), 82–85.

18. John Tracy Kidder, *The Soul of a New Machine* (Boston, 1981), pp. 64, 153.

19. Graham T. Allison, *Essence of Decision* (Boston, 1971), p. 81. Allison proposes three models of cause and effect to serve as possible explanations for the way in which U.S. authorities handled the Cuban missile crisis: (1) the rational-actor model, in which decisions were made on the basis of calculated choices to serve national interests; (2) the organizational-process model, in which decisions reflected the outputs of established procedures for participation (protocols as to who would be involved and how); and (3) the political model, in which decisions were a result of various bargaining games among players in the national government. These three models bear some resemblance to the leadership styles under discussion.

20. "General Electric Company: Dr. John F. Welch, Jr.," Harvard Business School videotape 882–024, 1982.

21. Michel Crozier, *The Bureaucratic Phenomenon* (Chicago, 1964), pp. 163, 164.

22. Joseph Badaracco and Richard Ellsworth, "Incremental Leadership," Harvard Business School publication 0–385–106, 1984, p. 2. They elaborate on this discussion in *Leadership and the Quest for Integrity* (Boston, 1988), pp. 17–37.

23. Morgan W. McCall, Jr., and Michael M. Lombardo, "Off the Track: Why and How Successful Executives Get Derailed" (Greensboro, N.C., Center for Creative Leadership, Technical Report 21, January 1983), p. 9.

24. Ibid., p. 11.

25. Ibid., p. 5.

26. Selznick, *Leadership in Administration*, p. 151.

6

Meeting the Global Business Challenge

In a 1990 listing of the world's ten largest public companies, only three were U.S. enterprises.[1] While the significance of this list could be questioned for including financial institutions as well as industrial companies and for ranking on the basis of market value instead of sales, the impression it gives of dispersed economic power is nonetheless valid. Twenty years ago, any list of largest industrial or financial firms would have been dominated by U.S. entities. Today, General Motors and Ford share automotive world leadership with Toyota and Nissan. Goodyear, the sole major survivor of the formerly dominant U.S. tire industry, must now compete with Michelin (France) and Bridgestone (Japan). Caterpillar has had to cede much of the earth moving equipment market to Komatsu. And in consumer electronics, the once proud leaders, GE and RCA, have given up the field to Matsushita, Sony, and other Japanese and Korean firms.

The trend toward internationalization has also affected individual corporations. For example, with standards for innovation, productivity, and service increasingly being set by Asian and European companies, the overwhelming domestic focus of many U.S. corporations has given way to a growing concern with global business considerations. In the 1980s, firms like Procter & Gamble, Eli Lilly, and General Electric made fundamental strategic commitments to develop strong competitive positions in the Far East, Western Europe, and other parts of the globe. The growing significance of global competition became increasingly clear to U.S. managers as foreign firms moved from exporting, to establishing plants and field sales operations in the United States, and even to engaging in friendly and unfriendly takeovers of U.S. firms.[2] Table 6.1 gives some idea of this last activity in listing the value and dates of the largest acquisitions of U.S. firms by Japanese firms. It also shows how foreign firms have taken over a major part of the U.S. entertainment industry through acquisitions. To fill out this picture, one must also consider the growing pace of

Table 6.1 Acquisitions of U.S. Firms by Foreign Companies.

U.S. Firms	Acquirer	Date	Value ($Million)
A. Largest U.S. Acquisitions by Japanese Companies			
MCA, Inc.	Matsushita Electric Ind.	Dec. '90	$6,590
Columbia Pictures	Sony Corporation	Nov. '89	3,410
Firestone Tire	Bridgestone	May '88	2,650
Intercontinental Hotels	Seibu Saison	Dec. '88	2,270
CBS Records	Sony Corporation	Jan. '88	2,000
Western Hotels and Resorts	Aoki Corp. (& Robt. Bass Gp.)	Oct. '87	1,530
CIT Group	Dai-Ichi Kangyo Bank	Dec. '89	1,280
Gould, Inc.	Nippon Mining	Nov. '88	1,050
Aristech Chemical Corp.	Mitsubishi Corporation	Jan. '90	859
Rockefeller Group	Mitsubishi Estate	May '90	850
Union Bank (Calif.)	Bank of Tokyo	June '88	750
Lyphomed, Inc.	Fujisawa Pharmaceutical	Oct. '89	670
B. Major Acquisitions of U.S. Entertainment Firms by Foreign Companies			
Motion Picture Studios			
Universal/MCA	Matsushita Electric (Japan)	Dec. '90	$6,590
MGM/UA	Pathe Communications (Italy)	Nov. '90	1,300
Columbia Pictures	Sony (Japan)	Nov. '89	3,400
20th Century Fox	News Corporation (Australia)	Mar. '85	575
Record Companies			
MCA/Geffen	Matsushita Electric (Japan)	(Part of Universal/ MCA Deal)	
A&M Records	Polygram/Philips (Neth.)	Oct. '89	460
Columbia	Sony (Japan)	Nov. '87	2,000
RCA	BMG/Bertelsmann (Germany)	Sep. '86	300
Technical Services			
Technicolor	Carlton Communications (U.K.)	Sep. '88	$ 780

Source: Wall Street Journal, November 27, 1990, pp. A3, A9, and *Boston Globe*, November 27, 1990, p. 5. Part A was attributed to IDD Information Services, Part B to BASELINE, Inc.

U.S. acquisitions by European firms—such as Norton (abrasives) by St. Gobain (France), SCM (chemicals) by Hanson (United Kingdom), and several of the transactions in part B of Table 6.1—and the other industries where many or most of the major U.S. competitors were acquired by foreign firms, such as consumer electronics and tires.

Many of the same forces for internationalization found in the United States are also at work in Western Europe and the Pacific-rim nations. The outcome of these developments is the creation of new strategic and organizational concepts. One of the many possible illustrations is Asea Brown Boveri, formed in 1980 by the merger of two venerable European manufacturers of electrical power systems and equipment. The global nature of this new entity is captured in the following comment by Percy Barnevik, president and chief executive officer:

> ABB is a company with no geographic center, no national ax to grind. We are a federation of national companies with a global coordination center. Are we a Swiss company? Our headquarters is in Zurich, but only 100 professionals work at headquarters and we will not increase that number. Are we a Swedish company? I'm the CEO, and I was born and educated in Sweden. But our headquarters is not in Sweden, and only two of the eight members of our board of directors are Swedes. Perhaps we are an American company. We report our financial results in U.S. dollars, and English is ABB's official language. We conduct all high-level meetings in English.
>
> My point is that ABB is none of those things—and all of those things. We are not homeless. We are a company with many homes.[3]

This chapter discusses the evolving scene in global business activities and the growing need for general managers to strive for *world-class* competitive advantage.

Pressures for Internationalization of Business Operations

What motivates large business organizations to expand international operations? For many, the most powerful inducement is the opportunity to increase sales and profits by extending successful business operations into new national markets. This impetus is often driven by a company's need to cover increasing product development and process technology costs. Other firms mount overseas operations to lower the costs of manufacturing, examples of which can be found in the sizable exodus of manufacturing operations from U.S. facilities to Taiwan, Singapore, Malaysia, and Mexico. Still other firms seek a window on technology, such as the Japanese and European firms that have set up operations in Silicon Valley, California, or on Route 128 near Boston. In a survey of CEOs representing over 400 North American, Western European, Japanese, and Asian Pacific corporations, at least 80 percent indicated access to larger and faster-growing markets as a reason for their firm's globalization efforts, 33 percent cited lower operating costs (inexpensive labor and raw materials), and 17 percent were seeking access to technology.[4]

Expanding international operations also enables a company to retaliate against competitive attacks. By having a business operation in its competitor's most profitable markets, a firm is in a position to dissuade aggressive forays into its own favored markets by threatening retaliation. For example, Unilever would be less likely to undercut Procter & Gamble's pricing for detergents in Brazil if P&G can strike back in Europe where Unilever has large market shares. A related reason is simply to be in a position to observe closely a major competitor's actions in an important base of operations.

When product specifications must be standardized, as in the design of consumer electronic items or aircraft communications equipment, a global presence can prove vital for a firm to get its favored approach adopted. As more firms assume global proportions, such standards are increasingly negotiated early in the development cycle. (The costly battle between Sony and Matsushita to establish respectively Beta and VHS configurations for VCR equipment and video tapes serves as a powerful lesson in this regard.) Gaining access to skillful people can also motivate an international move, as when U.S. technical firms set up operations in the United Kingdom during the 1960s to employ highly skilled engineers. And in some industries, having operations in certain centers of activity around the world offers important advantages; for example, New York, London, Tokyo for international finance and Paris, London, New York, and Rome for high fashion clothing accessories.

Besides obvious differences—such as size—the international business environment differs from the purely domestic one in that institutional and cultural factors often serve as powerful impediments to employing a single approach for a given business.[5] Sales promotion, service, product mix, and even product design might have to be altered to reflect local requirements. A second distinguishing characteristic is that factor costs, such as wages and the costs of materials and financing, can differ greatly from one country to another. A third is that language, time differences, and physical distance all complicate administrative and managerial functions.

While these variations present obstacles that complicate the managerial task, for the firm with worldwide business operations they also present opportunities for arbitrage and leverage that can result in competitive advantage.[6] For example, labor-intensive manufacturing operations might be placed in countries with low-cost labor, and high-technology manufacturing facilities can be set up in an area where critical support functions are readily available. Similarly, research can move to where skilled technical personnel are able to function most effectively. The firm with worldwide business operations also has an opportunity to lower its tax bill by its handling of transfer pricing and its choice of remittance payments (between royalties, fees, dividends, interest, and the repayment of principal). In a celebrated court case, Hoffman LaRoche was accused of charging £1,962 in the United Kingdom per kilo of active ingredient for producing the tranquilizer Valium, which cost only £77 to manufacture in Italy. In this instance, the high transfer price allegedly resulted in a higher retail price as well as a lower United Kingdom tax.[7]

Another opportunity for firms with worldwide business operations comes from their broadened access to capital markets and to financial incentives— such as subsidized loans, tax holidays, duty relief, and special credits—from countries promoting business investment. Both factors can contribute to lowering the cost of capital. Exposure to more and different sources of information and ideas can provide yet another competitive advantage to the internationally active firm. Technical innovations can arise in any country, as can innovations in marketing, product design, financing, and administrative practices. The firm with a wide array of observation posts is positioned to learn about such developments early and to benefit by introducing them to other parts of the world. In effect, a powerful advantage the international firm has over the domestic one is its greater ability to recognize innovative changes and to exploit the resulting opportunities.

The Changing World Business Scene

The growth of international competition reflects fundamental changes in underlying business conditions. The principal factors include markets, technology, capital, national and international policies, and events.

Markets

The growing post–World War II affluence of the countries of Western Europe and the Pacific-rim has transformed a global economic structure dominated by the United States into one with three dominant industrial and consumer regions, comparable in population and gross national product.[8] This transformation has had a profound effect on business. Large U.S. corporations can no longer assume that technical advantage or financial strength will ensure access to other markets. European and Japanese firms, in turn, have had to alter their competitive approaches to reflect the strengthening of their home markets and the growing business opportunities in other parts of the world.

Since the mid-1970s, the United States, Western Europe, and Japan have had to face problems associated with an uncertain oil supply, escalating social problems, aging populations, and expanding segments of economic stagnation. International expansion, which was motivated initially by the diminution of local business opportunities, was spurred on by the consequent appearance of new foreign competitors in a company's home territory. The difficulty of expanding abroad was eased somewhat by the increasing standardization of industrial product specifications (such as for machine tools, construction equipment, and chemicals) and the universal appeal of many new consumer products (such as for television sets, health care items, and detergents)—coupled with the emergent influence of television advertising. Growing purchasing power, increasing levels of education, and the development of worldwide news and advertising networks also have contributed to a homogenization of markets. As major end-product manufacturing firms expanded geographically, supplier firms—such as for automotive parts, chemicals, and electronic components—were motivated to follow suit.

Technology

Technological developments with respect to products and processes have altered patterns of comparative advantage (the use and cost of factors of production) and of product leadership. As high technology products mature, competitive advantage can shift from firms or nations with R&D strengths to those with manufacturing strengths or low factor costs. For example, the superior ability of Japanese firms to commercialize electronic innovations originating to a large extent in the United States, starting with the transistor in the 1950s and continuing through subsequent developments, resulted in their dominance of consumer electronics to a degree that would have been unthinkable twenty years ago. The early 1990s similarly finds Japanese firms maneuvering to compete in all segments of the computer market and to position themselves favorably in the emerging biochemical field.

Generally, technology-related costs have risen. Product development has become more expensive both because of the increasing complexity of the technologies involved and because of the increasing pace of product innovation. Process technology costs associated with automation, flexible manufacturing, and computer-aided design and manufacturing (CAD/CAM) have mounted. Meanwhile, the opportunities for recovering investments and making profits have diminished as the time for competing firms to copy or leapfrog innovations has declined. With increasing costs and a shorter product life, firms are compelled to find ways to spread their technology costs. The chances for a company to do so by expanding sales, sharing technology costs with another firm, or selling the innovations to noncompeting firms are enhanced by going beyond national boundaries. Also important is the fact that technology continues to facilitate international business operations through improvements in communications, data transfer, information handling, and air transportation.

Capital

Capital markets developed globally in support of expanding business operations. Some, like the Eurodollar bond market, have provided easy access to relatively inexpensive funds.[9] At the same time, a variety of derivative securities has evolved to assist firms in reducing risks associated with fluctuations of currency exchange rates and interest rates. Stock markets have grown in size and activity in Japan, Germany, and other countries, giving local firms greater access to equity capital, and foreign firms an expanded means for developing local ownership and presence. In apparent reaction to these developments, William H. Donaldson, chairman of the New York Stock Exchange, emphasized the need to expand greatly the number of foreign stocks trading on the "Big Board" as U.S. investors include more European and Far Eastern securities in their portfolios.[10] As advances in information networking technology lead to further integration of financial markets around the world, opportunities for innovative financing arrangements unfold, providing competitive advantage to those companies best able to exploit them.

National and International Policies

National industrial policies in Japan, Korea, and other nations have had a major impact on the evolution of international trade and of business in general. For example, the efforts by Japan's Ministry of International Trade and Industry (MITI) to gain leadership positions in industry after industry (e.g., steel, shipbuilding, automobiles, and consumer electronics in the early years and advanced computers and biotechnology in the 1980s) has helped to apply the nation's limited resources by focusing the business community's activities. Other countries—notably Argentina, the United Kingdom, the former German Democratic Republic, Poland, and Hungary—have strengthened the private sector of the economy by divesting state-owned enterprises. This movement toward "privatization" is most notable in Eastern Europe, where countries are attempting to convert from planned to market economies. Defense and social policies can also shape a nation's economic profile by creating markets for certain business activities and divesting funds from other business investments and consumption.

International concords to promote free trade, most notably the General Agreement on Tariffs and Trade (GATT), have improved conditions for worldwide business operations.[11] Trading blocs, such as the European Economic Community (EEC) and the European Free Trade Association (EFTA), also favored international expansion by coalescing fractured markets. European economic integration during the early 1990s is likely to result in major and long-lasting consequences favoring global business operations.

Events

General conditions and specific events can also shape the evolution of global business operations. For example, the strength of the U.S. dollar between 1981 and mid-1985 opened U.S. markets to imports while severely constraining the ability of U.S. firms to export. As the dollar weakened in subsequent years, many foreign firms were motivated to set up shop in the United States. Similarly, the economic downturn in 1990, coupled with a weakening of the dollar exchange rate, prompted and helped many U.S. firms to increase exports and to expand marketing operations abroad. The absence of a major war that could disrupt international trade has been another important favorable factor.[12] Finally, the surprisingly rapid end of the cold war and the opening of Eastern Europe have opened up many opportunities for international business operations.

Strategic Response

As discussed in chapter 4, at the most fundamental level of strategy senior management must concern itself with the *fit* between the dominant industry requirements and the firm's dominant capabilities. The need for fit is as true for a global business as it is for a domestic one. Some industries—where national preferences and tastes strongly favor distinctive products, such as furniture and prepared foods, or where governments demand direct control, such as telecommunications or defense—call for local responsiveness. Other industries—where cost savings based on economies of scale or comparative advantage outweigh idiosyncratic preferences, such as electronic components or athletic shoes—call for global integration. The classic responses to these archetypical competitive situations were the *multinational* (or multidomestic) strategy, in which each national organization is given considerable autonomy to facilitate local responsiveness, and the *global* strategy, in which operations for a product or business are integrated on a worldwide basis. Companies employing the multinational strategy typically organize along geographical lines, and those employing a global strategy along product lines. See Figure 6.1 for typical organizational structures.

In the multinational organization, each national unit is to be responsive to local requirements. As such, the organization can be characterized as a decentralized federation of assets and responsibilities managed as a portfolio of independent businesses.[13] The assemblage is typically coordinated through informal personal relationships and simple financial controls. The multinational structure was favored by many European firms, such as Philips and Unilever, that developed their overseas operations during a period of high tariffs and that were faced with the threat and the reality of dismemberment in two world wars. The global configuration, in contrast, is based on a centralization of assets, resources, and responsibilities. Management treats overseas operations as

Typical Product Divisional Organization

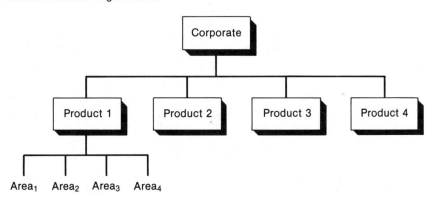

Typical Country or Area Organization

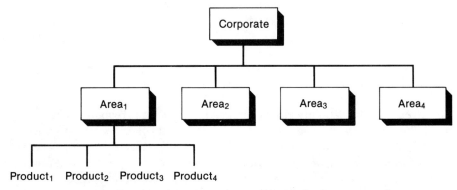

Figure 6.1 . Typical organizational structure for worldwide business operations.

delivery pipelines to a unified global market. This structure was favored by Japanese industrial firms entering the global arena primarily because the industries were those benefiting from mass production, continual product development requiring close coordination between engineering and manufacturing, and stringent quality controls. Moreover, Japan offered a comparative advantage with respect to wages, tariffs were relatively low, and management lacked experience with overseas operations. By way of analogy, the global structure can be likened to the use of a mainframe computer at headquarters with connections to dumb remote terminals in the field operations, while the multinational is comparable to the use of independent minicomputers for each operating unit.

While worldwide strategy is often characterized as a choice between global integration and local responsiveness, the general manager is rarely faced with such a straightforward choice. One reason is that most large companies offer products and services that are likely to differ in their requirements, with some calling for a global strategy, some a multinational approach, and some in between. A second reason is that different functional responsibilities are likely to face different requirements with respect to local sensitivity versus integration. For example, finance can benefit from being centralized, marketing is likely to be decentralized, and manufacturing might require both integration and local responsiveness. The functional organizational structures for some 100 international corporations, as depicted in Table 6.2, clearly show this effect.[14] This distinction can also be made in connection with the value chain discussed in chapter 2, where upstream activities (inbound logistics, operations, and outbound logistics in part, as well as the more fundamental aspects of technology, procurement, and human resource management) are more likely to benefit from integration, and downstream activities (marketing, after-sales service, outbound logistics, and those aspects of the support functions most closely tied to country operations) are more likely to relate to local responsiveness.[15] Finally, for any given functional responsibility, certain tasks are more likely to benefit from centralized handling and others are more closely connected to local responsiveness.[16] For example, for finance, raising equity funds is likely to be a headquarters responsibility, whereas acquiring seasonal funds is typically a local affair. Similarly, for marketing, product policy might best be handled centrally and promotional policies in the field.

Multifocal Organizations

The need to achieve both global integration and local responsiveness complicates the problem for the general manager. One of the early organizational responses was the *international* structure.[17] This structure features a strong headquarters capable of transferring knowledge and expertise to foreign units that are less advanced in technology and marketing expertise.[18] Many resources and responsibilities are decentralized but remain closely linked to

Table 6.2 Managerial Functional Areas (percent).

	Finance	Human Resource	Manufacturing	Sales and Distribution
Based in home country	57	44	25	9
Organized by region or center of excellence	22	22	45	25
Decentralized	21	34	30	66

headquarters through formal management planning and control systems. The international structure appealed to U.S. firms because of their strong domestic activities and their ability to exercise control through sophisticated management systems and specialist corporate staffs.[19]

As international competition heated up during the 1960s, 1970s, and 1980s, pressures for integration and for local responsiveness continued to mount. The international organization structure was unable to provide an adequate response where different parts of the business needed to adopt different organizational strategies and where the particular requirements were continually changing over time. Business practitioners began to look for a more flexible structure. An early attempt to provide this flexibility was the global matrix or grid, in which each business unit reported to a world product manager and to a country manager so that the demands for integration and for local responsiveness could both be taken into account in making strategic and operating decisions. Dow Chemical and other well-known companies championed this approach for years. However, the practice of reporting up two chains of command often had the effect of magnifying conflicts rather than resolving them, and ultimately the global matrix lost much of its appeal as a formal organizational structure.[20]

Companies like Procter & Gamble, Unilever, Ericsson, and Matsushita in the meantime had begun to adopt an approach that incorporates a diversity of arrangements within an overall structure.[21] Each found advantage in utilizing concurrently and selectively all three traditional strategies, centralizing some resources and responsibilities (global), distributing other resources and responsibilities to the national organizations (multinational), and maintaining centers of excellence that provide innovation and expertise to other units (international). Moreover, the assets and operations that are integrated for global economies and the centers of excellence are located and managed wherever greatest advantage is to be found, not necessarily in the home country. For example, a European company might have its research headquarters in the United States and its manufacturing center in Taiwan for one business and these functions at home for another. These moves reflect a recognition of the need to adopt different strategies and structures for different business operations within a single corporation. The resulting worldwide multifocal structure functions as a differentiated, interdependent network with large flows of components, products, resources, people, and information among the units. To continue the earlier computer analogy, the international structure can be likened to the use of a central mainframe connected to PCs capable of manipulating data and adopting solutions for local applications, and the emergent multifocal structure to the use of distributed powerful workstations connected in a network permitting different locations to play various lead roles in the systems.

This multifocal approach, which will be referred to as *transnational* to distinguish it from the matrix concept, can provide three important benefits.[22] One is efficiency. By organizing activities in accordance with the particular demands each faces—integration where economies can be gained or a critical mass is required (such as for research), and local responsiveness where called for—a transnational company can gain competitive advantage over firms emphasizing one approach or the other. The multinational firm risks offering appealing products at too high a price; the global firm risks offering low-priced products that are unappealing or that fail to conform to government restriction.

A second potential benefit is flexibility. As depicted in part A of Figure 6.2, traditionally structured corporations have their assets, skills, and relationships (supplier, customer, industry) locked into separate compartments—whether product or geographic divisions—that are possessive in their control and largely self-centered in their use of these elements. Cross-divisional cooperation and learning tend to be the exception rather than commonplace. The transnational approach attempts to free up these scarce resources so that they can be redeployed as competitive conditions change. As part B of Figure 6.2 illustrates, the corporate deployment of assets, skills, and relationships that were suitable for competing in 1992 can be reconfigured to adapt to altered competitive requirements in 1997. Moreover, by having in place a diversity of structure and the managerial capabilities for directing and linking the different elements, the transnational firm can adapt to changing circumstances far more quickly and effectively than can a firm with narrowly focused resources and experience. For example, if the balance between integration and local responsiveness were to shift toward the latter because of technological developments, such as CAD/CAM and flexible manufacturing, the general managers in a multifocal firm are more likely to be able to respond with actions that fall within their competencies.

A third advantage is with respect to sensitivity and learning. By having general managers in positions of leadership in different parts of the world, the transnational firm is better positioned to encounter and to act upon far more stimuli than a firm with senior managers all functioning in a single locality. In some cases the information gleaned, such as a new approach to selling a specific product, might initially be applied to a single activity and later be transferred and adapted to other locations and products. In other cases, the learning might apply to the entire organization, as when managers discover ways to improve internal communications or to inspire employee commitment.

Faced with a turbulent world, the transnational firm should be able to detect changes, opportunities, and threats early and to rearrange and recombine its assets, human skills and capabilities, organizational know-how (procedures,

A. Traditional Organizational Structure

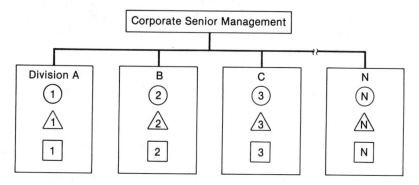

B. Transnational Organizational Structure

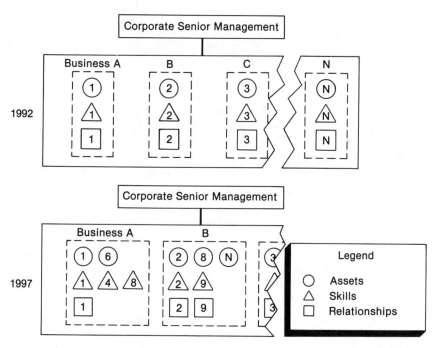

Figure 6.2 Competitive flexibility resulting from the redeployment of resources.

practices, proprietary information, and the like), and relationships (with suppliers, capital markets, governmental agencies, customers, and the public) to greatest effect. In contrast, the predecessor structures (multidomestic, global, international), highly effective for stable environments, lose their competitive advantage as conditions change. The strength and appeal of the transnational approach is adaptiveness, integrating resources and responsibilities where economics or critical mass are needed, dispersing resources and responsibilities when local responsiveness or local accountability are required, and modifying the organization's intelligence system (the structure and process by which vital strategic information is acquired, interpreted, and distributed) as global circumstances change.

Coordinating the Transnational Firm

The ability to adapt calls for a high degree of coordination. To operate as an effective strategic whole, the transnational firm must be able to coordinate the roles and responsibilities it deliberately differentiates and the assets and resources it deliberately disperses. More specifically, management must coordinate the flow of goods, resources, and information both vertically and horizontally within the corporation. The flow of goods includes the purchase of raw materials, the movement of supplies and work-in-process through various stages of manufacturing and assembly, and the distribution of finished goods for sale. The flow of resources embraces people, money, and technology. And the flow of information concerns proprietary know-how, internal operating data, competitors' moves, governmental policies, and any other intelligence that enables managers to make better decisions.

Coordinating such flows encompasses several challenges, not the least of which is the sheer volume and complexity of the task for companies offering many products and serving many countries. For example, in 1990 Reebok International had to order 66 million pairs of shoes in 650 different styles, sizes, and colors (stockkeeping units or SKUs) from fifty contracting factories located in six different countries for delivery to markets around the world at specified times. National quotas, plant capacities, and each factory's flexibility with respect to which styles it could produce complicated the coordination task, as did changing market demand and changing factor costs. Reebok also had to coordinate its production and sale of sport clothing, its human resources, and its cash flows on a worldwide basis. Firms like Philips and Matsushita have to coordinate a dozen or so diverse global businesses, each of which is more complex than athletic shoes and clothing.

Another aspect of the complexity such companies face is the need to coordinate the decision-making apparatus. Exchange-rate shifts, for example, have different effects on organizational units.[23] First, they can alter the financial statements of foreign subsidiaries (transaction exposure), the amount of funds repatriated or invested abroad (conversion), and even a firm's competitive advantage when its costs increase or decrease relative to competitors' costs. Second, organizations can deal with exchange rate exposure in a variety of ways, including hedging, arranging operations to lessen vulnerability, and making strategic decisions regarding a firm's involvement in specific businesses. These decisions concern financial experts, operating unit general managers, and corporate-level general managers respectively. A third difficulty is that these people are likely to be dispersed throughout the organization—that is, in different parts of the world—and to have different priorities and even competing professional and personal interests. While linear programming and other quantitative decision algorithms can assist Reebok with its sourcing problem, no similar opportunity exists to centralize or otherwise structure by a priori planning or analysis the complicated decision making for the unpredictable changes in exchange rates. What is needed for problems of the latter nature is a flexible organizational context that permits experts in different parts of the organization to recognize the need for joint efforts and provides incentives that encourage this behavior.

Major and rapid changes in technology, in national political and economic orientations, and in other relevant structural factors also complicate the coordination task. Advances in computer networking, data transmission, and other facets of information technology, CAD/CAM, and flexible manufacturing processes are just some of the technological developments that enable managers to decentralize (or centralize) specific operations in response to existing or new competitive requirements in ways that would not have been feasible under earlier conditions. Similarly, the collapse of the Soviet regime and the related opening of Eastern European countries, the restructuring of the European Community, and the emergence of other regional trading blocs also can invalidate existing patterns of coordination as market constraints are altered in ways that entice or even require firms to reconfigure their strategies and operations.[24]

Finally, the degree of coordination required of firms continues to go up as more competitors improve their ability to be responsive and adaptive to changing global conditions. Moreover, as times goes on, this upgrading of the standards of acceptable industry performance generally is becoming more frequent and pronounced. Half measures that could meet requirements in earlier times are no longer adequate. The growing consequences of inefficient or ineffective operations reflect the intensification of worldwide competition.

Coordination Mechanisms

Each of the early organizational approaches in support of worldwide business operations depends on its own principal means of coordination. For the global model, it is centralization: key decision makers are located near each other, facilitating the interactions needed to coordinate all activities. For the international model, it is the use of formal systems and procedures: detailed policies, planning, and control connect decision makers located far from each other. For the multinational model, it is a form of socialization: the operating requirements for the different business units are often so distinctive that no one set of rules can be applied, making the management process dependent on managers' understanding of corporate mission and on their close personal relationships.

Since the transnational corporation generally incorporates all three models simultaneously—certain business units are centralized, others given considerable autonomy, and still others dispersed with strong formal interconnections—its senior managers need to implement all three coordinating approaches and to coordinate across them. The fact that they must take direct charge in some businesses, limit their role to providing guidance and oversight in others, and not interfere in still others (except to ensure that good decisions are reached) makes clear the challenge they face in practice. Adding to this challenge is the fact that transnational corporations are in a constant state of flux. As assets, people, and relationships are reshuffled and the various flows adjusted to meet a changing competitive situation, the requirements for coordination—and the coordinating mechanisms—are also likely to change.

Corporate policies and structures alone cannot bring about the coordination needed to function effectively as a transnational. Ultimately, such coordination must rely on the active commitment and skilled actions of involved managers throughout the organization. Such commitment requires that people understand what needs to be done and are motivated to act accordingly.

To foster the necessary understanding, senior management has to ensure a clarity of purpose and means. Objectives should be explicit and concrete, continuous over time, and consistent with each other. Coordinating mechanisms have to be in place and easy to carry out. The earlier reference to managing shifting exchange rates gives some idea of how difficult and confusing such coordination can be. Senior management also has to ensure that people are well instructed about these matters through a combination of on-the-job and special training. Moving people around an organization in the course of their career also helps them to understand the coordination issues by exposing them to different aspects of the activities involved.

Willingness to act must accompany ability to act (see chapter 3), and so senior management must also concern itself with motivating people to coordinate their decision making and their actions. Such coordination across organizational boundaries is generally very difficult to achieve. Policies and exhortations promoting coordination are needed, but they are not likely to suffice by themselves. Stronger measures are normally required, such as evaluating and rewarding performance with respect to coordinating activities. Moving responsible managers around an organization also can motivate cooperation and coordination to the extent that they recognize a likelihood of being in the other person's position sometime in the future. For example, country managers in Philips, knowing that they might be assigned to a product division (or vice versa), tend to be more solicitous of their counterpart's position. Moving senior managers who have organizational influence and power to different important units in the corporate structure, as when Japanese and European firms send high-level executives to head U.S. operations, can also play an important role in legitimizing and motivating coordination. These "champions' ensure that their unit's perspectives and interests are taken into account in important corporate-wide strategic and operating decisions.

The task of coordinating corporate actions and decision making in a transnational organizational structure is sufficiently difficult to bring about and to sustain over time that not every company competing in world markets should attempt this approach. For corporations primarily engaged in businesses for which global, multinational, or international structures work reasonably well, the added cost (in terms of time, confusion, and morale as well as money) of adopting a transnational structure is likely to outweigh the benefits that might be gained in flexibility. But for firms operating in rapidly changing business environments and facing world-class competitors that are successfully building organizational flexibility, the need to follow suit is apparent.

Home Country

A major consideration in configuring worldwide business organizations concerns the location of assets and leadership responsibility.[25] With the possible exception of purely domestic or multidomestic industries, every business unit within a corporation is likely to have its own home base, where strategy is set, core product and process development takes place, and the essential proprietary skills reside. Particular countries can provide settings that are advantageous for particular industries; thus, for many global industries the leading firms are located in a single country. Prime examples of this clustering phenomenon include consumer electronics (Japan), the mass entertainment industry (United States), cartography (Switzerland), and dress shoes and jewelry (Italy). Relatedly, a multibusiness corporation might have good reason to locate its various business headquarters in different countries to avail itself of the competitive advantage each has to offer. IBM's decision to transfer the headquarters of its sizable communications business to Europe and the 1990 prediction by Chairman and CEO John Akers that IBM would relocate all of its PC development to the Far East within a few years are indicative of this latter point.[26]

Determinants of National Advantage

A nation's ability to provide world-class competitive advantage to an industry depends on the dynamic interplay of certain elements, especially: (1) relative position with respect to factors of production (including raw materials, human resources, and capital); (2) home demand; (3) strength of supplier and related industries; (4) nature of domestic competition; and (5) general attitudes of managers and workers toward the business, including such considerations as pride, confidence, and ambition.[27]

Factor Conditions

Factors of production, which can be defined as the inputs necessary to compete in an industry, comprise human resources, physical resources, knowledge resources (such as scientific, technical, marketing, and managerial), capital resources, and infrastructure (including transportation, communications, legal and political institutions, and health care). The mix of factors that are critical to business success differs greatly from one industry to another. A nation's firms gain a competitive edge to the extent that the country offers advantages in those factors most significant to the industry.

A nation's factor advantage depends, first, on the relative exclusivity of the factor. The fewer the countries with comparable offerings, the greater the advantage for a country with a critical factor. Another consideration is the inherent longevity of the factor advantage, that is, whether it is transient or enduring. For example, the advantage of low labor costs is likely to dissipate as wages rise with national prosperity and as less developed countries step in to provide cheaper labor. In contrast, an advantage in low-cost risk capital or in expert knowledge is more likely to be self-reinforcing and sustainable over time. A third consideration is the ease of transferability. Many basic factors—such as raw materials and unskilled or semiskilled labor—can be easily transferred either by physical removal (exporting copper or timber) or by using it in place as needed (such as U.S. firms using factories in Mexico for low-cost manufacturing and assembly operations). Other factors—such as highly skilled personnel, research institutes, infrastructure, and favorable altitudes—cannot be so easily moved elsewhere or used in place from a distant home base.

All three factor conditions—exclusivity, durability, immobility—must be met simultaneously to provide a sustainable national advantage for an industry. For example, in the early twentieth century, Chile possessed the finest source of nitrates, which were important ingredients for explosives and fertilizers (thereby satisfying the exclusivity condition). But the guano, which had been deposited by seabirds for centuries, was easily transported to other countries. As a result, Chile offered little advantage as a home-base location for an explosives industry. In time, German scientists synthesized the nitrates, eliminating the need for guano.

As a general rule, a nation with an advantage based on factors that are complex or specialized is more likely to sustain its preeminence over time than one favored with factors that are basic or general in nature. So it is not surprising to find far more business headquarters in countries with centers of technology, strong supplier industries, and good communications than in countries with raw materials and cheap labor. This phenomenon explains why nations strengthen their competitive advantage when they move over time from basic factors to more advanced ones. For example, in countries like Japan and South Korea, firms that first relied on low-cost labor to compete internationally have shifted the basis for their industry leadership to superior manufacturing operations and technological innovations.

The more complex and specialized factors that are most likely to provide sustainable competitive advantage are generally created rather than endowed by virtue of location. Consequently, a nation's factor-creating mechanisms—including educational institutions, research institutes, and port and highway authorities—play a critical role in sustaining that country's competitive advantage. Ironically, an abundance of basic factors can lull an area into complacency and deter the creation of more advanced and specialized factors. Conversely, a nation's factor-creating efforts can be stimulated by a disadvantage in some basic factor. For example, if a country lacks a low-wage, semiskilled labor pool, firms will be motivated to develop automated manufacturing processes to reduce or eliminate the need for such inputs. In doing so, they might also lower production costs, improve quality, or otherwise significantly enhance product performance. As noted earlier, German chemical firms, lacking any advantage in their access to natural nitrate supplies, were motivated to develop synthetic replacements. The skills that these firms developed to automate manufacturing and to synthesize natural chemical compounds are factors that are likely to be more advantageous and long-lasting than the basic factors they replaced.

Home Demand

A home demand that is large enough to justify investments is generally acknowledged as conferring some competitive advantage to a nation.[28] This advantage is likely to be greater where scale economies can be achieved in a home market, thereby giving firms in that country an edge over foreign firms with less opportunity to lower costs or improve features. Large home demand can also be a weakness when it leaves little incentive to look beyond. Generally, for comparative advantage, demand should be of greater relative significance in the home country than in other countries so that the industry will receive more attention, have greater prestige, and attract additional resources.

More important than size of demand is its makeup and nature. For example, a large number of independent buyers is likely to stimulate more reinvestment and improvement than if one or two customers were to dominate the home market. The commanding consideration, in this regard, is how sophisticated and demanding the customers are. If customers are complacent and compliant, firms have little incentive from this quarter. But if they are knowledgeable about product features and quality and discriminating in their purchases, firms are driven to improve their offerings. The excellence of German luxury automobiles and of Japanese consumer electronics can be traced in large part to the high expectations of home-market consumers. But for these pressures to result in global competitive advantage the home-market needs and demands must be relevant to other markets as well. Firms will gain little competitive muscle abroad if the product features demanded at home are not needed or valued elsewhere, as was true in the case of U.S. automobile manufacturers concentrating on domestic consumer demand for large, powerful cars during the 1950s and 1960s.

The presence of local customers who have significant business activities in other countries can encourage firms to expand internationally. U.S. and Japanese auto-parts suppliers followed their compatriot automobile manufacturing customers abroad. Similarly, firms serving consumers who travel to other countries might find opportunities to follow along, using this link to support beachheads for international expansion. Hotel chains, credit cards, car rental service, and certain brands of cigarettes all followed U.S. tourists abroad after World War II.

Supporting Industries

A third determinant of national advantage in an industry is the presence of world-class supplier industries and of other internationally competitive industries that are related through common technology, marketing, manufacturing, or other basis. Close physical proximity, the absence of national and linguistic barriers, and the motivations connected with local pride foster beneficial interactions and even common purpose.

Firms with this kind of access to internationally competitive suppliers can benefit in several important ways. One is in obtaining preferential treatment with respect to delivery, service, price, and allocation priorities. Just-in-time supply arrangements, for example, depend on close coordination that is made easier by proximity. New items of a complex nature, such as software or production systems, are likely to be initially offered locally to facilitate dealing with application difficulties and other unforeseen complications. Another advantage is the added opportunity for firms to influence the product development of a local supplier. For example, U.S. and Canadian paper-making firms strongly influence the design objectives of the North American paper-machine industry as well as the development of chemicals used for paper making. Notwithstanding the global nature of the paper industry, the requirements for manufacturing differ from one locality to another because of differences in the kind and quality of wood supplies. A third, related potential advantage is the stimulation of product development that can result from firms gaining early information about the expected performance characteristics of future-generation supply inputs.

Related industries that are internationally competitive can also provide important benefits. Industries can be related by product use (computer hardware and software, printing ink and coated paper), by technology (VCRs and facsimile machines), by raw materials (petroleum products and petrochemicals), by marketing and distribution (cigarettes and food, copier paper and office supplies), or by regulation (waste-water treatment and chemical manufacturing, air pollution equipment and electric utilities). These relationships can benefit firms in a variety of ways. Innovations in one industry can stimulate innovations in another. Vital information about customers, technology, government regulations, and international developments is likely to be shared. In many cases, the combined needs of related local industries accelerate the formation of commonly employed factors such as technology, people with special training and education, transportation and communication facilities, and special services (e.g., waste disposal).

Because of the many opportunities for mutual reinforcement, individual countries usually develop clusters of interrelated industries that are internationally competitive.[29] One example of a national cluster is the presence in Japan of leading firms in television, video games, audio equipment, VCRs, facsimile machines, computer hardware, memory chips, and integrated circuits. Clusters are often concentrated in a region (computer technology of Silicon Valley and machine tools in the American Midwest) or even in a city (supercomputers in Minneapolis and financial services in New York). This reflects in part how the clusters are formed. Resource or locational advantages can initially attract related industries. Spinoffs from established firms often remain in the locality for personal and business reasons. Entrants to supply new, distinctive input requirements or to exploit new applications often find it advantageous to locate near the core activities. This formation process is reinforced in that interaction among related firms is aided by geographical concentration. The vital information flows more easily as a result of personal relationships and more frequent contacts.

Domestic Rivalry

Competitive rivalry puts pressure on firms to improve their operations and offerings. Domestic rivalry plays an especially important role in creating competitive advantage for two reasons. First, strong local competitors are highly visible to each other and thereby command early and serious attention. Competition in the marketplace often is exacerbated by added rivalries in recruiting the most talented people, in obtaining preferential treatment from suppliers, and in gaining local prestige. Second, a local industry's efforts to improve operations and products is bound to stimulate improvements in local supplier and related industries, which in turn provides grist for additional innovative efforts in the originating industry. For example, the intense rivalry among U.S. telecommunications equipment manufacturers has led to advances in complex logic chips (a supplier industry) and in computer networking (a related industry). These advances open new opportunities for innovations in telecommunications equipment. The combination of imitation and stimulation that occurs in connection with domestic rivalry is self-reinforcing, leading to advances in knowledge and improvements that are difficult to replicate elsewhere.

To play a constructive role, domestic rivalry needs to motivate firms to improve their operations and offerings. Local competition that is excessive (as can happen when troubled firms find it difficult to exit the industry), destructive (involving unfair or illegal tactics), mindless (characterized by irrational behavior), or otherwise inappropriate (possibly based on false assumptions or wrong information) can undermine such motivation and subvert industry performance. Enlightened self-interest, industry norms, and public policy are common guards against dysfunctional rivalry.

Attitudes

The final determinant of national advantage has to do with dominant attitudes of the people involved. Relevant are attitudes toward work, authority, risk taking, rewards, short-term versus long-term consequences, ethical considerations, and other factors affecting enthusiasm, pride, confidence, commitment, and general approach to conducting the business in question. These attitudes shape business goals and strategies and have important consequences with respect to operations and the innovative process. The Swiss's renowned attention to detail is commonly cited as a reason for that country's success in banking and watch manufacture. The flair for showmanship in certain communities probably serves the United States well in the advertising, movie, and television industries.

Attitudes are determined by education, culture, history, policies, and events. People who entered the labor market during the Depression tend to be less willing to take risks than are those who grew up in the boom years after World War II. Koreans, with a strong sense of national pride, are driven by a need to compensate for over half a century of subjugation and war. The prestige attached to science and technology in Germany fosters excellence in a variety of high-technology businesses. Over time, attitudes change as experiences and conditions evolve. For the successful nation and for the successful firm, overconfidence and complacency loom as constant threats. Not surprisingly, people tend to lose their drive when everything seems to be going well and rewards are abundant. If a firm lacks external pressures from customers or rivals, the general manager needs to create pressures for innovation and quality performance from within.[30]

Two additional factors that influence the relative advantage a nation offers as home base for an industry are government and chance. Government can make a country more or less attractive by the policies it promotes and the degree of its stability. It can serve as a prime mover for certain industries, as when the United States subsidized the fledgling airline and airplane-manufacturing industries early in the twentieth century with mail contracts, or as in the case of defense and related products in the United States and Israel and nuclear power in France. It also can foster favorable economic conditions and trade relations. Finally, it plays an important role in factor creation through its power to influence education, research, and similar basic institutions.

Likewise, the vicissitudes of war, inventions, trade disruptions (such as for oil), financial perturbations, industrial accidents, business scandals, and other events capable of affecting the status quo can compromise a country's leadership position. For example, a major industrial mishap, such as occurred at the Three Mile Island nuclear plant near Harrisburg, Pennsylvania, in 1979, can incite enough public hostility to overwhelm any advantages a nation offers to an industry. Similarly, innovators like Edwin Land and Seymour Cray (pioneers in instant photography and supercomputers, respectively) can spawn new industries wherever they happen to reside, even when other locations offer greater competitive advantages.

National Competitive Advantage

For relatively simple industries, a national competitive edge can rest on comparative advantage with respect to one or more key basic factors of production. Saudi Arabia holds a commanding position in the petroleum industry because it has an enormous quantity of petroleum that is easily accessible. Similarly, countries where reasonably capable workers earn low wages attract mature labor-intensive industries such as textiles, shipbuilding, and consumer electronics product assembly. More complex, knowledge-based industries—such as computers, pharmaceuticals, investment banking, and medical electronics—depend on factors that are created. As such, these factors can be unique, difficult to replicate, and in a continuous state of being upgraded. For example, the Silicon Valley region in California provides competitive advantages to the computer and semiconductor industries in having skilled scientists and technicians, supporting industries that can provide needed services and products, world-class universities that provide research facilities and graduates dedicated to the field, venture capitalists who are familiar with the business, and communities with experience in handling the difficult safety and ethical issues that might arise. Few locations can offer this combination of factors, and efforts to assemble them may be stymied by the prevailing site's ability to improve and elaborate its factor advantages over time. In effect, sustained competitive advantage depends on a nation's ability to stimulate the creation and development of those factors that in turn lead to innovative advances in the industry.

As noted earlier, a demanding local market and strong domestic rivalry also are important determinants of the competitive advantage a nation can offer. In practice, the individual determinants generally are mutually reinforcing because the effect of one often depends on the state of others. For example, a favorable demand condition in and of itself will not motivate firms to strive for improved competitive strategies and operations without the added pressures of strong competitive rivalry. (A firm with monopoly power has much less motivation to innovate than one constantly engaged in robust competition.) Consequently, if a country is to provide an environment conducive to sustainable competitive advantage, it should offer advantage in more than one or two factors, thereby increasing both the synergistic benefits of mutual reinforcement and the cost and difficulty for another country to replicate the favorable conditions.

On the eve of the twenty-first century, long-standing economic structures are being transformed, industry leaders are being challenged and even supplanted by other firms, new industries are emerging, and most notably, business activities in general are increasingly international in nature. Advances in communications and transportation continue to shrink the globe, making people more aware and demanding of what can be made available and corporations increasingly capable of operating over great distances. The many changes taking place offer great opportunities and pose major threats to corporations everywhere. They also create a climate of uncertainty for the general manager.

In this swirl of disquiet and confusion, general managers everywhere are finding the standards of competition being redefined on a global scale. The "enemy" for a metal working machinery manufacturer in Cincinnati, Ohio, is no longer in South Bend, Indiana, or Providence, Rhode Island, but in Japan and Korea. Toyota, Honda, Volkswagen, Volvo, BMW, and Hyundai are names that have become as commonplace in the U.S. automobile market as Chevrolet,

Ford, Plymouth, Buick, Dodge, Lincoln, and Cadillac. Similarly, P&G (with Tide), General Electric (with medical imaging equipment), and Lotus (with personal computer spreadsheet software) have become major players in foreign markets.

To meet the resulting world-class standards for industry competition, corporations are attempting to adopt new organizational structures and processes that permit the realignment of resources, skills, and relationships as conditions change. The home base for each business would reside where conditions were most favorable for advancing operational performance and product offerings. The multifocal nature of the emerging approach to worldwide competition, however, poses very difficult coordination problems that are likely to result in practical limitations for some time to come.

Notes

1. *Wall Street Journal*, September 21, 1990, p. R28. The companies, ranked by market value as of June 30, 1990 (in millions of U.S. dollars), were: (1) NTT (Japan) $112,164; (2) IBM (U.S.) $67,529; (3) Royal Dutch/Shell (Netherlands, U.K.) $66,827; (4) General Electric (U.S.) $62,656; (5) Industrial Bank of Japan $60,493; (6) Exxon (U.S.) $59,844; (7) Toyota Motor (Japan) $59,019; (8) Fuji Bank (Japan) $51,325; (9) Sumitomo Bank (Japan) $51,098; (10) Dai-Ichi Kangyo Bank (Japan) $49,192.
2. The value of foreign sales dominates foreign trade for multinational firms. In 1988, American (and European) multinationals reportedly sold three times more overseas through their majority-owned subsidiaries than they exported to the world. Japanese firms reported foreign sales two times larger than their worldwide exports (this ratio is two-and-a-half times their sales in the United States). See Dennis J. Encarnation, *Beyond Trade: Foreign Investment in the U.S.–Japan Rivalry* (Ithaca, N.Y., 1992).
3. William Taylor, "The Logic of Global Business," *Harvard Business Review* 69, no.2 (March–April 1991), 92.
4. *Globalization, A Survey of Chief Executives* (New York: Booz Allen & Hamilton, 1990), p. 14. The survey was conducted by the *Wall Street Journal*, *Nikon Keizai Shimbun* and Booz Allen & Hamilton, Inc.
5. Bruce Kogut, "Designing Global Strategies: Comparative and Competitive Value-Added Chains," *Sloan Management Review* 26, no. 4 (Summer 1985), 15–28.
6. Bruce Kogut, "Designing Global Strategies: Profiting from Operational Flexibility," *Sloan Management Review* 27, no. 1 (Fall 1985), 27–38.
7. Francis Aguilar, "F. Hoffman-LaRoche & Co. A.G.," Harvard Business School case number 374–201.
8. See Kenichi Ohmae, *Triad Power* (New York, 1985). When zones of primary economic influence are added to the centers of industrial power, the resulting world economic structure comprises Asia, the Western Hemisphere, and Europe coupled with Africa and the Middle East (pp. 121–22).
9. Eurodollar bonds are dollar-denominated (all cash flows are in U.S. dollars) and are traded primarily outside the United States. Issued by U.S. corporations and U.S. government-sponsored agencies, these securities are underwritten by international syndicates of commercial banks or investment banks and are not registered with the Securities and Exchange Commission. See Frank J. Fabozzi and T. Dessa Fabozzi, *Bond Markets, Analysis and Strategies* (Englewood Cliffs, N.J., 1989), pp. 140–42.

10. *Wall Street Journal,* December 21, 1990, pp. C-1, C-17. The New York Stock Exchange lists about 100 foreign stocks for trading, many in the form of American depository receipts (ADRs), which represent an interest in shares that are kept in the custody of a foreign bank.

11. Carla Hills, U.S. trade representative for the Uruguay Round of negotiations in Geneva, gave an indication of GATT's importance in estimating that a successful agreement could increase world trade from $6 trillion to $10 trillion over the next decade (*Wall Street Journal,* December 3, 1990, p. 1).

12. The Persian Gulf conflict's potential to influence the evolution of global business was more attributable to its impact on the price of oil than on trading patterns.

13. The definitions for multinational and global organizations in this paragraph are from Christopher A. Bartlett and Sumantra Ghoshal, *Managing Across Borders* (Boston, 1989), pp. 49–52.

14. The data are from *Globalization,* p. 23.

15. Michael E. Porter, "Competition in Global Industries: A Conceptual Framework," in Michael E. Porter, ed., *Competition in Global Industries* (Boston, 1980), pp. 23–24.

16. Bartlett and Ghoshal, *Managing Across Borders,* p. 96.

17. In the literature on international business, the international organizational structure is commonly grouped with multinational and global structures as one of the three basic, traditional models.

18. For further discussion of the international organizational model, see Bartlett and Ghoshal, *Managing Across Borders,* pp. 49–51.

19. While an approximation at best, the multinational structure is generally associated with Europe, international with the United States, and global with Japan. This reflects the circumstances that prevailed at the time firms from the region were first expanding abroad.

20. Managers still advocate matrix relationships in connection with activities and systems that motivate people to work in the best interests not only of their particular business unit, but of the corporation as a whole. The means for achieving cooperation among business units in a corporation, as discussed in chapter 4, can include task forces, interconnected strategic plans, and moving managers through different business units during their careers.

21. This discussion, and the next section, draws from Bartlett and Ghoshal, *Managing Across Borders.*

22. The emerging complex structure has been given a variety of names by different observers, such as geocentric, multifocal, horizontal, heterarchy, and transnational. The *geocentric* structure was described by H. V. Perlmutter, "The Tortuous Evolution of the Multinational Corporation," *Columbia Journal of World Business* 4, no. 1 (January–February, 1969), 9–19; the *multifocal* organization by C. K. Prahaled and Yves L. Doz *The Multinational Mission: Balancing Local Demands and Global Vision* (New York, 1987); the *horizontal* form by Roderick F. White and Thomas A. Paynter, "Organizing for Worldwide Advantage," in Christopher A. Bartlett, Yves L. Doz, and Gunnar Hedlund, eds., *Managing the Global Firm* (London, 1990), pp. 95–113; the *heterarchy* model by Gunnar Hedlund, "Autonomy of Subsidiaries and Formalization of Headquarters—Subsidiary Relations in Swedish MNCs," in *The Management of Headquarters—Subsidiary Relationships in Multinational Corporations,* edited by Lars Otterbeck (Aldershot, U.K., 1981), pp. 25–78; and the *transnational* concept by Bartlett and Ghoshal, *Managing Across Borders.*

23. This discussion is based on a perceptive study by Donald R. Lessard and Nitin Nohria, "Rediscovering Functions in the MNC: The Role of Expertise in Firms' Responses to Shifting Exchange Rates," in Bartlett, Doz, and Hedlund, eds., *Managing the Global Firm,* pp. 186–212.

24. Coordination is greatly complicated by the need to reconcile conflicting economic and political considerations. For a discussion of how different corporate organizational structures relate to political risks, where political risk is generally defined as home and host government intervention in business activities, see Peter Smith Ring, Stefanie Ann Lenway, and Michele Govekar, "Management of the Political Imperative in International Business," *Strategic Management Journal* 11, no. 2 (February 1990), 141–51.

25. This section draws on Michael E. Porter, *The Competitive Advantage of Nations* (New York, 1990).

26. *Wall Street Journal,* December 4, 1990, p. A11, and an address by John Akers to MBA students at the Harvard Business School, November 19, 1990.

27. Porter combines the last two factors (domestic rivalry and attitudes) and, diagrammatically

arranging the resulting four factors into a diamond-shaped configuration, refers to a national "diamond."

28. Switzerland's preeminence in the watch and chocolate industries and Philips' major role in the lighting and consumer electronics industries, despite being heavily concentrated in the Netherlands for much of its history, provide notable exceptions to this rule and point to the importance of other advantages.

29. In *The Competitive Advantage of Nations*, Porter reports the phenomenon of industry clustering to be so pervasive as to appear a central feature of advanced national economies (p. 179).

30. This point is illustrated in a two-part *New Yorker* article by Ken Auletta, "A Certain Poetry," June 6 and 13, 1983. Auletta describes how Jean Ribound, then CEO of Schlumberger, a company with a commanding grip on the highly profitable oil field wire logging service, moved to combat complacency by changing managerial assignments radically and by challenging conventional wisdom.

7

Corporate Finance and the General Manager

Gone are the days when corporate finance was a relatively simple cookbook affair that could be left to the administrations of an honest, conservative and detail-minded treasurer. As time went on, greater volatility of interest rates added uncertainty to financing and cash management. Many firms were increasingly exposed to the effects of exchange-rate movements as they expanded their international operations. The traditionally close and congenial relationship corporations had had with commercial and investment banks eroded as these long-term commitments gave way to pressures for competitive proposals and deals based on who offered the best terms for a particular transaction. And the threats and realities of corporate takeovers superimposed requirements on a corporation's capital structure beyond those associated with sound business operations.

At the same time, financial opportunities have multiplied. More creative financing is possible with the development of global capital markets and the increasingly wide choice of financial instruments. New techniques for managing risks continue to emerge. Financial considerations can even drive corporate strategic and organizational choices, as when firms make strategic alliances in order to pursue ventures requiring investments beyond the capabilities of either party. The legacy of recent years compels senior general managers to take greater care than ever to ensure that the corporation is alert and skillful in handling its financial affairs, exploiting opportunities while averting dangerous and costly pitfalls. This chapter focuses on major concerns general managers face in deciding how to ensure sound financial policies and structure in the context of the firm's overall corporate strategy.

The New Financial Environment

While finance traditionally has been a core managerial function, two interrelated developments in recent years have transformed it from a relatively uncomplicated and benign activity to a tumultuous, high-stakes affair. Any senior manager of a publicly owned corporation must now come to terms with radical changes in capital markets and with changes in the relationships between corporations and the financial community.

Changes in the Capital Market

The plain vanilla common shares and debt arrangements that had so dominated the domestically oriented capital market of the early postwar years increasingly gave way to broader and more complex financing activities as access to funds went global and as new financial instruments were devised to meet special needs. According to one account, the Eurodollar bond market grew an astonishing 63 percent annually between 1975 and 1988, and U.S. firms' overseas borrowings rose from $30 million in 1975 to over $42 billion in 1985.[1] At the same time, the extraordinary growth of the high-yield (more popularly known as "junk") bond market—from $8 billion in 1976 to $180 billion in 1988—gave structure to an enormous pool of risk capital.[2] The rush of banks and insurance companies to supply mezzanine financing[3] and bridge loans provided vital intermediary funding that facilitated highly leveraged deals. Even with the setback of these markets at the close of the 1980s, they remain on the scene and are likely to take on new forms in the future.

Recent years have also witnessed rapid growth in the volume and variety of derivative securities—options, forwards, futures, and swaps. These financial instruments are typically used to alter the risks associated with foreign currency dealings, interest-rate fluctuations, commodity prices, and the underwriting of equity financing. Much of the recent growth in these markets has been abroad, further enriching the possibilities for customized hedging.[4] The increasing sophistication of foreign capital markets opens new opportunities to design complicated securities that shield companies from changes in interest rates and currency values.

Driving Forces

The forces propelling these changes include increased volatility in macroeconomic conditions, technological advances, deregulation, and the growth of global business operations. The impact of the macroeconomic changes was heightened by their nature and by the magnitude of the volatility increases. According to one observer, the most significant of these in recent years was the dramatic increase in the volatility of interest-rate movements.[5] As a case in point, the interest rate on three-month treasury bills fluctuated between 1 percent and 3.5 percent in the 1950s, between 4 percent and 11.5 percent in the 1970s, and between 5 percent to over 15 percent in the 1980s. At the same time, exchange rates experienced increasing uncertainty and volatility as abandonment of the Bretton Woods system of fixed exchange rates was accompanied by a sharp expansion of cross-border financial flows and by the increased variability of nominal and real exchange rates.[6] This increased volatility both in interest and exchange rates and in a variety of commodity prices (oil being among the most important) stimulated the development of new financial markets in futures, options, and related financial products.

Computer and communication technologies have had a profound effect on almost every aspect of the capital markets. Notable examples of this impact include the internationalization of financial markets, securitization (a process of transforming otherwise illiquid financial assets into marketable instruments), and program trading.[7] Improvements in telephone communications, the introduction of facsimile, advances in computer networking technology, and speedier air travel have helped to connect financial markets around the world, thereby giving corporations greater access and creating conditions for increased competition among financial institutions.[8] As for securitization, with computer record-keeping financial institutions have been able to bundle a portfolio of small loans—such as automobile loans, credit-card receivables, and commercial leases—collect the interest and principal payments, and pay them out to a third party. Computer technology has also led to the introduction of program trading. This controversial practice involves computer-directed trading between stock-index futures and the related stocks.[9]

A move toward deregulation in the United States beginning in the late 1970s had the effect of intensifying competition among financial institutions. London followed and triggered a wave of deregulation elsewhere, notably Tokyo, Paris, Frankfurt, and Zurich.[10] As a result, financing innovations emerged from more sources and spread more easily across the globe than in earlier years. Broadly viewed, the growth of global business operations joined increased volatility in macroeconomic conditions in defining new requirements for financing. Technology and deregulation in turn created new opportunities for financial institutions to satisfy these requirements. All together, these forces changed in important ways the relationships between business firms and the capital markets.

Changes in the Relationships Between Corporations and the Financial Community

During the 1970s and 1980s, the deregulation and globalization of financial markets created opportunities for financial institutions to compete in new ways. At the same time, high interest rates put pressure on corporations to search for low-cost loans. Similarly, increased interest-rate volatility called for innovative lending arrangements. The escalating risks and complexity of corporate takeover activities opened the door to firms with expertise in this field and resulted in financial institutions becoming increasingly aggressive in offering innovative securities and services that would allow them to attract new customers and to charge premium prices.[11]

One consequence of this development was a breaking down of traditional long-term relationships between financial institutions and their client companies. Relationship banking gave way to transaction banking, where the financial institution with the most attractive offering in terms of cost and features would be engaged. Corporate gains in lower fees and improved features, however, did not come without costs. The difficulty management faced in evaluating financing arrangements mounted as proposals became more inventive and complex and as rival financial institutions attempted to outmaneuver each other in selling their services. Past experience was no longer a reliable guide. Even more serious were the consequences of the breakdown of loyalty and trust that had traditionally characterized the banking relationship. As companies shopped around for financial services, they risked disclosing sensitive financial and business information to outsiders who inadvertently or purposely might violate confidentiality. With large fees at stake, financial advisors were motivated to serve competing client corporations, to take part in unfriendly takeover efforts, and even to put firms into play, notwithstanding industry ethical standards to the contrary. Senior corporate general and financial managers have had to exercise caution in this regard.

Another relevant change in the relationships between corporations and the financial community stems from the increasing proportion of equity shares in institutional hands as a result of the growth in mutual and pension funds. In recent years, as holdings became larger and consequently less liquid, U.S. fund managers have become more assertive, abandoning their traditional near-automatic support of management. Consequently, senior managers must dedicate more effort to shareholder relations than was necessary when institutions were passive or when less sophisticated shareholders, whose demands were often tempered by loyalty and apathy, played a greater role. On balance, the financial environment has become increasingly significant to corporate strategy, both as a discipline and as a source of advantage with respect to senior management's efforts to add value to the firm. More than ever, the general manager must be able and willing to provide effective leadership to the firm's financial strategy.

The Finance Role of the General Manager

Some senior general managers have come up the corporate finance ladder and are well qualified to provide active and effective financial leadership. There are other senior general managers who are also qualified by virtue of their keen interest and natural aptitude for such matters. Most chief executive officers, presidents, and chief operating officers, however, probably would not consider themselves as experts in finance. Some can even be remarkably naive on the subject.[12]

The job of the general manager, as discussed in chapter 1, is to ensure that the important work of the organization gets done in a timely, efficient, and effective manner. To carry out this responsibility with respect to the financial function, senior general managers need to enlist the help of experts. (Even general managers who are financial experts themselves need do this so that financial matters do not disproportionately occupy them or cause distractions from other important affairs.) General managers lacking financial expertise have an additional task of gaining sufficient understanding about financial matters so as to be able to provide strategic guidelines to the finance function, to judge its effectiveness, and to act sensibly on its recommendations.

The Financial Function

While the specific tasks of the financial function vary for different organizations and over time within an organization, they generally fall into the following broad categories: managing liquidity and working capital; financing; investing; managing risks; and internal administration. To this list must be added the need for senior managers to connect these separate functions by means of a cohesive set of financial objectives and policies that reflect the requirements of each tempered by any conflicts among these requirements.

Managing Liquidity and Working Capital.[13] One of the ongoing challenges for financial management is ensuring that a corporation has cash or its equivalent (e.g., credit) to meet its obligations while putting its money to work to the greatest extent possible. In effect, the benefits of liquidity have to be balanced with the costs of financing liquid assets—a task that relates to the management of working capital and requires interaction with the operating functions. Credit and collection policies, for example, must take into account the importance of customer credit to the corporation's marketing strategy and sales efforts as well as the company's financial ability to sustain such investments. Similarly, inventory policies must take into account manufacturing process requirements, and accounts payable policies the company's procurement strategy.

Financing. Business operations determine the kinds of assets that a corporation will need. The financing function is concerned with raising the necessary funds to acquire the needed assets and to sustain operations. Corporations normally have access to a wide variety of sources for funds. These include trade credit and unsecured bank loans for short-term needs, secured loans and term financing for medium-term needs, and securities (bonds, preferred equity stock, and common equity stock) for longer-term needs.[14] The choice of source depends on the length of time funds are needed for specific purposes and on the availability and cost of funds for each objective. The mix of funds a company uses to finance its operations (its capital structure) should reflect the risks inherent in the assets it holds and in its business operations. As shown in Figure 7.1, business considerations determine the contents of one side of the balance sheets (assets) and set requirements for the other side (liabilities). The actual financing is also determined by the kinds of financial instruments and terms available from the capital markets and the costs in effect. Managing a company's relationships with its bankers, its shareholders, and the investment community at large is an important part of the financing function.

Investing. Capital investments are a major concern for most companies. Investment proposals might have to do with introducing new products, expanding into new geographical markets, replacing equipment or adding buildings,

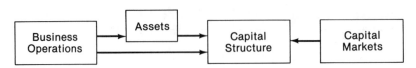

Figure 7.1

research and development, or upgrading management systems. While these decisions are defined and determined by strategic and operating considerations, the finance function generally plays a key role in administering the capital budgeting process and in setting financial criteria for selection. Successful administration of capital investments by a company requires the generation of attractive investment proposals, evaluation of cash flows, and the selection of projects based on suitable criteria (strategic, operational, and financial). A related task for the finance function is to invest any corporate funds that are not needed for business purposes. This requirement is generally temporary, as when capital funds that are raised for a large investment get used over time (building a plant) or are needed at some indeterminate future time (making an acquisition).

Managing Risks. Business inevitably requires taking risks. While management must be prepared to do this, it should avoid taking chances unnecessarily. Certain risks can be reduced or eliminated by operating and strategic decisions. For example, whether or not a company enters an unfamiliar business or market and whether it tries to lead or follow in technology fundamentally affects the risks it bears. Other risks involving liquidity and borrowing capacity are financial in nature and generally are managed by the finance staff. In addition, the increasing variety and availability of financial instruments for reducing risks associated with changes in commodity prices, interest rates, and currency exchange rates provide corporate financial managers with greater opportunities to reduce such operating risks.

Internal Administration. The corporate finance department of a large company is likely to have a sizable staff that must be organized and managed. In this administrative capacity, a chief financial officer functions as a general manager. The staff is usually divided into treasury and controller functions, with the treasurer the person most directly responsible for obtaining financing, managing relationships with bankers and investors, managing cash, and ensuring that the firm meets its obligations to investors holding its securities (such as interest and principal payments on loans and dividends for equity). The controller is the person most directly responsible for accounting, internal auditing, preparing budgets, and taxes.

Financial Experts

A CEO needs to assemble a team of qualified people who can provide the insight and expertise required to carry out successfully the corporation's financial function. The membership typically includes a chief financial officer (CFO), other financial managers, a public accounting firm, tax advisors, one or more investment bankers, commercial bankers, and members of the board of directors with financial expertise. Finding suitable in-house financial expertise is somewhat easier than finding marketing or technical expertise, because the pool of potential candidates is less restricted by industry-specific limitations. Moreover, the highly interactive financial community provides many readily available sources for information concerning suitable candidates.

In selecting financial experts, a general manager has to take into account experience, trustworthiness, ability to work harmoniously with others, and attitude toward risk taking. These criteria, of course, are common for recruiting experts in any functional area. The risk-taking attitude, which can be anywhere between ultraconservative and highly aggressive, takes on special importance, however, because the highly technical nature of corporate finance can obscure the risks associated with particular policies and practices.

In discussing the financial function with the author, Donald Melville, former chairman and CEO of Norton Company, observed, "In my experience, the second most important person in a corporation is the chief financial officer." While some senior managers might regard the ranking as hyperbole, few would disagree with Melville's essential assessment of the vital role that the CFO plays in the life of the public corporation. For example, a single smart move in raising capital can save or bring in millions of dollars—funds that can provide a valuable cushion against difficult times or a necessary springboard for a major strategic move. According to one study, the decisions made by corporate financial officers in raising funds, investing liquid balances, and controlling financial risks can have an impact on corporate profits that is as large as the earnings from operations.[15] Clearly, a CEO must be no less skillful and diligent in selecting a chief financial officer than he or she would be in choosing any other key member of the management team.

Financial Knowledge

General managers have to have a good understanding about finance and how the financial world functions for several reasons. First, to ensure that the firm has adequate financial expertise, general managers should be able to define the kinds of financial transactions that are likely to be of future relevance and the kind of financial experience and skills that pertain to such transactions. Second, general managers need to provide key financial people with strategic guidelines that would be likely to include performance objectives, investment opportunities, possible business risks, and investor relations goals. Indeed, corporate and business strategies are the driving force for any financial decisions, and general managers must guard against financial tactics taking precedence. *An active interaction between operational and financial considerations is one of the best ways to ensure that financial plans are compatible with business needs and that business plans rest on sound financing.*

Finally, general managers need to know enough about finance to be able to judge the merits of the financial advice and recommendations that they receive and to act on this information. Financial experts, like any other experts, can become overly influenced by what is popular at the time. Poison pills with flip-in and flip-over provisions were the rage one year.[16] ESOPs (employee share ownership programs), stock repurchase, leveraged buyouts, and other fads followed. Most of these techniques had become popular for valid reasons, and some firms benefited greatly. Many firms, however, simply followed the crowd without much thought to their own specific needs. The general manager has a special responsibility to guard against such herdlike behavior.

The level of understanding general managers need to have about finance is difficult to determine. In general, they need to be able to talk intelligently about financial considerations with the experts and to apply independent judgment on the decisions made. This ability, at the very least, presupposes a familiarity with financial statements and an understanding of what they reveal. There is no need, however, to have detailed knowledge about the mechanics of issuing stock or a mastery of Employee Retirement Income Security Act (ERISA) regulations concerning pensions. While specific areas for concern depend on a company's situation, setting financial goals, managing cash flows, and managing risk are topics of general interest to all senior general managers.

Managing Financial Goals

Chapter 2 dealt with how senior management, in setting corporate objectives, has to satisfy the parties on whom the corporation depends: customers, employees, shareholders, creditors, suppliers, and host communities. The obligation to these influential constituencies, however, is tempered by management's desire for organizational survival, independence, self-sufficiency, and personal fulfillment. As Gordon Donaldson notes, "[M]anagement must work to assure tradeoffs in the company's goals and performance which will retain all the constituencies' cooperation—if not their spontaneous loyalty. Nevertheless, even as these tradeoffs are made, management is watchful of constituency attempts to limit its prerogatives."[17] In effect, senior management's desire to *be in control* and to *stay in control* is likely to shape if not dominate corporate and financial strategy.

While these trade-offs manifest themselves in many ways, growth goals are generally a central issue. Rapid profitable growth can provide payoffs for all concerned parties. The increased demand for the firm's products and services indicates that customers are satisfied. For employees, growth generally involves financial rewards and enhances job security, opportunities for advancement, and professional development. Shareholders can benefit from higher stock prices, creditors from larger and more secure loan opportunities, suppliers from greater sales, and host communities from increased employment opportunities. Nor is the positive effect on senior management's reputation a trivial consequence. Of the twelve major U.S. corporations Donaldson studied, growth objectives ranged from 8 percent to 17 percent per annum, and respondents on average hoped to double in size every five years (15 percent per annum).[18]

Nonetheless, senior management's desire for self-preservation places limits on this compulsion to grow. For example, management might decide to forgo potential growth if it were determined that the additional business activities could give one or more customers or suppliers undue leverage over the fortunes of the firm. Similarly, management might restrain growth that makes the firm overly dependent on one or a few individuals (such as a preeminent scientist in a molecular biology firm or a superstar mutual fund manager) who could walk off with the business.

The incentives and limits to rapid profitable growth bear directly on financial goal setting. A history of rapid profitable growth can attract capital, often at a relatively appealing cost. But senior management must guard against becoming unduly beholden to creditors or causing significant shareholder dissatisfaction. Borrowings are purposely kept at a conservative level so that the firm can borrow more if needed at short notice or can meet its payment obligations in the event of unforeseen setbacks.[19] Similarly, dividends are set at a level that meets the investment community's expectation but is not likely to be burdensome under adverse conditions (since dividend cutbacks are generally viewed as an admission of serious trouble.) Rapid growth also risks giving shareholders an overly optimistic expectation for the future. Any setback causing disappointment could depress share prices. Managers generally prefer to grow at a rate that can be sustained over time and during most of the business cycle.

Long-Term Versus Short-Term Perspective

U.S. public corporations come under a great deal of criticism for overemphasizing short-term profits at the expense of long-term investments. Many business leaders deny these allegations, while those who concede that such behavior is prevalent often blame it on pressures from the investment community. According to a study on the effects of shareholders' trading practices on long-term corporate investments, managers' behavior in this regard tends to be a function of (1) their concern with current stock price; (2) the sensitivity of stock price to earnings; and (3) investors' confidence in reported earnings.[20]

One factor influencing managerial concern with current stock prices is the trading horizon of the firm's influential shareholders. Shareholders who expect to trade their shares within a year or two are likely to be concerned with near-term price performance and will communicate this concern to management. For most large public companies, institutional investors, whose trading horizon tends to be short-term, are heavily represented in this group. In contrast to Japan—where a significant share of equity is owned by a firm's customers, suppliers, and business partners[21]—and Germany, where a large percentage of equity voting rights are in the hands of the *Hausbank* (the principal banking connection), there is no large category of shareholders in the United States that can be counted on to hold shares for the long run. The threat of hostile takeover also influences management's concern with current share price. Higher current prices on the one hand make the company less vulnerable and on the other hand increase the payoff to shareholders in the event the company is taken over. The extent to which managerial compensation is based on share price can also be an important consideration.

The sensitivity of a firm's stock price to changes in earnings is a second factor influencing the trade-off senior managers make between short-term profits and long-term investments. The importance investors place on short-term earnings is influenced by, among other variables, the maturity of the company. In general, short-term earnings are less significant for start-up firms than for well-established, mature companies. Other relevant considerations include characteristics of the industry (such as whether it is cyclical, countercyclical, or noncyclical and the kinds of opportunities and threats it faces), the economic outlook, the past performance record of the firm in question, and the potential value of the firm's investment opportunities. These last two firm-related reasons obviously depend on investors' comfort with management and the company's financial projections.

Investors' confidence in reported earnings is a third factor affecting share price and consequently the likely balance between short-term and long-term investments. This confidence is a function in part of the complexity of the corporation's strategy and structure. A firm in a single business is easily understood by investors. A firm in many diverse businesses, like General Electric, is difficult to understand, and its price/earnings ratio can be depressed as a consequence. Investors' understanding of and confidence in reported earnings is also a function of the effectiveness of a firm's investor-relations efforts and of analysts' research efforts. Timely press releases and informative company reports coupled with well-planned road shows to the investment community can help give credibility to a firm's earnings numbers. Similarly, investors are likely to have more confidence in the earnings of a company followed by respected analysts than in one not covered.

Over the years, mature U.S. corporations have relied for financing almost exclusively on retained earnings and the additional debt that the internally generated equity could justify. The reason for this approach is corporate management's preference for sources that are readily and continuously available, that are reliable as to amount and timing, that bear a reasonable cost, and that do not lessen management's prerogatives. Raising new equity, on the other hand, is expensive (see subsequent discussion on the cost of capital) and unreliable, depending as it does on the vagaries of the stock market. Moreover, in mature firms, the necessity of turning to the equity market for supplemental funds is often interpreted as a public admission of poor management. Relying on retained earnings as the principal source of funds, as we shall see, also poses problems. It can inhibit a firm's ability to invest in attractive opportunities and consequently limit its rate of growth. The missed opportunities could possibly impair the company's competitive strength or its efforts to diversify its business operations.

The task of taking into account and balancing the interests of important stakeholders while preserving control is of central importance to the general manager. To do it well requires a firm understanding of how to manage cash flows and risks.

Managing Cash Flows

"Cash flow is what it's all about! Sales growth, profits, share of market are all important financial indicators, but cash is what really counts." With these words to a group of managers in training, John Rollwagen, chief executive officer and chairman of Cray Research, Inc., summed up his assessment of what is at the heart of corporate financial management. Notwithstanding widespread agreement among finance scholars that the value of a firm to shareholders is the net present value of its discounted future free cash flow, most U.S. managers continue to have a fixation on earnings per share (EPS) as the principal measure of performance. Many boards of directors agonize over quarterly earnings. Major projects are accelerated or deferred to help make the earnings pattern more favorable. And not without reason. As noted earlier, share prices do reflect earnings projections and earnings results. Financial analysts look to management to generate steady earnings growth and, above all, to avoid a negative earnings surprise.[22]

In recent years, more and more attention has been given to cash flows in valuing companies. The rash of takeovers and restructurings that began in the early 1970s provided strong impetus to this analytical focus, as cash reserves were cut back and higher leverage (debt to equity ratio) put a premium on cash flows for interest coverage and debt repayment. Further impetus was given in 1987 by the Financial Accounting Standard Board in requiring a cash-flow statement for public reporting as well as the traditional balance sheet and profit and loss statement.[23] The cash-flow statement, as evident in the example shown in Figure 7.2, breaks out the effects of operations, investments, and financing. This presentation reveals important information about the financial health and resiliency of a corporation not so readily apparent from the balance sheet and P&L statement. In the case of Abbot Laboratories, we see a firm that is generating more cash from operating activities each year. About one-half of the almost $1 billion for 1988 was used to acquire property and equipment. Much of the remainder was used to repurchase common shares and to pay dividends. This pattern was generally stable for the three years reported.

The cash flow statement highlights the need for senior managers to ensure that cash inflows are adequate to cover necessary cash outflows. This task involves both operating and financing decisions, generally in an interactive way. For example, in considering a business opportunity to enter a new market and to expand several related ongoing operations, senior management might ask the following business strategy questions: What are the viable approaches we might take? How fast should we move? What do we need in the way of resources (skills, technology, money)? The related financing questions would include: Where can we raise the funds? How quickly? At what cost? (A proper cost assessment goes beyond the interest charge or equity dilution of the im-

Figure 7.2　Typical cash flow statement for annual public reporting.

	Year ended December 31		
(dollars in thousands)	**1988**	1987	1986
Cash Flows From (Used in) Operating Activities:			
Net earnings	**$752,027**	$632,559	$540,460
Adjustments to reconcile net earnings to net cash flow from operating activities—			
Depreciation and amortization	**270,903**	243,683	199,502
Unrealized translation (gains) losses, net	**19,299**	455	(25,484)
Investing and financing (gains) losses, net	**14,145**	15,111	27,996
Trade receivables	**(87,920)**	(83,356)	(37,129)
Inventories	**(2,805)**	(64,662)	(49,731)
Prepaid expenses and other assets	**(107,584)**	(41,760)	(68,274)
Trade accounts payable and other liabilities	**107,296**	183,569	172,964
Net Cash Flow From Operating Activities	**965,361**	885,599	760,304
Cash Flow From (Used in) Investing Activities:			
Acquisitions of property and equipment	**(521,196)**	(432,736)	(383,389)
Purchases of investment securities	**(693,063)**	(604,376)	(665,016)
Proceeds from sales of investment securities	**778,699**	504,478	732,745
Other	**4,347**	5,108	5,195
Net Cash Used in Investing Activities	**(431,213)**	(527,526)	(319,465)
Cash Flow From (Used in) Financing Activities:			
Proceeds from (repayment of) borrowings with original maturities of 3 months or less, net	**(234,334)**	94,791	307,727
Proceeds from borrowings with original maturities of more than 3 months	**615,591**	372,903	169,169
Repayments of borrowings with original maturities of more than 3 months	**(398,146)**	(482,152)	(182,768)
Purchases of common shares	**(141,440)**	(175,599)	(487,563)
Proceeds from stock options exercised	**25,839**	20,174	19,625
Dividends paid	**(260,082)**	(218,736)	(188,559)
Net Cash Used in Financing Activities	**(392,572)**	(388,619)	(362,369)
Effect of exchange rate changes on cash and cash equivalents	**(591)**	7,630	639
Net Increase (Decrease) in Cash and Cash Equivalents	**140,985**	(22,916)	79,109
Cash and Cash Equivalents, Beginning of Year	**249,907**	272,823	193,714
Cash and Cash Equivalents, End of Year	**$390,892**	$249,907	$272,823
Supplemental Cash Flow Information:			
Interest paid	**$ 85,787**	$ 76,592	$ 95,743
Income taxes paid	**363,378**	235,852	149,982

The accompanying notes to consolidated financial statements are in integral part of this statement.

Source: Abbot Laboratories, 1988.

mediate transaction to include the future effect on the cost of capital). Every senior manager should recognize the task of balancing business opportunities and financial resources as an ongoing challenge.

Managing Growth

From a financial perspective, managing growth is primarily a matter of managing cash flows.[24] Rapid growth can put considerable strain on a company's financial resources. Since expansion often requires significant investment, a profitable firm that expands too rapidly can go broke.[25] Conversely, senior management of companies that grow too slowly run a risk of losing control to more aggressive outsider parties. The optimal rate of growth is one that takes full advantage of business opportunities to the extent permitted by sound financial policies. The maximum rate at which company sales can increase without increasing financial risk is known as a company's *sustainable growth rate* (SGR).

A key factor in determining SGR is a firm's ability to attract equity financing on favorable terms over time. For firms that are unable or unwilling to sell new equity and have a target capital structure and a target dividend policy, the controlling factor becomes the rate at which it is able to add to retained earnings on a continuing basis.[26] The following basic relationship must hold:

Asset increase = additions to retained earnings plus new borrowings. This relationship can be rearranged to express SGR as the product of four common financial ratios:

- Profit margin on sales (profit after tax/net sales)
- Asset turnover (net sales/total assets)
- 1 + debt to equity ratio
- 1 − dividend payout ratio (or dividend retention ratio)

The equation can be solved to show that relative growth in sales must be supported by a similar percentage growth in equity coming from retained earnings (i.e., SGR = Δ retained earnings/equity).[27]

A firm's sustainable growth rate is not likely to equal its growth opportunities as defined by its product or service markets. When a company has more investment opportunities to grow than can be sustained by the limits imposed by its financial policies and operating results (the four ratios), general management has a variety of ways to increase the firm's growth capacity. With respect to operations, it can try to raise the profitability margin by such means as raising prices, improving operating productivity, and pruning marginal and low-profit operations. It can raise the asset turnover ratio by, for instance, reducing inventories and accounts receivable. Shifting from in-house manufacturing to vendor sourcing can also improve asset turnover if plant and equipment assets are reduced. With respect to financial policies, management can reduce the dividend payout ratio and increase the debt to equity ratio. The former action could lead to a decline in stock price (at least temporarily), and as we shall see, there are significant costs and limits to debt financing. Moving beyond the four ratios, a firm can, of course, issue more equity. Alternatively, it can enter into some kind of partnership relationship with another firm to share the financial burden of growth. This arrangement can range from the loose strategic alliances that many small, rapidly growing biotech firms have arranged with large pharmaceutical firms to a full merger.

When a firm generates more cash than it can use to exploit attractive investment opportunities in its business, management faces the problem of deciding how to redeploy the excess. A common response is to diversify operations by investing in one or more new businesses. While some firms have been successful in this strategy, most have not. One reason for the failures is that the anticipated operating synergies tend to be elusive, if not illusory. For example, management might be operating in unfamiliar territory, management systems and standard operating procedures might be incompatible, or loyalties might clash. A second reason is that acquisition prices generally anticipate potential gains and add a premium for control, leaving the acquirer with, at best, a mediocre investment opportunity.

Another common response is for senior management to succumb to pressures from operating unit managers to invest in projects that might be only marginally attractive. When money is available, people can always come up with persuasive arguments for expanding into new markets or developing new technologies that are likely to be more appealing to senior managers than other uses for the money. One alternative is to invest the excess cash in marketable securities until needed. This once-common practice lost popularity during the takeover era because large holdings of cash and marketable securities generally make a company a more attractive target. The other alternative is to return the cash to shareholders through higher or special dividends. This action, however, flies in the face of senior management's predilection to increase the assets at its disposal. Senior management's inability to put the excess cash flow to good use—resulting in cash buildups, a deteriorating financial performance, or both—eventually increases a firm's vulnerability to takeover. A higher dividend yield, on the other hand, is likely to increase the company's common share price while leaving the balance sheet lean and trim. Finally, while probably less persuasive to corporate senior-level decision makers, the return of excess funds to shareholders can benefit the national economy by freeing funds for reinvestment in more promising and productive sectors.

Investment Decisions

Investment decisions are typically made with several criteria in mind. A major consideration is that of strategic fit: Is the proposal compatible with the company's business vision, perceived organizational strengths, and managerial preferences? This criterion often governs the investment decision. Also important are the project's expected benefits with respect to competitive position, organizational capabilities, and financial returns, including the effects on related ongoing business operations and possible future actions. Similarly germane is its feasibility, considering the skills, technology, physical assets (such as the availability of special equipment), and funding needed to ensure successful completion. While the financial analysis of complex investments can be daunting to a nonexpert, the general manager must never lose track of the effects on cash flows. Timing can be as important as the amounts involved. Steady returns are generally favored, but circumstances could favor accelerated or deferred cash flows. The relative uncertainty of cash flows is yet another important consideration.

The proper measure for selecting among alternative investment opportunities is *future or incremental* cash flow. In practice, such decisions are often made on the basis of financial accounting return on investment (ROI), profits, net present value of discounted cash flows (DCF), or some other measure, like return on sales (ROS).[28] Consider, for example, the three alternative and mutually exclusive business plans for exploiting a new market opportunity shown in Table 7.1, where the ROS, profit, and incremental cash flow are calculated for each. (For the purpose of simplification, taxes are ignored.) Alternative A results in the highest ROS, but in the lowest profit and cash flow. Unless investment funds are constrained, this approach would result in the poorest exploitation of the market opportunity. Alternative B shows the highest profits. But profits can be misleading because of the cost allocations that are based on cost accounting conventions and management control purposes. Costs that are fixed regardless of the alternative selected (for example, the costs for senior executives, general accounting, plant heat, and so forth) can make no real difference to the choice. The allocation of these costs, however, can alter quite differently the calculated profits for each alternative. By not allocating the fixed costs, we see that alternative C results in the largest net cash gain. Since everything else remains unchanged in this simple example, alternative C contributes $40,000 more to pay for fixed costs and to add profit than can alternative B, and $200,000 more than Alternative A. Thus, contrary to the impression given by the figures in the box, the company's profits would be highest by adopting alternative C.

The need for decision makers to consider cash flow rather than profits is vividly portrayed in Figure 7.3. By analyzing incremental cash flows (cash flows that change with a decision), we can see that each product makes a positive contribution to corporate profits. For example, product line A generates $90,000 if it is manufactured and sold, and nothing if it is discontinued. This cash flow is critical to the decision as to whether or not to produce product line A. The factory overhead costs remain unchanged whether or not product line A is produced, so that it is not relevant to this decision. By allocating costs on a proportional basis of the factory assets used (a common policy) and by requiring each product to be profitable (another common policy), management is driven to eliminate one cash-producing product after another until the entire operation—once capable of generating $220,000 in profits—is abandoned.

The risks associated with the cash flows for any investment need to be taken into account. A project with a certain, immediate payoff of $10,000 is clearly more attractive than a similar project with only a 70 percent probability

Table 7.1 Investment Decision Analysis ($ thousands).

	Alternative A	*Alternative B*	*Alternative C*
Sales	$450	$850	$800
Less Direct Expenses	230	470	380
Net Cash Flow	$220	$380	$420
Less Allocated Costs	100	170	240
Profit	$120	$210	$180
Return on Sales	26.7%	24.7%	22.5%

of paying as much as $10,000. For investments that extend over time, the time value of money must also be taken into account (see Box 7.1). Sound practice requires a firm to earn a return from its investments sufficient to cover the opportunity cost of the capital funds invested, which include both risk and the time value of money. In effect, this opportunity cost is what an investor could earn on another project with the same degree of risk and therefore is reflected directly in the cost of capital. The higher the cost of capital, the higher the expected required return. Setting the discount rate equal to the cost of capital recognizes that each investment should normally earn at least as much as the firm has to pay for the invested funds.[29]

Cost of Capital

The overall cost of capital of a firm comprises the costs of the various components of financing. The general relationship can be stated as follows:

$$\begin{Bmatrix} \text{Weighted} \\ \text{average cost} = \\ \text{of capital} \end{Bmatrix} \begin{Bmatrix} \text{After-tax} & \text{Debt as} \\ \text{cost of} \times \text{as \% of} \\ \text{debt} & \text{total capital} \end{Bmatrix} + \begin{Bmatrix} \text{Cost} & \text{Equity as} \\ \text{of} \times \text{\% of total} \\ \text{equity} & \text{capital} \end{Bmatrix}$$

For example, if a firm has a capital structure with 20 percent debt and 80 percent equity and a 10 percent average debt interest charge, a 15 percent cost of equity, and a 50 percent tax rate, then its weighted average cost of capital would be 13 percent:

$$\text{WACC} = [(.10 \times .50) \times .20] + [.15 \times .80] = 13\%$$

Given this equation, one might conclude that the firm could lower its cost of capital simply by carrying more debt and less equity as shown below for a 50 percent debt/50 percent equity structure:

$$\text{WACC} = [(.10 \times .50) \times .50] + [.15 \times .50] = 10\%$$

A division of a large corporation manufactures three product lines that share equally in the use of a factory and charges each one-third of the factory overhead costs. As shown in stage 1 below, if factory overhead costs increase from $240,000 to $300,000 because of inflationary pressures, product line A is no longer profitable. Since the corporation requires every product line to be profitable (a fairly common policy in practice), product line A is discontinued, and the fixed overheads are allocated to the remaining two products. As shown in stage 2, product line B can no longer show a profit with the higher allocation. As a result, it too is discontinued. At stage 3, product line C must carry the full overhead by itself. Unable to do so at a profit, it is discontinued, and the factory is closed down.

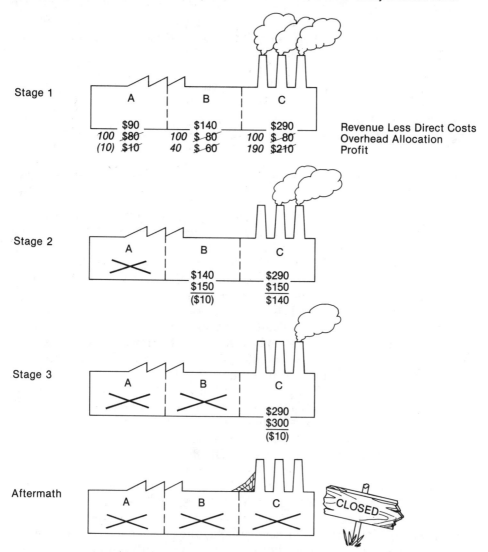

Incremental cash flow analysis would have shown the three product lines as generating $520,000 to cover fixed overheads and to contribute $220,000 to profits.

Figure 7.3 An example of how cost allocations can distort analysis.

Box 7.1   Time value of money.

The basic concept of net present value is that a dollar today is worth
more than a dollar in the future because it can be invested to earn
interest in the intervening time. For example, if you put $100 in a
bank account paying 10 percent annual interest, you will receive $110
in one year, or $121 in two years, and so on. Conversely, $121 two
years hence is worth $100 at present, given your opportunity to earn
10 percent interest for two years. If you could earn more than 10 percent, its present value would be less than $100. If you were not able
to earn as much as 10 percent, its present value would be greater
than $100. The present value of a delayed payoff can be found by
multiplying the payoff by a *discount factor*, which is expressed as the
reciprocal of 1 plus a rate of return: e.g., $1 \div (1 + r)$, where r is the re-
turn that the investor could otherwise earn. Thus $\$121 \times (1 \div 1.1) \times (1 \div 1.1) = \$100$.

But this calculation is wrong since the underlying assumption is valid only up
to a point. As shown in Figure 7.4, the weighted average cost of capital first
drops, then holds even, and eventually rises as debt increases as a percentage
of the total capital. Why is that?

   For a company with given prospects for future net cash inflows from operations, the greater the proportion of total capital in the form of debt obligations, the greater the financial risk. One reason is that debt obligates a company to future cash outflows (interest payments and the repayment of principal)
and equity does not (dividends can be discontinued). However, when the debt/
equity ratio is low, the effect of additional debt on a company's financial risk
is relatively small compared to the savings that the tax shield provides. The
effect is shown in the declining portion of the WACC curve on the left side of
the graph. As the debt/equity ratio becomes larger, the effect of the increase in
financial risk grows comparable to the incremental tax advantage for debt. This
effect is shown in the relatively flat portion of the cost curve. As debt continues
to increase as a percentage of total capital, financial risk mounts more and
more rapidly. A firm with a highly leveraged capital structure is more likely to
encounter difficulties in meeting its debt obligations than one with a low debt
to equity ratio should operating income falter for any reason, such as an unexpected economic downturn or the loss of market share to foreign competitors. A company's inability to service debt can give lenders a commanding
voice in how it is to be managed or else can lead it to bankruptcy.

   High financial risk results in a high WACC through its effect on both debt
and equity financing. As for debt, significant financial risk can cause a firm's
credit rating to deteriorate. As a firm's credit rating goes down, the rate of
interest it must pay for borrowed money goes up. An even more serious neg-

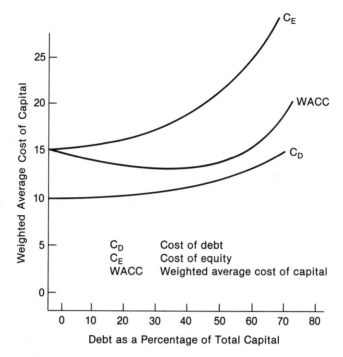

Figure 7.4 Weighted average cost of capital as a function of debt as a percentage of total capital.

ative consequence results from the inclusion of more severely restrictive cove-nants with respect to financial ratios and the use of cash that could put man-agement's control of the corporation in jeopardy.[30] As for equity, once again, the higher the risk, the higher the cost. According to modern portfolio theory, investors relate expected return (a company's cost of equity) to the risk they have to bear. As a firm's debt rises beyond accepted levels for its industry and its particular conditions, the cost of equity increases far more than the cost of debt. (Appendix A to this chapter describes one approach to calculating the cost of equity capital, the capital asset pricing model.) The net effect is for the WACC to rise as shown on the right side of the graph in Figure 7.4.[31]

To return to the earlier calculations, to compensate lenders for their higher financial risk the firm will have to pay a higher interest charge with 50 percent debt than if it had 20 percent debt. It will also have a higher cost of equity for the same reason. For example, the cost of debt might go from 10 percent to 12 percent and the cost of equity from 15 percent to 20 percent. Then,

$$WACC = [(.12 \times .50] + [.20 \times .50] = 13\%$$

Note that the weighted average cost of capital remained at 13 percent even though both the cost of debt and the cost of equity increased. As shown in Figure 7.4, a debt/equity ratio somewhere around 35 percent would have resulted in a somewhat lower WACC. In practice, each industry has a generally accepted range of debt/equity ratios that depends on the economic risks inherent in the business operations associated with that industry.

Managing Risk

Strategic choices and major operating decisions generally involve considerable uncertainty and risk. Since the consequences of these uncertainties and risks often can have a major bearing on the financial health of the firm, the general manager has to be sensitive to their existence and prepared to manage them. While risk management has advanced markedly as a field during the past two decades, many senior general managers have been slow to respond. Often, they are simply not accustomed to thinking systematically about uncertainty and are not aware that the insight gained from such information could help them in making major decisions. Consider the following example:

Financial projections for a major newsprint manufacturing company indicated that earnings per share for 1990 would drop from $4.00 to about $3.50 as a result of expected price declines for paper and pulp in a weakening economy. Senior management and the board of directors reviewed this projection and were comfortable that the limited earnings setback would have only a moderately adverse effect on the company's common stock price. Further analysis, however, would have revealed that while the price of newsprint was expected to drop from around $700 per ton to $625, there was one chance in ten that the price could actually rise to $780 or drop to $475 per ton. With this added information about uncertainties, senior management's assessment of the firm's situation would be likely to change dramatically. While a drop in earnings from $4.00 to $3.50 per share that would have resulted from the expected reduction in price from $700 to $625 per ton might be tolerable, a drop to $3.00 per share (should the price of newsprint drop to $550 per ton) might be viewed as cause for concern, and to below $2.50 per share (price below $475 per ton) as a potential crisis with respect to the effect on share price and ultimately to the firm's vulnerability to being forcibly taken over. In this case, as in many others, an explicit consideration of uncertainty can cause the general manager to redefine the firm's risk exposure and to alter decisions and plans concerning both strategy and operations.

Risk

In financial theory, risk can be defined as the possibility that the actual return will deviate from that which was expected.[32] As shown in Figure 7.5, the more spread out the possible returns, the higher the risk. In the above example, the greater the likelihood of earnings falling to $3.00 or below $2.50, the more threatening is the situation. If there is only one chance in 100 for earnings to fall below $2.50, management might consider the risk as sufficiently remote so as to ignore it. In contrast, if the chances for such a serious earnings decline

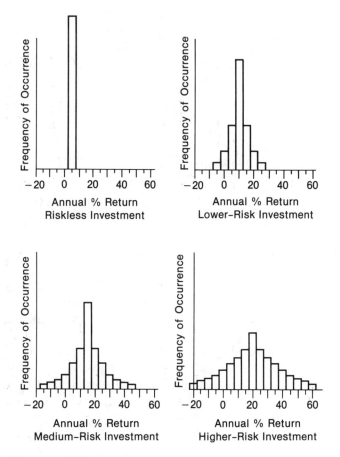

Figure 7.5　Risk as variability in return.

were as much as one in four, the risk is likely to be regarded as very high. In this situation, the general manager might reduce or defer costs or take other actions to cushion the effect of depressed prices on net earnings.

Business risks have many origins. Some are connected with normal business operations. Loss of assets in a fire, an employee wildcat strike, and lower-than-expected demand because of an economic downturn or because of a competitor's successful sales campaign are examples of operating risks. A firm's vulnerability with regard to servicing its debt and its exposure to changes in interest rates, foreign exchange rates, and commodity prices in turn are generally referred to as financial risks. For example, a U.S. firm that sells a commodity chemical abroad on the open market runs a risk that the spot price might drop from the projected price. It also runs a risk that the foreign currency will be devalued, reducing the dollars it receives in exchange.

The distinction between operating and financial risks breaks down when changes in interest rates, foreign exchange rates, and commodity prices affect a firm's competitiveness, such as when rising commodity prices make substi-

tute products more attractive to end users. The risks associated with such indirect consequences can be easily overlooked by management until the damage
is done. For example, the senior general managers of a small Indiana manufacturer of industrial tools and equipment with operations and sales exclusively
in the Midwest had never considered foreign exchange rates as relevant to the
company's fortunes. But when the dollar strengthened against the yen and
deutsche mark, foreign competitors entered its market and almost put it out of
business.[33]

Clearly, senior management has to be alert to threats of this nature. Indeed,
the starting point in risk management is to identify all of the significant risks
that the company is exposed to so that action might be taken to contain them.
The next step is to assess how sensitive the firm's earnings and cash flow are
to these uncertainties. For example, a financial model for the firm can be used
to answer such questions as "What will happen if the LIBOR (London Inter-
bank Borrowing Rate) were to increase by 0.5 percent? By 2 percent?" and
"What if copper prices were to drop 10 percent following the Chilean election
and at the same time the escudo were devalued by 8 percent?" By means of
simulation, probability distributions for relevant future interest rates, foreign
exchange, and commodity values can, in turn, generate probability distributions of the resulting earnings and cash flows similar to those shown in Figure
7.5.[34]

Alternatively, linear regression analysis can be used to examine the historical sensitivity of a firm's earnings and cash flows to changes in interest rates,
foreign exchange rates, and commodity prices. The regression model can also
be used to estimate the financial exposure of a competing firm, using public
data. Inexpensive and easy-to-use software programs that structure the analysis and perform the calculations are readily available for both simulation and
regression analysis.

The final step is to take appropriate offsetting actions.

Reducing Risk

Management has at its disposal many means of reducing business risk.[35] Insurance can be purchased to protect against certain losses. Operating risks can
also be lowered by prudent strategic choices, such as favoring stable business
lines over erratic ones, serving multiple independent markets, and avoiding
very risky projects or sharing them with one or more other parties. Alternatively, many financial transactions (e.g., forward contracts, swaps, options) can
be employed to hedge specific risk exposures. What is important is that management consider the alternative courses of action open to it. For example,
companies commonly use forward contracts, futures, and other financial hedging arrangements to protect against exchange-rate fluctuations. But several
business moves might prove more effective in dealing with this problem.[36] One
is to configure individual businesses to have the flexibility to shift production
and sourcing to countries that gain cost advantages due to changes in exchange
rates. Another is to reduce exchange-rate exposure by matching costs and rev-

enues in the foreign countries involved. A third is to select a portfolio of businesses with offsetting exposures. Firms face a similar set of choices in their marketing strategy for regulating their exposures to fluctuating exchange rates and their ability to respond to these changes.

Reducing operating risks normally incurs costs of some kind (actual expenditures in the case of insurance; opportunity costs—for example, foregone revenues—in the case of passing up or sharing attractive but risky projects). At some point, when these costs exceed the expected benefit, further reduction of operating-risk exposure becomes unsound. Since a firm's well-being depends on the combined effects of operating and financial risks, the level of operating risk serves as a major factor in determining the level of financial risk that the firm can comfortably tolerate. (Examples of financial risks would include large interest obligations and tight credit restrictions.) In general, the higher the operating risk, the lower the financial risk should be, and the lower the operating risk, the higher the financial risk can be. The debt/equity ratio is the major means by which senior management can control this relationship.

Some of the most important recent advances in risk management have involved reducing the financial risks associated with changes in interest rates, foreign exchange, and commodity prices. New financial instruments for hedging have emerged in recent years and are imaginatively blended to produce the desired risk exposure. Major segments of the business community, however, have been slow in adopting these powerful but unfamiliar techniques.[37] The principal reason for this reluctance, according to a 1986 survey of 193 of the *Fortune* 500 industrial companies, is a lack of knowledge coupled with resistance by senior management or the board of directors.[38]

Ignorance is not a valid reason for any company to fail to manage its financial risks in the most efficient and effective manner possible. To take unnecessary risks or to pass up attractive business opportunities so as to avoid risks that could be hedged are both irresponsible managerial actions. Responsible general managers must be adequately informed about risk management to ensure that it gets handled properly by competent people. Basic to this purpose, they need to have some familiarity with the range of financial instruments that are available for controlling risk.

Financial Instruments to Manage Financial Risks

Four fundamental financial instruments can be used to reduce financial risk: forward contracts, futures contracts, swap contracts, and option contracts (see Box 7.2 for a definition of each). While differing in detail and in specific application, they all allow one party to reduce financial risks in exchange for value to a second party. The exchange in the case of forward contracts, futures, and swaps[39] is to reduce a complementary risk for the other party. For example, with a forward contract, a U.S. company awaiting a payment in French francs can arrange with a French firm awaiting a similar payment in U.S. dollars (in terms of value and timing) to exchange the payments each is to receive at some agreed rate. In this way, both firms receive fixed payments in their own cur-

Box 7.2   Financial instruments to manage financial risks.

A *forward contract* is an agreement to buy or sell an asset at a certain future time for a certain price (known as the "exercise price"). A forward contract is settled entirely at maturity.

A *futures contract* is also an agreement to buy or sell an asset at a certain time in the future for a specified price. In contrast to forward contracts, a futures contract is normally traded on an exchange, does not usually specify an exact delivery date, is settled on a daily basis ("marking to market"), and requires a margin deposit. The last two features eliminate any risk of either party not making payment.

A *swap* involves a private agreement between two parties to exchange cash flows at certain times in the future according to some prearranged formula. It is in effect a bundle of forward contracts. The most common application is to swap floating-rate and fixed-rate interest obligations. The currency swap is also popular.

An *option* gives the holder a right to buy (call option) or to sell (put option) the underlying asset by a certain date for a cerain price. The holder does not have to exercise this right.

rency, no matter what happens to the exchange rate during the intervening period. With options, some or all of the risk associated with future uncertainty is exchanged for a fixed fee (the cost of the option).

The way a forward or futures contract reduces financial risk is illustrated in Figure 7.6. The firm's inherent risk profile is shown by the dotted line. The higher the future price (ΔP) of a commodity (or the higher the interest rate, or the stronger the dollar), the lower the transaction value (ΔV). A forward or futures contract can be arranged to have a complementary payoff with the resulting net exposure reduced to zero—that is, earnings will be unaffected by changes in the price of whatever was hedged.

The payoff profiles for various common hedging instruments are shown in Figure 7.7. Managing financial risk with these instruments is a matter of selecting the hedging payoff profile that produces a desired resulting exposure at an acceptable cost. For example, we have already seen how a forward or futures contract could neutralize the risk of a particular transaction. The problem with this arrangement is that the firm forgoes potential gains as well as potential losses. As shown in Figure 7.7, by buying a put option, management can retain upside gains while limiting downside exposure.[40] The reason purchased options do not drop in value is that they are only exercised under favorable circumstances.

The possible variations and special features of these hedging instruments

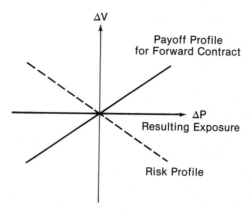

Figure 7.6 Forward contract effect on risk.

appear almost limitless. For example, variations of the standard forward contract include a *flexible forward* (or range forward) contract (that permits payment at spot rates between a ceiling and floor level), and a *break forward* (or cancelable) contract.[41] *Caps* guarantee that the rate on a loan will never go above a certain level. *Collars* guarantee that the rate will remain within a given range. There are even options on options, known as *compound options*. And the list goes on. The point is that managing financial risks is too complex and dynamic a field for most general managers ever to become proficient, let alone expert, in its execution. But the basic considerations of risk management are not so difficult so as to excuse managers from understanding the need for this critical task and from providing the necessary leadership and oversight to ensure that it is executed properly. One important oversight function is to ensure proper controls so that hedging arrangements are neither excessive nor so complex and confusing so as to inadvertently expose the company to major unforeseen cash-flow risks.

Managing financial goals, cash flows, and risk are vital to the health of the firm. As such, these tasks call for the active involvement of senior general managers who bear responsibility for the performance and well-being of the firm. This involvement requires general managers to understand the nature of the interrelationships between financial and business considerations. Earlier we saw an example of how exchange-rate exposure could be reduced by operating as well as financial arrangements. Similarly, cash flows and other aspects of financial performance are influenced by strategic and operating decisions as well as by financial policies and practices. General managers are responsible for ensuring that both business and financial considerations are taken fully into account. As circumstances become more complex, the focus of this task shifts from decision rules and standard operating procedures to organizational processes that involve people with the appropriate expertise—operating as well as financial—for anticipating and responding to problems and opportunities affecting the financial health of the firm.

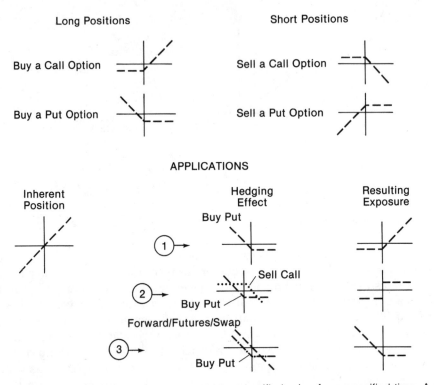

A *call option* gives the right to *buy* an asset at a specified price for a specified time. A *put option* gives the right to *sell* an asset at a specified price for a specified time.

Figure 7.7   Hedging effects of options.

   This involvement also requires general managers to have some understanding and skill in financial analysis. The requisite capability is not in understanding the mathematical concepts and being able to perform the calculations, but in knowing what the critical factors are and how to relate them to fundamental corporate strategic goals and commitments. For example, CEOs or division general managers do not need to know anything about the techniques of modeling or simulation. They should know, however, that financial models of the firm (such as the P&L and balance sheet statements) can be structured to permit "what if" questions to be tested. And they should be able to pose probing questions that are likely to uncover valuable information.

   The computer has transformed quantitative analysis. Techniques that used to be difficult and time-consuming—such as linear programming for scheduling constrained resources, multiple regression analysis for forecasting demand, or simulation for risk assessment—can now be performed quickly and easily. What this means for general managers at all levels of an organization is that quantitative analysis is increasingly accessible and useful. Not too many years ago, if a CEO wanted to know what would happen if the value of this or that variable were altered, days could pass before an answer was given (longer if the general manager only headed a small business unit). By then, everyone concerned would be off doing something else and the answer would probably be of little interest. Today, the CEO—and the small unit general manager—often can get the answer in a matter of minutes, when the information is most useful.

The changing capital-market scene continues to open new opportunities for companies to tailor financing so as to meet their special needs. The growing size and sophistication of international sources of funds, advancing computer network technology linking these markets, and the increasingly active role that banks and pension funds have taken in structuring financial arrangements are all helping to redefine traditional approaches to financing. As one indication, a growing number of firms are structuring their own deals and trades, eliminating the financial middleman. For example, British Petroleum issues commercial paper, performs interest-rate and currency swaps, and does mergers and acquisitions, and Eastman Kodak conducts up to $25 billion yearly in foreign exchange trading and hedging.[42] While the prospects for such do-it-yourself financial activities would seem limited largely to certain kinds of straightforward and recurring transactions for large companies, strong in-house financial expertise can benefit every firm in anticipating financial needs and opportunities, identifying the financial alternatives most suitable for these needs, exercising quality control over outside financial services, and preventing unnecessary or exorbitant fees. Any one of these benefits could more than justify senior management's devoted attention to the financial component of corporate strategy.

Finance has much to say about the broad aspects of company management. By its explication of risk, its focus on cash flows, and its concern with shareholders and creditors, corporate finance can help to direct general managers' attention to fundamental business considerations and to strengthen their thinking in these matters. Effective senior general managers actively exploit these valuable inputs.

Notes

1. Wayne Marr and John Trimble, "The Persistent Borrowing Advantage in Eurodollar Bonds: A Plausible Explanation," *Journal of Applied Corporate Finance* 1, no. 2 (Summer 1988), 65–70.
2. Much of this risk capital had been available previously in the form of private placements by insurance companies. The high-yield bond market, in effect, securitized this source and made it more flexible and more widely accessible.
3. A mezzanine issue occupies an intermediate position between senior debt and common equity. It is almost always placed privately, carries an intermediate term that ranges from five to twelve years, and generally includes equity participation in some form, whether as warrants, stock appreciation rights, or common stock.
4. The U.S. share of the growing futures and options worldwide trading volume declined from 80 percent in 1986 to 60 percent in 1990, according to a special report in *Business Week*, November 5, 1990, pp. 119–32.
5. Frederic S. Mishkin, "Financial Innovations and Current Trends in U.S. Financial Markets," National Bureau of Economic Research, Inc., working paper no. 3323, April 1990, p. 2. This increased volatility has led to the introduction of such instruments as the adjustable-rate mortgage in 1975, variable-rate certificates of deposit in 1977, and interest-rate swaps in 1981.

6. "Innovations and Institutional Changes in Major Financial Markets—A Ten-Year Perspective," in Maxwell Watson, Donald Mathieson, Russell Kincaid, David Folkerts-Landau, Klaus Regling, and Caroline Atkinson, *International Capital Markets—Developments and Prospects* (Washington, D.C., 1988), p. 40.

7. Frederic S. Mishkin, "Financial Innovations," pp. 8–11.

8. Many participants in international capital markets (investors, issuers, regulators) are concerned with the possible dysfunctional effects of diverse accounting rules. The International Accounting Standards Committee, reasoning that greater comparability among financial statements throughout the world would enhance their credibility and usefulness, is engaged in efforts to draft common standards and to raise minimum reporting requirements. In 1990, the U.S. Securities and Exchange Commission began supporting efforts to harmonize accounting rules so that more foreign corporations could qualify for listing on U.S. exchanges. (*Forbes*, March 18, 1991, p. 72). Others see diverse accounting rules as less of a problem for two reasons. First, many of the reported differences reflect real differences in business and structural conditions in different countries as opposed to the effects of reporting rules. For example, the relatively high market value of Japanese firms compared to U.S. firms reflects the high degree of cross-holdings in Japan (i.e., firm A owning shares of firm B and vice versa) and the generally stable nature of their share ownership. Second, the financial community relies on many sources of information other than financial statements to uncover the true economic condition of a firm. See Frederick D. S. Choi and Richard M. Levich, *The Capital Market Effects of International Accounting Diversity* (Homewood, Ill., 1990).

   Critics of program trading assert that it has led to substantial increases in trading volatility capable of destabilizing the market (e.g., the Black Monday crash of October 19, 1987). Many studies document a positive association between measures of volume and volatility on the equity market. For a survey of the literature, see Jonathan Karpoff, "The Relation Between Price Changes and Trading Volume: A Survey," *Journal of Financial and Quantitative Analysis* 22 (1987), 109–26. Advocates of program trading question the applicability of these findings on the grounds that stock-index futures reflect the same economic forces that move stock prices. This view was reinforced by a study showing innovations in trading technology to result in a reduction in short-run sluggishness for price adjustments and not in an increase in long-horizon volatility. See Kenneth A. Froot, André F. Perold, and Jeremy C. Stein, "Shareholder Trading Practices and Corporate Investment Horizons," National Bureau of Economic Research, Inc., working paper no. 3638, March 1991.

10. For a description of changes in the major financial markets around the world, see Julian Walmsley, *The New Financial Instruments* (New York, 1988), pp. 33–53.

11. According to John D. Finnerty, "An Analytical Framework for Evaluating Securities Innovations," *Journal of Corporate Finance*, (Winter 1987), p. 4, a new security is innovative only if it enables an investor to realize a higher after-tax, risk-adjusted rate of return and/or an issuer to realize a lower after-tax cost of funds than they could realize with previously existing securities. It is not enough just to be different; there must be some value added to the issuing company.

12. The lack of financial expertise typically has to do with experience rather than intelligence or aptitude. Many senior general managers have risen through the ranks of manufacturing, engineering, marketing, or even legal, with little or no exposure to financial activities. Very few of them would have had any exposure to such important financial matters as the treasury function, investor relations, and tax management. Many are unclear about financial accounting. As a rough indication of this last problem, approximately one-third of the executives attending the Harvard Business School's advanced management program have little familiarity with even the rudiments of financial accounting. These are people with an average of roughly twenty years successful experience in some of the world's leading corporations and with high prospects for advancement to senior-most positions.

13. Liquidity can be defined as the extent to which a corporation has assets that can be used to meet its obligations. It is a measure of the availability of cash (cash on hand and the conversion of other assets into cash). Working capital is the difference between current assets (e.g., cash, accounts receivable, and inventories) and current liabilities (e.g., accounts payable, wages payable, and current obligations for repaying bank loans).

14. Leasing represents another form of financing and can apply for any time period.
15. Ian Cooper and Julian Frank, "Treasury Performance Measurement," *Midland Corporate Finance Journal* 4, no. 4 (Winter 1987), 29–43.
16. To discourage an unfriendly takeover, some companies distribute rights to their shareholders, allowing them to purchase a new series of securities, typically convertible preferred stock, when any party acquires some percentage, frequently 15 or 20 percent, of its outstanding shares. This mechanism, known as a *poison pill*, is meant to force the potential acquirer into negotiating directly with the board of directors. Flip-in and flip-over provisions enable the shareholder to convert the preferred stock either into a multiple number of the company's shares (typically two) or an equivalent value of the surviving corporate entity's common stock.
17. Gordon Donaldson, *Managing Corporate Wealth* (New York, 1984), p. 155.
18. Ibid., p. 37. Donaldson went on to conclude, ". . . corporate growth objectives must equal or exceed anticipated industry growth for competitive strategy to be judged successful" (p. 40).
19. This reserve borrowing capacity, known as *financial slack*, helps to insulate a company from scrutiny by capital markets. See Jeremy C. Stein, "Efficient Capital Markets, Inefficient Forms: A Model of Myopic Corporate Behavior," *Quarterly Journal of Economics* 104 (November 1989), 664.
20. Froot, Perold, and Stein, "Shareholder Trading Practices and Corporate Investment Horizons."
21. James Abegglan and George Stalk, Jr., *Kaisha, The Japanese Corporation* (New York, 1985).
22. See Jeremy Stein, "Efficient Capital Markets, Inefficient Firms: A Model of Myopic Corporate Behavior," *Quarterly Journal of Economics* 104 (November 1989), 655–69. The stock market is said to use earnings as a basis for making a rational forecast of value for mature firms, whereby higher current earnings are correlated with higher future earnings. Managers are consequently motivated to pump up current earnings so as to increase the forecasted earnings and the resulting share price. Investors, anticipating this behavior, in turn discount the value of reported current earnings, thereby further motivating managers to report the most optimistic earnings when profit growth falls short of target.
23. SFAS 95, issued November 1987, requires the preparation of a cash flow statement for each accounting period that an income statement is presented. The cash flow statement replaced the statement of changes in financial position.
24. This section draws on Robert C. Higgins, *Analysis for Financial Management*, 2nd ed. (Homewood, Ill., 1989), chap. 4.
25. A general manager should never confuse profits and cash. A firm can show profits while losing cash or show losses while gaining cash. Inadequate cash, not financial accounting loss, is what forces a firm into bankruptcy.
26. In general usage, SGR analysis assumes no new external equity.
27.
$$\text{SGR} = \frac{\Delta \text{ Sales}}{\text{Sales}} = \frac{P}{S} \times \frac{S}{A} \times \left(1 + \frac{D}{E}\right) \times \left(1 - \frac{\text{dividend}}{P}\right)$$

where

P = profit after tax E = equity
S = net sales D = total debt
A = total assets Δ = change in (sales, for example)

The following two adaptations can be made:

1. $1 + \dfrac{D}{E} = \dfrac{E+D}{E} = \dfrac{A}{E}$

2. $1 - \dfrac{\text{dividend}}{P} = \dfrac{P - \text{dividend}}{P} = \dfrac{\Delta \text{RE}}{P}$ (where RE = retained earnings)

then

$$\text{SGR} = \frac{P}{S} \times \frac{S}{A} \times \frac{A}{E} \times \frac{\Delta \text{RE}}{P}$$

This equation can be further reduced to the following forms:

$$\text{SGR} = (1 - \text{payout ratio}) \times \text{return on equity} = \frac{\Delta \text{RE}}{E}$$

28. One of the simplest and possibly most popular methods for measuring the economic value of an investment is *payback period*. The payback period is defined as the length of time required for the stream of cash proceeds produced by an investment to equal the original cost outlay required by the investment. This approach has three weaknesses that disqualify it as a general method for ranking investments: (1) It fails to give any consideration to cash proceeds earned after the payback date; (2) It fails to take into account any differences in the timing of proceeds earned prior to the payback date; and (3) It fails to take risk differentials into account. See Harold Bierman, Jr., and Seymour Smidt, *The Capital Budgeting Decision*, 2nd ed. (New York, 1966), pp. 21–22.

29. A firm's overall cost of capital is often used for this purpose. A refinement is to use the cost of capital that would apply to the risk level of the specific project or business in question. The riskier the project, the higher the discount rate. For example, a holding company might use 12 percent as the discount rate for an electric power utility investment, 16 percent for a tire manufacturing project, and 19 percent for an airline venture, even though its overall cost of capital was 15 percent.

30. A *covenant* is a provision in a debt agreement requiring the borrower to do, or not do, something. In addition to the normal risks associated with a company's ability to service debt as leverage increases, debt-holders face another risk associated with a divergence of their interest with that of shareholders. The higher the proportion of debt, the more strongly management might be motivated to take on risky projects since shareholders stand to gain disproportionately from high returns and creditors stand to lose disproportionately from failures. See Michael C. Jensen and William H. Meckling, "Theory of the Firm: Managerial Behavior, Agency Costs and Ownership Structure," *Journal of Financial Economics* 3, no. 4 (October 1976), 305–60.

31. For highly leveraged capital structures—such as those employed for restructuring purposes and leveraged buyouts—the downside risk for debtors approaches that for shareholders. As a result, the cost of debt approaches that of equity. Moreover, some form of convertibility to equity is commonly included in the arrangements to give creditors an opportunity to divide the upside payoff with shareholders. For further comments about the limitations of the weighted-average formula for highly leveraged financial structures, see Richard A. Brealey and Stewart C. Myers, *Principles of Corporate Finance*, 3rd ed. (New York, 1988), pp. 454–55.

32. James C. Van Horne, *Financial Management and Policy*, 8th ed. (Englewood Cliffs, N.J., 1989), p. 13.

33. This tendency to define narrowly such risks holds as well for companies engaged in international business operations. According to one study, such firms often frame the problem of shifting exchange rates with a narrow focus on particular transactions or decisions where exchange rates have a critical and direct impact rather than on larger, less explicit competitive exposures for the business unit or firm as a whole. An example given was of firms emphasizing yen cost exposures in connection with sourcing a few components despite the fact that they faced Japanese competition virtually across the board in their product markets. See Donald R. Lessard and Nitin Nohria, "Rediscovering Functions in the MNC: The Role of Expertise in Firms' Responses to Shifting Exchange Rates," in Christopher A. Bartlett, Yves L. Doz, and Gunnar Hedlund, eds., *Managing the Global Firm*, (London, 1990), pp. 186–212.

34. Simulation is a technique that can be used to generate the full range of possible outcomes for a quantitative model of a firm's earnings or cash flow. The value of each variable is selected randomly in accordance with the probability of its likely occurrence. For example, on one run, the calculation might assume an interest rate of 9.2 percent and sales of $486 million. On the next, it might assume 8.7 percent and $512 million respectively. By running hundreds or even thousands of such "what if" scenarios, a likely outcome pattern emerges.

35. This section draws partly on Clifford W. Smith, Jr., Charles W. Smithson, and D. Sykes Wilford, *Managing Financial Risk* (New York, 1990).

36. This example is from Lessard and Nohria, "Rediscovering Functions in the MNC," p. 191.

37. According to a 1989 survey of 255 members of the Financial Executives Institute, 46 percent of the respondents reported that their company did not manage interest rate risk exposure (Henry Davis, "Financial Products for Medium-Sized Companies" [The Globecon Group, Ltd., 1989]).

38. Stanley B. Black and Timothy J. Gallagher, "The Use of Interest Rate Futures and Options by Corporate Financial Managers," *Financial Management* 15 (Autumn 1986) 73–78.

39. In addition to hedging a company's exposure to interest rates by altering the cash flows of an existing loan, swaps are also used to reduce the cost of a debt issuance by taking advantage of the relative costs two firms would have to incur for fixed-rate and floating-rate loans. For further information, see Laurie S. Goodman, "The Use of Interest Rate Swaps in Managing Corporate Liabilities," *Journal of Applied Corporate Finance* 2, no. 4 (Winter 1990), 35–47, and also John Hull, *Options, Futures, and other Derivative Securities* (Englewood Cliffs, N.J., 1989), pp. 17–21 and 283–302.

40. A *put option* gives the holder the right to *sell* a specified asset at a specified price for a specified time. A *call option* gives the holder the right to *buy* a specified asset at a specified price for a specified time.

41. In a break forward contract, the owner agrees to purchase the asset at a premium price for the privilege of being able to break the contract at a lower price. The effect is somewhat similar to that of buying a put option and selling a call. See Sam Srinivasulu, "Second-Generation Forwards: A Comparative Analysis," *Business International Money Report*, September 21, 1987.

42. *Business Week*, November 5, 1990, p. 125.

Appendix

Modern portfolio theory describes how investors and creditors value the firm and how the equity market determines expected returns. The central idea— first developed in 1952 by Harry Markowitz (who won the 1990 Nobel Prize in Economic Science)—is that investors relate expected return to the risk they have to bear. Since then, this concept has been refined and extended, resulting in several theories or models.[1] One of the more widely supported models since the 1960s is the capital asset pricing model (CAPM).

CAPM, representing an idealized view of how the market prices securities and determines expected returns, provides a measure of the risk premium. The model assumes that investors can eliminate *unsystematic* risk (relating to events peculiar to a specific firm) simply by holding large portfolios. As a result, investors holding large portfolios are exposed only to *systematic* (nondiversifiable) risk. Systematic risk includes market-related factors (such as political, social, and economic events that affect investors' expectations concerning corporate profits) and changes in purchasing power (inflation and deflation). It also includes indirectly the effect of interest-rate changes on corporate earnings and on margin trade costs, both of which influence share price.[2] Figure 7A.1 illustrates the reduction of total risk as securities are added to a portfolio. Unsystematic risk is virtually eliminated in portfolios of thirty or forty securities drawn from industries that are not closely related. Box 7A.1 gives examples of systematic and unsystematic risk factors.

CAPM provides a convenient measure of systematic risk. This measure, called beta (β), indicates a security's volatility relative to the market's volatility. A stock with a beta of 1.0 tends to rise and fall the same percentage as does

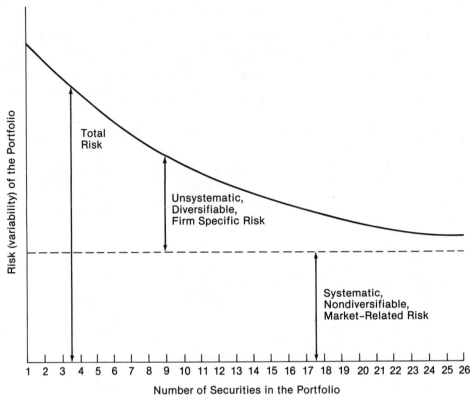

Figure 7A.1   Risk versus diversification.

Box 7A.1   Systematic and unsystematic risk factors.

Examples of unsystematic risk factors:

- A firm's technical wizard is killed in an auto accident.
- A wildcat strike is declared.
- A lower-cost foreign competitor unexpectedly enters a firm's product market.
- A pharmaceutical company's potential blockbuster drug receives early FDA approval.

Examples of systematic risk factors:

- Congress votes a massive tax cut.
- The Federal Reserve follows a restrictive monetary policy.
- There is a precipitous rise in long-term interest rates.
- Political developments ease a threat of major armed conflict.

Table 7A.1 Beta Coefficients for Common Stocks of Selected Companies, December 14, 1990.

Company	Coefficient	Company	Coefficient
AMR (American Airlines)	1.40	Georgia Pacific	1.25
Abbot Labs	1.05	Goodyear	1.15
Aetna Life and Casualty	.95	Hewlett-Packard	1.20
Akzo N.V. (ADR)*	.90	Humana	1.10
Allied Signal	.95	Intel	1.50
AMAX	1.25	Int'l Business Mach.	.90
American Express	1.30	Johnson & Johnson	1.05
Amer. Tel & Tel	.90	Lilly, Eli	1.15
Anheuser-Busch	1.00	Lotus Development	1.35
Apple Computer	1.25	McDonald's	1.00
ASEA AB (ADR)*	.85	Merck	1.00
Bard, C.R.	1.10	Merril Lynch	1.20
Biogen	1.70	Minnesota Mining	1.05
Boeing	1.00	NIKE	1.15
Boston Edison	.70	Polaroid	1.25
Bowater	1.25	Procter & Gamble	.95
Caterpillar	1.20	Sears, Roebuck	1.15
Citicorp	1.15	Spiegel (Catalog retailer)	1.90
Coca-Cola	1.00	Sun Microsystems	1.25
Cray Research	1.25	Toys "R" Us	1.30
Dayton Hudson	1.40	TransAlta Utilities	.50
Dow Chemical	1.20	USX	1.001
Exxon	.80	Unilever NV	.80
Ford Motor	1.15	United Technologies	1.15
General Electric	1.10	Xerox	1.15
General Mills	1.05		

Source: Value Line Investments.

*ADR = american depository receipt, representing an interest in shares of a foreign company that are kept in the custody of a foreign bank.

the market as a whole. Stocks with a β greater than 1.0 tend to rise and fall by a greater percentage than does the market and therefore have a greater than average systematic risk. Similarly, a stock with a β less than 1.0 has a lower than average level of systematic risk and is less sensitive to market swings. Beta coefficients for common stocks of selected companies are given in Table 7A.1.

An investor requires return to increase with unavoidable (systematic) risk. This risk/expected return trade-off with CAPM is called the security market line and is illustrated in Figure 7A.2. The expected return on a firm's stock—by definition its cost of equity capital—is consequently defined as follows:

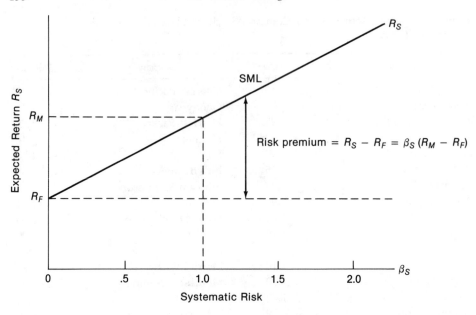

Figure 7A.2   The security market line: The risk/expected return trade-off with CAPM.

Firm's cost of equity capital =   Risk-free rate of return + {Firm's β × Risk premium for total market}

The risk-free rate of return can be estimated as the average or expected rate of return on U.S. treasury bills in the future. The risk premium for the total market is the expected return less the risk-free return. A firm's beta can be estimated by linear regression or by observing the stock's reaction to swings in the market. It is also available from investment advisory services for most established, publicly traded firms.[3]

As noted earlier, CAPM assumes the presence of perfect or efficient capital markets. When this assumption is relaxed to take account of real-world conditions, the unsystematic or residual risk of a stock becomes a factor in determining valuation. For example, the greater the residual risk for a company, the greater the possibility that bankruptcy costs might be incurred and therefore the higher the required rate of return. Similarly, small firm size also increases expected return. Such imperfections in the market and measurement problems cause the required rate of return to be higher than that indicated by CAPM.[4] Recently, conventional CAPM theory has undergone challenge from an alternative model of asset pricing—called the arbitrage pricing theory (APT)—that embraces several risk dimensions to explain market equilibrium.[5]

Notes

1. These models can be grouped into three main categories: versions of the market model, versions of the capital asset pricing model, and versions of the efficient market hypothesis. See Jason McQueen, "Beta is Dead, Long Live Beta," *Issues in Corporate Finance* (New York, 1983), pp. 36–41.

2. See Donald F. Fischer and Ronald J. Jordan, *Security Analysis and Portfolio Management*, 4th ed. (Englewood Cliffs, N.J., 1987), pp. 116–20.

3. For more information about CAPM, see David W. Mullins, Jr., "Does the Capital Asset Pricing Model Work?" *Harvard Business Review* 60, no. 1 (January–February 1982) 105–13, and Robert A. Haugen, *Modern Investment Theory* (Englewood Cliffs, N.J., 1986), pp. 155–206.

4. James C. Van Horne, *Financial Management and Policy*, 8th ed. (Englewood Cliffs, N.J., 1989,) pp. 230–31.

5. See Stephen A. Ross, "The Arbitrage Theory of Capital Asset Pricing," *Journal of Economic Theory* 13 (December 1976), 341–60.

8

Corporate Governance and the Board of Directors

Events over the past several decades have called into question traditional concepts of corporate governance.[1] During the 1960s, the U.S. business community came under attack regarding its public responsibilities. Ralph Nader epitomized the movement with his condemnation of General Motors' alleged disregard of product safety.[2] The goal for many critics was not simply to rectify objectionable practices, but to correct the problem at its source by changing the manner in which the corporation would be governed. They called for more regulations, for changes in the composition of board of directors' membership to represent important public interests, and for mechanisms to encourage internal policing, such as board committees to monitor corporate rectitude and laws to protect "whistle-blowers" (people who publicly reveal objectionable corporate actions). This chapter explores the often conflicting interests and responsibilities of general managers and boards of directors for U.S. publicly owned corporations as they face major and sometimes unprecedented changes in public expectations, in the laws that regulate corporate behavior, and in accepted business practice.

In addition to the battle over corporate public responsibilities, senior managers have had to contend with a near-epidemic of takeover activities. The relative security that incumbent management enjoyed during the 1940s and 1950s gave way in the 1960s as businesses began to bolster the slowing growth of internally generated earnings with the earnings of acquired companies. An infatuation with the perceived advantages of diversified operations provided the American business community with additional impetus for adopting increasingly aggressive merger and acquisition activities. Companies like Textron, Gulf & Western, and Litton Industries set the pattern, and others followed. As Alfred Chandler observed, "By the late 1960s, acquisitions and mergers had become almost a mania. The number rose from just over 2,000 in 1965 to over 6,000 in 1969."[3]

Changes in financial accounting rules that had the effect of reducing the tax and reporting advantages of acquisitions, along with a general failure to create lasting shareholder value from conglomerate business activities, brought this era to an end. But the allure of taking over companies that had excess cash or unrealized asset values continued unabated. Hostile tender offers became a dominant business feature of the 1970s and 1980s. Even size no longer protected corporate management as companies like Crown Zellerbach and Gulf Oil came under attack. As the 1980s progressed, so did the growth of leveraged buyouts (LBOs) and leveraged restructurings, culminating with the $25 billion LBO of RJR Nabisco. The 1990s, according to two senior corporate bankers, can expect to experience a continuation of this trend toward aggressive financial practices: "Asset and capital redeployment through restructuring transactions initiated by outside parties will characterize the financial environment for many years to come. That such restructuring will most certainly continue is ensured by the natural evolution of technology and market fundamentals, the growing pressure for greater efficiency, the expanding supply of capital to facilitate such transactions, and the large number of investors vigorously seeking to profit from such change."[4]

Meanwhile, new challenges regarding a corporation's public responsibility have forced senior executives and directors to redefine their roles and their relationships to each other as well as to powerful third parties. Two fundamental questions lie at the heart of these issues and are the subject of ongoing debate in public forums and in the courts: To whom is management accountable and by what means is management to be held accountable?

To Whom Is Management Accountable?

Based on principles associated with the ownership of private property, the traditional view of management accountability has held that top executives and directors are answerable solely to the owners of the business.[5] In the words of Milton Friedman: "In a free enterprise, private property system, a corporate executive is an employee of the owners of the business. He has direct responsibility to his employers. That responsibility is to conduct the business in accordance with their desires, which generally will be to make as much money as possible while conforming to the basic rules of the society, both those embodied in law and those embodied in ethical custom."[6] Friedman holds that any necessary constraints are imposed by the parties involved in a company's transactions (customers and suppliers can stop dealing with an excessively self-serving company; employees can leave an unfair employer or can retaliate in various ways) as well as by legal and political forces.

This view generally has been reflected in U.S. corporation law. The Supreme Court of Delaware, in its opinion in the case of *Unocal Corporation* v. *Mesa Petroleum Company* (1985), while opening a new era in the application of corporate governance principles to constituencies other than shareholders, nonetheless reiterated "the basic principle that corporate directors have a fiduciary duty to act in the best interests of the corporation's stockholders." This primacy of shareholders' interest was reaffirmed and elaborated the following year in the celebrated *Revlon, Inc.* v. *MacAndrews & Forbes Holdings* case, which centered on the propriety of Revlon's board in using such defensive tactics as poison pills and lockup options[7] to retard the bidding process and thereby thwart a takeover bid by Pantry Pride in favor of a management leveraged buyout. In ruling against Revlon, the Delaware court disallowed directors any action motivated by considerations other than the best interests of the corporation and its stockholders where a change of corporate controls was intended to be accomplished and the corporation in effect was up for sale.

The public responsibility of corporations has always been at issue. The widespread outcry against profiteering during the Civil War; the creation of the Interstate Commerce Commission in 1887 to regulate railroads; trust-busting, the enactment of the Sherman Antitrust Act in 1890, and its stiffening by the Clayton Antitrust Act in 1914; the Wagner Act (1935) and other laws to protect the labor movement; and the Food, Drug, and Cosmetic Act (1938) for consumer safety were notable manifestations of this concern over the years. During the 1960s and 1970s, the counterculture that arose largely in response to the Vietnam war challenged the establishment to a degree rarely experienced in U.S. history. Business corporations were challenged along with government, religion, and society itself. The civil rights movement called into question the corporation's treatment of and impact on blacks and other minority segments of the population. Ecologists called for more stringent regulations to protect the quality of water and air. Incited by Rachel Carson's *Silent Spring* (1962), the public decried alleged indiscriminate corporate promotion of dangerous pesticides, herbicides, and other noxious chemicals. The oil spill in 1969 at Santa Barbara, California, asbestos in the Duluth drinking water,[8] and the degradation of forests and water quality from industrial effluents were some of the major rallying points on this front.

A case for corporations participating actively in public affairs and assuming responsibility for the impact of business activity upon society was laid out by Kenneth Andrews.[9] He argued in 1971 that government regulations could not be an effective substitute for knowledgeable self-restraint; that corporations had the power to help or harm society; that corporations needed executives with enough integrity, intelligence, and humanity to realize that they could not confine themselves to narrow economic activities while ignoring the social consequences of corporate actions; and that the dangers and problems of corporate participation in public affairs could be dealt with through education, government control, and self-regulation.

During the ensuing years, changes have occurred on many fronts to lend support to this comprehensive view. The Occupational Safety and Health Administration (OSHA) develops and monitors workplace safety and health standards, and other government agencies issue regulations regarding air and water quality, pension plan management, and discriminatory human resource practices. Since the *Unocal* decision, over half the states have enacted changes in corporate statutes empowering directors specifically to consider constituencies other than shareholders in response to unfriendly takeover attempts and general business policy. Delaware broadened its *Revlon* and *Unocal* positions in the case of *Paramount* v. *Time* (1989), where the court observed, "Absent a limited set of circumstances, a board of directors, while always required to act in an informed manner, is not under any *per se* duty to maximize shareholder value in the short term, even in the context of a takeover." Moreover, the opinion ruled out any court attempt "to appraise and evaluate the relative merits of a long-term versus a short-term investment goal for shareholders." In effect, the Delaware court empowered directors to give precedent consideration to the fortunes of the corporation as such (as opposed to individual shareholders' interests) in pursuit of a strategic plan, so long as the firm had not been up for sale in the *Revlon* manner.

Consistent with these external changes, many larger corporations have included on their board of directors people who are expected to be sensitive to the concerns of certain special interest groups, such as minorities, environmentalists, and the public at large. In some cases, board committees have been charged with monitoring the company's performance with respect to its public responsibilities and ethical behavior. And a growing number of firms have taken steps to increase employees' awareness of and responsiveness to outside constituencies.

As the 1990s unfold, the debate on corporate, public, and social responsibility—and consequently the question as to whom management is accountable—remains largely unresolved. Complicating the issue has been the changing character of corporate ownership. Management could easily identify with shareholders when the vast majority were individuals, many holding shares for long periods of time. It is far less easy to feel empathy for institutional investors (pension funds, mutual funds, insurance companies) that are likely to trade the company's shares more quickly than would the average individual investor. Even more difficult for management is identifying with shareholders who invest for very short-term speculative purposes only. Such investors can hold a significant portion of a corporation's total equity in anticipation of a possible change in ownership control. Indeed, CEOs and directors openly and privately question just how accountable they should be to an arbitrageur who buys their company's shares during a takeover campaign with the intention of selling them as quickly as possible for a gain with little to no regard for the fortunes of the corporation itself.

Lack of agreement on accountability is likely to cause organizational confusion over time, especially during moments of crises. In the absence of an accepted norm in the business community, senior general managers have to decide for themselves (in collaboration with the board of directors) the corporation's position in these matters. The implications are far-reaching—from how the company deals with its employees, the environment, and product safety, to how it responds to a takeover attempt.

By What Means Is Management to Be Held Accountable?

While the question of *how* management is to be held accountable depends in part on determining *to whom* it is accountable, senior managers nonetheless have an opportunity to strengthen corporate governance by looking independently at the process for controlling corporate behavior.

Principal Controls on Senior Corporate Management

The principal control mechanism for senior managers of publicly owned corporations is the board of directors. Control is also exercised by other parties (through the board) and independently (especially in situations where a board fails to function effectively). Even those who are most strict in their adherence to the concept of management as agent for shareholders acknowledge that other constituencies must be satisfied for the corporation to succeed—and thereby reward shareholders. In broad terms, these sources of control include: (1) customers, suppliers, competitors, communities, and any other parties in the firm's business environment who can help or hinder its performance; (2) government regulations; (3) employees, including managers; and (4) capital markets; as well as the personal values and moral convictions of the senior managers themselves. In practice, these forces work independently and in concert.

As was discussed in earlier chapters, the expectations of customers, suppliers, employees, and other parties who are affected by a company's activities and who in turn can affect its performance have to be considered, and to some extent satisfied, if the company is to succeed. Inferior products or services are likely to result in lost customers and revenues. Shoddy treatment of suppliers can impair a firm's ability to procure necessary materials and services on favorable terms when shortages arise. The corporation's ability to function will suffer when its employees and managers are dissatisfied with how they are treated. Similarly, government regulations and incentives, reflecting public and private interests, can constrain and motivate general management's strategic and operational decisions. Capital markets also impose discipline on corporate management, but with a broader perspective than the aforementioned forces. Constituents like customers and employees impose controls on corporate activities that affect their particular interests. In contrast, creditors set standards for cash flow that reflect overall corporate operations, and shareholders evaluate the general quality of management, both in terms of achievements and future prospects; reward and punishment is expressed in the price of the common stock and ultimately in who is to control the corporation. Finally, the professional pride and sense of responsibility senior managers have in their work can prove a very effective means of control.

The board of directors, which exists explicitly for the purpose of corporate governance, is required by law to exercise prudent surveillance over all corporate affairs. Toward this goal, the board has access to inside information, making it potentially the most comprehensive and compelling external control of senior management. In fulfillment of its responsibilities, the board must be sensitive to the demands and expectations of the corporation's important constituencies.

How well do the controls on senior corporate management work? According to critics of the competitive performance of U.S. business, the answer would seem to be not well at all. These observers hold that the decline and failure of industry after industry over the past thirty years—such as steel, machine tools, automobiles, and consumer electronics—has been a failure of American management.[10] Even more pointed is the characterization of the mid-1960s and early 1970s as "an era of gross corporate waste and mismanagement."[11] According to some accounts, some chief executive officers seem more interested in their perks and in their golf scores than in running a corporation.[12]

To understand the reason for the apparent widespread failure in corporate governance, one must examine the individual mechanisms for control. Customers, suppliers, and competitors in many cases can be slow in exercising control and even slower in forcing change. As the histories of once-great firms like International Harvester, Johns Manville, and Pan American Airlines have so vividly illustrated, companies with strong brand names and deep pockets can coast on their momentum for decades before the mounting rejection of the marketplace takes effect. Employees, too, primarily because they are concerned almost exclusively with how they are treated by the corporation, are often insensitive to the need for change and slow to act. Government regulations, by their nature, tend to provide only crude or narrowly focused controls. When multifaceted agencies such as the OSHA, the Environmental Protection Agency, the Federal Aviation Administration, the Federal Communications Commission, or a utility commission—are required to enforce regulations, bureaucratic hassles and political machinations often distort and frustrate the process.

Self-policing by managers also has serious limitations. Professional pride and personal integrity can fall prey to overwhelming temptations, especially at the highest levels of authority. The nature of this corrupting influence was starkly laid out in a *Business Week* cover story: "Pampered, protected, and perked, the American CEO can know every indulgence. . . . It is a job that can easily go to one's head—and often does." The article continues: "With each higher step on the corporate ladder, an executive discovers fewer restraints: unlimited expense accounts, fewer performance appraisals, and the power, in some cases, to make decisions unchallenged by anyone. . . . The decreased supervision and increased power that coincide with success only reinforce and confirm the narcissist's already grandiose self-image."[13]

A board of directors, in contrast, can apply objective, timely, comprehensive, and direct controls on management. To do this, however, requires an independent body of people with good judgment and with time and motivation to perform this difficult task. The problem for many public corporations was that CEOs, in gaining control of the nominations process and of the meeting agenda, co-opted the boards to which they were supposed to be accountable. In the worst cases, board membership comprised a CEO's cronies or people otherwise beholden, and meetings—chaired by the CEO—were brief affairs that focused on routine matters. The board, in effect, functioned to provide window-dressing governance.[14] This degradation of the board as an effective governing body, according to critics, was what prompted investors to become more active and led to the upsurge of takeovers, LBOs, and other initiatives to change control. It has been argued that the active investor is the only reliable control over management and frequently the only means of dislodging an incompetent management before it has ruined the corporation.

The change-in-control approach to governance, not surprisingly, also has its detractors. These people, who view the takeover movement as motivated more by personal greed than by any concern for the well-being of the corporations involved, maintain that employees, communities, suppliers, and even customers (by virtue of reductions in research and development spending) are victims of the self-serving financial wheeling and dealing.[15] For some, the takeover climate is seen as motivating managers and board members alike to adopt a short-term perspective. Admiral Bobby R. Inman, former director of the nonprofit Microelectronic and Computer Technology Corporation and member of the President's Council on Competitiveness, notes, "I sit on six corporate boards, and I watch management decisions driven not by looking at the opportunities technology offers, but rather by a mandatory need to provide a quarterly return."[16]

During the 1980s, corporate governance was strengthened on several fronts. Increased global competition gave customers, suppliers, and competitors more leverage over the corporation's actions. Boards of directors became stronger and more independent as the number of outsiders increased and as board members were faced with more and more shareholder litigation. And, in many cases, unfriendly takeovers resulted in improved leadership. More important, the threat of takeover served as a control on senior managers and board members in every public company, at times motivating beneficial but painful actions that might not otherwise have been taken. Notwithstanding these advances in corporate governance, much more remains to be done.

The General Manager's Response

Top management is held accountable for its actions through the discipline of the marketplace, government regulations and the legal system in general, the board of directors, and the specter of a change in control (takeovers). Some observers argue that only change in control provides effective restraint on management performance. According to these critics, the marketplace works too slowly (especially for large, well-heeled corporations), government regulations and legal actions often penalize the wrong party (the corporations and shareholders rather than management), and boards of directors are largely ineffective in holding senior managers fully accountable. While not everyone would agree with such assertions, business leaders nonetheless need to consider the best way to ensure management accountability at the highest levels. For many corporations, the board of directors holds the greatest promise for improvements in this regard.

Board of Directors

The legal authority of a board of directors for a public corporation in the United States is broad.[17] Section 141 of Delaware General Corporation Law provides,

"The business and affairs of every corporation . . . shall be managed by or under the direction of a board of directors."[18] In carrying out these responsibilities, directors are expected to exercise the *duty of loyalty* (which concerns such matters as conflicts of interest) and the *duty of care* (which calls on directors to use diligence in being well-informed when making decisions and carrying out their duties).[19] Notwithstanding a corporate board's broad legal authority, its power can be severely limited in practice due to (1) a lack of clarity with respect to its principal tasks; (2) confusion concerning accountability; or (3) the power that the CEO holds. The first reason—lack of clarity with respect to tasks—stems from the practical need for a board to delegate the actual management of the business. As noted in the *Corporate Director's Guidebook*: "It is generally recognized that the board of directors is not expected to operate the business. Even under statutes providing that the business and affairs shall be 'managed' by the board of directors, it is recognized that actual operation is a function of management. The responsibility of the board is limited to overseeing such operation. . . ."[20]

The question remains as to just how a board and management should partition responsibilities and activities. One answer to what the duties of directors should be is provided by the American Law Institute:

1. Select, regularly evaluate, fix the compensation of, and, where appropriate, replace the principal senior executives.
2. Oversee the conduct of the corporation's business to evaluate whether the business is being properly managed.
3. Review, and, where appropriate, approve the corporation's financial objectives, major corporate plans and actions, and major changes and other major questions of choice respecting the appropriate auditing and accounting principles and practices to be used in the preparation of the corporation's financial statements.
4. Perform such other functions as are prescribed by law, or assigned to the board under a standard of the corporation.[21]

The difficulty with such a list is that not everyone agrees with it, and those who do are likely to interpret it differently.

According to the findings of an in-depth study of corporate boards, directors share a strong consensus about their duties under normal conditions.[22] The following three were identified as most important: selecting, assessing, rewarding, and, if necessary, replacing the CEO; determining strategic direction; and assuring ethical and legal conduct. Of these, determining strategic direction is most likely to cause difficulty in sorting out the roles of directors and managers and consequently has been the most controversial over the years.[23] During times of crisis, the potentially divisive issue of accountability is likely to complicate matters. Lack of agreement as to the board's responsibility to shareholders versus other constituencies can seriously impair a board's ability to function effectively under pressure.

In many corporations, the greatest limit on board power is the CEO's power.

One source of this power is the CEO's superior knowledge of the corporation and its business operations. Outside directors are keenly aware of their lesser grasp of company affairs. Another is the CEO's control of the board meeting. Generally, CEOs have a strong hand in creating the agenda, determining the information directors receive in advance, and, at the meeting, directing the flow of discussions. When the CEO also holds the position of board chairman, his or her opportunity to control board discussions is nearly total. A third source of CEOs' power is their ability to influence or control the selection of board members and the composition of board committees; they are able to pack the board with people who are sympathetic to their views or for other reasons unlikely to cause them trouble. Any potentially contrary-minded directors can be assigned to those committees where opportunities for criticism and interference are minimized. In the extreme, CEOs can attempt to achieve board support or submission through various forms of payoffs.[24] These levers of power are further enhanced by the norms that dictate actual board behavior. For example, outside board members are generally reluctant to contact fellow directors outside of meetings. Openly criticizing the CEO, or the CEO's position, at a meeting generally is not done under normal circumstances. Issues that are potentially embarrassing to management are artfully avoided. These and similar practices reduce a board's ability to function spontaneously and independently as a governing body. As Jay Lorsch aptly put it: "[D]irectors see most problems through the eyes of the CEO, who, like a multitalented filmmaker, writes the script, assigns the roles, directs the production, and has the starring role."[25]

Strengthening the Board of Directors

Responsible corporate management strives to ensure the presence of a countervailing force that can monitor and correct its performance as required. An independent, well-informed, and capable board of directors can go a long way toward providing this essential governing safeguard. The benefits of a strong board, of course, extend beyond this defensive consideration. Talented board members can contribute positively to corporate performance through the advice and counsel they give senior managers.[26]

While there is no single formula for ensuring that a board is independent, well-informed, and capable, certain practices regarding the selection of directors and the functioning of the board contribute to this end. For example, to reduce the CEO's involvement in the selection process, many corporations have created nominating committees, comprised entirely of outside directors, that are responsible for determining the desired qualifications for each new member and for screening and selecting candidates. The idea is to include people who will provide important skills and perspectives to the board and who can work together without compromising their independent judgment and voice.

The chairmanship of the board is probably the key consideration with regard to the functioning of the board. Sentiment appears to be growing that this position should be held by an outside director rather than by the CEO if the board is to maintain its independence. This step enables the board, and especially the outside directors, to control the agenda, committee membership, and even the amount and type of information they receive. The chairman, of course, should be someone with adequate time to perform this job. Devoting sufficient time to the job is also an important consideration for the board as a whole. Having a board meet two hours every other month might satisfy legal requirements and give suitable appearance of activity, but the diligent execution of board responsibilities is likely to require longer and more frequent sessions.

Board committees provide a valuable means for dealing with complex corporate affairs. To permit in-depth consideration of corporate strategy and other complex issues by the board as a whole, an increasing number of corporations schedule an annual board planning meeting that lasts from one to three days. Typically, considerable staff preparation is required to provide the information outside directors need to understand the issues. Outside experts can be brought in to provide independent judgments or to present alternative approaches to those recommended by management.

Board effectiveness also depends on the ability of its members to work in harmony. Personal compatibility is important. Also important is for the members to have unity of purpose. Confusion surrounding accountability, discussed earlier, makes it difficult for a board to assert itself forcefully. Efforts should be made to reduce this confusion as much as possible. For example, the issue can be discussed openly in connection with counsel specifying directors' accountability as indicated by relevant state (and, in some cases, federal) laws.

Beyond the Public Corporation?

Even if public corporations were to improve significantly the effectiveness of their boards, a small but growing number of critics of U.S. management would still consider the capital market as the only truly reliable source of corporate governance. Michael C. Jensen, a leading proponent of this school of thought, goes so far as to question the viability of the public corporation under certain circumstances: "The public corporation is not suitable in industries where long-term growth is slow, where internally generated funds outstrip the opportunities to invest them profitably, or where downsizing is the most productive long-term strategy. In these and other cash-rich, low-growth, or declining sectors, the pressures on management to waste cash flow through organizational slack or investments in unsound projects is often irresistible."[27] By implication, these pressures would be likely to overwhelm the board of directors as well.

Jensen goes on to identify a new model of general management. This model is built around highly leveraged financial structures, pay-for-performance compensation systems, substantial equity ownership by managers and directors, and contracts with owners and creditors that limit both cross-subsidization among business units and the waste of free cash flow.[28] The purpose of these conditions is to motivate the organization to maximize *value*, with a strong emphasis on cash flow, rather than to maximize earnings per share. Concerning any anxiety about the dangers of excessive borrowing, he argues, "Overleveraging creates the crisis atmosphere managers require to slash unsound investment programs, shrink overhead, and dispose of assets that are more valuable outside the company."[29] Without the discipline of the interest burden, management for a larger, well-established corporation is able to sustain wasteful conditions for a long period of time, destroying much of the enterprise's value in the process. Debt is the "mechanism to force managers to disgorge cash rather than spend it on empire-building projects with low or negative returns, bloated staffs, indulgent prerequisites, and organizational inefficiencies."[30]

The most common manifestation of the new corporate model, the LBO association, typically comprises: a partnership that sponsors conversions to private ownership and that counsels and monitors management in ongoing cooperative relationships; company managers who hold substantial equity stakes in their corporate unit; and institutional investors (insurance companies, pension funds, and money-management firms) who fund the limited partnerships that purchase equity and lend money (along with banks) to finance the transactions.[31]

According to this line of reasoning, by resolving the central weakness of the public corporation—the conflict between owners and managers over the control and use of corporate resources—LBO associations are making remarkable gains in operating efficiency, employee productivity, and shareholder value.[32] Critics dispute these claims and generally characterize the change-in-corporate-control movement as driven by the opportunism and personal aggrandizement of financial deal makers and a few favored senior executives.[33] The counterargument is that such personal gains, if considered wasteful of corporate assets, pale in comparison with the waste of corporate assets that uncontrolled management can and does incur.

Responsible Governance

The issue of corporate governance promises to remain highly controversial for years to come. Even under ideal conditions where a corporation enjoys healthy and thriving business activities, the issues of accountability and the proper division of responsibilities between those charged with management and those with oversight are difficult to resolve. With less favorable corporate conditions and performance, these issues are even harder to work out.

Responsible corporate leadership demands that senior general managers, in concert with the corporation's board of directors, address questions of accountability and responsibility directly and take whatever actions they find necessary to ensure well-informed and expeditious corporate control and governance. As people responsible for the performance and well-being of an enterprise, they need to consider how the corporation is to protect itself against failures in leadership. What are the safeguards against management's abuse or incompetence in its stewardship of the resources under its command? However sincere and accomplished they might be, the senior-most general managers need to address the difficult question of accountability as an integral part of their fundamental responsibility. To do less would be a serious breach of general management duty.

Notes

1. *Governance* (from the Latin *gubernare*, to govern, pilot) is defined as the exercise of authority and control.
2. Ralph Nader, *Unsafe at Any Speed: Design and Dangers of the American Automobile* (New York, 1964).
3. Alfred D. Chandler, "The Enduring Logic of Industrial Success," *Harvard Business Review* 68, no. 2 (March–April 1990), 139.
4. Michael J. Murray and Frank C. Reid, "Financial Style and Corporate Control," *Journal of Applied Corporate Finance*, 1, no. 1 (Spring 1988) 77–84. The collapse of the junk market and tightened credit conditions in the closing years of the 1980s prompted at least one knowledgeable observer to declare the era of unfriendly takeovers to be dead. Although the explosive pace of takeovers was cut short by these events, corporate managers could not afford to become entirely complacent regarding their control. The efforts by European and Japanese firms to take over U.S. companies continued unabated, serving as a reminder of the risks associated with less-than-excellent financial performance. Moreover, creative financiers could be expected to find ways to exploit opportunities for capturing unrealized asset values in poorly managed corporations. Like Humpty-Dumpty, the earlier near-sanctity of management control probably can never be put back together again, except as Security and Exchange Commission proxy rules are useful to rebuff unwelcome suitors.
5. In a narrow sense, for a U.S. corporation, the question of management accountability has a simple answer: management is accountable to its board of directors. In these cases, the pertinent question is to whom are management *and* the board accountable.
6. Milton Friedman, "The Social Responsibility of Business Is to Increase Its Profits," *New York Times Magazine*, September 13, 1970, pp. 32–33, 122–126. See also Milton Friedman, *Capitalism and Freedom* (Chicago, 1962).
7. A *lockup option* gives one party the right to purchase corporate properties at a specified price in the event of a successful takeover bid by another party. These properties are typically among the corporation's most valuable so as to make corporate control a less appealing prize for unwanted suitors. For a definition of *poison pill*, see chapter 7, note 16.
8. Termed by *Time* magazine "The Classic Pollution Case," the allegations concerned the daily discharge by Reserve Mining Company (a joint subsidiary of Republic and Armco Steel corporations) of 67,000 tons of taconite tailings (waste from iron ore production) that threatened the ecological balance of Lake Superior, the world's largest fresh-water body (*U.S.A., et al.,* v. *Reserve Mining Company, et al.,* U.S. District Court, District of Minnesota, Fifth District Civil Action, No. 5–72).
9. Kenneth R. Andrews, *The Concept of Corporate Strategy* (Homewood, Ill., 1971), pp. 118–77.
10. See, for example, Robert H. Hayes and William J. Abernathy, "Managing Our Way to Economic Decline," *Harvard Business Review* 58, no. 4 (July–August 1980), 67–77.
11. Michael C. Jensen, "Eclipse of the Public Corporation," *Harvard Business Review* 67, no. 5 (September–October 1989), 62.
12. See, for example, "CEO Disease," *Business Week*, April 1, 1991, pp. 52–60.
13. Ibid.
14. Adolf A. Berle, Jr., in his classic analysis *Power Without Property* (New York, 1959), traced the genesis of management's control of the corporation to the early 1930s. Noting the absence of large stockholders concerned with maintaining close working relationships with management, he concluded, "Thus they [management] need not consult with anyone when making up their

slates of directors, and may simply request their stockholders to sign and send in a ceremonial proxy. They select their own successors" (p. 73).

15. See, for example, William Lazonick, *Controlling the Market for Corporate Control*, unpublished paper presented at the Third International Joseph A. Schumpeter Society Conference, Airlie, Va., June 3–5, 1990.

16. *Wall Street Journal* January 28, 1991, p. 1.

17. The role and structure of boards of directors varies significantly among countries. However, the fundamental issues of governance, especially with respect to the partitioning of powers and responsibilities between boards and management, have broad application.

18. While the laws of incorporation differ in many respects among states, they are generally consistent on this basic premise. Delaware's corporation law is generally regarded as the most influential because of the preponderance of large publicly owned companies incorporated there. Section 3.5 of the Model Business Corporation Act recommends, "All corporate powers shall be exercised by or under authority of a board of directors."

19. The opinion of the Supreme Court of the State of Delaware in its review of *Mills Acquisition Co., et al.* v. *Macmillan, Inc., et al.* (May 3, 1989), appears to add a duty to be fair, at least with respect to the directors' treatment of parties bidding for control of the corporation.

20. *Corporate Director's Guidebook, Business Lawyer*, 1978, p. 1603. Similarly, the Business Roundtable's *Corporate Governance and American Competitiveness*, March 1990, comments: "It is plainly impossible for a board composed partly of 'outsiders,' that is partly of persons who are not full-time employees, to conduct . . . day-to-day [corporate] affairs." Although the board cannot effectively conduct day-to-day operations, it does have a major role in, and a major accountability for, the financial performance of the enterprise. This clearly requires a continuing check on corporate financial results and prospects, including profit and loss and cash flow by major business segments.

21. American Law Institute, *Principles of Corporate Governance: Analysis and Recommendation*, Draft 15 (April 1991), pp. 129–31. It goes on to state, "The board of directors of a publicly held corporation also has power to . . . (3) Manage the business of a corporation."

22. Jay W. Lorsch, *Pawns or Potentates* (Boston, 1989), pp. 63–74.

23. For one running account of this debate, see Kenneth R. Andrews, "Directors' Responsibility for Corporate Strategy," *Harvard Business Review* 58, no. 6 (November–December 1980), 104; "Replaying the Board's Role in Formulating Strategy," *Harvard Business Review* 59, no. 3 (May–June 1981), 109; and "Corporate Strategy as a Vital Function of the Board," *Harvard Business Review* 59, no. 6 (November–December 1981), 174.

24. For example, F. Ross Johnson, CEO of RJR Nabisco, reportedly ingratiated himself with his directors by providing them with free corporate jet transportation and celebrity-studded golf events. See Bryan Burrough and John Helgar, *Barbarians at the Gate: The Fall of RJR Nabisco* (New York, 1990). In some cases payoffs are made for specific purposes, as when outside directors of Macmillan, Inc. granted themselves a 25 percent increase in compensation and a retirement plan—which subsequently came to include severance benefits for *spouses* of directors—at a time when the CEO and several other senior corporate executives were attempting to take control of the corporation ownership through a sweetheart leveraged buyout arrangement. See *Mills Acquisition Co., et al.,* v. *Macmillan, Inc., et al.,* Supreme Court of the State of Delaware, May 3, 1989.

25. Lorsch, *Pawns or Potentates*, p. 82.

26. A statistically significant finding showing a positive correlation between strong boards and superior company performance—both with respect to the objective measures of earnings per share and financial strength and subjective judgments—was reported by John A. Pierce II and Shaker A. Zahra, "The Relative Power of CEOs and Boards of Directors: Associations with Corporate Performance," *Strategic Management Journal* 12, no. 2 (February 1991), 135–54.

27. Michael C. Jensen, "Eclipse of the Public Corporation," *Harvard Business Review* 67, no. 5 (September–October 1989), 61–74.

28. Ibid., p. 65.

29. Ibid., p. 67.

30. Ibid., p. 67.
31. Ibid., p. 68.
32. Ibid., p. 21.
33. Berle warns that the concentration of wealth in the hands of pension trustees, mutual fund managers, and insurance company managements might have the effect of transferring the "power of selecting boards of directors and managements from these managements themselves as self-perpetuating oligarchies, to a different and rising group of interests" that, in turn, becomes self-perpetuating. The true owners of the corporation (those who provide the funds) thereby remain disenfranchised. See *Power Without Property*, p. 59.

II

CASES ON
GENERAL MANAGEMENT,
CORPORATE STRATEGY,
AND
BUSINESS POLICY

THE CASE METHOD

. . . the root of the true practice of education must start from the particular fact, concrete and definite for individual apprehension, and must gradually evolve towards the general idea.

Alfred North Whitehead[1]

It can be said flatly that the mere act of listening to wise statements and sound advice does little for anyone. In the process of learning, the learner's dynamic cooperation is required.

Charles I. Gragg[2]

In these two statements are the educational underpinnings of the case method: inductive reasoning (from the particular to the general) and active participation. The validity of this approach for the study of the general manager rests on the nature of the subject matter and on the objectives of management education.

As the text has underscored and the cases will demonstrate, general management is an enormously complex subject, and the general manager has an enormously complex job. To rely on principle for either the study or the practice of general management is to stand on shaky ground for several reasons. First, any important challenge a general manager faces typically involves too many critical factors to yield to simple recipes. Several principles are likely to apply to a given situation, and they will often be at odds with one another. Second, innovative managerial actions repeatedly vitiate or alter the significance of business precedents and principles. Accepted routines and conventions are successfully broken every day in practice as enterprising managers find ingenious new ways to deal with obstacles and opportunities.

While these limitations to the use of principles as the basis for studying general management are severe, even more compelling is the lack of definition and clarity the general manager typically faces. As experience shows, one of the general manager's most critical challenges is to identify and define problems and opportunities. It does little good to act in accordance with principles in dealing with the wrong problem. As you will discover in reading the case studies, the problem is seldom exactly what you thought it to be. And a single modification in the definition of a problem can change the whole analysis and call for a radically different course of action. Only a skillful selection and analysis of the many facts and conjectures about a given situation can provide the general manager with the diagnosis effective action requires.

The case study approach is similar to the approach used in legal, medical, and other professional training, in which the aim is to develop practitioners skilled in diagnosing situations and acting accordingly. Arthur Dewing captures the essential nature of management education as preparation for the manager "to meet in action the problems arising out of new situations in an ever-changing environment."[3]

Drawing on some forty years of experience as a dedicated practitioner of case-method instruction, C. Roland Christensen connects these educational objectives to the need for students to participate actively in the learning process:

> In education for management, where knowledge and application skills must be related, student involvement is essential. One does not learn to play golf by reading a book, but by taking club in hand and actually hitting a golf ball, preferably under a pro's watchful eye. A practice green is not a golf game, and a case is not real life. Fortunes, reputations, and careers are not made or lost in the classroom. But case discussion is a useful subset of reality. It presents an opportunity for a student to practice the application of real-life administrative skills: observing, listening, diagnosing, deciding, and intervening in group processes to achieve desired collaboration.[4]

He goes on to describe some of the specific in-class experiences good case discussions should provide:

- a focus on understanding the specific situation;
- a focus on the total situation, as well as on the specific;
- sensitivity to interrelationships; the connectedness of all organizational functions and processes;
- examining and understanding any administrative situation from a multidimensional point of view;
- approaching problems as one responsible for the achievements of the organization; and
- an action orientation.[5]

Amplifying his last point, he characterizes "action orientation" as the following:

- an acceptance of institutional conflict;
- a sense for the possible;
- a sense for the critical, "the jugular";
- a willingness to make firm decisions;
- the skill of converting desired objectives into a program of action;
- an understanding that obtaining the commitment of personnel to the accomplishment of any plan is crucial;
- an appreciation of the limits of management action.[6]

Rarely, if ever, is there one correct solution to any major problem that the general manager faces. As Dewing points out, it would be surprising if any group of experienced businesspeople could offer an unequivocal solution with unanimous accord. He concludes:

> Cases should be used with the clear consciousness that the purpose of business education is not to teach truths—leaving aside for a moment a discussion of whether there are or are not such things as truths—but to teach men to think in the presence of new situations.[7]

In any learning experience, there is usually a direct relationship, in accordance with intelligence and aptitude, between a person's efforts and the learning that takes place. Unlike most lecture courses, the case method requires such efforts before and after classroom discussions as well as during.

How to Prepare a Case[8]

The starting point is individual preparation. You have to read the case, figure out what is at issue, do the necessary analysis, and draw whatever conclusions the assignment calls for.

While no single preparation method works best for everyone, you should consider the following generally useful guidelines:

1. Try to anticipate what is at issue by reviewing the assignment questions and by taking into account what major topic or topics your course is currently trying to address.
2. Skim the case quickly to ascertain the general nature of the situation and the kinds of information it provides for analysis.
3. Read the case carefully with respect to the issues under consideration, noting specific problems and the data germane to each.
4. Analyze each problem and issue, taking into account all the relevant data in the case and noting explicitly your assumptions.
5. Develop a set of recommendations supported by your analysis.

The next preparation step, when feasible, is to meet with about six other students to discuss the case. (Discussion groups may be formally organized.) This discussion, which typically might last thirty minutes to an hour, is an opportunity to get assistance on technical points that you might not understand or on other confusing matters, to present your arguments and test your reasoning, and to hear other viewpoints. This exchange is an important preparatory step for class discussion.

The purpose of the discussion group meeting is *not* to develop a consensus or a "group" position. Rather, it is to help each member refine his or her own thinking. It is not necessary, nor is it even productive, to continue spending time trying to convince the others to agree with your position once you have made it clear. The most constructive procedure is to exchange ideas on as many of the important issues as time permits, not to beat one to death.

Classroom Discussion

The guidelines for classroom discussion are few and simple. The first is to participate, participate, and participate. The second is to make a conscious effort to contribute to classroom discussion by adding new ideas to the debate and by introducing new dimensions and new issues at opportune moments.

Active participation is critical to case-method study not only because your comments can help your classmates learn, but also because it is one of the most effective ways for you to learn. Each of us has powerful defense mechanisms to protect our ego from getting bruised. One of these mechanisms is a proclivity to hear what we want to hear.[9] A student who only listens in class may hear only what reinforces his or her preconceptions, especially if they are broad and fuzzy. Taking a position and exposing your thinking to the questions and challenges of others is one of the best ways to discover inconsistencies or gaps in your understanding and flaws in your reasoning and judgment. This discovery can be a painful experience at times—after all, no one likes to be shown wrong—but it is undoubtedly better to make your mistakes in the classroom than on the job.

Participation works best for all concerned when the comments relate to the flow of the classroom discussion, adding new information and insight. Challenging or supporting recent speakers with different facts and new interpretations stimulates thinking and learning. The student who repeats earlier comments or simply recites case facts deadens the learning process. So does the student whose comment is off the point.

Introducing a new topic of discussion can be a constructive move at times, but runs the risk of being disruptive to the group's learning process. Inexperienced case students might do well to rely on the instructor for such transitional moves.

Debriefing

A good case discussion can generate a lot of intriguing ideas. These ideas do not always make their appearance in a logical sequence, nor are they always entirely consistent with each other. The student needs to take a little time after class to sort them out. Moreover, with normal classroom time pressures, rarely will a class cover all of the important implications of the key points. Thinking about these implications, particularly as they might relate to your own interest and experience, can be very productive.

You might ask yourself the following two general questions to get your debriefing started:

- What did I learn in class?
- What did I not learn that I wish I had?

In answering these questions, be modest in your expectations and reasonably charitable in your assessments. After all, much of the responsibility for what you learn in class is yours.

Notes

1. Alfred North Whitehead, *The Aims of Education* (New York, 1929), p. 97.
2. Charles I. Gragg, "Because Wisdom Can't be Told," in Malcolm P. McNair, ed., *The Case Method at the Harvard Business School* (New York, 1954), p. 6.
3. Arthur Stone Dewing, "An Introduction to the Use of Cases," in Cecil E. Fraser, ed., *The Case Method of Instruction* (New York, 1931).
4. C. Roland Christensen, *Teaching by the Case Method*, (Boston, 1981), p. 10.
5. *Ibid.*, p. 13.
6. *Ibid.*, pp. 13, 14.
7. Dewing, *op. cit.*
8. The content of this section was derived in part from a paper by E. Raymond Corey, "The Use of Cases in Management Education," Harvard Business School Publication 9–376–240.
9. Communication theory has something to tell us about unintentional distortions that arise from cognitive limitations to the human reception of information. As noted in Donald T. Campbell, "Systematic Error on the Part of Human Links in Communication Systems," *Information and Control* (December 1958), pp. 334–369:" This tendency to distort messages in the direction of identity with previous inputs is probably the most pervasive of the systematic biases. . . . It is also one of the most typically 'human' error tendencies."

GUIDE TO THE CASES

The cases presented here are comprehensive in nature and can be used in various sequences to emphasize different aspects of general management. Since the order of their use will depend on the design and objectives of the course and on the instructor's personal preference and judgment, they are arranged in alphabetical order.

Asahi Breweries, Ltd.

This case focuses on corporate renewal, strategic repositioning, and administrative leadership. One major issue concerns how a newly arrived general manager can revitalize a company and radically reposition it in the marketplace by reorganizing available resources both inside and outside the company. The case also calls for consideration of how organizational processes can be redesigned to allow norm-breaking decisions to be implemented. Industry and competitive information permits the analysis to consider future moves, starting with a major investment proposal to expand brewery capacity. Although the setting is in Japan, the critical issues that the company and its managers face are universal in nature.

Bard MedSystems Division

A middle-level general manager battles to turn around a troubled division. After several years of effort, he achieves some success, but still faces major challenges. This case examines general management from two perspectives. The first deals with the divisional manager in considering how he was able to devise a business strategy, build an organization, and create an upbeat divisional spirit against formidable odds. The second perspective concerns how the corporate culture might have influenced the division manager's performance. Senior management's attitudes and a number of corporate practices and systems are described for this purpose.

Bowater Computer Forms, Inc.

Bowater Computer Forms—the rapidly growing sole subsidiary of the large U.S. paper company, Bowater—was at a point of organizational transition as its management continued to implement a strategy of geographic roll-out with a goal of national coverage by 1990. The case describes the business operations of this dedicated forms manufacturer and the problems its general manager faced in trying to professionalize the organization as it became increasingly large and dispersed. His challenge was complicated by the need to deal with pressures from corporate management to accelerate expansion and to decentralize operations.

CEO Evaluation at Dayton Hudson

Corporate governance and the role of the board of directors in a publicly owned corporation are subjects likely to invite continuing debate throughout the 1990s and beyond. This case touches on one of the board's most important and sensitive duties, that of evaluating a CEO's performance. It describes the process by which this evaluation is performed at Dayton Hudson Corporation, a leading retailing firm. Various outside directors comment on some of the specific procedures followed and allude to conditions that might be necessary for such a process to be effective. The position statement for the company's seniormost executive also invites a reexamination of Chapter 1's definition of the general manager's job as it applies to a specific setting.

Coca-Cola Versus Pepsi-Cola and the Soft Drink Industry

A century of rivalry qualifies Coca-Cola versus Pepsi-Cola as one of the classic competitive battles of the twentieth century. This case provides an opportunity to practice industry analysis in a familiar consumer product setting. For this purpose, it describes the key players—producers of concentrate, bottlers, and retailers—and various changes in their relationships. The case also provides an opportunity for competitive analysis by describing the thrusts and counterthrusts of the two dominant firms during the 1960s, 1970s, and 1980s. Of interest are the barriers to entry that have frustrated consumer-savvy giants like Philip Morris, R. J. Reynolds, and Procter & Gamble in their attempts to enter this attractive business.

Cray Research, Inc.

The Cray Research case focuses on the problems facing corporate-level general managers in a rapidly growing high-technology company. It presents a rich mix of strategic, organizational, and administrative issues that can be analyzed from the perspective of the company's CEO, John Rollwagen.

The strategic issues center around Cray's choice between continuing to focus on state-of-the-art supercomputers for sophisticated government and university users (Cray's "classic customers") versus increasing emphasis on industrial markets with their larger sales potential. The organizational issues include the difficulties associated with preserving the enterpreneurial spirit and small-company atmosphere, which in Rollwagen's judgment contributed so vitally to the company's successful growth, in an ever larger and increasingly complex organizational entity.

The growing relative importance of software and marketing also poses problems for Rollwagen as he tries to increase the prominence of these functions without antagonizing the vitally important reigning stars, the supercomputer design engineers. Getting Cray's management to decide these issues and to implement the strategic and organizational changes needed to carry Cray Research forward presents a severe test to Rollwagen's administrative skills.

Cray Research: Preparing for the 1990s

This case is a sequel to Cray Research, Inc., describing the company's business activities until the decision in 1989 to spin off the Cray-3 developmental effort under Seymour Cray as a separate enterprise. During this period of time, John Rollwagen continues to redirect Cray Research in response to increased competition, the saturation of established markets, and the growing relative importance of software to supercomputers. He also continues his efforts to preserve an innovative corporate atmosphere while adding management structure to cope with the increasing size and complexity of operations. The creation of a new, second-in-command senior management post in late 1988 poses important administrative issues as Rollwagen and the newly appointed president and chief operating officer sort out their individual roles in a time of turbulence.

Daewoo Group

The Daewoo Group is one of several remarkable Korean firms that have experienced explosive growth, coming from nowhere in 1967 to emerge as a giant trading and manufacturing business empire. The case invites discussion about how this company was able to accomplish so much so quickly, about the problems and opportunities if faced in 1984, and about the actions management should take. Government-business relations, the limits and allocation of resources, corporate strategy, the role of Korean firms with respect to Japanese and Western businesses, and the leadership qualities of Chairman Kim Woo-Choong are salient issues for consideration. An invitation to purchase a government-owned large-scale integrated-circuit manufacturing plant serves to focus attention on the company's strategic direction as a unifying theme for the discussion.

Eli Lilly and Company: European Pharmaceutical Operations

Mounting costs for developing new products, increasing competition, and converging national regulatory practices are among a number of forces driving pharmaceutical companies to compete on a global basis. This case describes Eli Lilly's efforts to advance its competitive position in Europe as part of its worldwide strategy.

European market unification in 1992 poses both opportunities and problems for Lilly. Uncertainty characterizes future pricing and regulatory practices, and growing parallel trade (trade within the region by independent parties taking advantage of price differentials) greatly complicates matters. General managers at three levels—corporate, regional, and national—are challenged to sort out their respective roles in creating an organization that can become a leading pharmaceutical supplier to the Europe of the future and at the same time can play a major role in a cohesive global corporate structure.

General Electric: Reg Jones and Jack Welch

General Electric is widely acknowledged to be a world leader in strategic planning. The case, in describing the origins of some of today's most commonly employed planning concepts—such as the strategic business unit and the portfolio investment grid—invites discussion about the function of these particular planning constructs and what top management must do to operationalize them. In addition, the evolutionary nature of change at General Electric can be analyzed. The case also raises issues dealing with entrepreneurship in large companies, the appropriate role of planners vis-à-vis general managers in the planning process, and the impact of financial systems on managerial behavior.

Tracking Reg Jones's activities during the 1970s and Jack Welch's during the early 1980s gives students an opportunity to assess the job of the chief executive in a large diversified company over time and under different circumstances. Comparisons can be made between Jack Welch's leadership and accomplishments and those of Reginald Jones.

General Electric: Preparing for the 1990s

Frustrated by the price performance of GE's common stock, Jack Welch, chairman and CEO, articulates his views of the corporation's accomplishments during the 1980s and its promise for the 1990s in speeches and in the company's annual report. The case opens with his description of GE's corporate strategy and its efforts to carry it out. It goes on with Welch's image of GE as a "Growth Engine," highlighting the important cash-flow dimension of the corporation's strategy. The case concludes with a reference to the next phase of Welch's plans for change.

By almost any measure, the need for GE to renew itself easily ranks among the most difficult general management challenges of this nature in recent years. Still in the making, Welch's concept of the GE of the future invites questions concerning his objectives, the results to date, and the prospects for success.

Gold Star Co., Ltd.

Gold Star, the largest and most profitable firm in the Korean electronics industry, was a part of the giant Lucky-Goldstar group. The case issues are well summarized in its opening paragraph:

> On April 6, 1984, Mr. Chung Jang-Ho, the recently appointed executive managing director for exports for Gold Star, was informed of the U.S. International Trade Commission's determination that an "industry in the United States is materially injured by reason of imports of color television receivers from the Republic of Korea which are sold at less than fair value." The resulting antidumping penalty added another obstacle to an already difficult course for establishing Gold Star as a major premium brand name in the United States for home electronic products. In a climate of growing protectionism in Europe and the United States, Chung had to resolve the somewhat conflicting pressures from two even more pressing developments. One was an apparent effort by U.S. and Japanese electronics firms to dislodge Gold Star from its U.S. beachhead. The other, which had direct repercussions on export strategy, was a major challenge in Korea to Gold Star's domestic leadership position in home electronics products.

The situation can be analyzed from the perspectives of the U.S. general manager, the executive managing director for exports in Korea, and the Gold Star general manager—thereby permitting consideration of subsidiary-parent relationships and the special problems of a middle-level country manager.

Groen: A Dover Industries Company

Three months after taking over as president of Groen, an old-line manufacturer of commercial food processing and food service equipment (i.e., kettles, braisers, and steamers), Louise O'Sullivan had to contend with a major plant walkout. The case describes her efforts to reposition the company for rapid growth while dealing with serious operating problems of this nature. An apparently successful introduction of an exciting new product for commercial use opens the possibility for Groen to enter the consumer market for the first time. The potential rewards from such a move are accompanied by high risks.

The case also describes the extraordinary corporate context in which Groen operates. Company presidents are given wide latitude in setting goals and in making decisions. A generous three-year incentive compensation system and senior management's encouragements play a decisive role in motivating business initiatives and operating follow-through. As a senior professor of organizational behavior observed, "This is the kind of corporation that we teach about but so rarely see in practice."

Gurney Seed & Nursery Corp.

Gurney is a venerable mid-Western seed catalog and mail-order firm with sales of $35 million. The case examines a new management team's actions and plans shortly after its purchase of the troubled company through a leveraged buyout. Improving operations and setting a new strategic course for the company are vital issues for consideration. The company's cash flow is of particular importance because of the severe seasonal swings and the large bank loans outstanding.

Johnson & Johnson (A)

Johnson & Johnson is a successful company. Its chief executive officer, James Burke, credits the corporate culture for this success. The two J&J cases are designed to examine the power and limitations of a strong corporate belief system and how such a culture might be managed.

The thrust of the first case is to understand how a corporate culture is implanted and managed and how it can serve as a powerful motivational force in guiding and inspiring people. The second case introduces the dysfunctional consequences of a prized belief system—J&J's long delay in responding to a major competitive threat and the difficulty it has had in implementing a response—and focuses on the potential Achilles heel of a strong corporate culture: its power to limit organizational flexibility. When used in sequence, the apparent contradiction between the lessons associated with each case provides a powerful learning experience.

The principal topics of the (A) case include:

- the importance of a corporate culture or belief system in shaping and directing a firm;
- how culture works in J&J: the interplay between beliefs and management process;
- the dynamics by which a strong culture develops in a company: the role of executive leadership, symbolic actions, and external stimuli (e.g., Tylenol) in institutionalizing values.

Johnson & Johnson (B): Hospital Services

This case builds directly on the issues raised in the Johnson & Johnson (A) case, relating culture and management process. The source of the hospital-services problem has to do with the incompatibility of the environmental requirements for strategy and the cultural constraints of organization. The case describes the internal resistance to the proposed changes and top management's efforts to resolve the contradictory requirements of strategy and culture. A major case issue concerns the challenges facing a middle-level general manager who has been given responsibility for operationalizing the forced solution.

McCaw Cellular Communications, Inc. in 1990

As the largest cellular phone service company in the United States in 1990—
with almost 1 million subscribers, over 70 million potential customers in its
service territory, and over $500 million in revenues—McCaw Cellular Com-
munications faced strategic decisions that could influence the future structure
of the industry. Craig O. McCaw, the firm's forty-year old chairman and CEO,
was attempting to build a seamless national cellular phone system that could
charge premium rates for top-quality service. This vision faced an uncertain
and changing environment.

This case provides an opportunity for both industry and competitive analysis in a high-technology setting. Specifically, consideration can be given to how
such industries evolve, how industry standards can be influenced, how technological uncertainty might be managed, and the potential advantages and risks
of being a first mover in a rapidly evolving business. The challenge for McCaw
is complicated by the limitation the company faces in funding its strategy when
compared to the resources available to many of its large competitors. As an
entrepreneurial phenomenon of the 1980s, McCaw Cellular Communications
in the 1990s presents a challenge to create a sustainable competitive advantage.

Monsanto Company: The Queeny Division

The Monsanto Company: The Queeny Division case focuses on the administrative actions of a general manager, Chris Hubbard, as he attempts to implement
strategic changes for his division through a newly imposed corporate administrative system. The problem he faced was to determine the activities supporting the division's strategy and to develop a budget accordingly. His difficulty was increased by his and his colleagues' lack of familiarity with the new
budgeting system. The lessons to be learned in understanding the leadership
challenges faced by this young and relatively inexperienced general manager
have broad business relevance.

National Medical Enterprises

Only fifteen years after its founding, NME, one of the several for-profit
hospital-management companies that benefited from Medicare funding, reported 1984 sales in excess of $2.5 billion. The case examines management's
attempts to cope with this rapid growth and to deal with the pressures from
increased competition and the severe tightening of government payments. The
situations for two newly formed divisions are described to allow for an in-
depth consideration of the problems facing divisional general managers as they
deal in a large corporation with the complex interactions among related businesses.

The Philips Group: 1987

At the end of his first year as president of the Philips Group, Cor van der Klugt had made or announced a number of sweeping organizational and managerial changes that affected almost every aspect of the giant Dutch company's existence as it approached its centennial anniversary. He challenged his organization to become more global, innovative, and profitable. The case describes the forces for change that led management over two decades to focus on selected business sectors and to "tilt the matrix" away from national organizations to a global orientation. The proposed changes are viewed from the perspective of two contrasting operating units—lighting and medical systems—as well as headquarters. Philips presents a classical example of a corporation that has changed its strategy and structure to respond to an evolving competitive environment. The challenge for van der Klugt is to gain organizational support for his leadership and to complete the process of corporate renewal.

Richardson Hindustan Limited

The Richardson Hindustan Limited case deals with the job of a "country manager"—a general manager in charge of a foreign operation. It was written to highlight the problems in serving multiple constituencies with different and often opposing interests. This typical middle-management issue is complicated by distance (about 10,000 miles between Bombay, India, and Wilton, Connecticut), a difference in cultures, the significance of government-business relationships and, in this instance, outside ownership. Two specific projects call for decisions that help to sharpen the different perspectives.

T Cell Sciences, Inc.

In T Cell Sciences, the job of the chief executive officer is examined in some detail as James Grant, an experienced executive, takes over the position for a young biotechnology firm. He reveals his concerns with technological developments, organizational capabilities, FDA approvals, share price, and cash flows. He also describes his thinking about priorities and risks. The examination of Grant's thinking and actions occurs over time to reveal how priorities change as some issues get resolved and others arise.

This case also invites discussion of T Cell Sciences' corporate strategy. Important issues include which markets to go after, how fast to push research and development, the role of strategic alliances during the company's formative years, and the prospect of remaining independent versus being acquired by a larger firm.

Asahi Breweries, Ltd.

In mid-January 1989, President Hirotaro Higuchi of Asahi Breweries was faced with a major investment proposal. Implementation of the proposed investment plan would expand brewing and packaging capacity at Asahi up to 2,100,000 kilo liters per years in 1990 from the existing level of 880,000 kilo liters. This plant expansion would lay the foundations for Asahi to become the industry leader. At the same time, implementation of this plan would push the Japanese beer industry's overall capacity up by 30% between 1987 and 1990 (assuming competitors' capacity remained at the present level). Exhibits 1, 2, 3 and 4 show details of the investment and associated profit plans as well as related financial data.

Asahi Breweries and its president were two of the brightest lights of the Japanese business community in 1988. The company recorded a 71.9 percent sales volume increase in 1988 while the industry as a whole grew only 7.6 percent. This had pushed the company's market share from 10.5 percent to 20.6 percent between 1986 and 1988. Prior to Asahi's challenge, Japanese beer drinkers were said to be so brand loyal that the maximum market share gain for a company could only be around 1 percent per year. The dramatic shift in Asahi's market share, however, appeared to negate this presumption.

Much more than these numbers, the company seemed to have created a social phenomenon. The "dry" taste concept that the company introduced with its "Super Dry" beer had such appeal to the consumers that the competing beer manufacturers rushed to sell their own "dry" beers. Dry beer is a kind of draft beer that is fermented to a higher degree than ordinary beer. This gives it a lower sugar level, higher alcohol content and, consequently, a "sharper" taste.

Prior to Asahi's introduction of dry beer, there were two major kinds of beer sold in Japan: one was the more traditional, richer tasting lager beer; the other was the steadily growing and lighter tasting draft beer. The two were quite similar in their production processes, except that lager beer was heat pasteurized at the end whereas draft was not. By this traditional definition, the dry beer was merely a kind of draft beer. However, its growth and differentiated image were seemingly making it into an independent market segment.

Since long industry experience had shown that beer drinkers in Japan did

Exhibit 1 Operation and investment plan for Asahi Breweries (as of January 1, 1989).[a] (billions of yen)

	1986	1987	1988 (est.)	1989 (proj.)	1990 (proj.)	1987 Kirin	1987 Sapporo	1987 Suntory
Sales	259.4	345.1	545.0	780.0	1,000.0	1,266.3	467.0	780.0
Of which beer	200.0	271.2	460.0	670.0	870.0	1,182.4	440.0	215.7
Operating profit[b]	2.6	3.5	14.0	16.0	20.0	69.6	14.5	25.7
Ordinary profit[c]	5.3	9.4	14.0	16.0	20.0	80.8	13.1	47.4
Net profit[d]	1.5	2.5	4.8	6.0	7.0	34.1	5.3	16.4
Permanent employees (people)	2,747	2,944	3,160	3,340	3,700[e]	7,557	3,791	4,772
Depreciation expense	4.0	5.0	8.0	15.0	30.0	22.9	10.3	15.6
Investment in production capacity	10.0	20.0	70.0	100.0	130.0	—	—	—
Production capacity (thousand kl)	550.0	580.0	880.0	1,450.0	2,100.0	2,886.0	1,086.0	520.0
Advertising and promotional expense	27.0	38.0	50.0	—	—	54.0	24.0	81.0

Source: Company data.

a. Effects of projected tax changes are excluded.

b. Calculated as sales, minus cost of goods and SG&A.

c. Calculated as operating profit, plus nonoperating income, minus nonoperating expenses. Nonoperating income consisted mainly of interest and capital gains from investments while nonoperating expenses consisted mainly of interests on corporate debt. Asahi's profit plan assumed that for the years 1988 through 1990, nonoperating income and expenses would equal.

d. Profit before tax. Calculated as ordinary profit, plus extraordinary income less extraordinary expense.

e. In addition to its permanent work force, Asahi planned to hire 2,000 or so temporary employees to help increase sales.

Exhibit 2   Detailed breakdown of costs, 1987.

	1987	% of Sales
Costs of Goods Sold	267,214	77.4
Of which: liquor tax	158,445	45.9
raw material	74,571	21.6
labor	8,103	2.3
depreciation	3,850	1.1
power and light	1,545	0.4
other overhead	9,193	2.7
real estate	1,815	0.5
inventory adjustments	9,689	2.8
SG&A	74,389	21.6
Of which: promotional expense	19,222	5.6
advertising expense	18,902	5.5
logistics expense	10,584	3.1
provision for bad debt	72	0.0
salary	7,433	2.2
bonus	2,598	0.8
depreciation	1,227	0.4
other	14,347	4.2
Nonoperating expenses	8,497	2.5
Extraordinary expenses	1,748	0.5
Of which: writeoff	836	0.2

Source: Condensed from corporate financial reports.

not change their taste preferences very quickly, Asahi's decision to change the taste of its core product was considered an extremely risky proposition by most observers both inside and outside the industry. Not surprisingly, Asahi's initial success, based on its break with established beliefs and expectations, attracted wide attention.

Until 1986, Asahi Breweries was regarded as a marginal player, barely surviving in the stagnant and highly concentrated beer industry. In 1985, the Japanese beer industry was dominated by the giant Kirin, holding over a 60 percent share that left the three other manufacturers sharing the residual market. By 1985 Asahi had 9.9 percent share and was a distant number three in the industry. It was considered only a matter of time before the company would be taken over by Suntory, a whiskey giant that entered the industry as a latecomer. The story of Asahi's success, was thus one of a miraculous comeback by an underdog that charged on to challenge the invincible giant.

The most serious bottleneck for the company in pursuing further growth was the shortage of production capacity. During the summer of 1988, the company could supply only approximately 70 percent of the orders placed. This

Exhibit 3 Income statement, 1985–1987 (millions of yen).

Year ending December 31	1985	1986	1987
Sales	236,383	259,357	345,112
Cost of goods	186,187	202,867	267,214
Gross profit	50,195	56,489	77,897
SG&A	45,796	53,842	74,389
Operating profit	4,398	2,646	3,507
Nonoperating income[a]	3,283	8,348	14,378
Nonoperating expenses[a]	4,411	5,673	8,497
Ordinary profit	3,270	5,321	9,388
Extraordinary income[b]	2,776	15	19
Extraordinary expenses[c]	1,582	1,286	1,748
Profit before tax	4,464	4,050	7,659
Provision for tax	3,100	2,540	5,150
Net profit	1,364	1,510	2,509

Source: Condensed from corporate financial reports.

a. Nonoperating income and expenses consisted mainly of financial income and expenses.

b. Extraordinary income consisted mainly of profit from sales of assets.

c. Extraordinary expenses consisted mainly of a special provision for retirement pensions and a write-off of undepreciated assets.

had caused not only lost sales but, more importantly, failure to live up to distributors' expectations of the company.

The plan, then, was to invest 100 billion and 130 billion yen in 1989 and 1990, respectively, to expand production capacity. (The 1988 year-end exchange rate stood at $1 = ¥125.) Such an investment would push the depreciation expense from the 1988 level of 8 billion yen to 30 billion yen by 1990. This increase in cost would be greater than the expected 1988 net profit of 4.8 billion yen. Sales were projected to expand from 545 billion yen in 1988 to 1 trillion yen in 1990 to justify the fixed cost increase.

The competitive environment would be tougher for Asahi in the future than ever before. Its competitors were now recovering from the initial shock they experienced with the introduction of Asahi's "Super Dry" and were preparing to strike back. "Post Dry" campaigns were already being launched against Asahi, claiming that "dry" was simply a fad that would end soon. Subsequent generations of beer were apparently on their development paths within Asahi's competitors.

The History of the Japanese Beer Industry and the Kirin Legacy

The Japanese beer industry began in late nineteenth century. The industry was fragmented at the beginning but concentrated over the years. By the 1940s the industry had only two companies: Dai Nippon which held roughly 75 percent

Exhibit 4   Balance sheets, 1985–1987 (millions of yen).

Year (year-ends)	1985	1986	1987
Cash and securities[a]	18,197	42,801	78,312
Notes receivable	15,542	15,991	17,870
Accounts receivable	15,225	19,591	39,967
Inventory	21,328	18,419	20,400
Other	14,771	16,641	18,478
Total current assets	85,063	113,443	175,027
Tangible fixed assets	39,979	46,177	64,962
Intangible fixed assets	580	1,236	1,883
Investments and other[b]	14,116	20,702	24,362
Total fixed assets	54,676	63,116	91,208
Total Assets	139,739	181,560	266,235
Notes payable	5,529	7,753	4,408
Accounts payable	6,054	7,397	19,127
Short-term loan	17,699	5,921	24,481
Unpaid liquor tax	15,992	26,433	40,136
Deposit	31,368	33,623	40,322
Other	18,747	22,379	34,207
Total current liabilities	95,389	103,506	162,681
Bonds	4,600	7,060	4,540
Convertible bonds	0	20,000	5,333
Long-term loan	972	12,260	8,657
Total other[c]	5,934	5,511	5,170
Long-term liability	11,507	44,832	23,702
Paid-in capital	15,918	15,918	61,284
Retained earnings	16,923	17,302	18,566
Shareholders' equity	32,842	33,221	79,851
Total Liabilities and Shareholders' Equity	139,739	181,560	266,235

Source: Condensed from corporate financial reports.

a. Consisted of cash, deposits, and short-term investments in securities.

b. Consisted of long-term investments in securities, long-term loans, and other long-term investments.

c. Consisted mainly of provisions for retirement compensation fund.

of market, and Kirin. Dai Nippon was essentially a group of localized companies bound by common ownership.

During the second world war, emphasis was placed on supplying the soldiers fighting at the front. In this period, masses of Japanese were exposed to the taste of beer for the first time. Prior to the 1940s, beer was still a novel and expensive item. The generation that fought in the war subsequently formed the core of the first mass consumer segment after the war. This generation defined what the "right" kind of beer was in Japan. They preferred a richer, heavier, and more bitter taste compared to the present younger generations.

After the war, occupation forces implemented a policy of splitting up dominant companies in excessively concentrated industries. As a result, Dai Nippon Breweries was split into Sapporo Breweries (originally named Nippon Breweries) and Asahi Breweries in 1949. At the time of the division, Sapporo was the market share leader with 38.6 percent, followed by Asahi with 36.1 percent and Kirin with 25.3 percent.

The history of the Japanese beer industry since then until 1980s was essentially that of Kirin building a formidable empire. From its 25.3 percent share in 1949, Kirin had expanded to hold 63.8 percent of the market by 1976.

Many reasons were cited for Kirin's advance. First, when Dai Nippon was split, Kirin was left as the only national player. Dai Nippon's division was made geographically with Asahi inheriting mainly the factories and the brand and distribution channels in western Japan. Sapporo took those in the east. Since Dai Nippon was a group of localized brands, this meant that Sapporo and Asahi had to start as regional players.

Second, Kirin was credited with identifying the market trends effectively. Immediately after the war, beer was still an expensive item and the majority of consumption took place in restaurants and other commercial locations. Beer consumption at home was then only 25 percent of total industry sales. Sapporo and Asahi, who were traditionally strong in the commercial market, focused their efforts in expanding the sales in this market. Kirin, on the other hand, focused its attention on the home consumption market by developing an extensive distribution network. With rising incomes and the addition of refrigerators to most homes, beer consumption in the home grew rapidly, and so did Kirin.

Perhaps the most important achievement by Kirin in the period was developing its top-quality image as "the beer of beer lovers." The top 10 percent of beer drinkers were estimated to consume 50 percent of the total consumption, and when the next 10 percent was included, the number reached 75 percent. Kirin captured the heart of this heavy beer drinker market. In addition, according to market research conducted at the time, the top three reasons for choosing a brand was "quality," "what I have always drunk," and "reputation." This meant that once becoming the industry champion, Kirin could virtually lock up its commanding position, leveraging on its quality image and consumers' brand loyalty.

The perceived conservatism of consumers made beer manufacturers conservative about the taste of their products. Kirin's pasteurized lager beer became the industry standard, and competitors did not try to differentiate the taste of products very much.

An important exception to this was nonpasteurized draft beer. Draft beer was recognized by the consumers as good-tasting beer. However, because quality control of draft was difficult, draft was originally only served fresh during the summer at beer halls. Bottled or canned products for home use did not exist until the 1960s. Even after the introduction of bottled and canned draft beer, the perception remained in consumers' minds that draft was a summer-and-beer-hall-only product, and bottled/canned draft was somehow not real draft beer. Sales of canned and bottled draft beer nevertheless grew steadily, and by 1985 the draft segment was 41 percent of the total beer market. Sapporo, Asahi, and Suntory were all pushing draft beer for home consumption as a weapon against the Kirin legacy.

Kirin, on the other hand, maintained that, for bottles and cans, their pasteurized lager beer was the "right" formula. The thought within Kirin was that, since they had secured their industry champion's position through sales of lager, it was unwise for them to commit themselves to nonlager products. Kirin refused to market bottled draft beer for home consumption until 1985, when they decided that this segment was becoming too large to be ignored. In spite of draft's advance, however, Kirin's pasteurized lager beer still had a commanding 52.7 percent share in 1985, and Kirin as a whole had a 61.3 percent market share. The Kirin legacy was still alive in 1985. Exhibits 5, 6, 7 and 8 show the comparative production and performance data of Japan's beer manufacturers.

Consumers' conservatism with respect to taste was reflected in the trend in the late 1970s and early 1980s toward product differentiation based upon packaging and product image. Numerous sizes of beer cans and bottles were sold to address the different market segments, mini barrels for small group get-togethers being an example. In addition, characters such as penguins or raccoons were used to attract consumer attention. Advertising was focused on creating a product image rather than on explaining the product.

By the mid-1980s, however, it was becoming clear to the beer companies that consumers were bored with sales gimmicks. In addition, the tax increase and the consequent price hike of beer in 1984 had created a major shift of demand away from beer to other alcoholic beverages, namely shochu. Shochu was a traditional distilled liquor that had not only become price competitive, but also had succeeded in finding new markets through promotion as a cocktail base. As a result, the beer industry as a whole experienced negative growth in 1984. The industry was in need of a breakthrough.

Kirin, however, remained a very conservative player. As Kirin grew bigger and stronger, its power and market share became a burden. It became the favorite target for the promoters of strict antitrust-law implementation. Kirin at this point felt that any additional increase in market share would lead to a forced break-up of the corporation by the government. As a result, Kirin shifted its attention to diversifying into nonbeer businesses in order to maintain growth.

Industry Economics of the Modern Japanese Beer Industry

Production. The process of producing beer was basically uniform among all the beer companies. Malt and hops were used as primary raw materials with other grains, such as rice, added according to necessity and taste. The produc-

Exhibit 5 Comparative performance of Japanese beer producers, 1984–1987.

	Asahi				Sapporo			
	1984	*1985*	*1986*	*1987*	*1984*	*1985*	*1986*	*1987*
Sales (billion yen)	224.4	236.4	259.4	345.1	379.9	402.6	436.0	467.0
Of which beer	175.0	178.6	200.0	271.2	357.1	378.7	411.9	440.0
Sales per employee (million yen)	83.3	88.5	94.4	117.2	99.5	106.3	116.3	123.2
Operating profit (billion yen)	4.3	4.4	2.6	3.5	12.2	12.2	15.1	14.5
Ordinary profit	2.8	3.3	5.3	9.4	9.8	10.7	12.4	13.1
Shareholders' equity (billion yen)	32.6	32.8	33.2	79.9	47.5	50.5	76.6	108.6
Total assets	145.2	139.7	181.6	266.2	206.6	206.6	256.6	365.8
Equity/total assets (%)	22.5	23.5	18.3	30.0	23.0	24.5	29.8	29.7
Operating profit/ sales (%)	1.9	1.9	1.0	1.0	2.6	2.7	2.8	2.8
Personnel (persons)	2,695	2,672	2,747	2,944	3,819	3,787	3,749	3,791
Average age (years old)	41.0	41.4	41.3	40.8	40.4	41.0	41.6	41.1
Advertising expense (billion yen)	8.9	7.9	11.7	13.9	11.0	12.1	13.3	15.1
Promotional expense	10.8	11.7	14.9	19.2	6.6	7.2	9.3	8.7
Total marketing expenses	19.6	19.7	26.6	38.1	17.6	19.3	22.6	23.9
Marketing expenses/ sales (%)	8.8	8.3	10.3	11.0	4.6	4.8	5.2	5.1
Fixed assets (billion yen)	48.9	40.0	46.2	65.0	79.6	80.4	104.0	142.0
Stock price (year high, yen/share)	393	450	1,110	2,010	535	706	1,460	2,300

Source: Asahi Breweries.

tion process involved using yeast to ferment sugar content present in the primary raw materials. The invention of large outdoor tanks in late 1960s had added substantial economies of scale to the brewing process.

An important production-related issue was the dramatic seasonality of sales. Consumption of beer was heavily concentrated in the summer season. Since stale beer was extremely unpopular in Japan, this sales pattern created large

Exhibit 5   *(cont.)*

	Kirin				Suntory		
1984	*1985*	*1986*	*1987*	*1984*	*1985*	*1986*	*1987*
1,151.8	1,210.9	1,221.8	1,266.3	761.5	767.5	749.5	780.0
1,079.2	1,138.4	1,151.6	1,182.4	177.8	190.0	196.3	215.7
153.2	161.0	162.8	167.6	161.6	160.4	156.5	163.4
60.7	65.5	72.1	69.6	30.2	32.8	25.1	25.7
66.6	73.3	79.3	80.8	17.3	22.9	14.7	47.4
235.7	262.6	294.7	323.0	146.4	153.9	157.9	173.6
604.4	647.1	690.2	813.5	600.0	605.9	591.8	693.5
39.0	40.6	42.7	39.7	24.4	25.4	26.7	25.0
5.3	5.4	5.9	5.5	4.0	4.3	3.3	3.3
7,519	7,521	7,507	7,557	4,713	4,785	4,789	4,772
37.7	38.2	38.7	39.0	35.0	35.4	35.9	36.4
15.9	18.9	15.9	18.4	26.7	22.8	22.9	27.1
23.1	23.0	29.8	35.2	40.8	40.8	47.8	53.6
39.0	36.9	45.7	53.5	67.5	63.6	70.7	80.7
3.4	3.0	3.7	4.2	8.9	8.3	9.4	10.4
193.7	206.2	205.2	208.7	132.0	130.0	129.1	136.0
633	796	1,780	3,170	NA	NA	NA	NA

fluctuations in capacity utilization. (Exhibit 9 shows the seasonal demand patterns.) The effect of the seasonality was not identical across all competitors. In the past, Kirin, with its more popular product experienced relatively constant sales. Other competitors experienced larger fluctuations, absorbing the demand during the short-supply summer months, while being overwhelmed by

Exhibit 6 Sales volume of beer shipped in Japan by national brand manufacturers, 1975–1988 (thousand kl)

	Total (growth)	Kirin (share)	Sapporo (share)	Asahi (share)	Suntory (share)
1975	3,928.1	2,380.8	795.1	529.4	222.8
%	8.9	60.6	20.2	13.5	5.7
1976	3,639.3	2,321.9	669.6	429.4	218.4
%	(7.4)	63.8	18.4	11.8	6.0
1977	4,124.2	2,554.1	806.7	496.1	267.2
%	13.3	61.9	19.6	12.0	6.5
1978	4,430.4	2,751.3	868.4	513.9	296.8
%	7.4	62.1	19.6	11.6	6.7
1979	4,475.8	2,815.3	859.4	496.8	304.4
%	1.0	62.9	19.2	11.1	6.8
1980	4,513.8	2,807.6	889.2	496.5	320.5
%	0.8	62.2	19.7	11.0	7.1
1981	4,617.1	2,894.0	927.9	473.2	322.0
%	1.3	62.7	20.1	10.2	7.0
1982	4,733.5	2,946.6	946.5	473.1	367.3
%	2.5	62.2	20.0	10.0	7.8
1983	4,908.7	3,006.6	981.4	502.2	418.5
%	3.7	61.3	20.0	10.2	8.5
1984	4,645.8	2,858.7	904.8	464.6	417.6
%	(5.4)	61.5	19.5	10.0	9.0
1985	4,746.9	2,910.2	931.0	467.8	437.8
%	2.2	61.3	19.6	9.9	9.2
1986	4,930.3	2,946.6	1,012.0	516.9	454.8
%	3.9	59.8	20.5	10.5	9.2
1987	5,302.7	3,023.6	1,090.2	684.4	504.6
%	7.6	57.0	20.6	12.9	9.5
1988	NA	NA	NA	NA	NA
%	7.6[a]	50.5[b]	19.8[b]	20.6[a]	8.9[b]

Sources: 1975–87 data from Nikkan Keizai Tsushin. 1988 data from the following sources:

a. Asahi Breweries.

b. *Japan Economic Journal* (minor inconsistency with a, due to survey-method differences).

Note: Besides the national brands, one local brand, Orion Beer, sold only in Okinawa, had a 0.7% share of the national market in 1987. Also, figures include foreign brands, produced under license and shipped by each company.

Exhibit 7   Share of draft beer sales for nationally marketed brands, 1980–1987 (%).

	All Beers	Kirin	Sapporo	Asahi	Suntory
1980	21	3	45	46	100
1981	25	5	55	56	100
1982	30	5	65	64	100
1983	33	5	70	75	100
1984	37	9	73	80	97
1985	41	14	78	83	96
1986	44	15	81	85	95
1987	50	18	85	91	96

Source: Nikkan Keizai Tsushin.

the clout of Kirin during the off-peak season and running with substantial excess capacity.

In the course of its growth, Kirin aggressively sought to cover the nation with a network of production facilities. Since beer was a bulky product relative to its price, this gave Kirin a logistics cost advantage where sufficient sales were achieved in the markets surrounding the individual plants.

Distribution. Distribution was structured into a two-layered system of distributors and retailers. Both the distributors and retailers were licensed by the government, which strictly limited issues of new licenses.

There were basically two kinds of distributors. One was the general distributor, found primarily around the Tokyo area, that dealt with all four brands of beer. The other was the exclusive distributor that dealt with only one or a limited number of brands. Exclusive distributors were strongly represented in the Osaka area.

The distribution system tended to work as a barrier against new entrants to the industry, as well as against attempts by any player to gain a major share increase. With the widely held perception that beer was a commodity and that differentiation was not effective except in limited niche segments, the objective of beer producers had been to create a close personalized relationship with distributors who would constantly place orders with their preferred supplier. Kirin, in particular, had strong bargaining power over the distributors because of its historical popularity and product shortage. Takara, a distillery, attempted to enter the beer market in 1957 but was forced to retreat after failing to secure a distribution channel.

Retailers were typically liquor stores that sold to consumers and to commercial operations that served alcohol. Retailers independently selected which beers to sell.

One important element in the distribution of beer in Japan was the emphasis on "fresh rotation." As noted above, consumers preferred to drink beer as fresh as possible and could distinguish beers more than a few months old.

Exhibit 8 1988 monthly market share of nationally marketed brands consumed at home by major product category (% share of total beer market).

	January	February	March	April	May	June	July	August	September	October	November
Asahi	11.2	13.5	16.0	16.2	17.3	19.1	18.7	20.3	23.1	21.9	20.5
Sapporo	16.9	17.2	15.8	18.2	17.5	17.4	16.5	18.1	16.0	16.2	18.2
Kirin	66.0	64.1	61.8	59.7	59.1	57.8	58.5	56.4	56.3	55.9	56.2
Suntory	5.6	5.0	5.8	5.6	5.6	5.5	5.6	4.9	4.6	5.3	4.7
Dry Beer Subtotal	6.2	8.3	17.3	23.2	27.6	31.0	34.8	36.0	35.1	30.5	28.1
Asahi	6.2	7.8	10.3	11.3	12.8	15.3	15.4	17.0	19.3	17.7	17.3
Sapporo	—	0.2	1.4	3.5	4.2	3.9	4.6	4.9	4.4	3.7	3.3
Kirin	—	0.3	4.3	6.7	9.0	10.2	12.8	12.4	10.3	7.5	6.5
Suntory	—	0.0	1.3	1.7	1.6	1.6	2.0	1.7	1.1	1.7	1.0
Draft Beer Subtotal	—	33.4	30.0	29.6	27.3	26.8	25.8	25.5	23.5	24.7	24.6
Asahi	—	5.0	5.3	4.4	4.4	3.6	3.2	3.1	3.5	4.0	2.9
Sapporo	—	15.0	12.9	13.6	11.9	11.8	10.4	11.4	9.9	10.8	12.9
Kirin	—	8.7	7.6	7.9	8.0	8.3	9.1	8.5	7.9	7.3	6.4
Suntory	—	4.7	4.2	3.7	3.0	3.1	3.1	2.5	2.2	2.5	2.4
Lager Beer Subtotal	—	57.9	52.2	46.9	42.9	40.6	37.5	36.6	38.8	41.7	44.0
Asahi	—	0.6	0.5	0.4	0.1	0.1	0.2	0.3	0.2	0.2	0.2
Sapporo	—	2.0	1.5	1.2	0.8	0.8	0.8	1.1	0.9	0.9	1.3
Kirin	—	55.1	49.9	45.1	41.8	39.2	36.3	35.0	37.5	39.9	42.0
Suntory	—	0.2	0.3	0.2	0.2	0.3	0.2	0.2	0.2	0.2	0.3
Malt 100% Beer Subtotal	—	—	—	—	1.6	1.6	1.6	1.6	1.9	3.0	3.3
Asahi	—	—	—	—	0.0	0.0	0.0	0.0	0.0	0.0	0.0
Sapporo	—	—	—	—	0.6	0.8	0.8	0.7	0.7	0.8	0.8
Kirin	—	—	—	—	0.3	0.2	0.4	0.4	0.6	1.3	1.4
Suntory	—	—	—	—	0.7	0.6	0.4	0.5	0.6	1.0	1.1

Source: Shakai Chosa Kenkyusho Ltd.

Note: Data are compiled through a monthly survey using sampling methods. December data were not available.

69

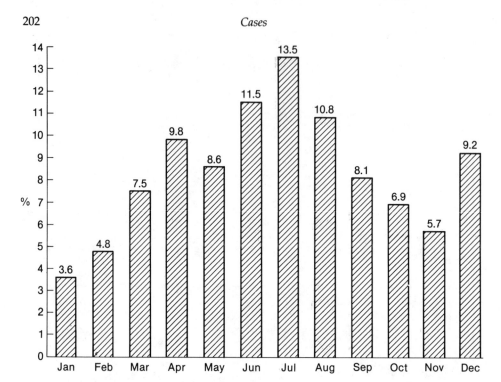

Exhibit 9 Monthly shipment of beer: % of year; 1977–1987 average. *Source:* HBS Estimates.

Marketing. Another important aspect of beer marketing in Japan was that the retail price of beer was virtually regulated at a uniform level by the Ministry of Finance. This reflected the government's policy of securing a stable source of revenue from domestic beer sales. As a result, beer was a heavily taxed item in Japan. Heavy dependence on beer tax revenue provided an incentive for the government to maintain healthy beer companies. Thus, maintenance of a minimum price level was perceived as necessary, because Kirin had the power to drive the smaller players into financial difficulty and monopolize the industry.

Price competition did, however, exist at the distribution level. There were both producer rebates to distributors and distributor rebates to retailers. The producer rebates to the distributors played a relatively small role, since transactions in this part of the distribution channel carried lower margins than distributor/retailer transactions. Distributors traditionally were forced to give retailers higher rebates for Asahi's products than for the more popular Kirin beer. This made Asahi's exclusive distributors financially weaker than Kirin's distributors. For general distributors, the rebate structure also made Asahi's beer less attractive to push.

On the advertising front, a minimum level of expense was necessary regardless of the size of the sales in order to maintain brand recognition. Thus, in 1985, for instance, Asahi's advertising budget was 62 percent of Kirin's while its sales were only 20 percent as large. (See Exhibit 5 for comparative financial data.)

Cost and Price Structure. Variable costs as a percent of sales could be estimated by adding logistics costs, promotion costs (rebates), and liquor tax to the raw materials cost. In Asahi's case this was around 76 percent in 1987. (See Exhibit 2.) All of the beer companies sold the standard large bottle (0.633 liters) to distributors at a uniform price of 4,756 yen per case (20 bottles). Distributors, in turn, sold a case of beer to retailers at 5,178 yen. The case price at retail to consumers was 6,200 yen. (Prices exclude rebates.)

Asahi Breweries, Ltd.

The breakup of Dai Nippon in 1949 left Asahi Breweries in a difficult competitive position. "The destructive force of the breakup was enormous. Asahi had to start with a negative tone and fell into vicious circle," recalled Executive Vice President Takanori Nakajo. Managing Director Mitsuro Matsuwake added, "Immediately after the breakup, Asahi brand was not sold in Tokyo. Sapporo was in the same position in Osaka. Kirin, on the other hand, had brand recognition and distribution capability in both places. Businesspeople who traveled between the two major business centers thus tended to choose Kirin constantly since consumers preferred to stick to one brand if they could."

After the breakup, Asahi went into a long period of decline as Kirin gradually increased its share. A mistake that had pushed Asahi below Sapporo in market share was its agreement to allow Suntory, a whiskey giant and a newcomer to the industry to use its distribution channel. Suntory, using its own financial power gained from the whiskey business, gradually pushed Asahi aside.

Another mistake, often pointed out by industry analysts, was Asahi's focus on the relatively stagnant commercial market instead of the growing home-consumption segment. Advisor Yoshio Oka, former managing director, claimed that that was all Asahi could do. "At the time of the breakup, the commercial market was both larger and more influential than the home consumption market. Asahi at the time was faced with the task of creating a marketing channel from scratch in eastern Japan. It was thus only natural for us to aim at the bigger segment in those markets where we needed to create initial sales volume."

Although Asahi stagnated, it did not mean that the company was inactive. Rather, Asahi was regarded as the innovator in the industry. Vice Chairman Tooru Takenawa explained, "We have always been trying new things, but we were always pushed back by the clout of Kirin. Asahi, for instance, was the first to start differentiating its product through packaging innovations as with the introduction of "Mini Barrel" in 1977." This was a small-sized barrel that could be used at home to serve draft beer. It became a sensation in the marketplace. "But this idea was copied by our competitors quickly," Takenawa added. The success induced others to come in, and when they did, they snatched the market away from Asahi. In addition, it triggered a proliferation of packaging types and thus increased industry-wide stock-keeping units. This worked to the disadvantage of Asahi, whose total volume was smaller and who could not secure as much shelf space as its competitors. With Kirin displaying a full line of beer products, little shelf space was kept for Asahi.

In addition to the beer business, Asahi provided soft drinks, pharmaceuticals, and specialty foods, and also ran a real estate business. Together, these nonbeer businesses generated 21.4 percent of corporate sales in 1987. These diversified businesses either used the by-products of brewing or exploited other assets and skills employed in the beer business. As the beer business stagnated, hopes grew that those businesses would help the company survive.

On the financial side, Asahi had the Sumitomo Bank as its primary source of financing and had kept close relations after the Dai Nippon break-up. Since 1971, and until 1989, the president of Asahi always came from Sumitomo. Each president invested substantial effort in restructuring Asahi. Executive Auditor Shigeji Nakakoji summarized Ashi's policy as follows: "In general, the focus was on cost cutting, trying to regain equilibrium by contraction. During this period, the whole company was managed by the accounting department."

Crisis Situation in the Early 1980s

By the late 1970s, Asahi was in a downward spiral. A mediocre image of both the company and its product led to slow sales. Slow sales in turn led to slow inventory turns which caused a deterioration in taste and product image. Lower sales necessitated steeper rebates and higher advertising costs per bottle.

The problem at Asahi was not that its sales personnel were lazy. The General Manager of Sales Division, Kazuo Takahashi said,

> On the contrary, we were trying much harder than our competitors' sales force. We might have depended too much, however, on personal relationships between the salespersons and buyers. This was a time consuming method, requiring our sales people to make very frequent visits. Also, because our product was not perceived as attractive, and those distributors carrying multiple company products did not push our products aggressively, our sales people had also been visiting retail stores and drinking places. Kirin's people just visited distributors and sold more than Asahi salespeople. The morale of the sales force was naturally low because they saw little progress, no matter how hard they tried.

The management control system malfunctioned, too. Because strong emphasis was placed on increasing sales and market share, there was a tendency to try to push products into the distribution channel at the end of the fiscal year. This not only resulted in a reactionary dip in sales in the subsequent nonth, but much more seriously, it caused deterioration of taste due to longer stocking.

Another controversial element of the control system was the productivity index. In order to acquire productivity data, the company used an index that showed plant efficiency "assuming the plant was running at full capacity." This assumption had to be made because otherwise sluggish sales would eclipse whatever improvements were achieved on the production line. Using this index, Asahi managed to eliminate sufficient personnel at the plants to make the company a low-cost producer during the late 1970s and early 1980s. There was, however, a downside to this. Executive Vice President Toshiomi Fukuchi explained, "Production originally started using this system to help generate sales. But, in reality, the index created such a mentality among production people toward cost that they ended up focusing, so to speak, on producing unsalable products efficiently."

Distrust among employees was perhaps the most serious problem of all. Many of the employees felt that since they were working as hard as any of the competitors' counterparts, it must be somebody else in the organization who was doing a mediocre job and ruining the company. The production people, for instance, felt that the products they produced were as good as any in the market and that it was the mediocre sales force who let the products sit idly in the distribution channel and deteriorate. On the other hand, the sales force felt that the engineers were egocentric and were not sensitive to the customers' tastes.

A particularly depressing year for Asahi employees was 1981. In this year, the company was forced to implement an early retirement program: 550 people had to leave an organization that only employed 3,200 persons. Another source of depression in 1981 was that Asahi became a target of a "greenmail" attempt. The company's shares were secretly acquired by a health care institution in the hope of higher repurchase price. Asahi was eventually saved by the Sumitomo Bank and a friendly chemical company that took over the aggressor's shares, but this incident left a negative image of Asahi in many customers' eyes.

The Murai Era

In 1982, Sumitomo Bank decided to send its executive vice president, Tsutomu Murai, to the troubled Asahi as president. Murai, who had a reputation as a turnaround manager, had been credited for going in as executive vice president and saving Mazda, an auto manufacturer that faced crisis shortly after the 1973 oil crisis.

Murai explained his initial impression upon arriving at Asahi as follows:

> I found at Asahi as at Mazda, a rigid, vertical organization. Everyone was looking upward—to the strong CEO. An organization cannot be effective on this basis because it will eventually become risk averse; distance will build up between top management and line management; divisions and departments within the organization will become self-chartered; and the central administrative function will begin to swallow up all the resources, both human and financial. These are all the signs of an organization in decline, and both Asahi and Mazda shared these characteristics. By the time I got to Asahi, I had seen it before.

Exhibit 10   Corporate philosophy of Asahi Breweries, Ltd.

We at Asahi Breweries, Ltd., through our business activities including alcoholic and nonalcoholic beverages, food and pharmaceuticals, wish to contribute to the health and well-being of people the world over. By thus contributing to society as a whole, the Company seeks to attain the trust and confidence of the consumer and develop still further.

1. **Consumer Orientation**
   Identifying the best interests of consumers, we endeavor to meet their demands by creating products suited for contemporary tastes and lifestyles.

2. **Quality First**
   Open to consumer opinion of our products, we consistently enhance quality level and extend technological capabilities in order to market the finest products in the industry.

3. **Respect for Human Values**
   Our Company firmly believes that human beings are the core of the business, and follows the principle of human values through developing human resources and implementing fair personnel management. Each employee is encouraged to fully utilize his or her own potential, and work to realize an open, positive-thinking corporate culture.

4. **True Partnership Between Labor and Management**
   Our Company aims to strengthen harmonious relations between labor and management based on mutual understanding and trust. Both parties work hand in hand for corporate development as well as the welfare of all employees.

5. **Cooperation with Business Associates**
   We seek to build strong relations with all our business associates and affiliates in a spirit of co-existence and co-prosperity based on mutual trust. At the same time, we are determined to accept and fulfill our responsibilities as the core of the Asahi group companies.

6. **Social Responsibilities**
   We at Asahi, through securing and expanding the base of our operations, desire to fulfill our responsibilities to stockholders and the local communities in which we operate. Also, in carrying out business activities, we sincerely observe the moral principles of management based on social standards.

One of Murai's first actions as president was to instruct his managers to formulate an explicit company credo. General managers of different functions were gathered to discuss the overall goals of the corporation. In this process, many of the conflicts that functional departments had with each other were discussed in light of overall corporate goals. See Exhibit 10 for the credo formulated at the time.

On a more personal basis, Murai frequently hosted small night-time gatherings at which managers were given the opportunity to talk directly with the president. To facilitate such communication, Murai often organized a study group of managers, who were assigned reading materials that would be discussed over drinks. A facility was located nearby to host such casual meetings.

Some of the most common words and phrases used by Asahi managers to describe Murai included "accessible," "good communicator," "dauntless," "cheerful," "prepares a positive environment and waits for subordinates to come up with the right idea," and "ignites the middle management." Murai described his initial goals as follows, "As a new CEO, I knew I had to do two things successfully: first, I had to be perceived as arriving without prejudice; second, I had to feel the organization with my own hands and avoid the "naked king" syndrome. A naked king is a CEO whose aides protect him from seeing the real picture."

During his effort to understand the company, Murai found out that there was a report prepared by McKinsey and Company in 1980 that analyzed Asahi's problems and gave four general recommendations: (1) improve corporate image; (2) have market needs instead of technology drive product development; (3) make efforts to convey the good aspects of Asahi and its products; and (4) guarantee that the fresh rotation of beer is maintained.

This report had been disregarded by the previous president, but Murai found the analysis to be credible and decided to ask for concrete action plans to implement these recommendations.

To facilitate the process, Murai created two cross-functional task forces: the Corporate Identity Introduction Team and the Total Quality Control Introduction Team. Reflecting Murai's philosophy that operating managers are the driving force behind a company, the members of the CI and TQC Introduction Teams were chosen from the deputy-general-manager and section-chief level. Each team consisted of seven to eight members.

The TQC Introduction Team began by reviewing various methodologies of TQC which focused on customer satisfaction and the scientific use of data. Subsequently, all 600 managers above the section chief level were brought in for training sessions, which were intentionally designed to encourage managers from different functional areas of the company to discuss the common topic of quality.

TQC activities began on a corporate-wide basis in January 1984. Quality Control Circles were set up on the shop floor, where employees were encouraged to make suggestions on how to guarantee the delivery of high-quality fresh beer to customers. At the corporate level, a quality assurance committee was organized by general managers of various functional departments to deal with suggestions from the field, complaints from customers, and other related issues.

In the meantime, corporate identity activities were also under way. CI was basically a set of activities aimed at improving the image of the company to the public, as well as raising the self-perception and expectations of the company's employees. Murai had experience in successfully implementing a CI program when he was with Mazda.

The CI Introduction Team started with a survey of how Asahi and its products were perceived by consumers. The result was summarized in the following three points.

1. The presence of Asahi in the marketplace was not felt by consumers.
2. Efforts by Asahi were not recognized by consumers.
3. The company lacked capability to communicate effectively with the public. It also lacked the capability to identify trends in the market.

Based on these findings, the CI team went ahead to discuss the future directions Asahi should take. To win the support from the rest of the organization, the process of formulating these points was purposefully designed to incorporate a wide range of employees.

Through the process of conceptualizing the present situation and the future direction, the need for a symbol to represent the efforts of Asahi was strongly felt. A proposal was made to change completely the corporate trademark and labels that were used on the products. This became an extremely controversial proposition. The conventional trademark of the rising sun had close to 100 years of history, and many employees, along with Asahi's distributors, felt proud of it. Strong opposition also came from branch managers, who claimed that there were many old fans of Asahi among consumers who identified with the traditional trademark.

An important development in the CI process that took place in parallel with the corporate trademark debate was the proposal for changing the taste of Asahi beer. This proposal stemmed from a separate study conducted by the marketing division, which had run market trials in conjunction with the product development division. A blindfold taste test involving 5,000 beer drinkers revealed that consumer preference was changing away from the bitter and rich taste represented by Kirin to a more refreshing, "sharper" taste.

This finding was turned into a new product proposal by the Corporate Identity team. This group was beginning to question whether Asahi's products really matched the needs of consumers. "We were very fortunate," Marketing Division General Manager Yasuo Matsui said, "that CI was under way. People were willing to question taboos." The beer industry was so conservative, the fear of losing existing market by changing taste so strong, and the pride of the engineers in the existing product so strong that it had always been a taboo to suggest changing taste.

During the fall of 1985, it was finally decided by the management committee to implement a full change in the corporate trademark in conjunction with a major taste revision. Taste was changed to emphasize sharper taste rather than richness and bitterness. Attention was paid, however, to the conservative attitudes toward richness. While "richness" and "sharpness" were technically contradictory, efforts by engineers brought about a product that seemed to meet both criteria. The all new "Asahi Draft" was born with completely new labels and a new taste that was designed to match contemporary beer lovers. This draft beer was to become an interim product that later led to the "dry" beer that further moved away from richness to sharpness.

"The reason why the organization was able to make such a daring decision in violation of industry norms," a number of executives explained, "was probably because Asahi was at the edge. People knew Asahi beer could not continue anyway if we did nothing and kept on losing. We had little left to lose, so we could bet it all."

Through these corporate-sponsored programs, the atmosphere of the corporation became more open and lively. This new spirit, however, was not translating into results. The 0.2 percent share increase that followed Murai's installation as president in 1983 soon started to slide. By 1985, it was at 9.9 percent, only 0.7 percent above Suntory's. Sympathetic distributors and retailers were starting to give up on Asahi. The number of retailers carrying Asahi were starting to drop sharply. Many executives pointed out that this was a most dreaded trend for any consumer products manufacturer, one that could lead to a total collapse. There was a strong feeling of crisis within the company.

Higuchi Comes In

In the spring of 1986, two events took place that turned the situation around for Asahi. First was the coming of a new president, Hirotaro Higuchi. Second was the official launch of its all-new Asahi Draft.

Higuchi was another Sumitomo banker who was following a fast track to become the youngest executive vice president in the bank's history. Murai and Higuchi knew each other well for a long time within the bank. In 1986, Murai was reaching the age of sixty-eight and requested the bank to send Higuchi to succeed him for what was expected to be the demanding battle of implementing the dramatic changes that had been planned.

Higuchi was described by his subordinates as a "quick-response person, always talking in concrete terms, hates abstract philosophy, high spirited, a romantic person who pursues ideals, comes up with his own ideas, does not wait for subordinates' coordinated decisions." Everybody interviewed by the casewriters agreed that his management style was top-down. Higuchi described his own management posture as follows: "Ensuring profit is the responsibility of the president, and the president only. The rest of the organization's members should be dreamers that suggest whatever they feel is worthwhile for themselves and the corporation. They shouldn't worry about numbers. It is then up to the president to decide which ideas should be implemented and to align the efforts into a profitable format. These decisions are ultimately mine."

Waiting for Higuchi immediately after he joined Asahi was the second major event, the launching of the new Asahi Draft. Higuchi made several significant policy decisions at this point. The first was recalling all the beer in the distribution channel that carried the old label. "This cost us 1.5 billion yen," Higuchi looked back and said "but we had to show our commitment to quality and the new image. I have learned through my experience at the bank that it generally pays to get rid of bad operation even if you have to throw in extra money just to do it." There were arguments against this action suggesting that if Asahi sold the old product in peripheral markets at steep discount, the product could be sold out. Higuchi's action had the risk of wiping out the company's net profit, which was at the 1.4 billion yen level in 1985. Higuchi's decision, however, was firm.

The second policy was the choice of raw materials. Higuchi instructed the organization to use the best quality malt available, even if it meant higher cost. As a result, Germany became its source of malt.

Third, Higuchi declared that the company would spend "as much money on advertising and promotion as necessary until operating profit dropped down to zero." This was a departure from the traditional policy of containing the advertising budget within a framework that ensured a certain level of operating profit.

Looking back to this period, the Engineering Division General Manager Yukio Tsukamura commented, "Mr. Higuchi came in and started telling us to spend as much money as we need on facilities to improve quality. Before then, we were really cost-focused and weren't used to spending that much. So in the end, we couldn't spend that much. I think Mr. Higuchi made his statements intentionally to change the way we think."

The advertising and promotion of the Asahi Draft was focused on conveying the "better taste" message. A caravan was organized that distributed mini-sized cans to 1 million people who would test-drink the product and hopefully spread the word of the new product. Heavy advertising was also implemented using mass media, particularly newspapers. It was expected that newspapers would logically convey Asahi's message on why new Asahi Draft tasted better than other beers.

In 1986, the sales of Asahi Breweries grew 9.7 percent over the previous year. In the beginning of this year everybody including the company's employees themselves was still skeptical about whether Asahi's revolutionary strategy would be successful. But signs of improvement soon began to appear. The firm's former Public Relations Director and a CI member Hirofumi Tange recalled, "After a while, the distribution people began to understand that Asahi's determination was for real. And we made a point in convincing all the 160,000 retailers to taste our beer. Then they started to push Asahi products seriously."

The Super Dry

In the summer of 1986, while Asahi Draft was gaining ground, a new plan was proposed but rejected by Higuchi in an executive meeting. The plan was to introduce a new product called Super Dry in 1987. Super Dry was a product that would further follow the general trend that Asahi Draft started toward emphasizing "sharpness" over "richness."

Director of Marketing Yasuo Matsui, who was the primary promoter of the proposal, explained his logic as follows:

> While Asahi had initial success with the strategy of emphasizing good taste, competitive response was mounting against it. If we sat idle and had tried to increase our share gradually with only Asahi Draft, we would have been squashed by the big guys. Therefore, we needed a strategic product, something that would make our step forward a firm one, something that would really boost the rate of market-share increases. The trend in the food industry is toward more sophisticated taste and higher purity. A refreshing, sharp taste is important. Strategically, lager beer, Kirin's main line, was suitable for emphasizing richness rather than sharpness. Thus, we had the chance of driving Kirin lager into obsolescence by emphasizing sharpness.

The basis for Higuchi's initial rejection of Super Dry was that it came too soon after launching the successful Asahi Draft. Introducing a new product was thought to dilute the image and effort expended on Asahi Draft. Higuchi explained, "I hesitated because I knew Asahi had the reputation among its distributors for launching lots of new products and giving up soon when they didn't work." Also, being in a similar line in terms of product concept, Super Dry was certain to cannibalize the Draft.

The Super Dry development team persisted, however. Higuchi later commented: "I originally rejected the idea. But the young guys kept on coming to me. Finally, they came to me and made me drink the product. I changed my mind. The new beer really tasted good." It was decided to market Super Dry from the beginning of the 1987 season.

In 1987, Asahi increased its sales by 33 percent with the boost from Super Dry. Vice Chairman Tooru Takenawa analyzed the success of Super Dry, saying that "The timing of several factors was right. Kirin's core supporters were getting older; people were bored with the packaging and the cute·mascots; draft was good but was already too old an idea to create a major change. Also, the boom over shochu was about to end. So, when Asahi presented consumers with Super Dry, a product that was developed through a careful analysis of their changing taste, the consumers were ready to react."

The Dry Wars

In 1987, when dry was initially introduced, Kirin ignored it, stating that it was a niche-and-fad item. They maintained that their product was the best-tasting beer and that consumers would come back to them soon after trying a novel item. After a while, however, Asahi's competitors started to recognize that dry was becoming more than a niche product. Furthermore, statistics showed Super Dry eating into Kirin's core market.

Seeing Asahi's large increase in share and the quick expansion of dry beer as a market segment, other beer companies decided to sell a dry beer of their own in early 1988. Following the tradition of the industry, these products were not differentiated in either concept, content, or packaging. Direct confrontation was at hand.

Sales General Manager Takahashi recalled, "We didn't mind others launching a similar product using dry as the name. What upset us was the fact that their design of packaging was almost identical to ours. Our competitors probably thought they could take over the dry market by launching an undistinguishable product which would eliminate the psychological link between Asahi and dry in the minds of consumers. Kirin boasted that they would become the top seller of dry."

Asahi responded to its competitor's moves by demanding that packaging and concept statements be changed in the spirit of protecting Asahi's development efforts. The active squabbling by the beer companies over packaging attracted the attention of the press as a fight over an intellectual property rights violation. Intellectual property rights were, at the time, becoming a focal point of trade conflict between the United States and Japan and had become a favorite topic of discussion. The confrontation was given the name of "Dry Wars."

This dispute had an effect of emphasizing to the consumers that Asahi was the one that originally introduced dry beer. Once the consumers recognized that Asahi Super Dry was the "real" dry beer, the competitors' advertisements for dry beer benefited Asahi more than themselves.

During the summer of 1988, it became increasingly clear that Asahi had established itself as the dominant player when it came to dry beer. It also seemed that dry beer was becoming a stable independent segment within the market. These developments pushed Asahi's competitors into changing their strategy. In a dramatic about-face, their new strategy focused on trying to convince consumers that dry beer was a fad product and that the taste was really not as great as Asahi claimed.

Asahi's competitors implemented their strategy in two ways. First, they went back to pushing their strongest product lines. Thus, Kirin started to reemphasize that lager was after all the best-tasting beer, while Sapporo pushed its popular "Black Label Draft" and Suntory its "100 percent malt beer." Second, they rushed the development of new products that were to become the next generation after dry. Already in the fall of 1988, Sapporo launched a new draft beer product, Fuyu Monogatari (Winter Tale), which was beginning to pick up in popularity.

At the end of 1988, consumers, retailers, distributors and industry watchers were all watching the development of the beer market with great curiosity. The *Wall Street Journal* reported on December 5 that "the losers in Japan's dry-beer war are striking back, hoping to create a 'post dry' era." Exhibit 8 shows competitors' market share figures by product category.

The Impact of Super Dry on the Asahi Organization

The rapid increase of Super Dry sales had a profound impact on the various functions of the company.

Production. Asked what was the most serious problem in October of 1988, Higuchi put shortage of capacity at the top of the list. During the peak-demand summer season of 1988, a supply shortage became so serious that delivery to distributors had to be rationed. Sales General Manager Takahashi said, "We used to dream that the day would come when products sold more quickly than we could produce them. But when the day actually came, we recognized how painful it was not to be able to supply distributors who desperately wanted the product. We were not living up to our responsibility as a manufacturer."

It was not that Asahi was timid about expanding capacity. On the contrary, Asahi's production capacity had been increased by 50 percent between 1987 and 1988. It was in March 1987 that Higuchi decided to invest 70 billion yen for this expansion. Corporate Planning General Manager Kenichiro Masui recalled, "The difficult thing about capacity planning is that it requires over a one year lead time from when you commit to an investment plan until the capacity comes on line. Thus in the spring of 1987, we had to make up our mind about 1988 capacity before looking at the 1987 sales data. So we made the plan for 1988 capacity based on 1986 data and came up with what we thought was a very aggressive plan of 30 percent capacity increase. But Higuchi didn't like it. At the top management meeting where the plan was presented, he asked the engineering people what the maximum capacity expansion they could handle was, and when they answered 50 percent, that became the plan. Sales General Manager Takahashi commented, "Had there not been the 50 percent increase decision, our success in 1988 would never have materialized. We would have been very short of supply. There was no hard number basis for the 50 percent. We can only say that it was the vision of the president that made the advance possible."

A complicating factor regarding capacity expansion was the existence of government regulation. Licenses for beer production were location-based, and it was necessary to acquire a license to open a plant at new locations. As Executive Vice President Takemasa Yoneyama explained: "The Ministry of Finance restricts the issuance of licenses when they see potential for industry-wide excess capacity." Thus, the past efforts in expanding production capacity were focused on increasing the capacity of existing plants. One of the important ways to achieve this was by adding shifts.

Staffing shift increases became a problem, however. The Production General Manager Hisashi Usuba explained, "We had been trying not to increase the number of workers. So we reduced the number of members in a shift when we increased the number of shifts. But there was still a shortage of technicians on the plant floor. We are now hiring from outside, but the availability is limited. Training of new hires is an additional problem."

Engineering the capacity expansion was another problem. Engineering General Manager Yukio Tsukamura commented, "The major capacity expansion for 1988 created a shortage of design engineers. We tried to hire from outside, but the supply is quite limited. As a result, right now, the mechanical and electrical engineers are concentrated in capacity expansion. We really ought to have some on the plant floor for maintenance and utility administration."

Tsukamura continued, "Procurement of equipment is also a constraint. The equipment for beer production is right now in high demand worldwide. The shortage is causing the delivery time to slow down. Delivery of stainless steel tanks, for instance, now takes eighteen months after an order is placed, and packaging machines take twelve months."

Managing director Yujiro Komiya stressed that Asahi was making a great effort to ensure quality during the expansion. "A decline in quality by an accident in the production line, for instance, could become a bigger threat than Kirin."

Personnel. Shortage of personnel was a problem for the whole company. Personnel General Manager Yutaka Tamino said, "Besides the engineers and technicians, there is a shortage of sales and administrative staffs, too. We had been limiting the number of new recruits in the past, and the number of people in their early thirties is particularly small. We are thus relying heavily on recruiting experienced job switchers. I recognize this sometimes creates cultural problems in Japanese companies which usually hire staffs straight out of college. But so far this has not been the case, probably because there is shortage of staff everywhere, and any help the departments get is a blessing."

Tamino continued, "We will not, however, increase the number of permanent employees more than we have to. We will have to increase the number somewhat, to fill the needs involved in opening a new plant. Our plan is to increase the number of permanent employees from 3,200 to 4,000 over the next three years. We will need additional help temporarily, while we continue our sales drive. But for this, we will be hiring many housewives on a temporary, part-time basis."

The morale of the employees was very high due to the success of the company. Higuchi made a specific point in sharing the success of the company with the employees. In the autumn of 1987, Asahi implemented a special wage increase without any demand from the union. This was unusual for a Japanese company that ordinarily implemented wage hikes only in the spring based on union demands. Asahi was subsequently criticized by a managers' association for breaking the norm. "However, this really made the employees trust Higuchi," Tamino explained.

"Higuchi pays close attention and gives detailed instruction about employees' well-being," Tamino added. "He emphasizes that the current success is based on the sweat and the tears of the people who struggled through the bad times. He thus put forth a policy that whoever had accepted early retirement and wished to return could do so. He added to this that if an eligible person was too old to work, their sons and daughters would be given priority hiring privilege in Asahi-related companies. Another thing he did was erect a memorial for all employees and other supporters of Asahi. He invited relatives of the deceased ones to ceremonies held to show gratitude to past contributors." A retired Asahi executive explained, "A special feature of this memorial is that outside supporters such as distributors, retailers, and suppliers are included. Flowers are given in their memory on the anniversaries of their death."

Finance. Higuchi's policy of spending aggressively on advertising resulted in operating profit falling from 4.4 billion yen in 1985 to 2.6 billion yen in 1986. In spite of this, Asahi managed to increase its ordinary profit to 5.3 billion in 1986 from 3.3 billion in 1985 (see Exhibit 3). A major contributor to this was the increased earnings from financial transactions, facilitated by an unprecedented boom in the Japanese stock and bond market in 1986. Higuchi explained, "Asahi managed to strengthen its balance sheet through equity financing in the favorable market. The liberalization of the financial market also allowed us to generate profit comparable to the conventional level by simply investing the funds wisely. Thus we could afford to put all of our operating profit back into operations and still report reasonable earnings." Higuchi personally managed the company's portfolio of investments.

Asked about the financial risks involved in the proposed investment, Finance Division General Manager Hiroshi Okada answered, "Asahi, being an old company, has a lot of securities and real estate that we purchased a long time ago at a low price. As a result, we have a large sum of undervalued assets. With the recent rise in stock and land prices, these undervalued assets grew to around 600 to 700 billion yen. So even if the expected sales do not materialize and we get stuck with excess capacity, there is no fear of bankruptcy. In addition, the number of shares outstanding for Asahi is relatively low because we have not been able to issue very much in the past. Consequently, dividend burden for us is low. So now that our stock price has risen to the 2,000-yen level, we can fund all of the investment with equity financing without the fear of seriously diluting our earnings. We have issued stock recently and secured 100 billion yen. All in all, we are pretty safe in terms of cash flow."

Okada continued, "We are aware that on an annual income statement basis, increased depreciation expense is certainly going to add risk to our profit level. So we have to be very careful about making large fixed-asset investments. When it comes to this project, however, it's not a numbers' game. You've got to think about whom the management is. Right now, we have a president who has made things work and is determined to do so in the future. And the employees are buying into it."

Distribution. Rapid expansion of the sales volume put a lot of pressure on the distribution channel. Logistics Division General Manager Yasuo Ogura explained, "So far, we have been able to manage the dramatic increase in volume because we now have an attractive product that sells steadily. Before, we had to ship products to wherever sales were made, and it was hard to predict how large sales would be. We now know the products sell constantly everywhere. We can now ship products with much higher efficiency. However, in the future, we will have to make investments in the hardware, particularly the distribution centers, to deal with the expected sales increase."

Ogura continued, "Logistics capacity is a problem not only for Asahi, but also to the distributors. For the general distributors that handle all the brands, it's not a big issue in a volume sense, because it is a matter of substituting one product for another with total volume roughly the same. Exclusive distributors, on the other hand, are experiencing a huge volume increase and are in need of funds and expertise to expand their physical capacity. We are trying our best to help them through consulting and referrals to financial institutions. We are also delivering products directly to retailers on an emergency basis in some urban areas."

Deputy Director of Tokyo Branch office Ryozo Mochizuki said that there were problems with general distributors, too. "Those distributors that were sympathetic to Asahi in the past were the smaller distributors, and they cannot catch up with the rapid expansion. So we have to increase our volume with the larger distributors. In reality, however, we have to consider the delicate balance between our volume goal and the important ties we have with those distributors that have been loyal to us through the bad times."

Mochizuki continued, "There is also the question of rebate policy. Traditionally, distributors had to give retailers larger rebates for Asahi product than for Kirin's. Now that Kirin is less popular, they are forced to give more for Kirin beer. This means they lose profit unless the total beer sales volume goes up or rebates on Asahi's product are squeezed. Asahi is trying its best to convince the distributors to keep the rebate at the current level for now because this is an important time for Asahi to advance, and we do not want to lose the momentum we've built."

The Organizational Process. "Decision making at Asahi accelerated after Higuchi came," Corporate Planning General Manager Masui said. "Higuchi gets mad when he finds that he is not informed, particularly of bad news. He doesn't want delays either."

Public Relations Section Manager Naoki Izumiya said, "There is a big contrast between Murai's style and Higuchi's. Murai tried to set the environment and wait for things to develop. Murai was also philosophical, and his words were conceptual. Higuchi on the other hand, is more action-oriented. He comes up with his own ideas, and his instructions are concrete and specific. At a meeting for instance, Murai would be the last to speak and Higuchi is the first to speak. Because Higuchi requires people to report anything substantial and to do so fast, he is quite busy. Murai was not so specific about reports."

A retired executive commented, "Higuchi's top down approach has been working well to turn things around and start the rapid growth. But at some point, when things become more stable, it would help to tap more people's wisdom. The president cannot keep on doing things alone. He needs support." Higuchi himself seemed to share this view. Many executives observed Higuchi consciously trying to delegate authority and develop managers. His basic style, however, remained top down.

The Future

Views were mixed about the future of Super Dry. While competitors and some industry watchers talked about "post dry" era, Asahi maintained that dry beer would last. Marketing Director Matsui said, "Dry is not a fad because it was created to match the long-term trend in the consumers' preferences. We should not overreact to competitors' moves. There will be some proliferation of products as segmentation progress. We are launching new products to address such needs. This spring, for instance, we are introducing a completely new type of draft beer, Super Yeast. But dry has the potential of establishing itself as the beer of beer lovers. We will make it that way."

Senior Managing Director Chikara Sano commented, "Kirin will have to stagnate for a while. It's clear, now that their lager beer is becoming obsolete. Yet they cannot push other concepts that would undermine lager, which still is their bread-and-butter product. But we have to be aware that they do have the money and technical resources to strike back." Asahi's management believed that Kirin was hesitant to take aggressive action that would sacrifice current profitability. They also observed that Kirin's financial strategy was relatively risk-averse.

Managing Director Koichiro Iwaki, in charge of corporate planning added, "Momentum is important. Higuchi came in, took advantage of Murai's improvement of corporate culture, broke the industry norms and started the huge advance. Since then, the organization has become better as we have won. Winning is the best way to improve the organization. Higuchi is anxious not to stop the momentum we have built up."

Iwaki continued, "The demand for beer as a whole seems encouraging for several reasons. One is a change in tax policy. There is a good chance that a substantial cut will be made on beer tax while other competing liquors' prices are expected to rise. Second is the rise in health consciousness and trends toward low-alcohol beverages. We can expect demand to shift to beer from stronger spirits. Third, the children of the baby boomers will be coming into the market shortly. Taking these into consideration, the industry sales volume has prospects for growing at around 7 percent for the next few years. Asahi's goal is to capture most of the increment. I know there are people who point out difficulties in our plan. But we should be trying to figure out how to accomplish our goal, rather than analyzing why it cannot be done."

The investment and profit plan also projected a 76 percent expansion of nonbeer sales between 1987 and 1990. Higuchi considered the soft drink business as a possible source of such growth. He was cautious, however, about moving into businesses that lacked synergy with the beer business.

Higuchi's staff generally supported a continuation of an aggressive expansion plan. There was a difference between the past two years' expansion and the future expansion plans in that the latter would require substantially greater investment in fixed assets. As he considered the investment proposal, Higuchi reminded himself of what he had often expressed to others, "My natural instinct as a manager tells me to grow, to become the biggest, the most powerful. I am, however, always telling my people that the goal of the corporation is not to become a big company but to become a good company. A good company is one which has good product and good culture as well as being recognized by the public to have good people who are courteous and humble. There is no value in our existence otherwise."

Bard MedSystems Division

Intrapreneurial Showcase

At an annual meeting of C.R. Bard's top management in May 1986, Robert McCaffrey, chief executive officer, announced a special award to the Med-Systems Division in recognition of its accomplishments. In his remarks, McCaffrey praised the division for the exemplary manner in which it had adhered to and successfully carried out the corporation's basic strategy of "decentralization, concentration, and innovation." The division's return from red ink to black and, more important, its strong prospects for future profitability were offered as evidence of the merits of providing distinctive products to a specific market segment where Bard could develop a competitive advantage.

In deciding to make a special award to this division, McCaffrey had not only wanted to give this struggling unit the recognition it deserved for its impressive accomplishments to date, but also to have it serve as a showcase, setting an example for other young managers to emulate and a standard to achieve. McCaffrey was clearly pleased with MedSystems' accomplishments, but even more delighted with the spirit and ingenuity which had led to these results.

This event came as a sweet moment of vindication for the division, which until recently had been viewed by many as the "corporate garbage dump," and especially for its general manager, Richard Klein, who was to have been fired two years earlier. Klein found the pleasure of this moment of glory somewhat attenuated by the daunting task his division still faced of transforming the recent turnaround they had accomplished into a truly successful Bard business operation.

C.R. Bard was a rapidly growing health care products company with emphasis on cardiovascular, urological, surgical, and general health applications. According to its 1985 annual report, hospitals, physicians and nursing homes purchased approximately 90 percent of its products, most of which were used once and discarded. The company, employing approximately 7,200 people worldwide, reported for 1986 revenues of $548 million and net income of $51.2 million. The appendix describes C.R. Bard. The body of this case focuses on the history and operations of the Bard MedSystems division.

An Inauspicious Start

In September 1978, Klein, then a 34-year-old plant manager in charge of producing plastic catheters and guidewires for Bard's USCI Division, was asked to meet with George Maloney, president of the corporation. At that meeting, Maloney, who saw Klein as "a young, eager-beaver manufacturing engineer", unexpectedly offered him an opportunity to head up the troubled MacBick Division, explaining that new product development was likely to be the unit's key challenge. Klein readily accepted.

While Klein did not hesitate in his decision, there was abundant reason to do so. A foreword to the 1977–79 three-year plan (prepared in 1976) had read:

> During the past five years, the MacBick Sales Division has been operated as a separate entity and as a consolidated, integrated part of Medical Products Division. MacBick has not operated as a profitable division of the company during this time period.
>
> MacBick product lines are sold direct to hospitals. They can generally be characterized as being low gross profit, mature, commodity in nature and fragmented as to in-use areas in the hospital. MacBick Sales Division has no strong customer identification.

Klein received other warning evidence as well. As he remembered the occasion, "When I told my friends about the new job, their reaction was 'You've got to be out of your mind. MacBick is Bard's garbage dump. Why would you want to go there?' " Indeed, MacBick had already run through two general managers since it had been spun out from the Medical Products Division only one year earlier to market steel hospital carts, pharmacy cabinetry, sterile packaging, non-woven products (masks, gowns), arterial blood gas kits, and other miscellaneous items.

This diverse line of unassociated products was a "collection of leftovers and discards", according to Dan Doyle, MedSystem's vice president of marketing, who had started as a MacBick sales representative in 1973. He explained:

> MacBick had been acquired by Bard in the late 1960's for its urological products. These were stripped out and joined to the company's core business, leaving the small and shrinking hospital cart business and an odd assortment of other items. Since MacBick was one of the few Bard units with a direct sales force, it became a dumping ground for other divisional losers on the grounds that direct selling might possibly be what was needed to increase sales. What we ended up with was a collection of dated commodity products in small, declining markets.

Klein's reasoning and response to Maloney's offer was characteristic of the man. He described his thinking at the time:

> MacBick really appealed to me because it was in such bad straits. The only direction it could go was up. Moreover, the president of the company asked me to do it. I'm a loyal employee, and when the president asks you to do something, you do it. I didn't even ask him what the new salary

would be. It was only later, when I was to relocate and needed to make out a mortgage application requiring such information, that I asked.

George Maloney described MacBick as an eclectic group of product lines and a good group of people. He said that he would like to see what I could do with them. Based on my earlier problem-solving successes with Raytheon and then with Bard, I considered myself a good technical generalist rather than an engineer. I guess I took on the job with a great deal of self confidence.

See Exhibit 1 for biographical information about Richard Klein.

Klein's self-confidence was soon to be put to the test. MacBick's sales manager had been reassigned to another division the Friday before he was to take over. Klein's recollection of the subsequent events was vivid even eight years later:

> I had heard from several people that there was really only one person in Bard who could step in and take over as sales manager, but that he had already declined the job offer from the group vice president responsible for MacBick. I wanted to try again and called my new boss to tell him of my intention. I guess he didn't like the implication that I thought that I could succeed where he had failed. In any case, he blew his stack and bawled me out so loudly that I had to hold the phone a foot away from my ear. Maloney, who just happened to be walking past the group VP's office at that moment, witnessed this event. The next thing I knew, I got a new boss as of the second day in the job. I was to report to Maloney.

The first day was to reveal another surprise. As Klein sorted through the division general manager's in-basket, he uncovered a set of instructions for requesting corporate R&D funds. Intrigued by this unfamiliar item, he soon discovered that every Bard division contributed one percent of its sales each year to an R&D kitty which was then reallocated to divisions, upon request, for specific projects. He also learned that MacBick had never made a request for funds.

Klein's immediate reaction was to try to get some money for the division. He and his top managers spent the next two weeks trying to identify some project for which they could ask money. This effort resulted in a proposal to conduct market research on medical packaging (one of the division's product lines) and an award of $49,000. Klein later observed, "From then on, we had never not asked for money."

One of Klein's first hires during his first week as divisional president was a commercial artist. He explained why he had accorded such high priority to this particular talent:

> Some people questioned this hire. They thought it was an odd place for a troubled division to be spending money. My view was that the division desperately needed to sell itself to insiders as well as to outsiders and that professional quality presentations were needed. We really had to make the best of what we had, which wasn't much. When we made presentations to the management committee, we injected humor and cartoons trying to get the people in a good frame of mind. I suppose we were trying to distract

Exhibit 1 Klein's intrapreneurial record.

Richard Klein, born June 10, 1944, the eldest of four children, grew up in Queens, New York. Following studies at Northeastern University, where he received a Bachelor of Science in Industrial Engineering degree in 1967, Klein went to work for Raytheon in Waltham, Massachusetts.

Klein remembered two "intrapreneurial successes" while at Raytheon. The first occurred shortly after he joined the company. At the time, the Raytheon name and other identifying information were epoxy-spray-painted on each electronic module. With a major increase in volume anticipated, Klein was asked to assess the paint booth requirements. His study showed the need to expand from two booths to thirty-two, a number which far exceeded available space.

Klein volunteered to solve the problem. After several months he devised a machine which could stamp the information on modules with fast-drying epoxy paint, something more senior engineers had said could not work. The process was so rapid that one machine would more than equal the capacity of the needed thirty-two paint booths. This accomplishment so impressed management that Klein was selected to participate in a special two-year manufacturing management training program just six months after joining the company.

Several years later, as manager of new business planning, Klein achieved his second enterprising success, creating an entire department which utilized time-sharing computing for sophisticated manufacturing planning and forecasting (years before the availability of minicomputers).

In 1974, faced with a divorce, Klein considered leaving Raytheon to become a consultant specializing in time-sharing computing techniques. Instead, faced with a severe economic downturn resulting from the first oil crisis, he joined C.R. Bard as a materials manager and was assigned to a division suffering from a one million dollar back order and from excessive inventories. In his first month he recognized the cause of the problem to be the lack of a good manufacturing planning system. In ten months, Klein was able to solve the problem by developing special software programs, (the algorithms were still in use in 1987). The back order was subsequently reduced to an acceptable $100,000 level and inventories also reached acceptable levels. This success, in his view, led to his promotion to plant manager in 1976. Two years later, Maloney asked him to head MacBick. By then, Klein had earned an MS in Engineering Management from Northeastern University and an MBA degree from Babson College. He had also remarried and started a family.

them from noticing that we had so little to offer in the way of real business
prospects.

In Search of a Mission

Klein quickly assigned top priority to finding products which could provide
the division with growth in sales and profits. He described the initial efforts:

> I first concentrated our attention on the products we had in hand to see
> if there might not be a diamond in the rough among them. I was convinced
> that we could come up with some winners if we tried hard enough. During
> the next six months, we must have considered every conceivable odd-ball
> way to breathe life into our tired product lines.

Klein went on to describe one of the more successful outcomes, a promotional campaign for MacBick's sterile packaging:

> One day between flights while prowling around the airport—I can't ever
> keep still. I'm the kind of guy who has to read while he eats or be doing
> something while he waits—anyway, I saw a cute little furry white seal in a
> gift shop and suddenly had an idea. So I bought one and wrote the manu-
> facturer for a quote to make a batch of seals with blue fur. Our plastic sterile
> bags and pouches turn blue when they are sealed by heat and pressure,
> and the blue seal stuffed animal seemed a good fit with our Blue Seal trade
> mark.
> We distributed blue seals at the trade shows and gave them to nurses.
> They were a great hit. We created a blue seal cartoon character for our ad-
> vertising and promotional materials. In time, we gained a disproportionate
> share of market awareness, when compared to our giant competitors, and
> sales increased nicely.

The blue seal also became an important device for improving divisional morale. Klein described this aspect of the Blue Seal campaign:

> At one of MacBick's national sales meetings, Dan [Doyle] dressed up as
> a blue seal and brought the house down. We then featured a photo of him
> clowning with Maloney on the front page of the division's house organ to
> create some excitement and a sense of corporate recognition of our efforts.

Notwithstanding the popularity of the Blue Seal campaign, MacBick's successes during the first year turned out to be modest and few. Most of Mac-
Bick's product development efforts were characterized by Klein as false starts
and outright failures. He described some of these disappointments:

> Flushed with the success of Blue Seal, we went on to create 'The Wizard'
> to promote unit dose packages and 'The Three Bears' for our hospital carts.
> Neither campaign ever took hold. The three bears idea, for which I have to
> take full credit, was the biggest disaster of them all. Luckily, these under-
> takings didn't cost us too much. Still, we were stymied. The sterile pack-
> aging was a small market, and nothing else seemed to work.

In 1980, Klein and his management team decided to propose *Medication
Management* as the division's charter. The idea was to develop a cohesive group

of "products for the formulation, preparation, storage, distribution, dispensing, and control of medication". At the time, only the steel carts, pharmacy cabinetry, and unit dose packaging, accounting for less than 40 percent of the division's sales, fit the target. Intentionally broad in scope, the charter aimed for new products which "were more sophisticated, had elements of disposability, and involved the pharmacy call point."

As soon as the management executive committee had approved this charter, MacBick began to introduce product line extensions to fill in the missing pieces of a yet-to-be defined total system. At the same time, it began divesting or discontinuing those product lines which did not fit the Medication Management concept.

Some product introductions, such as the new pharmaceutical carts, met with limited success. This product was a standard hospital linen cart with a closed container affixed so that drugs and medication could be kept under lock and key during a nurse's rounds. Most of the new product introductions—such as oral syringes and a computer system for preparing medication labels—turned out to be, in Klein's words, "fiascoes." Sales and profits lumbered on unimpressively through 1979 and 1980.

In June 1981, MacBick's long and increasingly desperate search for a winning product was to be rewarded. The breakthrough took place at a hospital pharmacist's convention where the division had assembled a panel of eight pharmacists to help MacBick's management assess eight new product proposals then under consideration. Klein described the event:

> When we finished our presentation, and it had become obvious that the proposed products were all pretty crummy, I turned to the panel and asked them for some ideas. There was no response. I should have thanked them for their efforts, paid them their honorarium, and called an end to the session. Instead, I became insistent and kept pushing them until one of them mumbled, 'Well, this probably is of no interest, but . . .' and went on to describe an experimental project in analgesia-on-demand being done at the University of Kentucky. That comment got a second pharmacist to tell of some development work a company called Auto-Syringe was doing with syringe pumps for infusing medication at his Rockville Center, New York hospital.
>
> That was it! I felt that we might be on to something big. So, shortly after the meeting ended, I sent one of my top managers straight to Kentucky, and I went to New York to look into what was going on.

As a result of this investigation, Klein was convinced that a syringe pump for infusing medications would be a great improvement over the common gravity feed, plastic mini-bag intravenous (IV) system. A small pump infuser could be more cost effective, more precise in the dosage given, less wasteful of medicine, and in certain circumstances more convenient for the patient. Klein was particularly mindful of this last point when he remembered the frustration he had experienced the year before in trying to conduct management meetings while tied down to his hospital bed by the conventional IV apparatus used in the treatment of an infection.

The concept of "patient controlled" analgesia was equally exciting since patients were anxious about pain throughout their hospital stay. Moreover, reasoned Klein, since pain was a subjective phenomenon, who could better control it than the patient.

Klein's enthusiasm for the new products was not universally shared at Bard. He recalled some of the initial reactions:

> When I began to talk about the possible products with people back at Bard, the response was very negative. "It's crazy. You can never succeed in that area. The major companies have a stranglehold on the infusion pump and mini-bag businesses," were the discouraging words of one corporate officer. Another thought that we could never get the idea of patients dispensing morphine analgesics through a machine accepted by the doctors. They would see it as an infringement on their work and possibly unsafe.
>
> Whatever merit these arguments of discouragement might have had, as I saw it, we had no choice. Our backs were up agains the wall. When I went to the management committee I had a cartoon which showed a tall evergreen with all the branches cut off with the exception of a small sprout at the top which was labeled "infusion pumping and control." Also in this cartoon was a lumberjack identified as George Maloney with an ax ready to cut down the tree and a lumber truck ready to cart it off. [See Exhibit 2.] I pleaded that the infusion pump was our last chance. If it didn't succeed, George would and probably should cut us down.

A number of people involved with the decision questioned the proposal, wondering if this was not just another false trail leading to another dead end. In the end, possibly swayed by Klein's enthusiasm and the recognition that this was MacBick's last chance, the management executive committee voted in favor. Maloney gave some insight into how the decision was made: "When the committee is faced with difficult investment or allocation situations, McCaffrey will often end the debate with the comment, 'Let them play another nine'. Over the years, MacBick had gotten to play the extra nine time and again, and this was one such occasion." McCaffrey later recalled being favorably impressed by the "sheer persistence of the man."

Birth of Bard MedSystems

Klein set out to acquire Auto-Syringe. Bard bid up to $12 million but eventually lost to Baxter Travenol, which purportedly paid $17 million for the company. By then, Klein had identified two other potential acquisitions for entering the infusion pump business. One of these, Harvard Apparatus, a small company in Eastern Massachusetts producing old-style syringe pumps, became Bard's next target. The company had sales of about $2 million, split evenly between syringe pumps for medical and bioscience applications. After some difficult negotiations, Klein and Maloney were able to settle on an acquisition price of 2\frac{1}{2}$ million plus a conditional payment of 1\frac{1}{2}$ million, which subsequently failed to materialize. Klein remarked, "What we got was an established name in the business, a safe—albeit somewhat antiquated—product, and some good technical people. A year later we sold the bioscience portion of the company back

Exhibit 2 A typical MedSystems' presentation slide.

to the original owners for over $1 million, so that our total cost for Harvard Infusion Pumps roughly totalled a little over one million dollars.

With the acquisition completed, Klein had the division's name changed to Bard MedSystems, retaining MacBick as a product brand name for hospital carts and cabinetry and Harvard for infusion pumps. Fifteen months of intensive product development resulted in a new generation syringe pump called a Mini-Infuser. Exhibit 3A is an advertisement for this product.

The Mini-Infuser posed a much more complex sales challenge than anything the division had ever faced. The point of sales for its traditional products typically had been in only one or two hospital departments. Since Mini-Infusers would be used throughout the hospital and would infringe on the practices of physicians, nurses and pharmacists, the decision to change IV systems would involve many people and departments. Doyle and Klein knew that it would be necessary to start with a prestigious hospital as a showcase.

The first successful sale was to Beth Israel Hospital in Boston. According to Klein, this hospital had 400 beds and a need for 100 to 150 pumps. He calculated that the hospital could save from $100,000 to $150,000 a year by replacing the mini-bags holding intravenous solutions with the new infusion pump. Each bag cost $1.25, and a patient required four per day. By using the intravenous pump, the hospital only paid 10 cents per application. These savings would enable the hospital to recuperate its investment in pumps in four to five months. The prospects of improved accuracy of drug delivery and increased convenience for the patients and nurses had also been important considerations in Beth Israel's decision to try the Mini-Infuser.

According to Doyle, the big companies supplying solution bags soon acted to thwart MedSystems' sales campaign. Their price for a bag was eventually reduced to 85 cents, and their large field sales forces made a concerted effort to convince hospitals not to switch. Doyle remarked, "We were threatening a very profitable product for companies like Abbott and Baxter Travenol. They were not about to lie down and roll over for us."

Building a Management Team

Closely related to Klein's concerns over the years with discovering and developing new products was that of building a strong management team. When he took over MacBick, he got a small sales force with the department manager's position recently vacated and an even smaller marketing group headed by his unsuccessful predecessor. A sister division manufactured its products and handled its financial accounting.

After six months, Klein succeeded in having the plant that manufactured hospital carts reassigned to his unit. A few months later top management approved his request to add a controller to his management team.

One of Klein's major concerns was upgrading his key department heads. In 1980, he replaced the plant manager with Don Martin, a plant engineer who showed broad talents. The following year he promoted his strongest product

manager, Dan Doyle, to head marketing. And when he got another good plant manager, Don Johanson, with the Harvard Apparatus acquisition, he convinced him to take charge of engineering and product development. Klein saw these moves as crucial to the division's success:

> I believe that if you get the right team, you can do anything. So right from the beginning I spent a lot of time building my own management team. By the end of the first year I had the nucleus of a staff. When Johanson agreed to take over engineering, that put the last key piece in place.
>
> While I am pretty outspoken as a person, my style is really participative. I see myself as coaching a team on which there are good players.

Don Martin described one assignment which was a revealing example of Klein's interest in developing people:

> In 1980 and 1981, Dick insisted that everyone on his staff go out with the sales force and make sales calls for five days each year. It was an eye opener for me. I could see that this was where the action was and the experience broadened my interests beyond manufacturing. I also got a better idea about what manufacturing meant in this division.

The PCA: A Second Major Product

As efforts to market the Mini-Infuser mounted, the division continued to work on the development of the second infusion pumping and control (IPAC) product idea, patient controlled analgesia (PCA). The device would allow a patient to self-administer morphine or other narcotic drugs within permissible dosage levels. As a result, a patient could counter pain with timely small dosages, reducing both discomfort and drug usage.

Because of the stringent requirements for safeguards and controls on drug dispensing, it took two years to develop the first PCA device. In April 1984, the morning Klein was to present to the management executive committee MedSystems' plan for launching this new product, it was featured on *Good Morning America*. Klein had the televised discussion videotaped and, 45 minutes later, opened the presentation with it. He later remarked, "It was lucky timing and great showmanship."

The MedSystems managers were elated with their situation and prospects. The division had launched a distinctive product—the Mini-Infuser—which had a market potential greater than that of all of its then existing products together. It now had a second product coming on stream with equal if not greater potential. See Exhibit 3B. As one Bard executive remarked, "MedSystems was the ugly duckling turning into a beautiful swan."

A Rocky Road

The division's success had not come easily. Its relations with corporate staff had been a major source of friction over the years. Klein described the problem:

Exhibit 3B Advertisement for the patient controlled analgesia device.

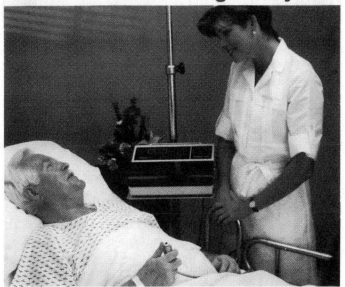
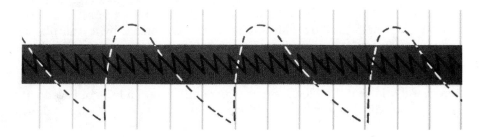
229

It was really frustrating trying to work with the corporate staff. Part of the problem was that we were too small and too unimportant for them to bother much with us. On top of that, they were forever seeing why something or other couldn't or shouldn't be done. It was difficult to get any real support from them.

A senior staff executive described the source of the problem differently: "Klein was always very intense and dogged. The only time you heard from him was when he wanted something. Whatever it was, he would want it right away and just his way. He would never stop pestering you to the point that his behavior became irritating and counterproductive. To put it simply, he was generally regarded as a real pain in the ass." Klein knew of his reputation, explaining. "I can be outspoken, persistent, and even pushy when necessary. The staff's obvious disdain for our ragtag operation probably brought out the worst in me. My aggressiveness and MacBick's unimportance within Bard combined to increase their enmity and resistance."

Klein's relationships with his direct line superiors had also posed difficulties. After a year with Maloney, he was assigned to a group vice president who more or less ignored him. In 1981, MacBick was reassigned to a group vice president who was later characterized by a senior Bard executive as a manager who just could not fit into the Bard culture.

In 1983, Bill Little, a New Zealander who had started as a sales trainee in Johnson & Johnson and joined Bard ten years later to head its U.K. operations, was given group responsibility for MedSystems. Little, who was also responsible for two other larger divisions, described his early relationship with Klein:

Klein and I just didn't get along. Part of it might have been that we had been peers as divisional presidents and the new relationship was awkward. The biggest problem though was his unpredictability. One day we would agree on a strategy. The next day Klein would spark other ideas and be off on another tack. This would drive me crazy. When somebody promises to do something, I expect it to get done. This was not always the way Klein operated. Moreover, he was often bucking the system. He was not a corporate player. He always knew best. Often it was true, but not always. He would fight the way things were done even if such a fight were counterproductive. In short, Klein was a nonconformist.

In Bard, each division had to pay its own way. In 1984, MedSystems was experiencing a significant net loss. According to Little, "Klein's biggest single mistake was to let his enthusiasm run away with him. He was always out too far ahead of himself." Little's philosophy was characterized by a wall plaque, which read, "Yesterday is cancelled. Tomorrow is a promissory note. Today is cash in hand."

By early 1984, Little, frustrated by his inability to work with Klein, went to Maloney and said that the MedSystems general manager had to go. Faced with the many complaints senior staff executives had voiced about Klein, Maloney finally concluded, albeit reluctantly, to acquiesce to Little's request.

McCaffrey, who had the final say, quashed the decision with the comment, "Bull ___! I don't know Klein from Adam, but he is the only guy around here trying to build a new product area. There's no way we are going to fire him just because people find him hard to work with." McCaffrey was later to remark, "I have always understood that thoroughbreds are hard to ride. Klein, in his own way, was a thoroughbred."

Loss of the PCA

The sense of recovery and even jubilation that Klein had experienced in connection with the coming launch of MedSystems' second major new product was to be short lived. At the April 1984 Three-Year Plan presentation, Med-Systems' management announced that the PCA System would be released nationally later that year. However, the division, at the same time, expressed concern over its limited number of experienced sales representatives.

Later, when reviewing this presentation, the management executive committee concluded that a simultaneous launching of two new product concepts through MedSystems would be a mistake. The decision was then made to transfer the PCA line to the Electro Medical Division (Bard EMS) to insure that the product would receive adequate support.

When Klein was informed of this action at the May 1984 annual Bard Management meeting, he was devastated. He recalled:

> The decision to take PCA away hit me like a bolt of lightning. It was my pet project—something we had been working toward for four years. And then to have it taken away like that—oh, they gave me reasons like the PCA requiring surgeons calls and MedSystems' lack of selling resources. But having a product that would allow us to call on doctors was exactly what we were trying to do.

Klein thought seriously of offering his resignation and expressed this intention to management. He was told that he was reacting to his feelings and not thinking rationally about the situation. He was advised to take a week to think the matter through.

Within 24 hours, he told corporate management that he would stay and began to prepare a resume. He later added, "In 1984, if the right opportunity had come along, I would have left Bard."

Klein described his subsequent actions:

> We were now a one-product company again and desperately needed critical mass. We had to find an area where no other division had a charter. So with the management executive committee's concurrence, we picked "anesthesia." We tried to go for an acquisition, but management said no to the deal we came up with. We proposed that MedSystems merge with Bard's small Critical Care Division which had some products positioned in anesthesia. Senior management again vetoed the idea. I began to feel like I was walking through a gauntlet. At the same time, I never stopped trying to get back PCA.

Recovery in 1986

Early in 1985, George Maloney met with the senior management of American Hospital Supply Corporation, and a discussion ensued about the prospect of one of their divisions, American McGaw, selling Mini-Infusers. Maloney discussed this idea with other Bard corporate personnel, and it was agreed that Klein should endeavor to negotiate an agreement with McGaw, which had a sales force of 130 specializing in selling intravenous therapy products. An agreement resulted which specified that McGaw would purchase 15,000 units per year for two years.

The agreement went into effect in September 1985.

At the same time, Klein and his management team developed a rationale and strategy for returning the PCA to their division. In effect, MedSystems argued that the PCA was central to its long-term development of specialty drug delivery pumps. With McGaw assuming the responsibility for selling Mini-Infusers, Little and Maloney were convinced that this was a good strategy, and the concept was endorsed by the management executive committee during the budget review for 1986.

On January 1, 1986, the responsibility for the Harvard PCA system was transferred back to Bard MedSystems, along with an ambitious $10.5 million sales goal that Bard EMS had set for 1986. PCA pump sales for the last six months of 1985 had totalled $2.75 million.

In early 1986, MedSystems proposed to Janssen Pharmaceuticals, a major Johnson & Johnson company, the development of a specialty pump to use with its promising new narcotic anesthesia, Alfenta. According to Doyle, Janssen was attracted to the proposition because of the need for a simple and safe method of administering the drug in the operating room. Subsequent discussions led to the concept of the Alfenta pump, which, according to Doyle, was to be "tremendously user-friendly and indestructible" and the first hospital pump to be designed for one specific drug.

In December 1986 Janssen received FDA approval for Alfenta. Under the marketing arrangement, the new pump would be jointly sold by the 120-person Janssen and 23-person MedSystems sales forces. MedSystems was responsible for producing the units and for providing sales support to assist Janssen's drug salespeople handle this unfamiliar device. Doyle estimated that up to 10,000 of the approximately 35,000 operating rooms in the United States were potential customers for at least one pump each. The overseas market would require a reconfigured pump design because different protocols were followed in administering drugs for anesthesia.

During 1986, Klein also began a campaign to broaden MedSystems' presence in the drug delivery field. The 1987–89 Three-Year Strategic Plan, submitted in May 1986, identified Cormed, Inc. as an acquisition candidate for MedSystems' entry into the rapidly growing outpatient/home drug infusion market.

While Cormed enjoyed the position of number one market share for ambulatory pumps and number two for associated implantable access ports, the company was widely regarded as being troubled with old technology products and inadequate R&D. When questioned about these deficiencies, Klein responded that Bard was buying an established name, a market position, and a flow of sales, much as it had done with Harvard Apparatus four years earlier. Klein also decided to go after Cormed because of his conviction that it was easier in Bard to get approval for an acquisition than for internal development when entering a new field, since management could see an operating cash inflow as of the time the investment was made. In September 1986, Bard acquired Cormed for $9½ million.

One of Klein's first actions was to instruct Cormed's management to develop in 1987 a new pump incorporating the latest microprocessor technology. MedSystems' technology group would provide support in the development of the product concept and engineering to the extent possible. While the technology from the motor to the control system was familiar ground to MedSystems' engineers, the pump itself employed peristaltic action (contractions that force the fluid along, like squeezing a tube), which involved different technology than that of driving syringes. The advantages of peristaltic technology for ambulatory care were that the pump could be made smaller and could deal with larger applications (up to 200 milliliters of drug versus a maximum of 60 milliliters for syringes), permitting more time between refillings. (The syringe pump could administer small doses more accurately, an important advantage for many hospital applications.) By January 1987, Klein had also reached an agreement with a Swiss firm to supply Cormed with the world's smallest ambulatory pump, the size of a credit card.

Success and Respectability

As 1986 progressed, it became increasingly apparent that MedSystems would make its first profit in years. The division's financial results are shown below in Table A. The most pleasing element in the 1986 results for MedSystems management was PCA's $11.7 million new sales for the year, exceeding what was thought to be the ambitious target of $10.5 million.

Klein's relationships with corporate headquarters also improved markedly in 1986. Group vice president Little, who seemed at ease in discussing the subject, said, "I get along fine with Klein now. We've worked out a comfort-

Table A MedSystems' sales and net income,[a] 1977–86.

	1977	1978	1979	1980	1981	1982	1983	1984	1985	1986
Sales ($ millions)	22.4	21.4	21.4	23.5	26.1	30.1	26.8	22.1	22.2	39.6
Net Income ($000)	356	916	442	578	632	(296)	416	(1854)	(1622)	1608

a. Financial figures disguised to protect confidentiality of the data.

able relationship." Klein, in turn remarked, "I have developed a good relationship with Bill. As it works, 75 percent of the time we agree, 20 percent of the time I convince him to go my way, and 5 percent of the time he insists I go his way." And Maloney later observed, "Little now knows how to tell Klein in no uncertain terms when to stop."

The increasingly constructive nature of the relationship between the two men was indicated in a controversial divisional appointment. In December 1986, Klein put Doyle in charge of sales and marketing to give Doyle broader management responsibilities and to free himself to devote more attention to the recent Cormed acquisition. He had previously cleared this move with Gene Schultz, the corporate vice president for personnel, with his group vice president Little, and with Maloney. Doyle's new title was vice president and business manager. When McCaffrey later discovered the intention of the title change, he rescinded the promotion in no uncertain terms. In his view, the sales function was too important in Bard to report to anyone other than the divisional general manager. Klein recalled Little's role in the incident: "One thing I'll have to say for Bill, he stood up on my behalf and made clear that I had gone through all the right channels on this one. I appreciated that."

Klein's relationships with corporate staff had also improved considerably in 1986. Klein remarked on this change, "In part, I've toned down and learned to live more with the system. In part, it's just easier to have a good relationship when you're respected and have credibility. The growing recognition top management has given our division has certainly helped create a more favorable climate."

Divisional Challenges

The management award announced by McCaffrey was in recognition of outstanding performance; it did not mark the successful completion of Klein's mission. Indeed, Klein felt that the pressures and risks were mounting as the stakes grew larger and expectations grew higher. He remarked, "Before we were a penny-ante operation with little in the way of risk, accomplishment, or promise. To exaggerate a bit, we could get by with wild promises, frenetic action, and funny presentations. That is no longer the case."

The senior MedSystems managers identified several issues which they considered as major challenges before them.

A Secure Business Base

In 1986, the MedSystems division had made its first profit in years. Klein felt a need to prove that it had not been the result of accident or luck. What worried him most was the division's heavy dependence on one product, the PCA pump. (Mini-Infuser sales growth had stalled under the McGaw arrangement.) The division risked a major setback should any serious problem arise with PCA's performance. To illustrate this risk, Klein mentioned that one patient had died while connected to a Harvard PCA pump. Fortunately for Med-Systems, the cause of death was not clear and could not be attributed to the pump. He went on to assess the division's vulnerability within Bard: "Should we be required to recall our devices, divisional gains to date could be wiped out overnight. However, I think that we have gained enough credibility in Bard to weather the storm."

Klein saw the Alfenta pump as broadening the division's product base and reducing this risk. The new Cormed pump would provide additional security, and Klein was eager to introduce even more products to reduce the risk of failure as well as to fuel the rapid growth he was planning.

The risk of product failure or misuse was not the only threat to the security of MedSystems' performance. Competitive pressures were also increasing rapidly. Klein noted:

> When we started pushing the Mini-Infuser, we were the only one trying to do something in the field. We created a new exciting business out of what was a backwater. Now, industry giants like Becton-Dickenson, Abbott Laboratories, and Baxter Travenol have all become very interested. To give you an example, one of these firms recently introduced a new infuser pump that is a direct copy of our Mini-Infuser. We are suing them for patent infringement, and while we will probably win this skirmish, the future challenges are not likely to be so easy to defend.
>
> Not only do these firms have more resources than Bard, they are more committed. They have been long involved in this business with their profitable IV feeding systems and are 100 percent committed. Bard is new to the field and is still not sure what investment to make. The problem for us is to remain number one. I see our situation as somewhat analogous to that experienced by Apple Computers. They created the personal computer field only to be out-muscled by IBM when the prize became attractive enough.

Managing Technology

Distinctive high quality infusion pumps and controls had been at the heart of MedSystems' remarkable recovery. As the division broadened its scope and as competitive products proliferated, the challenge MedSystems faced in managing new product development grew with the increasing number of products under consideration, level of sophistication, range of technologies, and time pressures.

Investments in new product development had increased each year, reaching a planned level in excess of $4.5 million in 1987. Highest priority was given to a family of "smart pumps." The Medsystems 1987–89 Three-Year Strategic Plan described these products as follows:

> . . . Computer-based delivery systems with microprocessors capable of interpreting complex pharmacokinetic algorithms which will automatically adjust the drug dosage over time.
>
> The Harvard Chronofusor System will be the first self-contained pump with the capability to deliver drugs pharmacokinetically. Algorithms devel-

oped by drug companies for their specific products or by researchers at major medical institutions can be input to the device manually or through preprogrammed, Bard-supplied cartridges.

Anesthesia Drug Intravenous Administration System (ADIAS), available in late 1987, will semiautomate the delivery of anesthesia narcotics and vasoactive drugs in the operating room. Pump modules will permit uninterrupted drug therapy as they can be moved, with the patient, through the postoperative recovery room and intensive care.

Closed loop systems, the "ultimate" in drug delivery, is a 1987/88 project currently in the earliest, definition phase and, therefore, not budgeted. Consisting of a "smart pump," like the Chronofusor, a catheter(s), and a sensor(s), this system will measure a patient's specific physiological feedback (e.g., blood pressure) for the real time control of medication delivery. IVAC, a division of Lilly, recently introduced such a system.

New and possibly competing technologies were also under scrutiny. Transdermal infusion, which supplied medication directly through the skin, was one example. According to the division's plan, "potential applications included therapies for many chronic illnesses, such as pain management, alcoholism, drug addiction, hypertension."

The pressures for new product development posed a management problem for the division. Doyle was concerned that these pressures might divert the division from maintaining product leadership in its established lines. As he explained the situation, MedSystems had one engineering group responsible for the maintenance of existing product lines, for line extensions, and for the development of new products. The product managers generally put pressure on this group to improve existing products and, to some extent, to develop product line extensions. R&D management was inclined to favor new product development. Doyle commented on the problem of maintaining a proper balance between these competing demands:

> These days we have more good ideas than we can handle. A big challenge is to get the right priorities. What really concerns me is that the division will worry too much about tomorrow's products and not enough about today's. The PCA, for example, has tremendous opportunities. Its market saturation is less than 10 percent. Since it is doing so well in the marketplace there are some who believe that our development work should focus elsewhere. That's wrong. In my view, the division needs to devote a major part of its engineering resources to this product.

The Mini-Infuser Arrangement

The Kendall-McGaw arrangement also posed some difficult problems for MedSystems' management. The 1987–89 Strategic Plan described the situation as follows:

> When MedSystems signed the Supply and Distribution Agreement with McGaw, effective October 1, 1985, little did we know how agonizingly slow they would be to capitalize on the Mini-Infuser opportunity.
> Our analysis of McGaw activity indicated a multiplicity of problems:

- Upper management's preoccupation with their acquisition by Kendall [from American Hospital Supply Corporation] during the fourth quarter, 1985.
- A good marketing strategy but weak sales action plan, i.e., the inability of management to communicate an effective "how to" strategy to the field.
- Competing field priorities, i.e., some major, high gross profit McGaw products compete directly with the Mini-Infuser so their representatives are prohibited from selling to current McGaw accounts.
- Novice product managers assigned to Mini-Infuser System. Three turned over in six months.
- For the first six months, McGaw did not advertise or develop new support literature.
- Underestimation of the effort and follow-up needed to sell this "concept."

To support McGaw, we have introduced additional sales incentives to the MedSystems sales force to help convert trials, loaned them additional trial pumps to lift the ban on new trials, and forced a closer relationship between our Mini-Infuser product manager and his new McGaw counterpart(s).

With second-year contract negotiations to take place in August/September, Bard has several viable alternatives:

1. Stay with McGaw but reduce future annual purchase commitments; for example, 15,000 pumps to 6,000 pumps. They would demand that we give them the right to manufacture disposables, but then we would demand a sizeable, fixed-percentage royalty.
2. Terminate contract with McGaw and distribute Harvard Mini-Infuser System through our Harvard PCA dealer network. Compete against McGaw as it unloads excess pump/set inventory on marketplace. Take back all disposables contracts as provided for in the current agreement.
3. Same as (2) . . . but assumes that Bard and McGaw agree on equitable penalty for cancellation of current 15,000 pump purchase commitment. McGaw, therefore, would have no products to unload on market. Harvard PCA dealer network could sell more pumps and sets. Reasonable sales volume is based on 8,000 pumps.
4. Transition year. Terminate contract with McGaw. McGaw unloads excess inventory of pumps/sets on market. MedSystems sells existing microbore tubing sets direct, and looks to Harvard PCA dealer network to increase sales volume of Harvard Mini-Infuser System incrementally. Assume no new pump sales.

Alternative	Pumps (Units)	Total Sales ($)	Gross Profit* ($)
1	6,000	5,200K	2,100K
2	2,500	3,800K	2,000K
3	8,000	7,400K	4,000K
4	0	3,500K	2,200K

*Disguised

The McGaw contact also complicated the situation for Klein in developing an idea he had for supplying prefilled syringes for Mini-Infuser applications. He explained:

> Pharmacists don't like to fill syringes if they don't have to. We consequently saw an opportunity for supplying prefilled syringes, for use with the Mini-Infuser.
>
> When we first proposed this idea to McGaw, they disagreed and would not support such a program. That stymied us for a year. When we threatened to go forward ourselves, McGaw finally came around. Now we are trying to work out an arrangement in which a drug company prefills syringes to be sold by the McGaw sales force in connection with Mini-Infusers. What complicates the negotiations is to find a way for Bard to get a piece of the payoff as a non-operating partner in a three-way agreement.

Divisional Charter

As MedSystems grew in size and scope, conflicts between its business interests and those of other Bard divisions were likely to increase. According to Klein, the distinctive nature of his division's charter exacerbated the problem. While the other divisions tended to focus on particular hospital departments (such as urology, cardiology, and surgery), the customer base for MedSystems' products cut across hospital organizational lines. The competition for PCA within Bard had reflected in part this problem of overlapping interests.

With the acquisition of Cormed, MedSystems obtained a line of indwelling catheters and ports (implantable devices to provide long-term drug delivery into the body). This put it in direct competition with Bard's Davol division, which also produced and sold these items as part of its newly developed mission aimed at the oncology (relating to cancer) market.

Klein believed that MedSystems was justified in laying claim to these products, explaining,

> After Davol was acquired in 1980, its charter became "wound management." It was a good organization, but in need of new products. So when Evermed (market leader for indwelling catheters) was acquired in 1983, the group vice president, who had come from Davol, came up with the idea of adding oncology to Davol's charter and gave the new unit to it instead of to us. This was a mistake, in my opinion, because these products fit so closely with our pumps.

From that time on, Klein began a campaign to communicate within Bard that MedSystems was more than "a pump company." The 1987–89 Three-Year Strategic Plan stressed this point, illustrating it on page one:

> Harvard's product line consisted entirely of syringe pumps which, at that time, represented only the tiny "small-volume" niche of the infusion pumping and control (IPAC) market, an arena dominated by several large competitors, e.g., IMED, IVAC, Abbott, Travenol. To the uninitiated, IPAC means intravenous (IV) therapy; but the development and proliferation of new drug delivery products for hospital, outpatient, and home infusion validate the concept of IPAC as a MULTI-MODALITY, TOTAL SYSTEM . . .

IT IS SHORTSIGHTED TO THINK OF MEDSYSTEMS AS JUST A "PUMP COMPANY."

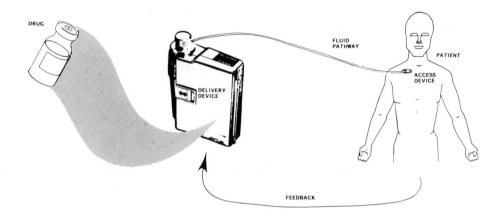

Martin gave some idea of MedSystems' competitive drive in speaking about the product overlap with Davol:

> To have two divisions in Bard manufacture and sell the same products could be questioned. Internal competition, however, also has motivational benefits. We are all psyched up to clean out Davol's clock. Of course, they probably would like to do the same to us. But we have the advantage of supplying an integrated system. In time these operations might be consolidated, but for now, its up to both divisions to show their stuff.

Klein as Manager and Intrapreneur

In assessing Klein as a general manager, his direct reports made the following list of strengths and weaknesses:

- He sets high standards. You will either gear up or gear out. If you don't meet his expectations, he drives you crazy.
- He is very optimistic, with a tendency to see opportunities instead of problems.
- He works closely with his people and gives them opportunities to grow.
- He is very creative, often coming up with unusual solutions.
- He sometimes runs too fast for the group with a flood of ideas.
- He comes up with a lot of bad ideas—as well as good ideas. Since he is so persistent, blunt, and even domineering by nature, it takes a lot of skill and patience to turn him around without having a knock-down, drag-out battle.

In connection with this last point, one of MedSystems' executives described the key role he and his colleagues had to play:

We have to serve as a foil for Klein, trying to keep him on the right path. He is good at talking to people and generating ideas. Our job is to evaluate these ideas without slowing down his aggressive and inquisitive nature. Even if there is only one good idea in a hundred, it is important to uncover it. I just hope that we don't begin to lose this ability as the division gets bigger.

Klein was described as hard to work for, but those who had learned how indicated a great deal of respect for him. Klein in turn described himself as changing over time:

I used to go after everything with no give. But I've learned that I cannot fight every battle. Now I'm more selective. Sometimes I'll even give up on an issue to gain position for another.

He went on to describe some of the lessons he had learned as a general manager:

One thing I've learned is that one person cannot accomplish all that much by himself. You need good people to make a division succeed. A corollary lesson is that you have to help other people to succeed for them to help you to succeed. The third lesson is that you have to be able to deal with setbacks and failures. I've certainly experienced lots of failures along the way.

In the May 1986 corporate top management meeting, Klein gave a presentation about intrapreneuring. He might have had himself in mind when he opened with the following definition for intrapreneur from Gifford Pinchot's book *Intrapreneuring*:

Any of the "dreamers who do". Those who take hands-on responsibility for creating innovation of any kind within an organization. The intrapreneur may be the creator or inventor but is always the dreamer who figures out how to turn an idea into a profitable reality.

In a series of statements accompanied by cartoons, he identified some of the key attributes of such a person:

- Intrapreneurs *are* different. (See Exhibit 4.)
- Intrapreneurs have dogged determination, intensity, and a sense of urgency.
- "Popularity" is often a casualty of intrapreneuring.
- Intrapreneurs *are* highly visible.

On another occasion, he described the importance of an organization being able to deal with deviant behavior:

I kept running into the reaction, "Why can't you do things like everyone else?" What an organization has to be able to do is to put a leash on its people and then to allow them to do their own things. In my opinion, nothing overwhelms creativity more completely than excessive structure.

George Maloney has been great in this respect. He gives me advice and then lets me learn from experience.

Exhibit 4 Cartoon used in defining intrapreneurs.

*"Why can't you just shit in the woods like
every other bear?"*

When asked about his future career plans, Klein responded:

I receive calls every few months from people who are checking on my availability. The money offered almost always exceeds what I am currently receiving, sometimes by a factor of two. But I am not a job jumper, moving from one company to another. I like Bard, and I feel it takes time in one place to accomplish something worthwhile.

On the other hand, I've been at this job for eight years, and 1 m ready to do something else. I realized recently that I am one of the senior division general managers in terms of years in office. I'm also older than most. Their average age is forty; I'm forty-two.

I've been a good general manager. McCaffrey once said, "You're nobody until you know how to make money." Now I've made money. I'm becoming less interested in the nitty gritty details. My value to the company is in coming up with strategies, building management teams, and motivating people. The company really needs me beyond this particular division.

I would like to take on the broader responsibilities of a group vice presidency. I am trying to show my ability and maturity. I am trying to prove that I can operate in a corporate environment.

I've been with the company thirteen years; there is a risk of becoming stereotyped and pigeonholed if you stay in a job too long. I think it's important for me to move on pretty soon, or my opportunities are going to dry up.

Klein spoke about his career ambitions with a touch of the same dogged determination and optimistic expectation that had marked his behavior in managing the Bard MedSystems division over the past eight years.

The Importance of Corporate Context

In reviewing the events of MedSystems' impressive performance, McCaffrey observed:

Klein deserves a lot of credit for MedSystems' turnaround, but it is important to recognize the other important contributors to this outcome. As he himself pointed out, his key people also deserve much credit. It was, and continues to be, a team effort.

Perhaps less obvious, but no less vital to MedSystems' results, was Bard's deep commitment to decentralized management, to a market focus, and to providing distinctive products of value to the customer. This core concept served to guide Klein and his team in their decisions and to aid corporate management in assessing their proposals. Everyone involved had a common framework which gave direction and which allowed for experimentation and failures along the way.

McCaffrey continued:

Klein seemed to think that his showmanship presentations were a decisive factor in winning top management support. Actually, the cartoons and hype had the effect of putting me off more than winning me over. What really gained top management's attention and support was the division's dedication to finding and building a business that would focus on specific markets and supply differentiated, quality products. As a result, we were willing to make exceptions for MedSystems. For example, the corporate management would probably have said no to another division had it requested R&D funding for the kind of market research project proposed by Klein in 1978. We let MedSystems go with other questionable proposals when it seemed important to divisional morale to do so. Everyone involved—MedSystems' management and senior management—had to take some risks and had to have a measured faith in our abilities to learn from our mistakes and to capitalize on our breaks. That, it seems to me, is an important part of what management is really about.

Appendix: C.R. Bard, Inc.

C.R. Bard founded his company in 1907 to sell catheters for the emerging medical specialty of urology. Catheters were devices for draining a person's bladder when an obstruction of the urinary tract prevented its normal functioning. The introduction in the 1930's of a catheter with a balloon on the end to hold it in place greatly expanded the use of these devices, and Bard's sales multiplied from $150,000 in 1929 to over $45 million in 1968 under the able leadership of Harris Willits. With reference to the balloon (Foley) catheter, which, in 1987, continued to be the most widely used bladder drainage device, Willits remarked, "That product made this company, and we had the best one made!"

Under Wendell Crain, who succeeded Willits as Bard's president and CEO in 1968, the company introduced many new medical equipment and supply products and expanded international operations. Crain also set out to reduce costs by expanding the company's manufacturing operations and by instituting asset and expense control programs. Over the next seven years, sales rose to $131 million and profits from $3.5 million to $9.7 million.

In 1975, Bard's board of directors became concerned that excessive attention to manufacturing and control had seriously weakened Bard's traditional strength in marketing. As a result, the board decided to change the leadership of C.R. Bard.

New Leadership

On February 9, 1976, Bob McCaffrey was appointed Bard's president and CEO. An outside member of the board explained his selection: "He's a salesman. He is intelligent, widely read, has a good feel for managing people, and has some experience in manufacturing . . . [but] the key factor in his selection was that he was a marketing man."

McCaffrey had started as a salesman for Johnson & Johnson, rising to become president of one of its small companies. In 1966 he left Johnson & Johnson to join Howmedica, a company making orthopedic cement and implants, rising to the positions of executive vice president and chief operating officer in 1974. Commenting on his decision to leave that company for Bard, McCaffrey said, "You can't tell yourself you're a professional manager and turn down a crack at being the CEO of a publicly held company."

During McCaffrey's first year, marketing and product development expenditures were increased. To strengthen management's marketing perspective, he promoted George Maloney, a divisional president who had joined Bard in 1959 as a sales representative, to group vice president.

In June 1977, McCaffrey presented his written analysis of the situation to the board, excerpts of which follow:

> Bard began strictly as a marketing company and started, about a decade ago, to enter manufacturing. As so often happens, in the intervening ten years, the manufacturing influence at Bard has become the dominant one

with a waning influence on the part of marketing. As a result, there is a conglomeration of product in a couple of divisions which makes for very ineffective sales concentration.

The ideal organization for Bard should be properly decentralized. Product lines should give a good opportunity for salesman concentration. The marketing and manufacturing of a product [should] be in a single division to avoid intercompany pricing problems.

The story (in the field) is that Bard is a monolith which isn't going anywhere . . . It is our plan to develop divisional alignments in Bard adhering to very clearly defined product areas. We expect to staff each division with the best possible people, to be selected either inside the company or out. We expect division's management to develop a thoroughly thought-out and lucid charter. This will enable them to focus on building share of market on existing products and strengthen their franchise by developing other products within the dictates of their charter.[1]

McCaffrey lost no time in implementing the proposed reorganization. Operations were restructured to achieve specialization by markets. To reassert Bard's traditional marketing strength, salespeople focused on these markets, each of which was defined by a particular medical specialty.

To spearhead the reorganization, Maloney was promoted to executive vice president in charge of operations and was also elected to the board of directors. By the end of 1977, Bard had been reorganized into ten domestic and five international divisions. This structure, with minor modifications, continued to be employed in 1987. Exhibit 5 contains a company organization chart. Exhibits 6 and 7 show C.R. Bard's financial results for selected years.

Decentralization, Concentration, Innovation

Over the years, McCaffrey continued to emphasize the need for divisions to focus on attractive markets and to provide distinctive products of value to the customer. This general strategic idea gradually was refined into a core concept of "decentralization, concentration, and innovation."

In McCaffrey's opinion, the effective decentralization of operating authority had to be coupled with strong corporate oversight and control. Accordingly, Bard had developed strong financial controls and an active management executive committee. This committee of eight people—comprising the CEO, COO, CFO, controller, vice chairman, and three group vice presidents—reviewed all major operating issues. Each division general manager would come before the committee to present the division's three-year plan, to initiate discussion of the divisional budget, to review management resources, and to discuss major actions and problems. Corporate staff units were purposely kept small to prevent them from getting overly involved in divisional affairs. As Gene Schultz, vice

---

1. Source: Harvard University case, *C.R. Bard, Inc.*, 381-180

Exhibit 5 C.R. Bard, Inc., company organization chart, 1986.

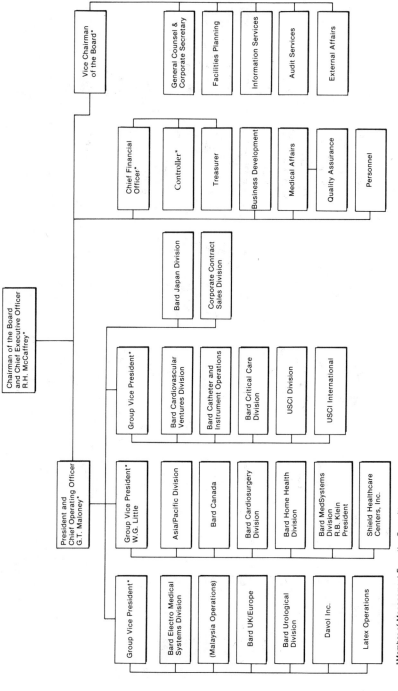

*Member of Management Executive Committee

Source: company document

Exhibit 6 C.R. Bard, selected financial results 1979–86 ($ million, except per share amounts).

	1979	1980	1981	1982	1983	1984	1985	1986
Net sales	160	219	295	343	397	417	465	548
Net operating income	22	34	46	56	64	64	74	89
Net income	14	15	23	27	33	35	42	51
Total assets	141	204	223	256	287	329	385	423
Working capital	73	83	94	110	129	149	173	153[a]
Net property, plant, equipment	38	53	60	70	75	83	92	90
Long-term debt	2	34	33	38	37	41	39	36
Shareholders' equity	113	125	144	168	194	222	257	266[b]
Return on average share-holder's equity (%)	12.5	12.6	16.7	17.4	18.3	16.9	17.5	19.6[b]
Debt/equity ratio (%)	—	—	22.9	22.6	19.3	18.3	15.3	13.6
Share price high	5¼	8⅛	11	17½	23⅜	18⅞	22	40⅜
Share price low (adjusted for splits)	3⅝	3½	6⅝	9⅛	13⅝	9½	10⅞	18¾
Number of employees	3,900	5,500	6,135	6,360	6,200	6,000	6,350	7,200

Source: C.R. Bard Annual Reports.
a. Excludes $25 million short-term investments placed in 1986.
b. A significant number of shares were repurchased by the company in 1986.

Exhibit 7 Bard sales by medical specialty ($ million).

	1980	1981	1982	1983	1984	1985	1986	Six-Year Growth
Cardiovascular	45	64	83	107	129	153	190	4.2x
Urological	74	88	103	106	90	100	109	1.5x
Surgical	23	51	60	68	70	80	94	4.1x
General Health (includes MedSystems division)	32	36	36	44	57	58	60	1.9x
Foreign and Export	46	57	61	72	71	76	94	2.0x

Sources: 1985 annual report and 1986 fourth quarter report.

president of personnel, noted, "That way we can't get in peoples' way. There is no time to make work for others."

Bard had a policy of promoting from within whenever possible. Top management spent one week each year assessing strengths and weaknesses of each manager. As Schultz noted, "We are small enough to know the people in the trenches."

Salaries were generally above average for the industry. Bard also had a widespread stock incentive scheme which for operating managers was based on a discretionary assessment of corporate earnings, divisional profits, and an individual manager's performance. Turnover among salaried personnel was low.

In a presentation to security analysts in Europe during October 1986, McCaffrey summed up his views of the importance of Bard's management approach with the following comment:

> I truly believe that Bard's management ability and style are most important in differentiating us from our competitors.
>
> An important element of Bard management is the exceptionally strong spirit of teamwork—within Bard divisions, and between Bard divisions and the corporate staff.
>
> The word teamwork is used frequently—by perhaps every corporation or group—but teamwork really means something at Bard because Bard's people really make it happen. This has a lot to do with our continuing success. It also makes Bard an enjoyable place to work, and we have fun to boot.

Bowater Computer Forms, Inc.

> When we decided to go into the computer forms business, I looked at a lot of companies with the thought of buying our way in. After a careful search I decided that given our strategy we had best go from the ground up. So then we decided to find the best person in the field to run the operation, and we did—we found Bill Detwiler, who had had a similar idea while he was working at Willamette, a major forms supplier.

Ron Toelle, the vice president of corporate development for Bowater Inc., leaned forward in his chair to describe the situation at Bowater's subsidiary, Bowater Computer Forms, Inc. (BCFI).

> Bill has done a superb job of creating this organization. He's a real entrepreneur. The question we now have is whether the skills that are needed for running a start-up can be carried into the new, large organization, and whether the centralized decision making that characterized the start-up can be decentralized. Bill is Swiss by background and is a very autocratic guy. He's been trying valiantly to change his attitudes and behavior and get his hands off the machines. However, even though he professes great democracy, he still tends to have all the answers himself.

The Parent

Bowater, Inc., was the largest domestic producer of newsprint in the United States, and a major producer of coated publication paper. Through most of its history it had been the American subsidiary of the British corporation Bowater, Ltd. In 1984, a decision was reached that it would be in the shareholders' best interest to separate the North American and British operations. At the time the company was earning a net income of $72 million on sales of $887 million from two large paper mills in Tennessee and South Carolina and two medium-sized mills in Canada.

Management attributed Bowater's success in the United States over the years to its strategy. The company had focused on the highly efficient manufacture of a limited number of commoditylike products (see Table A). Scale economies and a favorable location in the Southeast (which had low raw material costs and a growing market) resulted in some of the best operating margins in the industry.

Table A Bowater financial results by sector, 1984.

	Sales	Profits
Newsprint	66%	72%
Pulp	11	5
Coated paper	10	23
Other	13	small loss

Source: Merrill Lynch.

Concerned with the possible negative impact that television and other forms of electronic communication might have on the volume of newspapers, periodicals, and other printed materials that used Bowater's products, U.S. management began in the late 1970s to consider a strategy of diversification. The ten-year plan in 1979 described management's views on diversification in the context of the company's overall objectives:

> Bowater North America seeks to accomplish the following objectives:
>
> 1. Generate increased profits and cash flows
> 2. Continue to develop U.S. pulp and paper operations
> 3. Diversify into a limited number of new businesses
> 4. Achieve superior performance

The company's first move was to enter the rapidly growing computer forms business, concentrating on the large-volume, commoditylike stock continuous forms (the blue- or green-barred paper to record output from computers). A year later, in 1981, Bowater's managers selected the expanding home-center retail business as the second diversification target. One of its appeals was the opportunity to integrate backwards into the manufacture of building products.

In 1984, A. P. Gammie, chairman, president, and CEO of Bowater Inc., reaffirmed the company's diversification strategy in a memorandum to the board of directors:

> As indicated in our Business Plan, the strategic direction for Bowater favored by the Executive Committee comprises two principal elements. One is to realize the growth potential in the pulp and paper business without increasing our dependence on newsprint. The other is to diversify into related businesses which require less capital than pulp and paper operations. In this way, Bowater would reduce its exposure to any future setback which newsprint might encounter and, at the same time, broaden its opportunities for maintaining the high returns on assets and equity that it has generated in the past.
>
> It is useful to consider, in a conceptual sense, the sort of company we want Bowater to be ten years from now. Ideally, we would like to have a third or more of the company's profits to be generated from activities outside pulp and paper within ten years.

Exhibit 1   Total forms industry, 1985 estimate ($6.0 billion).

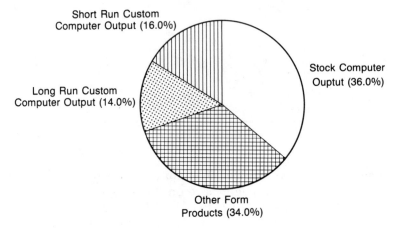

Short Run Custom
Computer Output (16.0%)

Stock Computer
Ouptut (36.0%)

Long Run Custom
Computer Output (14.0%)

Other Form
Products (34.0%)

The Computer Forms Industry and BCFI Strategy

The business forms industry, estimated to have an annual domestic market of $6 billion in 1985, produced a wide variety of business paper products including register forms, carbonless forms, custom and stock unit forms, sales books, stock computer output paper, and long-run and short-run custom output paper. (See Exhibit 1 for a breakdown of major product sales.)

The appeal of the business forms industry to Bowater management rested on several industry factors. First, the business forms market was growing at a higher rate than any other segment of the printing industry and at a much higher rate than the GNP. Second, long-run continuous computer output paper accounted for the bulk of that growth as a result of the huge data-processing demands of large firms such as banks, airlines, and oil companies. (See Exhibit 2.)

Though forms-industry analysts fretted in the 1970s over claims that America was moving toward a paperless society, in which data would be processed purely on video displays, by 1986 this outcome appeared increasingly unlikely. Bowater management believed that the computer forms market would enjoy healthy growth well into the 1990s, because IBM and other computer manufacturers had made a major and enduring commitment to line-hole continuous-output paper.

Due to the high shipping costs of paper and the degree of required customization, the forms industry had been characterized for many years by a fragmented structure with as many as 600 small regional "converters." Most of these firms, attempting to sell a very broad line of products, ran their factories as job shops. Approximately seventy-five firms competed in the computer-output paper segment and, according to BCFI's management, only one national and four regional firms had sought to specialize to any degree within that segment. See Table B for the sales figures of the major forms suppliers.

Exhibit 2 Business forms industry, sales (1970–85).

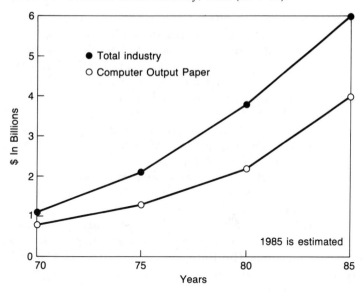

Table B Total 1984 estimated sales for major U.S. forms suppliers (in millions of dollars).

Company	Stock Computer Output Paper	Long-Run Computer Output Paper[a]	Total U.S. Forms[a]
Moore	300	450	1,200
Willamette	105	155	155
Standard Register	65	100	340
Uarco	60	95	325
Duplex Products	60	60	342
Chicago Stock Tab	60	60	60
SCM Allied Egry	50	70	150
Data Documents	45	70	150
Star Business Forms	45	45	60
Wallace Comp. Serv.	40	80	170
Total	830	1,185	2,952
Total Industry	2,000	3,700	5,600
BCFI	44	56	56

a. Stock computer output paper is included in the long-run computer output paper figure, which in turn is included in the Total U.S. Forms column.

Source: BCFI 1985 Strategic Plan.

The Entrepreneurial Phase

When Detwiler was hired in January 1980 he had a strategic concept, a corporate name, a corporate name, a bank account—and that was all. Within three months he hired a team of people he had known over the years. He first took on Marty Allan to assist him in administration, then Larry Hatfield to head sales, and Norm Pellegrine to run manufacturing. The only member of the initial team to come from Bowater, Inc., was the controller, Denis Tontodonato.

Toelle had told Detwiler that he could put the corporate headquarters "anywhere East of the Rockies," so Detwiler selected a site in Plano, Texas, a sprawling northern suburb of Dallas dotted with industrial plants and crisscrossed with expressways. This location was desirable, because land was inexpensive, unions were rare, persons with manufacturing experience were readily available, and it was in a region of the sunbelt that was both centrally located and economically booming.

Detwiler immediately began construction of the first plant and brought it on line in December 1980. A second plant in Scottsburg, Indiana, began production in December 1982. The third plant, in Sparks, Nevada (a suburb of Reno), was nearing completion for start-up in July 1986, and two more were planned before the end of the decade.

Manufacturing

The manufacturing strategy of BCFI was to bring economies of scale to the converter industry by minimizing short- and customized-production runs. As Toelle described it, "We get the best equipment possible, and we run the blazes out of it, 24 hours a day, 349 days a years." The employees in BCFI's plants worked twelve-hour shifts—four days on, then four off, three on, then three off.

The actual production process was simple. Large rolls of paper weighing from 1,000 to 2,500 pounds were brought by rail from paper mills to the BCFI plants. The rolls were fed into machines that cut the paper to the proper width, printed lines (if necessary), punched holes in the sides, and folded it—all at a speed of almost fifty miles an hour. Indeed, the process was so elementary that the cost of the raw material—the paper rolls—accounted for approximately 60 percent of total costs, as shown in Table C.

Plant personnel paid close attention to quality. Samples of the paper shipped from the mills were tested for moisture content and other key variables; rolls that did not meet the standard were returned. This attention to quality extended throughout the manufacturing process. As Detwiler described it:

> We are working to have the reputation as a top-quality house. Every box that goes out of the plant has the initials of the operator who produced it. We can tell when it was made, and on what machine, and by whom. We can even identify the roll it came from and go back to the paper mill if a problem arises which is tied to raw material.

Table C Percentage of total cost of delivered product.

	12" x 8½" IBM 3800	14⅞" Two-part stock
Paper	66	56
Labor	8	10
Carbon paper	—	12
Other manufacturing	5	4
Distribution	6	5
Sales	8	7
General and administrative	7	6
	100	100

Source: BCFI 1985 Strategic Plan.

Because of the importance of the quality and cost of paper to producers of converted goods, some firms, such as Willamette, were vertically integrated. Detwiler explained why Bowater favored purchasing paper supplies on the open market:

> Though on the surface it might seem advantageous to have a secure, in-house supply of paper, in practice the benefits are illusory. For one thing, paper is normally transferred at market prices, so that the paper mills can show a normal profit. Moreover, when the paper mills have old plants, the costs can be higher than is available on the open market. But the biggest problem is that the mill tends to focus attention on outside customers rather than on internal transfers, which are taken for granted. So we can get better treatment from paper companies in an arm's-length transaction than if we had to rely on a sister operation.

Detwiler personally conducted many of the purchasing negotiations with BCFI's large paper suppliers.

> I get heavily involved with the paper because it represents such a large part of our total costs that any price changes affect us directly on the bottom line. I also do it, because having the president of the company involved gives us more clout with the paper companies. We enter into long-term contracts; we sit down with suppliers and show them the three-year demand growth curve. These contracts protect our supply requirements for our rapid growth. We are already an important customer for paper suppliers.

Sales

With its strategy of focusing on large-volume orders of stock forms, BCFI management regarded national accounts as a prime target that would eventually account for over 50 percent of its total sales. By 1986, national accounts represented about 35 percent of total sales. National accounts differed greatly in their practices: about 10 percent were fully centralized, controlling orders and inventories for all their operating units; about 60 percent centralized the purchase order and allowed required units to order their supplies as needed; and 30 percent only approved suppliers, permitting individual units to purchase supplies from a selected list of suppliers. The sales force worked out of twenty-three district offices, each of which had its own warehouse and distribution center.

In contrast to the rest of the industry, salespersons were paid on salary (combined with annual bonus incentives based on contribution) rather than on commission. Hatfield attributed much of the firm's success to this compensation policy, since it encouraged cooperation rather than competition within the sales force and enabled the company to provide coordinated service to a firm with facilities and offices throughout the country.

> The commission system is designed to get people to take lots of little, bad orders rather than to look for good ones, ones which enable us to have long production runs. It also creates a lot of fighting over territory. We don't have that. We have a team and the people we hire have to be willing to be team players. But it's hard to teach new people that they don't have to take every order that comes their way!

Although Bowater had had no difficulty recruiting experienced salespeople from other companies, the time required to educate and transform new recruits into "team players" was seen by management as a significant constraint on the rapid growth of the company. Experience had shown that salespeople who refused to learn eventually clashed with the others and usually chose to leave.

There were fifty-four salespeople in all, fifty-one men and three women, and Detwiler and Hatfield expected to recruit ten salespeople with industry experience each year for the next five years. Each salesperson was expected to generate $3.5 million in sales per year.

To land a national account with a major firm took patience, experience, and much direct personal contact. As David McBride, vice president of sales, described it, "Some people just think that all you have to do to make a sale in this industry is to hire a gorilla, burn a price on his chest, and send him out to take orders. But price is not the most important thing—it's service to the customer."

Detwiler concurred:

> We are a supply item for most companies, and though in some ways we are a commodity, we represent a critical link in their entire system. Their computers can't print output without our paper and so they want no stockouts. So we have to maintain quality, make deliveries on time, and respond quickly to problems 100 percent of the time.

The salespeople were encouraged to make cold-call sales visits to firms to try to identify key decision makers and major competitors. Sometimes the key person would be a manager of the company's computer data-processing division. These people tended to be concerned about quality and availability. Other times the key person was the purchasing agent, who, as long as he or she received no complaints about a product, focused on price. When a "sponsor"—someone within the firm who would like to see the business go to BCFI—was located, that person was carefully nurtured and provided with samples to test. BCFI salespersons also had entertainment allowances, in contrast to competitors, whose salespeople had to pay for entertainment out of their commissions. When an account was finally landed, the salesperson was responsible for maintaining close contact—usually weekly—to monitor any quality problems and to prevent stock-outs.

Hatfield said:

> When I was in the field I used to have coffee with the purchasing guys from my major accounts every Monday morning. After they trusted me, I was often able to do the inventory and ordering for them, and I would make sure that they never ran out. It really got so that I knew their needs better than they did.

Such personal contacts also helped the sales force cope with a recurring problem in the industry: the great volatility in paper prices that had to be passed immediately along to customers in order to maintain desired profitability levels. Although some customers negotiated fixed annual prices or capped increases, most continued to follow the traditional industry practice of purchasing at market price. Maintaining good relations with these latter customers could be a problem at times when prices increased. BCFI salespersons worked hard to educate them about raw material price trends and to build trust.

As BCFI expanded its operations, it encountered increasingly severe competitive resistance. As a result, establishing a position on the West Coast proved to be more difficult than originally forecasted. In Detwiler's view, the competitors had come to recognize BCFI as a committed contender who had to be taken seriously and whose progress must be impeded as much as possible.

Prices were kept in line through national pricing guidelines. The "A" price was the lowest a salesperson could go without approval of the district manager; "B" was the lowest a district manager could go without consulting the regional manager; and "C" was the lowest a regional manager could go without talking to the vice president. District and regional sales managers were also responsible in their areas for expense control, account and market sales strategies, sales forecasting, hiring and firing, and training.

BCFI had also initiated a small reseller program in 1985 to promote Bowater products with retail stores for personal computer users. The program was handled through manufacturers' representatives and guided by the vice president of retail sales, Marty Allan.

Production Scheduling and Inventory Control

To minimize delivery time, BCFI tried to supply customers from inventory in the distribution center. Production scheduling was largely dedicated to replenishing and adding to inventory in accordance with forecasted needs. According to Detwiler:

BCFI currently handles better than 98 percent of its business from inventory, including contract jobs. We find this approach works very well in our established markets. The new market regions pose some problems because of the rapid change in the volume and mix of orders.

The complex task of coordinating the needs of the sales force with the constraints of manufacturing and of balancing inventory levels in distribution centers fell to several staff persons, most notably Ray McDowell, the vice president for technical services, who was responsible for production scheduling. Virtually all of the firm's production reporting, inventory systems, accounting records, sales data, and other data-processing needs were handled centrally by a single IBM 38 computer in Plano, under the supervision of MIS manager Patty Dockery.

Under McDowell's guidance, BCFI maintained a close watch on stock inventory levels and used these to prepare production orders. The central computer would keep a record of the approximately 125 items sold to some 2,000 customers over the previous sixteen weeks and would identify both the peak and trend in sales. Since demand was expected to continue to grow at a rapid rate, the peak sale of the earlier period was selected as the "safety stock" level for the next, so that an order of the same size could automatically be filled from inventory. Salespersons also filed Volume Change Notices to signal significant changes in sales; these were entered from terminals in the sales regional offices directly into the computer in Plano.

The desired safety stock levels were then compared to current inventory levels and the difference was categorized as "commit jobs" within a certain week—that is, an order for a production run in a plant. These orders were compiled and assigned to presses in the plants by McDowell's office. The plant managers in Plano and Scottsburg had the option of rearranging the order of runs or the use of the machines, as long as by the end of each week all of the assigned orders had been produced.

McDowell's job was not always smooth, because the sales and production function had different objectives when it came to scheduling. People in sales wanted to make sure that their delivery dates were met, while the plant managers wanted the longest possible runs in order to maximize efficiency and tons per hour. As a result, the size and location of finished-goods inventories were critical issues. Some persons in production, including vice president for manufacturing Norm Pellegrine, believed that production scheduling should be handled by the manufacturing function. McDowell, an engineer and M.B.A., did not seem to mind. As he put it, smiling, "I work on the principle that if you have everybody—sales, manufacturing, and finance—equally angry with you, then you are probably doing a good job."

Challenges of the Professional Phase

In the first six years of its existence, Bowater Computer Forms had grown from a tiny start-up to a firm of 350 employees and $76 million in sales (see Exhibit 3

Exhibit 3 Financial data, 1985 ($ millions).

Sales	$77	Cash	a
Cost of sales	59	Inventories	$17
Depreciation	2	Accounts receivable	8
Gross margin	16	Fixed assets, net	18
Distribution	5	Total assets	$44
GS&A	8	Accounts payable	4
Operating income	3	Deferred tax	3
		Bowater ownership	37
		Total liabilities	$44

Selected financial ratios

Gross fixed assets per sales dollars	8.2%
Inventory turnover	5.4X
Days sales outstanding	40
Operating profit as percentage of sales	4.3%

a. Less than $500,000.

for financial data). Everyone expected the growth to continue, and probably to accelerate, as the applications for computer technology expanded not only within large firms but within small companies and individual homes. The 1985 Bowater Strategic Plan projected that by 1993, when the market was expected to begin showing the first signs of maturation, the firm would have expanded to five plants and forty-five district offices around the country.

To make the heady transition from a relatively small firm to one that would break into the ranks of the *Fortune* 500 with hundreds of millions in sales by 1990 required the adept handling of several delicate management problems—the degree of centralization to maintain, the development and professionalization of managers, and the selection of proper distribution methods to reach the dynamic and diversifying market.

Centralization versus Decentralization

From the beginning Detwiler's strategy called for a tightly coordinated interplay between production and sales so that a local salesperson would have the authority and ability to commit the company to produce and deliver large orders to a national account at multiple delivery points within price guidelines. Under his strategy, the centralized authority over sales guidelines, production schedules, and inventories was the key to BCFI's competitive edge. In his view, to decentralize would be to create confusion. Said Detwiler:

> The only time I ever hear about decentralization is from Connecticut. They keep talking about it, but I don't know what they mean. At first I thought they meant having functions represented at each regional plant—

but that had been tried at other forms companies and I know it has not been successful. For example, I know of one company that has multiple plants and each one was a different division and had its own sales force. The division was a god unto itself! If there was a transfer, there was a $7\frac{1}{2}$ percent margin for each plant. Each plant had different equipment, and a different cost system. This structure was a deterrent to trying to sell national accounts.

While most of Detwiler's senior managers seemed to agree with him, there were some feelings in Scottsburg and at headquarters in Darien that Detwiler was holding the reins too tightly. Jim Ginter, the new plant manager in Scottsburg, described the situation from his point of view:

> We are committed to centralization. I see both sides of the issue. From one standpoint, it's great; I only have to worry about inventories in and manufacturing out. On the other hand, we are a thousand miles from Texas. We could react quicker to some situations—for example, problems in transportation—if we didn't have to find the person responsible in Plano before we could act.
>
> I don't know that some person punching buttons on a computer in Plano is really sensitive to production issues. I am not sure he or she knows the business well enough. We see green paper already running on this machine, and they are telling us also to run it on that machine. We could make the shift, but that would foul up the computer.
>
> And what if the rolls of paper don't come in on time? Then what? The schedule goes out the window. We get all our shipping orders from Plano; if the computer doesn't spit out shipping orders for a couple of hundred pallets before 5 P.M., the stuff just piles up. The scheduler is a thousand miles away, and stuff is coming off the line, and the shippers are standing around with nothing to do. And if the computer line goes down, then what do I do? It happens all the time.
>
> I don't know the answers. We just have to make things work. Bill Detwiler believes in this system, and so I have to believe in it too! He has built sales from nothing to $100 million so he must know what he is doing. I'm not really a proponent of decentralization, but I guess in some ways I am, because I know that we could control some areas more efficiently since we could react quicker when changes or unpredictable situations occur.

Pellegrine agreed:

> I am not a great believer in centralized management. This is the third company I have been with, and I have had good and bad experiences with it. I'd like to see the plant managers and regional vice president of sales work together to solve problems in inventory, particularly in finished goods inventory, rather than funnel all this through headquarters. I think centralization in certain areas—accounting, finance, purchasing—is good. Bill, on the other hand, has had bad experiences with decentralization. If left to him, Bill would make every decision; he would schedule every press. He's very good. He knows the manufacturing side and the marketing side and he's got that entrepreneurial spirit.

Said Toelle:

Bill is a very centralized kind of guy. He likes to make decisions himself and to control things from the top. He was so used to going into the plant and checking things that he and I finally decided that we had to move him and the other senior people out of the front office at the plant and into a corporate office in the RepublicBank building. And at first, he didn't want to go. So the degree of centralization is still an open question. That's a decision to be made down the pike.

Managerial Development and Promotion

The senior managers of BCFI also cited the challenge of developing managers fast enough to meet the demands of the rapidly expanding firm as a pressing problem. Three aspects of the company's approach aggravated the situation. First, the preoccupation with the day-to-day crises of a new company had blunted the managers' ability to take time to develop their subordinates. Second, in striving to achieve break-even performance as rapidly as possible, BCFI managers had deliberately held down administrative costs. Third, the centralized structure and strategy meant that the plants were judged on production costs and the sales offices on revenues and profit contribution, leaving the total profit responsibility—and the broad outlook of a general manager—to Detwiler alone.

By the spring of 1986 the senior managers had taken several steps to address the need: They had moved the corporate offices away from the plant, hired a human resources director, and brought up a new layer of managers to handle operating issues.

The Move to the New Office. In February 1986 the senior managers moved out of their offices in the front of the Plano plant and into a large suite occupying the entire eleventh floor of the modern RepublicBank office building several miles away. In conversations with the casewriter, several of the senior managers jovially suggested that they had made the move with relative ease compared to their colleagues. Sitting in his new, spacious, blue corner office Detwiler said:

> I have a great team, very fired up, very hands-on. But they didn't want to move over here to the new office. I had to drag them kicking! My Finance VP said to me, "But who's going to close the books at the end of the month?" and I told him, "You're going to have to train someone else! What if you were sick?"

In a later conversation, Finance Vice President Denis Tontodonato said:

> The four of us who started the business—Bill, Norm, Larry, and I—are really cut from the same mold. The move here and the transition to a professional mode was not as difficult for me, because I was the corporate controller for the Bowater parent before I came down here and I'm glad to roll my sleeves back down and do the work I used to do. But Bill by his nature just loves to get involved, and it was tough for him. We even kid him about it.

The Human Resources Manager. During the first five years, BCFI had employed an outside consultant to develop a detailed performance appraisal system for all employees based on weighted combinations of productivity, achievement of goals, and absenteeism. In January 1986, Bill Detwiler hired Michael Anders, formerly a human resources manager for the Harris Corporation, as the new director of human resources and charged him with the task of improving the managerial development within the firm.

Said Anders:

> It's going to be painful to move the company from one stage to the next; it's going to require a lot of detail management. In the entrepreneurial stage, if the senior managers needed a price quote, they would just decide it themselves. Now they can't do that because they have set up price guidelines.
>
> Bill tended to be involved in every aspect of the business and had the reputation of being pretty domineering. He's working hard to make the transition to a new style. If he's able to pull it off, he will be one of the few who has. But he is making a great effort. He is allowing people to make more decisions.
>
> One good thing about Bill is that he will not tolerate "yes" people. He'll play devil's advocate just to make sure you can support your opinion. He tests people. He'll pick a fight to see if you are strong in your resolution. So people tend to speak their minds in meetings.

In February 1986, six weeks after he had joined the firm, Anders was in the process of assessing BCFI's needs and planning his first steps.

Establishing a New Mid-Management Layer. To strengthen the operating management ranks and to free up the senior managers to deal with broader issues, Detwiler had authorized establishing a secondary level of managers, including a set of regional sales vice presidents and a new inventory manager. (See Exhibit 4 for an organizational chart.) This move, however, had created some tension within the company, because despite management's stated policy of promoting from within, Detwiler had felt obliged to hire some of these people from outside the firm to acquire the necessary expertise.

As McDowell described it:

> A lot of people joined the firm with high expectations. They were told that this was a growth company with a bright future and real potential for advancement. But the future has arrived, and it doesn't look so bright. There's only one president and the slots below him are filled by relatively young managers. The pyramid has gotten tight.

McDowell was particularly aware of the problem, since he had recently had to confront the disappointment of one of his employees in inventory control. This employee was upset that despite her five-year tenure as an inventory and production scheduler at the company, she had been passed over for promotion in favor of an outsider. This employee commented:

> From the moment you get hired here they dangle the policy of promotion from within like a carrot before your face, but then they don't take the

Exhibit 4 Organizational chart.

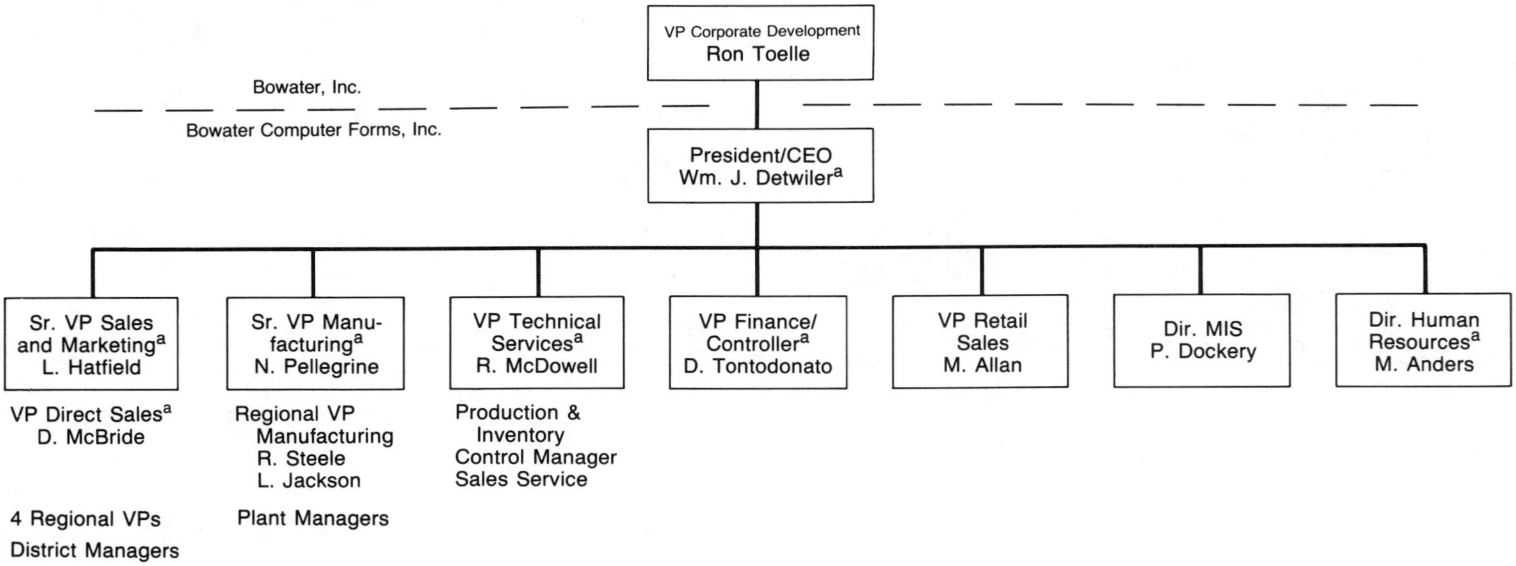

Bowater, Inc.

- -

Bowater Computer Forms, Inc.

VP Corporate Development
Ron Toelle

President/CEO
Wm. J. Detwiler[a]

Sr. VP Sales
and Marketing[a]
L. Hatfield

VP Direct Sales[a]
D. McBride

4 Regional VPs
District Managers

Sr. VP Manu-
facturing[a]
N. Pellegrine

Regional VP
Manufacturing
R. Steele
L. Jackson

Plant Managers

VP Technical
Services[a]
R. McDowell

Production &
Inventory
Control Manager
Sales Service

VP Finance/
Controller[a]
D. Tontodonato

VP Retail
Sales
M. Allan

Dir. MIS
P. Dockery

Dir. Human
Resources[a]
M. Anders

[a]Office in new building.

time to develop people within the company and they go to the outside. So a lot of people are discouraged.

Now Ray has said he will help me with career planning and I am hopeful that it will help. There are other people who are unhappy here; they feel the company did me wrong. They ask me, "Why are you staying?" I tell them, "I still believe that if I pay my dues I will get what's coming to me."

Dissatisfaction with the promotion policy was also expressed in the plant. Said one operator:

The policy of promotion from within is a bunch of BS. I had a lot of hope when I came here. They told me it's a growth company with a lot of potential. I even took a few management courses. But they won't develop you, and they won't promote you. There's people out there who have been stuffing boxes for five long years!

Maybe if you scratch their backs, you'll do all right. But in a pinch Detwiler is going to go hire his buddies from the outside. And you know something? Ninety percent of the workers agree with me.

Said another, a lead man who had been promoted:

There is opportunity here, if you work. But they don't give you a lot a training; they just pop you in the new job and then it's sink or swim. I was lucky because I had a good manager.

According to Anders, the percentage of employees promoted to their current position from within the company, as of January 30, 1986, was as follows: executive staff, 80 percent; mid-management (administration), 67 percent; mid-management (sales), 53 percent; regional management, 100 percent; and supervisors, 86 percent. The over-all average for these categories was 74 percent. The company's total workforce comprised 81 percent male/19 percent female and 73 percent non-exempt hourly/27 percent salaried employees.

Dispute over the Reseller Program

An additional problem for BCFI was the simmering debate over policy between Hatfield, senior vice president of sales and marketing in charge of the national account direct-sales force, and Allan, vice president of retail sales in charge of the reseller program. The reseller program had been started in November 1984, after a market research study had projected that individual and small business owners of personal computers would account for over 45 percent of the market for continuous computer paper by the mid-1990s.

Allan had served for several years as the vice president of administration, coordinating production scheduling, purchasing, and inventories. In 1984 Allan switched full time to the reseller program, and tasks formerly under his control were divided between Hatfield's and McDowell's departments.

Allan had begun in 1982 by attempting to sell directly to personal computer owners through direct mail. The sales pitch included lower prices, because the product would be purchased "direct from the factory," innovative packaging (in the form of a container that turned into a sturdy "dead files" storage box), and promotional add-ons such as a free diskette with every box of paper.

The direct-mail campaign turned out to be less successful than anticipated, because the lists of computer owners were chronically out of date. Allan then persuaded Detwiler to move to a full-fledged reseller program that would seek to place BCFI's products with wholesalers and retailers. Sales would be directed to large accounts such as discount mass merchandisers, computer store chains, department stores, book store chains, and the like. Detwiler agreed on the condition that the program would be profitable by the end of the first year.

Sales in the reseller program were made through eighteen manufacturer's representative firms and had totaled $1.7 million in 1985, the program's first year. Allan projected that sales from this program would be significant to BCFI within five years.

Hatfield was opposed to the reseller program on the grounds that it undermined and confused BCFI's principal marketing thrust. He noted:

> You can't control the reps; in fact, they control you, because they tinker with price and demand. It's against what we set out to do—go for long runs and big accounts. Instead they shoot for small numbers and volumes.
>
> Moreover, they aren't Bowater employees, and yet they make themselves out to be. They have Bowater cards and Bowater stationery. But they aren't really loyal; in fact, they are following the historic route of trying to break down the sales force.

Allan saw it differently:

> The charge that the reps aren't loyal isn't fair. They have given up other lines to handle ours exclusively. And they aren't selling at low prices and volumes—since they are on commission, the higher the volume and price, the higher the amount of money they make.
>
> We have two different marketing problems and two different solutions. We have a direct sales force to focus on the *Fortune* 2000, and we have a group of reps to sell to retailers such as Computerland, Target stores, or IBM product centers.

The two men were particularly disturbed at reports from the West Coast about a large retail chain that had been approached by both the direct sales force and the reps. The reps were trying to place BCFI paper in the stores, while the direct salespeople were trying to sell for the company's own data-processing needs. A vice-president of the chain had called BCFI headquarters to inquire why the reps were quoting a much higher price than the direct sales force.

To Allan, this problem was one that could be solved through more effective management of the boundaries; to Hatfield, it was a sign that, the larger the reseller program became, the more it would undermine the BCFI direct-sales strategy. Said Hatfield:

> I don't think the reseller program is a good idea because it is not sanctioned by sales. It's really one of Bill's special projects. History has shown that you cannot split your organization like this.

Detwiler had sided squarely with Allan. As he told a casewriter:

> The small-user segment of the market is going to be big, and we need to
> be in there. Hatfield is just going to have to get religion on this one. We are
> going to have to persuade him.
>
> *Casewriter:* And if he genuinely believes it's a bad idea and won't be
> persuaded?
>
> *Detwiler:* It could affect my opinion about his qualifications to be con-
> sidered as one of my potential successors.

Pressures and Problems of Rapid Growth

The final challenge of the new phase was deciding how to respond to pressure
on BCFI to accelerate its expansion. The industry was expanding at such a rate
that most of BCFI's growth was coming from the increase in demand rather
than from taking sales away from competitors. The relatively small capital investment required by each plant (only $12–15 million per plant, compared to
$250 million or more for a paper machine) combined with the robust profit
projections were prompting members of the parent company's board to encourage Detwiler to consider expanding into new product lines and to accelerate the schedule for bringing the new plants on-line.

As one board member put it:

> The growth is there, the business is there, the money is there—why not
> move faster? The slower we move, the more time we give competitors to
> copy our approach or to find ways of stopping or outflanking us.

Detwiler was reluctant to have BCFI move any faster than it was already
doing. He vividly recalled how, in the face of a forecast upturn in industry
demand, it had been decided to open the Scottsburg plant several years ahead
of schedule, to his eventual dismay. The accelerated expansion had caught
BCFI short of qualified staff, and the necessary transfers of people to Scottsburg disrupted the Plano operation. By the time the Scottsburg plant had come
on stream, demand had subsided, and BCFI losses had increased. This deterioration of performance occurred before the BCFI strategy had proven itself
and, consequently, Bowater senior managers' confidence in the subsidiary was
shaken.

In the second quarter of 1984, as monthly losses were mounting, Toelle
began to pressure Detwiler to pursue margins rather than volume. This shift,
under the black cloud of headquarters' dissatisfaction, caused considerable
consternation in BCFI's ranks, especially among the sales personnel. Many
salespeople felt that the new objectives were premature and unrealistic, and
that the rug had been pulled out from under them. Toelle argued, and Detwiler concurred, that proving the viability of BCFI's strategy was of paramount importance.

Detwiler launched an all-out drive to achieve break-even results in 1984. As
shown in Table D, BCFI achieved that goal, and recaptured the parent company's confidence and enthusiasm.

Table D BCFI actual operating profit (000s of dollars).

	Actual
1982	(2,820)
1983	(3,465)
1984	925
1985	3,061

Apart from the caution induced by his earlier experiences, Detwiler was reluctant to overtax BCFI's human resources capabilities. In his view the company was limited in the number of experienced managers who could supervise the start-up and operation of new plants, and it took time to develop and promote supervisors and plant managers to take on tasks as the plants came on-line. Moreover, as Bill pointed out, a strategy of accelerating the rate of growth contained some hidden dangers.

> We keep getting pressure from Connecticut to bring the plants on fast and to look at cut sheets [8½″ – 11″ individual pages], labels, and other products. We hear them, and then we sit in our strategic planning meetings and ask ourselves: Should we do this? Do we want to risk spreading ourselves so thin? Do we really want a guy who is taking $10,000 orders for stock to stop and spend the extra time taking a $500 order for labels? And how fast can we push the growth of our manufacturing capacity before quality begins to suffer? Success in this industry depends on maintaining a tight strategic focus and a reputation for quality and service. How far and how fast can we go before these things suffer?
>
> For my part, I would like to see BCFI increase its sales over the next five years at an average 21 percent annual rate—which is just half of what we averaged these past three years—and to earn by the end of this period 15 to 17 percent operating profit and 30 percent return on investment. Based on the information flowing down to me, those targets might not be ambitious enough for some people.

CEO Evaluation
at Dayton Hudson

*If I were to become the Chief Executive Officer of another corporation, I would
want there to be a review process. As CEO of Dayton Hudson Corporation, I
can attest to the advantages of a partnership with a strong independent board,
and the evaluation process helps forge that partnership.*

> Kenneth A. Macke,
> Chairman and CEO, Dayton Hudson

*Several of our board members were surprised when we said this review process
is what we want to do, but to me, it really was a fulfillment of that which is
really the heart and soul of Dayton Hudson. So its presence at the board level
is really an outflow of what Dayton Hudson is throughout, rather than an
invention by and for the board.*

> Edwin H. Wingate,
> Senior Vice President of Personnel, Dayton Hudson

By 1990, Dayton Hudson Corporation was one of America's stellar companies.
Founded in 1902 by George Draper Dayton, the "Dayton Company" evolved
from a single downtown department store to a multibillion-dollar retailer, operating such well-known chains as Target, Mervyn's, Dayton's, Hudson's, and
the recently acquired Marshall Field's. The Minneapolis-based company went
public in 1969, and was managed from 1950 to 1975 by George Draper Dayton's
five grandsons. By the early 1980s, the final two Daytons, Kenneth and Bruce,
left the company and retired.

According to Dayton Hudson management, Kenneth and Bruce Dayton felt
one of their contributions to corporate America rested in their ideas concerning
corporate governance. At Dayton Hudson, that meant a methodically conceived and implemented process for the board. But perhaps the Daytons' most
unique contribution to corporate governance was their system for review of
the performance of the chairman of the board and the Chief Executive Officer.

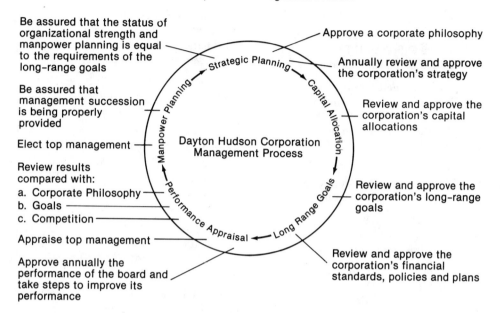

BOARD OF DIRECTORS—DUTIES

Relationship to the Management Process

Be assured that the status of organizational strength and manpower planning is equal to the requirements of the long-range goals

Be assured that management succession is being properly provided

Elect top management

Review results compared with:
a. Corporate Philosophy
b. Goals
c. Competition

Appraise top management

Approve annually the performance of the board and take steps to improve its performance

Strategic Planning

Manpower Planning

Performance Appraisal

Long Range Goals

Capital Allocation

Dayton Hudson Corporation Management Process

Approve a corporate philosophy

Annually review and approve the corporation's strategy

Review and approve the corporation's capital allocations

Review and approve the corporation's long-range goals

Review and approve the corporation's financial standards, policies and plans

Exhibit 1   Dayton Hudson "Wheel" of board of directors duties

The CEO Review Process

The Dayton Hudson CEO review process was one element in a system of corporate governance at the retail giant. Management and directors spoke of "cycles" instead of "years," in order to emphasize the ongoing nature and interconnectedness of their activities. At Dayton Hudson, the board approved strategy and allocations of capital in the fall, conducted its review of the CEO and chairman of the board in the spring, and reviewed corporate financial standards, policies, and plans in the summer. (See Exhibit 1 for Dayton Hudson "wheel" of board duties.)

In 1990, the Dayton Hudson board consisted of fifteen members, thirteen of whom were outside directors. (See Exhibit 2 for list of Dayton Hudson board of directors.) According to Kenneth Macke, to be selected as an inside director, one must either be the CEO or a candidate for that position. Although at times in Dayton Hudson's history the chairman of the board and the CEO were different people, Macke performed both jobs. He explained: "I personally believe it is important for the chairman to be involved in the management of the company."

The Executive Committee of the Dayton Hudson board was composed of all of the outside directors plus the chairman of the board. Bruce MacLaury, a board member since 1977, had served as vice chairman of the Executive Com-

Exhibit 2 Dayton Hudson Board of Directors

Rand Araskog (1982)
Chairman of the Board and Chief Executive Officer of ITT Corporation, a diversified multinational company.

Robert Burnett (1983)
Former Chief Executive Officer and current Chairman of the Board of Meredith Corporation, a media company.

Livio DeSimone (1987)
Executive Vice President of 3M Company, a diversified manufacturer.

Roger Enrico (1990)
Chairman and Chief Executive Officer of Frito-Lay, Inc., a subsidiary of PepsiCo, Inc.

Roger Hale (1982)
President and Chief Executive Officer of Tennant Company, an industrial equipment manufacturer.

Donald Hall (1978)
Chairman of the Board of Hallmark Cards, Inc., a greeting card manufacturer.

Betty Ruth Hollander (1986)
Chairman of the Board and Chief Executive Officer of the Omega Group, Inc., a manufacturer of scientific measurement and control devices and systems.

Michele Hooper (1990)
President of Baxter Corporation, a subsidiary of Baxter International, a health care supply company.

David Kearns (1987)
Former Chief Executive Officer and current Chairman of Xerox Corporation.

Kenneth Macke (1979)
Chairman of the Board, Chief Executive Officer, and Chairman of the Executive Committee of Dayton Hudson Corporation.

Bruce MacLaury (1977)
President of the Brookings Institution, a research and education organization.

David McLaughlin (1976)
President of the Aspen Institute, an institute for leadership development.

Mary Patterson McPherson (1988)
President of Bryn Mawr College.

John Rollwagen (1986)
Chairman of the Board and Chief Executive Officer of Cray Research, Inc., a manufacturer of supercomputers.

Stephen Watson (1990)
President of Dayton Hudson Corporation.

Date in parentheses indicates year director was elected to board.

mittee since 1987, and chaired the CEO review meetings, during which the CEO excused himself from the proceedings.

Management believed that the CEO review process was inextricably linked with other board activities. To Bruce MacLaury, this emphasis was apparent to him from the moment he joined the board:

> The CEO review process struck me as one part of a very highly thought through and articulated policy of corporate governance, because there was a whole dimension of processes that the board and the CEO and the senior

management went through on an annual schedule. CEO performance was one important part, but only one part, of a very well thought through process. . . . I was impressed when I came on board that somebody had given a great deal of thought to how a corporation ought to be run.

In the first formal step of the CEO review process, the CEO prepared a self-evaluation for the Dayton Hudson board meeting. This "prereview" followed the format of the job description for the chairman and the CEO. (See Exhibit 3 for chairman and CEO job descriptions.) In his prereview, Kenneth Macke commented on those sections of the job description that he felt he needed to discuss. He took his previous year's evaluation and began from there, attempting to report progress on comments made in that review:

> If the board had commented the prior year that: 'You need to represent the corporation more in society,' I would update them on how I had responded to that challenge. So these things flow from one year to the next, and from objective to objective.

Macke then discussed the company's objectives outlined in the strategic plan prepared the previous autumn, and described how well those objectives were being met. For Macke, this was the opportunity to present his own view of the health of the corporation, as well as highlight some of his concerns. "I strive to create dialogue," said Macke, about some of the points he might raise in his prereview.

For most board members, the prereview was used as a starting point for their own comments on the CEO's performance. But it had an additional function. Bruce MacLaury felt:

> [The prereview] highlights where the CEO's perception is different from that of the board. It's important to know that. . . . The procedure is designed to make sure that a misunderstanding, or gap, if it exists, would be made known.

Kenneth Macke presented the prereview, which was usually six to eight pages long, in a meeting of the Executive Committee of the board. His presentations, in which Macke would be expected to do the majority of the talking, would last about an hour. After the prereview had been presented, the CEO would leave the meeting and the Executive Committee would move into "executive session," with the vice chairman presiding. When the company was generally recognized to be in good shape and doing well relative to its competitors, there would be little discussion at this point. However, as David McLaughlin, a board member since 1976, pointed out:

> When the company wasn't doing well, this became a vehicle for the board to have a very tough discussion about where the company was going. The board itself really got into a serious discussion on a number of issues during those years.

In good times, lengthy discussion became "unnecessary," according to McLaughlin. But, he believed, if there was a serious question of governance of

Exhibit 3   Chairman and CEO Job Descriptions.

DAYTON HUDSON CORPORATION

Position Description

Chairman of the Executive Committee,
Chairman of the Board and CEO

I.   FUNCTION

A. Serve as Chief Executive Officer of the Corporation, reporting to the Board of Directors, accepting responsibility for the success or failure of the Corporation.

B. Serve as Chairman of the Board and Chairman of the Executive Committee enabling both the Board of Directors and the Executive Committee to fulfill their corporate governance functions, and facilitate the optimum interaction between Management and the Board of Directors.

C. Give direction to the formulation and leadership to the achievement of the Corporation's philosophy, mission, strategy, financial objectives and goals.

II.   RESPONSIBILITIES

A. Governance

1. Chair meetings of the Board. See that it functions effectively, interacts with management optimally, and fulfills all of its duties.

2. Develop agenda for meetings so that the Board can fulfill all its responsibilities effectively.

3. See that the Board is kept fully informed on the condition of the Corporation and each of the Corporation's businesses and on all important factors influencing them.

4. Get the best thinking of each Board member.

5. Work to maintain and periodically renew list of potential directors and work to make the committee structure of the Board function effectively.

6. Recommend to the Board the composition of the Board and its committees.

7. Be accountable to the Board of Directors of Dayton Hudson Corporation and responsible to the Executive Committee on matters of corporate governance.

8. Chair meetings of the Executive Committee so that it can fulfill its responsibilities in matters of organization and compensation.

9. Present to the Executive Committee his evaluation of the pace, direction, and organizational strength of the Corporation.

10. Annually focus the Executive Committee's attention on matters of corporate governance which relate to its own structure, role and relationship to the Board of Directors and Management.

11. Present to the Board any concerns management has in regard to the role of the Board of Directors or individual members.

12. Preside at shareholders' meetings.

B. Chief Executive Officer

1. Be responsible for the Corporation's consistent achievement of its financial objectives and goals.

2. Make certain that the Corporation's philosophy and mission statements are pertinent and practiced throughout the Corporation.

3. Assure that the Corporation has a long-range strategy which maximizes its opportunities, and toward which we make consistent and timely progress.

4. Make certain that the allocation of capital reflects the Corporation's current strengths and future potential.

5. See that the Corporation has an effective top management team, with provision for succession.

6. Ensure the development and implementation of personal training and development plans and programs which will provide the human resources necessary for the achievement of the Corporation's goals.

7. Maintain a climate which attracts, keeps and motivates top quality managers.

8. Formulate and administer all major corporate policies.

9. Provide supervision to the President of DHC and the Chief Executive Officers of Target and Mervyn's.

10. Serve as the chief spokesman of the Corporation, and thereby see that the Corporation is properly marketed to its various publics.

March 1, 1989

───────────────────────────────

the company or the direction the company was headed, "That dialogue would come back."

After this discussion, MacLaury would then remind the board members of the evaluation process and hand out blank rating sheets for the positions of chairman and Chief Executive Officer. (See Exhibit 4 for rating sheets.) It was important to all at Dayton Hudson that the chairman and CEO roles were defined and evaluated separately. Ed Wingate explained:

Exhibit 4 Chairman and CEO rating sheets

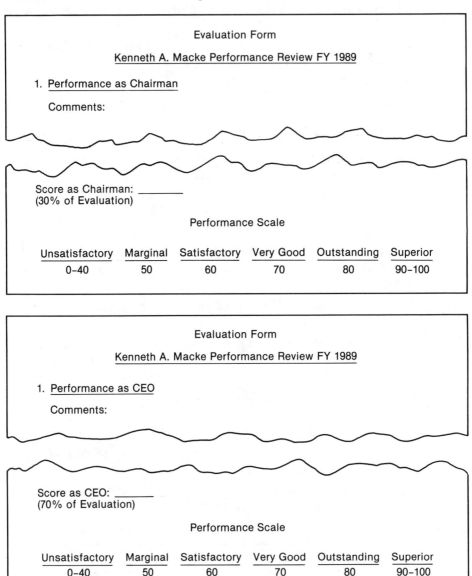

Evaluation Form

Kenneth A. Macke Performance Review FY 1989

1. Performance as Chairman

    Comments:

Score as Chairman: _____
(30% of Evaluation)

Performance Scale

Unsatisfactory	Marginal	Satisfactory	Very Good	Outstanding	Superior
0–40	50	60	70	80	90–100

Evaluation Form

Kenneth A. Macke Performance Review FY 1989

1. Performance as CEO

    Comments:

Score as CEO: _____
(70% of Evaluation)

Performance Scale

Unsatisfactory	Marginal	Satisfactory	Very Good	Outstanding	Superior
0–40	50	60	70	80	90–100

The chairman of the board is responsible for the functioning of the board, succession of the board, and committee orchestration. But we want our CEO to know that by far the lion's share of his duty is to run this company well, to earn a return for its shareholders, and to deal well with its customers, its public, and its financial investors.

Each director had his or her own method of developing comments. Bruce MacLaury described how he measured the CEO's performance:

> There are two scorecards. One is the objectives that are set for the company by the CEO, with the approval of the board, which are discussed at the beginning of the cycle. . . . The other is the standing scorecard of the position description of the CEO. And so we have an annually changing set of objectives, and a static, persisting, position description.

While he was actually making his comments, MacLaury would review the list of responsibilities in the position descriptions, while keeping the set of objectives in mind: "If there is an element in that list where I think that there is something worth noting, that will become a comment."

Roger Hale, a director since 1982, had his own method:

> My bias is to write the comments about the CEO without having his prereview in front of me, or in fact of having heard the prereview first, because you come to a board meeting so many times a year, you're on several boards, you've got your own business to run, and it's pretty easy to get swept up in—'Let's see now, he says that he did this or did that; that's pretty good, so I'll write down he did this or that.' It's sort of like if you're writing a book review. I prefer to always do it not having seen any other book reviews. Pretty soon, I'm commenting on the comment. So my bias is to try to go with what I feel, and then maybe to look at the thing and say, 'Oh, I forgot about that point. That is an important point.'

David McLaughlin used as input the CEO's prereview, the company's objectives, the position descriptions, the previous year's CEO review, and the CEO's assessment of the senior management team. McLaughlin said:

> It's not something which I've ever taken away from a meeting and filled out on the plane, and then mailed it in. It's a process where I look at it, sit back and reflect, not just on the specific questions, but on the overall impression I have of where the company is, the CEO is, and then direct whatever constructive comments to quite specific things which are important to the future of the company. I don't think I ever mentioned an issue that I haven't raised either privately or publicly at a board meeting. . . . If I came away from that process and was downgrading performance for an issue that I hadn't already raised, I would think that was my failure, and not the CEO's.

Bruce MacLaury felt the same way:

> There is so much opportunity during the year for discussion, we don't wait for the evaluation to spring something that nobody's ever heard about. This is an opportunity to summarize, and look back, and consolidate. It is not normal that one would bring up something unprecedented and never heard of before in an evaluation.

Each director sent their comments and ratings to Ed Wingate, who synthesized them into a narrative form. Wingate also took the numerical ratings and averaged them. The CEO/chairman was graded 70 percent on his performance as CEO and 30 percent on his performance as chairman. After averaging the weighted scores together, one number was reached. This number comprised 50 percent of the CEO's score. The other 50 percent was dependent on a calculation of Dayton Hudson's performance compared to their control group of retailing companies in earnings growth and return on investment. A final score would be reached after the mathematics was completed, which would become the official rating of the CEO.

The final rating of the CEO was used both as a performance measure and for compensation purposes. The CEO salary and bonus structure was designed so that, for example, a "75" rating would put the compensation of the Dayton Hudson CEO at the seventy-fifth percentile of the compensation of the CEOs of Dayton Hudson's retail control group.

Roger Hale discussed the numerical rating of the CEO:

> Some board members object to that and say that's silly, to have a numerical score. And what's more, how can I rate someone a 4 or 6 or 7; that implies too much precision. All that is true. But, it really has a value, because what happens is you can see a pattern, and so I may feel awkward rating a certain category 7 instead of 9, or 6 instead of 8, or something like that. . . . It's so subjective. But the fact is what will happen is that I put that down, director B puts that down, and pretty soon you see a pattern so that you're going along at 8 or 9 up here, and all of the sudden one thing is 6 or 7. And it tells the CEO that there is obviously some kind of fire there, because there is the smoke. And it really is very effective. And I would argue for having the numerical score every time.

For the narrative portion, board members typically made five to seven comments. Since Wingate would see all the comments and ratings by the board, and also see who made them, this meant a staff member of the CEO was responsible for material concerning the CEO to which the CEO would not have access. Bruce MacLaury commented:

> This is unusual in itself—to have the CEO of a major corporation have sufficient confidence in the discretion of his director of human resources, and similarly for the board to have that confidence, to allow that individual to consolidate their comments about his boss. And it would not work in many different kinds of corporations. In other places, I would have to do that process personally. That is unusual, but for us it works very well.

David McLaughlin felt that Ed Wingate provided a check on the system, by virtue of being a staff member playing a role in the process:

> The Wingate position is absolutely critical. . . . That kind of an auditor of the process enhances the trust that the CEO can have in the process, knowing that if it starts to get off track, he's going to know about it. And the board takes comfort in knowing that there's somebody there that knows the systems and can reflect the sensitivities in case the board starts to get off track.

With a prepared narrative and the directors' comments in hand, Ed Wingate traveled to Washington to meet with Bruce MacLaury. They then reviewed the narrative and made changes, sometimes, according to MacLaury, of a "substantial" nature, but at other times the changes included only minor editing. After the meeting, Wingate would send the revised evaluation to each of the Executive Committee members, who would then review the entire document before the April board meeting.

At the April board meeting, the Executive Committee reviewed the CEO evaluation. With the evaluation in nearly final form, only a few points were added or modified, said MacLaury, and perhaps a point might be deleted. While any changes in the document were being made by Wingate, the board began its regular meeting. After normal board business concluded, Macke and MacLaury sat down alone and MacLaury presented the evaluation. Macke explained: "For balance and objectivity, the review is best handled with one person presenting the evaluation."

MacLaury would read through the evaluation line by line, taking time to elaborate on certain points or answer the CEO's questions. MacLaury said he was aware of the sensitive nature of the discussion:

> Obviously, it's a much tougher deal when the world is not going well than when it is going well, because tougher things need to be said and discussed, and that is not easy for either side of this process. But it is candid.

The CEO might feel compelled to respond to a point or two contained in the evaluation at the succeeding board meeting, but that rarely happened, according to MacLaury.

Benefits to the CEO

Dayton Hudson officials universally described the CEO review process as a positive one for their CEO. From his standpoint, Kenneth Macke said he wouldn't work under any other system, and relied on the CEO review to communicate important information to him about his performance:

> I don't think this is just in the interest of good governance. As CEO, I want to know where I stand. I can't envision not having a review. Some things in the review I'm not going to like. But what a marvelous opportunity to have that out on the table instead of festering underneath.

When Macke first became CEO, the company held two-day strategy sessions for the board of directors in the fall, at a site that had been popular with previous management. During Macke's presentation of his prereview the following spring, one of the directors casually mentioned that he disliked the location of the strategy session. When this was mentioned (while Macke was discussing his efforts at stimulating communication between management and the board), several other directors spoke up and made clear their dislike of that location. Macke said:

> I don't know how long that had been under their bonnet. But I would guess that without the review system, that those feelings may not have

been made known. Communication isn't open when someone is where they don't like to be. Now that's not going to make or break corporate America, but perhaps some of the communication that results from little things like that being addressed has given boards new opportunities for open discussion of other issues.

Bruce MacLaury cited the improved relationship between the CEO and the board as a dividend of the review process:

> The CEO knows where he stands with the board, all of the time. He is not guessing. He is not uncertain. It is an important part of building a rapport between the CEO and the board, that I think is unlikely to arise in other ways.
>
> Now, it can arise over cocktails at dinner, but that's superficial. This is really quite profound and fundamental, because there should be no possibility of misunderstanding [between the board and CEO].

David McLaughlin also believed the review process helped to improve the relationship between the CEO and the board. Directors, said McLaughlin, react to CEOs not just based on the performance of the company, but also on the style of the CEO. And the board needs to feel like it can get through to the CEO:

> Often if [boards] don't have a way to express themselves and communicate, then you get to some cataclysmic point where they fire the CEO and make other precipitous changes. It seems to me that this system has more potential for increasing the longevity of CEOs in a job because there's a constant way to make midterm corrections, and not just let them all be pushed ahead until you really get a major problem between the board and the CEO.

MacLaury felt also that if the board had a particular concern, and mentioned it in its review, that the CEO would concentrate his energies a bit more in that area in the following year—and then report on his progress in the next year's prereview. MacLaury felt that if there was a critical remark, for instance, in the area of getting the most out of individual board members:

> That's not the end of the day, that's the beginning of the day. The beginning of the day is that the CEO will make an extra effort in the succeeding year to leave time within the agenda to call upon individual board members to have their say.

Kenneth Macke believed that the reassurance he was leading the corporation in a direction of which the board approved was the most significant aspect of the review to him personally:

> I feel rewarded and reinforced by what the board views as positive for the corporation. I think that gives you confidence. All CEOs are somewhat insecure, so reinforcement is a big factor. You know where you stand.

The CEO Review Process and Corporate Governance

Virtually all involved with the Dayton Hudson CEO review system believed that the review served as more than just a tool for the improvement of the CEO. They considered the system as one of the important aspects of corporate governance at Dayton Hudson. David McLaughlin stated:

> The board has got to make certain that there are objectives and goals for the company that are reflective of the interests of the stakeholders, and that the policies of the company are supportive of those goals, and that there's a commitment on the part of management to conduct the company in a way that's consistent with that. The board has critical stewardship over that process, and is responsible for it. But the board invests a huge amount of that responsibility in the CEO. . . . If the board acknowledges its responsibilities, and there are already clearly defined objectives of what the company is trying to do, then it must have a way of communicating clearly and honestly with the CEO, or the board will not be able to perform that function. To me, this process fits in that matrix in a very critical way.

Roger Hale believed that the review process helped directors break down barriers to participation:

> The process facilitates discussion. It is a format by which you can talk about issues that are there, but often times don't get talked about because of all the norms that prevail in a board atmosphere, the rules of the game. There are certain things you do and don't do unless you're very obstreperous. That's a very inhibiting atmosphere in the board room.

Hale also believed that some directors—especially, although not limited to, ones who lacked expertise in corporate finance—might be intimidated by other directors. The CEO review process, then, was an avenue for them to communicate their opinions about the company:

> This is a less threatening way for a director to express his or her thoughts about a CEO, and then get into a discussion where you see all these comments laid out on the table, and so you realize you're not alone with this comment and this idea you had. And if the person who runs that executive session discussion has any skill at all, he or she can draw out these comments and give you a chance to express yourself more without fear that you're going to be put down by some other directors. . . . The peer pressure, the pecking order, has an awful lot to do with the way a board works.

From a human resources standpoint, Ed Wingate believed the CEO appraisal system served several functions. Board members would be attracted to Dayton Hudson, according to Wingate, because they would see that their time would be put to good use, and their work taken seriously by management. Wingate also saw beneficial ripple effects in the organization. Performance appraisals were a hallmark of Dayton Hudson at every level, and review of the CEO perpetuated the importance of appraisals throughout the company.

Exhibit 5 Dayton Hudson Corporation selected financial data.

Consolidated Results of Operations (Millions of dollars, except per-share data)	1989	1988	1987
Revenues	$13,644	$12,204	$10,677
Costs and expenses			
Cost of retail sales, buying and occupancy	9,890	8,980	7,950
Selling, publicity and administrative	2,264	2,038	1,769
Depreciation	315	290	231
Interest expense, net	267	218	152
Taxes other than income taxes	230	206	176
Total costs and expenses	12,966	11,732	10,278
Earnings before income taxes	678	472	399
Provision for income taxes	268	185	171
Net earnings	410	287	228
Earnings per share:			
Primary	$ 5.37	$ 3.45	$ 2.41
Fully diluted	$ 5.35	$ 3.45	$ 2.41
Average common shares outstanding (millions):			
Primary	76.3	83.3	94.8
Fully diluted	76.6	83.3	94.8

Analysis of Operations

Business Segment Comparisons (Millions of dollars)	1989*	1988	1987	1986	1985	1984*
Revenues						
Target	$ 7,519	$ 6,331	$ 5,306	$4,355	$3,931	$3,550
Mervyn's	3,858	3,411	3,183	2,862	2,527	2,141
Dayton Hudson Department Store Company	1,801	1,693	1,552	1,566	1,448	1,396
Other	466	769	636	476	349	432
Total	$13,644	$12,204	$10,677	$9,259	$8,255	$7,519

Operating profit						
Target	$ 449	$ 341	$ 323	$ 311	$ 278	$ 236
Mervyn's	358	256	150	160	245	223
Dayton Hudson Department Store Company	179	159	122	166	122	107
Total	$ 986	$ 756	$ 595	$ 637	$ 645	$ 566
Interest expense, net	267	218	152	118	100	98
Corporate and other	41	66	44	25	27	15
Earnings from continuing operations before income taxes and extraordinary charge	$ 678	$ 472	$ 399	$ 494	$ 518	$ 453
Operating profit as a percent of revenues						
Target	6.0	5.4	6.1	7.1	7.1	6.6
Mervyn's	9.3	7.5	4.7	5.6	9.7	10.4
Dayton Hudson Department Store Company	10.0	9.4	7.9	10.6	8.4	6.9
Assets						
Target	$ 3,505	$ 2,982	$ 2,638	$2,179	$1,519	$1,375
Mervyn's	2,260	2,166	2,114	1,817	1,615	1,329
Dayton Hudson Department Store Company	838	808	761	739	738	727
Corporate and other	81	567	563	547	546	369
Total	$ 6,684	$ 6,523	$ 6,076	$5,282	$4,418	$3,800
Depreciation						
Target	$ 170	$ 146	$ 103	$ 76	$ 70	$ 66
Mervyn's	98	91	82	68	54	43
Dayton Hudson Department Store Company	34	33	30	28	27	32
Corporate and other	13	20	16	11	7	4
Total	$ 315	$ 290	$ 231	$ 183	$ 158	$ 145
Capital Expenditures						
Target	$ 414	$ 457	$ 501	$ 598	$ 138	$ 110
Mervyn's	133	154	207	243	177	165
Dayton Hudson Department Store Company	37	31	49	31	37	33
Corporate and other	19	39	82	69	51	28
Total	$ 603	$ 681	$ 839	$ 941	$ 403	$ 336

*Consisted of 53 weeks.

Other includes Diamond's and John A. Brown through September 1984 and Lechmere through September 1989.

Wingate also felt that the CEO review, and all performance reviews within Dayton Hudson, allowed the company to set priorities:

> It allows us to focus on the most important issues. We don't change our minds during the year because our performance has changed. I can't suddenly decide that health care cost containment isn't important if I don't do a good job on that issue. We've got agreement on what the job is, and I have a chance to argue my point of view before they become measured and measurable. So I think it creates a clarity in directing the company's efforts.

Bruce MacLaury agreed that the process had significant positive spillover effects:

> If it were simply an appraisal of an individual, that would be useful, but that isn't all that can be gotten out of the process. The appraisal of the CEO is part of the whole governance structure. . . . The position description of the CEO says that he's supposed to be taking care of the various elements of the corporation throughout the year. We, the board, meeting seven times a year, have divided up this process so we cover all the bases during the course of the year.

A Model for Corporate Governance?

As Ed Wingate said above, the CEO review process was both an outgrowth of and a model for review processes at all levels of the company. Every Dayton Hudson employee, from secretaries to Vice Presidents, had a prereview and a written appraisal. This culture of performance reviews ensured that the CEO and the top staff would be well used to the system. The "strengthful dependence" on the system by Dayton Hudson employees was, according the company's management, one of the primary reasons for the success of Dayton Hudson.

One of the ramifications of this emphasis on performance appraisal was that by the time an individual rose to the position of Chief Executive Officer, he would be accustomed to Dayton Hudson's appraisal process. Kenneth Macke felt that other CEO's might be skeptical about such a system if they weren't used to it: "I think the change is more threatening to other CEO's, because of the fact that they haven't had one. The fear of the unknown is greater than the actuality."

David McLaughlin felt that a comprehensive CEO review was a significant enough change in a board's relationship with the CEO that such a process would be difficult to implement except at a transition time: "It's very hard to [implement] when you're in the middle of the soup. You have to stand back and get people to evaluate [events objectively]."

The best time to install a comprehensive system of CEO review, according to McLaughlin, would be when there was a new CEO. Bruce MacLaury felt the same way:

> It would be very difficult to impose a CEO review unless the CEO *sincerely* wanted the kind of openness and frankness and a scorecard that a

performance appraisal entails. . . . The only time that a board can insist on it is the time a new body sits in the CEO's chair. And they *can* insist on it, as a condition of employment.

From time to time, outside directors of Dayton Hudson would ask each other or wonder to themselves whether they should try to introduce such a system in other boards where they served. One Dayton Hudson outside director had seen a situation in which the evaluation process was implemented in the midst of a CEO's tenure, and felt it was very constructive:

> I'm quite familiar with the system and have seen it work in a couple of circumstances where the company and the relationship between the board and the CEO was very troubled. In fact, I think it saved the relationship between the board and the CEO at another company where I serve as a director. My guess is that if we hadn't gone through a formal evaluation, and worked with it, that the board would have fired the CEO, which would have been a very grave mistake. He turned out to be an excellent CEO, and is now a strong advocate of the system. We put it in when relations between the board and the CEO were at their nadir. I have a very strong bias towards this CEO evaluation system. I have seen it work under dire circumstances.

Ed Wingate believed aspects of Dayton Hudson's process were translatable to other corporations:

> But it would start at a different point of evolution. There is no question that the best answers are those that are developed by the group affected. So rather than saying here's a cookbook on how to go about having a CEO appraisal process, it seems to me the important thing is for a board and a CEO to agree that it would be helpful in terms of performance of the corporation and the development of the individual to have a methodology for getting honest feedback.

(Exhibit 5 provides selected financial data for Dayton Hudson.)

Coca-Cola Versus Pepsi-Cola
and the Soft Drink Industry

In 1986, the Coca-Cola Company was celebrating its 100th anniversary. The Coca-Cola name had become a part of American folklore and was considered by many to be the best-known brand name in the world. In 1985, however, regular Pepsi-Cola had become the single most popular soft drink in the United States.

The competition between Coca-Cola and Pepsi-Cola was ninety-three years old in 1986, but had intensified at an ever increasing pace during the previous thirty-five years. By the mid-1970s, this competition was regularly labeled by business journalists as "The Cola Wars." The wars had continued into the 1980s, and the landscape of the soft drink industry had been vastly altered.

Industry Structure

With retail revenues estimated to exceed $30 billion in 1985, the U.S. soft drink industry had become an integral part of the American way of life. Soft drinks consisted of a flavor base, a sweetener, and carbonated water. Some products also contained caffeine and artificial coloring. Cola-flavored drinks accounted for approximately 63 percent of the market in 1985 and lemon-lime, 13 percent. Diet and caffeine-free products were taking a growing share of the market. The number of product introductions, nearly all from established producers, had proliferated dramatically in the 1980s.

Soft drink consumption had been increasing at a rate of 6 percent per year. Per capita soft drink consumption had risen from 0.6 gallons per year in 1889 to 3.3 gallons in 1929, 23.4 gallons in 1969, and 44.5 gallons in 1985. The 15–24 and 25–34 age groups had been primarily responsible for this growth.

The prospects for future growth in U.S. soft drink consumption were being actively debated in 1986. Some had argued for years that U.S. soft drink consumption was approaching its limits, especially given the aging of the "baby boom" generation (approximately 26–40 years old in 1986). Other observers believed that industry innovation in product development, packaging, advertising, and distribution would fuel continued industry growth.

Exhibit 1 Soft drink industry structure, 1986

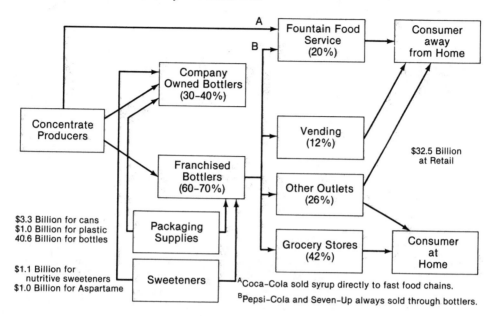

There were three major participants involved in the production and distribution of soft drinks: concentrate and syrup producers, bottlers, and retail outlets. Exhibit 1 diagrams the industry with estimates where available of the size of different parts of the system in 1986.

Concentrate Producers

Concentrate producers manufactured the basic flavors and sold them to franchised or to company-owned bottlers. Although there were over fifty concentrate producers in the United States at the end of 1985, the bulk of industry sales were accounted for by a few firms, notably Coca-Cola and Pepsi-Cola (Exhibit 2).

In addition to Coke and Pepsi were several other national producers, including Seven-Up, Dr Pepper, and Royal Crown. There were also several dozen regional and private-label producers, such as Canada Dry, Polar, and White Rock, with modest shares of their regional markets. They sold a wide line of soft drink flavors—such as cola, grape, orange, cream soda, and ginger ale—usually only to major food chains. Their products were distributed through the chains' warehouse systems. Financial results for leading soft drink producers are given in Exhibit 3.

Early in their history, Coca-Cola and Pepsi-Cola had both begun to grant franchises for the right to bottle their soft drinks, and the practice had spread to other leading concentrate producers. Franchisees were granted, in perpetuity, the exclusive right to bottle and distribute a concentrate company's line of

Exhibit 2   U.S. soft drink market shares by case volume, selected years.

	Market Shares (%) by Volume						
	1977	*1978*	*1980*	*1982*	*1984*	*1985*	*1986*
Coca-Cola Co.							
Classic	—	—	—	—	—	6.1	19.1
Coca-Cola	26.3	25.8	25.3	24.6	22.5	15.0	2.5
Diet Coke	—	—	—	0.3	5.2	6.6	7.3
Sprite and Diet Sprite	3.0	3.0	3.0	3.3	3.8	4.3	4.3
Cherry Coke[a]	—	—	—	—	—	1.7	1.9
Tab	2.8	2.9	3.3	4.0	1.6	1.1	0.6
Caffeine Free Coke, Diet Coke and Tab	—	—	—	—	1.8	1.7	1.7
Others	4.2	4.0	4.3	2.5	2.6	2.0	2.5
Total	36.3	35.7	35.9	34.7	37.5	38.5	39.9
PepsiCo, Inc.							
Pepsi-Cola	20.0	20.4	20.4	20.3	19.1	18.9	18.6
Diet Pepsi	2.4	2.7	3.0	3.3	3.2	3.9	4.4
Mountain Dew	2.2	2.7	3.3	3.2	3.0	3.0	3.0
Pepsi-Free and Sugar-Free Pepsi-Free	—	—	—	0.4	2.7	2.4	2.0
Slice	—	—	—	—	—	0.7	1.5
Diet Slice	—	—	—	—	—	0.7	1.0
Others	—	1.2	1.1	0.9	0.7	0.1	0.1
Total	24.6	27.0	27.8	28.1	28.7	29.7	30.6
Seven-Up	7.3	7.0	6.3	6.7	6.8	5.9	5.0
Dr Pepper	5.6	6.0	6.0	5.2	5.0	4.9	4.8
Royal Crown Co.	4.6	4.3	4.7	3.9	3.1	3.0	2.9
Other Companies	20.2	20.0	19.4	20.5	18.9	17.7	16.6

Source: John C. Maxwell, Jr. and *Beverage Industry*.

a. Regular and sugar-free.

branded soft drinks in a defined territory as long as conditions of the franchise agreement were met. Franchisees were not allowed to market a directly competitive brand; for example, a Coca-Cola bottler could not sell Royal Crown (RC) Cola. However, franchisees could sell noncompetitive brands and could decline to market a concentrate producer's secondary lines. For example, a Coca-Cola bottler could decide to turn down the Coca-Cola lemon-lime drink Sprite in order to bottle Seven-Up.

Concentrate producers sold only flavor concentrate in the case of regular soft drinks. Bottlers purchased the sweetener themselves. Coca-Cola, the exception, had traditionally sold syrup (already containing regular sweetener) to its bottlers. Coca-Cola charged its bottlers for the concentrate plus the list sweetener price. In 1980, Coca-Cola began to sell concentrate only to its largest bottlers.

For diet drinks, concentrate was always sold together with artificial sweetener. The early artificial sweetener, derived from natural ingredients, was cyclamate,[1] followed by saccharin. By 1985, a new artificial sweetener, named aspartame, had become the industry standard, raising fewer health concerns. Aspartame, with 180 times the sweetness of sugar, was marketed under NutraSweet brand by G.D. Searle Company, which held a patent expiring in 1992. Aspartame was far more expensive than saccharin. At the list price of $80/pound, it was almost twice as expensive as the equivalent amount of sugar.

Manufacturing concentrate was a simple process requiring little capital investment. The cost of concentrate represented approximately 20 percent of a concentrate producer's selling price to bottlers. A concentrate producer's most significant costs were for advertising, promotion, market research, and bottler relations. (See Exhibit 4 for data on advertising spending.) Concentrate producers employed extensive sales and marketing support staff to work with, and help improve the performance of, their franchised bottlers. They set standards for their bottlers and suggested operating procedures. Concentrate producers also negotiated directly with their bottlers' major suppliers—particularly sweetener and packaging suppliers—to encourage reliable supply, faster delivery, and lower prices.

Marketing programs were jointly implemented and financed by concentrate producers and bottlers. The concentrate producers usually took the lead in developing the programs, particularly in product planning, market research, and advertising. Bottlers assumed a larger role in developing trade and consumer promotions. Bottlers usually paid for two-thirds of promotional costs, while advertising costs were usually split fifty–fifty.

Bottlers

Bottlers added carbonated water and sometimes sweetener to the concentrate, bottled or canned the soft drink, and delivered it to customer accounts. All the major concentrate producers utilized direct-store delivery. Soft drinks were delivered directly to individual retail outlets, bypassing retailers' warehouses. Bottler-route salespeople stocked and maintained food store shelves.

Shasta and Faygo, small national brands, distributed through food-store warehouses. Retailers earned higher gross margins on the few warehouse-delivered soft drinks than on the store-door-delivered products. However, store-door delivery reduced the retailers' in-store handling costs and increased

1. This sweetener (in addition to saccharin), was removed from the Food and Drug Administration's list of approved food additives in 1969 when tests revealed that this product caused cancer in laboratory animals.

Exhibit 3 Financial data for the leading soft drink competitors, 1972 to 1985 ($ millions).

	1972	1973	1974	1975	1976	1977	1978	1979	1980	1981	1982	1983	1984	1985
Coca-Cola														
Corporate sales	$1,876	$2,145	$2,522	$2,773	$2,928	$3,328	$4,013	$4,588	$5,475	$5,699	$6,021	$6,829	$7,364	$7,904
Corporate net income	190	215	196	249	294	331	375	420	422	482	512	559	629	722
Income/sales	10.1%	10.0%	7.8%	9.0%	10.0%	9.9%	9.3%	9.2%	7.7%	8.5%	8.5%	8.2%	8.5%	9.1%
ROE	21.5%	21.0%	19.1%	20.9%	20.5%	21.0%	21.6%	21.9%	20.3%	21.2%	18.4%	19.1%	22.6%	24.2%
L.T. debt/total capital	4.8%	5.0%	5.5%	3.1%	3.5%	3.5%	3.8%	6.8%	9.9%	9.3%	17.3%	17.5%	17.9%	23.0%
Soft drink sales	NA	NA	NA	NA	NA	$2,702	$3,306	$3,765	$4,522	$4,683	$4,516	$4,695	$5,015	$5,510
Soft drink operating income	NA	NA	NA	NA	NA	562	634	676	732	804	873	859	880	881
Operating income/soft drink sales	NA	NA	NA	NA	NA	20.8%	19.2%	18.2%	16.2%	17.2%	19.3%	18.3%	17.5%	16.0%
Soft drink identifiable assets	NA	NA	NA	NA	NA	$1,518	$1,806	$2,106	$2,436	$2,472	$2,521	$2,671	$3,010	$3,680
Soft drink operating income/ identifiable assets	NA	NA	NA	NA	NA	37.1%	35.1%	32.1%	30.0%	32.5%	34.6%	32.2%	29.2%	23.9%
Soft drink capital expenditures	NA	NA	NA	NA	NA	187	241	294	224	251	249	238	295	326
Pepsico[a]														
Corporate sales	$1,560	$1,913	$2,409	$2,709	$3,109	$3,649	$4,300	$5,089	$5,975	$7,027	$6,811	$7,166	$7,699	$8,057
Corporate net income	80	87	100	124	162	197	223	251	261	298	224	284	213	544
Income/sales	5.1%	4.5%	4.2%	4.6%	5.2%	5.4%	5.2%	4.9%	4.4%	4.2%	3.3%	4.0%	2.8%	6.8%
ROE	16.3%	15.8%	16.8%	18.3%	20.4%	21.0%	20.6%	20.8%	19.8%	20.3%	14.0%	16.5%	11.5%	29.6%
L.T. debt/total capital	33.5%	37.8%	36.3%	34.9%	30.6%	29.2%	26.3%	29.2%	31.4%	27.2%	28.4%	23.7%	23.0%	36.0%
Soft drink sales	$ 661	$ 829	$ 982	$1,065	$1,161	$1,407	$1,698	$2,014	$2,768	$2,772	$2,908	$2,940	$2,908	$3,129
Soft drink operating income	85	101	114	111	144	180	227	254	244	252	218	126	247	264
Operating income/soft drink sales	12.9%	12.2%	11.6%	10.4%	12.4%	12.8%	13.4%	12.6%	8.8%	9.1%	7.5%	4.3%	8.5%	8.4%
Soft drink identifiable assets	NA	NA	NA	NA	476	567	750	959	1,266	1,355	1,389	1,249	1,039	1,319
Soft drink operating income/ identifiable assets	NA	NA	NA	NA	NA	31.7%	30.3%	26.4%	19.3%	18.6%	15.7%	10.1%	23.8%	20.0%
Soft drink capital expenditures	NA	NA	NA	NA	NA	69	124	101	140	127	111	94	84	161

The Seven-Up Company[b]

Sales	$ 133	$ 147	$ 191	$ 214	$ 233	$ 251	$ 186	$ 296	$ 353	$ 432	$ 531	$ 650	$ 734	$ 678
Net income	12.0	14.1	16.6	20.3	24.8	25.8	—	—	—	—	—	—	—	—
Operating income	—	—	—	—	—	—	26.0	7.0	(7.1)	(1.7)	(1.2)	(10.8)	5.3	10.0
Net income/sales	9.1%	9.6%	8.7%	9.5%	10.6%	10.3%	—	—	—	—	—	—	—	—
Operating income/sales	—	—	—	—	—	—	14.0%	2.4%	(2.0%)	(0.4%)	(0.2%)	(1.7%)	0.7%	1.5%
ROE	23.7%	23.6%	23.9%	23.6%	24.0%	23.1%	—	—	—	—	—	—	—	—
L.T. debt capital/total capital	4.1%	4.5%	3.4%	2.3%	3.1%	4.2%	—	—	—	—	—	—	—	—

Dr Pepper Company[c]

Sales	$ 77	$ 99	$ 128	$ 138	$ 152	$ 227	$ 271	$ 292	$ 333	$ 364	$ 516	NA	NA	NA
Net income	8.1	9.7	9.9	11.9	15.5	20.3	23.6	23.6	26.5	29.4	12.5	NA	NA	NA
Income/sales	10.5%	9.8%	7.7%	8.6%	10.2%	8.9%	8.7%	8.1%	8.0%	8.1%	2.4%	NA	NA	NA
ROE	26.0%	25.4%	22.7%	24.0%	27.0%	26.5%	26.9%	24.5%	25.5%	25.2%	9.2%	NA	NA	NA
L.T. debt/total capital	0.0%	0.0%	0.0%	0.0%	0.0%	0.0%	0.0%	0.0%	0.0%	0.0%	0.0%	NA	NA	NA

Royal Crown Company[d]

Sales	$191.4	$195.4	$223.2	$257.5	$295.1	$349.6	$390.7	$421.4	$438.1	$450.4	NA	NA	NA	NA
Net income	11.7	12.2	8.2	13.3	15.2	18.6	1.4	16.4	10.1	15.5	NA	NA	NA	NA
Income/sales	6.1%	6.2%	3.7%	5.2%	5.2%	5.2%	0.4%	3.9%	2.3%	3.4%	NA	NA	NA	NA
ROE	22.1%	19.8%	12.0%	17.4%	15.4%	18.8%	1.5%	16.4%	9.9%	14.2%	NA	NA	NA	NA
L.T. debt/total capital	NA	NA	NA	NA	NA	28.3%	38.3%	38.3%	38.2%	34.3%	NA	NA	NA	NA
Soft drink sales	NA	NA	NA	NA	NA	202.7	213.0	204.0	221.0	230.0	NA	NA	NA	NA
Soft drink operating income	NA	NA	NA	NA	NA	21.0	11.1	14.8	13.9	22.7	NA	NA	NA	NA
Operating income/sales	NA	NA	NA	NA	NA	10.4%	5.2%	7.3%	6.3%	9.9%	NA	NA	NA	NA

a. In 1982, PepsiCo incurred an unusual charge of $79.4 million due to problems in its Philippine and Mexican operations. In 1983, international soft drink losses, resulting largely from devaluations of the Mexican and Venezuelan currencies, offset strong results from Pepsi-Cola U.S. operations.

b. Philip Morris purchased the Seven-Up Company in 1979 and sold it to PepsiCo in 1986.

c. Acquired Welch's and Barrelhead in 1976; Canada Dry in 1982 went private through a leveraged buyout in 1983. In 1984, sold Canada Dry to R.J. Reynolds.

d. In 1984, Victor Posner purchased Royal Crown Cola.

Exhibit 4 Advertising spending by brand ($ millions).

	1985[a]	1984	1983	1982	1981	1980	1979	1978	1977	1976	1975	1974
Coca-Cola Company												
Coca-Cola	64.6	64.1	41.7	44.9	38.3	35.6	41.7	35.0	25.0	22.1	20.3	22.1
Diet Coke	40.8	48.3	20.9	38.0	—	—	—	—	—	—	—	—
Cherry Coke	8.4	—	—	—	—	—	—	—	—	—	—	—
Sprite	31.7	35.3	21.2	16.2	11.5	10.7	9.6	7.9	4.5	2.7	2.6	2.5
Tab	14.8	31.8	25.2	22.0	15.2	12.6	12.6	8.6	4.2	5.2	6.5	5.3
Fresca	—	—	—	0.6	3.7	7.3	6.3	6.1	1.3	2.0	2.4	2.6
Others	0.2	1.7	10.7	3.3	4.8	4.9	3.5	2.1	1.3	2.8	2.6	2.9
Total	160.5	181.2	119.7	125.0	73.5	71.1	73.7	59.7	36.3	34.8	34.4	35.4
Pepsi-Cola USA												
Pepsi-Cola	48.3	47.8	22.8	39.1	31.2	39.7	35.0	25.7	24.5	17.5	15.0	14.9
Diet Pepsi	36.8	44.7	20.6	15.0	13.8	11.6	8.7	6.4	6.4	4.1	3.7	4.1
Pepsi Free (Reg & SF)	17.5	20.6	23.0	4.2	—	—	—	—	—	—	—	—
Mountain Dew	10.1	11.2	8.4	8.4	13.0	10.2	8.4	6.8	4.5	3.3	2.8	0.6
Pepsi Light	0.5	0.3	6.2	5.4	5.1	5.2	6.3	3.7	6.5	2.9	0.9	—
Teem	—	—	—	—	0.1	0.1	0.6	0.5	0.2	0.1	0.1	—
Others	22.6	—	3.2	3.2	2.5	0.5	1.5	0.4	0.1	1.6	2.9	5.5
Total	135.8	124.6	84.2	75.3	65.7	67.3	60.5	43.5	42.2	29.5	25.4	25.1
Dr Pepper Company[b]												
Dr Pepper	8.7	11.7	6.0	10.0	9.7	11.0	9.0	10.2	7.0	5.2	4.9	5.4
Pepper Free	0.5	1.3	2.6	—	—	—	—	—	—	—	—	—

Diet Dr Pepper	5.7	5.6	3.5	4.5	3.1	2.9	2.8	1.9	1.8	1.6	1.6	1.8
Barrelhead	—	0.1	0.1	0.1	0.8	1.3	0.7	1.0	1.2	1.4	1.3	0.6
Welch's	—	0.1	0.1	0.3	1.6	2.6	2.3	1.8	1.5	—	—	—
Others	—	—	—	—	—	0.2	0.4	0.3	—	—	—	—
Total	14.9	18.8	12.3	14.9	15.2	18.0	15.2	15.2	11.5	8.2	7.8	7.8
Seven-Up Company												
7-Up	37.1	29.7	21.2	19.6	23.4	25.5	24.6	15.6	13.2	11.1	10.2	10.4
Diet 7-Up	16.4	15.5	11.9	7.8	7.1	7.9	5.7	3.7	1.5	3.0	3.3	2.0
Like	2.0	9.1	9.0	3.7	—	—	—	—	—	—	—	—
Others	—	—	2.6	1.1	—	—	1.2	1.1	—	—	—	—
Total	55.5	54.3	44.7	32.2	30.5	33.4	31.5	20.4	14.7	14.1	13.5	12.4
Royal Crown Company												
Royal Crown	5.9	6.5	4.0	6.2	3.0	6.5	7.3	7.3	7.6	11.7	10.5	5.7
Diet Rite Cola	4.5	5.7	5.4	4.2	5.1	3.4	3.0	3.1	2.3	4.2	3.5	2.1
Others	—	2.0	5.6	6.0	0.1	0.1	0.6	0.5	0.4	0.4	0.4	0.3
Total	10.4	14.4	15.0	16.4	8.2	10.0	10.9	10.9	10.3	16.3	14.4	8.1
Canada Dry[c]	12.1	15.5	0.8	8.9	7.9	10.1	4.6	5.5	4.5	5.1	5.2	4.9
Shasta	5.6	6.3	6.1	6.1	4.1	4.4	4.6	4.1	4.1	3.0	2.8	2.3
All Others	30.4	75.3	24.0	38.4	29.5	26.3	25.0	21.2	11.4	11.0	10.5	10.1
Industry Total	$425.2	$490.4	$306.8	$317.2	$234.6	$240.6	$226.0	$180.5	$135.0	$122.0	$114.0	$106.1

Sources: *Beverage Industry*, *Advertising Age*, and company annual reports.

a. 1985 figures reflect TV media expenditures only; TV as a percent of total advertising averaged 89% in 1984.

b. Acquired Barrelhead and Welch's in 1976.

c. Canada Dry acquired by Dr Pepper in 1983; then purchased by R.J. Reynolds from Dr Pepper in 1984.

inventory turns more than three times, yielding a higher profit to the retailer on the allocated space.

Bottling was a capital-intensive process, involving high-speed lines. Bottling and canning lines cost from $100,000 to several million dollars depending on volume and packaging type. Each package type required separate bottling equipment, as lines were interchangeable only for packages of similar size and construction. Economies of scale and capital costs in bottling had been increasing. During the 1950s, 1960s, and 1970s, larger bottlers earned substantially higher profits than their smaller counterparts.

In 1960, returnable glass bottles had accounted for 94 percent of soft drink volume, nonreturnable glass bottles accounted for 2 percent, and steel and aluminum cans for 4 percent. Throughout the 1960s, 1970s, and 1980s, a host of new packages had been introduced. Glass bottles had been supplemented by tin cans, aluminum cans, and plastic bottles.

Five glass-container manufacturers dominated sales to the soft drink industry. Five can companies, including Crown Cork and Seal, accounted for 98 percent of the cans sold to the soft drink industry. Most sales were made to individual bottlers, although each of the concentrate producers negotiated with the canning suppliers about the design, availability, and price of cans. Coca-Cola also operated its own canning company, supplying some of its bottlers with canned soft drinks. Plastic containers were supplied primarily by three firms. Concentrate producers negotiated directly with plastic packaging suppliers to obtain lower prices and to ensure that items were quickly available in sufficient quantity for their bottlers. In 1985, the concentrate producers were seeking new suppliers of the new three-liter package for their bottlers, and some large bottlers were beginning to invest in plastic extrusion machines to make two-liter bottles in their own plants.

In addition to packaging, bottlers purchased nutritive (or caloric) sweeteners such as sugar and high fructose corn syrup (HFCS) for use in regular soft drinks. The soft drink industry accounted for 31 percent of total U.S. consumption of nutritive sweeteners in 1984.

Concentrate accounted for approximately 20 percent of bottlers' cost of goods sold, packaging approximately 35 percent, and nutritive sweeteners approximately 10 percent. Labor and fuel accounted for most of the remaining variable costs. The cost structures of a typical concentrate producer and bottler are shown in Table A.

Soft drink bottlers could be divided into four types. The first were independent, privately owned bottlers. Many of these were small and marketed only Coca-Cola or Pepsi-Cola products. Some private bottlers had achieved substantial growth by buying up franchises in contiguous areas and by taking on secondary brands such as Dr Pepper or Seven-Up. J.T. Lupton, a Texas-based private company holding multiple Coca-Cola franchises, accounted for 15 percent of Coca-Cola's U.S. volume. The number of independent bottling franchises had fallen approximately 15 percent between 1974 and 1984, and the average size of the franchise territory had increased. The number of bottling plants had fallen from 2,613 to 1,522 during the same period.

Table A Comparative cost structure and financial structure (per standard 8-oz./24-bottle case).

	Concentrate producer		Bottler	
	Dollars per Case	Percent of Total	Dollars per Case	Percent of Total
Profit and loss data				
Net sales	.55	100	3.80	100
Cost of sales	.15	27	2.30	60
Gross profit	.40	73	1.50	40
Selling and delivery	.01	2	.95	25
Advertising and marketing	.24	42	.10	3
General and administration	.05	11	.12	3
Pretax profit	.10	18	.35	9
Balance Sheet Data				
Cash, investments	.14		.05	
Receivables	.01		.18	
Inventories	.05		.10	
Net property, plant and equipment	.05		.62[a]	
Total	.25		.95	
Pretax profit as % of assets				

a. 80% = equipment

A second group of bottlers consisted of large, publicly owned, multibrand franchise firms, based in major metropolitan areas. The financial performance of the large public bottlers varied. MEI, a company that owned several Pepsi-Cola franchises and that operated twenty-four plants in nineteen states, had an average ROE (return on equity) of 23 percent over the five years prior to its being acquired by PepsiCo in early 1986. Coca-Cola Bottling Company of New York, which operated twenty-four plants in five states, was another example. It had an average ROE of 10 percent over the five years prior to 1982.

The third category of bottlers were the diversified companies—such as Beatrice Foods, IC Industries, General Cinema, and Procter & Gamble—which owned bottling franchises of Coca-Cola and Pepsi-Cola. Beatrice, for example, owned Coca-Cola franchises in nine states, and its bottling operations accounted for $880 million in sales in 1983.

The fourth category was the bottling operations of concentrate producers themselves. Coca-Cola had owned a number of bottling operations through the 1970s. Between 1980 and 1985, however, Coke refranchised (through buying and reselling franchises) most of the country and sold off most of its company-owned bottlers through leveraged buyouts. By 1985, Coca-Cola had only 11 percent of its U.S. volume in company-owned bottlers. PepsiCo, in contrast, had embarked on an acquisition program in 1970 to expand its ownership base, steadily increasing the percentage of volume sold through its Bottling Group

Table B Retail outlets for soft drinks, 1982.

	Food Stores	Fountain	Vending	Other[a]
Percent of industry volume				
1982	42	20	12	26
1972	39	18	12	31
Share of channel (percent)				
Coca-Cola (all brands)	29	59	41	27
Pepsi-Cola (all brands)	30	22	26	24
Other brands	41	19	33	49

a. Includes restaurants that served soft drinks in bottles or cans, and convenience stores.

to 21 percent by 1985. Seven-Up, Dr Pepper, and Royal Crown had historically owned some bottlers as well, though accounting for a small fraction of volume.

Retail Outlets

Industry analysts divided the retail channels for soft drinks into four types: food stores, fountain, vending, and other. Distribution of sales by channel is shown in Table B.

Soft drinks were a major product category for food stores, traditionally yielding a 20 percent gross margin (about average for food products) but accounting for 4.5 percent of food-store revenues in 1983. In food stores, rival bottler sales forces fought fiercely for shelf space to ensure maximum visibility, accessibility, and support for the product line.

Fountain sales involved the sales of syrup to retail outlets, who mixed the syrup with carbonated water on site for immediate consumption by the end customer. Soft drink sales were extremely profitable for fountain outlets, with gross margins in the range of 75 percent. Large fast-food chains accounted for one-third of fountain sales and were one of the fastest growing channels for soft drinks.

Coca-Cola had historically dominated fountain sales and controlled the important McDonald's account. Coca-Cola sold syrup directly to the outlets of large chains with a dedicated fountain sales force, bypassing the local bottler. Local Pepsi bottlers handled the fountain accounts in their respective territories, selling syrup to the fast-food outlets that belonged to national chains that carried Pepsi. Pepsi-Cola had won the Burger King account from Coca-Cola in 1982. PepsiCo's purchase of Pizza Hut, Taco Bell, and Kentucky Fried Chicken, had made it the world's largest fast-food company, and helped it achieve a stronger position in the fountain market.

In the vending channel, bottlers purchased, installed, and supplied machines. Concentrate producers often offered rebates to encourage their bottlers to invest in vending machines and to allocate all or most of the slots (usually four to six per machine) to their products. One source estimated that Coca-

Cola bottlers owned 50 percent more vending machines in the United States than did Pepsi bottlers. On average, bottlers obtained significantly higher margins through vending machines than from food stores. Coca-Cola bottlers, for example, often earned over half their total profits through vending.

There were also a host of other smaller channels for soft drinks. Restaurants, caterers, and institutional buyers such as airlines often served soft drinks in bottles and cans rather than from a fountain. Convenience stores were accounting for an increasing volume, especially through "single serve" cold cases. Their percentage of soft drink distribution had increased to 20 percent in 1986. Some mass merchandisers also allocated shelf space to soft drinks. Sales to these diverse outlets were handled by local bottlers.

International Markets

The soft drink industry outside the United States also consisted of concentrate producers, independent local bottlers, and retail outlets. Product lines tended to be narrower and channels less developed, but this varied by country. During the 1960s and 1970s, growth in the consumption of soft drinks internationally was greater than in the United States. In the first half of the 1980s, U.S. growth had exceeded that in the international markets because of economic problems in many countries. The international profits of all the concentrate producers had fallen in the early 1980s.

By the mid-1980s, both Coca-Cola and Pepsi-Cola had company-owned or franchised bottling operations in over 140 countries. Coca-Cola had enjoyed a substantial head start in the establishment of international bottling activities and held a strong lead overseas. The company estimated in its 1984 annual report that even including local soft drinks unique to particular countries, Coca-Cola held the leading market share with 38 percent of the worldwide market. Coca-Cola's lead was particularly strong in Europe where it outsold Pepsi-Cola, its nearest competitor, by four to one. Coca-Cola obtained 62 percent of its soft drink revenues from outside the United States in 1984. Pepsi's strongest positions were in Latin America and the Middle East, where it held the market-share leads in a number of countries. Approximately 20 percent of Pepsi-Cola's soft drink revenues came from outside the United States.

History of the Leading Soft Drink
Concentrate Producers

Soft drinks had existed since the early 1800s, when many U.S. druggists concocted blends of fruit syrups and carbonated soda water that they sold at their soda fountains.

Coca-Cola

Coca-Cola was formulated in 1886 by Dr. John Pemberton, a pharmacist in Atlanta, Georgia. The drink was sold as a refreshing elixir at the fountain counter of Jacobs' Pharmacy, of which Dr. Pemberton was part owner. Eventually, Mr. Asa Candler became sole owner of the pharmacy and of the rights to the soft drink. Candler began selling the syrup for the drink to other pharmacies, established a sales force, and began advertising the drink on signs placed in train stations and town squares. The advertising budget reached $100,000 in 1901. Candler granted the first bottling franchise for the drink in 1899 for $1, believing that the main future of the drink rested with fountain sales.

Coca-Cola's franchise bottler network grew quickly, and a standard 6½-ounce "skirt" bottle was designed in 1916 to be used by all franchisees. This bottle eventually became one of the best-known images in the world. In 1920, U.S. Supreme Court Justice Oliver Wendell Holmes ruled that the nickname "Coke" could only mean Coca-Cola, because "it means a single thing coming from a single source, and well-known to the community. Coca-Cola probably means to most persons the plaintiff's familiar product to be had everywhere."

In 1919, Ernest Woodruff purchased the Coca-Cola Company from Asa Candler for $25 million. In 1923, his son, Robert W. Woodruff, who was to become the most dominant figure in Coca-Cola's history, was made CEO. Woodruff began working with the company's franchised bottlers to make Coca-Cola available everywhere, any time a consumer might want it. Woodruff tried to motivate the bottlers to place the beverage "in arm's reach of desire," arguing that if Coke were not conveniently available when the consumer was thirsty the sale was lost forever. In 1929, Coca-Cola and its bottlers began to offer an open-top cooler for bottled Coca-Cola to storekeepers and gasoline-station operators at extremely low prices. In 1937, the company introduced the first coin-operated vending machine. Woodruff also initiated "life-style" advertising for Coca-Cola, which emphasized the product's role in a consumer's life rather than its product attributes. The product's famous motto, launched during the 1920s, was "The Pause that Refreshes." The company continued to own its original bottling operations around Atlanta and began to buy back a few franchises that were underperforming.

Woodruff also began to develop Coca-Cola's international business, principally through export. The international division was led by James A. Farley, who later became a close aide to President Franklin Roosevelt. The Coca-Cola Company was viewed as closely connected to the Roosevelt Administration.

Woodruff's most memorable action may have been his decision, made at the request of General Dwight Eisenhower at the beginning of World War II, to see, as Woodruff said "that every man in uniform gets a bottle of Coca-Cola for five cents wherever he is and whatever it costs." Coca-Cola bottling plants followed the march of American troops around the world. This action established for Coca-Cola the dominant market share in most European and Asian countries, a lead the company still held in 1986. Robert Woodruff remained on the board of directors and an influential figure in major decisions until his retirement in 1982.

In the years immediately following World War II, Coca-Cola outsold its closest rival Pepsi-Cola by ten to one, and held 70 percent of the cola segment of the market. Hundreds of small regional soft drink producers continued to market a wide assortment of flavors.

In 1954, Coca-Cola sales declined 3 percent and profits dipped 8 percent, the first declines since before World War II. In 1955, the company made the first change in its bottle since 1916, increasing its size to 12 ounces. Later in the 1950s, Coca-Cola introduced even larger bottle sizes to be sold through food stores. The company also changed its advertising motto to "Be Really Refreshed" and in 1960 to "No Wonder Coke Refreshes Best." Coca-Cola executives never voiced the name Pepsi-Cola in meetings with Coca-Cola bottlers, but rather discussed only the growth of their own brand. Industry observers often referred to Coca-Cola as "Mother Coke."

Pepsi-Cola

Pepsi-Cola was invented in 1893 in New Bern, North Carolina, by a pharmacist, Caleb Bradham. Pepsi-Cola followed a pattern similar to Coca-Cola of expansion through franchised bottlers. Its growth in the early 1900s was not nearly as significant, however, and the company was on the brink of bankruptcy several times. Pepsi-Cola designed a standard twelve-ounce bottle, which its bottlers sold at a retail price of ten cents compared to Coca-Cola's five cents for its 6½-ounce unit. In 1933, Pepsi-Cola lowered the price to five cents, and in 1939 it launched its radio advertising jingle, "Twice as much for a nickel, too. Pepsi-Cola is the one for you." In 1940, that jingle was rated by the radio industry as the second best-known song in America, behind only the Star Spangled Banner.

In 1950, Alfred Steele accepted an offer to become CEO at Pepsi-Cola. A former Coca-Cola marketing executive, he had apparently irritated Robert Woodruff with his style. Pepsi was nearly bankrupt, having lost during the 1940s much of the market position it had gained in the 1930s. Steele later stated, "When I arrived at Pepsi, the vice presidents figured I had come to liquidate the company."[2]

Steele made "Beat Coke" his theme and claimed that he saw the day when Pepsi would outsell Coke. Pepsi introduced several new bottle sizes, including the first 24-ounce bottle for family consumption at home. Pepsi executives emphasized take-home sales through the supermarkets that were springing up in the growing suburbs as the appropriate focus of Pepsi bottlers' efforts. New advertising campaigns were developed. In 1955, Steele married the actress Joan Crawford, who then began touring as guest speaker at regional Pepsi bottler meetings. Pepsi-Cola revenues increased over 300 percent between 1950 and 1958. Pepsi also began to expand its international operations in earnest during this period.

Other Competitors

Dr Pepper was formulated by a fountain clerk in Waco, Texas, in 1885. Dr Pepper produced a uniquely flavored drink, based on a combination of juices. It enjoyed intense consumer loyalty, though it was said that a consumer had

---

2. J. C. Louis and Harvey Z. Yazijian, *The Cola Wars* (New York: Everest House, 1980).

to try Dr Pepper several times to become accustomed to it. Dr Pepper had historically been a regional producer in the Southwest, where it maintained a network of franchised bottlers for which Dr Pepper was the primary brand. In 1962, a U.S. court ruled that Dr Pepper was not a cola, and therefore Coca-Cola or Pepsi-Cola bottlers were able to carry it. Dr Pepper began moving aggressively to expand from its Southwest base by signing up Coca-Cola or Pepsi-Cola bottlers across the country.

Dr Pepper placed great emphasis on providing excellent support to its bottlers. By the mid-1970s, Dr Pepper had secured nationwide distribution. Through creative advertising and bottler support, its sales had grown from $17 million in 1962 to $152 million in 1976. Dr Pepper also did well with Diet Dr Pepper, which masked the taste of saccharin better than colas.

Royal Crown Cola, which was the fifth leading concentrate producer and a specialist in cola drinks, was introduced in 1935. It also employed independent franchise bottlers, who also often marketed Seven-Up, Dr Pepper, and other smaller brands. Royal Crown was strongest in the midwestern U.S., where its bottlers were most numerous. Many analysts considered RC the most innovative concentrate producer. It had introduced the first diet soft drink, Diet Rite, in 1962, and the first decaffeinated diet cola in 1980.

The Seven-Up Company specialized in a lemon-lime drink that had been packaged in a distinctive green bottle since its introduction in 1929. Seven-Up managers took pride in the close, cooperative relations that they established with their bottlers, who were referred to as "developers." The vast majority of Seven-Up developers also bottled Coca-Cola, Pepsi-Cola, or RC Cola. By the 1950s, Seven-Up had achieved national distribution through its franchise network. Seven-Up also established and owned a small number of bottling operations.

In the post–World War II period, Seven-Up emphasized its product's medicinal benefits, both for children (with such slogans as "Tune Tiny Tummies") and adults (with such slogans as "Cure for Seven Hangovers"). The product was also widely used as a mixer with alcoholic beverages. Seven-Up and Seagrams Seven Crown whiskey became a particularly popular drink. Seven-Up sold its concentrate for approximately 15 percent more than Coca-Cola, because Seven-Up used less sugar and thus saved its bottlers some sweetener cost. Seven-Up sold at prices comparable to Coca-Cola at retail.

In the 1960s, the company found that its sales were significantly skewed toward older buyers and that the product was frequently viewed as an aid for indigestion or as a mixer but not a soft drink. In 1968, Seven-Up launched its "Uncola" advertising campaign, designed to position Seven-Up as the soft drink alternative to colas for the 16- to 24-year-old age group. In 1970, Seven-Up also introduced a diet version of its product, containing saccharin. Consumer taste surveys regularly indicated that Diet Seven-Up had less aftertaste than did the various diet colas containing saccharin that were marketed in the 1970s. Both moves were highly successful, and Seven-Up became the dominant soft drink in the lemon-lime category, which comprised approximately 12 percent of the total soft drink market during the 1960s and 1970s. The second best-selling lemon-lime soft drink was Sprite, introduced by Coca-Cola in 1961.

Seven-Up did not enter the fountain market until 1960. However, fountain sales represented 12 percent by 1974. Seven-Up succeeded in convincing most of the major fast-food chains to allocate one or two fountain dispensers (out of the four to six) to Seven-Up products. In 1975, Seven-Up persuaded McDonald's to carry Diet Seven-Up, the first time a major chain had taken on a diet drink. By 1976, Seven-Up was sold in nine of the top ten fast-food chains.

Coke Versus Pepsi in the 1960s and Early 1970s

Coca-Cola

In the 1960s, Coke continued to expand distribution and availability of its own product in the United States and internationally. Coca-Cola also began in 1961 to offer its soft drinks in cans as well as bottles. In 1960, Coca-Cola purchased the Minute Maid Corporation, the world's largest producer of citrus concentrates, as its first diversification effort. It subsequently diversified into other beverages, including coffee (1964), wine (1977), and spring water.

In the 1960s and 1970s, new products such as the lemon-lime drink Sprite (1961) and the diet drinks Tab (1973), Fresca (1966), and Diet Sprite (1974) were introduced. Coca-Cola introduced a drink tasting similar to Dr Pepper, called Mr. Pibb, testing it first in Waco, Texas, in 1972. The company said that it would not extend the Coca-Cola or Coke names to any other products.

Throughout the 1960s and 1970s, Coca-Cola continued to increase its unit sales and profits, although at a rate slower than Pepsi. Advertising expenditures were steadily increased, and Coca-Cola commercials in the United States were designed to portray a positive image of Coke as part of American life. Coca-Cola executives maintained their policy of not mentioning Pepsi-Cola at bottlers' meetings.

In 1976, Paul Austin, CEO of Coca-Cola, stated in an article that U.S. soft drink consumption had matured and that Coca-Cola's largest growth would come from the international market. International sales by 1980 accounted for 62 percent of Coca-Cola's soft drink volume, in contrast to 20 percent of PepsiCo's.

Pepsi-Cola

In 1963, Donald Kendall became CEO of Pepsi-Cola. Kendall, a former Pepsi sales manager and later head of the international operation, had gained fame in 1959 when he convinced Vice President Richard Nixon to bring Soviet Premier Nikita Khrushchev by the Pepsi booth at the American Exhibition in Moscow in 1959. Under Kendall, the Pepsi-Cola Company was renamed PepsiCo and diversified into several new lines of businesses, including snack foods (Frito-Lay), restaurants (Pizza Hut and Taco Bell), trucking, and sporting goods.

In the 1960s, Pepsi-Cola began to expand its product line, introducing both Diet Pepsi and Mountain Dew in 1964. Pepsi Light, a semidiet drink, was introduced in 1977. Also in the 1960s, Pepsi launched its "Pepsi Generation" advertising theme, positioning the product as the choice of the young and "young at heart." Pepsi bottlers were praised at meetings as "veterans in the war against Coca-Cola" who "invaded" Coke markets with new "sales weapons."[3]

PepsiCo also moved to improve the management of its store-door delivery operations, in which Pepsi bottlers delivered soft drinks directly to individual grocery stores. (Both Pepsi beverages and Frito-Lay snacks were distributed through this method, although PepsiCo owned all the delivery operations for Frito-Lay.) Andrall E. Pearson, a McKinsey director who had consulted for Kendall from 1967 to 1970, became president and chief operating officer of PepsiCo in 1971. Pearson established stringent standards by which Pepsi and Frito-Lay store door salespeople were to gain, keep, and maintain in good form the retail shelf space for PepsiCo products. Salespeople were to secure an exclusive primary shelf-space site and to strive to maintain a "permanent" secondary site like an end-aisle display. In the mid-1960s, industry executives had tended to accept that both soft drink and snack food sections of food stores would be frequently in disarray because of high product turnover. By the end of the 1970s, as both Pepsi and its competitors improved their standards, these sections were widely regarded as the best-maintained parts of most food stores.

The price that Pepsi-Cola charged its bottlers for concentrate was approximately 20 percent below the Coca-Cola price throughout the 1950s and 1960s. Pepsi's franchise agreement permitted renegotiation of the price, however, and Pepsi raised the price to a level equal to that of Coca-Cola in the early 1970s. Pepsi secured the price increases without fierce bottler opposition because it promised to use the extra margin to increase advertising and promotion for Pepsi brands. In 1975, the Pepsi-Cola brand for the first time gained the market share lead in food stores from Coca-Cola, according to Nielsen audits.

The Pepsi Challenge

In Dallas, Texas, Pepsi-Cola was the third largest-selling soft drink in 1974, behind both Coke and Dr Pepper. The sales manager for that district had seen the Pepsi market research that indicated that the majority of consumers in blind taste tests preferred Pepsi over Coke by approximately 58 percent to 42 percent. The Pepsi manager initiated in-store "Challenge Booths" to persuade consumers to take the blind taste test themselves. Pepsi-Cola began immediately to move up in share and eventually became the number-two brand.

In 1975, Victor Bonomo, president of Pepsi U.S.A., decided to employ the Pepsi Challenge in other markets in which Pepsi was weak. The challenge was extended to all company-owned bottlers, which meant that it was employed in markets accounting for over 20 percent of Pepsi's sales, including New York, Los Angeles, and Detroit. Advertising, store displays, the message that the bottlers' salespeople conveyed to the trade, and in-store Challenge Booths all highlighted the Challenge.

3. Pat Watters, *Coca-Cola: An Illustrated History* (New York: Doubleday, 1978).

Pepsi launched the Pepsi Challenge nationwide in 1977. By 1980, the regular Pepsi brand had gained an additional 1.3 percent share of market lead over the Coca-Cola brand in food stores. Pepsi-Cola worked to exploit the success of the Pepsi Challenge to motivate and improve the performance of its bottlers. John Sculley, who succeeded Bonomo as president of Pepsi U.S.A. in 1980, urged Pepsi bottlers to expand sales through vending and fountain outlets. Sculley was quoted in 1980 as saying, "I want our bottlers to defend their competitive position in food stores but also to go for the competitors' jugular by attacking its high-margin vending business." Sculley also increased the price of the concentrate for Diet Pepsi and used the greater margin to increase advertising in the growing diet segment.

Coca-Cola responded to the broadened Pepsi Challenge by initiating major retail price discounts in selected markets where Pepsi was weak, the Pepsi bottler was an independent franchisee, and the Coca-Cola bottler was company owned. Coca-Cola used price only selectively as a competitive weapon during the remainder of the 1970s. The cost of price promotions continued to be split approximately two-thirds to the bottler and one-third to the concentrate producer. Advertising expenditures for both Coca-Cola and Pepsi-Cola, however, increased significantly during the late 1970s.

New Leadership at Coke

Industry observers were surprised in 1980 when Roberto Goizueta, a Cuban immigrant, was tapped to become CEO of Coca-Cola. As one of his first acts, Goizueta issued a 1,200-word strategy statement that called for dramatic changes at Coca-Cola. Coca-Cola was to look for growth in the U.S. soft drink market. Price discounting would be used when necessary to retain Coke's dominant position in that market.

As a result, price discounting began to reach a new level of intensity in 1980 as Coca-Cola and its bottlers increased discounts. By the end of 1980, approximately 50 percent of Coke and Pepsi in the food-store channel were sold at discount. In 1981, Nielsen audits indicated that Coca-Cola cost an average of fifteen cents less per 192-ounce case than Pepsi-Cola.

Coca-Cola would also seek to "amend" its franchise agreement, permitting the price of Coca-Cola concentrate, which had been frozen by the agreements for sixty years despite inflation, to be increased. Coca-Cola would use the increased gross margins for advertising and promotions. In exchange, Coca-Cola agreed to sell concentrate rather than syrup (including sweetener) to some of its largest bottlers. The company would use the Coca-Cola brand name as competitive "equity" and would no longer treat it as sacrosanct.

In 1980, Coca-Cola began the effort to influence the ownership and management of its franchised bottlers. While Coca-Cola would remain committed to independent bottlers, the company would replace bottlers in key markets where they were deemed not "sufficiently aggressive," sometimes taking an equity position in the new ownership. Between 1980 and 1984, franchises that represented 50 percent of Coca-Cola volume changed ownership. The president of Coca-Cola U.S.A. stated that the Coca-Cola Company had had some role in each purchase. In several cases, it even offered to raise capital for certain potential buyers.

One of the most dramatic examples of this effort was Coca-Cola's decision in 1982 to make Coca-Cola Bottling of New York a private corporation. Coca-Cola Bottling of New York was a $700 million corporation, publicly traded on the New York Stock Exchange, that had diversified into several smaller operations besides bottling. It had an average ROE of 10 percent in the five years prior to 1982. The Coca-Cola Company (of Atlanta) acquired 35 percent of Coca-Cola of New York and arranged for private investors (including Bill Cosby, the entertainer, who was then the advertising spokesperson for the Coca-Cola brand) to acquire the other 65 percent. Charles Millard, CEO of Coca-Cola of New York, later said, "We became a born-again bottler, as we focused again on our mainline business of selling soft drinks."[4]

Coca-Cola also changed its advertising theme in 1982. Goizueta stated, "With our new slogan—Coke is it—we're saying we're Number One and not ashamed of it. Our former slogan—Have a Coke and a smile—was wonderful but we were in a fight, and our slogan was a ballad. The momentum has now shifted from Purchase, New York (headquarters of PepsiCo) to Atlanta."[5]

In July 1982, Coca-Cola announced plans to introduce Diet Coke on a national basis. Surveys showed that most consumers found the Diet Coke formula far superior to Tab. Many observers believed that Coca-Cola had developed the Diet Coke formula years earlier and had the formula sitting on its shelves. Yet management was said to have hurriedly decided to introduce it. The advertising spending levels for Diet Coke were set at $50 million annually.

Some Coca-Cola bottlers voiced strong resistance to the use of the Coke brand name. However, the introduction of Diet Coke in New York City proved successful beyond even the company's expectations. Diet Coke had gained national distribution by early 1983.

Coca-Cola also extended its corporate strategy in 1982. Columbia Pictures was acquired in 1982, and Goizueta stated that Coca-Cola would become a "beverage and entertainment enterprise, strong in both businesses."

Industry Developments in the Late 1970s and Early 1980s

Philip Morris, a leading cigarette and beer producer, acquired Seven-Up in 1978 for $520 million, or about twenty times earnings. Philip Morris embarked on a restructuring and upgrading program to arrest the slow decline in Seven-Up's market share that had taken place since 1974. Seven-Up cut back on its promotional support to the bottlers and chain stores. Marketing expenditures were increased substantially, and a new ad campaign. "America's Turning Seven-Up," was designed to boost consumer awareness. Experienced Philip Morris

4. *Beverage World*, July 1984.
5. *Industry Week*, November 1982.

executives from the cigarette and beer industries filled key posts. While sales grew, however, Seven-Up recorded losses in 1980, 1981, and 1982.

In 1980, surveys indicated that approximately 15 to 20 percent of American consumers expressed a serious concern about caffeine consumption. In addition, the diet segment of the soft drink market had been growing at three times the rate of regular soft drinks, accounting for 18 percent of the market by 1982.

Royal Crown announced RC/100, a diet caffeine-free cola, in 1980. In 1981, Seven-Up decided to exploit the fact that Seven-Up had never contained caffeine. Its advertising was changed to the theme "Never Had It, Never Will." It also ran ads showing other soft drink brands, including Pepsi-Cola, stating that they contained caffeine and implying that caffeine was bad for the consumer. Pepsi-Cola management wrote an angry letter to its franchise bottlers who marketed both Pepsi-Cola and Seven-Up, demanding that they not run the ads disparaging Pepsi-Cola. Some bottlers complied; some did not.

Seven-Up attempted to carry this theme further by introducing "Like" in March 1982. Like was a caffeine-free regular cola. Philip Morris's $12 million advertising budget for Like consisted of network television, spot TV, radio, point-of-purchase, and other merchandising concepts. Like gained a 0.3 percent market share in 1982, and Seven-Up's lemon-lime market share increased by the same amount. Nevertheless, Seven-Up found it difficult to gain national distribution for its new product. In addition, McDonald's, which had been the first fast-food chain ever to take on a diet drink in 1975, dropped Diet Seven-Up in favor of Diet Sprite in 1983. Losses at Seven-Up continued. In response to a suit initiated by Coca-Cola, a U.S. court determined that Like was in fact a cola, and therefore bottlers of Coca-Cola, Pepsi-Cola, and RC Cola could not market it unless they gave up their other cola brands.

Soft drink producers had competed primarily through advertising, new products, and bottler relations throughout most of the postwar period. Widespread price discounting began in the industry in the late 1970s. Price discounting grew more intense in 1982. The trend was led by Coca-Cola, particularly in the early months of the year. By 1984, all Coke and Pepsi products were sold at a discount at virtually all times in every major food store.

Victor Posner, a financier, acquired the Royal Crown Company in 1984. In early 1984, Forstmann Little & Company engineered a leveraged buyout of Dr Pepper for $622.5 million. Later that year, Forstmann sold the Canada Dry brand, which had been purchased by Dr Pepper, to R.J. Reynolds and sold the remaining company-owned Dr Pepper bottlers to various investors. In 1984, R.J. Reynolds ($16.6 billion in sales in 1985) bought the Sunkist brand from General Cinema. Reynolds had already owned the Del Monte Division's Hawaiian Punch and Cott Beverages. All these brands combined to give Reynolds 4.6 percent of the U.S. soft drink market in 1985.

Coke and Pepsi Jockey for Position

Pepsi introduced Pepsi Free and Sugar Free Pepsi Free, both caffeine-free colas, in 1983. Pepsi planned $100 million in annual advertising for the caffeine-free colas, heavily weighted toward television. The company announced that it intended these products to become the leaders in the caffeine-free segment. Pepsi's ad campaign was so successful that it captured about half of the caffeine-free segment by the end of 1983.

In June 1983, following Pepsi's national rollout of Pepsi Free, Coca-Cola introduced Caffeine-Free Coke, Diet Coke, and Tab. Each brand was supported by TV advertising. In August 1983, Coke announced that it would incorporate aspartame, a new sweetener, in its diet drinks before year end in a proportion of slightly less than 50 percent of the overall sweetener content. Diet Coke had become the largest-selling diet soft drink by the end of 1983. Coca-Cola also introduced Diet Coke in twenty countries in 1984.

In 1984, Pepsi-Cola introduced a new marketing campaign using the slogan "Choice of a New Generation." It secured endorsements from the singers Michael Jackson and Lionel Richie (1984), former Democratic vice presidential candidate Geraldine Ferraro (1985), and actor Michael J. Fox (1986). These endorsements gained extensive free publicity and were used to generate excitement at the large conventions of Pepsi-Cola bottlers. Many advertising executives believed that this new advertising campaign had proved particularly successful in building loyalty for Pepsi among teenagers. Regular Pepsi became the single most popular soft drink in the United States in 1985.

In late 1984, Pepsi-Cola launched two new lemon-lime drinks, Slice and Diet Slice, which contained 10 percent fruit juice, distinguishing them from both Seven-Up and Sprite, which contained no fruit juice. Spurred by the innovation of one of its bottlers, Pepsi-Cola was also the first to introduce the three-liter plastic bottle in 1984, gaining a four-month window before Coca-Cola could secure supplies from Owens, Illinois, for its own bottlers. Pepsi-Cola and Coca-Cola products packaged in three-liter bottles sold at retail for significantly less per ounce than the same products packaged in two-liter bottles, though the packaging cost for three-liter bottles was slightly more expensive per ounce than for two-liter bottles.

Pepsi-Cola moved in late 1984 to be the first to use 100 percent aspartame in its diet beverages. All major concentrate producers followed within months. (Industry sources believed that they had all secured significant, but varying, discounts off the list price.) Pepsi-Cola was able to obtain delivery of aspartame from G.D. Searle before Coca-Cola did, and undertook a concerted effort to use its six-week lead to promote Diet Pepsi against Diet Coke. Industry sources indicated that the growth of Diet Pepsi exceeded that of Diet Coke during this period.

Coca-Cola quickly launched a national advertising campaign stating that Diet Coke had 100 percent aspartame, even though 100 percent aspartame was available only in certain packages and areas. Pepsi-Cola immediately reacted to this claim by emphasizing at the point of purchase that the labels of its Diet Pepsi actually contained the announcement of "100 percent NutraSweet" (the brand name of Searle's aspartame), while the Coca-Cola labels could not make this claim.

In mid-1984, Brian Dyson, president of Coca-Cola U.S.A., declared that Diet Coke had become the third largest-selling soft drink in the United States, surpassing both the regular Seven-Up brand and the regular Dr Pepper. Dyson predicted that Diet Coke would become the second largest-selling soft drink in the United States. Some industry observers believed that this statement was intended to motivate Coca-Cola bottlers.

Cherry Coke, a blend of Coca-Cola and cherry flavoring, was introduced in March 1985. Cherry Coke was supported with a substantial advertising campaign and began to gain share rapidly.

The Coca-Cola Reformulation

In April 1985, Coca-Cola announced that it would change the formula for the 99-year-old Coca-Cola brand. While Coke's soft drink sales had grown rapidly in 1984 in response to the Diet Coke introduction, regular Coke sales had suffered.

The reformulation was the lead story on all three network evening news programs on the day of the announcement. Surveys indicated that over 90 percent of Americans had heard the news within twenty-four hours and that 70 percent had tried the new drink within a month. The new Coke contained more sweetener, and consumers indicated that they believed the new Coke tasted more like Pepsi. Groups of consumers organized themselves to resist the change, and they received extensive news coverage. Southern bottlers added to the negative feedback; Coke's classic formula was synonymous with motherhood and apple pie.

The day Coke announced its reformulation, Pepsi held a press conference declaring a holiday for its employees. To make Coke drinkers aware that new Coke was more like Pepsi, the company ran national ads inviting disgruntled Coca-Cola drinkers to Pepsi-Cola, saying: "For 87 years Coke and Pepsi have been eyeball to eyeball. It looks like they just blinked. . . . We welcome the new Pepsi drinkers to the new Pepsi generation." Pepsi's case sales rose 10 percent in 1985 versus the industry's gain of 5.7 percent.

In June 1985, Coca-Cola introduced Minute Maid Orange and Diet Minute Maid Orange, sodas with 10 percent juice. Coke's entry into the juice-market category precipitated a proliferation of juice offerings among the two giants in the following year. PepsiCo expanded its Slice line to include mandarin orange. Pepsi also introduced Cherry Pepsi in Canada and the United Kingdom. Coca-Cola responded with another addition to its Minute-Maid line, a lemon-lime flavor. Pepsi countered with Apple Slice and Cherry Cola Slice.

Original Coca-Cola Returns

In July 1985, Coca-Cola announced that it would bring back the original formula, named Coca-Cola Classic, while retaining the new formula in a product to be named Coke. The new Coke was to be the company's flagship brand, and the company would emphasize it in its sales to fountain outlets. The company also said that new Coke would be introduced in all international markets.

Table C Share of take-
home market (percent)

Coca-Cola	31
Pepsi-Cola	31
Seven-Up	6
Dr Pepper	5
RC	2
Others	25
Total	100

In August 1985, Coca-Cola adopted a "Megabrand" strategy for Coca-Cola Classic and new Coke. Advertising was introduced with the theme "We've Got a Taste for You." Nielsen audits indicated that in the third quarter of 1985 Coca-Cola Classic was outselling Coke approximately three-to-one in food stores. Across all brands, however, Coca-Cola was running neck-and-neck with Pepsi in the take-home market (see Table C).

In September 1985, the Kentucky Fried Chicken fast-food chain decided that it would sell Coca-Cola Classic rather than new Coke. McDonald's and most other fast food-chains and restaurants that sold Coca-Cola products were still selling new Coke as of March 1986.

In January 1986, the Coca-Cola Company hired separate advertising agencies for Coca-Cola Classic and new Coke. In early 1986, commercials for Coca-Cola Classic ran with the theme "Red, White and You." Commercials for new Coke had the theme "Catch the Wave." The company also stated that Coca-Cola Classic would henceforth be considered its flagship brand. In early 1986, some Coca-Cola franchised bottlers said publicly that the Coca-Cola Company should drop the word "Classic" from the Coca-Cola name. Some industry analysts were questioning whether new Coke would survive.

Recent Industry Developments

Advertising increased significantly in the 1980s. Whereas, in the past, margins were relatively stable across all brands, products with aspartame and the newer juice offerings increased a bottler's costs per case by 10 to 15 percent over regular soft drink brands. Increased product-line breadth forced bottler costs higher. Grocery chains fought any retail price increases. Shelf space limitations were forcing more choices among the many brands, line extensions, and package types. Many bottlers had sold out by 1986, unable to cope with industry changes. A wave of acquisitions took place as multiple franchise owners and concentrate producers bought up most of the bottling system. Bottlers commanded acquisition prices as high as $5.00 per case in 1986 versus $2.50 per case in 1980, despite the fact that bottler operating profit per case had not increased.

With declining share and minimal profits, rumors abounded that Philip Morris would sell its soft drink operations. These were made more credible by the October 1985 announcement that Philip Morris was to purchase General Foods for $5.7 billion. Shortly thereafter, PepsiCo approached Philip Morris seeking to acquire Seven-Up. In late 1986, Pepsi announced that it would purchase Seven-Up for $380 million, the purchase not to include any of Seven-Up's company-owned bottlers. The FTC intervened in the sale, and Pepsi eventually purchased only Seven-Up's Canadian and international operations for $246 million.

In 1986, PepsiCo also acquired MEI for $600 million and Allegheny Beverages for $168 million, both PepsiCo franchises and accounting for 8 percent and 3 percent respectively of Pepsi's U.S. volume. These acquisitions increased PepsiCo's owned bottling to 32 percent of its total volume.

In February 1986, the Coca-Cola Company announced that it would purchase Dr Pepper Company for $470 million from Forstmann Little & Company. Once PepsiCo lost its bid for Seven-Up's domestic operations, however, Coke dropped its pursuit of Dr Pepper. Also in 1986, Coca-Cola acquired T.J. Lupton, a private Coca-Cola bottler accounting for 15 percent of Coca-Cola's U.S. volume. Lupton also bottled approximately 40 percent of Dr Pepper's volume. The acquisition sparked a series of additional bottling-company takeovers, increasing Coke's total bottling-company ownership from 11 percent to 38 percent of its total volume in a matter of weeks. Coke's actions culminated in the creation and subsequent sale of 51 percent of Coca-Cola Enterprises, Inc., a group of bottling operations, to the public in November 1986.

R.J. Reynolds, which once had aspirations to become a non-cola soft drink power, sold both its Canada Dry and Sunkist soft drink operations to Cadbury-Schweppes in June 1986. In August 1986, following closely on the heels of a $75 million buyout of A&W Brands Inc.'s root beer concern, an investment firm led by the partners Hicks & Haas engineered a leveraged buyout of the concentrate business of Dr Pepper Company for $416 million. Hicks & Haas was a company specializing in leveraged buyouts of small- to mid-sized companies. Philip Morris sold its domestic Seven-Up soft drink operations to Hicks & Haas in October 1986 for $240 million. Philip Morris retained only three bottlers, valued between $100 and $200 million (Philip Morris had invested an estimated $350 million in Seven-Up since its acquisition). Hicks & Haas's acquisition of Seven-Up's domestic business made it the third largest U.S. soft drink maker, with a 13.5 percent share of the domestic market. Terrence Hicks indicated that the soft drink industry was "an ideal industry" for leveraged buyouts because of its strong cash flow, steady growth, and lack of foreign competition.

Cray Research, Inc.

> The purpose of my new company is to design and build a larger, more
> powerful computer than anyone now has.
>
> Seymour Cray, *Chippewa Falls Herald Telegram*, May 1972

Cray Research was dedicated to making the fastest computer in the world. In
1976, four years after its founding, the company installed its first system, the
Cray-1 Serial One. Within a few years, Cray Research dominated the world of
supercomputers, so called because of the speed at which they operated. Sixty-
five of its systems had been installed worldwide by January 1, 1984, and annual revenues were $170 million.

Cray Research had clearly achieved the objective of its founder, Seymour
Cray, and had done so with entrepreneurial flair. Seed money had been raised
on the strength of Seymour Cray's reputation as the world's leading designer
of supercomputers. The first Cray employees were expatriates from other computer companies who had followed Seymour in pursuit of his goal. The first
machine was assembled in a rented storefront in Chippewa Falls, Wisconsin.

The company's very success, however, created pressures that ran counter
to Seymour Cray's desire to have a few engineers sitting in a clean, quiet room
thinking up ways to make computers run faster. Success challenged Cray Research's strategy, management, and culture.

Public ownership, which had been necessary to finance the fledgling enterprise, brought pressure for growth in earnings. Continued growth could be
achieved only by serving a broader market than the limited number of high-
powered scientific laboratories that valued Cray's raw computer power. Hardware design was the vital consideration for these classic supercomputer customers. Other users were somewhat more concerned with software, service,
and price, and these requirements called for a different way of doing business.

With growth had come administrative complexity. Faced with this personal
bête noire, Seymour Cray resigned from Cray Research in 1981, bringing to the
fore an issue that had haunted the firm over the years: "Is there life after
Seymour Cray?" On resigning, he agreed to serve as an independent contractor to his own company. Cray Research had the right of first refusal on his
designs until 1985.

Another problem taking up a good deal of management's attention was
how to preserve the entrepreneurial spirit that had been key to Cray's success.

The organizational philosophy had been to work in small groups, but by 1984 Cray had more than 1,500 employees and was still growing.

As if the problems of success were not sufficient to try Cray Research's young management team, the company also faced worldwide competition dedicated to toppling the Cray supercomputer from its throne. This threat was summed up in a *Newsweek* article in July 1983:

> The Japanese have announced a two-pronged plan to build advanced computer technologies. One project is the $100 million eight-year National Superspeed Computer project, which aims at producing machines 1,000 times faster than the existing Cray-1 built by Cray Research of Minneapolis. The other, the $500 million, 10-year Fifth Generation Computer project, is focusing on artificial intelligence. Both are now being countered by American efforts, including a Pentagon request for up to $1 billion over the next five years for superspeed and artificial intelligence technologies. Although behind, Great Britain and France have also launched national supercomputer projects.

With such interest in advanced computer technology mounting, Cray management could not afford to take its leadership in the industry for granted.

Cray: The Man and the Company

Seymour Cray had one professional goal: to design and build the fastest, most powerful computer in the world. Several times in his thirty-year career, he traded his position as a company's key computer designer for the freedom to sit in his cottage on Lake Wissota in Wisconsin with pencil and graph paper, writing the Boolean algebraic equations that would be translated into one of his phenomenal machines. The founding of Cray Research was one such move for freedom.

Seymour, as he was called by the press and by his employees, already had established a reputation as a computer genius and as the "father of the supercomputer" when he struck out on his own. *Forbes* magazine described him as "not just another scientist, but a national resource."

The First Supercomputer

It was at Control Data Corporation (CDC) in Minneapolis that Seymour was credited with the birth of the supercomputer and earned his reputation. The evolution toward speed began with the replacement of vacuum tubes by germanium transistors in the CDC 1604. In the 6600, Seymour pioneered the use of silicon transistors to increase the speed over that possible with germanium. But it was the 7600 that qualified as a supercomputer and was responsible for CDC's dominant share of this market from its introduction in 1969 until its eclipse by the Cray-1 in the mid-1970s.

To earn the title of supercomputer by 1980, a system had to perform more than 20 million computations per second and be capable of vector as well as scalar processing. Vector processing involved simultaneous performance of many calculations; scalar processing performed one calculation at a time.

Cray Research, Inc.

The early 1970s brought a change in CDC's business strategy that ran counter to Seymour's philosophy. The company merged with Commercial Credit Co. and began to shift its emphasis and resources away from scientific toward commercial applications.

CDC's refusal to fund Seymour's proposal to develop a machine faster than the 7600, coupled with the seemingly inevitable increase in corporate duties, made Seymour decide to move on. He left CDC with the company's blessing and with four of his colleagues to start his own company.

Cray Research was funded with $500,000 of Seymour's own money, $500,000 from CDC's Commercial Credit Co., and $1.5 million from fourteen other investors. Seymour was president and chief executive officer, and as founder, he made the rules. His company would build and sell one machine at a time and each machine would be a supercomputer. All models would be compatible with each other. The sale price of each machine would include a margin to cover ongoing research and development. Most important, the organization would leave him free to devote his entire time and energy to the design of the next Cray supercomputer.

An additional $6.1 million in private financing was raised during the next three years. The financing depended wholly on Seymour's reputation, since the company had no product on the market. By the time the Cray-1 was ready to be introduced in 1976, however, all the seed money had been used up. Help came in the form of John Rollwagen, who had joined Cray the preceding year. Rollwagen had an engineering degree from MIT and a Harvard MBA, was a native Minnesotan, and had worked at CDC. At Cray he was first hired in the marketing area, but his real role soon became apparent. Seymour wanted him to raise more money.

In March 1976, Rollwagen arranged a public stock offering. Cray had no sales, no earnings, a $2.4 million deficit, and was faced with further losses. The market for supercomputers was projected at eighty users worldwide. Nevertheless, the financial community reaffirmed its faith in Seymour Cray: The offering raised $10 million. Later that month, the first Cray-1, five times faster than the CDC 7600, was installed at the Los Alamos National Laboratory, in New Mexico, on a trial basis.

When the third machine was sold for $8.8 million in December, 1977 (Seymour had dismantled the second because of a design problem that slowed the machine down), the company made good on its seed money and showed its first profit. From that moment, Cray was in a surge of rapid growth, selling five machines in 1978, five in 1979, and nine in 1980. (See Figure A for the growth of customer installations and Exhibit 1 for the resulting financial performance.)

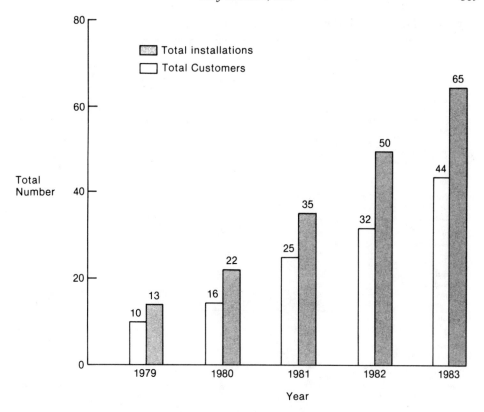

Figure A Growth of customer installations, 1979–83. *Source:* Cray Research, Inc.

Success

The year 1981 was pivotal. Cray had passed several milestones: revenues of $100 million, earnings of more than $1 per share, and employment of more than 1,000 people. Thirty-five Cray systems had been installed.

At the end of the year, Seymour announced his plans for developing the Cray-2. His new machine, performing 500 million to one billion calculations per second, would be six to ten times more powerful than the Cray-1 and its follow-on model, the Cray-1/S. The speed would be increased by shortening the wires through which the electronic signals traveled from four feet to sixteen inches. The central processing unit (CPU) would measure twenty-six inches high by thirty-eight inches long, compared with the Cray-1 CPU's dimensions of six by nine feet.

The miniaturization produced significant increases in heat as well as in speed. Most experts agreed that a rise of 18°C in junction temperatures halved the life of integrated circuits. The Cray-1 had been cooled by circulating freon, the refrigeration coolant, through channels surrounding the integrated circuit boards, but that method could not be applied to the smaller, more densely packed

Exhibit 1 Financial summary, 1972–83 ($ thousands).

	1972[a]	1973	1974	1975	1976	1977	1978	1979	1980	1981	1982	1983
Revenue:												
Sales	—	—	—	—	—	$ 8,816	$ 8,357	$26,496	$37,645	$ 65,207	$ 91,535	$125,008
Leased systems	—	—	—	—	450	2,261	7,349	12,545	17,558	27,604	35,623	26,151
Service fees	—	—	—	—	59	317	1,471	3,674	5,545	8,831	13,991	18,531
Total revenue	$	$	$	$	$ 509	$11,394	$17,177	$42,715	$60,748	$101,642	$141,149	$169,690
Net income (loss)	$ (72)	$ (527)	$ (944)	$ (887)	$(1,551)	$ 2,027	$ 3,501	$ 7,819	$10,900	$ 18,170	$ 19,000	$ 26,071
U.S. regions												
Revenue	—	—	—	—	—	—	$14,646	$14,293	$43,784	$ 90,852	$110,486	$ 87,443
Operating profit	—	—	—	—	—	—	7,448	3,259	20,225	49,926	51,191	37,772
International subsidiaries												
Revenue	—	—	—	—	—	—	2,531	28,422	16,964	10,790	30,663	82,247
Operating profit	—	—	—	—	—	—	1,042	19,817	10,280	2,482	15,531	39,383
Working capital	$2,375	$1,783	$3,314	$5,756	$10,786	$ 9,083	$ 7,498	$13,949	$53,543	$ 61,927	$98,600	$129,436
Long-term debt	—	—	—	2,720	2,720	3,321	4,670	3,029	7,876	12,360	33,741	37,612
Stockholders' equity	2,478	1,961	3,664	3,434	12,054	14,636	20,638	28,623	75,803	94,951	144,561	172,385
Operating and financial ratios:												
Return on stockholders' average equity	—	—	—	—	—	15.2%	19.9%	31.7%	25.6%	22.0%	18.6%	17.0%
Net income as % of revenue	—	—	—	—	—	17.8%	20.4%	18.3%	17.9%	17.9%	13.5%	15.4%
Current ratio	—	21.3:1	19.8:1	65.7:1	18.3:1	16.1:1	3.6:1	2.6:1	4.3:1	3.8:1	4.6:1	3.7:1
General data												
Cumulative systems installed	—	—	—	—	1	3	8	13	22	35	50	65
Number of employees at year end	12	21	30	45	124	199	321	524	761	1,079	1,352	1,551
Earnings (loss) per share	$(.04)	$(.18)	$(.20)	$(.18)	$(.17)	$.19	$.29	$.63	$.85	$1.32	$1.38	$1.77
Stock price												
High	—	—	—	—	2⅞	4⅛	11	16⅞	48½	48⅜	45¾	57⅛
Low	—	—	—	—	1⅞	2	3½	7¾	12¾	28	20	36⅜
Price/Earnings Ratio	—	—	—	—	NM[b]	43-21	51-16	27-12	57-15	37-21	33-14	32-21

a. April 6 (date of organization) to December 31.
b. Not meaningful.

Cray-2. Seymour solved the problem by immersing the entire computer in fluorocarbon, an inert liquid used for, among other things, artificial blood replacement in transfusions.

The Cray-2 would be priced over the Cray-1 and would require new software. The date of the first delivery was set for 1984.

Seymour had designed the Cray machines to be aesthetically appealing as well as functional. The Cray-1, pictured in Figure B, was shaped into an arc of columns containing modules and wiring surrounded by a knee-high padded bench housing the power supply. This configuration prompted the press to call this machine the "world's most expensive loveseat." When the Cray-2's liquid-immersion system was introduced, the machine was nicknamed the "world's most expensive aquarium."

Seymour's Independence

The year of accomplishment, 1981, was also the year Seymour moved to greater independence in his relationship with Cray Research. Aware of Seymour's

Figure B The Cray-1 Computer.

aversion to administrative problems, John Rollwagen sensed a need to face the implications of the company's rapid growth and increased complexity. As a result he initiated discussion with Seymour to see how the latter could avoid the kind of distractions that had caused him to sever his company connections in the past. Andrew Scott, one of Cray's founders and its legal counsel, soon joined the deliberations. Rollwagen explained, "There were no boundaries to our discussions. We explored all kinds of possibilities, such as Seymour quitting the company, stopping further growth, selling the company, and the like."

These discussions extending over several months finally led to an open-ended agreement, set forth in a two-page document that gave Cray Research the commercial rights to Seymour's designs through 1985 (later extended to 1987) in return for development funding. Andrew Scott, who had crafted the document, noted, "The agreement was intentionally brief and ambiguous. The relationship between Seymour and the company would have to flow from mutual decisions made in the light of changing conditions." John Rollwagen, who

Exhibit 2 Corporate organization chart, 1984.

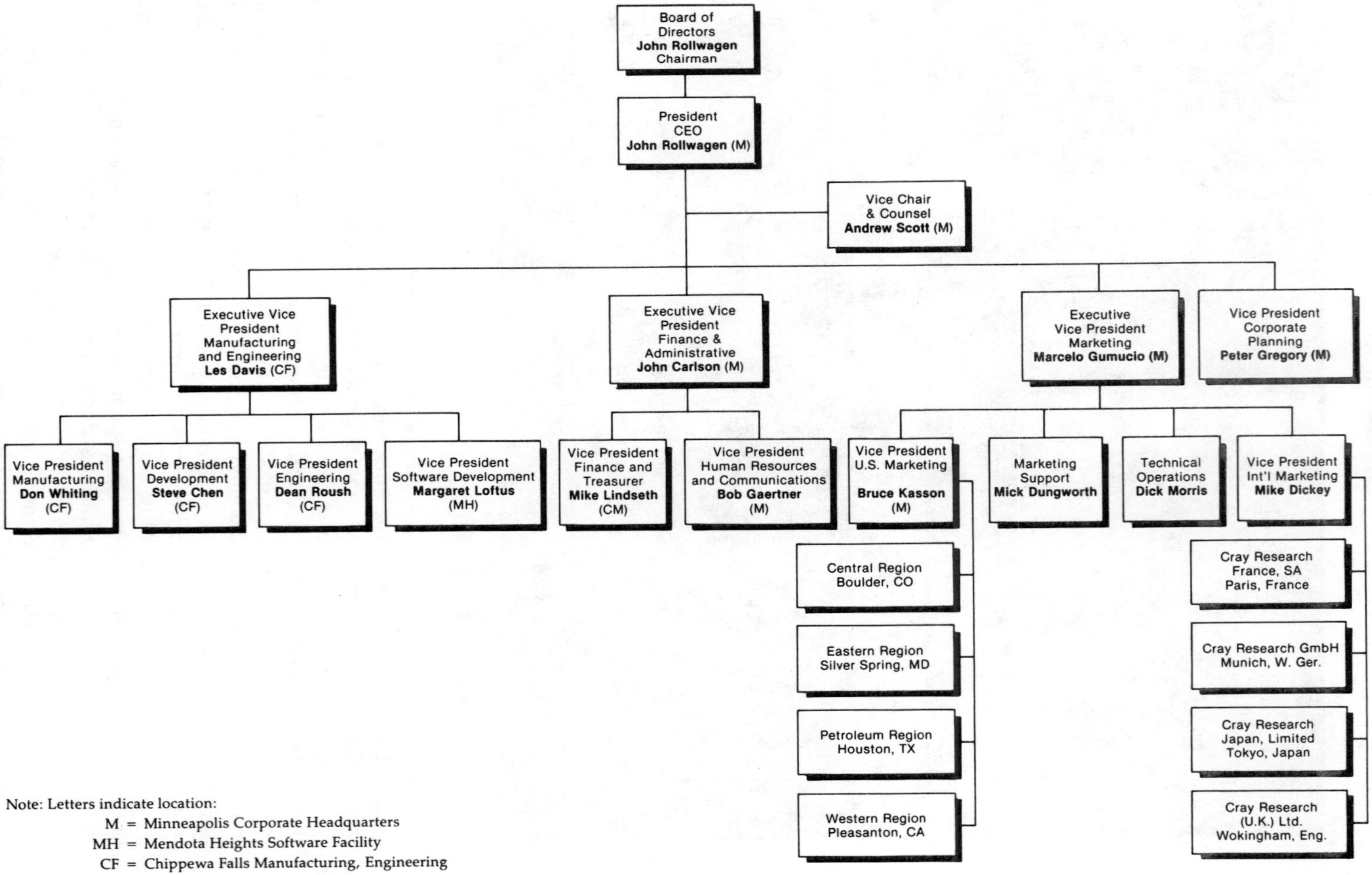

Board of Directors	**John Rollwagen** Chairman
President CEO	**John Rollwagen** (M)

Vice Chair & Counsel **Andrew Scott** (M)

Vice President Corporate Planning **Peter Gregory** (M)

Executive Vice President Marketing **Marcelo Gumucio** (M)

Executive Vice President Finance & Administrative **John Carlson** (M)

Executive Vice President Manufacturing and Engineering **Les Davis** (CF)

Vice President Int'l Marketing **Mike Dickey**

Technical Operations **Dick Morris**

Marketing Support **Mick Dungworth**

Vice President U.S. Marketing **Bruce Kasson** (M)

Vice President Human Resources and Communications **Bob Gaertner** (M)

Vice President Finance and Treasurer **Mike Lindseth** (CM)

Vice President Software Development **Margaret Loftus** (MH)

Vice President Engineering **Dean Roush** (CF)

Vice President Development **Steve Chen** (CF)

Vice President Manufacturing **Don Whiting** (CF)

Cray Research France, SA Paris, France

Cray Research GmbH Munich, W. Ger.

Cray Research Japan, Limited Tokyo, Japan

Cray Research (U.K.) Ltd. Wokingham, Eng.

Central Region Boulder, CO

Eastern Region Silver Spring, MD

Petroleum Region Houston, TX

Western Region Pleasanton, CA

Note: Letters indicate location:

M = Minneapolis Corporate Headquarters

MH = Mendota Heights Software Facility

CF = Chippewa Falls Manufacturing, Engineering

312

had already succeeded Seymour as president and CEO in 1977, would also assume the duties of chairman (Exhibit 2 shows Cray's organization chart). Seymour was free to spend his time finishing the Cray-2 and thinking about the next-generation supercomputer, the Cray-3.

The X-MP

In 1983, Cray Research introduced the X-MP a supercomputer that could operate at three to five times the speed of existing Cray models. The product was noteworthy in another regard: For the first time in more than two decades, the world's fastest computer was credited to someone other than Seymour Cray. Steve Chen, a computer designer who had joined Cray Research in 1980 and later became vice president of product development, had succeeded in multiplying the Cray-1's performance.

While Seymour had been increasing computer speed through miniaturization, Steve Chen took the alternative design route of parallel processing, or multiprocessing (the "MP" in the new machine's name). The method involved using a number of CPUs in a parallel configuration to solve different parts of a problem simultaneously. The X-MP's two Cray-1 processors were synchronized through clusters of shared registers in the CPU intercommunication section and through central memory. The X-MP also had as standard equipment a solid-state storage device with additional storage capacity that would allow more rapid access to large data files.

Unlike the revolutionary Cray-2, the X-MP had been designed to use software compatible with Cray's existing machines. In comparing his efforts with Seymour's, Chen said, "There is a different philosophy behind the X-MP. I deliberately settled between the Cray-1 and Cray-2. The reference point was to redesign everything by taking advantage of the existing software and the current technology."

The success of the X-MP came as a surprise to most people at Cray Research, including Seymour, who was reported to have said, "Well, you guys have *finally* learned how to do this," before returning to redesign the Cray-2 to operate at even faster speeds than originally planned. By early 1983, one X-MP had been installed, orders for several others had been booked, and Chen was working on the next model, which would have four processors.

Cray's rapid growth promised to accelerate with the successive phasing in of the X-MP, the Cray-2, and their even more powerful descendants.

The Growth Challenge

With the introduction of its first machine, Cray Research quickly dominated the narrow supercomputer market niche. The Cray-1 essentially knocked CDC out of its dominant position. According to a former CDC salesman, few, if any, CDC 7600s were sold after the Cray-1's introduction. CDC introduced its more powerful CYBER 205 in 1981, but by that time 35 Cray-1 systems had been installed. This rapid growth posed two quite different kinds of issues for management—one philosophical and the other strategic.

The philosophical issue had to do with how far the company would deviate from Seymour Cray's original concept of focusing on state-of-the-art applications. Over the years, Cray had broadened both its customer base and its product offering. The decision to expand had gained support from the professional managers hired to run the increasingly complex organization and was in effect ratified with Seymour's departure. John Carlson, Cray's chief financial officer, explained, "This company is driven by profitability. It's important to our investors to show a continued increase in earnings per share." Still, some senior managers had reservations and even misgivings. Top management continued to face the question of just how far to change the basic character of the business.

The strategic issues associated with rapid growth had to do with deciding where and how Cray Research should compete and with finding ways to preserve the entrepreneurial spirit that had contributed so vitally to the firm's success. To evaluate how to grow, top management continually assessed the markets, Cray's offerings, and the competition.

Markets

The 1976 projected total market of 80 supercomputer users soon expanded with a spreading awareness of the benefits to be gained from increased speed and power. By 1983 *Forbes* magazine estimated the worldwide market to be close to 400 potential customers, many of which might use more than one unit. Peter Gregory, Cray's director of corporate planning, set the long-term potential market at closer to 600 users, with about half designated as "probables." The growing demand for supercomputers was highlighted in the following *Fortune* account:

> A wave of technological change is poised to sweep over the computer industry. Faster and cheaper computers will allow users to do things they can't today. . . .
>
> The demand for faster but cheaper computers grows continuously. Sales of "supercomputers"—fast, specialized, hand-built, and expensive number-crunchers—have been taking off. Cray Research, Inc., a Minneapolis company (1983 sales: $170 million), got orders for 25 supercomputers last year vs. 16 in 1982. The burst of sales was ignited by technological advances that made possible deep price cuts—as much as $5 million on a $10-million Cray—and put the machines within reach of more users.
>
> Today's supercomputers are too slow for many potential tasks. Some jobs now take weeks or months—for example, simulating the airflow around an entire airplane in flight. Users have identified additional applications that would take hundreds or thousands of times longer; one would create a minutely detailed three-dimensional model of a fusion reactor's interior at work.[1]

Bob Walan, hired as Cray's first salesman in 1976 and manager of the central region since 1981, noted that buyers had changed over the years from the

---

1. "Reinventing the Computer," *Fortune*, March 5, 1984, p. 86.

"classic Cray customers" to a broader industrial market. The original classic customers were sophisticated, state-of-the-art scientific users who bought the basic hardware and developed their own software programs to take advantage of the machines' capabilities for their specific purposes.

Industrial customers included two groups distinguished by their software requirements. The petroleum industry, which Walan called "neoclassic," was similar to the classic customer in that it called for the most powerful Cray units to do scientific work. Petroleum industry users looked to Cray for assistance in developing support software to make their programs run faster and more easily on a Cray.

The other industrial customers typically added a Cray to an existing computer network and expected all the software to be supplied. Walan estimated that, in 1984, Cray's sales breakdown for the classic, neoclassic, and general industrial customer groups respectively would be 25 percent, 25 percent, and 50 percent in units and 40 percent, 30 percent, and 30 percent in dollars. Looking ahead, Peter Gregroy estimated that the long-term revenue potential for Cray supercomputers to these three markets might be something like 25 percent, 40 percent, and 35 percent, respectively.

Supercomputer users shared several common characteristics. First were their complex computational needs for large-scale research and development projects, which exceeded the power and speed supplied by conventional systems. An example was the nuclear research carried out by Cray's first customer, the Los Alamos Scientific Laboratory. Research included weapons design, laser fusion and isotope separation, magnetic fusion energy research, and nuclear reactor safety.

A second shared characteristic was the need to simulate a physical phenomenon. A supercomputer could be used to develop models of weather conditions, to simulate an event such as a space flight or a nuclear explosion, or to trace seismic activity connected with the underground flow of gas, water, and oil. John Rollwagen described the resulting advantage:

> Before, when an aeronautical engineer designed a wing, he or she had to slice it up in cross sections because the computers could only do a two-dimensional analysis of the wing. This meant the engineer had to be a very good mathematician, because dividing a wing into cross sections is not intuitive; it's fairly abstract. Now, with supercomputers, it's possible to do a three-dimensional analysis which means you can fly the whole wing in the computer mathematically and obtain three-dimensional graphics. This output conforms to concepts that the engineer is comfortable with and permits a greater play of creative intuition.

A worldwide effort to research weather and climatic conditions, the Global Atmospheric Research Program, resulted in a highly visible application of supercomputers. Massive amounts of data were transmitted from observation stations around the world to the European Center for Medium-Range Weather Forecasts (ECMWF) in Reading, England, which used a Cray-1. The Cray allowed ECMWF to produce ten-day forecasts within a few hours, based on the assimilation of millions of data elements gathered worldwide. The constantly updated forecasts extended the usual five- to six-day predictions on which industries such as agriculture, air service, shipping, construction, and energy relied.

A third customer characteristic was the ability to afford a large outlay for computer services. A single Cray machine was priced from $4 million to $17 million and required annual operating expenditures of close to half a million dollars.

Selling a Cray computer to a new customer in an established market took about two years. The first year included initial customer contact; benchmarking, which involved stringent performance capability tests; customer visits to see the manufacturing process in Chippewa Falls; working out the method of financing; and the signing of a letter of intent. Installation and acceptance of the system occurred during the second year. The customer had to accept or reject the system within thirty days of delivery. Revenue was recognized on acceptance.

Opening a new market was a slow process. The first calls to the petroleum and automotive industries were made in 1976. The initial contracts were not signed until 1981 for petroleum and 1983 for automotive.

Cray had eight regional offices to sell and service its products worldwide: four in the United States and four overseas. A typical U.S. sales office employed thirty-five site engineers, fifteen site analysts, seven sales analysts, three salespeople, four administrators, and five regional managers, for a total of around seventy people. This team was responsible for selling and servicing the product within its designated region and was expected to show a profit after installing two systems. Marketing fees, paid by headquarters, and service fees from customers provided revenues for each office.

Product Offerings: Hardware

In early 1984, Cray Research offered two basic computer models (Cray 1/M and X-MP) and two new peripheral machines (a solid-state storage device and an input-output subsystem). For most applications, the Cray computers were basically add-on rather than stand-alone products. Cray could interface with a wide variety of computer systems, including IBM, Honeywell, DEC, Date General, CDC, and Univac. (A CDC supercomputer, in contrast, could interface only with a CDC system.) (See Exhibit 3 for a description of the Cray system configuration.)

The S series had been introduced in 1979 as an improvement to the Cray-1. The 1/S had a larger memory and greater input/output capabilities. Late in 1982, this model was supplanted by an M series, which was equal to the S units in speed and power but used metal oxide semiconductor technology in the circuit design, allowing significant cost reductions. The M was offered in late 1982 at prices ranging from $4 to $7 million, compared with the $8–$13 million range for the S.

In addition to introducing the lower-priced M model, Cray had lowered 1983 prices on the X-MP from $11–$14 million to $9–$11 million. These pricing

Exhibit 3 Cray system configuration and glossary of terms. *Source:* Casewriter's interviews.

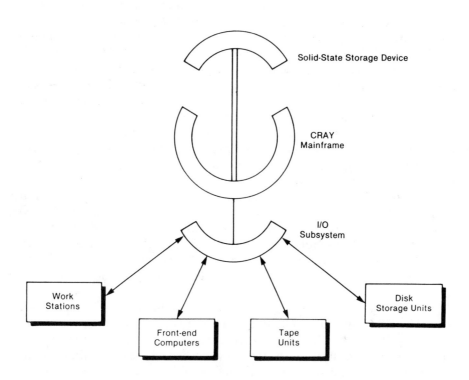

Solid-State Storage Device: Provides additional high-speed storage capacity like a disk file, but with performance improved by factors up to 100. Reduces input-output (I/O) time.

Mainframe: Contains the central processing unit (CPU), a core memory, and peripheral interfaces. The Cray-1 contained a single CPU; the X-MP had two in parallel.

I/O Subsystem: Acts as data concentrator for input to CPU and distributes output from CPU. Handles I/O for front-end computer systems and peripheral devices, such as disk and tape units. Contains multiple I/O processors and can contain additional buffer memory (secondary storage).

I/O Processors: Two required and two optional processors in the I/O subsystem designed to assist the CPU's I/O operations by "predigesting" data.

Work Stations: Locations of users' consoles which can be connected directly with the I/O subsystem or with the front-end computers.

Front-end Computers: Interface between mainframe and user. A Cray could interface with IBM, Honeywell, DEC, Data General, CDC, Systems Engineering Laboratories, and UNIVAC computers.

Tape Units: Mass storage device using magnetic tapes and requiring sequential access.

Disk Storage Units: Mass storage device using flexible (floppy) mylar disks to record information.

moves, which were attempts to broaden the market, initially disrupted sales by confusing customers. It took about eight months to reestablish orderly marketing. A year later, the *Wall Street Journal* reported that the strategy had successfully expanded Cray's market beyond its traditional base.

Each Cray computer was built to order, with a choice of memory sizes and number of input-output processors. It took two to three months to define the specific details of a system and to order and test the parts. Most components were designed specifically for Cray and were purchased from several outside sources. All hardware was then built, assembled, and tested in Chippewa Falls. Wiring and building modules took four months, and an additional four months were spent testing a machine on the floor.

About 80 percent of the manufacturing costs were for material and 20 percent for labor and overhead. Each machine was delivered with $250,000 worth of spare parts belonging to Cray. Maintenance was done on-site by Cray employees assigned to the unit on a full-time basis.

The Cray-2 and the next-generation X-MP were both scheduled for introduction in 1985. The new X-MP, using four CPUs in parallel, would be twice as powerful as the X-MP; the Cray-2 would, in turn, be four times as fast as the original X-MP, but would require new software. Because of these characteristics, the Cray-2 was expected to appeal to the classic customers (for whom raw power was critical), the next X-MP to the industrial customers (for whom proven software was important).

The X-MP and the Cray-2 were both breakthroughs in supercomputer technology. The X-MP was the first supercomputer capable of doing parallel processing. This design configuration represented a major achievement in supercomputer architecture. In contrast, the Cray-2 achieved increased speed through a new packaging of existing chip technology and the miniaturization of integrated circuit boards.

Seymour also had a project under way to increase the speed factor by using a new chip technology to replace silicon. His research team was experimenting with gallium arsenide, a substance whose electron mobility was four to five times that of silicon. He planned to use the new technology in the Cray-3.

Chen's and Seymour's differing approaches, parallelism and chip technology, were mirrored in industry research. There were close to fifty projects on parallelism in the United States in 1984, while chip technology was the prime focus of Japanese engineers.

Business Week reported that for 1982 Cray had been number one out of 776 companies in research and development (R&D) dollars per employee ($20,958) and number four in R&D as a percentage of sales (20.1 percent). The company's total R&D outlay for 1983 was more than $25 million.

Product Offerings: Software

Cray Research offered basic operating software with the hardware. This software included a Fortran compiler to gain access to the Cray internal logic and basic operating instructions for the Cray machines.

The proper amount of software programs and support had long been a point of contention in the Cray organization. Margaret Loftus, vice president in charge of software operations, explained her view of the problem: "This company was founded by hardware engineers whose main interest is in designing more powerful hardware. Software is a bother for them. What's changing, however, is the customer mix, with more and more users who need software to run their Crays. Before, we had difficulty selling software to the sophisticated scientific labs. Now, we have difficulty selling a Cray without software."

Loftus stayed in close touch with the regional and country managers to determine customer software needs. Major software requirements were the responsibility of the 260-person Mendota Heights, Minnesota, staff. On-site problems were handled by software field-support groups in each of the regional offices.

As the result of much lobbying, Loftus had succeeded in obtaining an increase in the software budget. The traditional 5 percent of operating profit would be expanded in 1984 to 7.5 percent, or about $15 million, for all software activities around the world. Loftus believed that software was, and would continue to be, the biggest constraint to the company's growth.

Financial Arrangements

With sales prices for Cray supercomputers in the millions, financing arrangements became an important element in the company's product offerings. Cray systems could be purchased or leased. Citicorp and U.S. Leasing handled all full-payout leases. These leases, amounting to $150 million in 1984, were not included in Cray's balance sheet. Cray financed directly all one-and three-year operating leases. Once installed, each system required a service contract amounting to about $25,000 to $50,000 per month.

John Carlson, Cray's chief financial officer, portrayed the company as having two businesses: manufacturing and financing. He ran the latter from Minneapolis, being involved in the financial arrangements for each machine.

Financing terms were arranged to result in a revenue breakdown of about 50 percent from sales, 40 percent from leases, and 10 percent from service fees. Carlson's aim was to have the cash flow from sales be used for production and that from leasing and service be sufficient to cover overhead costs, which comprised research and development, marketing, general and administrative, and customer engineering.

Research and development was the starting point for the budget, with first claim on 15 percent of total revenues. This amount was evenly divided, with the first 5 percent going to Seymour Cray, the second 5 percent going to other hardware development, and the third 5 percent going to software development. Expenditures for engineering and development and for marketing and administration in dollars and as a percentage of total revenues had been those figures shown in Table A.

For plant expansion and special projects, the company turned to external

Table A Expenditures in dollars and as a percentage of total revenues ($ thousands).

	1983		1982		1981		1980	
Engineering and development	$25,540	15.1%	$29,513	20.1%	$17,037	16.8%	$ 9,552	15.7%
Marketing and administration	$30,975	18.3%	$23,880	16.9%	$17,709	17.4%	$10,438	17.2%

financing. Because of Cray's needs for additional equity and debt financing, Carlson and Rollwagen devoted considerable attention to establishing and maintaining good relationships with the financial and investing communities. Assessing Cray's financial situation in 1984, Rollwagen concluded: "While raising money to finance growth is of essential importance to us, I do not see it as a constraint at this time. We believe that our debt/equity ratio could go as high as 50 percent. And our ability to raise equity funds is currently limited only by our own attitudes toward growth."

The Cultural Challenge

While rapid growth may have eased the financial officer's job, it resulted in serious problems for John Rollwagen and the other senior officers who were concerned with preserving the entrepreneurial spirit and small-company atmosphere they so valued. From the company's inception, management looked to the individual for accomplishing what had to be accomplished. Each person was allowed to define his or her own goals within the corporate mission. The growth in employee numbers and the geographic dispersion of activities, however, worked to undermine the Cray style of management.

In an attempt to capture the essence of what the Cray culture was all about, executives met in 1982 to write a one-page document called "The Cray Style" (see Exhibit 4). The in-house publication, *Interface*, introduced the statement as "an essay about our employees, our work relationships, our work environments, our attitude toward work and our belief in Cray products." It was described as an "attitude" to guide employees in everyday decisions and as a "style" that would evolve with the company.

Emphasizing Individual Initiative and Action

An organization could hardly have had a better role model for individual initiative and action than Seymour Cray. Seymour was his own man, whether designing new supercomputers or perfecting his skills as an accomplished windsurfer. This spirit was prized and practiced in management's ranks. Steve Chen's leadership in developing the X-MP and Margaret Loftus's efforts to multiply Cray's software capabilities were notable examples of individual

Exhibit 4 The Cray style. *Source:* 1982 annual report.

At Cray Research, we take what we do very seriously, but don't take ourselves very seriously.

We have a strong sense of quality—quality in our products and services, of course; but also quality in our working environment, in the people we work with, in the tools that we use to do our work, and in the components we choose to make what we make. Economy comes from high value, not from low cost. Aesthetics are part of quality. The effort to create quality extends to the communities in which we work and live as well.

The Cray approach is informal and nonbureaucratic. Verbal communication is key, not memos. "Call, don't write" is the watchword.

People are accessible at all levels.

People also have fun working at Cray Research. There is laughing in the halls, as well as serious discussion. More than anything else, the organization is personable and approachable, but still dedicated to getting the job done.

With informality, however, there is also a sense of confidence. Cray people feel like they are on the winning side. They feel successful, and they are. It is this sense of confidence that generates the attitude of "go ahead and try it, we'll make it work."

Also, there is a sense of pride at Cray. Professionalism is important. People are treated like and act like professionals. Cray people trust each other to do their jobs well and with the highest ethical standards. They take what they **do** very seriously. But Cray people are professional without being stuffy. They take a straightforward, even simple, approach. They don't take **themselves** too seriously.

Because the individual is key at Cray, there is a real diversity in the view of what Cray Research really is. In fact, Cray Research is many things to many people. The consistency comes in providing those diverse people with the opportunity to fulfill themselves and experience achievement. The creativity, then, that emerges from the company comes from the many ideas of the individuals who are here. And that is the real strength of Cray Research.

---

achievement, as was the company's reliance on one person to open its first commercial market. As President Rollwagen described it: "When we started to sell to the petroleum companies, just one man, George Stevenson, took on the industry. This idea of one man taking on a new industry is an attitude that goes through the company."

Management's preference for working in small groups where a personal touch could be maintained was borne out in the choice of locations for its principal organizational units. Headquarters was moved twenty miles from Mendota Heights to downtown Minneapolis in 1982, leaving the suburban facility to concentrate on software engineering and sales. In Chippewa Falls, Wisconsin, 120 miles from Minneapolis, research was carried out by several teams, and the manufacturing and engineering staffs worked in discrete groups.

A decision in 1982 to make profit centers of the four domestic regional sales offices represented another attempt to keep decision units small. This change moved operating responsibility from headquarters to the field sites, as had been done years earlier for the overseas offices.

A decision to create a new subsidiary was seen by John Rollwagen as another important way for Cray Research to encourage and reward individual initiative and action.

Circuit Tools, Inc.

In October 1983 Cray's board of directors voted to spin off a new, majority-owned subsidiary in a related field. The new venture was a vehicle for the firm to achieve growth while maintaining its focus on supercomputer hardware.

The new company, Circuit Tools, Inc. (CTI), was the result of a project conceived by John May, who had worked in the software-applications group at Mendota Heights. In an effort to tap the market potential in the semiconductor manufacturing industry, he set out to adapt for use on the Cray-1 a widely employed program called SPICE, which had been developed at the University of California, Berkeley, to verify the operational effectiveness of newly designed integrated circuits. A year's effort in rewriting the software resulted in a new program, C-SPICE (the "C" referring to Cray), which could take advantage of the supercomputer's speed.

Since none of the integrated circuit manufacturers owned Cray hardware, May came up with the idea of offering his applications software on a commercial time-sharing basis. He took his idea to Cray's development committee, which decided that C-SPICE fell outside the company's principal direction for software business.

May then considered marketing the product on his own and wrote a business plan. Subsequently, the development committee suggested that he submit a proposal. After several discussions, May's plans were approved. According to the final arrangements, Cray would invest about $1.5 million for 80 percent of the new company's shares. May was to receive 10 percent of the shares, and the remaining 10 percent would be available for distribution to his managers. "I had originally envisaged my own company to be much smaller than CTI is turning out to be," May said, "but Cray kept pushing me to think it out. In time I began to see more possibilities."

CTI was considered a prototype for other spin-off ventures that would motivate entrepreneurial efforts in Cray. If CTI succeeded, John May, who was in his mid-30s, could earn a great deal of money. If not, he could return to Cray.

Personal Incentives

Although the CTI arrangement might serve as a powerful incentive in special cases, it could not substitute for—nor was it designed to compete with—the more traditional incentives for Cray personnel. Financial compensation, exciting assignments, and an attractive work environment were seen by management as key considerations in attracting and keeping the talented people on whom Cray Research so depended.

According to John Rollwagen, the appeal of Cray's compensation scheme rested on two features. First, the company paid well by industry standards. In addition to high base-compensation levels, it offered a generous profit-sharing plan. Ten percent of pretax profits were distributed to all Cray employees, allocated in proportion to salary. In 1983, this bonus amounted to about 10 percent of an individual's base salary. As a special incentive, 8 to 10 percent of all Cray personnel were included in a leadership category of profit-sharing. This group was awarded two and one half times the general profit-sharing bonus. Company officers were eligible for a cash bonus of 40 percent of base salary, executive officers 55 percent, and the CEO 65 percent. These higher awards, however, were part of the target total-compensation package for managers, whereas the bonus awards for lower-level employees were incremental to their target salaries. For example, John Rollwagen's total compensation was decided by the board through the common practice of using as a reference the compensation received by CEOs of comparable companies. The bonus (at-risk) compensation was a component of this figure. Stock options were also employed, but had become an increasingly less important incentive over time.

The second important feature of Cray's compensation system was the "dual ladder" concept. Under this policy, a person devoted to technology could receive compensation comparable to someone in management. For example, Steve Chen's compensation in 1984 was close to the level for an executive vice-president.

Although management recognized compensation as an important motivational device, it considered other elements as even more powerful inducements to personal commitment. John Rollwagen explained:

> Association with Seymour Cray and with the world's most powerful computer provides a great deal of inspiration in our ranks. Maybe 90 percent of our employees have never met Seymour, but everyone knows Seymour stories. There's the one about Seymour building a new sailboat each spring, sailing it over the summer, and then burning it at the end of the season so that he wouldn't be bound by that year's mistakes when he sets about designing a more perfect craft for the following year. That's also the way Seymour approaches computer design. It says a great deal about innovation. Some of the Seymour stories probably aren't exactly true, but I wouldn't deny them for the world.
>
> In my judgment, the most powerful incentive we provide our people is recognition. Individuals are given responsibility, and they are given credit. We talk more about people than we do about functions. Individual people are the key to our success, and we try to make that clear.

The Technological Challenge

During the early years of the emerging supercomputer industry, Cray had little competition in the narrowly focused market. CDC had turned its attention elsewhere, and no one else had more than a passing interest in this esoteric extreme of the computer business. By the 1980s, however, commercial interest in supercomputers had begun to pick up. Technological advances in hardware and componentry had spurred industry growth. As of early 1984, Cray had supplied sixty supercomputers, Control Data, twenty-one, and Denelcor (largely U.S. government funded), four. So far, Cray had led the race, but competitors were beginning to snap at its heels.

The Race for Technological Supremacy

The race for technological supremacy implied more than commercial competition. As noted in *Fortune*, March 5, 1984, "With the fortunes of entire nations, not just companies, at risk, the race to dominate these 'information technologies' has become an international competition in which governments encourage and subsidize the participants." Salient among the national efforts were the $100 million supercomputer and $500 million artificial-intelligence projects in Japan and the Pentagon's corresponding request for $1 billion to counter the Japanese on both fronts.

The stakes and status of the contest were spelled out by a panel of fifteen U.S. scientists who returned from a trip to the Far East with the conclusion that "U.S. leadership in supercomputing is crucial for the advancement of science and technology and, therefore, for economic and national security. . . . [U]nder current conditions there is little likelihood that the United States will lead in the development and application of this new generation of machines."[2]

One unprecedented move in the U.S. private-sector technology race was the consolidation of research and development talent into the nonprofit Microelectronic and Computer Technology Corporation (MCC), organized in 1982 by CDC Chairman William Norris to develop state-of-the-art computer technology. MCC, which was based in Austin, Texas, had a staff drawn from eleven companies in 1983, with an annual budget of $75 million. Any company that wished to join this consortium would donate scientists and researchers for a period of up to four years and would fund research. In return, member companies would have the right to use the results. The consortium itself would not put out a product, but would own licenses and patents exclusively for three years. Individual member companies would manufacture and market the technological advances.

Newsweek called MCC a "bold departure from the way research is usually done" and brought up the issue of antitrust laws. The possibility of antitrust action had deterred IBM from joining. Cray, Texas Instruments, Intel, and several other companies also decided not to join. Cray's President Rollwagen said, "It really could be a yeasty place to work, but how the technology gets transferred back to the member companies is a mystery to me. There'll be a technological exchange—it may be positive for the country, but it probably won't be for the individual companies. Our system is based on individuality, not a sense of community as in Japan."

Norris's renewed interest in supercomputing was possibly the spur for CDC to spin off its supercomputer operations into a separate, publicly held subsidiary, ETA Systems, Inc. CDC would attempt to rise $100 million through public

2. *Science Digest*, September 1983, p. 49.

or private stock offerings, reducing its ownership to no more than 40 percent. The new firm would develop a 10-billion-calculations-per-second (10 gigaflop) computer for delivery by the end of 1986. "Control Data made the move because small, entrepreneurial companies can design, manufacture, and market such computers better than large companies," stated a company spokesman.

In response to CDC's announced plans, a manager at NEC, a Japanese computer company, was quoted in the October 17, 1983, issue of *Business Week* as saying, "We have the semiconductor technology to compete. We don't think Cray and Control Data have the capability to keep up. That's what success depends on and all the Japanese companies have it." A U.S. supercomputer authority in turn remarked, "The Japanese emphasis appears to be on device technology rather than on improved computer architectures. While faster components and innovative ways of arranging them are both necessary to push supercomputers to greater speeds, new architectures will likely be more important than faster devices. If the Japanese Superspeed Project doesn't exploit new architectures, it may not be much of a competitive factor."

Recent and impending Japanese supercomputer offerings were described in *High Technology* in May 1984:

> While Japan pursues its long-term development projects, three Japanese companies are making waves with several existing or soon-to-exist super-computers. Hitachi has already delivered its 630 megaflop (million-floating-point-operations-per-second) computer. . . . The forthcoming Fujitsu VP-200 will operate at 500 megaflops. Finally, NEC plans 1985 shipments of its SX-1, rated at 570 megaflops and its SX-2, rated at a staggering 1.3 gigaflops (billion floating-point operations per second).

Figure C shows the projected progress of supercomputer peak performance through 1992. The above article included the following caution about comparing supercomputer speeds:

> "The greatest threat is to our brochuremanship," says ETA's Lincoln, referring to the high peak performances claimed for the Japanese machines. . . . Thus, until the Japanese computers are tested with some real applications, it's difficult to evaluate their relative power.[3]

The competition that worried Cray corporate planner Peter Gregory was not the Japanese, MCC, or CDC; it was IBM. Gregory predicted IBM would introduce a machine in 1984 that would not only compute on the basis of perfor-

---

3. The variation between peak rating and actual performance resulted from a crucial division of labor between scalar and vector processing. A supercomputer with a fast vector mode but slow scalar mode would process some programs more slowly than a supercomputer having a lower peak (vector) rating but a fast scalar capability. It was for this reason that a Cray-1 offering a 250-megaflop peak rating and scaler processing at 80 MIPS, could outperform for many applications a Cyber 205 with a 400-megaflop peak rating and scalar processing at 50 MIPS. Other parameters determining a particular machine's ability to execute a particular program rapidly included component switching speeds, machine cycle times, memory size, compiler efficiency, pipelining capability (having repetitive sequential steps performed simultaneously), and peripheral-device capabilities. In effect, maximum machine speeds could be compared only for specific applications, and even then often only on the basis of actual trial runs.

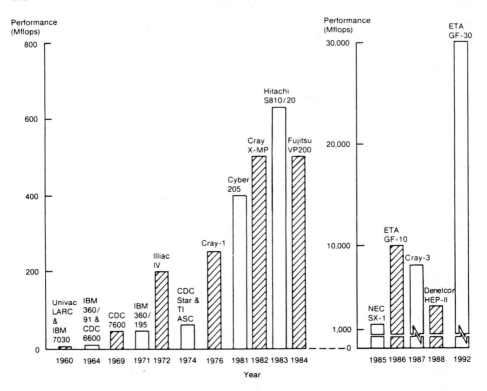

Figure C   Competing supercomputers' peak performance. This chart approximates each machine's theoretical peak mega-flop (million floating-point operations per second) rating, which is rarely attained in actual operations. For example, the 64-processor Illiac IV never came close to its theoretical peak performance. *Source: High Technology,* May 1984.

mance, but would appeal to organizations already committed to IBM systems.

Even Seymour voiced concern over the possibility that Cray might lose its lead in the supercomputer industry. In looking back at the company's impressive success record, he reflected: "We were fortunate in not having had any major things go wrong. I don't think we've been tried yet." To which John Rollwagen responded: "It is my job to make sure that nothing goes wrong."

A Strategic and Organizational Challenge

On May 14, 1984, members of Cray's top management attended a presentation on the company's performance in the petroleum industry that underscored an issue of great concern to them: Should the company change its strategic direction and emphasis?[4] If so, how far, how fast, and in what way? The report

4. The presentation concluded a field study by the following second-year Harvard MBA students: G. Eastman, D. Harding, K. Hollen, S. Mickel, M. Newlin, and S. Nyquist. Quoted material in this section was taken from an accompanying written report.

focused on actions Cray might have to take to protect and improve its enviable market position in light of some customer dissatisfaction and growing competitive threats.

As the report acknowledged, Cray had been remarkably successful in developing the petroleum market, selling ten machines to eight oil companies in just three years. This success was attributed to the company's ability to offer an "excellent product to an industry thirsty for computational power," essentially unencumbered by any competition.

The report went on to characterize the petroleum market by first comparing it with Cray's original customers:

> Cray has traditionally sold to government users who have purchased primarily on performance. They have demanded very little in the way of software support, IBM compatibility or hardware peripherals. They buy on the basis of speed.
>
> The petroleum companies, on the other hand, have huge existing investments in software and in IBM hardware. While they are interested in speed, they do not want speed at the expense of incompatibility. Petroleum companies are looking for trouble-free solutions to complex scientific problems.
>
> In the early 1980s, oil companies were swimming in cash and searching for attractive investments. Exploration production costs had been increasing rapidly, and reservoirs of new oil discoveries were declining in size compared to previous years. As a result, geologists, geophysicists, and reservoir engineers were encouraged to develop more sophisticated analytical techniques to evaluate oil investment projects. These techniques demand significant computational power to obtain reasonable accuracy. As a result, technically advanced reservoir engineers and state of the art geophysicists turned to the supercomputer industry to find the needed computational power. Although Cray's software support was limited, oil companies were able to solve significant engineering problems with the Cray. Oil companies regarded the Cray as a small exploration expense that paid off handsomely.
>
> Reservoir engineering demand is increasing 20–30 percent per year and seismic processing demand is increasing 30–50 percent per year by one customer's conservative estimates. Thus, the oil industry's thirst for computational power is large and growing.

Customer interviews led to the following findings on Cray's hardware, software, and responsiveness:

> We have found that Cray has generally met customers' price and performance expectations for hardware. However, customers believe Cray should expand memory capacity and improve networking capability to satisfy users in the petroleum industry. Finally, the Cray hardware is considered reliable, but not as good as IBM, which sets the standard for most users in petroleum industry data processing shops.
>
> Most Cray customers feel "software" was the weakest aspect of an otherwise highly attractive product. They are dissatisfied with the current software offerings as well as associated support.

Specifically, the software was criticized as not user-friendly, not well documented, and not designed for petroleum applications. The basis of comparison was IBM, since it set the standard for most users in the petroleum industry. According to several customers, the Cray software people were "too theoretical as a result of their experience with government labs and would have to become more practical if they are to meet petroleum customer needs."

This last remark touched on a broader concern about the extent to which Cray was really committed to serving the petroleum industry. The following customers' comments on this issue were reported:

- Cray is not as devoted as IBM to understanding the petroleum industry.
- There is no strategic commitment to the exploration industry from the top of Cray.
- We are looking for a supercomputer manufacturer to *serve* the oil industry.

The report went on to describe Cray's vulnerability and the dilemma management faced:

> Although switching costs are high (perhaps over $2 million to redevelop software for a new system), they do not represent an insurmountable barrier to entry given machine costs of $10 million or more. Thus, we see an opportunity for a competitive entry due to customer ambivalence or even dissatisfaction with Cray's software offerings. At the same time, there is an opportunity for Cray to respond to its customers' needs more aggressively and to build these entry barriers for itself.
>
> The nature of Cray's clientele is changing. More of Cray's sales will be to repeat customers and the management organization needed to maintain the petroleum region is growing. Furthermore, competitors are about to enter the market. This totals to a big demand for marketing dollars for the petroleum region.
>
> At the same time the company is facing the prospect of serious technological challenge to its position as maker of the world's fastest computers. The decision thus becomes how Cray will divide its resources (money, management, software, peripherals, manufacturing, etc.) in this new environment. If Cray continues to be a technology company, a maker of high speed boxes, that's fine, but the company may have to accept a slow-down in exploiting the commercial sector. If Cray wants to be more marketing driven, that's fine, too, but there probably will be technological sacrifices or delays that must be dealt with. Additionally, there will be an element of culture shock as the company moves away from being technology driven and toward being marketing driven.
>
> Can Cray be both technologically driven and marketing driven? Maybe, but management is going to have to clearly think through how it will balance the competing demands for resources.

Although the specific recommendations of the study dealt with changes within the existing Cray structure, the idea of creating an organizational unit with business reponsibility for the petroleum industry was raised for consideration. The students recognized that such a move was likely to exacerbate the problems management was facing in trying to maintain a cohesive, entrepreneurial company ambience. Although some differences might arise over future hardware requirements, the major potential source of conflict would be software development.

Competition for resources would arise between the applications-oriented software needs of the petroleum industry and the operating system-oriented software needs for Cray's new machines. This competition, in turn, would further complicate the existing software-hardware battle for funds.

Cray Research:
Preparing for the 1990s

Cray Research, Inc. said it plans to spin off the supercomputer design efforts of its founder and industry guru, Seymour Cray, as a separate company.

Wall Street Journal, May 16, 1989

This startling announcement brought to a head management's response to a number of mounting problems and changing conditions having to do with the slowing down of sales and profit growth, rising research and development costs, a changing competitive situation, and a growing disparity between the sizable scale and broad variety of operations and commitments that the company had to support and Seymour Cray's narrowly focused interest in using gallium arsenide integrated circuits to advance supercomputer hardware technology. In his comments at the annual stockholder's meeting on May 16, 1989, John Rollwagen, chairman and chief executive officer of Cray Research, explained these reasons and concluded, "So the action we are taking is to create two supercomputer companies in recognition of what is really going on inside Cray Research. We think this will provide benefits for everyone involved. In fact . . . in my way of thinking at least, all I could find was winners."

Winners or not, Rollwagen and Marcelo Gumucio, appointed president and chief operating officer of Cray Research in November 1988, faced a variety of issues in preparing to take the world's leading supercomputer manufacturing company into the 1990s. The proposed spin-off of Cray Computer (the provisional name for the new company) no doubt changed their situation and would alter their thinking. What would not change was their desire to recapture the rapid growth rate that in earlier years had made Cray Research a glamour stock for the investing community.

The Era of Rapid Growth

Founded by Seymour Cray in 1972 "to design and build a larger, more powerful computer than anyone now has," Cray Research installed its first supercomputer in 1976, showed its first profit in 1977, and moved into an era of rapid growth in 1978 as the Cray-1, five times faster than its only rival (the CDC 7600, which had also been designed by Seymour Cray), captured the acclaim of the scientific community. By 1981, Cray had revenues in excess of $100 million, earned more than $1 per share, employed more than 1,000 people, and had installed thirty-five systems. (The accelerating growth of sales, profits, employees, and installations is shown in Exhibit 1.)

Nineteen eighty-one was also the year when Seymour Cray moved to greater independence in his relationship with Cray Research. An agreement was fashioned by which the company would have commercial rights to Seymour's designs in return for development funding. At the end of that year, Seymour announced his plans for developing the Cray-2, a new machine that would be six to ten times more powerful than the Cray-1. This gain in speed would be attributable largely to making the central processing unit one-tenth its previous size.

In 1983, before the Cray-2 design had been completed, the X-MP, with a capability of operating at three to five times the speed of existing Cray models, was introduced. For the first time in more than twenty years, the world's fastest computer was credited to someone other than Seymour Cray. Steve Chen, vice president of product development, headed the technical team that had succeeded in multiplying performance by means of parallel processing (in contrast to Seymour Cray's emphasis on miniaturization). The X-MP synchronized two Cray-1 processors to solve simultaneously different parts of a complex problem.[1]

Product introductions and market development continued to fuel growth through the 1980s. The X-MP in 1982, followed by the Cray-2 in 1985 and the Y-MP in 1988, along with their derivative systems, spurred new and replacement sales. (See Exhibit 2 for a history of the principal Cray Research supercomputer systems.) Commercial applications expanded as the aerospace and automotive industries joined oil exploration in adopting supercomputers for technical analysis.

Aerospace. When Cray Research first sold a supercomputer system to an aerospace customer in 1980, the scientists saw it only as a tool that would allow them to move one step closer to the goal of calculating air flows around complex aerospace designs. As the accuracy of aerodynamic models improved, computational fluid dynamics became a leading experimental design tool. The supercomputer was soon applied to structural analysis and by 1989 was emerging as an integrated element in operational aerospace systems with prospects for next-generation satellite ground telemetry processing and complex real-time flight simulation. One newsworthy offshoot of the work in aerospace computational analysis was the use of an X-MP to design the hull of Stars & Stripes '87, the U.S. twelve-meter yacht that regained the America's Cup from Australia.

---

1. For more information about the company's early history, see, "Cray Research, Inc.," Harvard Business School Case number 385–011, 1984.

Exhibit 1 Financial and general data summary, 1978–1988 ($ millions).

	1978	1979	1980	1981	1982	1983	1984	1985	1986	1987	1988
Revenue											
Sales	$ 8.4	$26.5	$37.6	$ 65.2	$ 91.5	$125.0	$160.4	$227.5	$457.5	$515.8	$557.3
Leased systems	7.3	12.5	17.6	27.6	35.6	26.2	37.8	55.1	68.0	72.5	75.6
Service fees	1.5	3.7	5.5	8.8	14.0	18.5	30.6	47.6	71.2	99.0	123.4
Total revenues	17.2	42.7	60.7	101.6	141.1	169.7	228.8	380.2	596.7	687.3	756.3
Operating Costs											
Cost of revenue	7.0	15.3	22.2	36.5	55.5	69.8	82.0	133.3	202.7	245.4	289.1
Engineering and development	2.5	6.4	9.6	17.0	29.5	25.5	37.5	49.2	87.7	108.8	117.8
Marketing, G&A	2.7	6.0	10.4	17.7	23.9	31.0	45.1	65.3	89.7	111.9	131.5
Total operating costs	12.2	27.7	42.2	71.2	108.9	126.3	114.6	247.8	380.1	466.1	538.4
Operating income	5.0	15.0	18.6	30.5	32.3	43.4	64.1	132.4	216.6	221.2	218.0
Net earnings	3.5	7.8	10.9	18.2	19.0	26.1	45.4	75.6	124.8	147.1	156.6
Working capital	7.5	13.9	53.5	61.9	98.6	129.4	116.9	137.9	205.7	301.9	339.0
Long-term debt	4.7	3.0	7.9	12.4	33.7	37.6	15.6	11.8	122.6	108.7	109.9
Stockholders' equity	20.6	28.6	75.8	95.0	144.6	172.4	220.5	304.9	441.9	610.6	676.8
Return on stockholders' average equity (%)	19.9%	31.7%	25.6%	22.0%	18.6%	17.0%	23.6%	28.2%	33.0%	27.6%	23.9%
Number of installed systems	8	13	22	35	50	65	88	115	148	189	240
Number of employees (year end)	321	524	761	1,079	1,352	1,551	2,203	3,180	3,999	4,308	5,237
Stock price											
High	11.0	16.88	48.50	48.38	45.75	57.12	59.38	70.25	98.50	134.75	87.50
Low	3.50	7.75	12.75	28.00	20.00	36.38	38.50	25.12	59.88	54.25	53.33

Exhibit 2   History of principal Cray Research supercomputer systems.

System	Year Introduced	Number of Processors	Performance v. Cray-1	Technological Distinctiveness (When Introduced)
Cray-1	1976	1	1	Vector processing
Cray 1/S	1979	1	1	Increased memory and input/output capabilities
Cray 1/M	1982	1	1	Metal oxide semiconductor (MOS) technology
X-MP/2	1982	2	3–4	Two CPU parallel processing
X-MP/4	1984	4	6–10	Four CPU parallel processing
Cray-2	1985	4	6–12	Three-dimensional wiring, submergent cooling system
Y-MP	1988	8	30	2500-gate chip, eight CPU parallel processing
MP	Cancelled	64	100E	Parallel processing, fiber optics, laser technology
C-90	1991E	16	100E	10,000-gate chip, 16 CPU parallel processing
Cray-3*	1990	16	100E	Gallium-arsenide chip
Cray-4*	?	64	1000E	Refinements in Ga-As technology
FAST†	1995E	64	≥1000E	40,000-gate chip, 64 CPU parallel processing

*Transferred to Cray Computer

†Future Architecture Systems Technology

E = Estimated/Projected

Automotive. Since 1984, Cray systems had become important design tools for automotive companies around the world, including BMW, Chrysler, Daimler-Benz, Opel, Fiat, Ford, General Motors, Honda, Nissan, Peugot, Toyota, and Volkswagen. The Winter 1989 issue of *Cray Channels*, a quarterly publication intended for users of Cray computer systems and others interested in the company and its products, gave some idea of the range of applications in an edition devoted to the automotive field. The articles covered recent developments such as the emergence of side-impact simulation as an extension of the widely used front-impact crashworthiness simulation (which itself had only emerged in 1986), simulations in acoustics and vibrations to predict the comfort of car passengers, combustion chamber and inlet port modeling to yield efficient engine design, and tire design (Michelin). A November 1988 article in *Automation Engineering* extolled the virtues of the supercomputer with the glowing reference, "Indeed, researchers for one automaker recently suggested that the supercomputer is likely to revolutionize the automobile industry as much as the electron microscope did the fields of biology and medicine."

Table 1 Percent annual growth.

Year	Revenue	Net Earnings
1979	149	132
1980	42	39
1981	67	67
1982	39	5
1983	20	37
1984	35	74
1985	66	67
1986	57	15
1987	15	18
1988	10	6

A Slowdown in Growth

The heady growth of the 1980s decelerated sharply in 1987 and continued to lessen in 1988 (see Table 1). Early forecasts for 1989 indicated a continuation of the 1988 financial performance levels. The reasons for the slowdown included an approaching saturation of the markets for the more powerful (and higher margin) systems,[2] the increasing difficulty of maintaining a high-percentage growth rate for an ever-larger sales base, a less-certain world economy, and increased competition.

The slowdown in growth was to influence Cray Research in a number of profound ways. While not the only cause, nor even necessarily the principal cause, the consequent constraint on financial resources was a factor in a number of important decisions affecting the technological direction of the company and its leadership.

The MP Project Decision

On September 3, 1987, under a heading "Cray Research Cancels a Supercomputer Plan and Loses a Superstar," the *Wall Street Journal* disclosed the company's decision "cancelling its most advanced supercomputer project, an effort to create an exotic computer 100 times faster and more powerful than anything in existence," and the decision of the project leader, Steven Chen, to leave the firm. The forty-three-year-old Chen, who was credited with the design of the highly successful X-MP line and with the launch of the even more promising Y-MP system, had been widely viewed as the likely successor to sixty-one-year-old Seymour Cray.

This startling turn of events, following on earlier announcements about

2. Customers for the most powerful systems continued to trade up with each new generation. Market saturation, in this setting, reflected the increased percentage of trade-ins for established customers (reducing net margins) and the lower number of new sites.

projections of slower sales growth, caused Cray Research's share price to drop over the ensuing three weeks from $113 to $89.25—a loss of approximately $500 million in total market valuation—before rebounding to $94. While many specific concerns about technology and leadership were reported to explain the lowering of investors' confidence, the overriding reason might well have been that this setback came as the first major rent in the otherwise seamless public record of success and well-being that Cray Research had projected since its founding sixteen years earlier.

The MP project had been launched in 1985 to follow the Y-MP system, then under development and scheduled for delivery in 1988. Chen, who had been the project team leader for the X-MP and its successor Y-MP, was eager to push forward with new technology while the Y-MP development was carried to completion. In line with the company's tradition of encouraging individual initiative and innovation and in recognition of Chen's demonstrated design capability, senior management authorized the new undertaking. With formation of the MP project, Chen was promoted to senior vice president and reported directly to Rollwagen.

The original concept for the MP was to develop a 64-processor machine capable of running at one nanosecond clockspeed (compared to the projected clockspeed of two nanoseconds for the Cray-3).[3] The new system, with a budgeted development cost of $50 million, was to be introduced in 1991. In the fall of 1986, Chen requested a budget increase to $68 million and a year's delay in the target completion date. By early 1987, these projections had slipped further to $100 million and an additional year or so.

Faced with slower revenue growth and the need to reduce planned spending, senior management, after conducting an in depth review of the MP project, decided to terminate the effort. According to news accounts, Cray management judged the project as overambitious and out of control. The *Financial Times* on September 15, 1987, reported the principal concerns to be with Chen's determination to develop costly technologies in circuit integration and to use light and laser transmission for internal communication within the computer. In explaining the cancellation, Rollwagen concluded, "The project needs more money and involved more risk than the company is prepared to support."

Chen's departure created turmoil throughout the Cray organization. Almost fifty of the 204-member MP team left the company. Even more traumatic, according to Les Davis, executive vice president in charge of manufacturing and engineering, was the disorienting effect on the remaining members of the project and the unfavorable impact of the MP cancellation on the morale of the entire technical staff. He noted, "Many of our people felt that our company had let them down. We really had not thought through how to handle this situation and probably caused some unnecessary problems for ourselves."

Concerned with the growing perception that Cray Research might have abandoned its technological thrust in parallel processing with the departure of

---

3. A nanosecond is one billionth of a second. Light travels approximately one foot in that time. Clockspeed (or clock cycle) is a measure of the rate at which a computer executes an operation.

Chen,[4] Rollwagen disclosed on September 24, 1987, that the company had formed a new team early in the year to build a follow-up system to the Y-MP, long before top management had publicly acknowledged the discontinuation of the MP effort. The team's project, later to be known as C-90, would extend Cray's parallel processor architecture and was expected to make its debut in the early 1990s.

Under the terms of his separation arrangement with Cray Research, Chen had personal, nonexclusive licenses to technical developments that he had achieved in the company, so long as the work was not conducted in the employ of another firm. On December 22, 1987, IBM announced plans to forge an alliance with Chen's new company, Supercomputer Systems, Inc. IBM agreed to provide SSI with an undisclosed amount of funding[5] and access to its high-end technology in return for a nonexclusive right to market the resulting supercomputer. The unusual nature of this arrangement was noted by Carl Conti, IBM vice president and group executive of the information systems and storage group, as reported in the *Star Tribune* of Minneapolis on December 23, 1988: "This is probably different than anything we have done in the past . . . But Chen is a uniquely talented individual. . . . I think it maximizes our chances of success. I think we maximize Steve's chances of success as well."

On January 12, 1988, the *Wall Street Journal* reported Chen to be seeking additional support, "As Mr. Chen sees it, the new machine is so vital that besides his ballyhooed partnership with International Business Machines Corporation, he plans to seek other partners, including government, commercial users, and very likely more high-technology companies." He was said to be determined to construct within four years a supercomputer at least 100 times faster than anything in existence.

With almost six months perspective, *Fortune* softened the assessment of Chen's departure as a serious loss for Cray Research with the observation, "The company, however, is by no means crippled by Chen's defection. Says Jeffrey Canin, senior technology analyst at the Hambrecht and Quist brokerage firm in San Francisco: 'Cray is very, very deep in engineering and technology.' "[6] The reaction of many Cray managers to Chen's departure was reflected in the following remarks given in April 1989 by Greg Barnum, the director for finance and administration at the Colorado Springs site: "Chen's leaving was really no big deal. He was good, but not so good as we had made him out to be. He was given credit for what Les Davis and others did. Steve Chen

4. Viewed broadly, the work of Seymour Cray and that of Steven Chen were more closely related than commonly thought. Two divergent philosophies were shaping the development of parallel hardware architecture. One emphasized the sheer number of processors in a system and their interconnection. Many hundreds or thousands of relatively slow processors were linked in so-called "massively parallel processors." The other emphasized the power of individual processors primarily and the application of parallel processing secondarily (fewer units were connected in parallel). Both Cray and Chen labored in the second camp: the former placing more emphasis on improving processor power, the latter on improving parallel interconnections.

5. The January 7, 1988, edition of *Electronics* reported that an industry analyst "guesses that IBM funding will initially come to more than $20 million over two years."

6. Kenneth Labich, "The Shootout in Supercomputers," *Fortune*, February 29, 1988.

was billed as another Seymour Cray to symbolize to outsiders the company's depth and continuity of supercomputer technology leadership. That tactic turned out to be a big mistake."

The Ascendency of Software

Software, grudgingly tolerated as a necessary evil in the company's earliest days, had already become a major operation for Cray Research by the early 1980s. Its importance continued to grow as the company's systems moved increasingly into the oil, automotive, and aerospace industries. As prospects for future growth began to weaken, management recognized as increasingly compelling the need to develop new industrial applications for the established customer base and to open new industrial markets. The hardware existed or, as in the case of the Y-MP, was coming on stream. Software would be the constraining element.

The history of UNICOS provided one clear indication of the resulting speed-up in software development. To answer the need for an efficient, high-performance operating system that could be integrated into diverse computing environments, Cray Research began in 1982 to couple its proprietary Cray Operating System (COS) with the AT&T UNIX operating system that promised to become a standard for the scientific community. The resulting UNICOS 1.0 operating system was introduced in early 1985. Work to upgrade UNICOS continued, and a more powerful and versatile UNICOS 2.0 was announced in the spring of 1987. By the end of that year came an improved 3.0 version, some eight months later the 4.0, and in May 1989 the 5.0, said to provide "improved performance and functionality over previous releases."

To provide leadership for the expanding software operations, Robert Ewald was named vice president for software development in the fall of 1987. Ewald had joined Cray Research in 1984 (and was soon appointed vice president of commercial marketing) after seven years in computing and communications at the Los Alamos National Laboratory, one of Cray's largest and oldest customers. In November 1988, he was elevated to executive vice president, software, and was also made a member (along with Seymour Cray, Les Davis, and John Rollwagen as chairman) of the Technical Council. This newly created high-level body was responsible for determining the strategic technical direction for Cray Research.

Ewald gave the following account of the evolution that was taking place in supercomputer software:

> Cray initially employed the supercomputer for batch processing purposes. As a result, commercial customers originally viewed supercomputers as little more than specialized superchargers for their mainframe system. In contrast, the U.S. labs were using the supercomputer in an interactive mode for problem solving. It was not until the introduction of UNICOS for use with the Cray-2 that the company began to provide opportunities for interactive industrial applications. The evolution from batch processing to inter-

active operations is now extending to real-time applications. Each of these modes of operations in turn requires more complex software.

Another important dimension in software's evolution is its ability to make available to users the inherent power of the hardware architecture. In 1978, software was developed to help the user to employ the vector processing capability of the Cray 1. As multiple processor supercomputer systems were employed, users had to figure out how to split up the analysis. In 1988, Cray Research brought out an autotasking program that recognized some of the parallel parts of a problem and automatically spread them out for computation on up to sixteen processors.

He also described his view about the future use of supercomputers in the scientific and engineering field:

Engineers and scientists are going beyond traditional numerical analysis to pattern recognition and more symbolic workings of a problem. The implications for software are important. Numerical analysis depends on FORTRAN and C programs. For new expert systems, software has to incorporate artificial intelligence concepts and to incorporate more complex languages such as LISP. This development is likely to have repercussions on hardware as well. If LISP becomes the dominant language, then the machines will have to be designed to handle smaller chunks of data.

The increasing sophistication of workstations is another driving force for future software development. The engineer or scientist typically favors the use of a desktop workstation because of its advantages with respect to availability, control, and cost. The aim for Cray is to become an extension to a workstation, a window on its screen, so as to be readily accessible for the user at any time.

In 1989, the software division employed 500 people, including 350 professionals. Their major responsibilities were to develop operating-systems software, the compiler (translating FORTRAN into assembly language), a library of programs to facilitate user interface with the Cray, and increasingly, software connected with networking. About forty-five additional software people were assigned to marketing to work with third-party application software. One-half of Cray Research's total R&D budget was devoted to software. A new software and marketing center was under construction in Mendota Heights. The attractive, campuslike setting, scheduled to open in 1990, would include separate but interconnected buildings for software, marketing, training, technical support, and a computer center. The company's present computer center employed three X-MPs, a Cray-2, and a Y-MP, as well as three other Cray machines for software-use purposes.

Seymour Decamps

In March 1988, Cray Research announced that Seymour Cray would move the Cray-3 operations from Chippewa Falls, Wisconsin, to Colorado Springs, Colorado. The company had purchased an attractive manufacturing facility that was to be adapted for volume production of the new system. Rollwagen later described the events leading up to this surprising move:

Around January 1988, Seymour told me that things were not working out at Chippewa Falls and that he had to move his operations elsewhere. I agreed and asked him who he had in mind to run the operation for him. He suggested Neil Davenport, who was then the general manager of our U.K. operation with some 250 people. During a sales meeting in February, Neil was offered the job. He accepted on the spot and within ten minutes was given responsibility to decide on a new location anywhere in the world more than 1,000 miles from Minneapolis. We were prepared to move to Europe or even to Australia, where Neil planned to retire, but he quickly decided on a U.S. site because the dominant technology was here. A search committee—comprising Seymour, Neil, and their wives—soon after selected Colorado Springs. The new unit was operating by August and in full operation by the end of the year.

Seymour Cray explained his reason for the move, "I wanted to do something that couldn't be done at Chippewa Falls. I wanted to follow technology where it leads and found it difficult in the situation there." One problem had to do with the need for state-of-the-art robotics for manufacturing the new machine. According to Davenport, manufacturing a Cray-3 was like working on fine jewelry. Each machine had 200 modules, and each module required the precision placement and connection of some 12,000 almost-invisible, vertical connecting wires. These manufacturing skills were not available in the company's existing organization, and Seymour Cray had felt that it would not be right to bring in more people to a town where 3,000 out of 12,000 inhabitants were already Cray Research employees. Moreover, the need to share factory facilities with the Y-MP also was seen to pose a problem in getting the special attention the new machine required.

Davenport described his job as providing Seymour with a totally supportive environment, adding: "Seymour carries no baggage. I carry all the baggage." By April 1989, the factory was well on its way to being ready for a rapid manufacturing ramp-up. It was organized to have an initial output of fifty CPUs per quarter, or one machine (incorporating sixteen central processing units) per month, and to be able to double that capacity in nine months. In retrospect, Davenport identified his greatest accomplishment as the putting together of a team of over 100 persons in so short a time and with so few recruiting mistakes. Joe Blanchard, director of mechanical design who had left DEC West to join Cray Research on November 1, 1988, gave evidence of the new team's enthusiasm in creating a new machine: "I can't remember having a better time working so hard! After this job, I don't know what I would do next."

The initial impact of the Colorado Springs move on Chippewa Falls was far less positive. Learning from their mistakes in handling the MP termination and Chen's departure, Rollwagen and Davis worked hard to dispel the anxiety that was bound to arise among those left behind. Rollwagen later described the effects over time:

> The first reaction was one of enormous surprise. The second reaction was that of hurt. People were wondering if Seymour and maybe the company were abandoning them and leaving them to die. The next reaction was

anger against Seymour for having shown so little concern for them. Eventually, the people at Chippewa Falls came to accept the change when they found that their world had not fallen in. They still played a key role for the Cray-3 in providing the required printed circuit boards which could only be made there. Continuation of the C-90 project to follow the Y-MP also gave them a sense of independence. There is still some tenderness and nervousness at Chippewa Falls, but the hostility has been replaced by a growing determination to have the C-90 outperform the Cray-3.

A sense of competition with Colorado Springs was clearly evident at Chippewa Falls in early 1989.

Reinforcing Management and Policy

With the slowdown in growth and the related changes to the organization, Rollwagen recognized a need to reinforce the company's management and policy structure while preserving the innovative spirit that had played such a vital role in the past. In early 1988, he took the first of two major steps in this direction in hiring an experienced manager to strengthen Cray Research's human resources policies and practices. Then, in November 1988, he announced the promotion of Marcelo Gumucio as president and chief operating officer to provide needed leadership support as demands on his own time continued to increase.

Human Resources at Cray Research

Deborah Barber, formerly director of human resources for a major Honeywell division, joined Cray Research in January 1988 as vice president of human resources. A major part of her initial assignment was to align Cray Research's compensation, benefits, training, and related programs with the company's long-term business objectives. Fifteen months later she remarked, "I have tried to professionalize the human resources function. Much of what had been in place focused on the Cray style and was largely concerned with supporting a learning, growing, informal workplace environment." Some of the resulting efforts with respect to compensation, succession planning, and the Cray culture are discussed in turn.

Compensation. According to Barber, compensation was a means of attracting and keeping needed people and as a tool to focus employees' attention and efforts. To ensure that the motivation would tie directly to Cray Research's business needs, the HR staff organized eleven focus-group discussions (ninety-five participants representing all U.S. divisions) to determine prevailing attitudes toward compensation and senior managements' views of the firm's business objectives. Three guidelines emerged from these initial deliberations: (1) to reward performance and contribution; (2) to maintain a balanced emphasis

Table 2 Annual incentive award schedule†.

Group	Min Award	Target Range	Max Award	Base Salary % of mkt
1. Chairman	1.0	4.5–7.0	9	72
2. COO	1.0	4.0–6.5	8	76
3. EVP	1.0	3.5–6.0	7	80
4. Sr. VP	1.0	3.0–5.5	6.5	82
5. VP	1.0	2.5–5.0	6	85
6. *	1.0	2.0–4.0	5	88
7. *	1.0	1.5–3.0	4	92
8. *	1.0	1.2–2.0	3	96

†As a multiple of the distributed profit-sharing award.

*Various grades of technical and administrative employees.

on both long-term and annual performance considerations; and (3) to program cost control through variable compensation.

Barber pointed out: "The basic change to the compensation system was to have more pay at risk." This change was achieved with the introduction of an annual incentive-award plan. Its stated purpose was to recognize and reward key employees for significant contribution to the company's annual business performance. The plan supplemented the existing base salary and profit-sharing plan for all experienced engineers, administrators, and managers.[7] As shown in Table 2, the proportion of pay put at risk diminished with decreasing rank. For example, the COO was expected to receive an incentive award between 4 and 6.5 times the profit sharing award, vice president between 2.5 and 5 times, and a grade 8 software engineer between 1.2 and 2. At the same time, the base salary for the COO would be allowed to fall to 76 percent of the reference average for that position as industry salaries increased over time, to 85 percent of the industry average for the vice president, and only to 96 percent for the software engineer. According to the plan, the determination of individual awards was "based upon the participant's performance on predetermined objectives. Performance objectives should be set to stretch beyond the performance of normal job responsibilities and be based on company and division objectives."

The employee benefit stock plan was altered to increase the proportion of Cray employees eligible to receive long-term incentive awards from 20 percent to 35 percent. The plan was also altered to permit the awarding of small grants of up to twenty-five shares of unrestricted stock for purposes of recognizing outstanding performances at lower levels in the workforce.

Leadership and Management Succession Planning also received priority attention in 1988. The resulting program focused on future organizational needs and

7. The Cray Research profit-sharing plan distributed 10 percent of pretax profits to all employees, allocated in proportion to salary. A special profit-sharing program that awarded larger profit-sharing bonuses to the top 8 percent of all Cray personnel was discontinued.

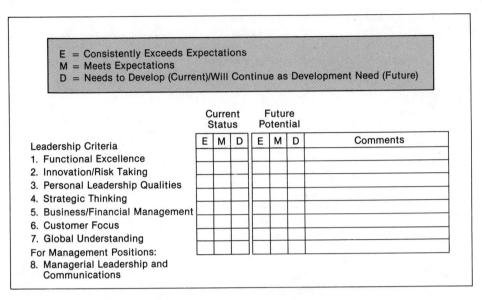

Figure 1 Leadership and management succession assessment

requirements. The heart of the assessment is shown in Figure 1. The leadership criteria were described in an accompanying guide, excerpts from which are included in Exhibit 3.

The assessment worksheet also called for a listing of the candidate's accomplishments, an explanation of how the person's strengths would contribute to the company's future needs, and an identification of areas for professional development. An additional form listed for each key position candidates for succession, indicating the year each person would be ready to move up and his or her development priorities. The succession-planning program was expected to provide important guidelines for developing internal talent, recruiting, and organizational design.

Cray Culture. Early in 1988, Rollwagen began to take an in-depth sounding of the organization's views of itself. Eighteen one-and-a-half hour sessions with an average attendance of fifteen people were held between February and July to get reactions to a document titled "Cray Vision—1995" (see Exhibit 4). Peoples' attitudes, questions, and concerns were recorded. The following quotes are illustrative of the information gathered:

- The company is talking to *customers* about future service support strategy before it talks to *its own people*.
- We need to have a little more polish with the outside world. . . . Chippewa and Seymour stories are good internally, but not outside!
- How do we keep the "small" in a big company?
- I'm impressed with top-down communication at Cray, but not across levels.

Exhibit 3   Excerpts from list of criteria for success at Cray

"Leaders at Cray are individuals who, by their vision and example, lead projects and people to shared success."

The following leadership and management criteria are proposed as the most critical capabilities required in Cray's functional leaders and managers. The criteria will not weigh equally for positions, but, in general, are considered to be important to individual and company success.

Innovation and Risk-Taking
- Challenges conventional wisdom and established belief systems.
- Has the courage to take significant risk and learn from failures as well as successes.
- Creates productive action out of tension and apparent contradictions.

Personal Leadership Qualities
- Creates and sustains a corporate vision and set of values.
- Engages the understanding and active support for the vision among all stakeholders.
- Demonstrates high level of energy and acts as a catalyst for action among peers and employees.
- Earns respect and trust from all constituents.
- Leads a balanced work and personal life and attends to his/her own total well-being.

Business/Financial Management
- Develops annual operating plans and budgets, and effectively uses the plans to measure performance on an ongoing basis.
- Plans for, secures, and allocates financial, people, and technological resources to meet strategic and operating objectives.
- Has a comprehensive understanding of key financial measures (profit and ROI) and is able to effectively manage these over the short and long term.
- Develops and uses project planning and management skills, when appropriate, to achieve desired strategic or operating-plan results.

- Why don't we mention the word "customer" in our mission statement?
- People have to realize that if we take risks, some won't work . . . there is no such thing as a guaranteed job.
- How do we keep what we're doing fun and exciting?

Exhibit 4   Cray Vision—1995.

A Clear Mission
Our simply stated mission is: "Cray Research designs, manufactures, markets, and supports the most powerful computer systems available." We recognize that "power" is defined not only in terms of hardware performance, but also in terms of systems and applications software, connectivity, service, support, ease-of-use, and more.

Unique Products
Cray Research is the worldwide leader in supercomputers. We understand and meet the needs of advanced computer users in science and engineering better than anyone else.

Worldwide Scope
Our products and capabilities are known and used around the world. We are truly an international company, with a real presence in all countries where we do business. As we grow, we maintain this presence by making sure the lines of communications remain open between Cray locations and between us and our customers.

Financial Performance
When we succeed technically, financial success follows. When we are financially successful, we can fund additional development projects to continue our tradition of technical success. The cycle is renewed.

We Are Individuals; We Share Common Values
Cray Research business is one-on-one. We are a company of individuals who choose to work together. We choose to do so because we are proud to share a single mission and the vision of the kind of place where we'd like to work.

Quality in Everything
As the Cray style says: "We have a strong sense of quality—quality in our products and services, of course; but also quality in our working environment, in the people we work with, in the tools that we use to do our work, and in the components we choose to make what we make. Economy comes from high value, not from low cost. Aesthetics are part of quality."

Trust
Again in referring to the Cray Style, we say: "Cray people trust each other to do their jobs well and with the highest ethical standards." Trust is earned and it's built through communication—openness, sharing of ideas and information, and getting to know one another.

Rollwagen found in these sessions a strong reinforcement of Cray's culture and "a tremendous commitment." He acknowledged that the task of maintaining the company's distinctive style was made more difficult by the growing number of employees and their geographic dispersement.

A novel way of expressing the special character of Cray's culture resulted from the efforts on compensation programs. In trying to identify the compa-

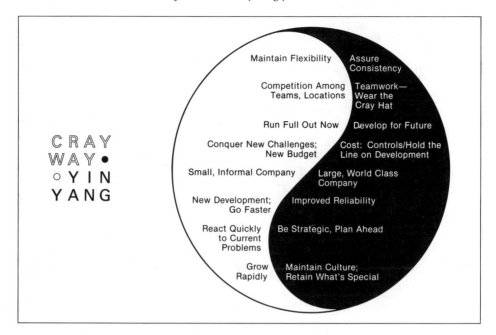

Figure 2

ny's objectives, Karen Clary, manager of compensation, received many contradictory views from different managers. When she confronted senior management with these inconsistencies, it simply acknowledged them. "The underlying message," realized Clary, "was that it all depended on circumstances. A favorite notion around here is the need to be consistently flexible and flexibly consistent." The sets of contrary concepts were subsequently depicted in a Yin/Yang fashion, and printed copies were distributed to employees (see Figure 2).

When asked why human resources reported to the CEO rather than to the new COO, Barber responded, "It might be to ensure that the company does not lose sight of its original vision and culture. These are critically important and might be vulnerable to operating pressures. In actual fact, I work more closely with Marcelo than with John." The organizational structure as of April 1989 is shown in Exhibit 5.

A Second in Command

As 1988 wore on and operating pressures mounted, Rollwagen decided to add depth to the general management function. He selected Marcelo Gumucio—who at age fifty-one had had general management experience at Hewlett-Packard, Memorex, and Northern Telecom before joining Cray Research in 1983 as head of marketing—to assume a newly created position of president and chief operating officer. As Rollwagen later acknowledged, Gumucio had the

Seymour Cray
Product Development

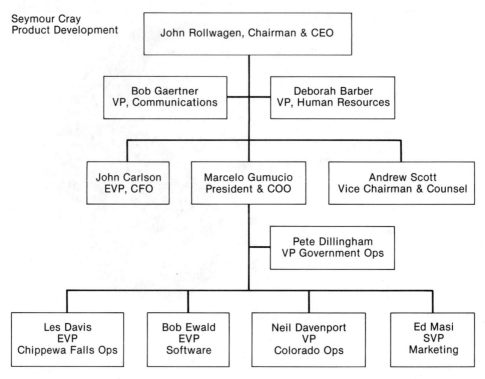

Exhibit 5 Cray Research corporate organization chart, April 1989. *Source:* Cray Research document

respect of his peers and the kind of hands-on, action-oriented disposition that would be needed.

On November 16, 1988, in an interoffice memorandum to all employees, Rollwagen explained the intended division of labor:

> We have done an excellent job expanding the supercomputer market to where we are today. But now we are entering an entirely new phase of market development, where supercomputers have much broader potential, and the definition of supercomputing involves much more than just the fastest computer. We need to understand how the market and the environment have changed, and to educate people about the real potential of supercomputing. This is quite a big task, and I am personally committed to leading it and very excited about it. At the same time, Cray Research is becoming much more visible, and as chairman and chief executive officer, I must represent our company to a worldwide audience of customers, government officials, and other leaders in research, education, and industry. I need to be able to focus on these two areas, and that's where Marcelo and his team come in.
>
> As president and chief operating officer, Marcelo will concentrate on the management of the day-to-day operations of the company and the accom-

plishment of objectives spanning one to three years—in effect, bringing the vision to reality.

In describing his new responsibilities, Gumucio noted the emphasis that he would place on current performance: "Each year we establish an operational plan and budget. This is our contract with ourselves, and my primary responsibility is to ensure that it is met." A committee of senior corporate line and staff executives was formed to assist him in this task. The Cray Management Committee met for the better part of a day every two weeks—alternatively at Minneapolis, Chippewa Falls, Mendota Heights, and Colorado Springs—to review key issues and to plan specific actions.

For all his concern with current performance, Gumucio had over the years played an important role in building Cray Research's management team. He explained his views on this point:

> Changes take place slowly in Cray because of its culture. Instead of changing organizational structure, I prefer to change the people and to get them to make changes over time. Bob Ewald and Ed Masi are some of the people that I brought on board for that purpose. It's important to rotate these people throughout the company to develop their abilities. . . . Personally, my own measure of success, besides profit and loss, will be how many people have grown under my leadership.

A Quest to Restore Rapid Growth

In March 1989, Gumucio identified as his principal challenge "to have Cray Research perform in the way it had performed in the past." This concern with restoring the company's rapid growth in sales and profits reflected Rollwagen's thinking, as indicated in his comment:

> In the past, I did not believe in growth for growth's sake. I have now come to modify my position significantly and to view growth as an essential ingredient at Cray Research. This growth has to come from the company's core strength, mainframe supercomputers, not from diversification. It is possible that the company might not grow or might not have an opportunity to grow. Personally, I would not want to continue leading the company under such circumstances.

To answer the question on growth, Gumucio asked Bob Ewald, executive vice president software, and Ed Masi, senior vice president marketing, jointly to identify and evaluate various growth opportunities for the company. For planning purposes, these new activities would be layered on a base case that assumed a 10 percent annual growth in existing core-related businesses with 30 percent pretax and 20 percent after-tax earnings. (The established business base, as of the end of 1988, is depicted in Exhibit 6. Of the total 220 installed systems, 142 or 65 percent were located in North America.) The five-year objective was to increase the annual growth rate to 20 percent. The computational

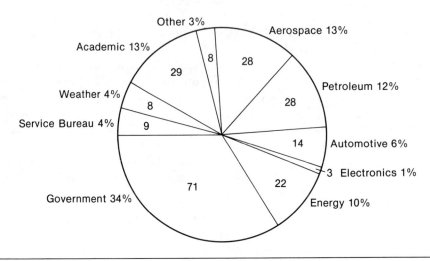

Installed Systems by Industry (4 Q/88)

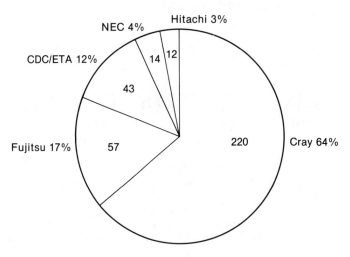

Worldwide Systems Installations (4 Q/88)

Exhibit 6 Installed by Cray Research systems, 1988

chemistry market, networking, and extending the lower end of the product line were among the principal opportunities under consideration.

Computational Chemistry

As efforts to develop the automotive and aerospace markets were underway, computational chemistry was singled out as a prime new target of opportunity. Chemical, pharmaceutical, and related bioengineering research and development were seen to provide a particularly rich field for supercomputing. Earlier experiences had demonstrated the importance of getting one or two leading firms in the target industry to adopt a Cray system as a means to demonstrate product value and to establish broad credibility in the new community. In 1986, Cray Research was successful in installing an X-MP in the National Cancer Institute and a used Cray-1A machine in DuPont (upgraded to a new X-MP in 1987).

The value of the supercomputer to the pioneering research on cancer and AIDS as well as to a broad spectrum of technical problem solving in chemistry and pharmaceuticals was clearly established by 1988. For Cray Research, the challenge was to make the computational power readily available to industrial users. The key to opening this or any other industrial-technology market was in the application software. John Carlson, chief financial officer, illustrated this point with reference to the automotive market breakthrough:

> Car manufacturers used to crash hundreds of new model cars to test for performance. With the development of PAM-CRASH©, an application software package that can simulate front-end collisions, they now do the testing on a Cray. Not only does the computer simulation save the companies the cost of wrecking so many new vehicles, it also permits the engineers to study the crash in slow motion. Previously, they would have to reconstruct the events after the fact, a slow and imprecise procedure.

Cray Research depended on third-party software houses to develop applications software for two reasons. First, the need to develop operating system software for the new machines as well as to upgrade the existing software itself imposed a full load on the company's software staff. Second, application software typically required intimate knowledge about the particular technology in question that was neither available nor easy to develop in-house. The limited market for supercomputer applications, however, tended to inhibit third-party interest in such programming.

To stimulate the development of application software for computational chemistry, Gumucio had entered into negotiations with a technological think-tank organization sponsored by companies in the chemical and pharmaceutical industries. The idea was to form a joint venture in which Cray Research would provide a Cray-2 system and its partner the know-how and software development effort. The sponsoring companies—including industry leaders such as Merck, DuPont, and Monsanto—would have access to any resulting application software. Users would be able to buy Cray computer time to run the program. As use increased, some were expected to purchase or lease their own Cray system.

Networking

In its struggle to introduce supercomputers to science and industry, Cray Research was counting on several interrelated developments to turn the tide. The first was the growing use of numerical simulation in science and engineering. The second was the rapidly spreading popularity in the scientific and engineering communities of the workstation as its power and versatility grew. Parallel advances in networking technology in turn would enable Cray Research to benefit from these other developments. In his presentation at the annual meeting on May 17, 1988, Rollwagen described the reasons for this connection and the commercial implications for supercomputers:

> An engineer will have on his desk [a workstation equivalent in power to] a CRAY-1 with very high resolution graphics that allow him to simulate physical phenomena very effectively. But no matter how powerful that computer is, it's going to be frustrating for him or her because it won't be powerful enough. With a network, it's possible for the engineer to leave his desk electronically . . . and to find the most powerful computer in the world that's available on the network.
>
> I think [networking] converts the supercomputer business into a personal computer business. This point was exemplified by a T-shirt that I saw at Apple. On the back was a MacIntosh. On the front it said, "My other computer is a Cray." So that in my view, we're not talking about eighty-six potential customers for supercomputers. We're not even talking about 860. We're talking about millions of customers around the world for Cray systems.

The appeal for a user to be able to tap into a Cray through his or her workstation or PC had been described in an Apple publication with the simile, "the interface is like starting up a Volkswagen and finding yourself flying a jet.[8] In May 1988, Apple Computer announced the election of John Rollwagen to its board of directors.

Rollwagen was active in supporting initiatives to create a national supercomputer network. The proposed network was described in the *New York Times* on December 29, 1988:

> Computer scientists and Government officials are urging the creation of a nationwide "data superhighway." . . . This highway would consist of a high-speed fiber-optic data network joining dozens of supercomputers at national laboratories and making them available to thousands of academic and industrial researchers around the country.
>
> The new network would cost about $400 million and could be in place by the mid-1990's, its proponents say. . . . Legislation introduced in October by Senator Albert Gore, Democrat of Tennessee, included initial financing for development and construction of a National Research Network.

For Gumucio, the prospective supercomputer network posed significant product-line issues. Referring to a schematic showing network supercomputing (see Exhibit 7), he queried, "Are we happy just to plug into a network or are there greater opportunities? For example, should we produce a file server that would be optimized to operate with Cray systems? What about the interconnectors between the hyperchannel and the supercomputers? Or even the terminals? In offering such ancillary products, we not only expand our revenue base, we also can provide better performance. In that sense, we would not be deviating from our traditional focus in offering the most powerful computing."

8. "McCray or CrayMac," *MacWorld*, January 1988.

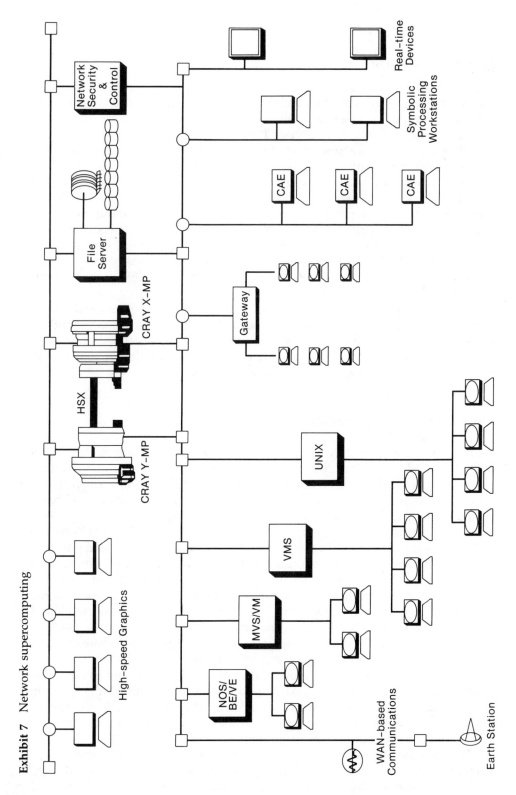

Exhibit 7 Network supercomputing

351

Lower-End Extension

The rapid growth of mini-supercomputers gave strong support to those who favored extending the Cray Research product line at the lower end. This market was estimated between $300 million and $400 million for 1989, with a potential to reach $1.2 billion by 1991 or 1992.

While the field was strewn with casualties, Cray Research could not help but notice the impressive success of the market leader, Convex Computer Corporation, which had introduced its first machine in 1984 and was projecting for 1989 revenues of $160 million and net profits of almost $12 million. Offering a machine a fourth the power at a tenth the cost of a supercomputer, Convex had succeeded in installing over 400 "Crayettes" for 260 customers in twenty-three countries. Another indicator of this market's attractiveness was the news report in July 1989 that Digital Equipment Corporation was showing mini-supercomputer prototypes to potential customers as a possible prelude to entering the market.

Rollwagen had publicly ruled out a Cray Research entry into mini-supercomputers. The possibility still remained for the company to expand its offerings at the lower end of its product line. Such a move offered opportunities to attract new customers and to lay claim to the uncontested ground still remaining between the minis and the true supercomputers.

The Cray-3 and C-90 Hardware Development Projects

As the 1988 slowdown showed signs of continuing and possibly worsening in 1989, the wisdom of Cray Research supporting two major machine developments at the same time came under increasing scrutiny. In 1987, when the C-90 was first authorized as a successor to the Y-MP, the expectation was that it would follow the Cray-3 by two or so years, continuing the dual design thrust that had characterized the company's recent offerings. (The Cray-1, X-MP, Y-MP, and C-90 had a common design lineage; the Cray-2, Cray-3, and a follow-up Cray-4 were viewed as a second family.) A year's slippage in the Cray-3 design and a speed-up in the C-90 largely eliminated the original staggered time phasing between the two introductions. Moreover, in the view of some managers, the distinction between the two lines was getting increasingly blurred as more software was developed in common.

While people differed with respect to issues of timing and performance, they shared concern with the growing financial pressures. Carlson explained this concern: "With 20 percent growth, the company could afford to carry two major R&D projects at one time. At 10 percent, we are hard-pressed, especially since the need to develop new growth areas for the company will require additional investments." Exacerbating this problem was an increase of some $15 million in the Cray-3 development budget.

The pressures for continuing both projects were also great. Seymour Cray was publicly committed to gallium arsenide. The company's core design-engineering staff at Chippewa Falls was similarly committed to the C-90. And

Rollwagen expressed concern with the risk of having the company "betting on only one technical thread."

Precipitating Events

Several events in early 1989 helped to bring the hardware product development issue to a head. Despite successful results in the development and testing of gallium arsenide chips, technical difficulties continued to disrupt the design schedule for the Cray-3 system. In March, Seymour Cray gave September as the point when a decision would be made on the viability of his team's efforts. This hiatus of six months left the future of the Cray-3 and the C-90 projects as well as of the Colorado Springs and Chippewa Falls facilities hanging in the balance.

On April 10, NEC Corporation announced a new series of multiprocessor supercomputer machines that was said to have a peak speed of 22 billion floating point operations per second (gigaflops), roughly eight times faster than the most powerful machine on the market. The SX-X was scheduled to be available in late 1990 and to sell from $5 million to $23 million. HNSX Supercomputers, a joint venture of NEC and Honeywell, would market the line in North America. While impressed with the SX-X, industry analysts were reported to be cautious about its commercial prospects. Peak performance numbers were notoriously unreliable indicators of a machine's problem-solving abilities. Further clouding the new machine's future was the successful challenge of NEC's proposed sale of a supercomputer to the Massachusetts Institute of Technology by the U.S. Department of Commerce the previous year. Notwithstanding the guarded reception generally accorded to the SX-X, Rollwagen acknowledged the potential threat, noting, "If we don't have a better machine when the time comes, we'll be in deep weeds."[9]

One week later, on April 17, Control Data Corporation announced the decision to close its supercomputer unit, ETA Systems, because of continued losses. According to the *New York Times* on May 1, 1989, Robert Price, Control Data chairman, disclosed that ETA had been losing $100 million per year and cited the prospect of Japanese competition as a major element in the company's decision. ETA's withdrawal left Cray Research as the only major supercomputer manufacturing company in the United States.

In reviewing recent and ongoing events in one of their frequent informal discussions, Gumucio and Carlson became intrigued with the idea of spinning off the Cray-3 operation as a possible way of dealing with the mounting financial pressures and with the unfolding competitive scene. Other senior officers were soon brought into the discussion. Rollwagen described the ensuing events: "The spin-off idea came to me in a planning meeting as just one of many alternatives. On April 26, I went to Colorado Springs to review our options with Seymour. We discussed the possibility of cancelling the C-90, of canceling the Cray-3—neither of which was being seriously considered—and of creating two divisions, among other possibilities. At the end, I introduced the idea of a

9. *Boston Sunday Globe*, April 2, 1989, p. A4.

spin-off, and we both got very excited." With all parties in general favor of this course of action, management proposed the spin-off to the board of directors and recommended that the proposed move be disclosed at the soon-to-be-held annual shareholders meeting.

The Spin-Off

In explaining at the annual shareholders meeting the decision to create Cray Computer Corporation, Rollwagen pointed to the heavy financial burden associated with developing both the Cray-3 and C-90 systems—". . . we are up 35 percent [in R&D costs] in an environment where the best we can hope for is a 10 percent increase in revenues"—and to the diminishing difference between the two in terms of expected performance and timing. He went on to say, "If we were a normal company, the logical thing to do would be to choose one or the other—the Cray-3 with the gallium arsenide work in Colorado or the silicon design and the momentum we have in Chippewa Falls. That clearly would work from a P&L standpoint. In fact, I think it would work well from a technical standpoint. But there would be some losers from that proposition."

One set of losers would be the people associated with the discontinued project. A second set of losers would be customers who would no longer have the opportunity to choose between the two technological thrusts. In this connection, Rollwagen had earlier mentioned ETA's withdrawal from the marketplace and the need for more than one company to comprise a viable industry. A third set of losers would be the company's shareholders. Rollwagen explained:

> You will have your exciting stock in Cray Research, Inc., just as it has been in size and kind of business, but with a much better focused operation [in terms of technology, software, field support, and marketing]. By the same token, you are going to get shares in what has to be one of the most exciting start-up companies in the decade. We've got another Cray Research on our hands with the company in Colorado, led by Seymour Cray, going after the same kind of goals that were set up in Cray Research in the mid-70s.

Seymour Cray, in turn, explained one important advantage of the new arrangement to his project:

> The goal that I accepted—to have production equipment and rapidly ramp up and deliver fifty machines a year—was meaningful for a billion-dollar corporation. We don't have to have that goal anymore. . . . We can now talk about, "Can we deliver ten machines in 1990?" The emphasis can be shifted from building of machinery, production, and inventory control to getting the prototype built. We should have done that before, but we were trying to do too much.

Under the proposed arrangements, Cray Research would license existing hardware and software technology to Cray Computer and would transfer assets valued at approximately $50 million and funds not to exceed $100 million for product development over a twenty-four-month period. According to Carlson, the transfers would be accounted for in a way that would avoid any impact on the earnings statement. Cray Research would distribute 90 percent of the stock in the new company to its shareholders, presumably on a tax-free basis, and would retain a 10 percent interest.

The Road Ahead

While wholly in favor of the spin-off, Rollwagen was nonetheless saddened by the need to break apart the enjoyable amalgam of business interests and close personal friendships that Cray Research has always been for him, and troubled by the need to choose one part or the other. He explained:

> My first emotional reaction was to join Seymour in Colorado Springs. But as I thought more about it, I came to realize that such a move was not right for Cray Research and not right for me. Cray Computer faces high risks and little uncertainty. The risk is in technology. If it develops a superior system, the market is there. In contrast, Cray Research faces less risk but great uncertainty. I can help with business uncertainty, not with technological risk. Moreover, I have already lived through that kind of experience. The challenges Cray Research faces are new to me and more exciting personally at this stage of my life.

While Rollwagen's role in providing strategic leadership and inspiration was indisputably vital to the future of Cray Research, the burden of implementing the separation plans and for reorganizing the residual operations would fall heavily on Gumucio's shoulders. His task was not made any easier by the deteriorating market conditions. On July 25, 1989, Gumucio announced a 77 percent earnings decline for the second quarter and the growing likelihood that revenues for 1989 would increase little, if any, over 1988.

Notwithstanding the performance setback Cray Research was facing, Gumucio believed the company had taken an important step in positioning itself for the future. In August, he remarked, "I feel a lot better today about our situation than I did twelve months ago. We are more streamlined, and we are less dependent on individual persons. We have a proven team in place to make Cray Research successful. I like to say 'Now mere mortals will make wonderful things happen.' " The challenge for the company, in his view, was to expand its market and still remain faithful to its mission.

On October 2, 1989, citing the continuing slowdown in demand for its larger systems, Cray Research announced the first layoffs in its seventeen-year history. According to press accounts, the company would reduce the work force at its main Wisconsin plants by 400 people, representing about 7 percent of overall employment or 18 percent of its manufacturing personnel. Gumucio was reported as saying, "This is going to be a tough year and we are taking the necessary steps to control costs."[10]

10. *Wall Street Journal*, October 3, 1989, p. A-6.

Daewoo Group

"If we work hard, there is no limit to what we can achieve. Hard work was a key to making our company as it is today. Hard work . . . and a sensitivity to the currents of business change. This sensitivity enabled us to position ourselves in line with the flow of opportunities in Korea and around the world." Kim Woo-Choong was explaining how in just sixteen years he had built one of the largest business empires in Korea.[1] In June 1984 Sweden's King Carl Gustaf XVI conferred on Kim, chairman of Daewoo Group, the International Business Award, a token of recognition awarded every three years by the International Chamber of Commerce to honor an "entrepreneur who has contributed to the idea of free enterprise by either creating or developing his own company."

Founded in 1967 by Kim with an initial investment of $18,000, Daewoo grew to become one of the four largest privately held group companies in Korea. In 1983 the group, with 77,240 employees, recorded $4.3 billion sales (of which exports accounted for $2.5 billion), $44.8 million profits, and $2.3 billion in total assets. (Exhibit 1 contains a record of financial performance.) Initially a textile and garment exporter, Daewoo's business activities had grown to include shipbuilding, construction, financial services, and the manufacture of machinery, automobiles, home appliances, and telecommunications devices.

That Daewoo had navigated a remarkable course of change and growth in its short life was evident. Less evident, perhaps, were the troubled waters that lay ahead. Growing worldwide trade protectionism had begun to impair the company's export opportunities. At the same time, rising wage rates in Korea were eroding a key competitive advantage that Daewoo and other Korean firms had held in the international arena. And the firm's very growth had brought with it problems of how to manage the increasingly complex organization. Among the important challenges were the need to find ways of preserving the employees' dedication to hard work and the managers' spirit of risk taking that had been so central to Daewoo's past success. Chairman Kim acknowledged these problems and challenges, while expressing confidence that Daewoo had strategies and resources to cope with them and to continue its remarkable record of growth.

1. In keeping with Korean custom, the surname is given first. After the first full use of names in this case, only surnames will be used.

Exhibit 1 Consolidated operating and financial statistics ($ millions).

	1983	1982	1981	1979	1978
Summary of operations and earnings					
Sales	$4,251	$3,346	$2,938	$1,871	$1,188
Operating income	142	174	223	136	101
Interest expense	76	77	115	76	47
Earnings before income taxes					
and minority interests	65	63	94	73	51
Income taxes	23	23	32	30	22
Net earnings	45	38	60	27	18
Summary of balance sheets					
Current assets	1,425	1,081	1,308	1,005	727
Investments and advances	242	189	147	178	101
Property, plant and equipment					
and other assets	622	588	433	692	426
Total assets	2,289	1,858	1,888	1,875	1,254
Current liabilities	1,327	1,078	1,290	1,105	726
Long-term debts and other accounts	697	586	461	658	424
Stockholders' equity	265	194	137	112	104
Key financial ratios					
Return on sales (%)	1.1	1.1	2.0	1.4	1.5
Return on equity (%)	17.0	19.6	43.8	24.1	17.3
Current ratio (%)	107.4	100.3	101.6	90.9	100.1
Debt/equity ratio (%)	762.6	857.7	1,278.1	1,574.1	1,105.7
Exchange rate (won/U.S. dollar)	795.5	748.8	700.0	485.0	485.0
Number consolidated companies	7	7	9	10	8

Note: The consolidated figures were for Daewoo Corporation and its subsidiaries in which it held 50% or more share ownership. In 1983, these subsidiaries comprised Koryo Leather, KOSCO, Daewoo Electronics Company, Korea Capital Corporation, Daewoo Development and Daewoo International (America) Corporation. Daewoo Motor, as a joint venture, was not included.

Daewoo Group did not publish its consolidated annual report in 1980.

Figures in U.S. dollars converted only for convenience.

Daewoo and Korean Industrial Policy

Daewoo's history reflected that of the Korean economy. As government policy in the late 1960s and early 1970s promoted the export of light goods, Daewoo became one of the nation's front-running exporters. When Korea began in the mid-1970s to shift its focus from light to heavy industries, Daewoo extended its domain from exporting textiles and other light goods to manufacturing heavy industrial goods. In the early 1980s, in line with the government's economic plan to emphasize electronics, Daewoo extended its business activities to home appliances, telecommunications, and other electronic equipment. In effect, Daewoo was at one and the same time a major beneficiary of and an important contributor to Korea's economic growth.

Light Industry Exports

With the successful completion of its first five-year economic plan (1962–66) emphasizing the development of import substitution industries such as oil refining, fertilizers, fibers and textiles, the Korean government was ready to move ahead with a new industrial policy of export-led economic growth. Korea's new commitment was set into motion in 1967 with the second five-year economic plan. The year 1967 also marked the birth of Daewoo.

At age 30, Kim, with the assistance of three business associates and a typist, founded Daewoo Industrial Company, Ltd., to export textiles. He came to this new venture with seven years' experience with a medium-sized garment manufacturing exporter and with half of the initial capital funds, which he had had to borrow from his partner. Although the title of president was conferred on one of his associates, who was several years his senior, Kim's leadership was obvious from the start. In Korean, the characters for *dae* and *woo* mean "great universe." But *woo* is also part of Kim's given name, Woo-Choong, pointing to the close identity of man and company.

Daewoo's first business was in exporting tricot fabrics to Singapore, where they were reexported to Indonesia and Africa. In 1968, as diplomatic relations between Indonesia and Singapore deteriorated, Kim promptly redirected Daewoo's exports directly to Indonesia. With this move, Daewoo soon gained a leading position as a textile exporter to Southeast Asia and Africa with export sales growing from $580,000 in 1967 to almost $4 million in 1969.

During this period, Daewoo made the decision to expand its manufacturing and marketing activities. In the 1960s, the Korean textile industry supplied cheap, unskilled labor based on CMT (cutting, making, and trimming). The Japanese trading houses supplied raw and submaterials and also sold the products to the overseas retail trade. As a result, Korean manufacturers had recourse only to a small part of the potential profits. Moreover, the scale of Korean operations was too small to supply large customers' requirements. Chairman Kim decided to go after the more profitable parts of the business through a number of what were then pioneering and bold moves for a Korean company. Central to his plan was the construction of a new textile factory with twenty lines of sewing capacity at a time when a factory with four to six lines was considered a large operation. To provide this factory with the needed raw materials, the company established a branch on Osaka, a center for supplies. Then in 1969, branch sales offices were opened in Singapore, New York, and London to market the output. Recognizing the importance of quality, Kim installed quality-control equipment identical to that used by Sears, Roebuck. Impressed with the new facilities and favorable prices, Sears became Daewoo's first major client to be followed by J.C. Penney, Montgomery Ward, and others.

Yoo Ki-Bum, an executive managing director who had begun his career at this time, described this important transformation of the young company: "I am still excited by what we were able to accomplish in those early years. We really worked very hard to make a success of our new business. Most employees worked from early in the morning until midnight to get the product out. It was during this period the Daewoo spirit of challenge, creativity, and sacrifice first blossomed."

The resulting clothing products were enthusiastically received by American consumers, and Daewoo's exports more than doubled in 1970 as a result. About this time, Kim became convinced that the U.S. government would sooner or later impose an import quota on textile products. He therefore set out to gain a favorable position for Daewoo by pushing its textile products into the United States with less regard to profitability. As a result of this action, Daewoo succeeded in increasing fivefold its exports into the United States, establishing itself as the leading supplier of textile products from Asia.

In 1972 the U.S. government imposed an import quota on textile products from Hong Kong, Taiwan, and Korea. Since the allocation of quota in Korea was in turn based on recent past exporting performance, Daewoo was awarded about 30 percent of the total. As a result, by the mid-1970s, Daewoo had become one of Korea's most profitable firms.

Public Ownership and Diversification

Based on its success in exporting textiles to the United States, Daewoo expanded its sales to Europe. Following this expansion, Daewoo management saw an opportunity to export other light-industry products to its markets, relying on its established reputation as a competitive supplier of quality products. At the time, a number of Korean manufacturing companies were in trouble due to a lack of expertise in overseas marketing. This situation enabled Daewoo to begin a round of acquisitions for expansion into other consumer products.

To support this expansion program, in 1973 Daewoo issued new common shares, amounting to 25 percent of the corporation's total issued shares, for sale on the Korean securities exchange. The issue sold at a premium of 330 percent over par value. One year later, the Korean government set in motion a new policy to encourage large Korean companies to go public in their ownership.

With funds secured from the sale of stock, with bank loans, and with cash flow from its flourishing textile exports to the United States, Daewoo acquired fourteen companies and took major positions in two other firms. By 1975 Daewoo had transformed itself from a solitary textile firm into a group of companies engaged in manufacturing and trading textiles, leather goods, and other light-industry products. Expansion was not limited to the manufacturing sector. During this phase of growth, Daewoo also began its diversification into banking and financing businesses.

In 1975 Daewoo Industrial Company was officially designated a general trading company. This designation, which had been initiated by the Korean government as a means of increasing and diversifying exports, gave the recipient special access to certain export financing and increased credibility in foreign markets.

Transition to Heavy Industry Manufacturing

By 1976, optimistic about the future world economy as well as the competitive potential of Korean companies, the Korean government began to promote the development of heavy industry sectors, such as machinery and shipbuilding. Generous bank financing was made available for investments in these sectors. In line with this objective, the government singled out a few of the most capable companies to develop heavy industry in Korea.

When Kim was asked in 1976 by the Korea Development Bank to take over the ailing Hankook Machinery, Ltd., one of Korea's largest producers of diesel engines, rolling stock, and industrial machinery, his executives opposed the move. The firm had not once shown a profit in thirty-eight years of operations under Japanese and then Korean ownership. Debts of the troubled firm exceeded Daewoo's total equity by twofold.

Chairman Kim nonetheless accepted the government bank's invitation. He changed the name of Hankook Machinery to Daewoo Heavy Industries, Ltd., made himself president, and took personal charge of turning around this new acquisition. He remarked on this experience: "I needed to get directly involved to make the right decisions. I often slept at the factory. One of the things I learned was that the workers were working overtime for the pay without adding much value. The machinery was turning, but it wasn't producing anything."

Instead of cutting back the workers' hours, Kim's response was to generate more business through aggressive marketing coupled with improved product quality. In this way, workers could be ensured of legitimate overtime work and job security. Production cost was lowered through the direct purchase of parts and components, and the company's original capital of $25 million was increased to $52 million. In the first year, Daewoo Heavy Industries achieved break-even operations. Small profits were made and dividends paid in the second year. This success enhanced Kim's reputation as a manager in the eyes of government officials and the public.

His reputation as a competent manager, coupled with his access to substantial funds through the financial institutions under his control, enabled Kim to acquire Korea Steel Chemical Company in 1977 and the Saehan Motor Company (a 50–50 joint venture with General Motors) and Okpo Shipbuilding Company in 1978. Daewoo's decision to take over the Okpo shipyard, a near-bankrupt enterprise, was prompted by the government's strong urging. The shipyard was to feature the largest dry dock in the world with a capacity to hold a one-million deadweight ton tanker. It was only 25 percent completed when Daewoo took it over, but the dry dock and yard were completed in 1981, and profits were recorded in 1983.

Chairman Kim

To understand Daewoo, one must first understand Kim Woo-Choong, its founder and chairman. Born in 1936, he experienced a youth of Japanese rule and war, followed by economic deprivation and then another war. His father, a professor, had been one of the few Koreans to receive a diploma from a Japanese national university, and his mother was one of the rare women of her day to obtain a university degree. "It was my mother, a devoted Christian,

who encouraged all of us to stand on our own feet and to go our own independent ways," explained Dr. Kim Duk-Choong, one of Kim's brothers and a
professor of economics.

The Korean War, 1950–53, forced Kim's mother to play the dominant role
in the upbringing of the family. His father and an elder brother, a physician,
were abducted by North Korean soldiers in July 1950 when Seoul was overrun.
"I saw my father taken away with my own eyes. I was thirteen at the time,"
Kim said. He never saw or heard from his father and brother again.

Chairman Kim remembered the days when he had to support his mother,
three brothers, and a sister on his earnings as a newspaper delivery boy. He
recalled: "One evening I returned home exhausted and hungry. There was
only a single bowl of rice available for the five of us. I fibbed that I had already
eaten. My mother told the young ones to eat the rice, also claiming to have
already eaten. Then each in turn urged the other to eat the rice. Of a sudden,
we all looked at each other, hugged and burst into tears. That was the happiest
moment in my life."

Following the Korean War, Kim attended Yonsei University with a schol-
arship covering tuition and a small stipend for books. Income from odd jobs
covered most of his living expenses.

At age forty-six, Chairman Kim projected an air of authority and boundless
drive. His belief in the virtue of hard work served to unify his actions and
thoughts. "Other than hard work," he once said, "I have no hobby." For him,
that meant a sixteen-hour workday, 365 days a year. Christmas and New Year's
would find him in the Middle East where business was unaffected by these
holidays.

This devotion to work was connected to Kim's pride in his heritage. In his
mind, Korea and its pride had almost fifty years of catching up to compensate
for the Japanese occupation from 1910 through 1945 and for another ten years
of turmoil during the Korean War as a battlefront in the East-West global struggle. Kim was not alone in this view. From times of antiquity, the people of the
Korean Peninsula have had to struggle to preserve their identity and cherished
culture from recurrent invasions by the Chinese, Mongols, and Japanese.
Chairman Kim conveyed this sense of mission in his thoughts about Daewoo:

> I am concerned about our standing as a country and as a society. Our
> culture used to be the source of Japanese learning. Under the Japanese rule
> during 1910 to 1945, however, Koreans were deprived of opportunities to
> obtain higher education. Nowadays, more than 300,000 college graduates
> enter the society every year. With 40 million people, 59 million if united,
> Korea can become as advanced as any country in the world. But to catch up
> with the rich countries, we must work as hard as the Americans and Japa-
> nese did when they built up their countries. One of my cherished dreams
> has been to show people around the world that Korea can produce the
> highest quality products at the lowest prices.

In 1983 Daewoo management launched a program for revitalizing the managerial spirit, stressing the need for creativity, challenge, and sacrifice as key
elements for continued success. Chairman Kim's reflections on these desired

managerial attributes helped to define the kind of company he wanted Daewoo to be:

> Creativity comes from hard work. To become wise, it's not how many books you read but how much you concentrate in your reading that is important. Business is the same. Traveling around the world, I can see money everywhere. It is in the street and in the houses. It is in America and in Africa. It is everywhere, but you have to work hard to see it and to get it. If you try hard enough, you will see more money than you could possibly collect in the time you have.

> Ten years ago we were a small company, but even then we felt a sense of challenge to become an important factor in our national scene. Since we had little money, the only way for us to grow was to rescue seriously troubled companies. And this we did by showing the workers what it meant to work hard.

> Many people point to the Japanese management systems as the reason for their success. But what can a system do without good people? You need people who are dedicated *and* experienced. The only advantage the Japanese firm has over a Korean firm is the experience of its people. You take shipbuilding, for example. The Japanese welder has 20 years' experience and our Korean welder about two years' experience. But that advantage will lessen over time.

> The American company is not what it used to be. In the old days, Americans worked hard to challenge new frontiers. But as their economy got mature, they became more interested in nice houses, jogging, and having a good time than in doing business. How can you compete without dedication? It is not the management system that is not working in American companies, it is the people not working hard.

> Korea is no exception to this cycle of hard work. As the standard of living improves in Korea, we shall eventually lose the spirit of working hard. Until we get to that stage, we have to keep growing our economy.

In October 1980, Kim announced his decision to donate all of his personal holdings in Daewoo Corporation, worth over $40 million, to a foundation dedicated to the Korean people. He explained that in a capitalistic society such as Korea, businessmen had a responsibility to become national leaders, and that only those who were willing to sacrifice their personal interests could truly take on such leadership roles. "When a businessman starts to count his own wealth, his life as a businessman comes to an end. After all, profits are for reinvestment, not for enjoyment." At the same time he declared his intention to dedicate himself to professional management. This move alone set him apart from other Korean business leaders.

Senior Management

Unlike other group companies, where members of the owner's family would typically fill key managerial positions, none of Daewoo's senior managers were related to Kim. As to the managers' abilities, he once said, "I always thought that I could achieve whatever I had set out to do on the strength of my own efforts. But Daewoo grew more rapidly than I expected, and this was possible only as a result of the efforts of the capable and dedicated managers within the group."

The senior management team shared two characteristics: their young age and their educational background. These commonalities served to create a tightly knit management group with strongly shared values. With the exception of Cho Dong-Jae, president of Daewoo's Pusan factory, and one of the founding members of Daewoo, all of the senior managers including Kim were born in the late 1930s. This age distribution reflected a result of historical events. Hong Soung-Bu, president and director of the group planning department explained:

> Men in their early forties are in some ways a special group in Korea. They are the people who had experienced the harsh years of the Korean War during their adolescence, and more important, are the first generation in many years to have received a regular education at the university level. As a result, they take nothing for granted and know how to get things right. Since many of their seniors were killed or injured in the war and few had the benefit of a proper education, the generation of the late thirties has had to step into important positions at a relatively young age.

The binding ties of school camaraderie were also readily apparent. Kim and six of the other ten senior executives in Daewoo had attended the prestigious Kyunggi High School. Since admission was based on the results of a rigorous entrance examination, preparation began early in life, even to the extent of taking special training before kindergarten so as to gain admission into the best school at each rung of the educational ladder. The students of Kyunggi High School could boast an average IQ somewhere between 130 and 140. The graduates were not only gifted individuals, but generally possessed self-confidence and an ability to persevere as a result of the gruelling preparatory training they had experienced. Similarly, eight of the eleven top Daewoo executives were graduates of the prestigious Seoul National University.

Although Daewoo considered itself to have gone much further than any other large Korean firm in developing professional management, Kim continued to dominate decision making on important issues. In recognition of his experience and personal dedication to Daewoo, managers would invariably turn to him for direction on all significant matters. When asked if his practice of centralized decision making might become unwieldy as Daewoo grew in size and complexity, Lee Kyung-Hoon, president of Daewoo Corporation's trading division, answered: "Strong leadership—even dictatorship, although one doesn't use this word in a corporate setting—is sometimes essential in the growth phase of any corporation."

Not everyone agreed. Another manager saw problems with the chairman's involvement in operations: "Although Chairman Kim has delegated considerable authority to the presidents of several group companies, he still gets involved with the operating decisions in many Daewoo units, causing some confusion among subordinates, and inhibiting the development of those presidents as field commanders."

In Kim's mind, the issue of leadership was tied in with that of succession:

> I know my strength as an entrepreneur; I also know my weakness as an organization builder. I can be an asset for Daewoo so long as it grows rapidly and a liability when it needs to be stabilized. When that time comes, I shall resign as chairman and hand over the job to a manager capable of structuring managerial systems in the group. Once my successor accomplishes stabilization, it will be time for him to turn over the chairmanship to someone else with entrepreneurial skills. This time, the entrepreneurial leadership would operate through a coordinated system.

Although not publicly announced, Kim had selected his successor and his successor's successor and was grooming them for the job. He had not set a specific date for stepping down.

Group Structure and Business Strategies

As of March, 1984, Daewoo Group comprised twenty-five companies in twelve industrial sectors as shown in Exhibit 2. Daewoo Corporation, which included the trading, textile, and construction activities as three divisions, performed the role of holding company for the group. Its shares were publicly traded, as were shares of Daewoo Heavy Industries and a few Daewoo financial companies. The complex ownership network is described in Exhibit 3.

The president for each of Daewoo's business units was responsible for its strategy and for its results. The appendix describes the major business units and their strategies. Although each business plan was tailored to the opportunities and challenges facing the particular business unit, there were several underlying strategies that characterized the overall direction of the group.

Higher Technology

A move to higher technology was perhaps the most pervasive change taking place in Daewoo. According to Lee Hun-Jae, an executive director in charge of strategic planning: "We started with the textile business, and gradually moved into more complex technology in shipbuilding, machinery and automobiles. In my opinion, the future of Daewoo, and of Korea, lies in high technology."

This move to higher technology was being implemented in two ways. First, there was a change in the mix of businesses. The transformation, which had begun with the diversification from textiles and light industries to shipbuilding and heavy industries, was now aimed at entering and building a capability in high-technology electronics. This latest phase was positioning Daewoo to compete in telecommunications, computers, robotics and the underlying electronics componentry, such as integrated circuits, digital switching, and optical fiber transmission. To gain these capabilities, Daewoo had entered into technology licensing agreements with firms such as Northern Telecommunications and Siemens.

Exhibit 2 Affiliated companies within Daewoo group, 1984.

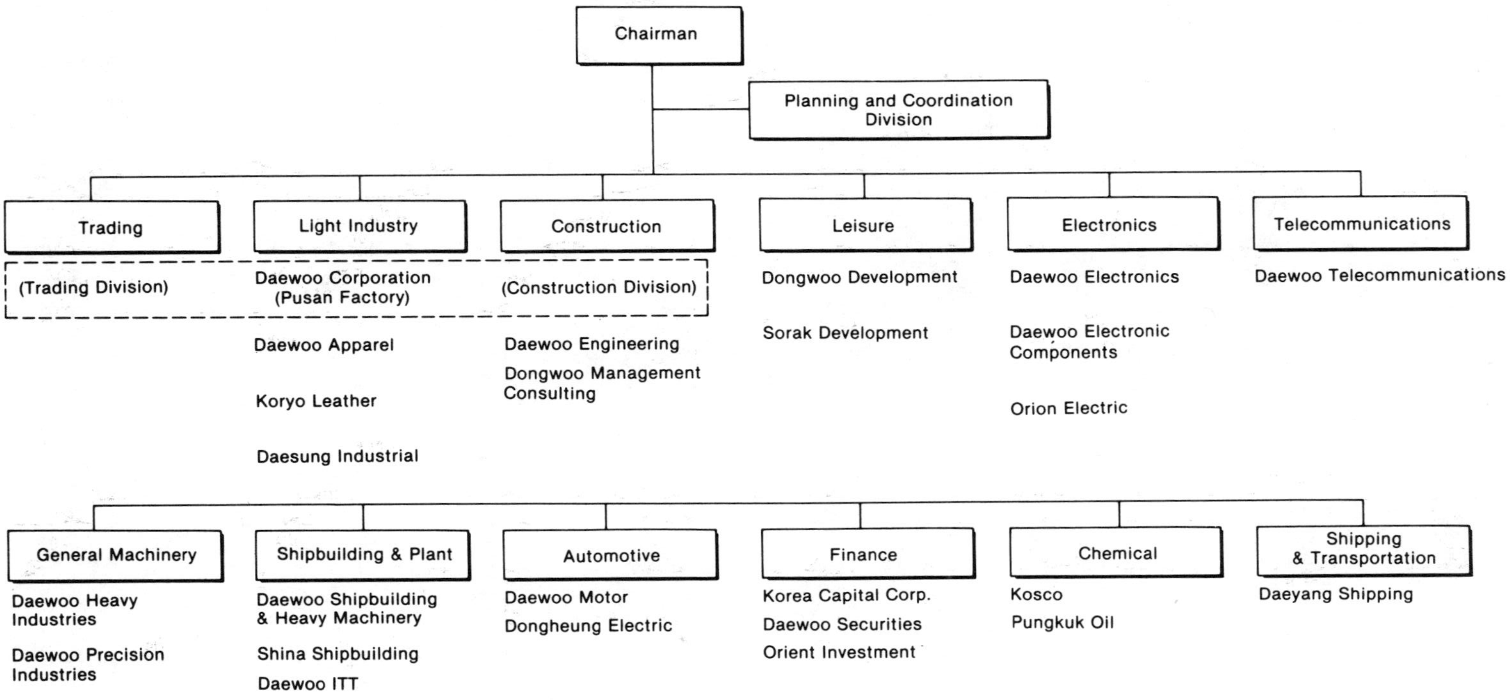

Note: Associated companies and overseas subsidiaries were not included.

365

Exhibit 3   Daewoo group companies' ownership structure (in %).

	Company					
Shareholder	Daewoo Corporation	Daewoo Apparel	Orion Electric	Daewoo Heavy Industries	Daewoo Securities	Orient Investment
Affiliated Companies						
Daewoo Corporation			9.99	31.86	9.15	10.14
Daewoo Apparel	0.58					
Daesung Industrial	0.38					
Daewoo Engineering				0.14		
Dongwoo Management Consulting	0.06					
Dongwoo Development	0.14					
Daewoo Electronics			6.68			
Daewoo Heavy Industries			17.05		3.48	2.80
Korea Capital Corp.	12.89					23.47
Orient Investment	0.60				1.47	
KOSCO					0.80	0.77
Pungkuk Oil				2.75		
Total Affiliated Companies	14.65		33.72	34.75	14.90	37.18
Associated Companies						
Shinsung Tongsang	0.71					
Foundations						
Daewoo Educational Foundation	3.26				4.17	
Daewoo Foundation	19.15	9.99		4.66	2.59	6.51
Seoul Press Foundation	0.37			0.35		
Total Foundations	22.78	9.99		5.01	6.76	6.51
Total Daewoo-related Companies	38.14	9.99	33.72	39.76	21.66	43.69
Non-Daewoo Owners	61.86	90.01	66.28	60.24	78.34	56.31
Total	100.0%	100.0%	100.0%	100.0%	100.0%	100.0%

Note: The exhibit shows ownership structures of publicly held companies only. Among the nonpublic companies, Daewoo Motor is 50% owned by Daewoo Corporation (50% by GMC). Daewoo Shipbuilding is 47.36% by Daewoo Corporation and 16.8% by other Daewoo related companies (35.84% by Korea Development Bank). Daewoo Electronics is 23.67% by Daewoo Corporation and 26.33% by other Daewoo related companies.

Second, technology in existing business operations was to be upgraded. The automation of textile manufacturing and computer-aided design and manufacturing (CAD/CAM) in the manufacture of heavy equipment were two examples of this change. An electronics planning committee had been set up to coordinate the efforts taking place within the various business units.

OEM Supply

A second common characteristic of the various business strategies was the emphasis placed on the OEM (original equipment manufacturers) supply business. Although Daewoo actively developed its own branded products, a large and growing proportion of its output was directed to supplying other firms with manufactured products bearing their names. Textile goods had always been manufactured to supply distributors such as Sears, Roebuck and branded lines such as Oleg Cassini, Christian Dior, London Fog, and Calvin Klein. In heavy machinery, much of the future growth would come from supplying firms such as Caterpillar with specific products for worldwide sales. For example, in April 1983 Daewoo signed a ten-year contract to manufacture fork-lift trucks in the 4,000–6,000-pound capability class for worldwide sales. Dale Turnbull, president of Towmotor, a wholly owned subsidiary of Caterpillar, said, "These all-new lift trucks will maintain Caterpillar quality standards in products offering high value at very competitive prices." Negotiations were under way in 1984 to extend this arrangement to include earth-moving equipment.

In automobiles, while Daewoo continued to compete in the Korean market with its own branded vehicles, management saw the company's major growth opportunity to be in supplying General Motors with parts and with a small, inexpensive automobile for worldwide distribution. Finally, Daewoo Electronics favored expanding its U.S. business by supplying leading U.S. distributors with television sets, microwave ovens, and other appliances rather than promoting its own branded items.

Yoon Young-Suk, president of Daewoo Heavy Industries, explained management's reasoning for this approach:

> Korea may not have new product development capability, but it does have a good manufacturing capability. I don't think this has really been understood in the international market. U.S. companies are now fighting against Japanese manufacturers worldwide. Korean companies can be used as an important building block in their global strategy.
>
> We can produce the same product at a price 25 percent lower than Americans and 10 percent lower than Japanese. They say it is because our labor is cheap. There is a certain truth in that. But it is not the whole story. We are achieving cost reduction not only in labor-intensive industries, but also in technology- and capital-intensive industries as well. One of the most important reasons is our relations with vendors. First of all, we can purchase parts locally at a very low price, because we pay them in cash instead of three-month promissory notes. Second, we lower their price by providing various services to them, such as providing them with quality control systems and free service in checking their measuring instruments. Then, we regularly invite our vendors to our factory and show them why precision is so important. As a result, defect rates of the parts supplied from outside went down from 25 percent to 3 percent this year, which allowed vendors to lower prices on parts by 17 percent. Right there, we were able to save $25 million. Another factor in our low price is overhead. We do not spend as much as our competitors in general and administrative expenses, and we do not add as high margins.

Daewoo management, however, saw limitations in the long run to its role as a contract supplier of parts and products. This strategy would be viable only so long as Daewoo could maintain a competitive advantage in manufacturing. Moreover, it placed Daewoo in a disadvantageous position in negotiating margins with the contracting company that held the trademark and the market franchise. As a result, management was exploring ways to control its own marketing networks and brands.

An Emphasis on People

Lee Woo-Bock, founding member and vice chairman of Daewoo Group, noted the manner in which Daewoo developed its human resources:

> Daewoo's commitment to its people is an important plus for morale. We believe every person has potential. If a person is doing poorly, we start with the assumption that the company is not employing that person in accordance with his or her talents. In line with this belief, we have never fired anyone from an acquired company. We work hard to motivate these people.
>
> We are also actively building the depth and quality of our managerial and technical capabilities. We began in 1976 to recruit many well-educated people from Europe and the United States. And about 5 years ago we began a program of sending 20 to 30 engineers and managers for study abroad.

When Yoo Ho-Min, a managing director of Daewoo Corporation, was asked what he considered to be the most important factor in Daewoo's success, he responded:

> The spirit of being in a family has made this company what it is. Every Daewoo Corporation employee receives a present on his or her birthday. If employees are sick at home or at the hospital, their boss and fellow workers will visit them just like relatives. You will see Chairman Kim staying overnight at the home of a Daewoo executive on the eve of a parent's funeral [a Korean custom for one's relatives and close friends]. When one of our general managers was killed in the tragic downing of a Korean airliner by the Soviet military near Murmansk in 1978, he was promoted posthumously to the rank of director, his wife was awarded 70 percent of his salary for the rest of her life, and his children received scholarships for college. We think of ourselves more as the Daewoo family than as the Daewoo Group.

Extensive Financial Sources

In view of their ambitious growth goals, Chairman Kim and Vice Chairman Lee had devoted considerable attention over the years to the task of expanding the firm's outside financing. As a result of their efforts, Daewoo was generally recognized as being the most sophisticated Korean firm in financial expertise and sourcing.

Suh Hyung-Suk, executive vice president of Daewoo Corporation, remarked on the company's financial structure:

> Daewoo Corporation has actively increased its equity base through the open market. Its debt-equity ratio of 7.6 would seem very high compared to an average American company, but such a comparison can be deceptive. For one thing, a general trading company requires substantial short-term

export financing. Also, the lack of consumer financing in Korea and Korean ExIm Bank's requirement for suppliers to carry consumer credit makes our obligation higher. In any event, we have a far more favorable financial structure compared to the typical Japanese trading company with its debt-equity ratio of between 20 and 30.

As of 1983, Daewoo's portfolio of financial companies included three companies, as shown in Exhibit 2, but the group indirectly exerted influence on a number of other financial companies through stock ownership and personal relationships with their management. This latter group included the First Bank of Korea, Korea Merchant Banking Corporation, and more recently, KorAm Bank.

KorAm Bank was opened in March 1983 as Korea's first joint-venture commercial bank. The Bank of America held 49.9 percent of the ownership; the remaining 50.1 percent was owned by eleven Korean companies, with Daewoo holding the largest share with 9 percent. This position reflected Daewoo's role in conceiving the idea and initiating discussions with the American partner.

Daewoo's involvement in off-shore financing was also expanding in the early 1980s. In the early 1970s, the group pioneered in establishing foreign subsidiaries to help gain access to local bank credit. Until 1981, the external financing of Daewoo Corporation and its foreign subsidiaries consisted exclusively of bank loans. Since 1982, Daewoo, assisted by Chemical Bank and Goldman Sachs, issued commercial paper on two occasions in the U.S. money market for a total of $100 million. The company also planned to tap the Eurobond market and then eventually to issue debentures and stocks in the U.S. capital market.

Having foreseen the necessity of diversifying its capital sources, Daewoo hired Peat, Marwick, Mitchell & Co. in 1976 to start producing consolidated financial statements by U.S. accounting rules. To a question of why Daewoo was not listed in *Fortune's* 500 largest companies outside the U.S. in which nine other Korean companies had appeared, Suh Hyung-Suk replied, "We didn't want to [be], because the figures of all the other Korean companies are combined, and ours are consolidated. It's like comparing the size of balloons and pebbles." Were Daewoo to report its financial results on a combined basis instead of consolidated basis, its 1982 sales of $6.1 billion would have placed it sixty-fifth on the *Fortune* list, behind Hyundai (forty-first) with $8 billion and the Sunkyong group (sixty-second) with $6.3 billion.

In contrast to most Korean companies, which sought little publicity, Daewoo was very active in promoting its image through advertising and press releases. A representative of Hill and Knowlton, a well-known U.S. public relations firm, served full time as an on-site consultant to help the company become better known to the financial community, especially in the United States. Excerpts from a six-page advertisement published widely in the U.S. business press in mid-1983 are shown in Exhibit 4.

Daewoo's financial constraints were undoubtedly connected with two other corporate strategies: growth by acquisitions and joint ventures; and limited risk exposure.

안녕하십니까.

대우는 16년이라는 짧은 역사에도 불구하고 연 매출액 33억 5천만불을 자랑하는 국제적인 대기업으로 성장했습니다. 이처럼 놀라운 성장의 원동력은 인재양성을 위한 대우의 꾸준한 노력에서 비롯하고 있습니다. 대우는 초창기부터 인재를 아끼고 키우는데 정성을 다해 왔으며 그 결과 오늘과 같은 단단한 저력을 갖추기에 이른 것입니다.

대우의 인재들은 오대양 육대주에서 일하고 있읍니다. 그들은 언어의 벽을 모릅니다. 영어, 불어, 독어, 중국어 등 다양한 언어를 사용하는 세계곳곳의 고객들에게 대우는 한결같이 깊은 신뢰를 얻고 있읍니다. 다음 페이지를 계속 읽어 보십시요. 그러면 대우가 얼마나 커다란 능력을 지니고 있으며 얼마나 깊은 신뢰감을 주는 기업인지를 알게 될 것입니다. 대우는 성실하고 유능한 인재들이 이끌어가는 기업입니다. 대우를 귀하의 파트너로 불러 주십시요.

감사합니다.

김우중

대표이사 회장

Language has never been a barrier to Daewoo.

In just 16 years, we've become a leading multinational company with $3.35 billion in sales. Because from the beginning, we've dedicated ourselves to developing the talent, ideas and energy of our people. So now, when a company needs the help of experts, we're able to offer them what they're looking for.

I'm proud to be Chairman of a company with that kind of reputation. If the contributions we've been making to industry haven't already come to your attention, read the following pages. They'll tell you more about our recent ventures.

You'll see how Daewoo people have earned the confidence of a wide range of companies around the world. Because whether you speak Korean, English or any other language, one fact is understood. Good people make good partners.

Woo-Choong Kim
Chairman

Growth by Acquisition and Collaborative Arrangements

Every major new business entry for Daewoo had involved the takeover of an existing troubled company. Daewoo acquired Hankook Machinery Company to form Daewoo Heavy Industries, Okpo Shipbuilding Company to form Daewoo Shipbuilding, Saehan Motor Company to form Daewoo Motors, and Taihan Electric Wire Company's Home Electronics Division to form Daewoo Electronics. This approach enabled the young firm to take a major position in each of these new business sectors with little or no call on its limited financial reserves, since the purchase price was low and in several cases the arrangements included the transfer of bank loans.

As a result of these experiences, Daewoo management had gained considerable confidence in its ability to turn around troubled companies. Chairman Kim also saw a social benefit from this approach: "Which is a better arrangement for the nation, to rescue failing companies and to put their facilities and people to work, or to let them collapse while starting brand-new ventures?"

Daewoo was also eager to participate in collaborative arrangements with foreign firms for the same financial reasons as well as for acquiring needed technology or distribution. These collaborative arrangements ranged from joint ventures (General Motors, Bank of America and ITT) to long-term production contracts (Caterpillar).

Limited Risk Exposure

Contrary to his reputation as a business leader willing to take big risks for the sake of growth, Kim believed he was cautious in his commitments:

> I always prepare a second and third alternative in case the preferred course of action fails to materialize. A number of companies have tried to emulate our growth pattern by taking big risks. They failed because they did not recognize our policy of never positioning ourselves in a live-or-die, bet-your-company situation.

Share of Market

Although not a deliberate strategic choice, Daewoo found itself in second or third position among Korean firms in many of its business fields, including overall exports. This result reflected Kim's decision to enter new fields with Daewoo's limited resources rather than to specialize in just one or two businesses. It also reflected, according to some managers, that most of the companies had had low market shares when acquired and were still in the process of moving to high market shares. Others argued that being No. 1 among Korean companies was irrelevant, at least for the important world markets, because Daewoo was really competing against larger Japanese and other foreign firms as well as its compatriots. Still, the market share ranking did raise the question in management's mind as to whether Daewoo should continue to

Exhibit 5 Major investment plans, 1984.

Company	Investment	1984 Capital Requirements ($ millions)
Daewoo Corporation	• resources project	6
	• plant project	9
	• computerized cutting and raw material handling system	10
		(Total Project)
Daewoo Heavy Industries	• Caterpillar project	12 (45–50)
	• defense industry project	20 (40)
	• technical center and aircraft project	26
Daewoo Shipbuilding and Heavy Machinery	• construction of a yard for steel structure manufacturing	39
	• expanding and improving manufacturing capability	30
Daewoo Motor	• manufacture of world car	86 (125)
	• parts manufacture	14
Daewood Electronics	• expanding and improving manufacturing capability	43
	• operating funds to produce microwave ovens and other new items	44
Others		227
Affiliated companies total[a]		566

a. Total capital requirement during 1984–1986 was approximately $1.2–1.3 billion dollars (based on fixed projects as of January 1984).

press ahead on all fronts or should focus its efforts so as to gain national or even world leadership in selected areas.

Resource Limitations

Whatever preferences Daewoo management might have as to which businesses to emphasize, it would have to take into account the resources available to it, both in financial and human terms. As shown in Exhibit 5 and in the appendix, the funds required to carry out the plans put forward by the group companies would amount to $1.2–$1.3 billion. Although creative and aggressive financing could be counted on to cover some of the shortfall between this figure and the funds available, Daewoo management would have to make some choices among the proposed investments.

The limits on human resources had to do with the need to bring on board the professional talent needed to compete in high-technology businesses. Chairman Kim had stated publicly that Daewoo would have over 1,000 scientific and engineering PhDs by 1990. Finding these people and learning how to manage them was recognized as a major challenge for Daewoo management.

Opportunity Knocks?

On February 15, 1984, Daewoo received an official invitation from the Korean Ministry of Commerce and Industries to participate in a competitive bid procedure for the sale of a government-owned, large-scale integrated circuit (LSI) plant. This opportunity brought into sharp focus the difficult strategic choices management faced as to the direction, emphasis, and timing of the company's commitments.

The Korean government had set up the plant in 1980 to develop national expertise in LSI technology. The subsequent entry by the Samsung and the Lucky-Goldstar groups into LSI operations removed the need for the government's continuing involvement. Although dedicated to research and development activities, the plant was capable of producing annually 150,000 four-inch diameter wafer starts, which could yield over 20 million integrated circuit chips. These chips were used for television sets, telecommunication equipment, and other industrial applications.

Daewoo management had reason to believe that it could win the award with a bid of $40 million. An additional $40 to $45 million would have to be invested in equipment to make the plant economic for mass production. This sum compared favorably with the $100+ million requirement Daewoo had been confronting in considering the possibility of leapfrogging the current LSI technology by moving directly to the newly emerging VLSI (very-large-scale integrated circuits) technology. Either move would require an additional annual investment in R&D of $10 to $15 million.

For Daewoo, the plant acquisition offered both advantages and disadvantages. The most important advantage was in getting some 200 workers and engineers with three to five years' experience. This acquisition of trained people coupled with existing operating equipment would help to speed up Daewoo's entry into high-technology electronics by two years.

Less favorable was the age of the equipment. In this rapidly changing field, three-year-old equipment was dated. The greatest disadvantage, however, was one of timing. Daewoo and General Motors were just bringing to a close lengthy negotiations that would require each partner to invest $125 million in new Korean facilities to build small cars for sale in the United States. This arrangement would place heavy demands on Daewoo's financial and managerial resources.

Daewoo management had two days to respond to the government concerning its intentions to bid or not.

Appendix: Major Affiliated Companies of the Daewoo Group

Among the twenty-five affiliated companies, five stood out in their importance to the Daewoo Group: Daewoo Corporation; Daewoo Heavy Industries, Ltd.; Daewoo Shipbuilding and Heavy Machinery, Ltd.; Daewoo Motor Company; and Daewoo Electronics Company. Each of the "Big Five," as they were commonly called, is described briefly below.

Daewoo Corporation

Daewoo Corporation was the senior unit in the group, given its history and role as the holding company for the other affiliated companies. It was formed in 1981 as a result of a merger of the Daewoo Industrial Company (trading and textiles) and Daewoo Development Company (construction). Its total sales of $4 billion and net income of $44 million in 1983 both ranked first among the 274 firms listed on the Korean securities exchange. Daewoo Corporation comprised three major divisions: trading, Pusan factory, and construction.

Trading division. Daewoo Industrial Company, which in 1981 became the trading division of the newly formed Daewoo Corporation, had been one of the ten Korean firms officially designated as a general trading company in 1975. Daewoo's trading business was concentrated on exports of textiles and garments (31 percent), ships and off-shore structures (28 percent), steel and metals (15 percent), machinery (6 percent), home appliances (5 percent), footwear (3 percent) and other products (12 percent).

The trading division's overseas network included fourteen subsidiaries and sixty-four offices engaged in selling, financing, and information gathering. In January, 1983, Daewoo was the first Korean company to open an office in Washington, D.C.

Although Daewoo's trading emphasis was expected to remain on exports, the company was seeking to expand with importing and overseas resource development. In 1983 the trading division imported $272 million of raw materials and merchandise, and was engaged in eight resource development projects. In May, 1983, Daewoo announced an agreement with a German firm for a joint uranium exploration and development project in Canada expected to produce annually 2,000 metric tons of yellow cake.

This move to imports and to overseas development reflected the increasingly gloomy outlook that Daewoo management saw for international trade because of growing protectionism. Lee Kyung-Hoon, president of Daewoo Corporation's Trading Division, expressed his concern: "In every single country of the world, scholars preach free trade, businessmen argue for free trade, and policy makers advocate free trade. But talking and doing are two different things. Despite the rhetoric, what we see is increasing protectionism in various forms. As it is, Korea's export volume amounts to only 1.3 percent of the world's total, and I am confident that it will continue to grow through counter-trade and other innovative means."

Pusan factory. Daewoo's Pusan factory was the world's largest textile plant. In 1982 it employed 8,600 workers and produced 72 million pieces of men's, women's, and children's clothing worth $203 million, representing 10.1 percent of Daewoo's total exports. Over the years, its customer emphasis had shifted from chain stores to brand manufacturers. In management's view, brand-name products not only increased the factory's value added, they also were less vulnerable to demand fluctuations.

Lee Yon-Ki, vice president in charge of the Pusan factory, was proud of the excellent labor relations the plant had enjoyed, pointing to the recent workers' vote against unionizing. However, he was concerned about Daewoo's weakening competitiveness against smaller firms with lower wages.

In light of the reduced growth opportunities in textiles, Daewoo management was seriously considering the possibility of setting up the Pusan factory as a separate concern with its own name.

Construction division. Daewoo's diversification into construction was as much by chance as by plan. In 1973, Daewoo purchased a half-constructed building in front of Seoul Railway Station to locate its headquarters. To complete the building, Daewoo acquired a small construction firm in order to obtain the necessary construction license. By 1983, the firm had advanced in its ranking among the Korean construction firms from 600th to second, next only to Hyundai.

In 1976 the company began overseas construction. At that time, the center of activity for the Korean construction industry was in the Middle Eastern countries of Saudi Arabia, Kuwait, Iran, and Iraq, where as many as ninety-seven Korean companies were competing. Instead of moving into this already congested arena, Daewoo focused on smaller but less competitive markets. Its first overseas business was initiated in Sudan when Daewoo was invited to build the National Guest House for $20 million. Daewoo was subsequently awarded an $88 million turnkey project to build a tire manufacturing plant. Daewoo soon expanded its operations into Sudan's neighboring countries—Libya, Morocco, and Tunisia.

In early 1983 the prospect of overseas construction business showed signs of waning. As OPEC's official oil price went down by $5 per barrel in March, so did construction activities in these countries. Chairman Kim, however, was undaunted by this trend:

> We can use such a slowdown in construction activities as an opportunity to increase market share. In a soft market, cost becomes a very important factor. With our dedicated people and efficient management system, we can outbid companies from advanced countries. It also gives us an opportunity to trim our overhead further, thereby increasing our international competitiveness. Our construction works used to aim at simple civil works. Now we are making every effort to raise value added by moving into sophisticated construction. We have formed a number of consortia with construction companies in advanced countries to get involved in such projects.

In 1983 Daewoo increased its construction orders by 50 percent over the previous year, with $2.3 billion worth of works to complete.

Along with other construction companies from Korea, Daewoo was actively looking for market diversification. In contrast to its competitors, which had moved to friendly countries such as Malaysia, Indonesia and Thailand, Daewoo was attempting to enter the markets traditionally less hospitable to Korea. Chairman Kim's target markets were Nigeria and Iran, both of which had big populations, large territories, and substantial oil money, but which were difficult to deal with because of the political situations. Kim explained the reason for his strategy:

> While the challenge is greater, so are the rewards. When you finally gain business in such difficult environments, you gain a protected market. We are willing to invest money on a long-term basis in order to enter such a market, and to lose money in one business if we can make it up in another. We have a concept of a total market approach in which all of our businesses get involved in a coordinated way.

Daewoo Heavy Industries, Ltd.

Daewoo Heavy Industries, Ltd., was created when Daewoo acquired deficit-ridden Hankook Machinery, Ltd., in 1976 and merged it with its previously acquired Dongkook Precision Machinery Company. The company produced diesel engines, rolling stocks, industrial machinery, earth-moving equipment, machine tools, and defense products.

In April 1983, the company signed a ten-year contract with Caterpillar Tractor Company to manufacture fork-lift trucks with a 4,000–6,000 pound capability for worldwide sale. The company was planning to invest $45–50 million for this project. Daewoo was also committed to a $25 million investment for defense products and another $25 million for strengthening the technology center, which was responsible for developing products such as robotics, laser-cutting machines, and automation systems. To provide the funds required, Daewoo Heavy Industries increased equity by $20 million in 1983, and it was planning an additional $25 million increase in equity and a bond issue of $20 million with a four-year maturity.

The company's main lines of business comprised machine tools, rolling stock, heavy machinery, and diesel engines for automotive uses. President Yoon Young-Suk was confident about his company's international competitiveness in the machine tool business with existing technologies. In three to five years, however, advanced countries were expected to bring out new technologies, such as intelligent machinery, which could make the existing technologies economically obsolete. Rolling stocks were big in volume and profitability, but future demand was difficult to project because of its dependence on government purchases. Heavy machinery promised the best potential in terms of growth and stability of demand, but the market was fragmented.

Daewoo Shipbuilding and Heavy Machinery, Ltd.

In its first year of operation, Daewoo received orders for and built a number of ships, including a 128,000 dwt shuttle tanker ($52 million) and four 22,500 dwt chemical tankers ($31 million each), simultaneously with construction of a one-million dwt dock. Since then, Daewoo completed construction of seven semi-submersible offshore rigs (worth $539 million), a 140,000 dwt bulk carrier ($38 million), a barge-mounted seawater treatment plant to be used in the Prudhoe Bay oilfields off Alaska for secondary recoveries by ARCO Alaska Inc. ($226 million), and a low-density polyethylene plant for Al-Jubail Petrochemical Company in Saudi Arabia ($120 million). In 1983, the company received the largest shipbuilding contract ever awarded, worth about $600 million, to build twelve container vessels for the U.S. Lines. It also completed construction of a second dry dock with a capacity to build 350,000 dwt vessels to accommodate the increased demand.

In spite of such brisk activities, in 1982, the first full year of operation, the company suffered a loss of $9 million on sales of $485 million. In 1983, the company made a net profit of $7.5 million on $517 million sales. Prospects for 1984 were much brighter, and the company expected to earn sizable returns from its operation. Explaining the reasons for the expected successful operation of the company, Managing Director Kim Tae-Koo singled out the existence of a vast pool of young people who worked twelve hours a day with a motivation to increase productivity to the level of Japanese workers.

Kaifu Hachiro, a leading authority in the shipbuilding industry and former vice president of Nissho-Iwai, one of the Japanese general trading companies with a strong position in the shipbuilding business, projected that worldwide market in the next fifteen years would belong to Korean shipbuilders. According to him, Korea would soon replace Japan as the leader in the industry. Such a remark would have been considered far-fetched in 1982 when Japanese shipbuilders took the lion's share with 48.5 percent of the world's total orders, while Korean shipbuilders were at a distant second with 9.3 percent. In 1983, however, the competition between the two became closer. Korean shipbuilders' share increased to 19 percent, while the Japanese share went to 57 percent.

Hong In-Kie, president of Daewoo Shipbuilding, shared Kaifu's views: "In Korea we expect to assume a leadership role in the world's shipbuilding industry. However, we are realistic enough to know that no one lasts at the top forever. Some developing countries such as China will become competitive sooner or later, and will eventually supplant Korea. In the meantime, we must work hard to realize our potential."

Although aggressively seeking shipbuilding contracts, Daewoo Shipbuilding had also expanded its offshore structures and plant equipment business. Chairman Kim related the two:

> In the long run shipbuilding is a better business for us than is offshore structures, such as oil rigs. Oil production is a relatively lucrative business, and the oil companies can afford to pay reasonable prices for oil rigs. But shipping companies have to complete on a global scale, and cost effective-

ness is the name of the game. So far as shipping companies are cost conscious, Korean shipbuilders have a definite advantage.

Today, however, the shipping business is slack and so is the shipbuilding business. Compared to 40 million dwt worth of orders per year in the past, there is only 15 million dwt worth of orders nowadays, 40 percent of which will be nationalized. So we are competing in a market with only 9 to 10 million dwt worth of orders. At best, Korea can capture 40 percent of the market, or about 4 million dwt. With our capacity and that of Hyundai's, that is not enough, so we have to move to other businesses to stay alive. The shipbuilding business is cyclical and will improve some day. When an upturn arrives, whether it is caused by a major international war or an economic boom, we can easily make money.

By the end of 1983, the company was in the process of constructing a skidway to accommodate construction of super-sized steel structures as big as 250 meters wide and 250 meters long. Daewoo's top management was also considering adding another dock with a capacity for building or repairing vessels up to 350,000 dwt in size. The required investment for the two projects was estimated at around $50–60 million.

Daewoo Motor Company

Shinjin Motor Company, the predecessor of Daewoo Motor Company, had been the industry front runner in Korea with over 50 percent of the domestic market in the 1960s. In 1972, the company entered into a 50–50 joint venture with General Motors, and changed its name to General Motors Korea (GMK). Beginning in 1975, its competitor Hyundai Motor Company captured the market with a subcompact called "Pony," which was domestically designed and produced. According to Choi Myung-Kul, president of Daewoo Motor Company, GMK was in a difficult position, since its engine facilities, constructed before the first energy shock of 1973, were geared primarily to making engines with a displacement suited for intermediate size cars. With the introduction of the fuel-efficient Pony by Hyundai, GMK's market position in the passenger car segment was eroded.

In 1976, the Shinjin group experienced financial difficulties and its shares in GMK were sold to the government-owned Korea Development Bank. The name of the company was subsequently changed to Saehan Motor. In 1978, the government requested Daewoo to acquire the Korean interests in the company. Mr. Choi said that Daewoo had wanted to acquire the company anyway, because of its strategic fit with the diesel-engine manufacturing capability of Daewoo Heavy Industries Ltd.

The motor industry, however, was heavily controlled by the government in Korea, whose policy was geared toward discouraging car ownership, because cars were seen as luxury items. The result of high taxes on ownership and gasoline was evident in the car-ownership figures: 7 units per 1,000 people in Korea, compared to 32 per 1,000 in Taiwan, 65 in Brazil, 70 in Mexico, and 115 in Argentina.

In August 1980, the government decided to restructure the industry. Daewoo was required to give up ownership of Saehan Motor Company only to have the edict nullified three months later. During this period, most of Daewoo Motor's inventories had been liquidated and many of the dealerships discontinued. At the same time, one of the worst recessionary periods hit the market during 1980 to 1982. Daewoo management, however, was constrained from action because investment decisions were in the hands of GMC expatriates.

In 1982, Daewoo negotiated with GMC for the latter to relinquish the right to manage the company. Under Daewoo direction the company changed its name to Daewoo Motor and launched a new small car that gained a 40 percent market share in 1983 in the small-car segment (which in turn represented roughly one-half of the total passenger-car market).

Although the domestic market remained small with 76,000 passenger vehicles until 1982, it was beginning to expand and was projected at 120,000 in 1983. Industry observers projected 20 percent plus growth rates over the next few years. Among the three automakers in Korea, Daewoo Motor's capacity of 90,000 units per year was the second (Hyundai's capacity was 175,000, and Kia's 75,000).

On March 7, 1984, the *Wall Street Journal* reported that General Motors and Daewoo had signed a "memorandum of understanding" to produce cars in Korea for export to the United States. The partners were said to be planning a $500 million expansion project to be financed by investments of $125 million by each partner and $250 million in loans. The resulting facilities would be capable in 1986 of producing 167,000 small, front-wheel-drive passenger cars that GM would design. GM would sell about 80,000 of these vehicles in the U.S. along with its lineup of small Japanese cars from Suzuki, Isuzu, and its proposed joint venture with Toyota.

An earlier report noted that Hyundai was constructing a factory capable of producing 300,000 front-wheel-drive passenger cars annually when completed in 1985. Like Daewoo, Hyundai planned to export half of its added capacity.

Daewoo Electronics Company

Daewoo acquired the troubled electronics division of Taihan Electric Wire Company early in 1983 and merged it with Daewoo Electronics Company, a small audio instrument maker. The new company manufactured most major home appliances—such as TVs, refrigerators, air conditioners, washers, and dryers—with a share of roughly 15 percent to 30 percent of the domestic market in each category.

Later in the year, the Ministry of Commerce and Industry (MCI) promulgated guidelines for electrical equipment manufacturers that would have them move into higher technology. According to these guidelines, these companies were to limit manufacture of home appliances and other consumer electronic products to 40 percent of their total output. The share of computers, electronic switching systems, and semiconductor memory chips was to be raised from the current 13 percent to 24 percent, while that of components and parts manufacturing would shrink from 45 percent to 36 percent by 1986.

Electronics manufacturers had anticipated the need for such a change. Daewoo Electronics, along with Samsung Electronics and Gold Star Electronics (a Lucky-Goldstar affiliate) had already begun to place more emphasis on the development of new products. In 1983 Hyundai Group joined the industry with a plan to invest $500 million in electronics over the following four years. This plan included setting up a subsidiary R&D firm in California's Silicon Valley.

Daewoo Group's future plans for expanding its high-technology electronics also involved its telecommunications unit. Daewoo Telecommunications was to look into the possibility of manufacturing semiconductors as well as computers and telecommunications. The initial stress with computers would be on the development of technology to manufacture and supply hardware to domestic and overseas mass markets. In the field of telecommunications, efforts would be made to develop such technologies as digital switching, pulse code modulation, optical communication, and bipolar metal-oxide silicon semiconductors. For this, Daewoo would need to invest substantially in R&D.

Eli Lilly and Company: European Pharmaceutical Operations

In the spring of 1990, Sidney Taurel, president of Eli Lilly International Corporation, described the objectives and challenges for Lilly's European operations.

> Our goals in Europe are clear. In 1986, when we were the thirty-first largest pharmaceuticals supplier in the European market, we set some aggressive growth objectives. By 1988, we'd moved up to twenty-fifth. By 1990, our goal was to reach the top twenty—and we're well on our way to achieving this immediate objective. Our goal for 1995 is to be in the top fifteen, and within the 1990s to reach the top ten. This is our real challenge, and achieving it will push all the resources we've been putting in place over the last five years.
>
> Our goals in Europe are important to the entire company. For decades, Lilly has been a leading U.S. pharmaceuticals supplier. We're now attempting to extend this position around the world. Given the changes taking place in Europe, especially the movement toward a unified market, there is an increasing interdependence among activities in the various countries. Because of these developments, we have to think carefully about our strategy for conducting business in Europe, including the appropriate roles for "Indy" [company name for corporate headquarters in Indianapolis], for "LEO" [the Lilly European Office], and for our affiliates.

Although Eli Lilly was the third largest pharmaceuticals supplier in the United States, the largest market in the world, it ranked eleventh worldwide. In the important European market, it ranked as the twenty-fifth largest supplier, putting it in the second or third tier in that region. Several of the company's leading competitors were significantly ahead in their overseas business activity.

In the last few years, the company had been making substantial investments to strengthen its position in key markets outside the United States. These investments were part of the company's long term strategy to seek global leadership in anticipation of the changes taking place in the industry. This case focuses on Lilly's efforts to advance its pharmaceutical business in Europe as part of its worldwide quest.

Pharmaceutical Industry

In 1988, the world market for pharmaceuticals totaled $154.2 billion, a 15.6 percent increase from 1987 and representing a compound annual growth rate of 14.3 percent over the prior five-year period. The market could be divided into two segments: retail and hospital. In all of the top eleven markets, except Japan, the retail percentage was more than 80 percent, whereas in Japan, this share was 52 percent. Due to concentrated buying decisions and more government regulation, competition in the hospital segment was more severe than in the retail sector. Exhibit 1 provides a breakdown of the market by region and country. The top eight markets accounted for 77 percent of the total world market. Exhibit 2 provides a breakdown of the ranking of leading pharmaceuticals suppliers around the world and by major region. In each major market, there were great differences in market share based on the supplier's nationality, as outlined in Exhibit 3.

Exhibit 4 shows a breakdown of the worldwide pharmaceuticals market by major therapeutic classes, including the share of total demand for each category by major geographical area. The markets for pharmaceutical products traditionally varied from country to country, reflecting differences in philosophies of medical practice, approaches to testing of health care products, and government programs for financing medical costs. Differences in health care markets were slowly but steadily diminishing. Although some medical conditions affected people in only a few parts of the world, the most serious problems were common in every major country. Traditionally, health officials took vastly different approaches to evaluating the safety and effectiveness of medical products, reflecting the preferences of local medical scientists and professionals. However, the occasion common for authorities throughout the world to communicate and develop common regulatory standards was on the increase.

The market for human health care products continued to show excellent opportunities for growth. Due to medical advancements, people throughout the world were living longer. In the United States in 1950, 8 percent of the population was sixty-five or older; by 1990, the proportion was expected to reach 13 percent. The same trend was found in other major developed markets. Typically, people over sixty-five required three to four times the medical support than did younger people. In addition, developments in modern health care technologies, including recombinant DNA and monoclonal antibodies, created entirely new approaches to diagnosis and treatment and were expected to produce a steady flow of major advances in medical technology. In total, the worldwide market for pharmaceutical products was expected to grow to $185 billion by 1993 in 1988 constant dollars, representing a real compound annual growth rate of 7.9 percent.

Despite the large growth potential of this industry, there were new obsta-

Exhibit 1 Total world pharmaceuticals market.

Region	1988 Market (mil.)	% of Total	87/88 Growth	83/88 CAGR
North America	$42,082	27.3%	+14.9%	+13.0%
Western Europe	$43,301	28.1%	+13.8%	+15.7%
Africa, Asia, Australia	$44,051	28.6%	+17.5%	+16.3%
Latin America	$ 6,817	4.4%	+ 9.5%	+ 4.2%
Eastern Europe	$18,000	11.7%		

Rank Market	Market (bil.)	87/88 Growth (US$)	87/88 Growth (LC)	87/88 Growth (real)	83/88 CAGR (US$)	83/88 CAGR (LC)	83/88 CAGR (real)
1 United States	$39.0	+15%	+ 15%	+ 7%	+12%	+ 12%	+ 4%
2 Japan	$30.6	+19%	+ 6%	+14%	+19%	+ 5%	+11%
3 Germany	$11.5	+11%	+ 8%	+ 6%	+16%	+ 6%	+ 5%
4 France	$ 8.7	+16%	+ 15%	+13%	+19%	+ 9%	+ 7%
5 Italy	$ 8.1	+15%	+ 15%	+12%	+20%	+ 15%	+ 9%
6 U.K.	$ 4.4	+22%	+ 13%	+9%	+11%	+ 9%	+ 8%
7 Canada	$ 3.0	+25%	+ 16%	+ 6%	+14%	+ 16%	+ 7%
8 Spain	$ 2.9	+22%	+ 16%	+13%	+15%	+ 10%	+ 7%
9 Brazil	$ 1.9	+ 8%	+607%	− 12%	+ 4%	+200%	+18%
10 India	$ 1.9						
11 Korea	$ 1.8	+32%	+ 18%	+18%	+ 4%	+ 5%	+ 6%
12 Mexico	$ 1.6	+24%	+103%	+14%	+ 3%	+288%	+15%
13 Argentina	$ 1.3	+ 6%	+387%	+ 8%	+ 3%	+288%	+15%
14 Belgium	$ 1.3	+10%	+ 9%	+ 7%	+16%	+ 7%	+ 4%
15 Australia	$ 1.1	+34%	+ 20%	+16%	+ 8%	+ 15%	+ 9%
16 Netherlands	$ 1.0	+ 8%	+ 5%	+ 4%	+19%	+ 9%	+ 7%
17 Switzerland	$ 1.0						
18 Sweden	$ 0.9	+16%	+ 12%	+ 9%	+14%	+ 9%	+ 5%
19 Austria	$ 0.8	+14%	+ 11%	+11%	+17%	+ 7%	+ 6%
20 South Asia	$ 0.8	+13%	+ 26%	+ 8%	+ 4%	+ 21%	+ 3%

Source: IMS International, Inc.

LC: local currency
Real: constant price

cles facing pharmaceuticals suppliers. The cost and time associated with developing, obtaining regulatory approval of, and introducing new products had grown substantially. Standard estimates of development costs of a new drug were $125 million. A revised industry estimate based on a statistical survey of major pharmaceutical companies increased this figure to $200 million for every new drug launched. The development and approval period had increased from

Exhibit 2 World pharmaceutical suppliers.

Company	Origin	1987 Pharm. Sales	5-Year Compnd. Growth	% of Corp. Sales	% Corp. Sales in Home Country	Ranking			Number of Top Seven Markets Ranked:		Corp. R&D Expenses (1988)	New Prod. Sales as % Total (1987)
						NA	EU	AAA	Top 10	Top 25		
Merck (MSD)	U.S.	$4,240	17%	84%	53%	1	5	9	6	7	$ 750	A
Glaxo	U.K.	$3,160	31%	98%	11%	5	2	—	4	6	$ 580	A
Cibo-Geigy	Switz.	$3,020	19%	29%	min.	9	3	—	6	7	$1,100	B
Hoechst	Germ.	$2,700	10%	18%	24%	—	1	15	3	6	$ 600	B
American Home	U.S.	$2,420	9%	47%	69%	2	—	—	2	4	$ 265	B
Bayer	Germ.	$2,370	18%	10%	20%	—	4	11	3	6	$1,400	B
J&J	U.S.	$2,350	12%	26%	51%	4	12	—	1	6	$ 675	B
Smithkline	U.S.	$2,300	10%	42%	61%	7	13	—	2	5	$ 495	C
Pfizer	U.S.	$2,260	9%	46%	54%	8	—	—	1	5	$ 475	C
Sandoz	Switz.	$2,230	14%	45%	min.	—	8	14	2	7	$ 400	A
Bristol-Myers	U.S.	$2,101	11%	33%	71%	6	—	—	1	3	$ 400	D
Eli Lilly	U.S.	$2,090	8%	70%	73%	3	—	—	1	3	$ 600	C
Roche	Switz.	$1,940	8%	40%	min.	—	10	—	1	4	$ 800	D
Squibb	U.S.	$1,710			54%	—	14	—	0	0	$ 290	
Schering	Germ.	$1,670		55%	20%	—	15	—	0	0	$ 360	
Upjohn	U.S.	$1,650	15%	59%	60%	9	—	—	2	2	$ 380	B

Source: Annual reports, company documents, and IMS International, Inc.

Data are estimates in millions of dollars.

Ranking

  NA = North America

  EU = Europe

  AAA = Asia, Africa, and Australia

  —not ranked in top 15 in the region

New Product Sales as % of Total

  A = >25%

  B = 15%–25%

  C = 10%–15%

  D = <10%

Exhibit 3 Market share by corporate nationality (market share percentage).

Supplier Origin	U.S.		Japan		Germany		France		Italy		U.K.		Canada	
	'83	'87	'83	'87	'83	'87	'83	'87	'83	'87	'83	'87	'83	'87
U.S.	80.0	75.8	10.7	9.6	18.8	18.0	21.6	23.1	20.1	22.0	37.3	32.9	64.3	60.8
Japan	—	—	80.3	79.9	—	—	—	—	—	—	—	—	—	—
W. Germany	4.2	4.3	4.7	5.1	55.6	56.3	10.7	10.6	15.1	13.8	9.4	10.5	4.9	6.0
France	—	—	—	—	3.9	3.8	51.3	48.8	3.3	2.6	3.7	3.5	2.0	2.2
Italy	0.5	0.6	0.1	0.1	1.2	1.5	—	—	43.0	43.0	—	—	—	—
U.K.	6.0	9.9	0.9	1.3	4.2	4.9	4.3	5.8	7.8	7.1	35.3	39.1	7.5	10.1
Canada	—	—	—	—	—	—	—	—	—	—	—	—	7.4	6.8
Switzerland	8.5	8.2	3.0	3.5	9.8	8.2	7.5	6.8	10.2	9.2	7.3	6.8	9.5	9.3
Sweden	0.4	0.5	0.1	0.2	1.6	2.4	—	—	0.9	0.6	1.7	2.1	1.8	1.4
Netherlands	0.2	0.3	0.2	0.2	—	—	1.3	1.3	—	—	—	—	—	—
Belgium	0.2	0.2	—	—	1.7	1.5	1.8	2.0	—	—	1.0	1.3	—	—
Denmark	—	—	—	—	—	—	0.5	0.5	—	—	2.4	2.1	1.7	2.6
Austria	—	—	—	—	—	—	—	—	0.4	0.5	—	—	—	—

Market (column group header)

Source: IMS International, Inc.

Exhibit 4   Major therapeutic classes, 1988.

Therapeutic Class	Sales	% of Total	Growth Rate	Europe	North America	AAA	Latin America
					Percent of Total		
Cardiovascular system	$18,862	17.4	+15%	44	30	23	3
Alimentary tract/metabolism	$17,995	16.6	+14%	34	28	33	5
General Anti-infectives	$15,339	14.1	+15%	27	28	41	5
Systematic antibiotics	$13,044	12.0	+14%	26	27	42	5
Cephalosporins	$ 5,723	5.3	+11%	17	29	53	2
Central nervous system	$11,862	10.9	+13%	35	41	20	5
Respiratory system	$ 8,875	8.2	+19%	37	33	24	6
Musculo-skeletal system	$ 7,322	6.7	+15%	32	29	34	5
Blood/blood-forming organs	$ 6,191	5.7	+22%	36	20	42	2
Dermatological	$ 5,053	4.6	+14%	36	37	21	7
Genito-urinary system	$ 4,487	4.1	+14%	34	45	16	6
Anticancer agents	$ 2,887	2.7	+19%	19	23	57	1
Sensory organs	$ 2,346	2.2	+15%	28	46	23	4
Systemic hormones	$ 1,728	1.6	+15%	44	21	31	5
Antiparasites	$ 346	0.3	+16%	18	29	26	26
Other	$ 5,417	5.0	+22%	35	24	38	4
Total Market	$108,709	100.0	+16%	35	31	30	5

Source: IMS International, Inc.

AAA = Asia, Africa, Australia

Sales in millions of U.S. dollars

ten to fifteen years from the initial discovery of a compound. One important reason for this delay was the expanding number of patients required for regulatory approvals. For example, 1,500 patients were involved in the clinical trial of a product introduced in the early 1980s. For a similar product being introduced at the end of the decade, the number of patients required was about 10,000. One consequence was to make it necessary for pharmaceutical companies to expand the pool of potential patients for these trails to include more than one country.

The lengthening development time was an important challenge given the limited patent life for each product. A patent application, typically filed one to two years before the submission of an investigational new drug application (IND), restricted competition for seventeen years after the patent was issued. (Exhibit 5 outlines the development process for a standard pharmaceutical drug product.) Finally, there was substantial risk associated with the entire R&D process. According to industry data, only one out of every 5,000 to 10,000 compounds discovered was developed into a marketable product. In addition, only one out of four products launched provided a return sufficient to cover its initial investment.

Exhibit 5   Drug discovery, approval, and marketing process

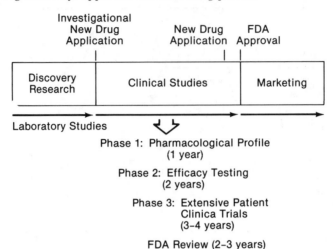

In addition, there were growing challenges even after a product was introduced. Because of spiraling health costs, there was in all major markets an
increasing emphasis on cost containment, including price controls, restrictive
reimbursement schemes, managed health care programs, and greater governmental involvement in medical and pharmaceutical reimbursement, especially
for the elderly, poor, and uninsured. These measures reduced the flexibility of
the pharmaceuticals suppliers in pricing decisions. Another significant aspect
of the changing market environment for pharmaceuticals was the growing
competition from generic drugs once a patent expired. It was not unusual for
sales of a drug to drop as a result of generic-drug competition by 35 percent to
50 percent in the first year and to continue to decline thereafter.

European Pharmaceuticals Market

In 1988, the European pharmaceuticals market totaled $43 billion, compared
with $42 billion in North America and $44 billion in Africa, Asia, and Australia.
From 1983 to 1988, the market grew at a compound annual rate of 15.7 percent,
compared with a worldwide growth rate of 14.3 percent. The European market
could be broken down into two segments: the five largest markets—West Germany ($11.5 billion), France ($8.7 billion), Italy ($8.1 billion), United Kingdom
($4.4 billion), and Spain ($3.0 billion)—and the smaller markets—Belgium ($1.3
billion), the Netherlands and Switzerland (each $1.0 billion), and other coun-
tries (each individually less than $1.0 billion). In 1988, the largest five countries
accounted for 85 percent of total European pharmaceutical sales.

Distribution channels for pharmaceutical products in Europe differed by
country, but in every market the primary channel was through wholesalers,
accounting for about 75 percent of product distribution. Typically, only sales

Exhibit 6   European Community: The sum of its parts.

Country	Area (thousand km)	Population (thousands)	GDP ($ billion)	Per Capita GDP
Belgium*	30.5	9,920	152.5	$15,376
Denmark**	43.1	5,130	101.3	19,751
France**	544.0	55,630	878.9	15,799
Greece**	132.0	9,990	47.2	4,722
Ireland**	68.9	3,540	29.4	8,313
Italy**	301.3	57,350	758.1	13,219
Luxembourg***	2.6	370	5.7	15,281
The Netherlands**	41.2	14,660	213.2	14,540
Portugal***	92.1	10,210	29.5	2,893
Spain***	504.8	38,670	259.8	6,719
United Kingdom**	244.1	56,890	669.6	11,769
West Germany**	248.7	61,170	1,124.0	18,374
EC	2,253.3	323,530	4,269.2	13,195
United States**	9,372.7	243,770	4,497.2	18,448
Japan**	372.3	122,090	2,373.1	19,436

Sources: IMF, *International Financial Statistics Yearbook 1988* and *New York Times*, December 12, 1988, p. 12 (reprinted from "Europe 1992," Harvard Business School case number 9–389–206, by Professor John B. Goodman and David Palmer.)

*   1988 data

**   1987 data

***1986 data

GDP = Gross Domestic Product

to hospitals were handled directly by the manufacturers. From the mid-1980s, there had been a significant trend toward concentration of wholesalers in many major markets. By 1989, three to four wholesalers handled the majority of distribution in France, West Germany, and the United Kingdom. In addition, there was a trend toward consolidation among wholesalers across countries.

Market Unification—"1992"

In 1985, the Commission of the European Community (EC) issued a "white paper" on the future of the community, recommending the removal of physical, technical, and fiscal barriers among EC member countries and leading to the passage later that year of the Single European Act. This Act sought to remove all barriers for the free movement of goods, services, capital, and people by 1992, hoping to make Europe the largest single market in the world. Exhibit 6 describes the EC membership as of 1989. Specific provisions of the Act included removing all border controls, standardizing of more than 100,000 regulations within the region, eliminating national preferences for all public procurement contracts, harmonizing value added tax and excise tax regulations, and establishing a common market in services.

Industry Regulation

National regulation of the pharmaceuticals industry evolved to ensure the safety of patients and to control product efficacy. The primary roles played by regulators were: (1) approving new products, including regulation of clinical trial processes and standards; (2) monitoring existing products; and (3) controling product standards, including the manufacturing processes. In addition, in a number of countries, local government controlled pricing of products.

Within the EC, there had been a history of movements toward developing a centralized regulatory approval process. These efforts took two general forms: mutual recognition and central regulation systems. Mutual recognition programs were based on the concept that a product, after receiving approval in one country, would receive automatic, or expedited, approval in others. This approach would not require any new regulatory organization, and it would allow some continued sovereignty by local regulatory bodies. A central regulation systems would entail a single organization replacing the efforts of each national government. Prior experience with central approval systems had not been successful due to an unwillingness on the part of governments to relinquish control of their markets.

In 1983, a multistate review process that represented a hybrid of the two approaches was introduced. Under this system, a company could submit an application to the Committee for Proprietary Medicinal Products (CPMP) in Brussels after having obtained product approval in one member country. The CPMP would then send to other governments the application, including the critical evaluation report prepared by the first country as a basis for review and approval. Individual countries would still have the right to approve products, but would have to do so within a fixed 120-day period. Due to delays in obtaining individual country approvals, companies had been increasingly turning to this system. They felt that national governments would more quickly approve products introduced through this system than through direct local applications.

By 1989, in some countries, the backlog of products awaiting regulatory approval had reached a crisis level. For example, in West Germany, the crisis was the result of not only an increasing number of new-product applications, including generics, but also a government-mandated review of all drugs approved before 1974. Some manufacturers claimed that it could take as long as six years to receive approval for a new product in West Germany.

Pricing and Reimbursement

Every European country had some kind of national health insurance system that paid for a majority of the cost of pharmaceutical products, ranging from 50 percent (Belgium, Denmark, Greece) to 65 percent (France, Italy, Portugal,

Exhibit 7   Public and private health care expenditures as a percentage of gross domestic product (1984).

Country	Total	Private	Public
United States	10.4%		
Sweden	9.4%	0.8%	8.6%
France	9.1%	2.6%	6.5%
The Netherlands	8.6%	1.8%	6.8%
West Germany	8.1%	1.7%	6.4%
Ireland	8.0%	1.1%	6.9%
Switzerland	7.8%		
Italy	7.2%	1.1%	6.1%
Denmark	6.3%	1.0%	5.3%
Belgium	6.2%	0.5%	5.7%
Great Britain	5.9%	0.6%	5.3%
Spain	5.8%	1.5%	4.3%

Source: OECD data

the Netherlands) to 76 percent (United Kingdom) of the total cost. Expenditures under these programs were becoming an increasing burden on each country's national budget. Exhibit 7 shows public and private health care expenditures as a percentage of gross domestic product.

Prescription and reimbursement programs were closely linked. In the United Kingdom, doctors earned a flat fee per patient, plus special expenses. In France, patients were reimbursed for all services rendered on a fixed-fee per category-of-service basis. In West Germany, doctors were reimbursed for all services up to a specified limit per quarter. These systems, along with various cultural influences, had a significant impact on prescription and drug consumption patterns among EC countries.

Through the national health insurance systems, the national governments were the largest customers for pharmaceutical products. As a result, all European governments, except those of West Germany and the Netherlands, had some form of price control that resulted in significant price differences among countries. Exhibit 8 shows a comparison of average price levels throughout the region. Governments exercised controls over prices through a variety of methods, ranging from required price approval (France, Italy, Belgium, Portugal, Spain) to controlling profits (United Kingdom). Although West Germany did not directly control price, it did exert influence through regulations regarding reimbursements.

Although governments had an interest in controlling prices to manage health care costs, they also had to consider the need to promote a strong local pharmaceuticals industry. In most European countries, a significant market share was supplied by local producers, and low prices reduced their ability to recapture development costs and to continue to invest the increasing R&D expenditures necessary to remain competitive in the world industry.

Exhibit 8 Comparison of European
pharmaceutical price levels
(scale: minimum = 100).

Country	Industry Average	Lilly Average
Spain	100	100
Portugal	107	125
France	113	120
Italy	118	116
Belgium	131	124
United Kingdom	201	138
The Netherlands	229	172
West Germany	251	177

Source: Company data

Parallel Trade

One serious threat facing pharmaceuticals suppliers in Europe was the rapid increase in so-called parallel trade, or trade within the region by independent parties taking advantage of price differentials. Barriers to parallel trade had been declining with the move toward market harmonization, with the increasing sophistication of parallel importers (including their ability to repackage products), and with the increasing willingness of governments to license parallel importers in an effort to reduce health care costs. Given the substantial variation in prices within Europe, government programs to promote parallel imports were under way in West Germany and the United Kingdom.

Estimates of the potential impact of parallel trade in Europe ranged from 5 percent to 20 percent reduction of the total market revenue. This reduction would result from products in low-priced markets flowing to high-priced ones. The companies most affected by parallel trade would be the large multinationals with sales throughout Europe of key products with substantial price differences in each market.

In 1989, the actual level of parallel imports taking place was estimated to account for between 3 percent and 10 percent of the U.K. market and 1 percent of the West German market. There was, however, the potential for these levels to rise significantly. In West Germany, sales of Eurimpharm, the leading parallel importer, had been increasing 20 percent to 30 percent per year.

One method for manufacturers to prevent parallel trade for future products would be to establish uniform European prices. However, given the price control systems in many markets, these prices would have to be substantially below the maximum level of such major markets as West Germany, thus adversely affecting profitability in these markets. Furthermore, there would be little incentive for low-priced countries to agree to a uniform price higher than their own approved price level. If the uniform price was not approved, a company could potentially withhold the product from its market. However, such action would entail two costs. First, there would be a substantial reduction in sales. Some low-priced markets, especially France and Italy, had significant volumes, and the loss of these sales would be damaging. In addition, in an extreme example, if a company withheld innovative new products, suppliers would fear a system of compulsory licensing to local producers. If such a system developed, it could lead to low-priced competitors, because the licensees would not have incurred development expenses.

Increasing Regulatory Controls

A number of national governments in Europe had introduced, or were considering, further legislation to control health care costs. As an example, in the United Kingdom, the government had introduced a controversial white paper, "Working for Patients," which proposed new regulations making doctors responsible for controlling health care costs. Under the proposed system, each doctor would receive a cash budget for pharmaceuticals expenditures. Any doctor exceeding such budget would face financial penalties. Unspent funds would be shared between the doctor and local family-practitioner committees. It was not determined how such funds could be spent.

This proposal had major implications on the profitability and method of operation for pharmaceuticals suppliers in the United Kingdom. Expected implications included an acceleration of generic prescriptions, increased price sensitivity on the part of physicians, reduction of over-the-counter prescriptions (referring patients instead to purchase products from retail outlets), a reduction in drug treatment for chronic diseases requiring long-term prescriptions, and a potential priority of diseases, reducing treatment for some in order to meet budgets.

Eli Lilly and Company

Eli Lilly traced its origins to 1876, when Colonel Eli Lilly founded a new business with four employees and a total capital of $1,400. Through the years, devotion to scientific and managerial excellence led to its becoming the largest pharmaceutical firm in the United States during the early 1940s, a position it maintained until 1985. According to Richard D. Wood, chairman (only the second nonfamily member to hold that position) and chief executive officer, "The Lilly family and its traditions and values guide our operations to this day. These principles have been the cornerstone of eleven decades of success, and they seem as relevant today as they were in 1876."

By 1990, Eli Lilly was engaged in the discovery, development, manufacture, and sale of a broad line of human health products. It was a world leader in oral and injectable antibiotics, marketing one of the broadest lines of cephalosporins in the industry, and in supplying insulin and related diabetic care products. In recent years, the company expanded its product line into chronic-

Exhibit 9 Summary of financial data, 1987–1989 ($ millions).

	1989	1988	1987
Net sales	$4,176	$3,607	$3,236
Cost of sales	1,256	1,125	1,087
Research and development	605	512	435
Marketing	795	690	565
General administration	355	330	335
Restructuring	—	—	272
Other income	(165)	(130)	(35)
Income from continuing operations			
before taxes	$1,330	$1,081	$ 579
Net income	$ 940	$ 761	$ 644
Geographic Information			
Net Sales			
United States	$3,052	$2,674	$2,448
Unaffiliated customers	2,659	2,308	2,103
Transfers to other regions	393	366	345
Europe, Middle East, Japan	$1,338	$1,165	$1,015
Unaffiliated customers	1,151	999	877
Transfers to other regions	187	166	138
Other	$ 371	$ 302	$ 257
Income from Continuing Operations			
United States	$ 945	$ 764	$ 355
Europe, Middle East, Japan	304	260	185
Other	94	$ 67	$ 42
Eliminations and adjustments	(13)	(10)	(3)
Total	$1,330	$1,081	$ 579
Total Assets			
United States	$4,449	$3,972	$4,116
Europe, Middle East, Japan	1,571	1,366	1,462
Other	268	238	235
Eliminations and adjustments	(440)	(313)	(558)
Total	$5,848	$5,263	$5,255

Source: Eli Lilly and Company, 1989 Annual Report.

care and retail segment products, with the highly successful antidepressant Prozac, the antiulcer agent Axid, and several other promising products. The company manufactured and sold its products in twenty-six and 130 countries respectively. Exhibit 9 contains recent financial results and supplementary data. The company was proud of its record of increasing reported sales and net annual income for twenty-nine consecutive years.

Exhibit 10   Description of Eli Lilly organizational structure (compiled version for case use)

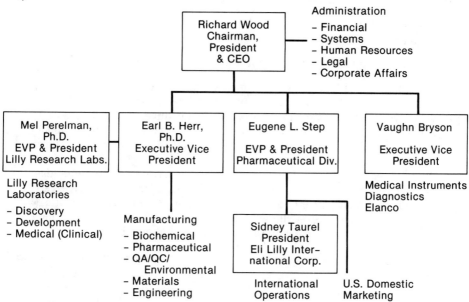

During the 1980s, Lilly's leadership recognized and responded to the many pressures for global operations that the pharmaceutical industry had begun to experience. According to a senior executive, "In 1985, a wave of new products for the future became clear. Richard Wood saw this wave coming and took steps to strengthen OUS operations [a Lilly term for "outside the United States"] to develop worldwide potential for products in the pipeline." In 1986, Wood put the International Division under Gene Step, president of the Pharmaceut-icals Division. This change created a pharmaceuticals business unit responsible for worldwide marketing activities of all pharmaceutical products. Under Step, one executive was responsible for U.S. marketing and another for OUS mar-keting. The purpose of these reorganizations was to orient each major business line to opportunities and markets throughout the world. Exhibit 10 describes the organizational structure of the company after these moves.

In addition to the reorganization, changes were made in the leadership of OUS operations, with the appointment in January 1987 of Sidney Taurel as president of the International Division, replacing Mel Perelman, who became executive vice president of the company, as well as president of Lilly Research Laboratories (LRL). Taurel, a 1971 Columbia MBA and the first international staff member to run OUS operations, had been executive vice president of International, stationed in the United Kingdom. While in this position, he had strengthened coordination within Europe, including initiating planning meet-ings for European country managers, medical directors, and marketing staff. These meetings were later expanded to include affiliates from throughout the world. Because of his experience, Taurel became recognized by top management as an expert in international business, and his selection indicated his expected role in leading an aggressive expansion of OUS activity.

International Personnel Policies

Dick Wood commented on the importance of management development.

> Constantly we have to work at developing our staff around the world, trying to find the right mix of staff and capabilities. I firmly believe that our value system is our single most important competitive edge and I am committed to spread it to all our operations. The most effective way we've found to do this is through interaction among our staff from different operations and backgrounds, especially when this interaction takes place at Indy where the total benefits of the culture are apparent. We have developed a number of programs to encourage these interactions. For example, we have very active formal management development programs for our managers at different levels from all over the world. I am also encouraged to see various functional groups now meeting regularly on a worldwide basis.

An important step in developing OUS human resources came about through several programs to hire, train, and develop foreign nationals. Initially, Lilly had hired foreign graduates of U.S. MBA programs. In 1986, it began hiring at major European business schools as well. New employees hired in Europe were typically assigned to their home country operations. In 1988 alone, a total of twenty-six European MBAs were hired, fourteen directly in Europe and twelve in the United States. Several major overseas affiliates were headed by executives who had participated in these programs.

Research Activity

R&D activity was key to the long-term success of Eli Lilly. According to Mel Perelman, president of Lilly Research Laboratories:

> We spend over $500 million on R&D activity, and there is an increasing need to ensure that we have gathered the best management and technology, as well as that we are betting on the right areas from both a science and market perspective. This requires a global approach in identifying and selecting the best prospects for major breakthroughs. Today, R&D activity, especially in the latter phases of clinical activity, is carried out on a global basis. Lilly used to conduct phases one and two only in the United States so that the results could be directly observed. We now use the world for clinical testing even before we know if a discovery will lead to a new product or not. This is necessary to move faster and use medical opinion leaders around the world; it subsequently helps in the marketing stage.

Before the 1980s, most Lilly clinical research and testing of chemicals had occurred in the United States, a pattern supported by the leading position held by the U.S. Food and Drug Administration (FDA). Regulatory authorities around the world had accepted FDA data in local applications. However, as a result of

Lilly concentrating these activities in the United States, key research physicians in other major markets, including Europe and Japan, did not recognize the company as a significant supplier. It had never approached these physicians with new drugs during the initial research and testing phase, and because they were excluded in the initial stages, they did not have much interest in studying the products when such studies were necessary for obtaining local approvals. In addition to affecting local regulatory approvals, this situation had a direct impact on subsequent marketing activities. Local investigators were typically important opinion leaders, who could impact subsequent demand for a product.

As an example of the progress made in clinical activities for three major new clinical testing programs under way in 1990, 50 percent of the test data originated in the United States and 50 percent in other markets. The data were generated using the same research protocol, and the applications for regulatory approval for these products throughout the world would incorporate these globally based data.

Lilly's European Operations

Sidney Taurel, as president of Eli Lilly International, was directly responsible for Lilly's international business. For business in Europe, Lilly maintained a regional headquarters, LEO, located in London, as well as affiliates in all major markets. The territory was divided into two regions, both of which reported to Gerhard Mayr, senior vice president of Eli Lilly International Corporation: the major European countries and the smaller affiliates in Africa, East Europe, the Middle East, and Scandinavia. The latter reported to George Baumer, area director, who in turn reported to Mayr.

One primary responsibility of the International Division was to ensure that the overseas operations were well coordinated in a strategy that met the corporate objectives for the region. Taurel described its mission:

> At Indy, we define the overall strategy, including the identification of our priority markets and allocation of our human and financial resources. There are a few major markets that account for the majority of pharmaceutical sales, and, of course, we want to make sure we focus our resources and activities in these markets. In the advanced markets, we have developed a strategy based on investing for the long term, and we try to ensure as much consistency with this basic posture as possible—even if we experience an off year from time to time in an individual market. We have to establish our position in these markets, and thus we have been investing heavily to build marketing and medical staff.

Much of the coordination of activities was accomplished through the unified planning system (UPS). In this system, Indy provided each affiliate with overall goals, and local management in turn was expected to prepare specific plans to meet these objectives, including additional resources requirements. In addition, affiliates were responsible for short-term planning and for imple-menting a strategy, once approved.

Affiliate management was measured based on both quantitative and subjec-tive factors. The quantitative measures included company-wide profitability for all activities related to their markets, local market share and rankings, and in-country profitability. Subjective measures emphasized personnel development activities. The objective of these measures was to have affiliate management promote total corporate objectives, not just local market interests.

Lilly European Office (LEO)

During the early 1970s the European regional office had been eliminated, with some company executives claiming it had become just another bureaucracy. However, during the late 1970s, the need for a regional office reemerged, and in 1979 LEO was reestablished. Taurel described the need for these LEO op-erations as follows:

> In the 1980s, as we began to commit greater resources to Europe in an-ticipation of new products, a new role for LEO began to emerge. In this process, we started to define areas where a regional office could add value to our total activities in Europe. We concentrated its efforts on medical and new-product-related activities, areas where we didn't have enough expertise at the affiliate level and where it made sense to build our capability on a pan-European basis. Since that time, we've constantly looked for areas where LEO could add value, not just another layer of management. Our concept for LEO has continued to evolve based on the concept of a lean, high-level organization guiding and influencing our affiliates in line with our regional objectives.

Gerhard Mayr, as head of LEO, oversaw all European operations, Mayr, who joined Lilly in 1972 after receiving an MBA from Stanford, described the role of LEO and its functions:

> The function of LEO is to lead and manage the growth of our business in Europe, including evaluating the therapeutic market and market oppor-tunities and recommending specific investments to maximize our growth potential. This function necessitates a three-year-plus outlook to manage within an overall affordable European plan. Such an outlook includes mar-keting, medical, financial, personnel, and production considerations.
>
> A key for our success is to move new products efficiently through the development phase to the market. We actively plan and coordinate product introductions and track the changing European registration requirements. We ensure that the European affiliates follow the same market research and planning processes. This allows exploiting synergies in increasingly homo-geneous markets. It also allows identifying local differences early and adapt-ing our strategy to them accordingly.
>
> Other important areas for LEO are "talent" hiring, tracking, and devel-opment to ensure the quality personnel needed for our rapidly expanding organizations. We are implementing programs to provide both multifunc-

tional and multinational growth experiences. In addition, we regularly re-evaluate the European production plan, considering the various incentives offered by national governments for new capital investments. And, we are actively building our European ISS systems structure to help manage our business today and our projected growth.

Apart from this multi-year outlook, the profit and loss responsibility requires an ongoing active involvement in setting key country objectives and measuring progress toward attaining them. We also want to ensure that the knowledge and expertise gained in one country is spread to others, where applicable, to take advantage of it.

If you look at these long- and short-term activities, you will see that we set performance targets and directions, serve as an agent of change, monitor performance, and help ensure that all possible help has been made available. We represent Europe to Indy, and corporate goals, values, and cultures to our affiliates.

At LEO, there were several staff functions reporting to Mayr to support his operation, including finance, personnel, and marketing. Given Lilly's traditional matrix structure, different functions both at LEO and at affiliates also informally reported to associated executives at Indy.

In marketing, LEO product managers visited affiliates to provide guidance and assistance in developing marketing plans. They also coordinated numerous medical events and symposia for regional opinion leaders and hosted Lilly European marketing meetings, which included staff from Indy. These meetings and visits were designed to ensure that affiliates took advantage of all successful marketing programs in Europe and that specific corporate and European management guidelines were followed. LEO marketing staff also represented Europe in key corporate committees that served as a linkage with other operations around the world.

Affiliate financial directors had a solid-line reporting channel to their general manager and a strong dotted-line relationship to the LEO financial director, who in turn reported to Mayr and had a strong dotted-line reporting relationship with Indy. After Lilly moved to a worldwide business structure in 1986, there were many demands placed on the affiliate financial staff. They often received direct requests for information from staff at Indy responsible for worldwide performance of specific products. Such requests caused some problems because these staff no longer had a single boss overseeing their activities.

One area LEO financial staff had been working on was putting more structure into its review process within Europe, including installing standardized reporting and planning formats. LEO staff considered this structure to be important, as it allowed them to review and communicate efficiently.

Some financial functions were highly centralized at Indy, including treasury, which was operated as a worldwide profit center responsible for cash flows, hedging, and other treasury functions. At the affiliate level, the primary treasury function was managing working capital, with authority limits restricted to borrowing or investing up to $5 million, with a commitment duration of up to one year. Indy also oversaw tax planning for each affiliate.

The affiliate financial director had traditionally been one of two directors dispatched from the United States. In the mid-1980s, this practice had started to change, and by 1989 there were mostly non-U.S. financial directors in Europe.

LEO's personnel department interacted with the European affiliates on all human resource matters. Several issues, including recruiting, succession planning, training, development, and corporate communication, were coordinated on a pan-European basis for all Lilly businesses.

One LEO personnel staff member described his function as being "both a facilitator and a stimulator, having responsibility without the traditional operational authority." A LEO personnel executive described the human challenges that management faced:

> What we are doing now in Europe is managing transition, from steady low growth to an organization trying to achieve heroic growth objectives in a very short period. One of the major challenges facing us is the recruitment and development of quality talent that will fuel the recognized needs we have for managing this growth.
>
> Another issue we face is that many of our affiliates have relatively young senior managers and directors. Although this is an outgrowth of the opportunities we provide, it can give new employees the perception of limited near-term growth. In addressing this issue, we work very hard to match talent with opportunities on a global basis. This process utilizes various training and development programs, including rotational assignments of increasing responsibility wherever they might exist in the Lilly organization.

In 1989, LEO formed a European Human Resource Planning Review Committee, which met for one full day with each affiliate to discuss all personnel issues. Through this process, LEO expected to link more effectively with Lilly's worldwide human resource planning process.

Affiliates

Lilly operated major affiliates in France, Italy, West Germany, and the United Kingdom. Traditionally, the company had concentrated its resources in the United Kingdom, which accounted for 70 percent of its capital base outside the United States. Specific operations in the United Kingdom included two production facilities (a dry-products manufacturing plant and a fermentation and biotechnology plant) and the only non-U.S. research facility at Erl Wood. (Although located in the United Kingdom, the research facility reported directly to Indy.) However, during the 1980s, the company had begun significantly expanding its operations in the other major countries, mainly France and Italy.

According to company executives, due to Lilly's increasing globalization efforts, the nature of the affiliate general manager role had begun to evolve. Affiliates began to receive more support from Indy in various functional areas, while other local requirements began to emerge. The following descriptions outline activities at the affiliates in France, Italy, and West Germany that typified the issues being faced by local management.

France. Lilly established a marketing and sales organization in France in 1962 and a manufacturing operation shortly thereafter. Before this date, Lilly had sold through local distributors. In 1989, France was the largest European affiliate in terms of sales. Total employment was about 1,000, with half at the production facility and half working at the headquarters in St. Cloud and in marketing. In addition, in 1989, Lilly announced its intention to increase its local presence by establishing a new human insulin production facility.

To introduce a new product in France, both technical and price approvals were required. For obtaining price approval, an application was submitted to a "transparency committee" to evaluate the relative contribution of the product compared with existing products. Suppliers requested a price level based upon their costs, prices in other markets, and efficacy, and then had to enter an "era of negotiations" with the government, often lasting from six months to several years, before fixing a final price. Several industry sources indicated that, for multinationals, these negotiations often included factors such as investment in local R&D and manufacturing facilities.

France typically had one of the lowest price levels in Europe, averaging about 60% of U.S. price levels. Such prices had led many multinationals to significantly delay launching products when they could not obtain satisfactory prices. For its last two major product launches, Lilly had spent more than a year in negotiations.

Felix Mosbacher, president and director general of Eli Lilly France and a 1962 Harvard MBA, joined Lilly in 1965. According to Mosbacher, "Given the degree of government intervention and controls here, our relations with government and civil servants are crucial elements of our business activity. This makes stability of leadership and understanding of French culture and how things are done here important to our operations." He continued describing how he viewed his functions:

> My job is to run our business here, making sure all critical decisions are made and implemented on time. Our main activities center around being an implementor for the core programs developed at Indy or LEO. General managers have very little autonomy, given Lilly's approval and planning systems. However, we are responsible for devising proposals to achieve our objectives. In France, one of my biggest challenges is to be close enough to the business to know detailed activities, while spending the time required on the external relations.
>
> We currently rank number thirty overall in the French market, being number four in the hospital segment and number sixty-five in the retail market. We've set some aggressive growth objectives and have recently increased our manpower as part of our effort to meet these goals. Now we need to make sure that we get the product approvals and price levels necessary to utilize the new resources and achieve our objectives. I have to manage these processes to make sure it happens.

Italy. Although Eli Lilly had operated in Italy since the late 1950s, the affiliate was a relatively young organization in 1989, with most executives in key positions having been in their posts for a relatively short time. Jean Bellin joined Lilly in 1979 and was appointed president and general manager of Eli Lilly Italia in August 1988. He described his market and operations as follows:

> Like many other countries in Europe, Italy has a system of price controls and has traditionally been one of the lower-priced markets in the region. There is a willingness on the part of the government to consider bringing local prices to average European levels, provided one does not treat the Italian market as a sales-only activity. Local production, capital investment, export, and co-marketing agreements are key elements of a successful long-term strategy. Co-marketing is important because it is one way to support the local economy and bring innovative molecules to a market that has not had a strong independent research tradition.
>
> Affiliate management here is responsible for the bottom-line results of all phases of our pharmaceuticals operations. Control over local manufacturing includes associated export activities, which account for about 25 percent of our total production.
>
> By nature, the pharmaceuticals industry tends to be centralized in order to ensure uniformity in the way we present our products to physicians. Our company is no exception, and affiliates work within a highly centralized system of frequent reporting and controls, based on approved three-year business plans, annual profit plans, and forecast reviews. In addition to the performance of individual products and operating-expense controls, there is close monitoring of management processes, ranging from sales-force activity, promotional strategies, and marketing trial plans to recruiting, salary administration, and personnel management.
>
> We look at LEO as a coordinating group for all the European affiliates. It provides a forum for us to meet with all the operations in the region to discuss issues of common concern. LEO also acts as a support group, especially for our medical and clinical areas.

Lilly Italia provided a good demonstration of the recent expansion of the company's infrastructure in Europe. In 1985, the medical group in Italy had fourteen staff members, including two medical doctors. By 1989, this group had increased to twenty-nine, including seven medical doctors. The group was then able to work as an interface between local authorities and opinion leaders and Lilly's medical group, helping to secure timely approval of new products and to provide information about the local markets to Indy. In the sales area, Lilly Italia expanded to almost 250 sales representatives.

West Germany. West Germany, the largest market in Europe, also had the highest prices for pharmaceutical products. As a result, all major competitors were active, with substantial resources to support their activities. Claude Bouchy, general manager of Lilly Deutschland GmbH and a 1974 Harvard MBA, described his function and activities:

> In general, Lilly is in the process of looking at the world as one marketplace. What this says about my role is that I should not be looking for independence, but rather for influence within our overall processes. The name

of the game for a general manager is to be able to influence global decisions and represent local interests.

On a consolidated basis, we ranked number thirty-five in 1988, and we want to get into the top ten. To do this, we will need both success with our new products and continued growth from existing products. All affiliates have been challenged to create plans to achieve the goals for their market. These plans were then approved in LEO and at Indy.

To meet our objectives, we took a two-stage approach. First, we expanded our retail sales force by 50 percent, while also expanding the use of co-marketing. For one product, we estimated we would need 200 to 300 sales representatives to be successful, but at the time we had only sixty sales staff in our entire retail sales force. One specific example was for Prozac, a product with great potential. We signed an agreement with Hoechst, the largest pharmaceuticals house in West Germany, whereby the product would be promoted jointly under a single trade name by Lilly and Hoechst. There is a cost associated with this agreement, from having to relinquish a significant portion of the price to the co-marketer, but we also can expand our sales volume significantly.

The second element of our strategy has been to concentrate our resources on the strategic products. In the past, we had all the product managers come in from Indy and tell us how to market their products. However, to be successful locally, we had to rank our products and put our resources behind those for which we had a competitive advantage, and then be the company with the strongest product marketing power for that product. One interesting thing we've found in going through this process is that our local priorities match fairly well with those of Indy. This was not the case in the past, when we were requested by individual product managers to actively market all our products.

Manufacturing Activities

Pharmaceutical manufacturing activities were broken down into three stages: development, bulk manufacturing, and formulation fill-and-finish operations. Development represented the linkage between R&D and manufacturing, and involved process development as well as the production of small quantities of products for use during clinical trials. Bulk manufacturing was the large-scale production of the pharmaceutical products, an activity tightly regulated by government authorities. According to industry sources, bulk-manufacturing location decisions were traditionally driven by tax considerations, where makers located the plants in "tax havens" and reduced tax liabilities through transfer-pricing mechanisms. Fill-and-finish facilities were smaller-scale operations that took materials from the bulk plants and supplied the final products. Traditionally, Lilly development and bulk-manufacturing activities reported directly to Indy, whereas many fill-and-finish operations reported through local affiliates. In late 1987, the company began to reconsider this approach.

Before the mid-1970s, Lilly had many small plants scattered throughout Europe, primarily serving their local markets. About 1975, it began a process of focusing these facilities along technological lines and building a pan-European manufacturing organization. There were three such plants: Basingstoke (United Kingdom), for dry products; Fegersheim (France), for injectables; and Giessen (West Germany), for liquids and ointments. Facilities in Madrid (Spain) and Florence (Italy) continued to supply products primarily for their local markets. This restructuring program, called REPO (Rationalization of European Production Organizations), continued to be implemented throughout most of the 1980s.

Manufacturing operations reported to the affiliate management and up through the international organization. Linkages to the U.S. manufacturing organization were informal and relatively weak. Performance measurement for these plants was incorporated into the measurement of the local affiliate, irrespective of the products' final destination. For example, at some U.K. plants, as much as 80 percent of the products were exported, but the plant's performance was measured as part of the local affiliate. According to some manufacturing executives, in some instances this evaluation caused problems because the affiliates were primarily marketing organizations and therefore not necessarily skilled concerning long-term production requirements.

In 1988, Lilly undertook another study of its manufacturing organization. This study pointed out the need to expand the linkage between manufacturing and product development so that a manufacturing strategy could be prepared during product development. It noted also the need for a global strategy for its manufacturing operations that would maximize the company's technology on a worldwide basis, while meeting with growing local requirements. The Manufacturing Strategy Committee at Indy, made up of senior executives of all major functional activities, was developing such a strategy.

In 1989, the committee began to look at what the company's European manufacturing structure should look like in the 1990s. By having representatives from various functional areas, the committee attempted to develop this strategy by taking into account all relevant factors, from optimal production economies to incentives for local investment. The concept that began to emerge was to develop a corporate-level mission for each plant to serve worldwide needs. In the mid-1970s, Lilly had begun the process of moving toward a pan-European structure. The Manufacturing Strategy Committee began to consider extending these roles worldwide.

Although each manufacturing plant continued to report to local affiliate management, support from Indy began to grow in 1990. According to one manufacturing executive at Indy:

> In terms of globalization, our manufacturing organization is just beginning to consider our opportunities and challenges. However, we have recognized the need to expand our scope, and, based on the Manufacturing Strategy Committee, we are starting to develop a company-wide consensus for the need for a global manufacturing strategy. This committee is acting as a vehicle for change to bring our manufacturing organization up to the same level of worldwide focus as that of our medical and marketing organizations.

According to several industry sources, it was a common requirement in this business to be sensitive to host-government-related matters in planning a manufacturing strategy. Given the industry economics, marketing advantages in terms of price differentials could easily overcome the benefits of manufacturing rationalization. As a result, most multinationals were attempting to balance these considerations.

1990 Status

Several executives commented on the status of operations in Europe. According to Gene Step, president of the Worldwide Pharmaceuticals Division:

> In our expansion in Europe, we are a little less than halfway there, and our future success will be based on the continuing flow of good products. In terms of our market share, we are only about a quarter of the way to achieving our objectives. But in terms of putting the basic infrastructure in place, we are about two-thirds of the way done. As we launch new products, we will continue to get better at it, and this will advance our drive toward being a world leader in our industry.

According to Gerhard Mayr:

> We have made significant investments in our European operations through a process of carefully controlled expansion tied to maximizing the sales potential of our new products. Looking ahead, the outlook for a "harmonized" Europe will likely change the economic and political structure of our markets. As our industry undergoes change and rationalization, a high premium will be placed on efficiency. Having implemented a pan-European process of managing our business and having a high degree of coordination between affiliates will be a great asset in facing these changes. Many European competitors still operate in each market as independent kingdoms. They are still struggling to develop a coordinated approach—and the multinational mindset necessary to run it.

According to Wally Lange, group vice president, Marketing Planning and Development:

> A major challenge we face in Europe is the issue of having qualified management at all levels of the organization to run our business. To be well run, a business needs to have a balance of skills and experiences at all levels; but with our recent rapid expansion, we have relatively inexperienced staff in many key positions. Building this infrastructure at all levels is critical. We have been actively working to install the programs necessary to develop this expertise, including personnel training and development programs, but it will take time. We will have to continue these efforts until we can build an organization comparable in experience and capability to our U.S. organization.

Challenges in the 1990s

Sidney Taurel described the status of operations as follows:

We've already invested heavily in our resources and organization in Europe. In the last three years, we've implemented a 50 percent increase in our sales organization and have significantly expanded our marketing and medical organizations. In markets where we didn't have the critical mass necessary for specific products, we've used co-marketing agreements. All these efforts have been successful. European profits have been growing at a rate significantly above that of our increases in costs.

With the evolving industry environment, we are continuing to feel the need for more coordination, and the way we run our business is gradually evolving. With our matrix structure and all the communication systems we've put in place, we have a good balance. However the environment will continue to be fluid until the mid 1990s.

Our key objective for each management layer is how it can add value to our operations. In this regard, we see some changes taking place in the role of our general managers, with their taking more active roles in local government and industry affairs. LEO's role is also evolving, given the growing benefits of pan-European-based activity. The success of our evolving structure will be dependent on having a truly globalized approach at all levels so that our local and regional operations can get the support they need while they expand their activities into these new dimensions.

The most significant immediate threat we now face is parallel trade. In the near term, it could significantly affect our profitability in the region, and, as a result, we are continuously monitoring our exposure and taking every effort to minimize it. In the longer term, this issue may be just an indication of the changes to come in many other areas.

General Electric:
Reg Jones and Jack Welch

On April 1, 1981, forty-five-year-old John F. Welch, Jr., became chairman and chief executive officer of the General Electric Company. Welch had spent twenty years in GE's operating organization—first in the plastics business, later in consumer products, and then as vice chairman. He was replacing the retiring Reginald H. Jones, a man described by some as a "legend." Indeed, the *Wall Street Journal* reported that GE had "decided to replace a legend with a live wire." Some wondered if the young dynamo could fill the elder statesman's very large shoes.

But Welch's first four years on the job convinced the skeptics that he had no intention of riding on his predecessor's coattails. By 1984, Welch had regrouped GE's sectors, redefined its core businesses, made massive investment and disinvestment decisions, changed the company's approach to planning, and drastically cut personnel. Despite a major recession in the world economy and flat sales, profits rose from $1.5 billion in 1980 to $2.3 billion in 1984.

Notwithstanding these accomplishments, Welch claimed at the time that he was only at the 15 percent mark of what he intended to do. He did not elaborate on the remaining 85 percent, but in the army of professional and amateur "GE watchers," there was no shortage of opinion and advice. This case chronicles the evolution of GE through the 1970s and early 1980s, focusing particularly on the changes wrought by Reg Jones and the way in which Jack Welch took that heritage and reshaped it to fit the demands of a new decade.

Part I: The Jones Legacy

When Jones was named as GE's new chairman and CEO in December 1972, he inherited a company undergoing a major reexamination of its management. A decade of lackluster profit performance in the 1960s came at the same time that three major ventures—commercial jet engines, mainframe computers, and nu-

This case draws material from General Electric's Strategic Planning: 1981 (copyright © 1981 by the President and Fellows of Harvard College, Harvard Business School case 9–381–174) and General Electric: 1984 (copyright © 1985 by the President and Fellows of Harvard College, Harvard Business School case 9–385–315).

clear power systems—were straining the company's financial resources. Pressure on corporate management was mounting, and GE's "sacred Triple A bond rating" was in jeopardy (see Exhibit 1).

Improving this financial situation was no easy task. In 1968 GE was widely diversified, competing in twenty-three of the twenty-six two-digit SIC industry categories, and was decentralized into ten groups, forty-six divisions, and over 190 departments. Indeed, diversification and decentralization had been the major strategic and organizational thrusts of GE's two prior CEOs—Ralph Cordiner, 1950 to 1963, and Fred Borch, 1963 to 1972. Under decentralization, GE's departments became organizational building blocks, each with its own product-market scope and its own marketing, finance, engineering, manufacturing, and employee-relations functions. One GE executive noted:

> In the 1950s, Cordiner led a massive decentralization of the company. This was absolutely necessary. GE had been highly centralized in the 1930s and 1940s. Cordiner broke the company down into departments that, as he used to say, "were a size that a man could get his arms around." And what the company would say after giving a man his department was, "Here, take this $50 million department and grow it into $125 million." Then the department would be split into two departments, like an amoeba.

In addition to decentralization, Cordiner pushed for expansion of GE's businesses and product lines. With growth and diversity, however, came problems of control:

> The case for Cordiner lies in his improvement of GE's numerators and in his creation of a truly remarkable "can-do" organization. He was the champion of volume and diversity and of make rather than buy. He built a company unmatched in American business history in the capacity to pursue those objectives. In the sense of home-grown know-how, GE *could* do almost anything; and, in the sense of in-house capacity, GE could do a lot of things simultaneously.
>
> But the very expansiveness and evangelism that were Cordiner's strengths were flawed by permissiveness and lack of proportion. "We can do it" too often became "we should do it." For example, massive investments with long payback periods were undertaken simultaneously in nuclear power, aerospace, and computers, with a blithe self-confidence in GE's ability to "do-it-ourselves." A sort of "marketing macropia" persisted in which previously constrained market segmentations and product definitions were escalated beyond experience or prudence.[1]

As Fred Borch faced the challenges of leading General Electric in the mid-1960s, internal studies of the company's problems began to proliferate. Finally, in 1969, Borch commissioned McKinsey & Company to study the effectiveness of GE's corporate staff and of the planning done at the operating level. He commented on McKinsey's study:

1. James P. Baughman, "Problems and Performance of the Role of Chief Executive in the General Electric Company, 1892–1974," mimeographed discussion paper, July 15, 1974.

Exhibit 1 Ten-year statistical summary, 1961–1970 ($ millions, except per share amounts).

	1970	1969	1968	1967	1966	1965	1964	1963	1962	1961
Sales of products and services	$8,726.7	$8,144.0	$8,381.6	$7,741.2	$7,177.3	$6,213.6	$5,319.2	$5,177.0	$4,986.1	$4,666.6
Net earnings	328.5	278.0	357.1	361.4	338.9	355.1	219.6	272.2	256.5	238.4
Earnings per common share	3.63	3.07	3.95	4.01	3.75	3.93	2.44	3.05	2.89	2.70
Earnings as a percentage of sales	3.8%	3.3%	4.3%	4.7%	4.7%	5.7%	4.1%	5.3%	5.1%	5.1%
Earned on share owners' equity	12.6%	11.0%	14.8%	15.9%	15.7%	17.5%	11.5%	14.9%	15.0%	14.8%
Cash dividends declared	$235.4	$235.2	$234.8	$234.2	$234.6	$216.7	$197.7	$183.1	$177.5	$176.4
Dividends declared per common share	2.60	2.60	2.60	2.60	2.60	2.40	2.20	2.05	2.00	2.00
Market price range per share	$94\frac{1}{2}$–$60\frac{1}{4}$	$98\frac{1}{4}$–$74\frac{1}{8}$	$100\frac{3}{8}$–$80\frac{1}{4}$	$115\frac{7}{8}$–$82\frac{1}{2}$	120–80	$120\frac{1}{4}$–91	$93\frac{5}{8}$–$78\frac{3}{4}$	$87\frac{1}{2}$–$71\frac{3}{4}$	$78\frac{1}{8}$–$54\frac{1}{4}$	$80\frac{1}{4}$–$60\frac{1}{2}$
Current assets	$3,334.8	$3,287.8	$3,311.1	$3,207.6	$3,013.0	$2,842.4	$2,543.8	2,321.0	$2,024.6	$1,859.7
Current liabilities	2,650.3	2,366.7	2,104.3	1,977.4	1,883.2	1,566.8	1,338.9	1,181.9	1,168.7	1,086.6
Total assets	6,309.9	6,007.5	5,743.8	5,743.8	5,347.2	4,851.7	4,300.4	3,856.0	3,349.9	3,143.4
Total share owners' equity	2,665.1	2,540.0	2,493.4	2,342.2	2,211.7	2,107.0	1,944.2	1,889.2	1,764.3	1,654.6
Plant and equipment additions	581.4	530.6	514.7	561.7	484.9	332.9	237.7	149.2	173.2	179.7
Depreciation	334.7	351.3	300.1	280.4	233.6	188.4	170.3	149.4	146.0	131.6
Total taxes and renegotiation	309.4	313.2	390.5	390.1	409.1	403.8	277.3	331.4	298.7	289.9
Provision for income taxes	220.6	231.5	312.3	320.5	347.4	352.2	233.8	286.7	254.0	248.9
Employees—average worldwide	396,583	410,126	395,691	384,864	375,852	332,991	308,233	297,726	290,682	279,547
Gross national product (current $ billions)	982	936	869	796	753	688	636	595	564	523

Source: General Electric annual reports; Business Statistics, U.S. Department of Commerce, p. 245, for GNP.

These problems included a highly fractured organizational structure, poor planning, a lack of business focus, and a corporate staff mired in ongoing operational issues rather than helping senior management to plan for the future of the company.

Strategic Business Units and Business Planning

The consultants' principal recommendation was for General Electric to reorganize on the basis of Strategic Business Units (SBUs). Each SBU would be characterized as having: a unique set of competitors, a unique business mission, an emphasis on competing in external markets (as opposed to being an internal supplier), the ability to accomplish integrated strategic planning, and the ability to "call the shots" on the variables crucial to the success of the business. A management task force was concerned that such a change might seriously jeopardize the successful functioning of GE's operational control system. To avoid this risk, management decided to superimpose the SBU structure on the existing line-reporting structure. For ongoing operations, managers would report according to the group-division-department structure. However, only units designated SBUs would prepare strategic plans.

As shown in Figure A, a group, division, or department could be desig-

Figure A   SBU overlay on existing organization.

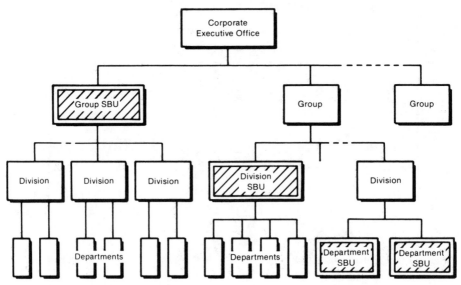

They were totally amazed at how the company ran as well as it did with the planning that was being done or not being done at various operating levels. But they saw some tremendous opportunities for moving the company ahead if we devoted the necessary competence and time to facing up to these, as they saw it, very critical problems.

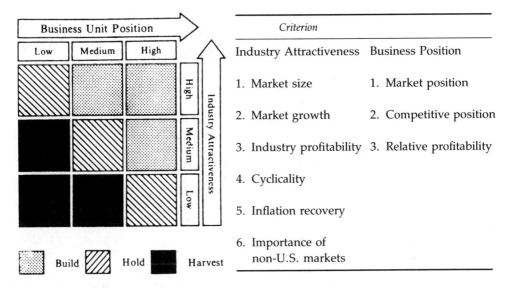

Figure B Investment priority screen.

nated an SBU. This overlay of a strategic planning structure on the operating structure resulted in a variety of reporting relationships. When a department was named an SBU, for example, the department manager would report directly to the CEO for planning purposes, but to a division manager for operating purposes. GE managers expressed the opinion that this approach provided the company with the best of both worlds—tight operational control on a comprehensive basis and planning at the relevant levels. One manager commented:

> In theory, the intervening layers of management were supposed to be transparent for planning purposes and opaque for control purposes. In practice, they were translucent for both. Even though the department or division SBU managers were to report directly to the CEO for planning, they would normally review their plans with the group executive. In a sense, we loosened the SBU structure to allow personal influence and power to shape the important strategic decisions.

Even with the reduction in the number of business plans from 190 departments to forty-three SBUs, the CEO faced a formidable task of review. One GE manager noted that "Borch had a sense that he wasn't looking for lots of data on each business unit, but really wanted fifteen terribly important and significant pages of data and analysis."

To deal with this problem, GE collaborated with McKinsey to compress all of the strategic planning data into an effective presentation by developing the nine-block summary of business and investment strategy shown in Figure B. One GE executive commented that "the nine-block summary had tremendous appeal to us not only because it compressed a lot of data, but also because it contained enough subjective evaluation to appeal to the thinking of GE management."

Jones added a proviso on how the plans were to be presented:

> At our general management conference in January 1973, I stirred up quite a few members of that audience when I said that I expected every SBU manager to be able to stand before a peer group and, without benefit of visual aids, give a clear and concise statement of his strategic plan. And that every manager reporting to him should fully understand that statement and be able to explain it to his troops. I meant it. When that happens, then you can say that planning has become a way of life.

Once the new SBU planning approach was in place, each SBU manager was required to hire a strategic planner. Because of the limited number of experienced strategic planners in the company, many were hired from the outside, an unusual practice for GE.[2] Both the SBU managers and their planners had to attend strategic planning seminars at GE's Management Development Center in Crotonville, New York. At the end of the courses, department and division managers (over 240 in number) were given a packaged slide-and-tape show to present to their subordinates.

Acceptance of Planning: 1972–77

In the 1950s and 1960s, a characteristic of GE was the belief that the company could succeed in all of the businesses in which it competed. A frequently voiced reaction to strategic planning and particularly to the nine-block analysis was that it legitimized exiting from certain businesses. According to *Fortune*, "GE stopped making vacuum cleaners, fans, phonographs, heart pacemakers, an industrial X-ray system, and numerous other products that failed to deliver the returns Jones demanded." During Jones's entire tenure as CEO, a total of seventy-three product lines were exited.

GE's successful exit from the mainframe computer business in May 1970 also played a pivotal role in legitimizing divestitures; as one manager commented:

> While the sale of GE's computer business actually preceded the adoption of strategic planning, somehow people began to connect the two. From then on it became fashionable to prune businesses. And Jones's subsequent promotion gave even more credibility to those managers who were willing to face up to the fact that certain businesses had to be exited.
>
> The planning system was just another tool which enabled a manager to face up to certain inevitabilities. Prior to this, we had really operated with a "floating J curve." In other words, businesses would forecast two or three years of flat or declining profitability, but then all of the numbers would

---

2. Over time, many of the SBUs developed planning staffs and the planning positions were filled internally. By 1980 there were approximately 200 senior level planners in GE. About half of these were career planners, while the others rotated through the position as part of their career development.

Table A GE's business mix (%).

	Sales		Earnings	
	1970	*1977*	*1970*	*1977*
Consumer products and services	22.8	23.5	29.6	29.6
Power systems	21.5	18.0	26.5	6.9
Industrial components and systems	23.1	20.6	28.4	17.6
Technical systems and materials	28.5	23.1	9.1	22.7
Natural resources	0.0	5.4	0.0	18.0
International	15.9	14.3	20.1	6.5
Corporate eliminations	(11.8)	(4.9)	(13.7)	(1.3)

Source: General Electric 10–K reports for 1970 (recast for organizational changes) and 1977.

point upward. What Jones did in selling the computer business and what strategic planning revealed was that the floating J curve was a fantasy.

Impact on the Business Mix. As shown in Table A, one impact on strategic planning was a shift in GE's mix of businesses. Reg Jones commented:

> Another source of confidence for us is the continued development of a strategic planning system that provides a strong discipline for differentiating the allocation of resources—that is, investing most heavily in areas of businesses that we identify as offering the greatest leverage for earnings growth, while minimizing our investments in sectors we see as growing more slowly or remaining static. [1973 annual report]

> Comparing the company today with the General Electric of only a few years ago shows that, in selectively allocating our resources to the growth opportunities identified through strategic planning, we have developed decidedly different sources of earnings and a different mix of businesses, whose potentials for profitable growth exceed those of our historic product lines. [1976 annual report]

As Table A illustrates, a major contributor to the shift in GE's business mix was the acquisition in 1976 of Utah International, a billion dollar mining company with substantial holdings of metallurgical coal.[3] Many saw in Utah a po-

3. General Electric's 1976 annual report related a pooling-of-interest exchange of 41 million shares of GE common stock for all outstanding shares of Utah International, effective December 20, 1976. Utah International's 1976 earnings were $181 million and sales were $1,001 million. The company's principal operations included the mining of coking coal, steam coal, uranium, iron ore, and copper. By far the most important contribution to 1976 earnings came from Australian coking coal supplied under long-term contracts to Japanese and European steel producers.

tential hedge against inflation and numerous opportunities for synergy with GE's other businesses. While not denying these benefits, in August 1977 *Fortune* reported:

> Jones wanted to make a lasting imprint on his corporation by providing a new source of earnings growth and creating what he likes to call "the new GE." Utah provided him with a means to make that concept credible. When the opportunity arose, he relied not on his hallowed planning staff, but rather seized the chance to personally lead his company into its biggest move in many years. As Jones himself now acknowledges: "Nothing in our strategic planning said that we should acquire Utah International."

Internal developments also contributed to the shift in business mix, as described by one of GE's senior executives:

> Much of the recent growth has come from the internal development of businesses brand new to GE. For example, engineered materials didn't even exist as a business in 1960. It was just a bunch of research projects. Now, it will have sales of $2 billion, it will make $200 million net, with an ROI of 18 percent, and it will have plants all over the world. The company's experiences with aircraft engines, information services, and several other businesses have been much the same.

Impact on Management Systems. Over time, GE's other management systems felt the impact of strategic planning. For example, manpower evaluation and selection were keyed to strategic plans. For the first time, the company could determine if managers really delivered what they said they would by checking their performance against previous plans.

Performance criteria were developed for incentive compensation that separated financial and nonfinancial business objectives. This was intended to provide greater emphasis on longer-term considerations, and it did to some extent, but as one manager noted, "It's a great theory, but in a crunch it's the financial results that matter."

Assessment of Strategic Planning. An internal audit reported that strategic planning had become ingrained at GE: 80 percent of those polled felt there would be no slippage and 16 percent felt there would be only minor slippage if corporate requirements for strategic planning were removed. The plans' flexible format provided room for some creativity and originality in the writing of the plans. Managers also appreciated the way that strategic planning helped them justify resources and gain the confidence of the people at the top of the organization.

Yet, complaints and criticism were also voiced. Some concerned the excessive effort devoted to cosmetics and upward merchandising of strategic plans. Others focused on the pressure for current earnings that undermined strategic planning. And several operations managers felt corporate-level reviewers did not understand their business well enough to be competent reviewers.

By the mid-1970s, SBU planning, while helping to strengthen GE's competitive positions and to improve profits, was also leading to a balkanization of the company. GE appeared to be moving in the direction of becoming a holding company—a development that ran directly counter to a basic GE management tenet. As early as 1973 Jones addressed management about the need to work "with the grain" rather than against it in reshaping the company. Prominent among the "abiding characteristics of General Electric," according to Jones, was "a strong preference for a single General Electric identity, despite our broad diversification." The world-famous GE monogram symbolized this core identity.

Coupled with the concept of a single GE identity was the notion of "value added." The recurrent attacks on big business, aimed at dismantling U.S. industry giants in the interest of increased competition, posed a serious potential threat to GE. As one senior GE executive explained: "The whole has got to be significantly greater than the sum of its parts. We have nothing to defend (against increasing external pressures to break up or, at a minimum, harass very large companies) unless we have a very effective, productive corporate level."

In Jones's mind, corporate review of SBU plans suffered from overload. He explained:

> Right from the start of SBU planning in 1972, the vice chairman and I tried to review each plan in great detail. This effort took untold hours and placed tremendous burden on the corporate executive office. After a while I began to realize that no matter how hard we would work, we could not achieve the necessary in-depth understanding of the forty-odd SBU plans. Somehow, the review burden had to be carried on more shoulders.

At the general management conference in January 1977, Reg Jones announced his intention to "revise GE's strategic planning system and to establish a 'sector' organization structure as the pivotal concept for the redesign effort." The proposed changes aimed to improve the strategic planning review process and to develop a cohesive plan for GE as a single, integrated entity.

Creating the sector structure was Jones's way of spreading the review load. The sector was defined as a new level of management that represented a macrobusiness or industry area. The sector executive would serve as the GE spokesperson for that industry and would be responsible for providing management direction to the member SBUs and for integrating the SBU strategies into a sector-strategic plan. The corporate executive office would thereafter focus its review on the strategic plans of the six sectors.

The new organizational line structure is depicted in Figure C. The dual organization in use since 1971—SBUs for planning; group, divisions, and departments for operations—was supplemented by the sector-SBU structure. The earlier designations of group, division, and department were retained to indicate the relative size of an SBU.

Along with improved review, the new sector structure was also seen as clarifying the responsibilities for business development in GE. According to a senior corporate strategic-planning staff executive: "Conceptually, SBUs are expected to develop new business opportunities by extending into contiguous

Figure C   Sector-SBU structure.

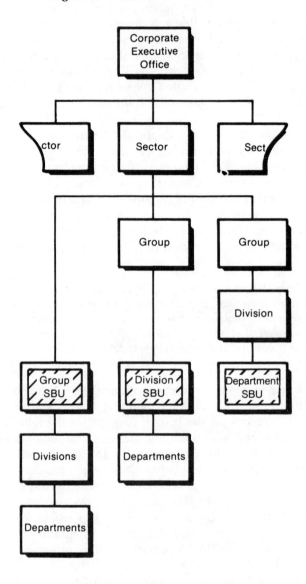

product-market areas. Sectors are expected to develop new SBUs by diversifying within their macroindustry scopes. And corporate is expected to develop new sectors by diversifying into unserved macroindustries."

Improving strategy review and business development were two visible reasons for the new sector structure. (Exhibit 2 shows the new sector structure and management assignments.) Jones also had a private reason for this organizational change:

Exhibit 2

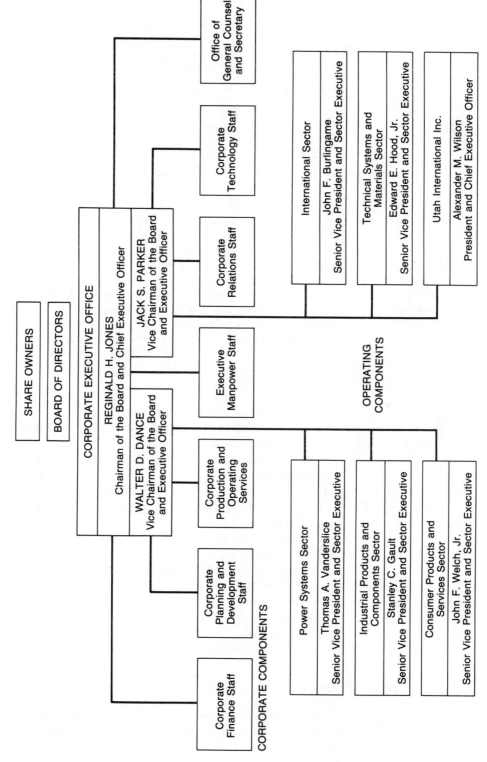

SHARE OWNERS

BOARD OF DIRECTORS

CORPORATE EXECUTIVE OFFICE

REGINALD H. JONES
Chairman of the Board and Chief Executive Officer

WALTER D. DANCE
Vice Chairman of the Board
and Executive Officer

JACK S. PARKER
Vice Chairman of the Board
and Executive Officer

Office of
General Counsel
and Secretary

Corporate Technology Staff

Corporate
Relations Staff

Executive
Manpower Staff

Corporate
Production and
Operating
Services

Corporate
Planning and
Development
Staff

Corporate
Finance Staff

CORPORATE COMPONENTS

OPERATING
COMPONENTS

International Sector
John F. Burlingame
Senior Vice President and Sector Executive

Technical Systems and
Materials Sector
Edward E. Hood, Jr.
Senior Vice President and Sector Executive

Utah International Inc.
Alexander M. Wilson
President and Chief Executive Officer

Power Systems Sector
Thomas A. Vanderslice
Senior Vice President and Sector Executive

Industrial Products and
Components Sector
Stanley C. Gault
Senior Vice President and Sector Executive

Consumer Products and
Services Sector
John F. Welch, Jr.
Senior Vice President and Sector Executive

417

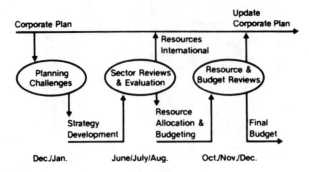

Figure D   Annual planning cycle.

I had a personal road map of the future and knew when I wanted to retire. Time was moving on, and I could see a need to put the key candidates for my job under a spotlight for the board to view. The sector executive positions would provide the visibility.

The men were assigned to sectors with businesses different from their past experience. I did this not only to broaden these individuals but also to leaven the businesses by introducing new bosses who had different perspectives. For example, major appliances had long been run by managers who had grown up in the business. I put Welch, whose previous experience had been with high-technology plastics, in charge to see if he could introduce new approaches.

Strategic Integration and Corporate Challenges. Jones also saw a need to develop a cohesive plan for GE as a single, integrated entity. In particular, he was concerned about uncoordinated actions and the lack of focus in connection with major opportunities and threats. "For example," he said, "I saw a need to push forward on the international front, a need to move from our electromechanical technology to electronics, and a need to respond to the problems of productivity. We needed a way to challenge our managers to respond to these pressing issues in an integrated fashion."

To provide corporate direction and impetus on such issues, Jones introduced the concept of corporate planning challenges. Each year he would issue a number of specific challenges that had to be addressed in the strategic plans of the SBUs and the sectors (see Figure D). For example, a 1980 corporate challenge called for a company-wide productivity increase of 6 percent. Each SBU and sector had to plan for improvements appropriate for their industry to counter worldwide competitive threats.

Jones saw the selection of challenges as a vital function of the chief executive officer:

> It's the job of the CEO to look ahead. Planning can be helpful, but it is really our job to look at the decade ahead. You look at the environment and couple that with your knowledge of the operations. You begin to see gaps that are beyond the plans. You have studies made to examine the possible shortcomings.

For example, as a defrocked bookkeeper, I have always had a concern about technology. In 1976, I commissioned a company-wide study of our strengths, weaknesses, and needs in technology. The findings—sixteen volumes of them—triggered a technological renaissance in GE. We stepped up our R&D budgets, built up our electronic capabilities and reoriented our recruiting and training activities. Now every SBU has a firm technological strategy integrated with its business strategy.

Implementing the New Structure. After allowing time for the new structure to take root, Jones made the following assessment three years later:

"The sector approach has turned out to be very successful. It even exceeded my expectations. Now I can look at six planning books and understand them well enough to ask the right questions. I could not do that before. The sectors also gave the board and me an excellent means for deciding on my successor. By 1979 the competition had been narrowed down to Burlingame, Hood, and Welch, and these men were moved up to vice chairman positions."

(See Exhibit 3 for biographical data.)

Jones was also pleased with the progress GE had made in responding to a number of corporate challenges. He pointed with particular pride to the "technological renaissance" that had begun to change the company's basic technology from electromechanical to electronics. Through acquisitions and increased R&D expenditures, there was a company-wide effort to apply the new microelectronics and the related information-based technologies to a wide range of GE products, services, and processes.

GE in 1980: A Call for Growth

In December 1979, Jones pointed to how GE was "positioned to achieve the objective of sustained earnings growth, faster than the growth of the U.S. economy, in the 1980s." But such growth had important implications for GE's traditional management approaches.

Challenging Forecasts and Realigning Resources. This public promise of rapid growth carried major implications for strategic planning. Early in 1980, Daniel Fink, the newly appointed senior vice president for corporate planning and development, questioned the adequacy of the existing strategic plans to meet Jones's growth challenge. After reviewing the recent and projected changes in business mix (see Table B), Fink suggested that GE's implied strategy seemed to be one of slowing the successful diversification of the previous decade (see Exhibit 4):

The vision of GE in 1984 that we get from the long-range forecasts is very much like GE in 1979—same product mix, same international mix, same strategy of leveraging earnings over sales growth. . . . It's that contradiction of a steady-state GE and a rapidly changing world that gives us, I think, the key strategic issue as we enter the eighties. How do we attain the vision

Exhibit 3 Biographical data

Reginald Harold Jones born Stoke-on-Trent, Staffordshire England, 1917. B.S. in Economics, University of Pennsylvania, 1939. Joined the General Electric Company in 1939 as a business trainee and traveling auditor, 1939–1950; assistant to controller, Apparatus Department, 1950–1956; general manager, Air Conditioning Division, 1956–1958; general manager, Supply Company Division, 1958–1961; vice president, General Electric, 1961; general manager, Construction Industries Division, 1964–1967; group executive, 1967–1968; vice president finance, 1968–1970; senior vice president, 1970–1972; vice chairman, 1972; president, 1972–1973; chairman of the board and chief executive officer, 1973–1981.

John F. Welch, Jr. born Massachusetts, 1935. BSCHE, University of Massachusetts, 1957; MSCHE, University of Illinois, 1958; Ph.D., 1960. Joined the General Electric Company in 1960 as a process development specialist for chemical development operations; process development group leader, 1962; manager, manufacturing polymer products and chemical development operations, 1963; general manager, Plastics Department, 1968; general manager, Chemical Division, then Chemical and Metallurgical Division, 1971; vice president and general manager, Chemical and Metallurgical Division, 1972; vice president and group executive, Components and Materials Group, 1973; senior vice president and sector executive, Consumer Products and Services Sector, 1977; vice chairman and executive officer, 1979; chairman of the board and chief executive officer, 1981–.

John Francis Burlingame born Massachusetts, 1922. B.S., Tufts University, 1942. Joined GE in 1946; vice president and general manager, Computer Systems Division, 1969–1971; vice president, employee relations, 1971–1973; vice president and group executive, International sector, 1973–1977; senior vice president, International sector, 1977–1979; vice chairman, 1979–.

Edward Exum Hood, Jr. born North Carolina, 1930. M.S., Nuclear Engineering, North Carolina State University, 1953. Joined GE in 1957 as a powerplant design engineer; vice president and general manager, Commercial Engine Division, 1968–1972; vice president and group executive, International, 1972–1973; vice president and group executive, Power Generation, 1973–1977; senior vice president and sector executive, Technical System and Materials Sector, 1977–1979; vice chairman, 1979– .

Table B GE's business mix (%).

	1968	1979	1984	Projected change
Electrical equipment	80	47	44	−3
Materials	6	27	27	0
Services	10	16	19	+3
Transportation	4	10	10	0
International	16	40	43	+3

now to reject that static forecast and then take the strategic actions that will move us forward in the eighties, just as we did in the seventies?

The first step to generating unprecedented business growth in the 1980s was to select the target areas with the greatest potential for GE. In-depth corporate planning staff analysis led to defining the following six broad business "arenas":

- Energy
- Communication, information, and sensing
- Energy applications-productivity
- Materials and resources
- Transportation and propulsion
- Pervasive services such as financial, distribution, and construction

Because the arenas cut across sector organizational lines, Fink saw a need for new management approaches:

> We're going to have to get our act together if we're to tackle some of these new opportunities. We're going to have to develop coventuring techniques, motivation and measurement techniques that have thus far eluded us. It won't come easy; it's nontraditional. It's not traditional for those of us who learned to manage at the John Wayne school of rugged individualism.

New Challenges for Welch. By 1981, Jones had decided on his successor. Jack Welch had attracted attention first as an engineer and then as general manager of GE's Pittsfield, Massachusetts, plastics plant, where he was credited with increasing earnings 33 percent annually for more than a decade. Beginning with a product with no market, he was soon selling millions of dollars of Lexan for computer casings and auto bodies, and eventually overtook the market leader, Dupont. On the marketing front, Welch went all out. "Pitching Lexan as a replacement for glass, he made a TV commercial with a bull in a china shop. Naturally, everything but Lexan broke. That image—rude havoc that reveals a Darwinian truth—is Welch in a nutshell."[4] His seventeen years in Pittsfield with a wide latitude to do what he wanted gave him a strong respect for the freedom of action of managers.

4. Stratford P. Sherman, "The Mind of Jack Welch," *Fortune*, March 27, 1989, p. 41.

Exhibit 4 Ten-year statistical summary, 1971–1980 ($ millions, except per share amounts).

	1980	1979	1978	1977	1976	1975	1974	1973	1972	1971 (2-for-1 stock split)
Summary of operations										
Sales of products and services to customers	$24,959	$22,461	$19,654	$17,519	$15,697	$14,105	$13,918	$11,945	$10,474	$9,557
Operating margin	2,243	2,130	1,958	1,698	1,528	1,187	1,171	1,070	877	772
Earnings before income taxes and minority interest	2,493	2,391	2,153	1,889	1,627	1,174	1,181	1,130	963	847
Taxes	958	953	894	773	668	460	458	457	385	333
Net earnings	1,514	1,409	1,230	1,088	931	688	705	661	573	510
Earnings per common share	$6.65	$6.20	$5.39	$4.79	$4.12	$3.07	$3.16	$2.97	$2.57	$2.30
Dividends declared per common share	$2.95	$2.75	$2.50	$2.10	$1.70	$1.60	$1.60	$1.50	$1.40	$1.38
Earnings as a percentage of sales	6.1%	6.3%	6.3%	6.2%	5.9%	4.9%	5.1%	5.5%	5.5%	5.3%
Earned on average share owners' equity	19.5%	20.2%	19.6%	19.4%	18.9%	15.7%	17.8%	18.4%	17.5%	17.2%
Dividends	$670	$624	$570	$477	$333	$293	$291	$273	$255	$250

Market price range per share	63 44	$55\frac{1}{8}$– 45	$57\frac{5}{8}$– $43\frac{5}{8}$	$57\frac{1}{4}$– $47\frac{3}{8}$	$59\frac{1}{4}$– 46	$52\frac{7}{8}$– $32\frac{3}{8}$	65– 30	$75\frac{7}{8}$– 55	73– $58\frac{1}{4}$	$66\frac{1}{2}$– $46\frac{1}{2}$
Price/earnings ratio range	9-7	9-7	11-8	12-10	14-11	17-10	19-9	24-17	25-20	26-18
Current assets	$9,883	$9,384	$8,755	$7,865	$6,685	$5,750	$5,334	$4,597	$4,057	$3,700
Current liabilities	7,592	6,872	6,175	5,417	4,605	4,163	4,032	3,588	2,921	2,894
Share owners' equity	8,200	7,362	6,587	5,943	5,253	4,617	4,172	3,774	3,420	3,106
Total capital invested	10,447	9,332	8,692	8,131	7,305	6,628	6,317	5,679	5,118	4,754
Earned on average total capital invested	17.3%	17.6%	16.3%	15.8%	15.1%	12.5%	13.4%	13.7%	12.7%	12.3%
Total assets	$18,511	$16,644	$15,036	$13,697	$12,050	$10,741	$10,220	$9,089	$8,051	$7,472
Property, plant and equipment additions	$1,948	$1,262	$1,055	$823	$740	$588	$813	$735	$501	$711
Employees—average worldwide	402,000	405,000	401,000	384,000	380,000	380,000	409,000	392,000	373,000	366,000
Gross national product (current $ billions)	2,626	2,414	2,128	1,900	1,702	1,529	1,413	1,307	1,171	1,063
Common stock performance	$44–63				General Electric common share price					$47–67
	759–1000				Dow Jones Industrial Index					798–950
	111–161				Standard & Poor's Industrial Index					99–116

Source: General Electric annual report, 1980; U.S. Department of Commerce for GNP; Moody's.

Lively discussions were being held throughout the company on what GE should do about the factory of the future, the office of the future, the house of the future, the electric car, synthetic fuel, and the like. The list of opportunities seemed endless. As Welch commented: "My biggest challenge will be to put enough money on the right gambles and to put no money on the wrong ones. But I don't want to sprinkle money over everything."

Part II: Jack Welch Takes Charge

When Jack Welch took office in April 1981 as the new chairman and chief executive officer of General Electric, he described his vision for the company he was going to lead:

> A decade from now I would like General Electric to be perceived as a unique, high-spirited, entrepreneurial enterprise . . . a company known around the world for its unmatched level of excellence. I want General Electric to be the most profitable, highly diversified company on earth, with world-quality leadership in every one of its product lines.

The Early Months

Jack Welch began his tenure as CEO by traveling throughout the $28-billion GE territory, meeting people, looking at operations, and asking questions. He proclaimed that everything was open to challenge. Such issues as the way strategic planning was done, the role corporate staff and the sectors would have, and the degree to which acquisitions would take precedence over internal development were fair game. After listening to many different views and proposals, he returned to corporate headquarters in Fairfield, Connecticut, with a firmer idea of how he would proceed.

In early August, Welch announced a restructuring of GE's organization, which had been in place since 1977. Two new sectors were created (see Exhibit 5A). The first, Technical Systems, combined all of GE's business units that made extensive use of microelectronics, such as industrial electronics, advanced microelectronics, medical systems, mobile communications, and aerospace. As such, it contained nearly all activities that were critically involved in GE's Factory-of-the-Future strategy.

The second new sector, Services and Materials, combined some of GE's fastest-growing businesses, including GE Credit Corporation (GECC), GE Information Services Company (GEISCO), and the Engineering Materials Group. Besides pursuing growth, the sector was to seek opportunities for integrating GE's credit and information services offerings and operations.

This change in the sector structure accompanied a new approach to planning. Welch believed that the planning system had evolved from being fresh, idea-oriented, and effective to becoming bureaucratic and inhibiting. To increase candor and constructive discussions, planning reviews were restruc-

Exhibit 5A Organization chart, 1981

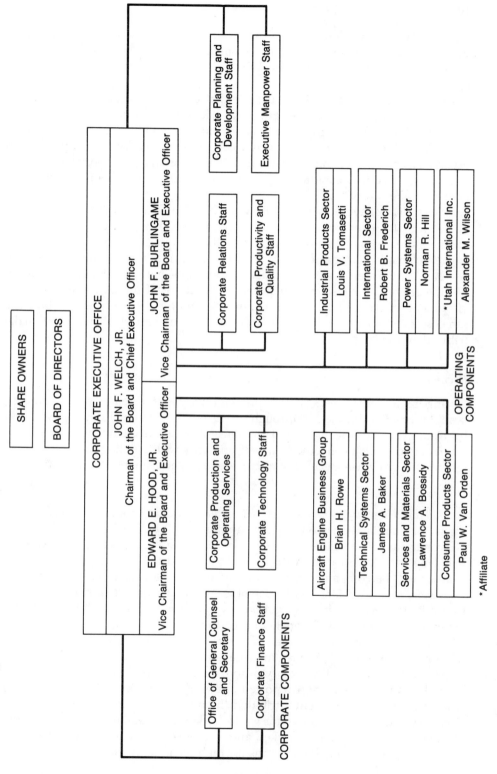

tured so Welch and two vice chairmen talked with individual SBU managers privately and informally. Rather than focusing on comprehensive strategic documentation or planning concepts, Welch directed the review around the key issues for each business.

At that time, Welch did not believe that an overall strategy could be described for a company like GE. He said, "How can you have a strategy for a company that in the last five months has committed a billion and a half dollars in Alabama for plastic plants, has put $300 million into Erie, Pennsylvania, to expand a locomotive operation, has built a North Carolina microelectronics center, and opened a copper exploration joint venture with Getty in Chile. There is no neat bow one can put on this."

Welch did believe that he could set an objective or central theme that would be relevant for everyone in GE: to be number one or number two in every business the company was in. Achieving this required the stressing of quality and excellence. "To me, quality and excellence mean being better than the best. . . . If we aren't, we should ask ourselves, 'What will it take?' then quantify the energy and resources required to get there. If the economics, the environment, or our abilities determine that we can't get there, we must take the same spirited action to disengage ourselves from that which we can't make better than the best."

Becoming Number One or Number Two

During his first four years, Welch pursued his plan for being "better than the best" by building businesses through acquisition and internal development and by exiting businesses that could not meet the test of being number one or number two. Welch concerned himself primarily with building those areas designated for growth—specifically microelectronics and financial/information services.

Building Growth Businesses. In 1981, after estimating that the world market for factory automation would grow rapidly to $30 billion by the early 1990s, GE committed $500 million to become a "world supermarket of automation." Believing that American industry would be forced to "automate, emigrate, or evaporate," the company was determined to create a Factory of the Future.

Several months before Welch took office, GE had acquired Calma, the world's fourth-largest manufacturer of CAD/CAM (computer-aided design and manufacturing) systems, and Intersil, one of the world's major manufacturers of state-of-the-art integrated circuits. The investment of over $400 million was justified by the enormous promise management saw in this market.

By 1984, however, the factory automation effort had stumbled. Revenues were flat, and the operation reported a loss of about $40 million after similar results in 1983. Management attributed the difficulty to large development expenses associated with its drive for world leadership in automation, slow growth of the industrial electronics market, and a slow economic recovery in general.

GE also targeted medical systems for high-technology growth. Already, the world's number one manufacturer of diagnostic imaging equipment (its old X-ray business had been revitalized by the introduction of the computerized axial tomography, or CAT scanner, in the 1970s), GE held great hopes for the new nuclear magnetic resonance (NMR) imaging device it had developed in the early 1980s. Total funds invested in the NMR device and a new, lower-cost CAT scanner topped $100 million. Welch was so willing to spend heavily to dominate the market that the president of Johnson & Johnson's Technicare Corporation conceded that competing against GE to be number one was unrealistic because matching GE's expenditures dollar for dollar could be "frivolous and very expensive."

In 1983 alone, Welch allocated $650 million for acquisitions and investments in the information service business, another priority growth area. To create a "supermarket of software services," GEISCO launched a program to acquire computer software companies focusing on five target areas: banking, manufacturing, financial services, management reporting, and energy.

Building Core Businesses. GE did not ignore special opportunities in its older, core businesses, however. In keeping with its high-technology thrust into the Factory of the Future, GE automated many of its own plants. As one sector executive noted, "We never appreciated just how profitable a 2 percent growth business could be when automated."

Between 1980 and 1983, the company spent $300 million to automate its seventy-year-old locomotive plant, and nearly $500 million to modernize its major appliance group. GE's locomotive and dishwasher plants were subsequently named by *Fortune* as being among America's ten best-managed, most efficient factories. Similar investments planned for the next four years amounted to $800 million. In some instances, entire manufacturing bases were shifted. For example, the decision to consolidate GE's lamp operations and invest $250 million to modernize production closed ten plants in five states and reduced the work force by 1,400 employees.

Exiting Businesses. While GE was building some businesses, it was exiting businesses that could not be number one or number two. If additional investments could not promote a good return and competitive success, the business unit in question was divested. In keeping with this policy, GE sold off 118 businesses from 1981 through 1983, for more than $3.5 billion.

The largest divestiture came in late 1983 when GE announced the sale of Utah International for $2.4 billion Although the business was highly profitable, Welch felt the money could be used better elsewhere. About the same time, GE sold its housewares division, which dominated the small-appliance market, to Black & Decker for $300 million. Profits were below company averages, and the money was used to help the consumer sector build the major-appliance line. GE also stopped taking orders for nuclear power plants, let go all but one of its broadcasting outfits, and sold its residential central-air-conditioning business to the Trane Company.

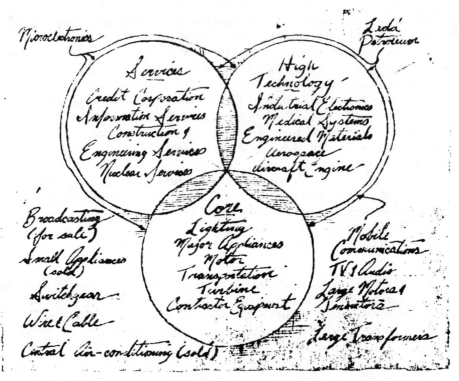

Figure E The shape of the new GE. Jack Welch's shorthand rundown of GE is based on three circles, covering the traditional "core" businesses (around 33% of profits), the high-technology businesses (30% but rising) and the services (29%). Around these main groupings lie the remainder of the businesses. Some are profitable, some lose money. Among them, they account for around 18% of sales. *Source: Forbes*, March 25, 1984. (Reprinted by permission of *Forbes* Magazine, © 1984 Forbes, Inc.)

The Three-Circle Concept

As GE built and exited businesses, Welch grappled to find a concise way to talk about GE to managers and outsiders. He wanted a concept that would have strategic meaning for GE. As Welch and corporate management looked at potential acquisitions and divestitures in 1983, a notion of GE as a configuration of three types of businesses began to emerge. In the three-circle concept, as it came to be called, all businesses were divided into (1) core, (2) high-technology, or (3) service areas. *Only* the fifteen businesses that dominated their markets would be placed in a circle (see Figure E). the businesses that did not meet the criteria of being number one or number two were placed outside the circles, and either had to come up with a strategy to get in a circle or be divested.

The three-circle concept came to dominate GE's investment planning philosophy. Welch decreed that core businesses were to focus on "reinvestment in productivity and quality," the high-tech businesses were to "stay on the leading edge" through acquisitions and large R&D investments, and the services were to grow by "adding outstanding people who often can create new ventures, and by making contiguous acquisitions." According to Welch: "We have our hands on a simple, understandable strategy for where we are, where we are not, where we can't find a solution, and where we have to disengage. We have to get used to the idea that disengaging does not mean bad people or bad management—it's a bad situation, and we can't tie up good resources, good dollars, chasing it."

In GE's thinking, the three circles were interrelated. The core businesses needed advanced process technology and strong service offerings to improve their competitiveness. High-tech companies served customers who were looking for solutions to problems as well as products, so that a linkage with services was important for maintaining a competitive edge in the industry. In turn, service businesses could not remain competitive without the benefits of the latest technology.

The Changing GE Organization

Besides the evolution of GE's strategy, structural and administrative changes occurred under Welch's chairmanship. Destaffing received the most press coverage, but he also made changes in planning, organization structure, and incentives.

Destaffing. When Welch took office, the U.S. economy was in its deepest decline since the Great Depression. To deal with a corporate bureaucracy that he sensed had grown too large, the new CEO emphasized what became known as destaffing. From 1980 to 1984, the total work force was reduced from 402,000 to 330,000, with 37 percent of the cutbacks due to lower sales volume, and the remainder representing a conscious effort to reduce staff and levels of organization.

The press nicknamed Welch "Neutron Jack," after the neutron bomb that wipes out people but leaves the buildings intact, a label he deemed to be exaggerated. He was convinced that a company the size of GE needed to stay "lean and agile" to be competitive, and acknowledged that becoming lean required destaffing. But he stated that GE had no intention of becoming "mean" in the process. He felt that GE had a responsibility to people who were not needed and that any action should "pass the fairness test that we'd like to be treated with ourselves." *Crain's Cleveland Business* of July 11, 1983, conceded that GE had used a "humane axe" in laying off 1,500 Ohio workers. The article pointed to the firm's offers of job counseling and placement alternatives and its efforts to explain "the inescapable necessity of it all."

Planning. By reinstating direct SBU reviews and focusing them on key issues, Welch had cut the 200-person corporate planning staff in half by 1984. His objective was to get "general managers talking to general managers about strategy, rather than planners talking to planners." Welch also dropped the requirement that every business have a strategy approved each year. A stable business with an approved strategy in place would only have to be reviewed every two to three years. A business in a dynamic environment with changing strategies would be under continuous review.

The newly hired vice president of corporate planning separated strategy and planning. He defined the former as the analysis of the elements of a business, while the latter was seen as the development of programs to support the strategies. He focused his staff's efforts on strategies, particularly seeking acquisitions and helping managers develop their strategy, while leaving the planning part to the managers themselves. To streamline the process, he stressed that his staff acted more as a consulting firm than as a police force.

Organization Structure. By 1984, Jones's six sectors had been reduced to four and several major businesses reported directly to the CEO. As shown in Exhibit 5B, medical systems, financial services, and plastics were among the businesses reporting to the CEO. A senior executive commented, "No one is quite sure what the role of the sectors will be in the future. My hunch is that they will slowly disappear and eventually the fifteen major businesses that fall within the three circles will all report directly to the Corporate Executive Office."

Welch considered choosing good people to be his most important job. Accordingly, he extended and increased his role in both the selection and review of key managers.

Incentives. Welch instituted new incentives that rewarded employees for their individual contributions. Corporate Executive Office (CEO) Awards were given for special one-time contributions. Special Stock Option Awards helped to build long-term identification with the company, retain key individuals, reward long-term contributions, and induce people to take unusually difficult or high-risk positions. Other incentives included restricted stock and special bonuses for meeting sales and income objectives in key positions in critical new businesses.

Welch's Philosophy

As he made his strategic and organizational changes, Welch forged a new management philosophy, that coalesced around ten key company values. Being number one or number two headed the list, followed by becoming and staying lean and agile. The remaining eight qualities fell into three categories: how to get to the top, how to behave as a company to stay there, and how to fund the process.

Getting to the Top: Ownership, Stewardship, and Entrepreneurship. Welch believed that one of the keys to GE's success was what he termed *ownership:* the willingness to take responsibility and make decisions down in the organization. To encourage the spirit of ownership he gave greater powers of delegation, raised capital appropriations levels, and held fewer and faster reviews. His aim was to drive the ability to act further down in the organization.

Exhibit 5B Organization chart, 1984.

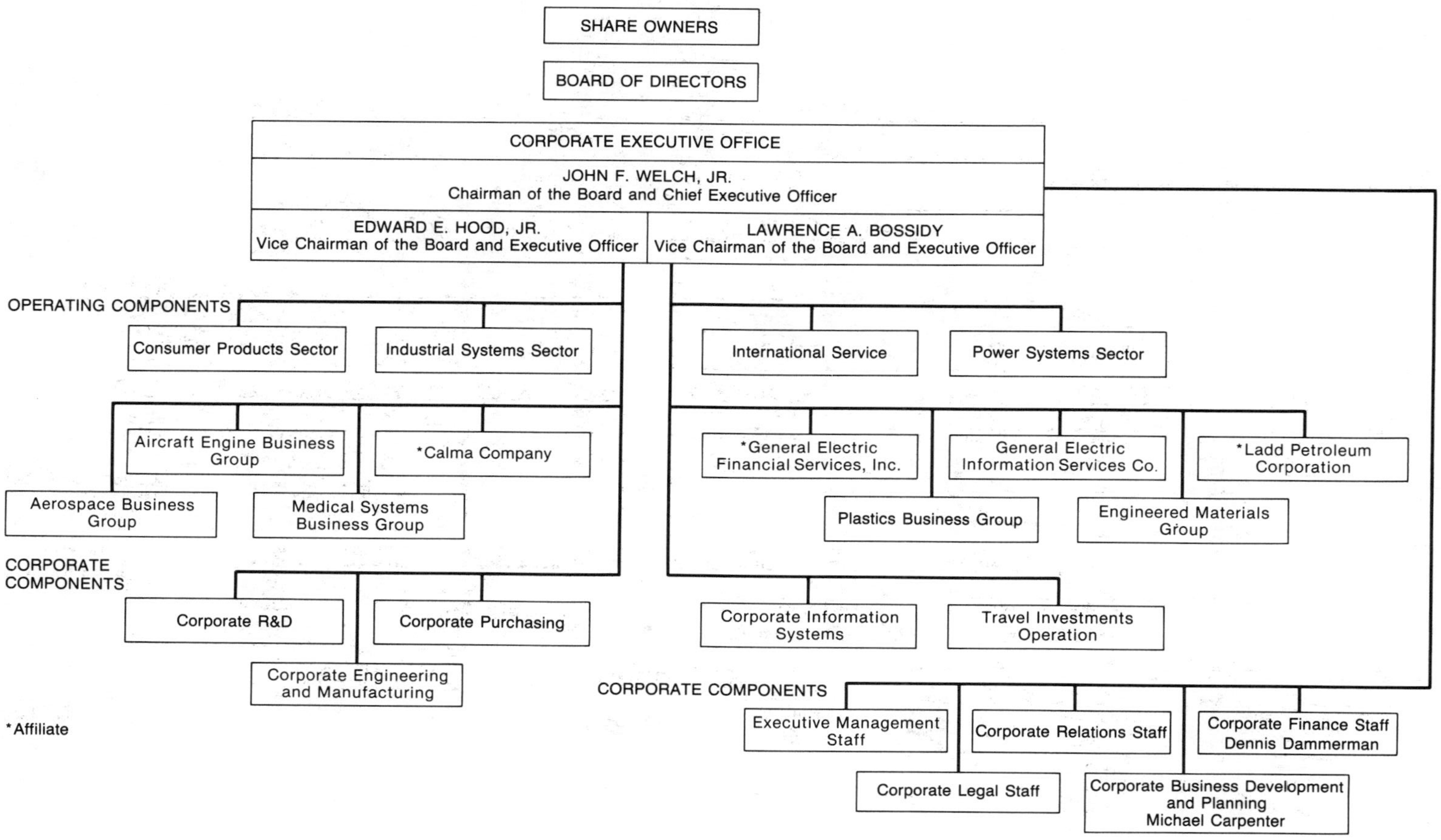

SHARE OWNERS

BOARD OF DIRECTORS

CORPORATE EXECUTIVE OFFICE

JOHN F. WELCH, JR.
Chairman of the Board and Chief Executive Officer

EDWARD E. HOOD, JR.
Vice Chairman of the Board and Executive Officer

LAWRENCE A. BOSSIDY
Vice Chairman of the Board and Executive Officer

OPERATING COMPONENTS

Consumer Products Sector

Industrial Systems Sector

International Service

Power Systems Sector

Aerospace Business Group

Aircraft Engine Business Group

*Calma Company

Medical Systems Business Group

*General Electric Financial Services, Inc.

Plastics Business Group

General Electric Information Services Co.

Engineered Materials Group

*Ladd Petroleum Corporation

CORPORATE COMPONENTS

Corporate R&D

Corporate Purchasing

Corporate Engineering and Manufacturing

Corporate Information Systems

Travel Investments Operation

CORPORATE COMPONENTS

Executive Management Staff

Corporate Legal Staff

Corporate Relations Staff

Corporate Finance Staff
Dennis Dammerman

Corporate Business Development and Planning
Michael Carpenter

*Affiliate

431

The responsibility that accompanied ownership was *stewardship:* an obligation to leverage GE's assets (i.e., people, buildings, balance sheets) through a willingness to work at full capacity. Welch stressed the need "to take the assets you have, and drive them to newer and better heights through excellence, through taking charge."

Welch wanted to use the spirit of *entrepreneurship* as "the kindling to start the fires leading to competitive success." To attain ownership and stewardship, he advocated that managers create and maintain an entrepreneurial environment and a sense of entrepreneurial responsibility. While conceding it was different in a $30 billion enterprise, Welch believed that the concept was essential to allow new ideas to surface and to create new ventures for the company.

How to Behave: Excellence, Quality, Reality and Candor, and Communications. Having a company ethic dedicated to ownership, stewardship, and entrepreneurship could get GE to the first spot in a tough, competitive world, according to Welch, but other values would keep it there.

Excellence, like ownership, was individual behavior that required each employee to pass what Welch called the "mirror test." He said, "Only you know whether or not the excellence is there. You can't be at this level at all times, but you've got to keep driving yourself."

Welch wanted to push *quality* beyond the product to instill a commitment to quality as a pervasive way of life. He saw it as an all-embracing concept that included products, services, fulfillment of citizen responsibilities, and communication to the outside world.

Welch's early move to meet directly with individual SBU managers was made to foster an atmosphere of *reality and candor* and develop trust in the corporate hierarchy. He believed that each employee should have enough trust in his or her boss to seek joint solutions to the problems, and enough self-confidence and belief in the company to approach that process with reality and candor.

Besides the internal dialogue necessary for successful operations, Welch felt that *communicating* GE's strengths and values to the outside world was central to implementing GE's philosophy. To understand and communicate GE's philosophy, Welch said, "You've got to embrace it, feel it, believe it. If you don't, you come back and recheck it and understand what we're doing."

Funding: The Investment Philosophy. The tenth value of Welch's management philosophy dealt with the *financial support* needed to pay for competitive success. Welch believed that all investments should be directed only to the markets that GE could dominate. Those markets that did not fit the long-term growth strategy would be abandoned. He set 15 percent as the overall annual growth rate, with the admonition that short-term investment decisions should not be made simply to meet the growth rate at the expense of long-term issues.

Reactions

Reactions to Welch's first four years as CEO were varied, as indicated by the following sample of comments by GE managers:

- There was a lot of resentment to the destaffing in my department and Welch was feared. But personally, I welcomed it. I knew we had deadwood, and I was happy that we were being forced to face up to it.
- All the words sound great—entrepreneurship, ownership, risk taking—but at my level [subsection manager] it's making budget that still counts.
- During the first two years, I didn't see much change. But then we got a new general manager who is right out of Welch's mold. Our business is now a different place—much more spirited, self-critical, and energetic.
- I don't see much change. My business has been in the fast-moving part of the company, and we've been managed this way for years. I think that some of the older parts of the company may be feeling some change, but for me it's been a continuation of the way things have always been and the way they should be.
- Welch has succeeded in keeping us from becoming complacent and is focusing our attention on worldwide competitors. That's an important accomplishment in a big company where we tend to become complacent and focus on our own organizations and promotions.
- Many of the changes [in planning] have been excellent. But we are relying almost totally on people. That's fine until some of those people make big mistakes. Then we miss not having those systematic plans.
- The key issue for me is what happens if you take a risk and fail. Welch is trying hard to convince us that it's OK, as with Halarc [an energy-efficient, $10 light bulb that failed to catch on with the public]. But I wonder. The people who get rewarded in a failure are those who recommend getting out, not those who recommend getting in.

Issues

Among the many issues faced by GE management since Welch became CEO in 1981, two had garnered extensive publicity. One addressed the huge funds GE had accumulated for investment: the other involved Welch's desire to increase the level of risk taking and entrepreneurship within the company.

The $5 Billion War Chest. By the end of 1984, GE's financial performance had changed dramatically (see Exhibits 6 and 7). The company had accumulated $5 billion in cash and securities, prompting questions about GE's acquisition intentions. Although Welch had said the money would not burn a hole in GE's pocket, he seemed to be having difficulty finding appropriate investment opportunities. GE's corporate staff had examined 6,000 potential acquisition candidates, of which it had completed in-depth analysis on more than 100. In the

Exhibit 6 Five-year statistical summary, 1980–1984 ($ millions, except per share amounts).

	1984	1983	1982	1981	1980
Sales of products and services to customers	$27,947	$26,797	$26,500	$27,240	$24,959
Operating margin	2,845	2,549	2,405	2,447	2,243
Operating margin as a percentage of sales	10.2%	9.5%	9.1%	9.0%	9.0%
Earnings before business restructurings, income taxes, and minority interest	3,501	3,063	2,753	2,660	2,493
Net earnings	2,280	2,024	1,817	1,652	1,514
Net earnings as a percentage of sales	8.2%	7.6%	6.9%	6.1%	6.1%
Net earnings on average share owners' equity	19.1%	18.9%	18.8%	19.1%	19.5%
Net earnings per share	$5.03	$4.45	$4.00	$3.63	$3.33
Dividends declared per share	2.05	1.875	1.675	1.575	1.475
Total assets	$24,730	$23,288	$21,615	$20,942	$18,511
Property, plant and equipment additions	$2,488	$1,721	$1,608	$2,025	$1,948
Average employment—worldwide	330,000	340,000	367,000	404,000	402,000
—United States	241,000	245,000	261,000	289,000	285,000
Gross national product (current $ billions)	$3,661	$3,305	$3,073	$2,938	$2,626
Common stock performance					
GE common share price	$59⅜–48¼	$58⅞–45⅜	$50–27½	$35–25⅝	$31½–22
Dow Jones Industrial Average	1287–1087	1287–1027	1070–777	1024–824	1000–759
Standard & Poor's Industrial Index	191–168	195–155	160–114	157–126	161–111

Source: General Electric annual report, 1984; U.S. Department of Commerce for GNP; Moody's.

434

end, however, only four candidates had been identified as strategically and financially attractive.

The most important acquisition consideration was that ownership would increase GE shareholder value by leveraging the acquired company's growth rate and profitability. It was difficult to find companies where GE could add sufficient value to justify the 50 percent acquisition premiums that were becoming the norm in 1984.

In the spring of 1984, GE Credit Corporation purchased Employers Reinsurance Corporation (ERC) for $1.08 billion. The reinsurance industry attracted GE because it had high growth, good return on investment, and because GE already knew the business through its Puritan Insurance Company [a subsidiary of GECC]. ERC was the number two or three reinsurer in the U.S. market but had grown more rapidly and earned higher returns that the leader, General Re. GE bought ERC from Texaco at an attractive price when the reinsurance industry was at a cyclical low point. Despite the ERC acquisition and numerous smaller acquisitions (GE had acquired over 50 businesses since 1981), it remained unclear how GE would spend its considerable cash reserves.

Internal Growth. Welch encouraged internal growth by emphasizing new business ventures within the corporation. In the *GE Monogram*, the company magazine, GE intentionally publicized venture activities to encourage managers to propose their own ventures.

On the financial side, however, new ventures had their limits. They faced the problems inherent in any start-up business, and they had the added problems of being part of a big company and having to deal across organizational boundaries. Perhaps the greatest limitation was size. As one executive noted, "We have a problem with ventures because of our need to think big. At GE, unless you can create a $150 million business it's not going to affect things much. We can create lots of small businesses. The problem is in creating the $150 million departments, and even more important, in creating the groups and sectors of the future."

Although they were not funded at the corporate level, the ventures focused attention on between sixty and eighty new business development efforts and their managers. Indeed, Welch often commented on the importance of ventures in developing managers:

> The ventures are far less important than the product of the processes, which are the people. By having high visibility on these people—each having their own P&L statement, their own game, competing against the world— we get a chance to look at how they perform. They can blow it and they can lose a little money, it doesn't matter. We get a feel for who they are and what they can manage. We get far more out of the people end of ventures than we do out of the earnings end.

Financial Systems. Although some of the problems in creating internal business development only pertained to new ventures, many managers indicated that GE's financial systems had a more pervasive negative effect on entrepre-

Exhibit 7 Industry and geographic segment information ($ millions).

	Total Revenues					Net Earnings	
	1984	*1983*	*1982*	*1981*	*1980*	*1984*	*1983*
Consumer products	$3,858	$3,741	$3,943	$4,202	$3,998	$228	$163
Major appliances	3,650	3,078	2,751	3,132	3,012	223	156
Industrial systems	4,274	4,228	4,705	5,364	4,907	73	84
Power systems	6,010	5,878	6,093	6,015	5,703	486	439
Aircraft engines	3,835	3,495	3,140	2,950	2,660	251	196
Materials	2,241	2,060	1,791	2,050	1,877	262	182
Technical products and services	4,803	3,825	3,546	3,005	2,424	232	210
Financial services[a]	448	397	286	239	193	336	285
Natural resources	609	1,579	1,575	1,722	1,374	117	301
Corporate items and eliminations	−792	−598	−638	−825	−625	72	8
Total	28,936	27,683	27,192	27,854	25,523	2,280	2,024
Outside the United States	7,703	9,148	9,412	10,190	9,597	419	668

a. Note 4 of 1984 and 1982 annual reports explain GE's income from financial services and other sources as follows:

Other Income ($ millions)	1984	1983	1982	1981	1980
GECC	$329	$271	$205	$129	$115
Marketable securities and bank deposits	323	239	239	230	229
Royalty and technical assets	83	58	60	59	52
Customer financing	75	69	58	80	72
Other items	179	247	130	116	95
Total	$989	$884	$692	$614	$563

neurship. Said one manager, "More than ever before, we are being told to innovate and invest for the long haul. But our financial system tells us to make our quarterly and annual projections. At times, the profit pressure is intense."

Traditionally, GE's financial systems had centered around the annual budget. Budget preparation began in July and involved extensive negotiation between the operating units, the intervening layers of management, and the corporate office. Once the budget was set, managers were locked in to meet it "at all costs," regardless of changes in the marketplace.

Management conceded that the system had undesirable consequences, such as game-playing to set low targets, or cutting long-term development to meet short-term targets. Welch's major objection was that the system locked management into figures prepared eighteen months before.

To address these problems, two changes were made. First, the controller's office prepared a set of financial objectives for each operating unit in order to more realistically reflect each unit's prospects and to reduce the amount of game-playing happening in the budgeting process. Second, the budgets were called operating plans, and line managers could propose financial revisions at

Net Earnings			Assets			Plant, Property, and Equipment Additions			Depreciation, Depletion, and Amortization		
1982	1981	1980	1984	1983	1982	1984	1983	1982	1984	1983	1982
$146	$225	$241	$2,382	$2,297	$1,997	$283	$235	$180	$143	$120	$124
79	82	104	1,370	1,030	1,101	111	80	78	75	68	73
148	212	218	2,670	2,569	2,478	264	228	251	151	158	139
384	242	223	3,689	3,242	3,574	243	252	228	179	173	185
161	149	141	3,317	2,523	2,174	356	218	140	136	129	93
148	189	170	2,362	2,030	1,682	425	231	243	149	147	120
218	144	99	2,778	2,052	1,698	340	216	198	166	124	106
203	145	126	2,312	1,929	1,634						
218	284	224	946	2,558	2,565	347	162	237	67	122	114
12	−20	−32	2,904	3,058	2,712	119	99	53	34	43	30
$1,717	$1,652	$1,514	$24,730	$23,288	$21,615	$2,488	$1,721	$1,608	$1,100	$1,084	$984
680	574	639									

any time that business conditions or the competitive situation had changed significantly from the original assumptions. Performance evaluation was made against the revised targets.

While some believed that the new budgeting rules helped GE to be responsive to new opportunities and industry changes, others felt its main impact was to encourage troubled units to try to renegotiate their targets to make them look better. GE's chief financial officer reported that most of the changes requested by operating managers were to lower revenue and profit projections, while expense levels remained the same. (This contrasted with the old system when managers had a greater commitment to fix their problems.) In addition, he felt that the operating units tended to ask for changes without providing upper management with adequate documentation. Despite these problems, GE remained committed to making the concept of operating plans work, because Welch was convinced that it would develop a more responsive and entrepreneurial spirit within the company.

General Electric—
Preparing for the 1990s

Nineteen eighty-eight was another exciting and successful year for GE. Earnings per share grew 17 percent. Earnings were $3.386 billion on revenues of $50.089 billion . . .

By virtually every measurement, it was a great year. But, as is usually the case in most years, a few thorns can be found among the roses—two, to be exact.

So began the letter to shareholders in the *GE 1988 Annual Report* that was to describe in some detail the company's strategy and accomplishments since Jack Welch assumed leadership in 1981. Following a brief comment concerning the problem GE had experienced with a new type of rotary compressor for refrigerators, the letter continued:

"The second disappointment of 1988 is one you, as share owners, are quite familiar with: the price of our stock. Those who had held GE shares from the early 1980s had been rewarded handsomely. Appreciation and yield provided a return averaging 20 percent per year, compounded from 1981 to 1988, even with the October 1987 correction, compared with a return of 15 percent for the S&P 500. But that's yesterday's performance. In 1988, the stock appreciation didn't keep pace with the Company's performance.

"We're not sure why this is the case, but it occurs to us that perhaps the pace and variety of our activity appear unfocused to those who view it from the outside. The general media and the financial press have, for the most part, been more than favorable in their appraisal of our performance, but as we've picked up the tempo, especially in 1988, we began hearing: GE is 'too difficult to understand' and 'portfolio managing.' We even heard ourselves described by the 'C' word—conglomerate—with its usual pejorative corollary: 'Who knows what they'll buy or sell next?'

"You get the idea. . .

Basic Premises

"There is no denying we are a diverse company. We are not a computer, or oil, or auto, or steel monolith. Those who track us in the financial analyst community or financial press have much more homework than do those who watch and report on our peers. We have businesses ranging from plastics to network broadcasting to the manufacture of jet engines to reinsurance. But the strategy, the management philosophy that drives the Company, is the essence of simplicity.

"We have two basic premises. The first is that we will run only businesses that are number one or number two in their global markets—or, in the case of services, that have a substantial position—and are of scale and potential appropriate to a $50 billion enterprise. Currently, there are 14 of these businesses, highly diverse in their pursuits, but closely knit by common values, shared technology and substantial resources; and they draw upon a pool of management talent we believe is unequaled in the world.

"The second premise is that in addition to the strength, resources and reach of a big company, which we have already built, we are committed to developing the sensitivity, the leanness, the simplicity and the agility of a small company. We want the best of both.

"These premises shape and explain everything we do. In acquisition philosophy, for example, being number one or number two dictates that we will only acquire companies that are a direct and enhancing graft onto one of our 14 key businesses or that are large, freestanding and in a position of leadership in their marketplaces. The RCA acquisition, while old news, illustrates this principle very well. NBC was a part of RCA and the nation's number one network. We kept it and added it to our other leadership businesses.

"The RCA Aerospace Group, on the other hand, was a natural fit with our own GE Aerospace business, so we merged them, strengthening our overall aerospace position. Several discrete RCA businesses that were not strategic to us, such as the carpet company, were neither graftable to our 14 key businesses nor large and freestanding, so we disposed of them almost immediately.

Mistaken Impressions

"But, for some reason, our trade of the merged GE/RCA television manufacturing business to Thomson of France in exchange for its medical diagnostic business and cash provoked some puzzling responses. Suddenly, the manufacture of televisions became something quintessentially American, like baseball. Some felt we had betrayed our heritage in our compulsion to 'do deals.' We heard phrases like: 'Un-American,' 'giving up on manufacturing,' 'exporting jobs.'

"The facts were these: the combined GE/RCA television business lost $125 million in the 1980s, was a cash drain and was number three or four in the global market with no way in sight of getting to number one or two. Thomson's television business, while profitable, was in a similar market-share situation—stuck in the middle of the pack. Our trade with Thomson produced the following results. Thomson, including its new employees from GE, broke out of the pack, doubled its volume and moved into a number one or two position in the industry. GE, by acquiring Thomson's medical business, with its $1 billion in sales, and grafting it onto the already strong GE Medical Systems business, became number one in a game central to our strategy. Exporting jobs? Some 21,000 of the 31,000 jobs in the television business had been overseas for a decade or more. Hurting employees? The employees in that business, form rly endangered by being part of an also-ran in a global market, now have the reach and volume that gives them a real shot at winning.

"We think it is one of the most important, logical and universally beneficial moves made anywhere in the 1980s—a win for the employees of the GE/RCA television business, a good deal for Thomson and a key victory for a high technology GE manufacturing business—Medical Systems—that is now the global technology and market leader.

Divestitures and Acquisitions

"The divestitures we've made in the 1980s have produced $9 billion in cash, which has been used for acquisitions to strengthen our 14 key businesses. In 1988, we purchased Borg-Warner's chemicals businesses to expand GE Plastics' global market basket. In addition, we bought the Roper Corporation to strengthen the position of GE Appliances in the domestic range market. GE Financial Services (GEFS) acquired the credit card business of Montgomery Ward, a move that effectively doubled our private label credit card assets and enhanced our number one position in that market segment. GEFS' 1988 integration of the 1987 Gelco acquisition created a leading position in automotive fleet leasing as well as in the cargo shipping container business.

"In all, we've invested some $16 billion in the 1980s on acquisitions. We would argue that some $15 billion of these funds has been very successfully invested. Only two niche electronics acquisitions—amounting to about $400 million—didn't pan out and were sold. Another $600 million invested in Kidder, Peabody has thus far had—for a variety of reasons—difficulty in reaching its potential. Even so, Kidder increased its 1988 earnings 20 percent to $46 million—admittedly a small part of the total GEFS net of $788 million; nevertheless, we see Kidder as a business with important synergies across GEFS that should become more significant in the 1990s.

"This track record gives us confidence in the acquisition process as one of the means to strengthen our global leadership positions.

"In addition to acquisitions, we continue to invest in alliances and joint ventures with other companies all over the globe to enhance our 14 key businesses. In 1988 alone, we concluded alliances between GE Motors and Bosch of West Germany, and we expanded an alliance between GE Electrical Distribution and Control and Fuji.

"Finally, in early 1989, we signed a series of historic agreements with GEC

of the United Kingdom that will open the door to increased European participation by four of our 14 businesses—Medical Systems, Appliances, Industrial
and Power Systems, and Electrical Distribution and Control. This move appears complicated on the surface because there are four businesses involved,
but it is driven, once again, by the simple strategy dictating that we advance
our 14 businesses, on a global basis, whenever we can, consistent with a consistent strategy.

Internal Development

"In addition to acquiring, divesting and forming alliances to support these key
businesses, we continue to supply them with resources to propel their internal
growth—investing close to $16 billion since 1981. In 1988, we made a multi-
year, $1.8 billion commitment to build a Spanish plastics complex that will
supply the European market, we committed another billion dollars to further
fuel the strong growth of GE Financial Services, and we spent a total of more
than $1.8 billion on new plant and equipment. Another $3.6 billion—about $1.2
billion funded by the Company—was spent on research and development, almost exclusively in support of these 14 key businesses.

"To those who perceive us as institutionally fickle, we would point to two
of our key 14 businesses—Transportation Systems, which is mainly locomotives, and Industrial and Power Systems; both went through purgatory in the
1980s, in the bottom of market troughs of several years' duration that saw few
orders in locomotives and none in large steam turbines.

"Instead of closing or selling these businesses, we reduced their costs consistent with the market, invested to make them more competitive ($300 million
in locomotives alone) and stuck with them through the lean years—not out of
sentimentality or inertia but because they are large, world-leading businesses
with big potential and because doing so fits our strategy. And in 1988, we saw
a significant market revival in areas of the turbine business.

"That, then, is the first part of our strategy: creating a company consisting
only of world-class global businesses that can compete and win in the 1990s
and beyond. The focus of our R&D, investment, acquisitions and alliances—
everything we do—is ensuring the growth and vitality of those businesses.

Lean and Agile

"The second part of the strategy, as we mentioned, is making this $50 billion
enterprise as lean, as agile and as light on its feet as a small company—a big
company with the heart and hunger of a small one.

"We've been grappling with how to achieve this unbeatable amalgam for
the entire decade, and, while we haven't yet achieved it, our progress is accelerating. Once again, the actions we have taken are totally consistent with our
oft-stated theory of the case.

"We believed layers of management were 'big-company' encumbrances—

so we reduced ours from nine to as few as four, from us in the Corporate Executive Office to the factory floor of any given business. In the mid-1980s, we made a calculated gamble and removed the entire second and third echelons of management in the Company—layers we called sectors and groups. The 14 key businesses now report not, as often in the past, to senior vice presidents who report to executive vice presidents—all with staff entourages—but directly to us three. This arrangement is dependent for its success on the quality of leadership at the business level. We gambled that we had that quality, and we won. The new arrangement has proved breathtakingly clean, simple, and effective. Ideas, initiatives and decisions move, often at the speed of sound—voices—where once they were muffled and garbled by a gauntlet of approvals and the oppressive ministrations of staff reviews.

"Secondly, we found ourselves in the early 1980s with corporate and business staffs that were viewed—and viewed themselves—as monitors, checkers, kibitzers and approvers. We changed that view and that mission to the point where staff now sees itself as facilitator, advisor and partner of operations—with a growing sense of satisfaction and cooperation on both sides. Territoriality has given way to a growing sense of unity and common purpose.

"The third step toward a small company management system began in 1988 when we formulated and began planning a project we call 'work-out.' This will be an intense and continuing program, conducted within the businesses and with support from the company's management institute, to 'liberate' the employees of our Company from the cramping artifacts that pile up in the dusty attics of century-old companies: the reports, meetings, rituals, approvals, controls and forests of paper that often seem necessary until they are removed.

Unleashing Creativity

"As we succeed over the next three years in ridding our Company of the tentacles of ritual and bureaucracy, we are now better able to attack the final, and perhaps the most difficult, challenge of all. And that is the empowering of our 300,000 people, the releasing of their creativity and ambition, to direct coupling of their jobs with some positive effect on the quality of a product or service. We want each man and woman in this Company to see a connection between what he or she does all day—and winning in the marketplace. Their roles, responsibilities and rewards must become clear to them and to everyone. Small companies thrive and grow on that sense of contribution and reward. We want it as well, and everything we do to evolve our management system will be consistent with getting it.

"Liberation and empowerment, as we use the concept, stems from what we believe is a very solidly grounded view of winning and losing around the world. We, as a globally competing company, have some serious disadvantages as we line up against our foreign competitors. Some of those competitors enjoy protection from foreign inroads into their markets; others are financially supported by their governments. Some are beneficiaries of nationally focused

R&D in key technologies. Others are part of regimented, paternalistic cultures that serve them well.

"We complain, on occasion, about all of this, but it is we who have the ultimate advantage, one that few of us, if pressed, would ever wish to trade. It is the fact that we are, despite our mix of global cultures and enterprises, an American company; and, as such, our system, while providing no guarantees, also has the fewest barriers to innovation, boldness and risk-taking—the stuff that will propel the real winners in the 1990s.

"And that's the 'why' behind our program of liberation and empowerment—more fulfilling work for all and greater competitiveness for our Company. The worst thing we could do is to stifle with bureaucracy our employees—the Americans and Germans, the French and Japanese, and the scores of other nationalities that are now part of the global GE. If we did, we would then have none of the advantages of our competitors—and many of the encumbrances that burden them all. We won't let that happen.

"If we can become that big company/small company hybrid while pursuing our global strategies and encouraging even more boldness in the leadership of our businesses, we will be within striking distance of the goal we set out in pursuit of eight years ago: We will be a more contemporary, more accessible, more responsive company, in touch with our customers, firmly in control of our own destiny, driven by more fulfilled people in control of theirs.

"We are on the brink of the most exciting and opportunity-rich decade in world business history. We approach it with a strategy that has been both consistent and very successful during the 1980s. If this summary of the strategy we have once again presented in this letter is clear, you will have no difficulty understanding everything we do in the 1990s . . .

"And we intend to do a lot."

The Quantum Leap Approach

The scope of GE's strategic redirection during the 1980s was clearly anticipated by Welch early in his tenure. The following excerpts from a 1984 speech entitled "Competitiveness from Within—Beyond Incrementalism" revealed his bias for bold moves, or what he called the quantum leap:

"For me, the idea is: shun the incremental and go for the leap.

"Most bureaucracies—and ours is no exception—unfortunately still think in incremental terms rather than in terms of fundamental change. They think incrementally primarily because they think internally.

"Changing the culture—opening it up to the quantum change—means constantly asking not how fast am I going, how well am I doing vs. how well I did a year or two before, but rather, how fast and how well am I doing vs. the world outside. Are we moving faster, are we doing better against that external standard?

John F. Welch, Jr.
Chairman of the Board and
Chief Executive Officer

Lawrence A. Bossidy
Vice Chairman of the Board and
Executive Officer

Edward E. Hood, Jr.
Vice Chairman of the Board and
Executive Officer

February 10, 1989

Chairman of the Board and Chief Executive
Officer John F. Welch, Jr. (center) is flanked by
Vice Chairman of the Board and Executive
Officer Lawrence A. Bossidy (left) and Vice
Chairman of the Board and Executive Officer
Edward E. Hood, Jr. (right).

Figure 1

An Example

"Take the case of two losing but closely allied businesses. One's losing $7 million, the other $5 million. Management comes up with a plan to merge the two and, by paring some costs, proposes to lose eight.

"The businesses have been merged, and the losses cut. Still a losing business, but better than last year. What is proposed in this case is nothing unusual. In fact, these managers had been trained all their lives to do just what had been done: make an improvement, make it better than it was. In another time, another place, cheers would have rung out. After all, the combined businesses had achieved a $4 million earnings improvement. That's one way of looking at it.

"The other way of looking at it is: How long can you sustain a losing business? The challenge is: How do we take the quantum move—improve the cost structure, halve the overhead, invest in modernization—to get it profitable, to get into a competitive position where it can fundamentally win. The move had to be decisive and bold.

"We've seen huge chunks of entire industries preside over their own orderly death, making what could be called incremental progress.

"How did it happen? How did we get that way?

Changing the Culture

"Companies have cultures. And the culture of today's large companies arose not in the '70s or '80s but after the Second World War; formed, in other words, in an age of plenty, of rapid growth, before the onset of world competition, when the opportunities exceeded the ability to produce. It was almost literally true that everything one could make, one could sell.

"Cultures were born and, with them, control and compensation systems. What was one of the objectives bred into the culture like this every year? 'Do better than you did the year before.' Incrementalism. The objectives didn't often enough contain expectations of the extraordinary effort, the innovation, the reach. Negotiated between supervisors and workers were things which were certainly—obviously—attainable in the eyes of both. Management objectives didn't demand the quantum leap.

"What can we do about it?

The Challenge Ahead

"The challenge is changing the culture. And that means changing the reward system, a big anchor to incrementalism.

"It means: First, big rewards for those who do things. And second, that we don't go after the scalps of those who reach for the big concept but fail. Punishing failure assures that no one dares.

"Changing the culture starts with an attitude. And I would suggest it starts at the top—with the CEOs and the boards of directors that are charged with leading our institutions.

"More boards have to be thinking how much can this organization take, how much can it absorb, is it being stressed too little or too much—constantly challenging the pace.

"How does an institution know when the pace is about right? I hope you won't think I'm being melodramatic if I say that the institution ought to stretch itself, ought to reach, to the point where it almost comes unglued."

The Restructuring of General Electric

Jack Welch was named chief executive officer and chairman of the board for GE in April 1981. Although GE made many acquisitions and divestitures during the first three years, none were of major significance to the company. The principal investments were for internal improvements ($300 million for locomotives and $500 million for large appliances). The first major move in restructuring GE occurred in 1984 with the acquisition of Employers Reinsurance Corporation for $1.1 billion. As described by Welch in his letter to the shareholders, this process then continued in earnest over the next five years with the acquisitions of RCA and several other major companies. The acquisitions were guided by Welch's concept of acquiring or strengthening GE's number one or two businesses.

The same concept guided Welch's strategy for divestitures. Many of these divestitures, however, caused controversy for GE. Critics characterized Welch as a financial wizard who was trying to achieve his goals and stay one step ahead of foreign competition by giving up on manufacturing businesses, GE's mainstay in the past. For his part, Welch described the divestitures as follows:

"Housewares and air conditioning combined in the good years made $20 million, in bad years they lost $20 million and their cash flow was about zero. So they gave us no earnings growth and no cash. When we sold them, we got $400 million of cash to restructure power systems and these other strong businesses.

"In consumer electronics, we sold our television business. It gave people a lot of grief . . . 'how could you do that?' Consumer electronics in the 1980s, the combined RCA and GE consumer electronics businesses, lost $150 million, and they used about $170 million of cash. They didn't give cash and they didn't give you any earnings. All they did was cause more grief in the stronger businesses.

"Power transformers was in the middle of GE's power business. It made everyone feel terrible when we sold power transformer. However to give you a feeling for the power transformer business, in 1985 its sales were lower than they were in 1970. In 13 of those 15 years, it lost money, cumulatively it lost over $100 million. It didn't belong. It made no sense. It just dragged the whole institution down, and those things put pressure on the other businesses. It makes you make the wrong decisions with the good businesses. So selling all those businesses, we got $8.5 billion of cash that we used in the [company] to do other things with."

Downsizing

Another element of Welch's transformation of GE was a substantial downsizing of the company, including a massive series of reductions in personnel. This also opened Welch to criticism, especially from labor. To some detractors, Welch was "Neutron Jack," the job killer creating a new breed of manager motivated by greed and contempt for its employees. One publication summarized labor's view of Welch: "There's not much doubt about what many union members think of GE Chairman Jack Welch. He's the consummate corporate villain, willing to sacrifice anyone's job to turn a higher profit—the consolidator who 'would reshape the future by obliterating the [union] contract.' "[1]

Welch stressed the need for the reductions and its essential contribution to GE's current performance:

"We started out with 411,000 employees. We acquired an additional 111,150 employees. Through divestitures, we reduced 122,700 employees. We restructured, or down-sized to get more efficient, reducing some 123,450 employees. Now we have 276,000. Enormous in and out. But we're doing 31 percent more volume with 31 percent fewer people. There was no way we could continue doing things the way we used to. Take 123,000 people, assume the whole mix of all the employees that are gone had an average salary of $35,000—and that's conservative. If you add benefits to that, you're up close to $50,000. Multiply that by 123,000 people, and you get over $6 billion, minus taxes of $2.4 billion, you get a final balance of almost $4 billion. GE would be losing close to a billion dollars today if we were operating in the same way we did in 1981. The option is not there to go back to the way we had it—the only option is to do it differently."

As for the well-publicized reference to "Neutron Jack," Welch rejected this slur, as quoted in *Fortune*, July 7, 1982: "Let me tell you why the name 'Neutron Jack' is wrong. Competitiveness means taking action. Nuking someone means you kill him. We start a renewal process. When people leave our company we provide a soft landing. People who have been removed for not performing may be angry, but not one will say he wasn't treated with dignity. I don't think anyone would say he was treated unfairly." Neither *Fortune* nor GE received any letters refuting this statement.

Exhibits 1A and 1B outlines GE's financial performance during the 1984 and 1988 period. (The company first broke out the financial data for GE Financial Services for public reporting purposes in 1987.) Figure 2A shows the result of the restructuring of GE.

Results: The "GE Growth Engine"

In 1988, Welch began to refer to the way the company worked as the "GE Growth Engine." The following excerpts from one of his numerous presentations on the subject explain this concept.

"On the left, we have what we do here at the headquarters, the corporate executives. We sell nothing. We make nothing. We're simply, if you will, over-

1. *Business Week*, December 14, 1987, p. 102.

Exhibit 1A   Selected financial data, 1984–1988 ($ millions, except per share amounts).

	1988	1987	1986	1985	1984
GE and consolidated affiliates					
Revenues	$50,089	$48,158	$42,013	$32,624	$31,442
Earnings before extraordinary loss and cumulative affect of accounting change	$3,386	$2,119	$2,492	$2,277	$2,239
Net earnings	$3,386	$2,915	$2,492	$2,277	$2,239
Dividend declared	$1,314	$1,209	$1,081	$1,020	$930
Earned on avg. shareowners' equity	19.4%	18.5%	17.3%	17.5%	19.0%
Net earnings per share	$3.75	$3.20	$2.73	$2.50	$2.47
Dividends declared per share	$1.460	$1.325	$1.185	$1.115	$1.025
Total assets	$110,865	$95,414	$84,818	$49,123	$43,860
Long term borrowings	$15,082	$12,517	$10,001	$5,577	$4,818
Shares outstanding—avg. (in thousands)	901,780	911,639	912,594	910,762	907,360
Total employees at year end	298,000	322,000	373,000	299,000	323,000
GE Data					
Short-term borrowings	$1,861	$1,110	$1,813	$1,297	$1,047
Long-term borrowings	$4,330	$4,491	$4,351	$753	$753
Minority interests	$228	$190	$189	$126	$128
Shareholders' equity	$18,466	$16,480	$15,109	$13,671	$12,398
Total capital invested	$24,885	$22,271	$21,462	$15,847	$14,326
Return of avg. total capital invested	16.4%	14.7%	13.9%	16.2%	17.6%
Borrowing as a percent of total capital invested	24.9%	25.1%	28.7%	12.9%	12.6%
Current assets	$15,499	$15,739	$14,288	$12,546	$11,552
Current liabilities	$13,419	$12,671	$11,461	$8,919	$8,607
Working capital	$2,080	$3,068	$2,827	$3,627	$2,945
Property, plant, and equipment additions (other than by RCA acquisition)	$2,288	$1,778	$2,042	$1,953	$2,419
Year-end orders backlog	$27,265	$22,737	$23,943	$23,117	$22,577
GEFS Data					
Earnings before extraordinary loss and cumulative affect of accounting change	$788	$552	$504	$413	$329
Net earnings	$788	$1,008	$504	$413	$329
Shareowner's equity	$4,819	$3,980	$2,994	$2,302	$1,874
Earned on average shareowner's equity	18.0%	18.0%	19.7%	19.9%	19.1%
Borrowings from others	$39,593	$30,885	$23,397	$16,393	$13,402
Ratio of debt to equity (GE capital)	7.67:1	7.98:1	7.83:1	7.89:1	7.97:1

	1988	*1987*	*1986*	*1985*	*1984*
Earnings assets of financing businesses	$42,173	$32,423	$25,169	$20,169	$17,054
Reserve coverage on financing receivables	2.63%	2.59%	2.59%	2.57%	2.54%
Insurance premiums written	$1,809	$1,729	$1,704	$1,092	$637
Securities broker-dealer earned income	$2,316	$2,491	$1,176	—	—
Market Data					
Gross national product (current $ bil.)	$4,881	$4,527	$4,240	$4,015	$3,715
Common stock performance					
GE common share price—High	$47\frac{7}{8}$	$66\frac{3}{8}$	$44\frac{3}{8}$	$36\frac{7}{8}$	$29\frac{5}{8}$
Low	$38\frac{3}{8}$	$38\frac{3}{4}$	$33\frac{1}{4}$	$27\frac{7}{8}$	$24\frac{1}{8}$
Dow Jones Industrial Average	2184–1879	2722–1739	1956–1502	1553–1185	1287–1087
S & P Industrial Index	327–278	393–255	283–225	236–182	191–168

Sources: General Electric Annual Report, 1988; International Financial Statistics; Moody's.

head. Our job is to multiply the resources we have, the human resources, the financial resources, and the best practices. We move people from business A to business B to add strength. We move the key people to the key jobs. We also allocate capital to the businesses. We give money where the growth is, where the opportunities are, and squeeze the money from those businesses that don't have [the growth opportunities]. And when someone has a good idea, we move it to all the other businesses. That's all our jobs are, to help those businesses really work. Our job is to help, it's to assist, it's to make these businesses stronger, to help them grow and be more powerful.

"We now have our 14 key number one and two businesses, and their job is to grow through market growth, volume, and productivity improvement. Their job is to give the company earnings. When we give them capital, its their job to decide which part of the business gets the capital and which part doesn't. These decisions eventually drive the earnings stream.

"We then take the cash to pay dividends, to make acquisitions, and take the excess cash and put it right back into the businesses. That's the fundamental way the company works.

Sales Growth

"Let's take a look at how all this is going. First there is sales growth. An often misunderstood thing about our company is that people feel we haven't had much top line growth. Well we've been disposing of a lot of businesses. If you look at the [key businesses] line, these are the businesses we have today. They

Exhibit 1B   Industry segment information ($ millions).

	Total Revenues				
	1988	1987	1986	1985	1984
GE					
Aerospace	$5,343	$5,262	$4,318	$3,085	$2,622
Aircraft engines	6,481	6,773	5,977	4,712	3,835
Broadcasting	3,638	3,241	1,888	51	104
Industrial	7,061	6,662	6,770	6,946	6,648
Major appliance	5,289	4,721	4,352	3,617	3,650
Materials	3,539	2,751	2,331	2,119	2,280
Power systems	4,805	4,995	5,262	5,824	6,289
Technical products & services	4,431	3,670	3,021	2,317	2,402
Earnings of GEFS	788	552	504	413	329
All Other	394	3,176	3,379	1,071	1,762
Corporate items & eliminations	(1,477)	(1,287)	(1,077)	(903)	(990)
Total GE	$40,292	$40,516	$36,725	$29,252	$28,931
GEFS					
Financing	$5,827	$3,507	$2,594	$2,469	$2,093
Insurance	2,469	2,206	2,017	1,329	831
Securities					
Broker-dealer	2,316	2,491	1,176	0	0
All others	43	21	27	7	9
Total GEFS	$10,655	$8,225	$5,814	$3,805	$2,933
Eliminations	($858)	($583)	($526)	($433)	($422)
Total	$50,089	$48,158	$42,013	$32,624	$31,442

Source: General Electric Annual Report, 1988.

have been growing from 1981 to 1988 at 8.5 percent a year. But the [as reported] line is how we've been reporting sales including those businesses we've sold off. [In 1987], we sold $3.5 billion of consumer electronics business that falls out of sales growth. So that year looked flat whereas in fact the remaining businesses have grown $3.5 billion. This [key businesses] line shows our real growth. We show projected growth rates through 1991. If the GNP grows at a 1 percent rate, our sales will be $47 billion. If the GNP grows at a 3 percent rate, we'll reach $52 billion. [See Figure 2, p. 452.]

"There's an interesting change taking place in our company. Look at the drivers that now determine our growth. The two most important drivers are totally different than GE ever had before. Plastics per auto around the world is probably the single most important driver to our earnings. Hospital outlays, how much people are spending on hospital equipment, is second, being critical to our medical business.

Operating Profit					Assets		
1988	*1987*	*1986*	*1985*	*1984*	*1988*	*1987*	*1986*
$640	$603	$608	$437	$332	$3,838	$3,943	$2,253
1,000	940	869	673	460	5,164	5,066	4,553
540	500	240	20	15	4,104	3,948	3,464
798	302	575	658	478	3,729	4,041	4,267
61	490	462	399	381	2,284	1,529	1,576
733	507	424	330	446	7,130	3,901	3,587
503	199	354	740	549	2,531	3,266	3,457
484	275	112	22	(8)	3,183	3,873	2,751
788	552	504	413	329	4,819	3,980	2,994
168	72	162	376	797	1,122	2,046	2,193
					3,379	2,707	3,316
$5,715	$4,440	$4,310	$4,068	$3,779	$41,283	$38,300	$34,411
$899	$636	($99)	$501	$444	$44,874	$34,163	$25,867
325	172	123	45	3	7,849	6,481	5,517
64	(23)	83	0	0	21,891	20,041	22,181
(261)	(213)	(168)	(122)	(93)	331	721	258
$1,027	$572	($61)	$424	$354	$74,945	$61,406	$53,823
($802)	($562)	($513)	($420)	($339)	($5,363)	($4,292)	($3,416)
$5,940	$4,450	$3,736	$4,072	$3,794	$110,865	$95,414	$84,818

Total Cost Productivity

"Our company is now [1987 results] up to about 5 percent total cost productivity, a remarkable job, up from around 1 percent just ten years ago. We have an ability to keep improving productivity by being even smarter. [See Figure 4, p. 453.]

Resource Allocation Dynamics

"Resource allocation dynamics is how we give out money to businesses that request it to do their job. In the 1980s, we poured money into aerospace and aircraft engines as President Reagan put a lot of money into the defense business. In these areas, earnings doubled or tripled, and employment went from 35,000 to 70,000. Everyone was well rewarded and it was a flourishing business. Going forward, this business is not the place we want to give a lot of

HOW A DOZEN GE BUSINESSES RANK ...		
	... IN THE U.S.	**... AND IN THE WORLD**
Aircraft engines	First	First
Broadcasting (NBC)	First	Not applicable
Circuit breakers	First tied with Square D and Westinghouse	First tied with Merlin Gerin, Siemens, Westinghouse
Defense electronics	**Second** behind GM's Hughes Electronics	**Second** behind GM's Hughes Electronics
Electric motors	First	First
Engineering plastics	First	First
Factory automation	Second behind Allen–Bradley	**Third** behind Siemens and Allen–Bradley
Industrial and power systems turbines, meters, drive systems, power transmission controls	First	First
Lighting	First	**Second** behind Philips
Locomotives	First	First tied with GM's Electro–Motive
Major appliances	First	**Second** behind Whirlpool tied with Electrolux
Medical diagnostic imaging	First	First

Figure 2A

money. In aerospace in particular, they've got to wrestle through some of the changes that are going to take place in the marketplace. As the U.S. balances its budget, it will have to cut back on defense. [See Figure 5, p. 454.]

"In power systems in the 1980s, we squeezed them because they had no market. Their employment went just the opposite, from 35,000 to 17,000. Their earnings also collapsed. But going into the 1990s, the outlook for power systems is clearly stronger than it is for aerospace. So we'll be giving more money to power systems, and we'll be squeezing the money out of aerospace.

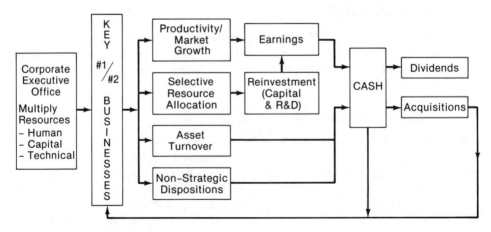

Figure 2B

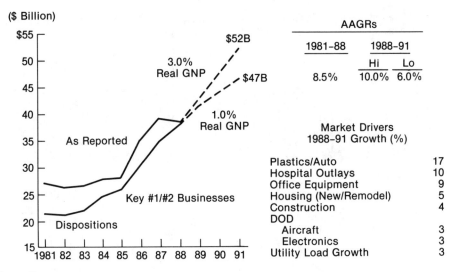

Figure 3

"In aerospace, unlike some of our other businesses, it is easier to explain to a broad audience. Everyone understands that defense budgets are going down. It's on the front pages of every newspaper and has been on television every night. Dealing with it won't feel any better, but everyone's aware of the reasons why.

"We've also poured money into financial services. GEFS has grown from under $100 million to a budget next year of $930 million, grown nine times in the last eight years. The same thing is true in plastics and medical as we've

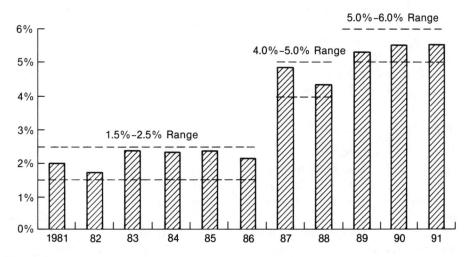

Figure 4

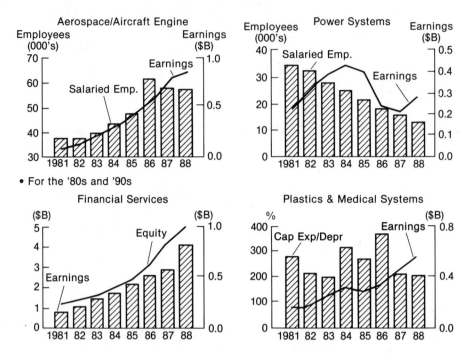

Figure 5

poured money into those businesses. These businesses have been getting people and resources to grow, the others have been squeezed.

Working Capital Turnover

"Working capital efficiency, asset turnover, inventories, receivables, how long
people take to pay. Working capital turnover in the 1970s was in the 3.5 range,
now we have it up to the 4.1 to 4.3 range, and we'll be at 4.5 next year. That's
just being more efficient, smarter. As a result, we freed up $2 billion of cash
that was just lying there dead because we had inventory all around the place
to make it easier to work. Freeing up $2 billion of cash essentially gave us a
free Borg-Warner. [See Figure 6, p. 455.]

GE Engine Performance

"Here's the engine's performance. Earnings in 1988 will be $3.4 billion. In 1991
they should be close to $5 billion. We'll give about 40 percent of that to share-
holders in dividends. GE Financial Services uses about $1 billion a year and we
give them that money to grow their business. Depreciation gives us cash of
about $1.6 billion. That's now equal to the cash we need with the businesses
we kept. Asset productivity, operating more efficiently, gives about $200 to
$400 million a year and that covers what we need for growth in volume. We're

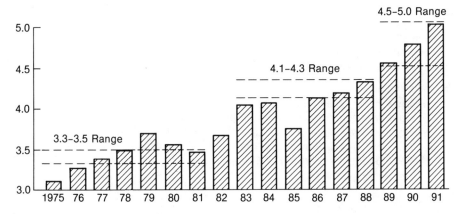

Figure 6

going to dispose of small things now, we're through with big dispositions, and that will give us a couple hundred million per year. Then there's the ratio of debt to capital. If you keep that constant, you can borrow $.5 to $1 billion. This says that every year the bottom line of these ins and outs is that this engine, after spending for plant, after investing $1 billion or more in R&D, is $2 to $3 billion of free cash flow, not being drained by other businesses. Everybody is giving cash now. We have $2 to $3 billion every year to do anything we want: buy a company, buy back stock, give dividends, do the things a company has to do to win in the world market. That's the critical part of what this engine produces.

Figure 6A

Sources	Usage
Earnings $3.4–$5.0B	Dividends (40%) $1.4–$2.0B
	GEFS $0.8–$1.0B
Depreciation $1.6B.	Capital Expenditures $1.6–$1.8B
Asset Productivity $0.2–$0.4B	Working Capital $0.2–$0.4B
Dispositions $0.2–$0.5B	
Additional Leverage $0.5–$0.9B	

GE Has $2–$3 Billion Each Year for
- **Strategic Acquisitions**
- **Other**

- Strategy
    - —Enhance #1 Businesses
    - —Acquire New #1 Business
- Major Actions
    - —CGR: Global Medical Systems
    - —Borg-Warner: Stronger/Broader Plastics
    - —Roper: 15 pt. Share in Core Line; Sears Penetration in Appliances
    - —RCA: NBC (New Service Business) and Leadership in Aerospace
    - —ERC/Kidder, Peabody/GELCO/Auto Auctions/Mont. Ward—Major Financial Service Expansion
- Lessons Learned
    - —Do's
        - —Direct Graft to Strong Business (Medical, GECC)
        - —Large & Independent with Leadership Position (ERC, NBC)
    - —Don'ts
        - —Small Graft without People Expertise (Software Int'l)
        - —Small Non-graftable Independent (Calma, Ceramics)
- Results
    - —$16.0 Billion Invested

Figure 6B

Acquisitions

"What do we do with all that cash? We buy companies, we buy businesses to enhance our number one position. We've learned what to do and what not to do. For example, we make complementary acquisitions—such as CGR for medical, Borg-Warner for plastics, Roper for appliances, and RCA for a whole series of businesses—or buy large independent businesses with leadership positions, like NBC, like Employers Reinsurance, a little company in Kansas City that will make $320 million this year. We don't buy little businesses and have them report to us here. That's an absolute one-act disaster. Fortunately we learned on little ones. If I had to say what had been good investments and what haven't, we've done well on $15 billion, $15 out of $16 billion have delivered enormous earnings. In RCA alone, we get $0.45 a share this year.

Short and Long Term Earnings

"We have wide discussions in our company about short term and long term. Are we too short term oriented? Is American business too short term oriented? The only reason anyone has the title of manager is to manage short and long, balancing resources, allocating yet to some and no to others, and no maybes.

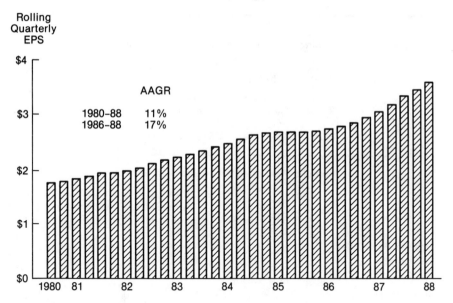

Rolling
Quarterly
EPS

AAGR

1980–88	11%
1986–88	17%

Figure 7

Weak management is about sprinkling it everywhere, lots of maybes. Win the popularity contest for the week, and sink the business.

"Over the last 8 years, every quarter, every year, we have improved our earnings. That's short term. Over this period, we have grown annually by 11 percent. In the last 2 years, we've grown 17 percent per year. It's been stronger at the end than it was in the beginning. That's long term. [See Figure 7.]

"Anybody can manage short. All you do is go in and for 2 years squeeze everything and look like a hero. Anybody can also manage for the long term, go in and say I'm going to delivery in 1995 and don't bother me until then. The hard game is balancing it and that's what our people have understood. We've been getting short term results while putting the long term plans in order.

Why GE is a Growth Company

"At 1 percent real GNP growth, we will have earnings growth of 8 percent to 14 percent, and at 3 percent real GNP growth, we will have growth of 11 percent to 18 percent. That's just arithmetic. Three businesses represent 40 percent of our company's earnings: GE Financial Services, plastics, and medical, three relatively new businesses. Their earnings growth over the next three years is somewhere between 15 percent and 25 percent. You multiply those two columns and you get 6 percent to 10 percent growth. Then these other businesses give slower growth, so you end up with earnings growth of 9 percent to 16 percent, depending on the growth rate of the GNP of 1 percent or 3 percent. Clearly we can grow at 1.5 to 2 times the GNP. We've done it the last

Earnings Growth Objective of 1.5–2.0 X GNP

Real GNP	Inflation	Nominal GNP	Earnings Growth
1.0%	4.5–6.0%	5.5–7.0%	8–14%
2.0%	4.5–6.0%	6.5–8.0%	10.–16%
3.0%	4.5–6.0%	7.5–9.0%	11–18%

Portfolio Positioned for Double Digit Growth

	% of GE Earnings	89–91 Earnings Growth Rate	Weighted Impact on Earnings Growth
Financial Services ⎱ Plastics ⎰ Medical Systems	40%	15–25%	6–10%
Aircraft Engine ⎱ NBC Aerospace Appliances GE Fanuc ⎰	40%	5–10%	2–4%
Power Systems ⎱ Lighting Communications & Services Motors ED&C Transportation ⎰	20%	5–9%	<u>1–2%</u> <u>9–16%</u>

Figure 8

two years and our forecast says we'll do it for the next three, making five straight years. We are a growth company."

Managing GE in the 1990s

With the major restructuring of GE's business lines completed, Welch was ready to move on to the next phase of his plan: increasing the productivity of all GE personnel. He considered productivity to be a key element for improving GE's competitive position in the 1990s, noting, "small changes in the growth rate [of productivity] can have phenomenal effects on profits. A single percentage point increase in productivity translates into an extra $300 million of pre-tax income."[2]

In a 1988 talk entitled "Speed, Simplicity, Self-Confidence: Keys to Leading

2. *Fortune*, March 27, 1989, p. 46.

in the '90s," excerpted below, Welch described the central managerial concepts that would take GE into the next decade:

"[N]ow it's time to look at the '90s and it is not a view for the faint of heart . . . for the environment and the events we see rushing toward us make the tough, tumultuous '80s look like a decade at the beach.

Global Competitors

"Our view as we entered the '80s focused, appropriately, on one powerful competitor: Japan, Inc. As we stand at the threshold of the '90s, we face not only an even more powerful Japan but a revitalized, confident Europe moving closer together and led by bold, aggressive entrepreneurs of the kind we simply didn't encounter in the '70s or early '80s. That huge Duke Power order that Gas Turbine won, if bid ten years ago probably would have been a domestic contest between GE and Westinghouse. To win it in 1989 we had to go to the mat with Asea/Brown Boveri, a Swedish/Swiss combination, Siemens of Germany, and a Westinghouse-Mitsubishi consortium.

"At the beginning of the '80s, Korea and Taiwan were principally sourcing centers for labor-intensive electronic products. They enter the '90s as innovative manufacturing powerhouses challenging the world in electronics, autos, steel and a dozen other industries. Behind them on the same path come other nations of the Far East. The global market pie is not growing at nearly the rate necessary to satisfy the hunger of all those after it.

"How do we get this Company ahead of change, ahead of these strong global players, permanently out in front in the '90s? How do we set the pace?

The People at GE

"The worst thing we could do is to stifle our employees with bureaucracy. If we did, we would then have none of the advantage of our competitors . . . and many of the encumbrances that burden them all. We won't let that happen.

"In the '80s while we grappled with the softer, human issues, with discussions of agility, ownership and the like, our main emphasis, by necessity, was on the very structure of the engine I referred to . . . the hardware of GE. In the '90s, while continuing to build and perfect the hardware, we'll be focusing even more on the human issues—the software of the Company.

"Just as 'number-one-or-number-two in every market' was the formula we used to construct the hardware of our company in the '80s, the key ingredients of the software with which we will guide it in the '90s will be speed, simplicity and self-confidence.

Speed

"We found in the '80s that speed increases in an organization as control decreases. We had constructed over the years a management apparatus that was right for its time, the toast of the business schools. Divisions, strategic business units, groups, sectors, all were designed to make meticulous, calculated decisions and move them smoothly forward and upward. This system produced highly polished work. It was right for the '70s . . . a growing handicap in the '80s . . . and it would have been a ticket to the boneyard in the '90s.

"So we got rid of it . . . along with a lot of reports, meetings and the endless paper that flowed like lava from the upper levels on the company. [Exhibit 2 contains an organizational chart for 1989.] When we did this we began to see people . . . who for years had spent half their time serving the system and the other half fighting it . . . suddenly come to life, making decisions in minutes, face to face, on matters that would have once produced months of staff gyrations and forests of paper. But this transformation, this rebirth, was largely confined to upper management. In the '90s we want to see it engulf and galvanize the entire company.

"We found in the '80s that becoming faster is tied to becoming simpler. Our businesses, with tens of thousands of employees, will not respond to visions that have sub-paragraphs and footnotes.

"If we're not simple we can't be fast . . . and if we're not fast we can't win.

Simplicity

"Simplicity, to an engineer, means clean, functional winning designs, no bells or whistles. In marketing it might manifest itself as clear, unencumbered proposals. For manufacturing people it would produce a logical process that makes sense to every individual on the line. And on an individual, interpersonal level, it would take the form of plain-speaking, directness, honesty.

"Defining this relationship, this bond—throughout the company—is a lot easier than making it real. But we believe the nexus between simplicity and speed is so important, so critical to winning in the '90s that we have embarked on a company-wide crusade we call 'Work-out.' Work-out will sequester the leaders of our business together with their teams. Assisted by our Management Institute people they will meet in monthly, multi-day sessions with no other objective than to exchange views on the vision of the business . . . and then go about attacking those things that stand in the way of its fulfillment: reports, meetings, approvals and all the other paraphernalia of bureaucracy. These sessions are designed to produce true teams passionately committed to simplifying and quickening the process of their business. Over 20,000 of our employees will participate in these sessions over the next year.

Self-confidence

"But just as surely as speed flows from simplicity, simplicity is grounded in self-confidence. Self-confidence does not grow in someone who is just another appendage on the bureaucracy . . . whose authority rests on little more than a title. People who are freed from the confines of their box on the organization

Exhibit 2 Organization chart, 1989

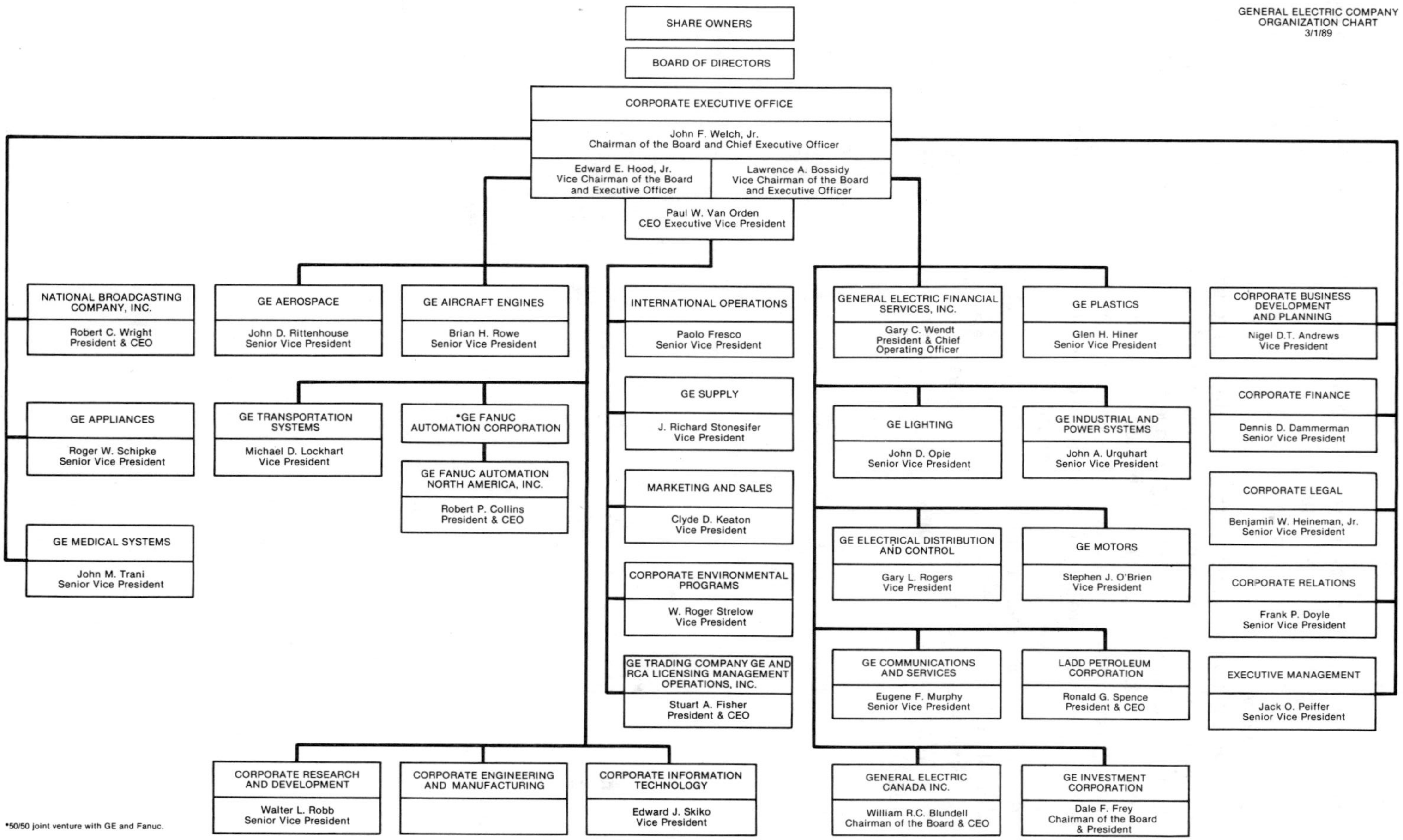

GENERAL ELECTRIC COMPANY
ORGANIZATION CHART
3/1/89

SHARE OWNERS

BOARD OF DIRECTORS

CORPORATE EXECUTIVE OFFICE

John F. Welch, Jr.
Chairman of the Board and Chief Executive Officer

Edward E. Hood, Jr.
Vice Chairman of the Board
and Executive Officer

Lawrence A. Bossidy
Vice Chairman of the Board
and Executive Officer

Paul W. Van Orden
CEO Executive Vice President

NATIONAL BROADCASTING
COMPANY, INC.
Robert C. Wright
President & CEO

GE APPLIANCES
Roger W. Schipke
Senior Vice President

GE MEDICAL SYSTEMS
John M. Trani
Senior Vice President

GE AEROSPACE
John D. Rittenhouse
Senior Vice President

GE AIRCRAFT ENGINES
Brian H. Rowe
Senior Vice President

GE TRANSPORTATION
SYSTEMS
Michael D. Lockhart
Vice President

*GE FANUC
AUTOMATION CORPORATION

GE FANUC AUTOMATION
NORTH AMERICA, INC.
Robert P. Collins
President & CEO

INTERNATIONAL OPERATIONS
Paolo Fresco
Senior Vice President

GE SUPPLY
J. Richard Stonesifer
Vice President

MARKETING AND SALES
Clyde D. Keaton
Vice President

CORPORATE ENVIRONMENTAL
PROGRAMS
W. Roger Strelow
Vice President

GE TRADING COMPANY GE AND
RCA LICENSING MANAGEMENT
OPERATIONS, INC.
Stuart A. Fisher
President & CEO

GENERAL ELECTRIC FINANCIAL
SERVICES, INC.
Gary C. Wendt
President & Chief
Operating Officer

GE LIGHTING
John D. Opie
Senior Vice President

GE ELECTRICAL DISTRIBUTION
AND CONTROL
Gary L. Rogers
Vice President

GE COMMUNICATIONS
AND SERVICES
Eugene F. Murphy
Senior Vice President

GENERAL ELECTRIC
CANADA INC.
William R.C. Blundell
Chairman of the Board & CEO

GE PLASTICS
Glen H. Hiner
Senior Vice President

GE INDUSTRIAL AND
POWER SYSTEMS
John A. Urquhart
Senior Vice President

GE MOTORS
Stephen J. O'Brien
Vice President

LADD PETROLEUM
CORPORATION
Ronald G. Spence
President & CEO

GE INVESTMENT
CORPORATION
Dale F. Frey
Chairman of the Board
& President

CORPORATE BUSINESS
DEVELOPMENT
AND PLANNING
Nigel D.T. Andrews
Vice President

CORPORATE FINANCE
Dennis D. Dammerman
Senior Vice President

CORPORATE LEGAL
Benjamin W. Heineman, Jr.
Senior Vice President

CORPORATE RELATIONS
Frank P. Doyle
Senior Vice President

EXECUTIVE MANAGEMENT
Jack O. Peiffer
Senior Vice President

CORPORATE INFORMATION
TECHNOLOGY
Edward J. Skiko
Vice President

CORPORATE ENGINEERING
AND MANUFACTURING

CORPORATE RESEARCH
AND DEVELOPMENT
Walter L. Robb
Senior Vice President

*50/50 joint venture with GE and Fanuc.

461

chart, whose status rests on real-world achievement . . . those are the people who develop the self-confidence to be simple, to share every bit of information available to them, to listen to those above, below and around them and then move boldly.

"But a company can't distribute self-confidence. What it can do . . . what we must do . . . is to give each of our people an opportunity to win, to contribute, and hence earn self-confidence themselves. They don't get that opportunity, they can't taste winning if they spend their days wandering in the muck of a self-absorbed bureaucracy. This is what our Work-out program is designed to help free them from. Work-out is designed to create an environment where every man and woman in the company can see and feel a connection between what he or she does all day . . . and winning in the marketplace . . . the ultimate job security.

"Speed . . . simplicity . . . self-confidence. We have it in increasing measure. We know where it comes from . . . and we have plans to increase it in the '90s."

Gold Star Co., Ltd.

On April 6, 1984, Chung Jang-Ho, the recently appointed executive managing director of exports for Gold Star, was informed of the U.S. International Trade Commission's determination that an "industry in the United States is materially injured by reason of imports of color television receivers from the Republic of Korea which are sold at less than fair value." The resulting antidumping penalty added another obstacle to an already difficult course for establishing Gold Star as a major premium brand name in the United States for home electronic products. Apart from a climate of growing protectionism in Europe and the United States, Chung had to resolve the somewhat conflicting pressures from two even more pressing developments. One was an apparent effort by U.S. and Japanese electronics firms to dislodge Gold Star from its U.S. beachhead. The other, which had direct repercussions on export strategy, was a major challenge in Korea to Gold Star's domestic leadership position in home electronics products.

Chung had returned from the Harvard Business School's Advanced Management Program in late December 1983 to assume his new position. An accountant by training, his previous position had been executive managing director of the corporate planning department for the Lucky-Goldstar group to which the Gold Star company belonged. In his new job, he reported to Huh Shin-Koo, the hard-driving and successful president of Gold Star, who was counting on exports to contribute significantly to the company's growth.

Lucky-Goldstar Group

The group's history dated back to 1931, when Koo In-Hwoi opened a dry-goods store in Chinju. In 1945, when Korea regained its independence, Koo moved from retailing to trade and subsequently, in 1947, into the manufacture of cosmetics and toiletries. His early success came with Lucky toothpaste, which enjoyed a virtual monopoly in the Korean market until the importation of consumer goods was liberalized in 1982. In the meantime, profits gained from this product were invested in the manufacture of chemical products, home electronics products (1958), a newspaper (1964), and oil refining (1967). Koo Cha-Kyung, the eldest son of the founder, succeeded to the chairmanship on his father's death in 1969.

In the 1970s, the Lucky group, as it was then called, concentrated on consolidating and strengthening its position in its key businesses, growing through capacity expansion and the development of related products. Exhibit 1 identifies the resulting portfolio of seven business areas and twenty-three principal companies for the group. In chemicals, oil refining, and electronic products, Lucky was the pioneer and undisputed industry leader in Korea.

Under Chairman Koo's direction, the group's sales and profits had grown from $164 million and $500,000 in 1970 to $7.2 billion and $71 million respectively in 1983. These results placed the Lucky-Goldstar group (renamed in September 1984 to reflect the increased importance of its Gold Star electronics business) in fiftieth position among the *Fortune* 500 largest industrial corporations outside the U.S. in 1983. Table A contains highlights of the group's recent financial results.

Group Management Philosophy

This growth reflected certain general values that had shaped management's approach to business. Any actions Chung might wish to take with respect to Gold Star's exports would need to conform to these values.

An Emphasis on Harmony. From the company's inception, its leaders cultivated *Inwha*, literally meaning harmony in human relations, as a guiding doctrine of management. In line with this principle, management sought harmony in making decisions and in formulating strategies. A senior executive described this credo:

> Having its roots in Confucian doctrine, *Inwha* is commonly understood as an important ethical order ruling interpersonal relationships. It was, however, Lucky-Goldstar's founder, Koo In-Hwoi, who first extended the application of this humanistic order to business and management. He perceived that unity, creativity, and excellence could be achieved through *Inwha*. The present chairman, Koo Cha-Kyung, has continued to regard the spirit of *Inwha* as essential to business management, recognizing that it is subject to reinterpretation as times change. His belief is based on a simple premise that business is carried out by people, is managed by people, and aims to serve the well-being of its people.

Even though many Korean companies were known to have adopted employee-oriented policies, the Lucky-Goldstar group was widely recognized as foremost in this regard. Group policies stated explicitly that no abrupt personnel changes were to be made that would cause employees unnecessary hardship. It was also well known that college graduates wishing to continue their MBA studies would choose Lucky-Goldstar group companies, because of their liberal and supportive policies regarding education for employees. Although some of the top executive spots were filled by members of the owners' families, all of these employees had risen to the top from entry levels, and only able family members survived.

Table A Major statistics of the Lucky-Goldstar group ($ million).

	1979	1980	1981	1982	1983
Sales	3,378	4,522	5,287	5,447	7,193
Exports	659	765	1,073	1,056	2,085
Net income	70	25	45	74	71
Total assets	2,601	2,994	3,198	3,745	4,266
Employees (000)	53	43	46	42	50
Overseas offices	37	43	52	58	62

Diversification Based on Related Products. Ever since the founding of Lucky Chemical Co. in 1947, the group had followed a course of safe, gradual diversification. Chairman Koo Cha-Kyung explained the group's successive moves into new business fields in the following way:

> My father and I started a cosmetic cream factory in the late 1940s. At the time, no company could supply us with plastic caps of adequate quality for cream jars, so we had to start a plastics business. Plastic caps alone were not sufficient to run the plastic molding plant, so we added combs, toothbrushes, and soap boxes. This plastics business also led us to manufacture electric fan blades and telephone cases, which in turn led us to manufacture electrical and electronic products and telecommunication equipment. The plastics business also took us into oil refining, which needed a tanker shipping company. The oil-refining company alone was paying an insurance premium amounting to more than half the total revenue of the then largest insurance company in Korea. Thus, an insurance company was started. This natural step-by-step evolution through related businesses resulted in the Lucky-Goldstar group as we see it today. For the future, we will base our growth primarily on chemicals, energy, and electronics. Our chemical business will continue to expand toward fine chemicals and genetic engineering, while the electronics business will grow in the direction of semiconductor manufacturing, fiber-optic telecommunications, and, eventually, satellite telecommunications.

Market Leadership Based on Technological Leadership. The Lucky-Goldstar management prided itself on the technological leadership it had maintained among Korean companies in each of its major businesses. This leadership had enabled the group to enjoy monopoly positions in new products over extended periods. In 1983, the government revealed a list of monopoly products in the Korean market, with Lucky-Goldstar accounting for twenty-one, the largest number held by any Korean company. Chairman Koo Cha-Kyung emphasized the role of technology development in the following way: "Outsiders may judge our group as ultraconservative because of our financial policies which emphasize stability over growth. Nevertheless, we have never neglected investing in technological development. On average, we have spent 6 percent of the group's

Exhibit 1 Lucky-Goldstar group's principal companies (1983).

Field	Company	Main Products or Activities	Established	Sales ($000)	Employees	Joint-Venture Partner
Chemicals	Lucky, Ltd.	Chemical products	1947	$ 473,341	5,600	
	Lucky Continental Carbon	Carbon black	1968	30,597	230	Continental Carbon Co., U.S.
Electricity, Electronics, and Communications	Gold Star Co. Ltd.	Electric and electronic products, minicomputers, mainframes	1958	967,312	14,200	
	Gold Star Cable	Electric wire and communication cable, heavy machinery	1969	228,838	4,030	Hitachi Cable, Ltd., Japan
	Gold Star Tele-Electric	Telecommunication equipment, computer peripherals, automatic-control systems, medical equipment	1969	76,307	2,650	Siemens A.G., West Germany
	Gold Star Electric	Telecommunication products	1970	67,717	2,600	Nippon Electric Co., Japan
	Gold Star Instrument & Electric	Electric and electronic equipment for industrial process-control systems	1974	62,344	1,700	Fuji Electric Co., Japan
	Gold Star Precision	Precision electronic equipment	1976	28,324	930	
	Shinyeong Electric	Electrical equipment	1971 (1978)[b]	47,429	1,450	Mitsubishi Electric Corp., Japan
	Gold Star Semiconductor	Transistors, ICs, LSIs, ESSs, computers, CAD/CAM	1976 (1979)	62,161	1,530	Western Electric Co., U.S.

Category	Company	Activity	Year established			Foreign partner
	Gold Star-Alps Electronics	Electronic equipment	1970	62,417	3,250	Alps Electric Co., Japan
Energy and Resources	Honam Oil Refinery	Refined petroleum products	1967	2,883,237	1,560	Caltex Petroleum, U.S.
	Korea Mining & Smelting	Nonferrous metal smelting	1936 (1971)	285,399	1,500	
Construction and Engineering	Lucky Development	General construction	1969	302,964	1,150	
	Lucky Engineering	Technical services	1978	6,999	220	
Securities, Insurance, and Finance	Lucky Securities	Brokerage, dealing, underwriting	1973	14,459	590	
	Pan Korea Insurance	insurance	1959 (1970)	46,986	680	
	Pusan Investment & Finance	Short-term finance	1973 (1980)	16,128	120	
	Gold Star Investment & Finance	Short-term finance	1982	16,942	90	
Trade and Distribution	Lucky-Goldstar International Corp.	Exporting, importing, manufacturing	1953	1,134,365	3,160	
	Hee Sung Co., Ltd.	Advertising and supermarket retailing	1971	48,226	510	
Public Services	Yonam Foundation[a]	Scholarships	1969	—	10	
	Yonam Educational Institute[a]	Education	1973	—	160	

a. Nonprofit entities.
b. Years in parentheses indicate when acquired by Lucky-Goldstar Group.

turnover in research and development. We will continue to spend a substantial amount of money in R&D in order to keep up with the rapidly changing nature of the business."

Joint Ventures. One way the group had developed its technology effectively over the years was by entering into joint ventures with foreign firms possessing advanced technologies. These arrangements gave Lucky-Goldstar an edge over rival companies at home and provided a channel for entry into new overseas markets. Six of the eight major joint ventures were in electronics and are described in Exhibit 1. In addition, Lucky Continental Carbon had been set up with Continental Carbon Company (a subsidiary of Conoco) in 1968 to produce carbon black (1983 sales: $30 million), and the Honam Oil Refinery was a 50–50 joint venture with Caltex Petroleum to produce petroleum products (1983 sales: $2.9 billion). Honam could process 380,000 barrels per day, accounting for 48 percent of Korea's total refining capacity in 1983. Chairman Koo explained how he had come to view joint ventures:

> Joint-venture partners typically want to make profits as quickly as possible, even at the expense of long-term growth potential. We as a Korean company, however, want to grow our business on a long-term basis. We recognize this difference in orientation, and therefore will form a joint venture where we do not have necessary technologies, and where we can make money quickly. On the other hand, we will form a wholly owned company where we expect long-term growth but not a quick profit.
>
> Based on our experience, I am generally disappointed with the way certain large companies behave as joint-venture partners. They are very slow to act, typically taking at least two years from the idea to the decision. Also, local managers have very little influence on the decisions made at headquarters. Smaller companies, on the other hand, are quick to act, and also very attentive to the local conditions here in Korea. Now we are more inclined to do business with smaller, tightly managed companies than with giant multinationals.

Gold Star Co., Ltd.

The Lucky-Goldstar group's electronics business started in 1958, when Gold Star Co., Ltd. began producing vacuum-tube radios, something no Korean company had done before. Thereafter, the company successively introduced electric fans (1960), refrigerators (1964), black-and-white TVs (1966), elevators and escalators (1968), room air conditioners (1968), washing machines (1969), package air-conditioning equipment (1975), cash registers (1977), color TVs (1977), electric typewriters (1980), microcomputers (1982), microwave ovens (1982), and compact disc players (1983), each a first for Korea. Gold Star was also the first in Korea to conduct electronics business abroad, with the export of radios to America (1962), licensing of color TV manufacturing technologies (1980), and foreign direct investment in the United States to establish manufacturing plants (1981).

Table B Major statistics of the Gold Star Co. Ltd. ($ million).

	1979	1980	1981	1982	1983
Sales	541	419	578	620	967
Exports	161	192	247	217	380
Net income	12	−15	15	13	34
Total assets	508	427	469	484	613
Employees (000)	16	11	10	9	12
Overseas offices	8	10	14	17	18

Starting in 1969, eight electronics-related firms were spun off from Gold Star to produce such products as wire and cable, industrial electronic equipment, and telecommunication equipment. In 1984, Gold Star Company continued to be the largest and most profitable firm in the Korean electronics industry. Table B shows the company's recent financial performance.

As can be seen in the financial figures, Gold Star's growth was not without interruption. 1980 was a particularly bad year in which the company experienced a cash drain serious enough to drive it to the brink of insolvency. This financial setback was attributed largely to two unforeseen disruptive events. First, in 1979, the second oil shock resulted in a sharp decrease in overseas and domestic demand, as well as an increase in manufacturing costs. Then, in October of that same year, Korean president Park Chung-Hee was assassinated. Political chaos ensued, leading to a severe depression in the domestic economy. A further disruption was the death of the company's president as a result of an automobile accident.

Recognizing the serious nature of Gold Star's financial position in the midst of the recession, Chairman Koo brought in Huh Shin-Koo to turn the electronics company around. Huh, a senior member of the owner family, was widely respected within the group as a tough and skillful marketer.

President Huh quickly took major steps to revive morale within Gold Star and to turn its finances around. His first move was to streamline manufacturing facilities by closing down inefficient plants and rationalizing manufacturing operations. The existing manufacturing facilities reflected the accumulation of piece-meal expansion moves that had been made over the years. As a result of the changes, each of the surviving plants specialized in a limited number of products, so as to benefit from scale economies.

Overhead costs were also drastically cut. At the same time, President Huh made major investments to strengthen the company's competitive position, including a decision to establish a sizable TV manufacturing plant in the United States. President Huh also sought to improve sales operations by cutting unnecessary expenses and improving after-sales services. Finally, he took measures to improve employee morale by eliminating internal bureaucratic red tape and improving intracompany communications.

In August 1981, the Korean government's decision to allow public broadcasting of color TV programs came as a welcome opportunity. (Color TV had been banned by the Park administration on the grounds that it would encourage conspicuous consumption and thus widen the disparity in consumption patterns between rich and poor.) Largely as a result of the new policy, Gold Star's 1981 domestic sales increased by 46 percent and the preceding year's loss figure of $15 million became a profit of $15 million. In 1982 domestic sales grew 22 percent and in 1983 another 46 percent.

Organization. Exhibit 2 shows Goldstar Co.'s organization in June 1984. Under President Huh Shin-Koo, two executive vice presidents were responsible for management and production, and two executive managing directors were responsible for domestic and export marketing of all the electronic products except computers, elevators, and package air-conditioning equipment.

Products and Production Facilities. Goldstar produced five major categories of products: video, audio, kitchen appliances, computers, and others. Video products included color TVs, black-and-white TVs, monitors, and VCRs. Audio products included audiocassette recorders and stereo components. Kitchen appliances included refrigerators, washing machines, and microwave ovens. Computers included personal computers (called FAMICOM), microcomputers (MIGHTY), minicomputers (DPS6), and mainframes (DPS8). Other products included room air conditioners, elevators, escalators, motors and industrial machinery. As shown in Exhibit 3, color TV was by far Gold Star's most important product in 1983.

Product development was prominent in Gold Star management's plans. The company's R&D facilities, located in Seoul, Pyungtaek, Gumi, and Changwon, employed about 330 engineers and supporting staff. In 1983, R&D expenses amounted to $47.8 million, which represented 4.9 percent of Gold Star's total sales. Regarding the role of R&D, President Huh explained:

> For the next ten years, it is obvious that we should move into computer-based intelligence equipment, laser-telecommunications, and semiconductors. All of these new businesses, however, require advanced technologies. Unlike the United States and Japan, in which private firms can easily tap well-educated human resources, we have an extra burden of educating our own people within the company in order to develop technologies. Each year we select 70–80 undergraduates, 40–50 graduates, and several postgraduate students and provide them with full scholarships. Upon graduation, they will come to work for us. Some of these talented people will be sent abroad for further advanced studies.

Gold Star's production facilities were scattered around Korea. The major plant manufacturing TVs was located in Gumi, a city (located about 170 miles from Seoul) which had been designated by the government in 1972 to become an electronics center. Computers, office equipment, VCRs, and audio equipment were manufactured in Seoul, while the Changwon plant (250 miles from Seoul) manufactured electrical appliances. In 1981, Gold Star established its

Exhibit 2 Gold Star Co.'s organization.

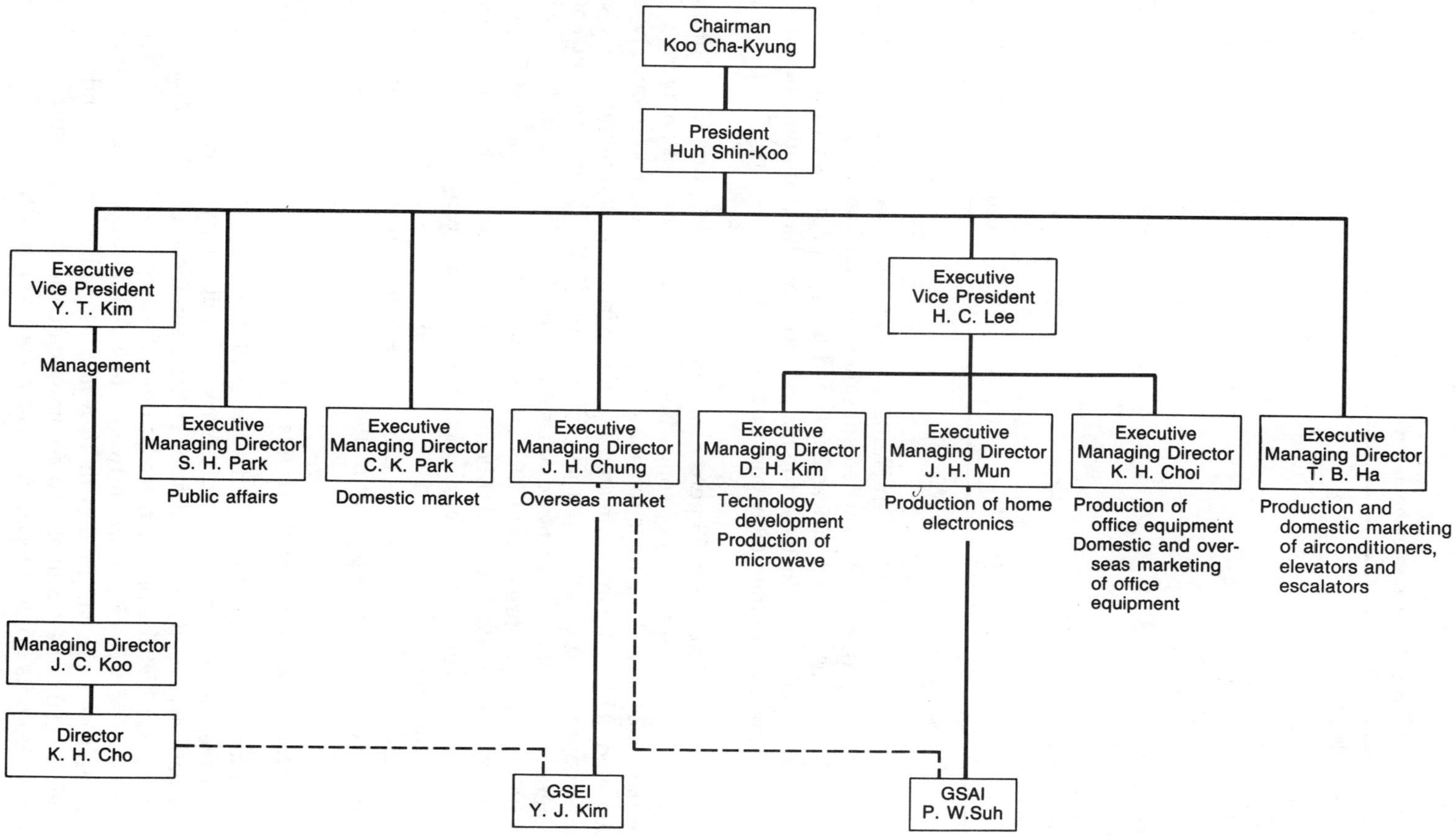

Exhibit 3   Gold Star Co.'s sales breakdown by product ($ million).

Product	1979	1980	1981	1982	1983	1983 (%)
Color TV	33	83	230	216	307	31.8
B&W TV	104	60	91	71	60	6.2
VTR	—	—	—	15	38	3.9
Audiocassette recorder	38	27	35	43	54	5.6
Stereo	16	38	26	11	10	1.0
Refrigerator	143	48	69	89	123	12.7
Washing machine	19	13	20	21	32	3.3
Microwave oven	—	—	—	6	30	3.1
Elevator/escalator	3	16	12	14	20	2.1
Others	186	144	95	134	293	30.3
Total	542	419	578	620	967	100.0%

first overseas assembly plant, in Huntsville, Alabama. Named Gold Star America Inc. (GSAI), this wholly-owned subsidiary had an initial capacity of 150,000 color TVs a year. In 1983, it was expanded to 300,000 units and then in May, 1984, to 450,000 units. In 1984, the manufacture of office equipment and VCRs was also initiated in the newly constructed Pyungtaek factory.

Markets. In 1983, over 60 percent of Gold Star's sales were to the domestic market. With a population of some nine million families and an average GNP per family of $8,700, markets for home appliances in Korea were quickly being saturated. The company estimated the following 1984 saturation levels for its most important products: color TV, 65 percent; B&W TV, over 90 percent; refrigerators, 80 percent; and audiocassette recorders, 88 percent. With respect to its new growth products, VCRs were expected to reach at least 50 percent of the Korean market by 1990. Microwave ovens, however, were not expected to become a major kitchen appliance, because they were not well suited for Korean cooking.

As shown in Exhibit 4, the U.S. market dominated Gold Star's overseas sales, accounting for 68 percent in 1983.

Gold Star's Operations in the United States

Gold Star first entered the U.S. market in 1961. However, it was not until 1978, when the company set up a U.S. marketing subsidiary, Gold Star Electronics International Inc. (GSEI), that sales became significant. Under GSEI, the number of local distributors increased from fifty-seven to 2,500 in 1982 and the number of service centers from twenty to 1,540 during the same period. Sales volume rose from $13 million in 1978 to $151 million in 1983 and net profits from $16,000 to $4.1 million. To accommodate the rapid growth, in 1981 GSEI moved from its original location in New York to larger facilities in New Jersey

Exhibit 4 Gold Star Co.'s sales breakdown by region (1983) ($ million).

Product	Total	Domestic (Korea)	USA	Canada	Latin and South America	Europe	Asia	Middle East	Africa	Others
Color TV	306.5	164.4	108.2	10.0	6.5	4.8	6.1	5.0	1.3	0.2
B&W TV	60.1	—	39.4	3.5	2.1	9.2	1.7	1.9	2.3	—
Combi TV	15.3	—	14.4	0.7	0.1	—	0.1	—	—	—
Audiocassette recorder	54.2	30.9	3.0	1.0	1.0	11.1	1.9	1.8	3.5	—
Refrigerator	122.8	109.3	9.1	0.7	—	—	1.8	1.9	—	—
Washing machine	31.9	30.9	0.4	—	0.3	—	0.3	—	—	—
Microwave oven	30.0	11.6	17.8	—	—	—	0.6	—	—	—
Fan	7.4	6.2	0.3	0.6	—	—	0.2	—	0.1	—
Others	338.8	233.7	65.5	5.5	3.7	13.3	9.4	4.6	3.1	—
Total	967.0	587.0	258.1	22.0	13.7	38.4	22.1	15.2	10.3	0.2
Percent	100.0	60.7	26.7	2.3	1.4	4.0	2.3	1.6	1.0	—

and opened local offices in Los Angeles, Chicago, and Dallas. The major products GSEI handled were color TVs, black-and-white TVs, microwave ovens, and audiocassette recorders. Color TVs were by far the most important item, accounting for 51 percent of sales in 1983. Headquarters in Korea continued to deal directly with major OEMs, (such as Zenith and GE), large retailing chains (such as Sears Roebuck), and large importers (such as Emerson).

One of the primary reasons for creating GSEI was to establish the Gold Star trademark in the United States. As a result, it was decided to sell only products carrying the Gold Star label through GSEI. While sales volume increased over time, this increase was less than hoped for. In the meantime, Gold Star's archrival, Samsung Electronics, chose the private-brand policy for its entire product line, and passed Gold Star in export volume. This setback caused Gold Star's top management to reconsider the GSEI's brand policy. Kang Kil-Won, a Gold Star executive vice president taking a sabbatical leave as a visiting professor of marketing at the University of Illinois, recalled this change of policy:

> We discussed at great length the merits and demerits of a private-brand policy. Some argued that the private-brand business would kill our hungry spirit and jeopardize our attentiveness to promoting the Gold Star brand. But others argued that the private-brand business would help us to increase sales volume quickly, without the burden of accounts receivables and after-sale services. They also pointed out that our corporate philosophy of *Inwha* would best be promoted by an international division of labor: manufacturing by us, marketing by them. The latter argument prevailed, and in 1980 we decided to seek private-label business through GSEI.

The flow of Gold Star's color TV sets to the U.S. market is shown in Figure A below. The OEM sets typically involved some particular design requirements by the purchaser; the private label sets were basic Gold Star units with another nameplate.

Figure A Gold Star Co.'s flow of color TVs to the U.S. market.

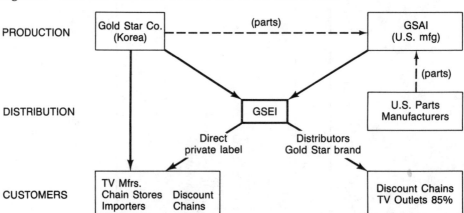

About 85 percent of GSEI's sales were to discount chains. To prevent destructive price cutting on Gold Star products, GSEI attempted to offer some exclusivity to its distributors. Gold Star labeled sets were sold only to noncompeting chains; private-label sets were not restricted in this way. For example, since Zayre carried Gold Star models, such sets were not made available to Caldor, a direct competitor. K-Mart, another competitor, carried Gold Star sets with a KMC label.

In 1984, GSEI had eleven salesmen (six Korean and five American) operating out of the New Jersey headquarters and branch offices in Chicago, Dallas, and Los Angeles.

U.S. Manufacturing. After two years of importing Korean products through GSEI, Gold Star management began to consider the possibility of manufacturing in the United States, for two reasons. The first was mounting trade barriers. U.S. restrictions on color TV imports from Korea started in late 1978 with the resolution of an Orderly Marketing Agreement (OMA) between the U.S. International Trade Commission (ITC) and the Korean government. Lee Hee-Chong, executive vice president, recalled the situation at the time. "The OMA agreement was originally planned for one year. But in 1979 the ITC extended it for another two years, and we recognized that some form of protectionism would continue. We then began to devise ways to cope with it." The second reason was that Gold Star could not easily respond to the rapid technological innovation in the U.S. and to the increasing design awareness of American consumers with the practice of manufacturing exclusively in Korea.

By 1980, seven Japanese TV manufacturers and one Taiwanese had located plants in the United States. Gold Star management began to consider a similar course of action. According to President Huh Shin-Koo:

> We were sharply divided concerning the pros and cons of setting up a manufacturing plant in the U.S. Some argued that such a move would be a big mistake, because we would have to deal with American workers without knowing how. Moreover, they questioned our ability to achieve costs and quality comparable to our Korean plant. Others stressed the need to have operations inside the trade barriers.

After considerable debate, President Huh decided in favor of investing in the United States. Lee Hun-Jo, president of the group's general trading company, Lucky-Goldstar International Corporation, and at that time president of the Chairman's Office, explained how top management thought about this investment:

> Korea was rapidly transformed from an agrarian to an industrial society in the 1960s. Because our domestic economy was still weak, we had to sell products overseas. With little experience in exporting, we relied on Japanese traders, who kept most of the profits and left us with almost nothing. This experience taught us that we should know foreign markets before we develop substantial business there. When the occasion arose for us to invest in the U.S., we considered it as an opportunity to learn about the U.S.

market. In that sense, our attitude concerning U.S. entry was a very humble one.

A careful site search led Gold Star to Huntsville, Alabama, where Dr. Werner Von Braun and some 200 other German scientists had helped to launch the NASA space exploration project in the 1950s. Alabama had initiated a program to develop Huntsville into an electronics center patterned after California's Silicon Valley and Boston's Route 128. The state supplied $10 million worth of industrial revenue bonds for GSAI, at about 8 percent annual interest. It also provided job training for new employees of the company.

President Huh explained how the plant capacity of 150,000 units a year had been decided:

> At the time, we had been exporting 400,000 units of color TVs to the U.S. market, 300,000 in the Gold Star brand, and the rest in private brands. We figured that at least half of the Gold Star branded TVs would find a market, even under depressed market conditions. In other words, 150,000 was an amount we could be sure of selling in the U.S. market.

Successful Operation

The Huntsville plant began operations in July 1982 and in 1983 produced 143,000 standard nineteen-inch manual rotary selector color TV sets. As shown in Table C, the net cost for the U.S. sets was comparable to that for sets imported from Korea. Some of the parts and materials used for U.S. production were shipped from Korea. Overall quality levels for the U.S.- and Korean-manufactured products were considered comparable.

Management had anticipated a loss for the first three years of operations. Unexpectedly, GSAI showed a profit of $1.1 million on sales of $24.5 million in 1983, and GSAI President Suh Pyung-Won saw even brighter prospects for 1984. He attributed this happy turn of events to a recovery of the U.S. TV market, close collaboration with the Korean operations reflecting Gold Star's *Inwha* philosophy, and the positive support provided by Alabama State.

Encouraged by the early results, Gold Star management authorized GSAI to expand its facilities. A second assembly line was completed in July, 1983, and construction of a second plant began a month later. President Huh Shin-Koo explained this expansion program as follows:

> Our business style is not to start with a giant plant and then get into trouble selling products, but to start with a small plant and develop manufacturing and marketing capabilities simultaneously on a step-by-step basis. Then, as our volume increases to about 250–300,000 units, we will split the existing workers into two groups and use the existing facility on a double-shift basis. When the volume exceeds 300,000 units, we will build the second 150,000-unit facility, and move the second-shift workers to that facility. As a result, the second facility would be run by a group of workers with the same expertise and dedication to the company as the first one. We do not believe in the merit of instant scale economies so much as in a slow and steady approach to a new business environment. We will learn American

Table C Comparison of U.S. costs for color TVs originating from Gold Star in Korea versus GSAI in the United States (based on 19″ rotary model in 1983).

	Korean Sets	*U.S. Sets*	*Difference*
Material	$133.86	$150.91	$17.05
Labor	3.39	6.18	2.79
Other	5.43	7.71	2.28
Manufacturing total	142.68	164.80	22.12
Transportation	7.69	—	− 7.69
Damage en route	varies	—	?
Duty	7.13	—	− 7.13
Total landed cost	$157.50+	$164.80	< $ 7.30

business through trial and error, but we will also make certain that we limit the business risk under our control.

A third assembly line, raising the first plant's capacity to 450,000 TV sets, was completed and staffed in April, 1984, and site preparation for a third plant began in June, 1984. The third plant would produce microwave ovens starting in 1985, and a projected fourth plant was scheduled for 1986 to produce "high tech" products such as VCRs and personal computers. Exhibit 5 shows a bird's-eye view of how the completed complex would look.

As of June 1984, GSAI employed about 200 workers. Employee morale was considered to be high. Several union attempts to organize the plant had failed to gain workers' support.

Color TV in the United States

The unions were not the only ones to notice Gold Star's presence in the U.S. According to Nam Yong, who had been associated with GSEI since its inception and now served as GSEI marketing vice president, "A number of established competitors—such as RCA, Zenith, Sanyo, and Sharp—are now attacking us with predatory prices for their basic TV models in an attempt to cut our market out from under us. They can afford to do this with the support of profits from their higher tech products. While we can make such products, we do not have the right distribution for them. Our problem is that our brand name is still weak in terms of awareness and that makes it difficult for us to get department stores and specialty shops to introduce our line."

Demand. In 1983, the U.S. demand for color TV sets increased to over 15.2 million sets, from the 11–12 million level in the previous three years. This market expansion took place in spite of the fact that over 99 percent of all U.S. households had at least one TV set. According to a report by the U.S. International Trade Commission, "Innovation in styling and technology, such as

Exhibit 5 Bird's-eye view of GSAI's proposed Huntsville plant complex.

478

wireless remote control and random-access channel selection, stimulated demand. In addition, the growing popularity of electronic games, videotape recorders, and videotape cassettes, which can be attached to television receivers, was having a positive influence on the demand for television receivers."

Consumption of color TVs in the U.S. market was concentrated in the nineteen-inch screen category, which accounted for 52 percent of the total sales in 1983. It was followed by 13-inch models with 19 percent of total demand, and large-sized models (20 inches and over) with 22 percent.

Channels of Distribution. Color TVs sold in the U.S. reached the ultimate consumer in two ways. In the two-step system, the producer or importer sold the merchandise to a wholesale/distributor, which then sold it to retail outlets. In the one-step system, the producer or importer sold directly to a retail outlet. Generally, only large accounts were involved in one-step distribution.

A substantial number of color TVs were sold under private-brand labels (i.e., the brand name of the retailer, not that of the producer). Private-label retailers such as Sears, Roebuck, J. C. Penny and K-Mart supplied prospective producers with specifications for a particular model television receiver or surveyed the specifications of sets currently being produced and picked the models that best suited their needs. Such private-label merchandisers would then solicit bids from producers and negotiate contracts for particular receivers for a model year. Such retailers typically purchased receivers from several producers, foreign and/or domestic. The percentage distribution of U.S.-produced and imported sets in 1983, as reported by the ITC, is shown in Table D.

Suppliers. Exhibit 6 lists the major brands in the U.S. color TV market. In 1983, 70.3 percent of the demand for color TV sets was supplied by seventeen domestic producers, and the remaining 29.7 percent by several hundred importers. As shown in Exhibit 7, domestic production increased 13.0 percent in 1983 to 10.7 million units, while imports more than doubled to 4.5 million units. As a result, the increased demand in 1983 (3.6 million sets) was largely

Table D   Distribution pattern of U.S. color TVs, 1983.

Market	U.S. produced	Imported
Private label	14.6%	10.8%
Discount	3.5	20.0
Department stores	4.7	6.8
Catalog	.7	.4
Full-service dealer	12.3	22.4
Buying groups	5.9	11.5
Wholesale distributor	44.7	12.7
Other	13.6	11.3
	100.0%	100.0%

Exhibit 6 Major color TV brands in the U.S. (%).

Rank	Brand	Estimated 1984	1983	1982	1981	1980	1979
1	RCA	19.0	20.0	20.0	20.0	21.0	21.0
2	Zenith	17.5	18.5	19.4	20.5	20.5	20.5
3	GE	7.6	8.1	8.0	7.7	7.5	6.9
4	Sears	7.1	7.1	7.25	7.2	7.5	7.9
5	Sony	6.5	7.0	7.0	7.0	6.5	6.5
6	Magnavox	5.7	6.0	6.5	6.9	7.0	7.2
7	Sylvania	4.2	4.5	4.0	4.0	4.0	3.9
8	Quasar	4.0	4.5	5.0	4.9	5.0	5.0
9	Panasonic	4.0	3.56	2.5	2.1	2.0	2.2
10	Hitachi	2.7	2.5	2.25	2.0	1.7	1.85
11	Sharp	2.5	2.0	1.5	1.5	1.5	1.5
12	Montgomery Ward	2.45	2.25	2.5	2.7	2.25	2.1
13	Mitsubishi	2.0	1.7	1.5	1.2	1.0	1.0
14	Sanyo	1.55	1.5	1.5	2.0	2.0	2.0
15	J. C. Penney	1.5	1.5	1.5	1.5	1.5	1.5
16	Toshiba	1.4	1.3	1.4	1.1	1.0	1.0
17	Samsung	1.2	0.6	0.45	0.4	—	—
18	Curtis Mathes	1.2	1.2	1.2	1.0	1.0	1.0
19	Philco	1.0	1.0	1.0	1.2	1.2	1.2
20	Gold Star	1.0	0.8	0.75	0.8	—	—
21	Emerson	1.0	—	—	—	—	—
22	Sampo	0.6	0.55	0.5	0.5	—	—
23	Capehart (NATM)	0.6	—	—	—	—	—
24	Portland	0.5	0.38	0.35	—	—	—
25	NEC	0.5	—	—	—	—	—
26	Teknika	0.4	0.5	0.5	—	—	—
27	AOC brand	0.4	—	—	—	—	—
28	Tatung	0.3	0.3	0.3	—	—	—
29	JVC	0.3	—	—	—	—	—
30	Fisher	0.25	—	—	—	—	—

Source: Company document.

met by imports. Although Japan increased its shipment by 67.5 percent to 1.4 million sets, it was displaced as the number one importer by Korea, with its shipment of 1.6 million sets.

Statistics of domestic shipments by company were not available, but Exhibit 8 shows that four U.S.-owned companies had a manufacturing capacity that stood at 9.5 million in 1983. Six Japanese-owned companies had 29.4 percent with 2.8 million units. The share of capacity, however, was not an appropriate indicator of each company's production, as some Japanese-owned firms operated more than one shift, according to the ITC report.

Exhibit 7 U.S. consumption of color TVs by sources of supply.

Item	1980	1981	1982	1983	Rate of growth 1982–83 (%)
			Quantity (1,000 units)		
Domestic shipments	9,731	10,085	9,482	10,718	13.0
Imports from					
Japan	435	734	813	1,362	67.5
Korea	293	391	621	1,573	153.3
Taiwan	303	457	446	1,056	136.8
All other	256	312	305	539	76.7
Total	1,288	1,895	2,184	4,530	107.4
Apparent U.S. consumption	11,019	11,980	11,666	15,248	30.7
			Relative Size (%)		
Domestic shipments	88.3	84.2	81.3	70.3	
Imports from					
Japan	3.9	6.1	7.0	9.0	
Korea	2.7	3.3	5.3	10.3	
Taiwan	2.7	3.8	3.8	6.9	
All others	2.3	2.6	2.6	3.5	
Total	11.7	15.8	18.7	29.7	

Source: USITC Publication 1514, "Color Television Receivers from the Republic of Korea and Taiwan," April 1984, p. A–37.

In recent years, two major developments had taken place in the domestic manufacturing sector of color TVs. First was a fundamental relocation of certain production operations, resulting in a new international division of labor. U.S. producers had either closed their plants entirely or had transferred an increasingly large portion of their production of labor-intensive components to other countries in an effort to cut labor costs. For example, RCA imported color chassis from its facilities in Taiwan and Mexico, Zenith imported color modules from Mexico and Taiwan, and GE produced color chassis and parts in Singapore. In addition, all black-and-white sets were obtained from their offshore plants. One source estimated that RCA, GE, and Zenith had an average of 50 percent of their value added from abroad. In contrast, Japanese and other foreign firms had started manufacturing operations in the U.S. to avoid import restrictions. The result was a reduction of the number of U.S.-owned firms from nine in 1976 to five in 1983, and an increase in the number of foreign-owned firms from four to twelve.

The second development was the adoption of technological improvements to reduce total labor content of TV manufacturing. Value added by direct labor

Exhibit 8 U.S. producers of color TVs.

Ownership and Firm	1976	1977	1978	1979	1980	1981	1982	1983	1983 U.S. Capacity (1,000)	Plant Location	Labor Unionized	Brand Names
U.S.-owned:												
Curtis-Mathes Manufacturing Co.	X	X	X	X	X	X	X	X	50	Athens, TX	?	Curtis Mathes
General Electric Co.	X	X	X	X	X	X	X	X	700	Portsmouth, VA	No	GE
RCA Corp.	X	X	X	X	X	X	X	X	2,000	Bloomington, IN and 2 others	Yes	RCA
Wells-Gardner Electronics Corp.	X	X	X	X	X	X	X	X	?	Chicago, IL	?	Teknika
Zenith Radio Corp.	X	X	X	X	X	X	X	X	2,000	Springfield, MO and 5 others	Yes	Zenith
GTE Sylvania, Inc.[a]	X	X	X	X	X							
Admiral Group	X	X	X									
Andrea Radio Corp.	X											
Warwick Electronics, Inc.[b]	X											
Dutch-owned:												
North American Philips Corp.	X	X	X	X	X	X	X	X	1,000	Greenville, TN Jefferson City, TN	Yes	Philips

Company									Employees	Location	Mfg. in U.S.	Brand
Japanese-owned:												
Sony Corp. of America	X	X	X	X	X	X	X	X	650	San Diego, CA and & other	No	Sony
Matsushita Industrial Co.	X	X	X	X	X	X			600	Chicago, IL	No	MIC, Panasonic, Quasar
Sanyo Manufacturing Corp.	X	X	X	X	X	X	X	X	800	Forrest City, AR	Yes	Sanyo
Mitsubishi Electric Sales	X	X	X	X	X	X			?	Santa Ana, CA	?	Mitsubishi
Toshiba America, Inc.	X		X	X	X	X			300	Lebanon, TN	Yes	Toshiba
Sharp Electronics Corp.			X	X	X	X			300	Memphis, TN	Yes	Sharp
Hitachi Consumer Products America, Inc.	X		X	X	X	X			150	Anaheim, CA	No	Hitachi
U.S. JVC Corp.				X	X	X			?	Elmwood Park, NJ	Yes	JVC
Taiwan-owned:												
Tatung Co. of America, Inc.			X	X	X	X			?	Long Beach, CA	Yes	Tatung
Sampo Corp. of America				X	X	X			240	Atlanta, GA	No	Sharp
Korean-owned:												
Gold Star of America, Inc.				X	X	X			300	Huntsville, AL	No	Gold Star

a. GTE Sylvania was purchased by North American Philips Corp. in January, 1981.

b. The television-manufacturing facilities of Warwick Electronics, Inc., were purchased by Sanyo Electric, Inc. (Japan), effective December 31, 1976.

Source: USITC Publication 1514, "Color Television Receivers from the Republic of Korea and Taiwan," April 1984, pp. A-8, A-9.

in the U.S., expressed as a share of the total value of domestically assembled color TV sets, decreased from 8.6 percent in 1980 to 7.4 percent in 1983.

Among the several hundred importers of TV apparatus in the United States, thirty to thirty-five firms were reported by ITC to account for over 80 percent of all imports. They were either producers of TVs themselves or private-label retailers.

GSEI's Strategy. From the beginning, Gold Star management had had in mind positioning the company's brand name in the U.S. as one of high quality and good value. But the need to build volume quickly so as to obtain economies of scale for exporting and later for the new U.S. plant required an early emphasis on selling low-cost standard models through discount chains. GSEI management was convinced, however, that for the long run, Gold Star would have to sell higher margin products through department stores and specialty shops. As price competition for the basic color TV models intensified, management felt the need to act on its strategy to move upscale. Kim Young-Joon, GSEI president, described his plan of action:

> To upgrade our position in the U.S. market, we have to do three things more or less at the same time. These are to increase brand awareness through advertising, to introduce higher margin products, and to sell through outlets where higher margins can be sustained. Here, for example, is an ad we are using to support our upscale move [see Exhibit 9]. In line with this plan, we have raised our advertising expenditures from less than $1 million to $8 million [amounts disguised] for 1983. This amount is still small compared to our competitors—RCA, Panasonic, and Sanyo probably spend over $30 million each—but it's all we can really handle to start with.
>
> As for products, we are looking to introduce twenty-five-inch color TV consoles and monitors in 1984 and VCRs the following year. These higher margin items are necessary to interest higher margin outlets to carry us. We shall also put a few more features on the basic models for these stores to distinguish the products they receive from the ones now carried by discount chains. Finally, we are busy trying to line up department stores like Macy's and Federated in L.A. and specialty stores like Lechmere's in Boston to handle our line of products. We have already gained entry into Fredder's Department Store in Chicago where Gold Star will serve as a step-up model from a competitor's discounted TV.

Confident that this strategy made sense and would work, GSEI management found itself beset on another front. Pressures for a major increase in volume were mounting from Gold Star in Korea as the parent company faced increasing competitive pressures from other Korean firms. The only way for GSEI to increase sales volume quickly would be through discount chains where it was currently geared to operate. GSEI management was reluctant to do so. In its opinion, such a move would interfere with its program to upgrade Gold Star's position in the U.S. market. Even more seriously, such a move would force GSEI to abandon its policy of selective distribution, with an effect of further weakening margins and ultimately Gold Star's image as a quality product.

The rising star in electronics is not from the land of the rising sun.

It's not Sony. Or Panasonic. Or Toshiba. Or Sanyo. Or Mitsubishi. Or Hitachi. Or Sharp. Or Sansui. Or TEAC. Or NEC.

It's not one of them, even though those well known Japanese electronics companies have earned a well deserved reputation for excellence.

But, in all fairness, they've had their day in the sun.

And it's time for the rising sun to make way for the rising star.

Goldstar Electronics.

We're part of a 7.5 billion dollar Korean company.

And we manufacture a line of TV's, VCR's, microwave ovens, radio cassette players, computer monitors, and other electronic products

that are giving our competitors fits.

For they can't figure out how we can offer such state-of-the-art quality at such reasonable and affordable prices.

The fact is, we don't do it with mirrors. Or magic.

We do it with young, aggressive and creative management.

We do it with inspired engineering.

And we do it with the very latest production techniques.

Then we pull all these elements together at our plant in Huntsville, Alabama, where we produce hundreds of thousands of quality color TV's and microwave ovens annually.

You can see the end result of all this talent and effort in our sales. For it seems that consumers just can't get

enough of Goldstar products.

Last year, our TV sales alone were up 50%. We sold 2.5 million radio cassette players. And we sold over 1 million microwave ovens.

We're going to continue this success in the years ahead by introducing some of the most innovative products you could imagine.

And we're confident we'll succeed because we've got the products, the leadership and, perhaps, most importantly, a commitment to settle for nothing less than success.

So, if in the very near future, the rising sun doesn't seem as bright as it once was, you'll know why.

It's been eclipsed by the rising star. Goldstar.

GoldStar

Expensive electronics. Without the expense.

©1984 GoldStar Electronics, Int'l., Inc.

485

Korean Consumer Electronics Industry

For ten years, Gold Star had the Korean electronics field largely to itself. In 1968, Samsung (one of the four largest diversified group companies in Korea, along with Gold Star, Hyundai, and Daewoo) entered this attractive business. As a latecomer to the Korean market where the Gold Star name was almost synonymous with consumer electronic products, Samsung emphasized exports as its avenue for growth. The competitive battle between these Korean giants would play itself out years later in the lucrative color TV arena.

The Korean color TV industry which was launched in 1973 grew rapidly in its pioneer days. A 17 percent revaluation of the yen against the U.S. dollar in the mid-1970s and U.S. restrictions on Japanese imports of color TVs through an orderly marketing agreement (OMA) led to a rapid expansion of exports from Korea. The opportunity presented by the Japanese OMA spurred a major color TV capacity expansion among Korea manufacturers.

Then, with total color TV unit capacity approaching nearly 2 million, Korea came under U.S. restrictions to limit its 1979 imports to 298,000 sets. Political disruptions (President Park's assassination) depressed the Korean home market at the same time. The resulting shock to the Korean consumer electronics industry eventually led to the entry of another powerful group company, Daewoo, as it acquired these insolvent business interests from Taihan Electric Wire. Finally, in 1982, Hyundai, the largest and most profitable Korean group company, announced its intention to enter the electronics field with an investment of $500 million and the establishment of an advanced technology unit in Silicon Valley, California.

While Daewoo and Hyundai potentially posed formidable competitive threats for the future, it was Samsung that drew Gold Star management's immediate attention. As U.S. trade restrictions eased, Korean color TV imports increased from 293,000 to 1979 to 621,000 in 1982 and then jumped to 1.6 million sets in 1983. Samsung, which had adopted an aggressive pricing policy, led Gold Star by a small margin in the battle for U.S. market share. As shown in Table E, Gold Star held the leadership share position in the most important Korean consumer electronic product markets.

Gold Star's brand awareness in Korea was even stronger than its volume share. A recent consumer survey had indicated that over 80 percent of the respondents had selected Gold Star as the best Korean color TV set available.

The ITC Ruling

On May 2, 1983, the U.S. International Trade Commission received a petition alleging dumping by Korean and Taiwanese color TV suppliers. The U.S. Department of Commerce instituted its investigations of the alleged dumping of color TVs in the U.S. by Korean and Taiwanese suppliers on October 27, 1983, following a preliminary determination by the International Trade Commission that such sets were being sold at less than fair value. The following excerpt

Table E Market shares of major consumer electronic products in Korea (1983).

	Gold Star	*Samsung*	*Daewoo*	*Others*
Color TV	45.0	36.8	12.5	5.7
Refrigerator	48.9	41.9	9.2	—
Washing machine	50.7	35.9	13.4	—
Microwave oven	45.7	54.3	—	—

from the *Federal Register* (March 1, 1984) gives some indication of the complexity of the issues involved:

> Gold Star argues that its trademark creates a significant commercial difference between merchandise sold in Korea and to the U.S. Purchasers [in Korea] are willing to pay a higher price because of the presence of a trademark. . . . Without an adjustment for the effect of a trademark on market value, the Department cannot ensure an "apples to apples" fair-value comparison.
>
> Zenith argues that a trademark's value is a function of the success of the seller's advertising, sales promotion, and after-sale servicing in convincing customers of the quality of the trademarked merchandise. Commerce should not adjust twice for the effect on value of those efforts.
>
> DOC Response: To the extent there was a value of the trademark, over and above the cost of creating the trademark recognition, it is an intangible. A company would have to show us how it took that intangible into account in setting its prices . . . before we would grant such an adjustment.

On April 5, 1984, the ITC issued its report finding the largest Korean and Taiwanese color TV suppliers guilty of dumping. The following report appeared in the *Asian Wall Street Journal* on April 6:

> The International Trade Commission rules Thursday that imports of color television receivers from South Korea and Taiwan are injuring domestic producers. Earlier, the U.S. Commerce Department determined that nearly all color TVs made in Korea and Taiwan have been exported to the U.S. at unfairly low prices, generally below the "home-market" prices for the same products.
>
> According to the ITC, the penalty duties to be assessed by the Commerce Department against the Korea sets will average about 14.64 percent of the import price, while the antidumping duties on the sets from Taiwan will average 5.56 percent.[1] The duties will vary widely from company to company, however.

Korean manufacturers generally were astonished by the size of the penalty. The earlier DOC determination had recommended 3–4 percent. The ITC penalty essentially removed Korea's cost advantage with respect to the Japanese.

---

1. The average penalty imposed on Gold Star's imports was 14.77 percent.

In *News Review* (April 7, 1984), a columnist noted how the Japanese would most benefit from the ITC ruling and speculated as to Japan's possible role in instigating the ITC petition. During the following period of crises among Korean suppliers, it was reported that Japanese manufacturers dramatically increased the exports of complete TV sets to the U.S. market by 169 percent.

Gold Star's response to the DOC ruling was one of the issues Chung was still trying to hammer out in late December 1984. Gold Star had already raised its minimum price for U.S. TV imports by 5 percent, and an expansion of GSAI's manufacturing plant that would double capacity was under way.

Chung's Dilemma

The contradiction of pressures in the U.S. were multiplied for Chung Jang-Ho when he considered the Gold Star export strategy as a whole. The interests of his subordinates, superiors, and peers all seemed to be at odds.

GSEI's managers were most concerned about the attack by American and Japanese suppliers that threatened to undermine Gold Star's still somewhat precarious position in the United States. Consequently, they assigned a high priority to implementing the program of upgrading Gold Star's market segment with higher margin products and distributors. As an indication of this priority, Chung had learned informally that GSEI marketing favored raising the 1985 advertising budget to $20 million instead of the originally planned $12 million [figures disguised]. He also knew that, in GSEI's judgment, to abandon its policy of selective distribution for discount chains would undermine its upscaling strategy.

Product supplies for the U.S. posed another problem for Chung. GSEI president Kim was known to favor shifting his source of supply from Korea to GSAI (the U.S. manufacturing plant in Alabama) as soon as possible. For obvious reasons, Chung's Gold Star colleagues in manufacturing wanted to retain in Korea as much of this volume as possible. Kim's position was that U.S. sourcing would eliminate the trade-protection problems that consumed so much management time and constrained GSEI's options. Moreover, the lead time necessary to change products in the Korean facilities had averaged 90 to 120 days, whereas GSAI claimed the Huntsville complex capable of making such conversions in half that time. The shorter lead time was seen as an increasingly important capability for GSEI as it moved to higher margin products where the novelty of design features became a key competitive weapon. Although he was not directly responsible for manufacturing decisions, Chung was nonetheless involved by virtue of his active role in coordinating all the U.S. field operations.

Groen: A Dover Industries Company

On Monday, July 13, 1987, Groen's management spent from 8:00 A.M. until 10:00 P.M. discussing how the company would compete in its industry through technological leadership. This discussion covered just a small part of the two-page agenda that Louise O'Sullivan had prepared for the one-day, off-premise staff meeting that was to help her chart her coming third year as Groen president. The focus on technology and product value-added was entirely in keeping with O'Sullivan's primary concerns, as she had earlier described them:

> There are two issues constantly on my mind: Do we have the right products? Do we have low-cost operations? In a way, I want to know if Groen is ready for possible Japanese competition. They are already supplying industrial refrigerators, microwave ovens, and ice machines in the United States. They have not yet entered with steam food service equipment, but are certainly capable of doing so.

The broad consideration of technical leadership encompassed a host of important subsidiary issues. These included redefining the firm's manufacturing policies, avoiding renewed labor strife, preparing for a possible breakthrough purchase order for the division's most exciting new product, and building research and development capabilities in an organization that had been weak in that function. A self-imposed sales target of $100 million by 1990 was ambitious, looking from the 1986 sales base of $42 million. But for the forty-one-year-old chief executive—described by her peers as "bright and articulate"—the goal was real and doable.

Groen and O'Sullivan

Founded by Fred Groen in 1907 to produce copper vessels for the dairy and brewing industries in the Midwest, the Groen Company continued to be a coppersmith job shop until the 1940s, when raw-material shortages and war-related demands encouraged it to begin manufacturing stainless steel kettles for the food processing industry. Although hundreds of models of kettles were available, it was not until 1967, the year that Groen was acquired by Dover Corporation, that the company introduced its second major product, a commercial braiser (a device that cooked by browning and then simmering in a covered container).

According to various accounts, the company had been manufacturing-driven from its founding until 1975, with management believing that the firm's products sold themselves on their quality. In 1976, Lewis Burns, then vice president of Groen, saw a need to place emphasis on marketing, as competitors began to reduce its quality advantage. O'Sullivan was hired as part of a build-up of the marketing function.

Louise O'Sullivan, who had earned a bachelors degree in teaching in 1967 and a masters degree in child guidance in 1970, taught third grade until the birth of her first child in 1971. From 1971 to 1976, she ran a parents' co-op preschool, did home-bound tutoring, and was a substitute teacher. In 1976, she began to work part-time for Groen, writing case studies at home in which she analyzed customers' comments as to why they had purchased Groen equipment. Soon after, she began to spend two days a week at the company preparing advertising copy and product specification sheets. In 1978, she was given the title of eastern sales manager and the job of covering the eastern half of the country, calling with sales representatives on restaurants, architects, consultants, schools, and others, still on a part-time basis.

Enjoying her work, O'Sullivan spoke to Burns about her interest in a career with Groen. She reasoned that it would be necessary to get a solid foundation in business concepts if she wanted to advance in the company and mentioned a small, local college where she could study for an MBA. Burns agreed, adding that if she wanted to take on such training, she should do it first-class and attend the executive MBA program at the University of Chicago, where he had gone. He then offered to cover her expenses. Years later, she remarked on the incident: "This spontaneously generous response by Lew told me a lot about the man and about the company. They believed in me, and believed in going first-class."

After receiving an MBA degree in 1980, O'Sullivan began to work full-time for Groen. At the time, Burns had begun to divide the company's operations because of the differences in manufacturing as well as in the markets served for food processing and food service. Processing equipment, sold in small numbers to food manufacturing firms, tended to be large and highly customized, calling for artisan skills and a job-shop setting. Food service equipment— sold to restaurants, fast-food chains, and other institutions where food was prepared for large numbers of people—was increasingly standardized and called for mass production techniques. In 1981, O'Sullivan was given responsibility for direct sales of food service equipment. In 1983, she received the title of vice president along with added responsibilities for food service engineering. The food service business accounted for about 80 percent of the company's sales at the time.

In line with Burns's new strategy, the company began in early 1984 to manufacture food service equipment in a temporary facility in Jackson, Mississippi, moving into a new plant in early 1985. The manufacture of food processing equipment and headquarters offices remained in the company's Elk Grove, Illinois, facility, located close to the perimeter of Chicago's O'Hare International Airport.

The Combo Oven Introduction

During the early 1980s, Burns initiated efforts to add new items to the company's limited product line. In 1981, Groen introduced its third major product, a steamer. More exciting to O'Sullivan, however, was the prospect of bringing the revolutionary combination oven into the United States from Europe, where it had been available for some seven or eight years. This combined convection oven and steamer reduced the cooking time for two twelve-pound turkeys from four or five hours to sixty-eight minutes and produced a more juicy and tender meat.

Groen originally sought to become a distributor for one of the European combination oven manufacturers and eventually entered negotiations with two German firms. In testing the equipment, Groen technicians saw the need for certain product modifications for U.S. usage. For example, automatic drainage was highly desirable since the equipment would be used by inexperienced kitchen helpers in contrast to Europe, where chefs ensured careful and proper handling.

The reluctance of the German companies to make design changes led Burns to look into having Groen develop its own combination oven as a possible fall-back position. O'Sullivan described this experience:

> At the time, the company only had a few young design engineers and a consultant who was strong in ideas but lacked resources in translating them into commercial products. A search for a person capable of designing the new equipment was unsuccessful since the industry was low-tech and had not attracted any top-quality engineers. Lew [Burns] then turned to my husband, who had a strong mechanical engineering background with prior experience in Control Data and RCA and who was running his own consulting business, to help in the search. When Bob failed to identify anyone, Lew urged Bob to help the company as a technical consultant.

In January 1985, O'Sullivan's husband, G. Robert Oslin began directing the design and development of a combination oven for the U.S. market. As negotiations with the German firms ground to a halt, this effort was accelerated. By September 1985, Groen showed a prototype of the new unit at the biennial NAFEM (National Association of Food Equipment Manufacturers) show. The german combination ovens were also introduced at this trade show. What most distinguished the Groen Combo™ unit were the solid-state electronic controls for ease of use and maintenance, the steam boiler placed inside the oven cavity, and the reversible doors. The advanced technology of the Groen oven was readily apparent when compared to the German units.

Taking Charge

In mid-1985, Dover Corporation created five wholly owned subsidiaries to manage most of its forty-six companies. Burns, who had been president of Groen since 1979, was asked to head one of these units, and O'Sullivan was selected to succeed him as president of Groen as of July 1.

Nineteen eighty five was a tough year for Groen. Sales, which had grown dramatically for food service equipment over the past four years, flattened, jeopardizing the company's ability to meet its annual target. Moreover, negotiations with the union at the Elk Grove plant, which had started in February in anticipation of the October contract date, had become strained. The company had taken the stance that no wage increase would be possible under the existing business circumstances, and an employee cutback in April further agitated the discussions.

O'Sullivan spent a great deal of time during her first months as president on the manufacturing floor in Elk Grove talking to workers. (She had already established a reasonably good relationship with the all-male work force in taking customers through the plant over the years.) She would meet with different groups of workers to explain the difficult problems the company faced in trying to compete with a wage structure averaging $3 per hour higher than the industry average and to reassure them that she and the company really did care about them.

When asked if the men resented having a woman in charge, O'Sullivan responded:

> Quite the opposite. In many ways it seemed as if they were trying to protect me from the nastiness of the situation. For example, they would often excuse me from culpability by saying that I couldn't know about this or that management provocation.

By September, O'Sullivan was heartened by the favorable feedback she was receiving from the plant supervisor, who had had thirty years experience in the plant and had even been a union leader years earlier. He reassured her that there would be no strike. "We felt pretty upbeat going into the vote," she later reported. "We were dead wrong." On October 1, the workers walked out.

The principal reason for this unexpected turn of events, according to the plant supervisor, was that the union officials had called for a stand-up vote, using peer pressure to intimidate many workers who had indicated a preference to settle. He predicted that the strike would be over in two weeks. Based on that assessment, O'Sullivan decided not to inform the sales representatives of the strike so as not to upset the marketplace.

Once again, poor information hurt the company. When the strike continued beyond two weeks, an embarrassed O'Sullivan had to tell the representatives what had happened. Orders were subsequently lost, in her opinion, not only because of a lack of supply, but also because of the ill will resulting from her failure to inform salespeople earlier. She later ruefully admitted, "I truly believed that most of the workers wanted to return to work and that the strike would end quickly. That just shows how naive I was."

The strike was a difficult experience for O'Sullivan. One unpleasant aspect had been the anonymous phone calls, some threatening and some obscene, she had received at home as well as at the office. In keeping with Dover's highly decentralized management philosophy, no help was offered. The strike was hers to handle. Burns only asked to be kept informed of the situation.

During the strike, O'Sullivan was invited to join the Young Presidents Organization. At her first meeting, one of the YPOers referred her to a labor consultant whom she quickly contacted. Pointing out numerous mistakes the company had made, he helped management to launch a program for winning support of the workers. The strike was ended in early November.

O'Sullivan was now free to address a number of other pressing issues, including the putting together of a strong management team. (When asked for an organization chart, she responded, "The company doesn't have one. Defining people's jobs tends to limit what they feel responsible for.") O'Sullivan summed up her situation in November 1985 in the following way: "Once I had survived the strike, the big question for senior management was 'Can she turn this company into a working team again?' "

Manufacturing

When the manufacturing vice president quit for not being selected to replace Burns as Groen president, O'Sullivan put the Elk Grove plant manager in charge of manufacturing. During and subsequent to the strike, she concluded that the challenge of managing two factories and improving production operations was too great for her new appointment. While meeting with some success in reducing costs, he had failed to solve serious delivery problems that had plagued the company for years. Whereas competitors delivered products within two to four weeks, Groen needed six to ten weeks, and even then occasionally failed to meet delivery dates.

It took O'Sullivan the first six months of 1986 to find Al Bruks, who had had extensive manufacturing experience with OMC Corporation, manufacturers of Johnson and Evinrude outboard motors and the Lawnboy line of mowers. The first goal that she assigned Bruks was to reduce delivery time and to restore the company's credibility concerning delivery dates. By December 1986, Bruks was able to achieve a delivery time equal to or better than the industry norm by improving production scheduling and increasing finished goods inventory appropriately.

Delivery time was not the only pressing problem for manufacturing during Bruks' first six months on the job. In October 1986, the union attempted to organize the Jackson plant. With a painful memory of the recent strike still vividly in mind, O'Sullivan spent significant time in Jackson to convince the men and women workers there that it would be a mistake on their part to vote in a union. After several weeks of intensive campaigning, the company narrowly won the vote, thirty-nine to thirty-six.

Looking into the future, Bruks saw the high wages and fringe benefits in Elk Grove as a fundamental manufacturing handicap for Groen. (Labor accounted for about 12 percent of the cost of goods. This figure was somewhat higher for the food process equipment manufactured in Elk Grove.) He described the source of the problem:

> Groen had been a family-owned business run very paternalistically. Succeeding generations worked there for all their lives and consequently had lost perspective with respect to the outside world. The workers produced high-quality products and received high wages in return. The trouble is that others can now match us in quality at a lower cost.

When the mid-contract renegotiation period arrived in January 1987, Bruks proposed to the union an expanded pay scale system to include additional job grades. All of the present work force would continue to remain on the existing pay schedule, ranging from $8.50 to $16.50 per hour (average $11.50). New hires would be placed on a second schedule, with wages ranging from $6.50 to $8.50 per hour. After lengthy negotiations, the union committee agreed to the concept. When Bruks added that it might be necessary to reclassify some jobs to the second schedule, the union balked. Negotiations collapsed when Bruks rejected the union's counterproposal to limit the two-tier system to the lowest end of the wage scale.

Bruks explained the problem:

> False perceptions are a part of the difficulty. The workers did not believe that they were overpaid or had overly generous fringe benefits. The union committee has some thirty-year people who had never experienced adversity and thought that Groen simply coins money year after year.
>
> To deal with this problem, we got the union to agree to a study comparing Groen's compensation to that of regional and national companies. About halfway through, when data began to show this discrepancy, the union shelved the effort. We then tried to get them to consider job classifications, arguing that Groen was two grades higher than comparable firms. Once again, the study was aborted as evidence mounted.
>
> While the union was aggressive, I did not feel any animosity in the bargaining. One possible problem with the dual-wage structure proposed was that it had been a bargaining issue before the strike, and the workers probably retained a negative feeling about the concept. Another problem was that the workers probably had viewed me as the new kid on the block who was trying to be a hero at their expense.

With Groen experiencing less than expected sales, Bruks's next move was to reduce substantially overtime work in the Elk Grove plant as of April 1, 1987. For many of the senior workers, this action cut take-home pay almost in half. At the same time, the company laid off eleven office workers at Elk Grove and nineteen production workers at Jackson in response to less-than-expected sales. This cutback, representing almost 10 percent of Groen's entire work force, reduced the total number to 265.

Bruks also moved to reestablish shop rules, putting an end to what was referred to as "constant coffee breaks throughout the shop." Despite these moves and increased use of outside vendors, Bruks felt that he was beginning to develop a rapport with the workers. He said:

> There is no way to avoid pain in changing from a smug, self-indulgent situation to become competitive in today's environment. So, we are making our moves in a very careful and deliberate manner, making sure that each one is totally understood and will become permanent. As a result, the workers have come to recognize that I will tell them the truth about my thoughts and intentions.

To get the workers to appreciate the increased competition the company faced, a large display of competitors' product brochures, indicating how each of these companies was trying to take business from Groen, was mounted above the time clocks.

Summing up his view of the labor-relations challenge as of July 1987, Bruks remarked:

> We have an ethical obligation to help these people change. At the same time, we have an obligation to make a successful business. On a scale of one to ten, we are probably at one with respect to our progress. We still face a nonreceptive audience. Someday, maybe, something will happen to help us get the message through. I certainly hope so.

Manufacturing Renewal. A second major challenge for Bruks was to improve Groen's manufacturing practices for producing the higher-volume food service equipment. He felt that the company had made a few mistakes in starting up the Jackson plant. One of the principal problems had been the failure to document the manufacturing process in sufficient detail. He attributed this failure to the company's job-shop heritage:

> In making customized process equipment, the engineers came up with a design and let the craftsmen on the floor work out the details. Some of that thinking was carried over to Jackson. As a result, too many people were hired and the start-up stretched out too long. These early mistakes hurt management's credibility.

A major effort to document and improve manufacturing procedures and processes was underway at Jackson. Mentioning his success in getting one of Groen's vendors, the 3M Company, to look into improved grinding techniques and into employing robotic welding, Bruks lamented the limited equipment and tooling available to the "small and sleepy" food equipment industry.

Upgraded manufacturing also meant developing the company's ability to manufacture the growing amount of electronic controls embedded in food equipment. Bruks described the dilemma he faced on this front:

Our experienced people are welders, grinders, and heavy metal benders. The company tried moving people from dusty grinding jobs to clean electronics assembly work, hoping to please the workers with improved work conditions. As it turned out, the older workers were uncomfortable with the new work and asked to return to their old, dirty jobs.

An Added Challenge. In September 1987, Groen was awaiting a decision by a major chicken restaurant chain concerning the possible purchase of Combo units for its U.S. franchise system. If the order were placed, the company would have to produce a large number of units in a concentrated period and with a short lead time. Bruks described his thinking about this special situation:

First, I have to decide if it is a bulge in production or one of many orders. On the current assumption that the order is likely to result in a bulge, we have lined up one outside vendor for assembly and will soon add a second vendor. We are also alerting our piece vendors, and are even building some component inventories in advance. Two administrative specialists in purchasing and manufacturing engineering are also being assigned to this project.

Elk Grove will serve as backup only. If the bulge turns into a long-term volume increase, we will probably consider the possibility of moving the operations to Jackson. We are now talking about 600 to 1,000 units per year, which comes down to nominally five units per day. If we ever get up to 20,000 per year, we might even consider going offshore. We are spending $16 per hour in fully loaded labor costs here and could get $1 per hour labor costs in Juarez, Mexico.

Marketing

Terry Crouch, who had joined Groen in 1984 to start a European operation for food processing equipment, was brought back to headquarters in early 1985 as food service national accounts manager with the idea of replacing O'Sullivan a year later as head of that unit's marketing function. When she and Burns unexpectedly moved up to their new positions in July, he was named director of marketing for food service equipment. Eighteen months later, he became vice president of marketing for food service and food processing products. An Englishman, Crouch began his career in 1966 working for Unilever in the United Kingdom. In 1977, he joined FMC in the United States, where he continued marketing to the food processing industry until he left for Groen.

Crouch spent much of his time training sales representatives. To distribute food service equipment in the United States, Groen had twenty-eight representatives. These representatives were independent agents with multiple product lines who were responsible for contacting: food service consultants, who specified equipment for certain applications; dealers, who took title of the equipment and installed the units; and end-users—chains, supermarkets, and the like. About 85 percent of the company's sales went through 1,500 to 2,000 dealers; the remainder were handled as direct national accounts. For food processing equipment, the company employed fifteen manufacturer's representative groups to deal with the food, cosmetic, confectionary, and dairy manufacturing firms. Crouch summed up one of his objectives for both businesses as "getting more than his share of the representatives' time. To achieve that, Groen has to be number one or two in terms of income for each representative."

According to O'Sullivan, there were almost 700 food service equipment manufacturing firms with median sales of about $4 million. Several large competitors had sales ranging between $200 and $600 million. A flurry of acquisitions in recent years was reducing the number of independent companies serving this almost $5 billion equipment market.

Because Crouch's experience had been primarily with the food processing side of the business, O'Sullivan continued to play an active supportive role in food service marketing. To keep in touch with the new developments, she continued field travel, attended industry trade shows, and participated in focus group meetings that the company organized about four times each year in different important markets. These groups, called Consumer Advisory Councils, usually comprised two food equipment consultants, two architects, two chain restaurateurs, one independent restaurateur, representatives from a school system and a hospital, one or two dealer distributors, service agents, O'Sullivan, and Crouch or someone else from Groen. O'Sullivan explained how the gathering, which ran four hours in the afternoon followed by cocktails and dinner, was conducted: "We make every effort to encourage criticisms and complaints as well as inquiries, suggestions, and complaints. We try not to be defensive or to make a sales promotion. By dinner, after drinks, our guests can be very informative. They are impressed that we're willing to listen."

Product Lines. Food service equipment accounted for about 90 percent of Groen's sales in 1987. The company's base product line comprised a variety of kettles, braisers, steamers, mixers, and accessories. Exhibit 1 shows a display of some of these items from a product brochure. While these base products had long accounted for the bulk of Groen's sales, two new products were particularly exciting to the marketing staff.

CapKold®—a central commissary system for cooking, packaging, chilling, storing, and reheating portions—had become a major growth item for the company. According to the product brochure, it provided the following benefits:

> The CapKold System is a revolutionary approach to food service production. It delivers quality meals with just-cooked flavor—prepared in a central commissary—days or even weeks before serving. Special preparation equipment and packaging methods provide extended [45 day] refrigerated storage, which increases the economies possible with centralized food preparation.

These systems, priced between $120,000 and $750,000 each, accounted for about 12 percent of Groen's sales.

The Combo oven promised an even greater impact. With growing sales through normal channels, Groen faced the prospect of a giant order were it to

Exhibit 1 Typical Groen food services equipment

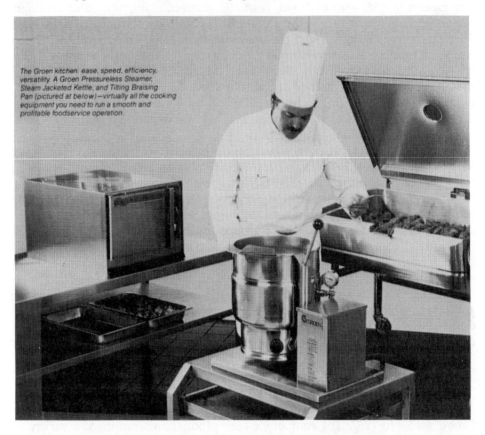

The Groen kitchen: ease, speed, efficiency, versatility. A Groen Pressureless Steamer, Steam Jacketed Kettle, and Tilting Braising Pan (pictured at below)—virtually all the cooking equipment you need to run a smooth and profitable foodservice operation.

win a runoff competition arranged by a major chicken chain. Rick Zuehlke, Combo product manager reporting to Crouch, described the situation:

> Last September, six companies were called in to submit proposals and demonstration models for preparing a possible new product—an oven-roasted chicken. Following a two-month evaluation, Groen and one other firm were asked to continue in the competition as potential suppliers. The ———— chain typically relies on one supplier for 99 percent of its needs and orders a token volume from the second for insurance. I feel almost certain that we'll win because of our built-in capacity to handle software. Our competitor has a German-made unit that has to add the computer software to what is basically a manual control.

If selected principal supplier, Groen could receive an order on January 1, 1988, to deliver 1,800 units to the corporate-owned stores starting the following March. Orders for another 3,000 or so units for U.S. franchise operations were likely to follow, and there was a further possibility for orders from 1,700 foreign units. This order could add $23 million to Groen's 1988 sales and would also have value in giving added credibility to its Combo oven.

Zuehlke described the challenges he would face if Groen won the order:

> My number one concern would be to ensure the successful handling of this big order. As product manager, I worry about getting the ovens out, since we would have a commitment for 500 per month. My second concern has to do with our ability to supply our other customers. We have 100 representatives selling Combos to smaller chains and individual restaurants who depend on us. These sales might total 1,000 units this year, 1,500 in 1988, and 2,000 in 1989. My third concern is "What's the encore?" We are already testing with a major hamburger chain to see about using the Combo for biscuits, roast beef, and steamed vegetables. The potential is to replace four convection ovens in 2,000 stores. We are also exploring possibilities with other smaller chains.

The Groen Combo was a half-size, electric unit (see Exhibit 2). The company planned to introduce a full-size, electric unit in September 1987 for sale to large institutions—such as schools, prisons, and hospitals—and a half-size, gas unit in 1988 for use in Florida, Texas, and other locations where electrical power was more expensive than gas. According to Zuehlke, eleven other food service equipment firms already were offering combination ovens, and three more had announced their plans for entry. Only one of them was not importing foreign products.

The food processing equipment business, accounting for about 10 percent of Groen's sales, was under review as to its future viability. This operating unit faced low margins as a result of the high manufacturing costs in Elk Grove, and a small market compared to food services. On the positive side, it had a new piece of equipment to handle large particulate foods in an aseptic manner, which showed good sales potential. According to O'Sullivan, "Customers are clamoring to test the Particon™ and are even willing to pay for the privilege. The units will go for $36,000 to $72,000, and we should sell ten to twelve in the first year."

In assessing Groen's future sales prospects for food equipment, Crouch saw product engineering as a key to success. He felt that the company had made great progress in new product introductions, exclaiming, "Getting the Combo from an idea to the marketplace in eighteen months was a fantastic achievement." But he saw a lack of product improvement for existing equipment as one of Groen's biggest problems. He believed that the company's long success with kettles and braising pans had removed any pressures for improvement.

Product Development

The development and improvement of Groen's standard products, manufacturing process engineering, and field service engineering were the responsibil-

Exhibit 2   The Groen combo.

Standard Features <u>No</u> Other Oven Or Steamer Can Match...

Can be ordered with right or left door swing...field reversible too!

Solid insulated door keeps cooler, is safer and reduces heat into kitchen

Pan rack guides center pans for maximum air flow

True 4 steamer pan capacity (2½" deep) or 7 U.S. Bake Pans per cavity

Hidden magnetic switch cuts power to unit when door opens

Dependable all solid state control system

Cavity and Turbo Fan™ design provides superior air flow

Fully automatic steam generator blowdown

Cavity accessible steam generator for easy inspection, cleaning, maintenance and trouble free service

Strong 'Continuous' hinge eliminates sagging doors, misalignment

Modular "plug-in" electrical components simplify service

Single action positive door latch with "no-hands" easy open design

Simple, Dependable Solid State Controls...With Self-Diagnostic Trouble Shooting

Bright, easy to read digital timer display

Large touch pads...can set 1 minute to 99 hours

One touch repeat of last cook time set

Oven status lights help operator, save time (WAIT, HOT, READY & SERVICE)

Simple one touch choice of cooking mode... Steam, Combo or Oven Cooking

Exclusive "Rapid Cool" feature allows fast oven cool down with door open

Built-in self-diagnostic system simplifies service

Automatic boiler flush when unit shuts down or switched to Oven Mode

Temperature displayed in either °F or °C with flip of switch

Bright easy to read digital temperature display

Precise temperature set in 5° increments, up to 575°F maximum

ity of John Jurkowski, a mechanical engineer with additional training in metallurgy who was also halfway through the University of Chicago's executive MBA program. He had ten people in his department, several of whom had recently joined the company. In addition to training, he saw a need for his department to develop a capability in electronics, mentioning that the industry as a whole lacked this expertise.

Groen's expenditures for engineering had doubled since 1985—going from 2.6 percent to 5.2 percent of sales for the first six months of 1987. The dollar level was expected to increase substantially during the next few years. These increases led Groen's financial officer, John English, to remark:

> We know that engineering is important and that it should be done. The question is how far and in what way? We have to specify what the payoff will be from this added expenditure. Obviously, we cannot do things without incurring costs. And we have to recognize that there are no guarantees of success.

New food service products were developed by an R&D department reporting to G. Robert Oslin. He described how his initial temporary assignment had evolved into a three-year, near-full-time job:

> As the likelihood of cooperation with a German supplier diminished, Burns put more pressure on me to see through the Combo development. Louise and I had some long discussions about what such an arrangement might mean for her. I was concerned that it could look bad for her and saw a big down-side risk. But it was clear that the company needed help.
>
> As it turned out, my close relationship with Louise was of great benefit to me since she knew the market so well. I spent the first several months talking with her, Terry Crouch, and several sales representatives in whom I had confidence, to gain an understanding of what the customers wanted and needed. This was key to the product's design. Little things, like not putting knobs on the unit because they would get knocked off, were uncovered during this process.

The resulting design, in the words of an observer, "was something never seen before in the industry." The solid-state electronics controls became a key selling point.

By mid-1987, Oslin had become involved in seven other design efforts and had built up a staff of nine. He spoke about the future: "I'm trying to establish a group that I can walk away from. I am working on instilling a philosophy and a right way of designing products. Unfortunately, the ability to invent is not something you can just hire off the street."

Oslin characterized himself as an aggressive, combatant person whose goal was to run his own company. He saw himself as an inventor and wanted a greater payoff than he could get as an employee. He described a dilemma he faced: "I would like to do my own thing, but at this point I can't just quit and leave the R&D group hanging. I also cannot do work for any firm that might compete with Groen." Oslin's reputation in the food equipment business gave him many opportunities to work for large companies in the industry. O'Sullivan described her view of the situation this way: "He'd like to leave and go back on his own. We would like to keep him forever."

Acquisitions

Acquiring small food service equipment manufacturers served as another avenue for adding new items to Groen's product line. With the encouragement of Burns, O'Sullivan acquired American Metal Ware Company in late 1986. This manufacturer of high-quality coffee brewing equipment for commercial and industrial usage, founded in 1883, had sales of $6.7* million. In March, the president of American Metal Ware, who had been with the company for seventeen years, quit on short notice and had to be replaced. As a result of this unexpected loss of management, O'Sullivan was obliged to interact more intensively with that unit than she had anticipated.

In June 1987, Groen acquired a small salad bar manufacturing company located in Savannah, Tennessee, about 100 miles from Memphis. Started in 1983, the company employed 170 people and had sales of $13.5* million in 1986 and was negotiating a contract with Kraft that could increase its sales to $29* million by 1990. O'Sullivan described her thinking about this investment:

> The company had good profit margins and an excellent growth history. As you might imagine, there were also some challenges. Management was essentially a one-man show. A major portion of sales came from one customer. It was involved in litigation for patent infringement with one of Groen's largest customers. What swung our decision was that this product would move Groen more closely to supermarkets, where equipment sales were growing more rapidly than was true for our traditional markets. From 1954 to 1987, the amount of the food dollar spent on food prepared away from home has increased from $.25 to almost $.50, and supermarkets are trying to capture this money through in-store restaurants and take-out-order facilities.

O'Sullivan had plans in July to look over a competitive coffee-making equipment company with sales of $13.5* million for possible acquisition. The owner of this family-owned firm wished to retire, but his sons would stay on to manage the company. This acquisition would raise Groen's share of market for coffee urns from about 30 percent to 60 percent, would strengthen its West Coast presence, and would add commercial glass pour-over coffeemakers (an industrial Mr. Coffee–type appliance) as a new product line with sales of $7* million.

The acquisitions remained independent units and reported directly to O'Sullivan. This arrangement posed a potential problem in that Groen managers were rewarded on the basis of the company's total results, but did not control the acquisitions' activities. This discrepancy could create problems as more companies were acquired. While there were many ways that her staff

*All dollar figures disguised.

could help the small acquired companies, any imposed intervention would run counter to Dover's philosophy of letting each unit run by itself.

The Combo Home Unit

Introducing a Combo unit for home use posed a major issue for O'Sullivan in mid-1987. She explained:

> The Combo is a natural for the home. You just can't believe what it does to food. If we don't move on this opportunity, someone else will. The home Combo has the potential of increasing Groen's sales from $100 million to half a billion.
>
> One problem is that Groen—and for that matter, Dover in general—has no experience in dealing with the consumer market. Another big challenge will be to design a unit that can be priced much lower than the $4,000 ticket for our present industrial model.

Groen's decision on how to approach this market depended in part on the strength of its patents. If its six patent applications were deemed strong, O'Sullivan would be open to discussing possible joint ventures or licensing arrangements with a large appliance manufacturer, such as KitchenAid or General Electric. Otherwise, the company might have to go on its own or with a smaller partner in order to guard its proprietary information.

Groen management was concerned that the home Combo could divert attention from the industrial product. Because of this risk, Crouch and Zuehlke spoke in terms of eighteen months to deal with the home Combo decision. O'Sullivan disagreed:

> Timing is key. We have to move fast with the home Combo before someone else walks off with the idea. The problem is that we are babes in the woods on this one. We are not sure how to protect ourselves from being outmaneuvered or outmuscled in negotiating arrangements with others. At the same time, we don't want to be so guarded and protective that nothing ever happens.

O'Sullivan knew that Burns and Dover management were negative about Groen's direct involvement in the home market. She also knew that the decision was hers to make in the hands-off, its-your-show style of management Dover practiced.

An Assessment of Groen's Growth Goals

English, Groen's treasurer and controller for the past five years, saw difficulties in the higher levels of investment projected for product development, manufacturing improvements, acquisitions, and launching a Combo home unit, noting:

How much can we invest in the company's long-term future when these outlays detract from short-term results? Where is the balance point? Is it correct to reduce ROI from 30 percent to 25 percent in order to develop market share? Should we be pursuing acquisitions, given that they typically lower our ROI?

This tradeoff is not just a theoretical issue for us. All the senior managers have a great deal at stake in the company's annual performance. In effect, as a result of Dover's emphasis on incentive compensation, each of us has to pay out of our pockets for these investments.

He went on to voice his support of O'Sullivan:

While I might question Louise on the pace of our investments and the ambitiousness of our growth goals, I am otherwise very comfortable with her leadership of the company. She is able to get to issues quickly and can be tough in asking searching questions. She might still be feeling her way, but she has a knack for distinguishing between fact and baloney.

On the subject of investments and profits, O'Sullivan had the following to say:

Dover's philosophy is to invest for profitable growth. In our case, the payoff can be three to tenfold as great as we would have otherwise gotten. If this were not the case, then we shouldn't be making those investments. We are making them because the opportunities for profitable growth are there.

Groen's Corporate Context

Dover Corporation comprised almost fifty firms manufacturing a wide range of industrial equipment. As a result of acquisitions and internal growth, sales had increased from $362 million in 1976 to $1.4 billion in 1986, earnings from $31 million to $88 million (down from $100 million in 1985), and cash flow from $37 million to $140 million. Dover's return on average equity had exceeded the S&P 400 industrials average every year since 1976, and the company's price/earnings ratio in mid-1987 was almost thirty times 1986 earnings.

In a speech to security analysts on April 30, 1987, Gary Roubos, president and chief executive officer, attributed Dover Corporation's success to its philosophy:

While we are generally referred to as a diversified company, we have stuck very close to our industrial product origin and have consciously avoided investing in types of businesses where we do not have considerable management knowledge. Automotive lifts and toggle clamps are different—but they have much more in common than, say, investment banking and selling soap.

We are firm believers in the concept of small, independent, niche companies. . . . With very few exceptions, each of these companies is the leader in its marketplace. It is rare for us to have as little as 25 percent of a particular market. Our businesses are generally very profitable, by which I mean pretax margins in the mid-teens and in some instances much better. After-tax-return typically averages 25 percent or more on operating investment. . . . Our culture is customer-driven and operations-oriented. We try to keep staff activities small. The corporate office has only 20 people in it. . . .

Let me add a few words about our company presidents. We believe we have excellent people in these jobs and that they are the key to our business success. . . . Our company presidents are well paid, but not lavishly. They have strong long-term incentive programs based upon the results of their own companies, and they receive 100 percent of the psychic income that comes from running a successful business. They don't get second guessed, they don't get harassed by a lot of staff, and they don't find their bosses running in to steal their glory when things are going well. I believe our company *is* well managed, but the reference is to the operating people within our company. This is the management level where we especially want to be good and are.

The following Shearson Lehman Brothers assessment of Dover Corporation—from its January 2, 1987, equity research report—was typical: "We continue to have the highest regard for Dover's management and for its longer-term record and prospects."

In 1985, Dover divided most of its business operations among five newly formed subsidiary groups to replicate the corporation as it had been twenty years earlier. Burns was named president and chief executive officer of Dover Industries, Inc. and assigned six companies including Groen. His unit subsequently acquired a seventh company, and in addition to Groen's acquisitions, two of Dover Industries' other companies acquired three companies in total. In 1987, Burns had a staff of two full-time people and one part-time person to oversee these businesses and to search for possible acquisitions. Burns described his views on management:

> The president for each of our companies knows more about the business than I do. I have to know just enough about the market to be able to check his or her judgment. If I feel uncomfortable about something, I make more visits and surround the president with questions.
>
> One of our biggest jobs is to help people to see the possibilities open to them. People often are not imaginative and aggressive enough. Buy a competitor? My managers thought that was out of bounds. We asked, "Why not?" and we went ahead and did it. Many big companies suppress initiative and imagination. There is little energy left when you finish fighting the bureaucracy. Dover doesn't operate that way. I see my job as being a cheerleader and making people think big.

He went on to comment on the limits to his direct intervention:

> In case of serious trouble, the ultimate recourse I have is to change the company president. But we are careful not to make management changes too quickly. It calls for patience; you have to give a top manager time to show his stuff. Moreover, there is a big cost in changing people. It can take two to four years for a new person to analyze market niches, scope out strengths and weaknesses, and initiate programs to maximize those strengths.

Of course, when you find a race horse in charge of one of your companies, you don't get in the way. You just let them make money for the stockholders and employees.

To motivate the company's top management teams, Dover had stock option
plans and an incentive compensation system. The stock option plan allowed
vesting after three years and provided a window of seven additional years for
exercising the options. The incentive compensation, which was above and beyond Groen's annual company bonus, was based on an operating company's
three-year average return on investment and three-year real earnings growth
performance. Burns explained the reason for these measures in the plan: "Many
of Dover's operations were family-owned companies where the managers got
big payoffs in good times and had to skinny down in bad. That's the real
world. We want our managers to think like owners."

A new three-year incentive compensation plan was implemented each year.
As a result, each executive would eventually have three plans running simultaneously. Exhibit 3 contains an illustrative performance award table. For a
company with a three-year average return on capital employed of 22 percent
and an inflation adjusted earnings growth of 6 percent, each vice president
would receive an award of $18,968. The company president would receive as
much as two and one half times this amount, or $47,420. (The incentive com-
pensation payout table was recast each year.) Total payout was capped at 20
percent of the total inflationary adjusted earnings increase for the three-year
period. According to Burns, acquisitions depressed incentive compensation in
the short run since the decreased ROI usually outweighed any growth in earnings.

To emphasize the extent to which Dover practiced hands-off management,
Burns added:

> A company's annual budget is not imposed or even approved; it is ac-
> cepted as submitted. If there is a budget shortfall during the year, nothing
> happens. We all feel bad, but the company managers usually feel worse
> about it. What really counts is the track record of real accomplishments.

O'Sullivan confirmed these comments when asked what kind of pressure
the group put on her for Groen's goals and performance:

> None directly. Ninety-nine percent of the pressure on me comes when
> the monthly "white book" comes out from Dover Industries comparing
> Groen's performance to the other companies in the group and to its plans.
> Our standing as managers rests on our performance.

Groen had had the following five-year sales record*: $26 million in 1982,
$37 million in 1984, $33 million in 1985, $42 million in 1986, and a projected
$57 million for 1987. Earnings had been projected to grow almost threefold

*All dollar figures disguised.

Exhibit 3 Abridged illustrative performance award table for divisional incentive compensation.

Average earnings growth	Average Return on Capital Employed										
	<10%	10%	12%	14%	16%	18%	20%	22%	24%	25%	60%
<-5%	0	0	0	0	0	0	0	0	0	0	0
-4%	0	0	0	0	0	0	663	663	1,194	1,326	24,539
-2%	0	0	663	663	1,592	1,857	2,388	2,785	3,183	3,183	26,395
0%	0	0	1,724	2,785	3,714	4,642	5,836	6,897	7,561	7,693	30,905
2%	0	796	2,785	4,377	5,306	7,295	9,152	10,877	12,070	12,336	35,548
4%	0	1,194	4,245	6,101	8,091	10,081	12,601	14,988	16,580	16,845	40,057
6%	0	1,592	5,571	7,958	10,213	12,734	16,050	18,968	20,957	21,355	44,567
8%	0	1,857	6,499	9,550	12,336	15,519	19,366	23,079	25,467	25,998	49,210
10%	0	2,255	7,826	11,274	14,458	18,172	22,814	27,059	29,844	30,507	53,719
12%	0	2,586	9,020	12,999	16,713	20,597	26,528	31,171	34,354	35,017	58,229
14%	0	2,918	10,346	14,590	18,835	23,610	29,579	35,150	38,863	39,527	62,739
16%	0	3,316	11,407	16,315	20,957	26,395	33,028	39,262	43,241	44,169	67,281
18%	0	3,648	12,734	18,039	23,212	29,048	36,476	43,241	47,751	48,679	71,891
20%	0	3,979	13,927	19,763	25,334	31,834	39,792	47,353	52,260	53,189	76,401
35%	0	6,969	19,896	29,712	35,282	41,782	49,740	57,301	62,208	63,137	86,349

over this period, and return on investment ranged between 30 percent and 50 percent, except for a low of 23 percent in 1985. The earnings performance for 1987 was under considerable pressure because of less than expected demand in the food service sector and the extra investment required by the Combo sales drive.

Gurney Seed & Nursery Corp.

"Cash flow is our number one concern today!" With these words, John Kemp, chief financial officer of Gurney Seed & Nursery Corp., sought to indicate management's priorities for its first budget since having acquired ownership of the venerable mail-order company seven months earlier through a leveraged buy-out arrangement. With him were Major General Harry W. Brooks (ret.), chairman and CEO, and Keith Price, president and COO. The company's vice president of finance, who reported to Kemp, also attended. The November 8, 1984, meeting was the final step in a four-month-long effort to establish a budget for the new corporation. Working from recommendations put forward by Gurney's staff, the four corporate officers were preparing a final operational plan for submission to the Bank of New York, the firm's major lending institution.

The basic issue underlying all other considerations concerned how the company should go about paying off the large debt that had been incurred to buy Gurney from Amfac, a *Fortune* 500 conglomerate located in San Francisco. Within this broad context, two questions received considerable attention. Would the forecast for 1985 bear out and provide the company with the cash needed to pay the interest on the debt? What could be done to reassure employees who had seen three different managements in five years, and who, because of management's decision to scale down operations, faced a lay-off of forty-two workers?

Gurney's History

Gurney Seed and Nursery Company was founded in 1866 by Colonel C. W. Gurney in Monticello, Iowa, as a retail and mail-order establishment specializing in seeds and plants. In 1897, headquarters were moved to Yankton, South Dakota. While the colonel and his son proved to be astute businessmen, successive generations did not, and the company went bankrupt in 1940. Revived and sold in 1942, Gurney became profitable again until 1969, when it was sold to a speculator named Jack Hesse.

Hesse was the first owner of Gurney to have no interest in running the operation. Instead, his focus was on building a business empire, and to that end he diverted Gurney's cash flow, leveraging the company to fund new acquisitions. In 1980, with Gurney deep in debt, Hesse sold out to Amfac, a company engaged in wholesale distribution, food processing, retailing, hotels and resorts, Hawaiian sugar, and land operations. A year later, Amfac also acquired Henry Field, one of Gurney's closest rivals, and created two new support companies, Dakota Advertising and Dakota Data Resources to form a Mail Order Division. This division in turn was then joined with several large nurseries and some other related businesses to make up the Horticulture Group with 1981 sales of about $85 million. See Exhibit 1 for an organization chart of the Mail Order Division within the group and corporate structure.

Amfac viewed the horticultural business as a vehicle for rapid growth. Sales of the Mail Order Division alone were projected to increase from $36.6 million in 1981 to more than $300 million by the end of the decade. Contrary to such optimistic projections, however, the group soon experienced rapid sales and profit declines in its nursery business. In 1982, the recession began to affect its mail-order business as well. Exhibit 2 shows selected financial data for Gurney from 1977 to 1980, and for Gurney with Henry Field from 1981 to 1982.

In May 1982, General Harry W. Brooks (then age fifty-three), a thirty-year veteran of the U.S. Army who had been a senior vice president and director of public relations with Amfac for four years, was put in charge of straightening out the ailing Horticulture Group. Later that year, Brooks hired John Kemp (then age forty), a Harvard MBA with seventeen years of prior management experience with Xerox, General Foods, and Chrysler, as vice president of strategic planning for the Horticulture Group. Kemp remarked on this decision, "As a black, the chance to work with Harry Brooks in the Horticulture Group personally appealed to me. Brooks was one of the few blacks I knew who really had senior-level line-management responsibility in a large corporation."

When the full impact of the recession hit in 1983, revenues from the Mail Order Division dropped to $33.1 million, and the Horticulture Group as a whole experienced a $55.3 million loss, primarily due to the write-offs of excessive crops planted prior to 1982. With the need to improve overall corporate financial performance (Amfac experienced a net loss of $68 million on sales of $2.3 billion in 1983), corporate management decided to divest the entire Horticulture Group in line with its new strategy (as stated in the 1983 annual report) "to focus on core businesses that show the greatest promise for future growth."

Brooks, Price, and Kemp were convinced that the mail-order business was an inherently attractive one that had suffered in a corporate environment geared to manage big-business operations. As Amfac entered negotiations with several potential buyers, these three men, and Donald Miller, a friend of General Brooks and a graduate of the Harvard Advanced Management Program, who was not associated with the business, teamed up to propose a leveraged buyout of Gurney, Field, and the Dakota subunits. With some reluctance, Amfac management was finally persuaded to sell the Mail Order Division to this group for $16.5 million. The four men put up $250,000 of their own money and borrowed the rest to make the purchase.

Exhibit 1 1983 AMFAC organizational chart.

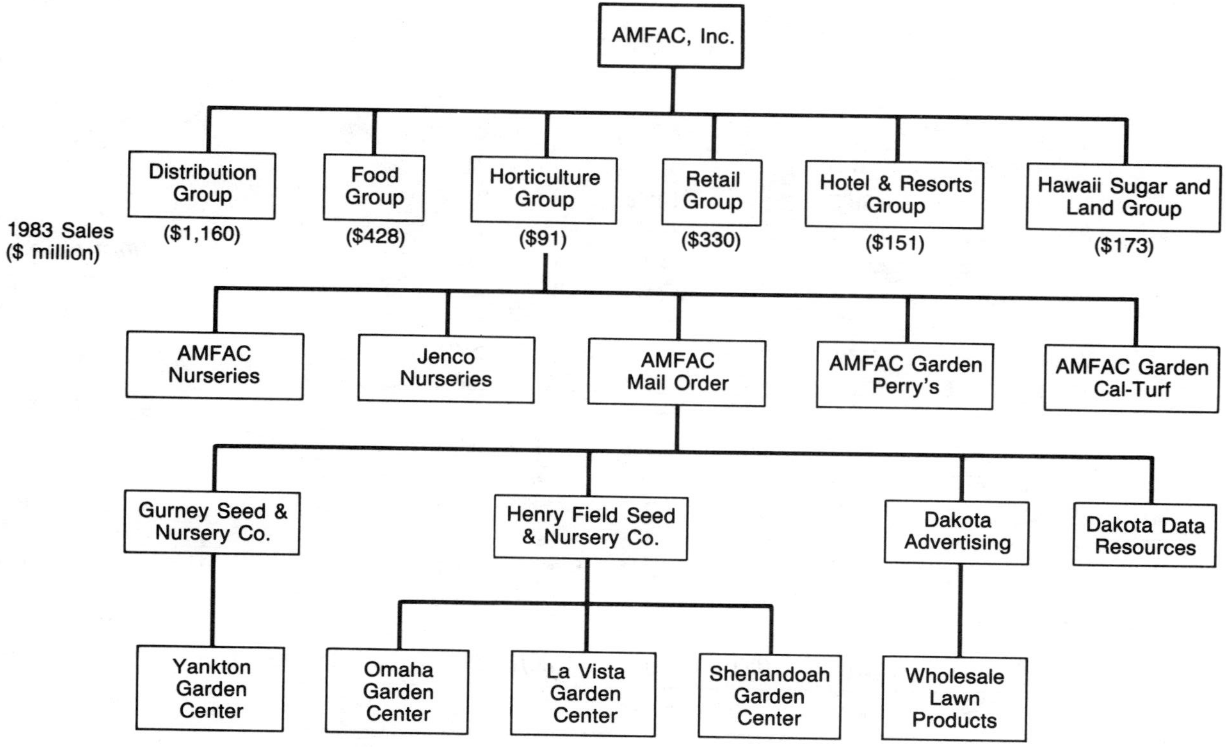

1983 Sales
($ million)

AMFAC, Inc.

Distribution Group ($1,160)
Food Group ($428)
Horticulture Group ($91)
Retail Group ($330)
Hotel & Resorts Group ($151)
Hawaii Sugar and Land Group ($173)

AMFAC Nurseries
Jenco Nurseries
AMFAC Mail Order
AMFAC Garden Perry's
AMFAC Garden Cal-Turf

Gurney Seed & Nursery Co.
Henry Field Seed & Nursery Co.
Dakota Advertising
Dakota Data Resources

Yankton Garden Center
Omaha Garden Center
La Vista Garden Center
Shenandoah Garden Center
Wholesale Lawn Products

Exhibit 2 Selected Gurney and Henry Field financial data (1977–82) ($ thousands).

	Gurney only								Gurney and Henry Field			
	1977	(%)	1978	(%)	1979	(%)	1980	(%)	1981	(%)	1982	(%)
Revenues	13,950	100.0	14,687	100.0	17,954	100.0	21,415	100.0	36,578	100.0	34,892	100.0
% Base mail order	93.4%		94.1%		93.9%		95.3%		87.7%		88.4%	
% Other	6.6%		5.9%		6.1%		4.7%		12.3%		11.6%	
Cost of sales	5,090	36.5	4,980	33.9	5,503	30.7	6,502	30.4	12,112	33.1	10,981	31.5
Gross margin	8,860	63.5	9,707	66.1	12,451	69.3	14,913	69.6	24,466	66.9	23,911	68.5
Distribution	2,106	15.1	2,138	14.5	2,471	13.7	3,207	15.0	5,006	13.7	4,782	13.7
Selling	4,273	30.6	4,613	31.4	4,989	27.8	6,683	31.2	12,017	32.9	13,397	38.4
G&A	1,628	11.7	1,669	11.4	2,114	11.8	1,627	7.6	2,906	7.9	3,019	8.6
Group allocation	—		—		—		174	0.8	350	1.0	496	1.4
Contribution	853	6.1	1,287	8.8	2,877	16.0	3,222	15.0	4,187	11.4	2,217	6.4
Gurney	853		1,287		2,877		3,222		3,747		2,438	
Henry Field									440		(221)	
Allocated charges	107	0.8	630	4.3	(23)	(0.1)	205	0.9	350	0.9	472	1.4
Income tax provision	299	2.1	290	2.0	1,043	5.8	1,497	7.0	1,858	5.1	801	2.3
Net income	447	3.2	367	2.5	1,857	10.3	1,520	7.1	1,979	5.4	944	2.7
Average total capital	2,539		2,251		2,401		2,881		6,171		6,744	
ROTC	12.5%		24.3%		53.3%		55.6%		34.4%		16.9%	
Gurney	12.5%		24.3%		53.3%		55.6%		60.1%		33.9%	
Henry Field							—		7.5%		(3.0%)	
Cash generated												
Gurney	28		1,589		1,088		(1,044)		677		(58)	
Henry Field	28		1,589		1,088		(1,044)[a]		1,762		208	
									(1,085)		(266)	
Simple Cash Generation (before corporate charges)	434		2,509		2,108		832		4,320		1,711	

a. Caused by fiscal year change at time of acquisition.

512

The Mail-Order Business

The first mail-order customers in the U.S. were farmers and trappers who were unable to travel long distances to retail outlets, but their selection of goods was limited to a narrow range of products at premium prices. Capitalizing on the improvement of rail transportation, Aaron Montgomery Ward set up a business in 1872 to bypass retail middlemen, cut prices, and offer a wide range of durable goods by mail, for cash. Montgomery Ward was followed into the general merchandise mail order business by Sears, Roebuck & Co. in 1886. By the early twentieth century, Sears, Roebuck proclaimed itself as "the Cheapest Supply House on Earth," and its catalog was known to farm families as the "wish book."

Changing population patterns in the United States in the mid-1920s prompted the largest two catalog companies, Sears and Montgomery Ward, to open hundreds of retail stores. Those outlets began to generate more profits than their mail-order operations, as automobile travel to stores became easier and faster than shopping by mail. As a result, mail-order shopping began to wane.

The spiraling price of gasoline, the rapid increase in the number of households with two working spouses, and the mounting traffic congestion in urban and suburban centers all worked to reverse this downward trend during the 1970s. As noted in *Forbes* (May 7, 1984):

> Sears was offering a variety of goods, mostly to people who lived a half day away from the nearest big store. Now, of course, it's just the opposite: The shelves are only minutes away. But high labor costs, . . . parking, traffic and crime are obstacles. So the ordeal of shopping takes half a day.

Technology in the 1980s played an increasingly important role in reducing the time required to process and distribute orders. Powerful computers that recorded inventory and electronically routed orders through automated warehouses were employed by major catalogers to speed products to customers. The use of toll-free telephone numbers and around-the-clock staffs to operate the electronic information systems further improved customer service.

This growth in technology in time increased both the business potential and the capital costs associated with efficient mail-order operations. By 1984, the mail-order industry, with total sales of $150 billion and growing at a rate of 15 percent annually, had become dominated by big players. The largest U.S. catalog companies included Sears with 1983 sales in excess of $2 billion, J. C. Penney ($1.7 billion), Montgomery Ward ($1.2 billion), and Fingerhut (over $500 million).

The mail-order seed and nursery business in 1985 was a highly competitive market, characterized by dozens of small regional catalogers and three national companies. Geography played an important role in segmenting the business. The seed and plant requirements were distinctive for different areas of the country, because of temperature, rainfall, and customer preferences. Furthermore, each company tried to project a distinctive image that would appeal to special mail-order audiences. As reported in *The Boston Globe* (February 8, 1985):

Rob Johnston, President of Johnny's Selected Seed, notes, "Every seed company has its own personality and it comes across in the catalog." The Johnny's catalog, filled with graphs and information geared toward organic horticultural methods, is earnest and educational. On the other hand, Gurney's looks and reads like a colorful Sunday comic strip with photos of 307-pound giant squash with captions such as "this balloon won't fly."

Gurney's management competed most directly on the national level with the Burpee and Park Seed companies. A June 1983 strategic analysis sized up the competition this way:

Burpee [a subsidiary of ITT]—Even though their primary appeal is to a slightly different market segment [more emphasis on flower seeds as compared to Gurney's emphasis on vegetable seeds], Burpee is our major competitor. Over the last several years they have appeared indecisive as to business direction and are certainly several years behind the industry in mail-order techniques. However, they will remain stiff competition on the east coast and throughout the northeast for the next several years just on the strength of their name.

Park Seed Company—Like Burpee, their appeal is to a slightly different market segment. However, with their base in the South and Southeast, they overlap our market and represent the second strongest competitor. Under family ownership, they tend to be conservative and behind the industry in many areas.

We strongly believe neither of these companies has grown as rapidly nor been as profitable as Gurney in the last five years, including 1983. We further believe that with the exception of the southern U.S., we have captured the biggest share of the market.

In 1985, ITT was reported to have included Burpee among the businesses that were being considered for divestment as part of a major move to generate funds.

Gurney's Products and Market

Gurney and Field both offered a full range of over 4,000 garden-related items in their catalogs. These items fell into three broad categories: garden seed, nursery goods, and merchandise (garden-related equipment and supplies). Table A shows the relative importance of each of these categories.

Customers. Gurney had an active customer list (i.e., persons who had made a purchase within three years) of approximately 2.7 million names and Field of 1.3 million names. Since management considered customer loyalty a potent force in buying behavior, the two lists were not commingled. Kemp noted, "Gardening involves a big investment in time and effort before you see the results. Therefore, people tend to stick with a company which has provided consistent satisfaction over the years." He estimated a 25 percent overlap in customers in 1984.

Demographically, Gurney and Field customers were about the same. Their

Table A Gurney's 1984 sales and margin statistics.

	Sales ($)	% of Sales	Gross Margin (%)
Garden Seed	9,900,000	33	81.5
Nursery	15,900,000	53	67.4
Other (catalog merchandise, retail & wholesale sales, and list rental)	4,200,000	14	50.0
Total	30,000,000	100	

median age was fifty years, and median family income was $21,000. Some 94 percent were homeowners, with an average garden size of 2,500 square feet. Geographically, customers lived in midwest and western states, with the heaviest concentration in Illinois, Minnesota, and Wisconsin. They tended to stay put: 90 percent lived in the same town they had lived in ten years earlier. Although most of the customers were not farmers, they were predominately rural, and were dependent upon farm income. Any drop in retail food prices or increase in the price of seed or nursery products also had a significant negative impact on the quantities ordered.

Catalogs

The principal means by which Gurney reached its customers was through catalogs sent out several times a year. The critical success factor in getting a good response from a catalog mailing was in having the catalogs in the customers' hands well before the start of the growing season.

Active customers were mailed a sixty-four-page spring catalog in December. If this catalog failed to elicit a response by late February, another copy was mailed to serve as a reminder. A smaller version (forty-four pages) was sent to prospective customers. In late March, another sixty-four-page special sale catalog featuring new products and sell-out prices was mailed to active customers. In August, a smaller fall planting catalog was mailed.

Management regarded Gurney's catalogs as more "folksy" than those offered by competing firms. In physical make-up the company's catalog had always been *Life* magazine size (11" x 16"), printed on stock paper, in contrast to the 8 ½" x 11" glossy paper catalogs generally used in the industry. Exhibit 3 displays a typical page from a Gurney catalog.

Gurney's Business Cycle

Production of the spring catalog, which began on August 1, marked the start of Gurney's business cycle. Sizable outlays of cash were required for layout, printing, artwork, and photography from August through November. In fall, production costs also began to increase as seasonal workers were hired to pre-

Exhibit 3   Page from 1985 Gurney catalog.

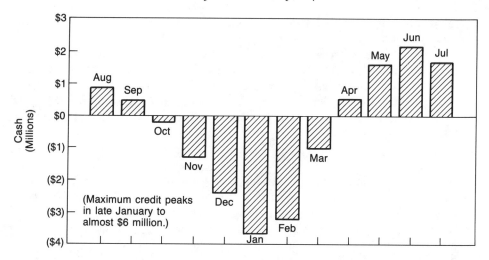

Figure A Typical cash position cycle for Gurney operations (monthly average).

pare and package seeds and other nursery items. Postage alone for mailing spring catalogs amounted to over $1 million. As a result of these activities, working capital requirements usually peaked in January.

As orders with cash payments began to arrive in mid-January, the company began to reduce its short-term debt. Cash inflows were typically great enough to retire all of Gurney's short-term debt by April 1.

As a general rule, about 85 percent of the entire year's cash inflows were received from February through July (50 percent in March and April). The remaining 15 percent were received in late summer in connection with the fall catalog. (Sales were recognized when the product was shipped; cash receipts when received with the order.) Figure A shows the seasonal impact on Gurney's cash position.

Operations

The company's principal operations included the preparation of catalogs, the production (farming) and purchasing of products, packaging, order taking, shipping, and customer service. Apart from catalog production and data processing, Gurney and Field were independently run.

Located near the banks of the Missouri River in Yankton, South Dakota, Gurney's farming facilities consisted of 525 acres of owned, and 67 acres of leased land. Twenty percent of its catalog products were produced on its own farm, including small flowering plants and vegetable seeds. Outside wholesale vendors provided the remaining 80 percent of catalog items, including all merchandise and such exotic nursery items as bulbs imported from Holland.

During the planting and harvesting seasons, the base crew of 220 farm workers ballooned to about 650 workers. During spring, several hundred seasonal workers were added to handle order taking, packaging, and shipping. All seasonal and full-time employees were nonunion and, except for those doing manual labor, most were women who had been with Gurney for many years.

Dakota Data Resources (DDR), a wholly owned subsidiary of Gurney, maintained the mailing lists, processed orders, tracked sales of catalog items, and collected financial data for both Gurney and Field. The company, located in its own building in downtown Yankton, used IBM 4300 series hardware and 150 IBM 3277-2 display terminals that were operated by part-time seasonal workers. During the peak season, DDR was capable of processing 30,000 mail orders daily.

Also located in downtown Yankton was Dakota Advertising, Gurney's in-house agency. This unit, employing a full-time staff of writers, artists, copy editors, and printers, did lay-out, design, graphic production, printing, and mailing of all Gurney's and Field's catalogs. Like DDR, Dakota Advertising hired additional workers during the peak season.

Henry Field's operating facility in Shenandoah, Iowa, performed many of the same functions as Gurney's facility, such as planting, harvesting, and shipping orders to customers. The company owned 135 acres, and leased 400 acres in the immediate area on which 25 percent of its products were grown. In addition to its mail-order operations, Field owned three retail garden centers (two in Omaha, Nebraska, and one in Shenandoah) that provided 15 percent of its annual revenue.

Keith Price, in charge of operations, had his office in Yankton. Harvesting, packaging, and shipping operations in South Dakota and Iowa were controlled by nursery managers who were responsible for meeting production schedules, stocking adequate inventory, and shipping orders in a timely fashion.

Harry W. Brooks, John Kemp, and two staff assistants occupied Gurney's corporate headquarters in San Bruno, California. By establishing headquarters near San Francisco, Brooks believed that the corporation would make itself more accessible to financial resources, as well as give top management a broader perspective on the marketplace. Another reason for putting headquarters in San Francisco was Brooks's confidence in Keith Price as the chief operating officer. Price had been Gurney's executive vice president in charge of marketing, and he was selected by Brooks in 1983 to assume the presidency of Amfac Mail Order Division.

By separating headquarters from operations, Brooks believed it would facilitate entering new businesses over time. Plans were under way to create, as of December 1, 1984, a new holding company, Advanced Consumer Marketing Corporation, to provide an organizational structure for such expansion in the future. See Exhibit 4 for the new organization chart.

The Leveraged Buy-out

Following lengthy negotiations, the four owners reached an agreement with Amfac management to purchase the seed and nursery mail-order business for $16.5 million through a leveraged buy-out arrangement. The exchange of own-

Exhibit 4 Gurney's revised organizational chart (December 1984).

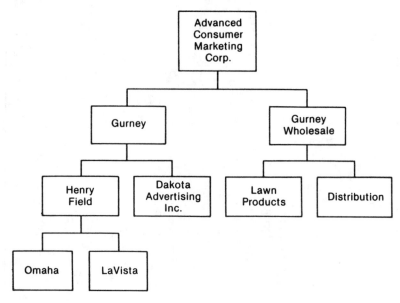

ership took place on Monday, April 30, 1984, and involved the following financial transactions (in $ million):

Amfac's Considerations			New Owner's Financing	
free cash flow from			free cash flow	$5.2
operations, Jan. 1–Apr. 30	$5.2		long-term debt	8.0
cash	10.1		short-term debt	1.85
note	0.5		note to Amfac	0.5
transfer of debt			other debt	0.7
to new owners	0.7		equity	0.25
Total	$16.5		Total	$16.5

The short-term debt was further reduced on that day by $700,000 from orders received over the weekend. A summary of the new company's debt is shown in Exhibit 5.

The 1985 Budget

John Kemp saw the main objective for Gurney's 1985 budget to be the reduction of short- and long-term debt. The firm's short-term debt position was of particular concern to him, standing at a million dollars at a time when the company should have had substantial cash on hand. Complicating the situation was the need Kemp saw to change the loan's restrictive covenants and the difficulty management had in forecasting 1985 conditions for the seed and nursery

Exhibit 5 Summary of debt and interest expense.

Payee	Description of debt	Principal Amount (as of 10/1/84)	Interest Rate and Payment Schedule	Estimated Total Interest to be Paid 10/84 to 10/85[a]
Amfac	Five-year subordinated note	$500,000	12%; yearly payments	$60,000
American State Bank	Existing loan on fixed assets due in 1988	663,943	9.75%; semi-annual payments	65,092
Bank of New York	Principal term loan to buy the company	8,000,000	Prime rate to 6/30/87; .25% + prime to 6/30/90; .50% + prime to 6/30/94 Thirty-two consecutive quarterly installments of principal beginning 9/86	960,000 (assuming 12% interest rate for 1985)
Bank of New York	Facility fee (an additional compensation to the bank for entering into the loan agreement)	1,999,998	Twelve consecutive quarterly installments of $166,667 beginning 3/31/89	—
Bank of New York	Short-term debt	up to 8,000,000	Variable	—
Other	Loan from Harry Brooks, due in 12/85 (for sub-chapter S purposes)	233,000	12% (three payments in 1985 with principal due 12/85)	20,970
	Lucille Foster Trust, due 1992	71,793	8%; monthly payments	4,946
				Total $1,449,508

a. No repayment of principal was scheduled for this reporting period (10/84 to 10/85).

520

mail order business. (A restrictive covenant imposes specific constraints upon the borrower to protect the lender's interests.)

Kemp explained his reasons for wanting to change the loan covenants: "At the time of the closing, many facts regarding the ultimate balance sheet, the accounting policies, and the size of inventory were unknown to the Bank of New York and to Gurney. Since then, we have had unexpected tax write-offs for inventory and catalogs. We have also decided to remove from the balance sheet about $3.4 million in prepaid expenses for catalogs and to recognize marketing expenses as period costs. The major thrust of our proposed changes is to emphasize cash flow over profits so as to minimize our tax exposure. As a result, the original covenants no longer make any sense."

Kemp sought to make the following specific changes in the bank loan agreement terms:

1. Minimum net worth covenant:

	as agreed	proposed
October 31, 1985	$ 750,000	$(3,600,000)
October 31, 1986	2,250,000	(2,800,000)
October 31, 1987	4,250,000	(1,700,000)
October 31, 1988	7,050,000	300,000

2. Short-term line of credit:

> Elimination of the requirement that short-term credit be limited to the sum of 90 percent of accounts receivable plus 80 percent of inventory plus 50 percent of net prepaid expenses. With management's decision to reduce inventories and to eliminate most prepaid expenses, the short-term funds available under this formula fell well below the $8 million ceiling. The bank was also to remove a stipulation requiring Gurney to have ninety consecutive debt-free days in its short-term line of credit account.

In preparing an economic overview for the business, Kemp had found 1984 to be a confusing year from which to project. Some of the sources of confusion included the following considerations: The U.S. was experiencing a high growth in GNP, but farm income had sagged; interest rates had declined during the first quarter, risen during the second and third quarters, and were again declining at year end; and unemployment had decreased but was still above the 1981 level of 7.5 percent. Moreover, according to Kemp, the industry's overall catalog sales had been dropping 10 percent per annum over the depressed 1981–84 period. His report to management concluded, "All of these factors make predicting 1985 all but impossible."

Notwithstanding these difficulties, Kemp had had to make several major assumptions in order to prepare pro forma financial projections. First, a prime rate of 11.25 percent was assumed for 1985, 12.75 percent for 1986, and 12 percent thereafter. A shift of 100 basis points (1 percent) in the prime rate would change Gurney's annual interest burden by $120,000.

The projections also assumed a low and stable general inflation rate of 4 percent for 1985. Because food prices were a major component in the inflation rate, a high inflation rate generally meant rising food prices. For Gurney's, higher inflation meant that more people would want to grow their own food, hence increasing demand. A second bonus from inflation was that it reduced the real interest rate that the company had to pay. The projections for inflation and interest rates were thought to be on the conservative side. Finally, Kemp assumed that the recession had bottomed out for the segment of the population served by the mail-order horticultural industry. Although the reelection of President Reagan and the likely resulting cutback on farm-support programs had been anticipated, the full impact of such changes on future farm income was difficult to predict.

As Kemp worked on the 1985 economic overview, operating managers were busy preparing operational plans. Kemp describes how management had set them to work on this assignment:

> No longer do we have a parent company around to bail us out at the end of the year. That means that we have to get our people to think in new ways. For example, we told our marketing people to put together a marketing plan with reduced costs. But we didn't tell them how to reduce those costs, nor did we tell them how much to reduce them. Even though we have a figure in mind of what those costs should be, we want them to propose cost reductions and to show what happens as those cuts are made. Then we'll sit down and talk.

When the various projections and proposals had been reviewed and adjusted, Kemp then began to prepare a variety of detailed financial projections. Monthly financial data for the 1985 base case are contained in Exhibits 6 and 7. This model was based on the following assumptions: a 25 percent reduction in catalog mailings for 1985; effective price increases of 4.5 percent for Gurney's products and 2.5 percent for Field's; no change in response rate or average order size when compared to 1984; labor and benefits cost reductions totaling $757,000; and an inventory reduction of $1.7 million. A sensitivity analysis with respect to response rate is given in Exhibit 8. Base case projections through 1988 are included in Exhibits 9 and 10.

The budget document concluded that (1) the company could withstand another year of lower than anticipated results, and (2) the upside potential was great. However, the financial projections incorporated policies concerning price increases and cost reductions that still had to be examined and decided in the budget meeting under way.

Price Increases

Product price increases were up for final approval in the November budget meeting. Gurney's prices were to rise by 4.5 percent and Henry Field's prices by 2.5 percent. Field's increase was less, because its prices were already comparatively higher than Gurney's. The net effect of those increases was an expected increase in average order revenues of 2 percent for Gurney and 1 percent for Field.

Part of the price increase would have to cover an anticipated 10 percent increase in postal and United Parcel Service shipping charges. In 1984, Gurney's postage expenses were about $1.5 million and UPS shipping about $1.7 million. Commenting on the price hike as a whole, Kemp noted, "We sell value. We're not the cheapest, but we're also not the most expensive. Our customers know that."

In addition to raising prices, management was thinking of increasing the average order size as a way of increasing revenues. Adding new products to the present catalogs was one approach under active consideration.

Cost Reductions

Kemp saw a major job for the new owners to be one of making the organization more cost and cash conscious. He remarked:

> Amfac had programmed people to think about rapid growth. Investments in staffing and facilities were made in anticipation of much larger and more complex operations. The pockets were deep and not too much attention was paid to cash. But when you are dealing with a small, privately owned company, P&L is meaningless. Cash is king.
>
> In a large organization, sometimes you would have to put a sunroof, automatic windows, and tinted glass on a proposal to get it through. You knew that they were going to strip off those layers, and you hoped that enough of your proposal would remain to recognize it when they got through. If the boss didn't like the numbers you brought him, you went away and brought him back some new numbers that he would like.
>
> That kind of game playing just doesn't make any sense for us. Our job now is to peel down the onion to its essence and to make people very concerned with cash flow. For example, under Amfac, Gurney always paid vendors within thirty days. Now, we slow down such payments. Labor and benefits were two other areas where we saw a need to reduce expenditures.

The seed and nursery business was highly labor intensive. Gurney and Field had spent nearly $4 million on wages and salaries in 1983, exclusive of advertising and data-processing labor costs. In October, 1984, management decided to cut the line work force by forty-two workers, based on a careful analysis of the expected business outlook for 1985. The resulting annual savings were projected to be $453,000.

The health plan was also targeted for savings. Kemp wanted to introduce a new plan that would provide a more comprehensive health coverage and would also include seasonal workers. At the same time, he proposed that employees pay a monthly fee and be liable for a $200 deductible. The net effect would be to save the company $206,000 annually.

In line with these moves, Amfac's practice of supplying many executives with a company car was discontinued, resulting in an expected savings of $39,000 for 1985.

Management's efforts to improve the economics of the company was strongly influenced by its concern that value be given for dollars spent and that muscle

Exhibit 6 1985 end of month pro forma balance sheets for base case (11.25% interest rate).

	Beginning Balance	Nov.	Dec.	Jan.	Feb.	Mar.	Apr.	May	Jun.	Jul.	Aug.	Sept.	Oct.
Current Assets													
Cash	$100	$100	$100	$100	$100	$100	$100	$613	$688	$100	$100	$100	$100
Accounts receivable	563	509	399	442	678	839	1,052	944	407	318	298	291	356
Inventory	3,986	4,250	5,298	6,263	5,774	4,423	3,211	2,717	2,640	2,874	3,011	3,286	3,523
Net prepaid expenses	184	141	145	180	245	219	178	141	129	132	143	158	193
Total current assets	4,833	5,000	5,942	6,985	6,797	5,581	4,541	4,415	3,864	3,424	3,552	3,835	4,172
Fixed Assets													
Property & equipment (at cost)	7,833	7,849	7,853	7,863	7,933	7,950	7,958	7,958	8,023	8,109	8,111	8,111	8,119
Less accum. depreciation	(344)	(405)	(466)	(527)	(588)	(649)	(710)	(771)	(832)	(893)	(954)	(1,015)	(1,076)
Net property & equipment	7,489	7,444	7,387	7,336	7,345	7,301	7,248	7,187	7,191	7,216	7,157	7,096	7,043
Other Assets													
Noncurrent receivables*	34	34	34	34	34	34	34	34	34	34	34	34	34
Other assets	61	61	61	61	61	61	61	61	61	61	61	61	61
Prepaid interest	935	924	913	902	891	880	869	858	847	836	825	814	803
Total other assets	1,030	1,019	1,008	997	986	975	964	953	942	931	920	909	898
TOTAL ASSETS	13,352	13,463	14,337	15,318	15,128	13,857	12,753	12,555	11,997	11,571	11,629	11,840	12,113

524

Current Liabilities

Short-term debt (Bank of N.Y.)	$2,667	$3,445	$4,530	$5,994	$3,579	$1,549	$515	$0	$0	$348	$1,012	$1,205	$2,228
Current interest due	150	274	403	185	323	438	156	185	273	98	190	288	129
AP & accrued expenses	886	1,788	4,141	4,172	3,878	2,392	1,043	890	912	1,182	691	837	952
Current portion of long-term debt	38	38	38	39	39	39	39	40	40	40	41	41	41
Income taxes payable (receivable)	0	0	0	0	0	0	0	0	0	0	0	0	0
Unfilled orders	734	447	535	1,465	3,062	2,375	1,218	569	427	482	912	1,187	679
Total current liabilities	4,475	5,992	9,647	11,855	10,882	6,793	2,971	1,684	1,652	2,150	2,846	3,558	4,028
	500	500	500	500	500	500	500	500	500	500	500	500	500

Long-Term Liabilities

Deferred interest (Bank of N.Y.)	1,057	1,067	1,076	1,086	1,096	1,106	1,116	1,127	1,137	1,147	1,158	1,169	1,179
Long-term debt (Bank of N.Y.)	8,000	8,000	8,000	8,000	8,000	8,000	8,000	8,000	8,000	8,000	8,000	8,000	8,000
Other long-term debt	1,439	1,439	1,439	1,438	1,438	1,438	1,402	1,401	1,168	1,168	1,167	1,167	1,131
Total long-term liabilities	10,496	10,506	10,515	10,524	10,534	10,544	10,518	10,528	10,305	10,315	10,325	10,336	10,310
TOTAL LIABILITIES	15,471	16,998	20,663	22,880	21,917	17,837	13,990	12,712	12,457	12,965	13,671	14,393	14,839

Stockholder's Equity

Common stock	250	250	250	250	250	250	250	250	250	250	250	250	250
BEGINNING retained earnings	n/a	(2,369)	(3,784)	(6,575)	(7,811)	(7,038)	(4,230)	(1,486)	(407)	(709)	(1,644)	(2,292)	(2,803)
Net income for the period	n/a	(1,415)	(2,791)	(1,236)	773	2,808	2,744	1,080	(303)	(935)	(648)	(511)	(173)
ENDING retained earnings	(2,369)	(3,784)	(6,575)	(7,811)	(7,038)	(4,230)	(1,486)	(407)	(709)	(1,644)	(2,292)	(2,803)	(2,976)
Total stockholder's equity	(2,119)	(3,534)	(6,325)	(7,561)	(6,788)	(3,980)	(1,236)	(157)	(459)	(1,394)	(2,042)	(2,553)	(2,726)
TOTAL EQUITY & LIABILITY	13,352	13,464	14,338	15,318	15,128	13,857	12,753	12,555	11,997	11,571	11,629	11,840	12,113

*Long-Term Deferred Tax

Exhibit 7 1985 monthly pro forma profit and loss statements for base case (11.25% interest rate).

	Nov.	Dec.	Jan.	Feb.	Mar.
Sales					
Mail order	497	141	800	2,872	6,043
Wholesale products	36	8	71	362	184
Retail stores	65	171	25	43	120
Other	100	44	144	57	144
Total sales	708	364	1,040	3,334	6,491
Cost of Goods Sold					
Mail order	138	39	222	796	1,674
Whole products	18	4	36	181	92
Retail stores	42	111	16	28	78
Other	55	22	72	29	72
Total COGS	253	176	345	1,033	1,916
Gross Margin					
($)	455	188	695	2,301	4,575
(%)	64.28%	51.57%	66.79%	69.02%	70.48%
Expenses					
Selling	1,274	2,464	1,320	662	499
Shipping & distribution	89	44	127	387	786
General & administrative	222	222	222	222	222
S.F.H.Q. expense	38	38	38	38	38
Prepaid expense amort.	43	0	0	0	26
Depreciation	61	61	61	61	61
Total expenses	1,727	2,829	1,768	1,370	1,632
Income before Interest					
and Taxes	(1,272)	(2,641)	(1,073)	931	2,943
Deferred interest	21	21	21	21	21
Interest expense	123	130	143	138	115
Interest income	1	1	1	1	1
Income before Taxes	(1,415)	(2,791)	(1,236)	773	2,808
0% Effective tax rate	0	0	0	0	0
Net Income					
Period	(1,416)	(2,791)	(1,236)	773	2,808
Cumulative	($1,415)	($4,206)	($5,442)	($4,669)	($1,861)

Apr.	May	Jun.	Jul.	Aug.	Sept.	Oct.	Total
5,593	2,684	714	183	187	359	880	20,952
286	28	11	0	1	2	1	990
490	867	418	169	129	211	146	2,854
138	119	99	65	38	65	165	1,188
6,507	3,698	1,242	417	355	637	1,192	25,984
1,549	743	198	51	52	99	244	5,804
143	14	6	0	1	1	1	495
319	564	272	110	84	137	95	1,855
69	60	50	33	19	33	83	593
2,080	1,380	524	193	155	270	422	8,748
4,427	2,317	717	224	200	367	770	17,236
68.04%	62.67%	57.77%	53.69%	56.30%	57.60%	64.63%	66.33%
473	405	465	685	365	366	358	9,337
729	364	116	49	50	73	140	2,954
222	222	222	222	222	222	222	2,668
38	38	38	38	38	38	38	450
41	37	12	0	0	0	0	159
61	61	61	61	61	61	61	732
1,564	1,127	914	1,055	737	759	819	16,299
2,863	1,191	(196)	(831)	(537)	(393)	(49)	937
21	21	21	21	22	22	22	254
99	91	88	88	93	97	104	1,309
1	1	3	5	3	1	1	19
2,744	1,080	(303)	(935)	(648)	(511)	(173)	(607)
0	0	0	0	0	0	0	0
2,744	1,080	(303)	(935)	(648)	(511)	(173)	(607)
$883	$1,962	$1,660	$725	$77	($434)	($607)	

Exhibit 8 1985 sensitivity analysis (Nov. 1, 1984 to Oct. 31, 1985) ($ thousands).

	90% Resp. CASE	95% Resp. CASE	BASE CASE	105% Resp. CASE	110% Resp. CASE
Total sales	23,895	24,940	25,984	27,029	28,074
Net income	(1,885)	(1,245)	(607)	31	666
Stockholder's equity					
Common stock	250	250	250	250	250
Ending retained earnings	(4,254)	(3,614)	(2,976)	(2,338)	(1,703)
Total stockholder's equity	(4,004)	(3,364)	(2,726)	(2,088)	(1,453)
Net increase in funds	(835)	(197)	439	1,075	1,708

not be cut with fat. This led it to investigate the areas of catalog production and customer service.

One of the largest expenses in Gurney's annual budget was the cost of putting together catalogs. Dakota Advertising, the in-house agency, had a $10 million ($1 million in overhead) operating budget. Although John Kemp considered these expenses to be high, he and his partners had not resolved whether they could or should be cut. Kemp described the dilemma they faced:

> Our catalogs don't really change much. The prices are changed, the pages are moved around a little, but it's pretty much the same from year to year. Right now I'm asking myself this: If we reduce staff at Dakota and just use pages from last year's catalog, change prices, and move things around, would we generate the same revenue? Will our customers notice or care? Dakota needs to justify that $1 million in labor and overhead as we go forward.

With respect to customer service, each year the company received some 60,000 letters of complaint (in connection with 1.4 million orders). While many complaints were due to incorrect addresses or quantities, others were due to orders that were delayed until a customer's full order could be filled, or because substitutions were made for out-of-stock goods. Keith Price favored a policy of filling orders as soon as merchandise became available, instead of waiting for a shipment to become complete. He estimated that such a policy might incur additional postal expenses of about $10,000, but he noted, "In the past we have made poor decisions on substitutions, deliveries, processing and right down the line. Customer dissatisfaction leaves us open to the competition. Therefore, we're doing all we can to improve in this area."

Strengthening the Company

In Kemp's view, one major reason for management's difficulties in putting together a tight budget was an inadequate management-accounting system. He remarked:

Exhibit 9 Base case balance sheet projections (Oct. 31, 1985 to 1988).

	Beginning Balance	Ending 1985	Ending 1986	Ending 1987	Ending 1988
Current Assets					
Cash	$100	$100	$100	$943	$3,553
Accounts receivable	563	356	404	414	432
Inventory	3,986	3,523	3,523	3,523	3,523
Net prepaid expenses	184	193	193	193	193
Total current assets	4,833	4,172	4,220	5,073	7,702
Fixed Assets					
Property & equipment (at cost)	7,833	8,119	8,405	8,691	8,977
Less: accum. depreciation	(344)	(1,076)	(1,808)	(2,540)	(3,272)
Net property & equipment	7,489	7,043	6,597	6,151	5,705
Other Assets					
Noncurrent receivables*	34	34	34	34	34
Other assets*	61	61	61	61	61
Prepaid interest	935	803	690	592	509
Total other assets	1,030	898	785	687	604
TOTAL ASSETS	13,352	12,113	11,602	11,911	14,010
Current Liabilities					
Short-term debt (Bank of N.Y.)	$2,667	$2,228	$794	$0	$0
Current interest due	150	129	124	115	114
AP & accrued expenses	886	952	1,091	1,125	1,149
Current portion of long-term debt	38	41	41	41	41
Income taxes payable (receivable)	0	0	0	0	0
Unfilled orders	734	679	699	713	713
Total current liabilities	4,475	4,028	2,750	1,994	2,017
Long-term Liabilities					
Deferred interest (Bank of N.Y.)	1,057	1,179	1,316	1,468	1,638
Long-term debt (Bank of N.Y.)	8,000	8,000	8,000	8,000	8,000
Other long-term debt	1,439	1,131	1,059	987	915
Total long-term liabilities	10,496	10,310	10,375	10,455	10,553
TOTAL LIABILITIES	15,471	14,839	13,625	12,949	13,070
Stockholder's Equity					
Common stock	250	250	250	250	250
Retained earnings	(2,369)	(2,976)	(2,272)	(1,287)	691
Total stockholder's equity	(2,119)	(2,726)	(2,022)	(1,037)	941
TOTAL EQUITY & LIABILITY	13,352	12,113	11,602	11,912	14,010

*Long-term deferred tax

Exhibit 10   Base case funds flow projections (1985 to 1988) (fiscal year Nov. 1 to Oct. 31).

	1985	1986	1987	1988
Funds Provided				
Net income	(607)	703	985	1,978
Depreciation	732	732	732	732
Deferred taxes	0	0	0	0
Prepaid interest	132	113	97	84
Deferred interest	122	136	152	170
Subtotal	379	1,685	1,967	2,963
Funds Applied				
Increase (decrease) working capital	(654)	(106)	(29)	(5)
Increase (decrease) fixed assets	286	286	286	286
Decrease (increase) long-term debt	308	72	72	72
Subtotal	(60)	252	329	353
Net increase in funds	439	1,434	1,637	2,610

Amfac's reporting system was near worthless for management purposes. It was based on a return-on-total capital concept, and it lacked the analytical tools for a manager to make any reasonable decisions.

We want to watch every penny going out and every purchase coming in. One of my high-priority efforts is to introduce a management-information system which will help management and employees to know exactly what is going on in the company. We're in a situation now where strategy is mixed up with day-to-day operations. We have to solve our internal reporting problems first, and then we can work on strategic planning.

Improving employee relations was also high on Harry Brooks' list of priority objectives. Kemp described the initial efforts:

At a series of meetings, Harry Brooks sat down with all of Gurney and Henry Field employees. The question he asked was, "If you had the power to change anything in the company, what would you change?" Out of this came employee-action groups to research particular problems. Some of the complaints were easily correctable. For example, one complaint heard repeatedly was about the conditions of the ladies' rooms of our hourly employees. We fixed that and generated some goodwill. We have a very low turnover rate among our employees and that says a lot. We have an obligation to them not to mess things up.

Bonuses were given to hourly employees. Incentives for managers and other wage earners, however, were considered inadequate. As a result, Kemp was developing with outside assistance a pension and profit-sharing plan for these individuals. Management decided, however, that it would be a bad move to introduce such a plan at a time when employees were being dismissed. Brooks observed, "What we need first is an upsurge in orders. When we beat plan, then we can talk about profit sharing. We'll delay the pension plan until the business gets turned around."

Management was also considering reintroducing credit cards as a way of increasing order size. An earlier attempt to use credit cards had to be discontinued when the customer-service department was flooded with calls and letters of complaint. Gurney's customers objected on the grounds that prices would have to be increased to cover the cost of credit.

Since Gurney was the only major mail-order seed company that did not offer credit, Brooks planned to test the idea again in 1985. He felt that a careful low-key introduction of the credit card would be necessary for its acceptance. Brooks was willing to risk alienating some customers to gain the advantages of a credit card. Not only would credit enable some customers to increase their order size, the cards would also permit the company to take telephone orders. Up to this point, all orders had to be accompanied by cash, check, or money order.

New Businesses

Improving Gurney's present operations dominated management's thinking in 1984, but preliminary discussions were also under way on how to offset the strong seasonality of the business. The initial focus of these deliberations was on expanding the current customer base through extending geographic coverage, and by introducing new product lines. Consideration was being given to the possibility of putting out a Christmas catalog that might include such items as mail-order needlepoint kits, horticultural products for urban dwellers, high-quality gardening tools, and popcorn makers or other types of home gadgets. A second possibility under consideration was a joint venture with another mail-order house, such as L. L. Bean, to sell its clothing in Gurney's catalogs. Management's enthusiasm for these avenues of diversification was somewhat tempered by the poor outcome associated with an earlier attempt to sell vitamins by mail.

For 1985, the company had budgeted $200,000 for developing new mail-order products. For Gurney, development meant finding and testing available products. This policy applied to horticultural items as well. According to Price, "We can go to any good agricultural college, say the University of Nebraska or Iowa, and buy new seed varieties for less than Burpee spends on developing their own seed strains."

An example of a related venture was expansion of the company's wholesale lawn program. It involved the sale of lawn fertilizer and garden products through 580 Gurney authorized distributors. Kemp estimated the annual sales potential for the business at between $1 and $2 million.

Further out in management's thinking was to enter entirely new businesses that could temper Gurney's seasonal cycle. Examples of possible businesses included radio stations, TV stations, and other kinds of mail order. Redefining

Dakota Advertising's role as a stand-alone business serving other clients as well as Gurney presented another possibility. The new organizational structure (Exhibit 4) had been put in place to permit adding such new businesses as separate divisions.

The Bottom Line

For Brooks, Price, and Kemp, Gurney was an adventure, a challenge, and even a "chance of a lifetime." Whether their efforts would ultimately lead to success or failure, in November, 1984, these three men were all "having fun" and were excited about future prospects. John Kemp summed up his feelings:

> We have a chance to do something really meaningful with the business. Look, all of us potentially are going to be rich. All we have to do is pay off the bills, and we can sit back and watch the money roll in. We'd like to do something with that money like set up a scholarship program for disadvantaged kids in South Dakota, and give more to our employees.
>
> We can control our destiny. We have a free rein to exercise creativity and imagination. But, this first year we have to think about survival. I believe that if we are patient and get our act together first, we will be successful in this venture.
>
> Success to me is enjoying what you do and being good at it. It has nothing to do with money or title. People who feel successful . . . are!

Johnson & Johnson (A)

> We believe the consistency of our overall performance as a corporation is due to our unique form of decentralized management, our adherence to the ethical principles embodied in our Credo, and our emphasis on managing the business for the long term.
>
> Statement of Strategic Direction

> Our culture is really it. That's what brought us together when the Tylenol tragedies hit. Without it, we would not have been able to manage the crisis as effectively as we did.
>
> James E. Burke, Chairman & CEO

In 1983, Johnson & Johnson (J&J) was widely regarded as one of the world's most successful health care companies. Over a twenty-year period, sales had grown at a compound annual rate of 14 percent, and earnings per share (EPS) at 17 percent. (During the 1970s, J&J's EPS growth rate was approximately double the average for the *Fortune* 100 largest industrial companies.) By 1982, J&J's worldwide revenues exceeded $5.7 billion and net income $473 million, placing it 55th in sales and 28th in net income on the *Fortune* 500 list of industrial companies. The underlying operations employed over 77,000 people based in fifty countries and sold products in 149 nations (see Exhibit 1 for financial data).

The company had also acquired a reputation for management excellence. A *Fortune* survey of industry executives to rank the management excellence of the 200 largest U.S. corporations placed J&J third overall and first among health care companies. This case describes the distinctive philosophy J&J espoused and the managerial systems and practices employed to put it into operation.

Company Background

J&J began with Robert Wood Johnson, an apothecary by training. At age thirty-one Johnson attended a seminar offered by Sir Joseph Lister, a noted English surgeon, who propounded the theory of "antisepsis." The year was 1876 and postoperative mortality rates were as high as 90 percent. The following account typified accepted surgical procedures at that time: "Unclean cotton, collected

Exhibit 1   Financial information, 1972–82, selected years ($ millions except per share figures).

	1972	1977	1980	1981	1982
Operating Statement					
Sales Revenues					
Domestic	880	1,714	2,634	3,026	3,304
Foreign	438	1,200	2,204	2,373	2,457
Total	1,318	2,914	4,838	5,399	5,761
Net earnings (after taxes)	121	247	401	468	523[b]
Percentage of sales revenues	9.2	8.5	8.3	8.7	9.1[b]
Per shara data[a]					
Earnings	0.72	1.41	2.17	2.51	2.79[b]
Dividends	0.15	0.47	0.74	0.85	0.97
Balance Sheet					
Cash and marketable securities	83	368	359	427	365
Other current assets	564	912	1,612	1,775	1,888
Fixed and other assets	334	740	1,372	1,618	1,956
Total	981	2,020	3,342	3,820	4,209
Current liabilities	179	383	774	881	900
Certificates of extra compensation	23	30	33	38	43
Long-term Debt	31	37	70	92	142
Deferred credits and others	15	91	197	281	325
Stockholders' equity	733	1,479	2,269	2,528	2,799
Total	981	2,020	3,342	3,820	4,209
Ratios and Other Information					
Return on equity	17.8%	17.8%	18.8%	19.5%	19.6%[b]
Number of employees (000's)	43.3	60.5	74.3	77.1	79.7
Number of stockholders (000's)	28.6	31.2	35.6	38.2	43
Average shares outstanding					
(millions)[a]	168.6	175.2	184.8	186.4	188.0

a. Per share data adjusted to reflect three-for-one common stock split in 1981.
b. Excluded, in 1982, an extraordinary charge of $100 million ($50 million after taxes or $0.27 per share) associated with the withdrawal of Tylenol capsules.

from sweepings on the floors of textile mills, was used for surgical dressings; surgeons operated in street clothes and wore a blood-spattered frock coat like a badge of honor."

Robert Johnson, then a partner in a small firm manufacturing pharmaceutical preparations, was impressed with Lister's theories and nurtured the idea of applying them. For this purpose, he joined with his two brothers, James and Edward, in establishing Johnson & Johnson to "manufacture and sell medical, pharmaceutical, surgical and antiseptic specialties and analgesic goods."

Table A Sales and operating profits (in %).

	Consumer	Professional	Pharmaceutical	Industrial
Sales	43.0	33.5	19.4	4.1
Operating profits	42.4	17.9	36.9	2.8

The firm was incorporated in 1887 with $100,000 of capital and began operations with fourteen employees on the fourth floor of what had been a wallpaper factory.

When the founder and first president died in 1910, J&J was already firmly established as a leader in the health care field. During Robert Johnson's tenure, the company had introduced revolutionary surgical dressings, established a bacteriological laboratory, and, in 1888, even published a book, *Modern Methods of Antiseptic Wound Treatment*, which for many years remained the standard text on antiseptic practices.

The company grew rapidly over the years as the result of new-product introductions and international expansion. New health care products were added through internal development and through the acquisition of established companies. One measure of the firm's recent performance in this regard was given by an independent nationwide survey in 1982 comparing the ten-year record of successful new-product launchings for eighteen major health and beauty aid manufacturers, including Bristol-Meyers, Procter & Gamble, and Kimberly-Clark. J&J was at the top of the list.

In 1982, J&J's products spanned four major groupings: consumer (baby care, surgical dressings, first aid, nonprescription drugs); professional (surgical dressings, sutures, diagnostic products); ethical (prescription) pharmaceutical; and industrial (nonwoven fabrics, edible sausage casings). The percentage sales and operating profits for these product groups in 1982 are shown in Table A.

International expansion began with the establishment of an affiliate in Canada in 1919 and one in Great Britain in 1924. By 1982, almost half of J&J's revenues and earnings were produced overseas.

The challenge of managing rapid growth in J&J was to do it in a way that would preserve the familylike atmosphere so valued in the company. When asked what it was like to work in J&J, a senior executive described it as follows:

> The prime motivator in J&J is the opportunity to grow with more responsibility. It runs through the entire organization. When we look at people in comparable jobs in other high-quality companies, we find that they are typically three to five years older than our managers.
>
> Another motivator is the climate. There is both respect for the individual and concern for the team. This is evident in our decision making. Everyone is free to argue his or her point of view. But once a decision is made, everyone is expected to do his or her best to make it work. In that way, even if a plan isn't exactly optimal, we make it succeed. In short, it's a nice company. People are nice to each other . . . and it's a nice place to work.

J&J's Philosophy and Culture

Robert Wood Johnson, the "General," son of the founder, and chairman of J&J from 1938 to 1963, was generally credited as the individual most responsible for shaping the company's philosophy and culture. Widely exposed as a young man to business around the world, he developed strong convictions about the merits of free enterprise and the ineffectiveness of large, ponderous organizations. Jim Burke, chairman and CEO since 1976, recounted: "He was convinced that if you have sensible people who know each other, in a small enough group, somehow or other problems would get worked out."

The General also held strong convictions about the public and social responsibilities that any business firm must assume. In 1947 he expressed his thoughts in a book, *Or Forfeit Freedom:*

> The evidence on this point is clear. . . . Institutions, both public and private, exist because the people want them, believe in them, or at least are willing to tolerate them. The day has passed when business is a private matter—if it ever really was. In a business society, every act of business has social consequences and may arouse public interest. Every time business hires, builds, sells, or buys, it is acting for the . . . people as well as for itself, and it must be prepared to accept full responsibility for its acts.

These convictions about enterprise and social responsibility were reflected in J&J's decentralization and in its enduring statement of beliefs, the Credo.

Decentralization

General Johnson's firm belief about the inherent superiority of small, autonomous units led J&J on a consistent path toward decentralization. Autonomy was preserved for new acquisitions, and new independent units were spun off from existing organizations whenever they appeared ready to respond to new market opportunities on their own. This process continued over the years, leading to an assemblage of some 150 companies.

The nature and purpose of J&J's decentralization were described in the 1981 annual report:

> Johnson & Johnson is not one company but many. . . . The largest has 6,300 employees; the smallest, at year-end had six. . . .
>
> Whatever their size or location, they share a commitment to meeting the special needs of a well-defined customer. In doing so, they create a wide variety of innovative ways to successfully run their businesses.
>
> We feel that the secret to liberating that productivity is decentralization—granting each company sufficient autonomy to conduct its business without unnecessary constraints. In short, we believe decentralization = creativity = productivity.

Jim Burke elaborated on the concept:

> The basic concept behind the decentralization philosophy is to try to organize each business around a given market need and a given set of cus-

tomers. It's easier said than done but that's really it. . . . Ethicon is an example of a business that's built around the needs of the surgeon sewing people together . . . and their success is based upon their understanding that what they are is an extension of the skills in the hands of the surgeon. With this approach they built this business out of nothing.

The Credo

General Johnson's views on public and social responsibility were formalized in the 1940s as the company's Credo. This statement underscored the company's responsibilities to its customers, to its employees, to the communities in which it operated, and finally to its stockholders. Described by J&J managers as the underlying and unifying philosophy guiding all important decisions, the Credo was prominently displayed in every manager's office (see Figure A).

Burke described the influence of the Credo on J&J managers as follows:

> All of our management is geared to profit on a day-by-day basis. That's part of the business of being in business. But too often, in this and other businesses, people are inclined to think, "We'd better do this because if we don't, it's going to show up on the figures over the the short term." This document allows them to say, "Wait a minute. I don't *have* to do that. The management has told me that they're really interested in the long term, and they're interested in me operating under this set of principles. So I won't."

One expression of the Credo was "Live for Life," a positive health program for J&J employees. In 1976, Burke asked a senior line-operating manager to figure out how the company could mount a program to make J&J employees the healthiest in the world. The findings of an exhaustive two-year study led to the introduction of a program focusing on four principal areas: exercise, nutrition, stress control, and the cessation of smoking. "Live for Life" was designed to encourage employees "to create their own programs for improving their life styles and getting rid of bad health practices that lead to illness and disability." In support of this plan, flextime arrangements permitted employees to use new in-house health fitness facilities daily, and a variety of programs— such as "kick the smoking habit" group sessions, classes on weight control and nutrition, and yoga—were offered. As one senior executive noted, "It's a great program for the participants. The company also benefits from the feeling it engenders among our people that J&J really cares for its employees."

Notwithstanding the universal acknowledgement accorded the Credo within J&J, Jim Burke perceived some degree of tokenism and a need to inculcate in the managers the values underlying this statement. He described his actions in 1979:

> People like my predecessor believed the Credo with a passion, but the operating unit managers were not universally committed to it. There seemed to be a growing attitude that it was there but that nobody had to do any-thing about it. So I called a meeting of some 20 key executives and chal-lenged them. I said, "Here's the Credo. If we're not going to live by it, let's

Our Credo

We believe our first responsibility is to the doctors, nurses and patients,
to mothers and all others who use our products and services.
In meeting their needs everything we do must be of high quality.
We must constantly strive to reduce our costs
in order to maintain reasonable prices.
Customers' orders must be serviced promptly and accurately.
Our suppliers and distributors must have an opportunity
to make a fair profit.

We are responsible to our employees,
the men and women who work with us throughout the world.
Everyone must be considered as an individual.
We must respect their dignity and recognize their merit.
They must have a sense of security in their jobs.
Compensation must be fair and adequate,
and working conditions clean, orderly and safe.
Employees must feel free to make suggestions and complaints.
There must be equal opportunity for employment, development
and advancement for those qualified.
We must provide competent management,
and their actions must be just and ethical.

We are responsible to the communities in which we live and work
and to the world community as well.
We must be good citizens — support good works and charities
and bear our fair share of taxes.
We must encourage civic improvements and better health and education.
We must maintain in good order
the property we are privileged to use,
protecting the environment and natural resources.

Our final responsibility is to our stockholders.
Business must make a sound profit.
We must experiment with new ideas.
Research must be carried on, innovative programs developed
and mistakes paid for.
New equipment must be purchased, new facilities provided
and new products launched.
Reserves must be created to provide for adverse times.
When we operate according to these principles,
the stockholders should realize a fair return.

Johnson & Johnson

Figure A   The Johnson & Johnson credo.

tear it off the wall. If you want to change it, tell us how to change it. We either ought to commit to it or get rid of it."

The meeting was a turn-on, because we were challenging people's own personal values. By the end of the session, the managers had gained a great deal of understanding about and enthusiasm for the beliefs in the Credo. Subsequently, Dave Clare and I have met with small groups of J&J managers all over the world to challenge the Credo.

Now, I don't really think that you can impose convictions or beliefs on someone else. However, I do believe that if I really understand what makes the business work, then I can prompt you to think through the facts and come to see just how pragmatic the philosophy is when it comes to running a business successfully. . . . And I think that's what happened here.

For some J&J managers, the strongest evidence of the Credo's power was in the company's response to the Tylenol crisis. In 1982, seven people died after ingesting Tylenol capsules that had been laced with cyanide. Even though the poisoning had occurred outside J&J premises and was limited to the Chicago area, J&J withdrew all Tylenol capsules from the U.S. market at an estimated cost of $100 million. At the same time, the company initiated with the medical and pharmaceutical communities a comprehensive communication effort involving 2,500 employees throughout the J&J organization. This response prompted the *Washington Post* to write that "Johnson & Johnson has succeeded in portraying itself to the public as a company willing to do what's right, regardless of cost."

Putting the J&J Philosophy into Operation

The key organizational units for J&J were the operating company at the business level and the executive committee at the corporate level. The relationship between these two units was carefully managed to produce the cohesive independence that had become a cultural hallmark of J&J's operating structure. Strategic planning, compensation systems, and human resource management were among the major support systems to this relationship.

The Operating Companies

J&J's 150 operating units were for the most part integral, autonomous, and wholly owned subsidiaries. Each company had a well-defined mission (or "franchise") and submitted monthly, quarterly, and annual financial reports, as well as dividends. The importance of the company mission was described by the Codman & Shurtleff Company president:

> We spend a lot of time talking about mission, not from the point of view of protecting our turf but to ensure that the mission of the business is defined well enough so that we can see that we're not going at it helter-skelter. Our mission is to develop, on a worldwide basis, electromechanical and electro-optical equipment and devices to aid the physician in performing least-invasive surgery.

What this mission statement does is to make it very clear to us what fits into our business and what would merely diffuse our resources. We think of our franchise as one that is snug enough and neat enough in terms of technological requirements to be managed on a worldwide basis and not implicate other J&J companies, beyond the fact that what we're doing here may speed up the use of their products or, for that matter, the demise of their products.

To keep established missions reasonably focused, a new company was created when any new or peripheral product or market handled by an operating company was deemed important enough to warrant a separate dedicated effort. For example, McNeil Consumer Products Company was created in 1976 to focus exclusively on the consumer product opportunity for Tylenol. It did so with great success, guiding the brand to a preeminent position in the over-the-counter analgesic business. McNeil Pharmaceutical was left free to concentrate on prescription products, including Tylenol with codeine, which became the industry leader in number of new prescriptions in the United States.

In similar fashion, Ortho Diagnostic Systems, Inc., became a separate company in the 1970s to focus on products for blood banks and clinical laboratories, while Ortho Pharmaceutical concentrated on its products for family planning, dermatology, and other fields. In 1982 Technicare Ultrasound was split off from Technicare Corporation to concentrate on ultrasound medical diagnostics. Technicare Corporation continued its activities in CT scanning, nuclear medicine, and the newest modality, nuclear magnetic resonance. One senior executive described his personal experience with this process of setting apart new businesses:

> I started with what was then called the Hospital and Professional Division. Over the years, that unit was a source for some eight or nine spinoffs. Every time we identified a new major market opportunity, we would test it and then split it off as a new company. Our handling of disposable surgical soft goods, including gowns, linen, and face masks is a good case in point. Originally, these products were included in our broad product line. Along the way, we began to see a huge potential for these disposable items. So we developed a dedicated business approach within our unit, tested it and then spun it off, creating Surgikos, with its own mission. That's a good example of what has happened eight other times in just this one company, and the same thing is happening throughout J&J.
>
> In each of these cases, growth opportunity was the driving force for creating a separate organization. In effect, two companies were able to develop greater sales volume and opportunities than a single company could have done by itself.

Among the 150 J&J companies, some 20 to 25 were referred to as source companies. These companies were leaders in developing products and markets that were the basis for new-company formation. Table B lists the principal J&J companies and their major products.

As the number of companies continued to grow, senior management began

Table B Principal domestic operations, 1982.

Company	Major Products
Chicopee	Fabrics for commercial and industrial customers.
Codman & Shurtleff, Inc.	Surgical supplies including instruments, equipment and disposables.
Critikon, Inc.	Products for hospital critical care units, such as oxygen monitoring systems, and cardiovascular catheters.
Devro	Edible natural protein sausage casings and other collagen-based products used by food processors.
Ethicon	Products for precise wound closure, including sutures, ligatures and mechanical wound closure instruments.
Extracorporeal, Inc.	Dialysis fitters and machines for endstage renal disease; oxygenators for open heart surgery, and heart valves.
Iolab Corporation	Intraocular lenses for cataract surgery.
Janssen Pharmaceutica, Inc.	Pharmaceutical products used for anesthesiology and systemic fungal pathogens.
Johnson & Johnson Baby Products Company	Consumer baby products including powder, shampoo, oil, cream and lotion.
Johnson & Johnson Dental Products Company	Serves dentists and dental laboratories with a broad range of restorative products (e.g., porcelain for crowns and bridges) and preventive products (e.g.: Prophylaxis paste).
Johnson & Johnson Products, Inc.	The Health Care Division provides consumers with wound and oral care products; the Patient Care Division offers wound care products to hospitals; the Orthopaedic Division markets surgical implants and fracture immobilization products.
McNeil Consumer Products Company	Line of acetaminophen-related products, including Tylenol, CoTylenol Cold Formula, and Sine-Aid.
McNeil Pharmaceutical	Prescription drugs for the medical profession including analgesics, major tranquilizers, anti-inflammatory agents and muscle relaxants.
Ortho Diagnostic Systems	Products for blood analysis in blood banks and clinical laboratories.
Ortho Pharmaceutical	Prescription and nonprescription contraception products and dermatological products for professional skin treatment.
Personal Products	Products for female hygiene.
Pitman-Moore	Products for animal health.
Surgikos	Disposable packs, crowns, and surgical specialty products for use in major operative procedures.
Technicare	Products in diagnostic imaging—computer tomography (CT) scanning, ultrasonic images, nuclear medicine systems and digital X-ray.
Xanar	CO_2 surgical laser systems.

to look for ways to bring some order to what otherwise might become an un-manageable hodgepodge. Jim Burke described his thinking on this issue:

> What we want to do is to look at each of those businesses that appear to have a worldwide franchise opportunity and to run them as world businesses. The ideal arrangement would be, for example, to have a world Ethicon business [surgical sutures]. Ethicon would have independent, product-related companies in 30 or 40 countries. Where the business in a particular country wasn't large enough to justify a separate company, the products would be sold by a so-called umbrella company in that country.
>
> So, 10 or 15 years from now, we would like to have a collection of global J&Js. It won't be easy to do because a number of our businesses are not so simple to segregate as is Ethicon.

Each operating company was headed by a president, general manager, or managing director, who reported directly or through a company group chairman to a member of the executive committee. J&J had fourteen company group chairmen. The J&J organization structure is shown in Figure B.

Dave Clare, J&J president and chairman of the executive committee, described how this management structure had evolved:

> Years ago, each operating company reported directly to one of the executive committee members. As the number of individual units multiplied around the world, we were faced with the dilemma of how to maintain a line organization relationship between each of the managements and the executive committee members. We had two choices. We could expand the executive committee, or we could transfer to another group of individuals much of the operating responsibilities which had historically been handled by the executive committee. We chose the latter approach.

Each company group chairman reported to a member of the executive committee and was responsible for an assigned group of operating units. Where the assigned group included a number of smaller overseas units, the latter reported to a vice president under the company group chairman. Some managers were concerned that this layering of management responsibilities might slow company reaction time or reduce the autonomy traditionally accorded each operating company. Burke acknowledged this concern:

> Some of the operating managers do make the argument that there are too many layers of decision making within the company. In some cases a company reports to a vice president, a company group chairman, and the executive committee.
>
> The real key is what these layers do. If they become operationally oriented—and there are instances where they do—then we have a real problem. But there are plenty of other instances where that's not the case at all.

Dave Clare was on record as stating:

> We don't want the managing director of any unit, any place in the world, to feel that he hasn't the right, the responsibility, or the ability to go direct to his executive committee member with his problems and his challenges.

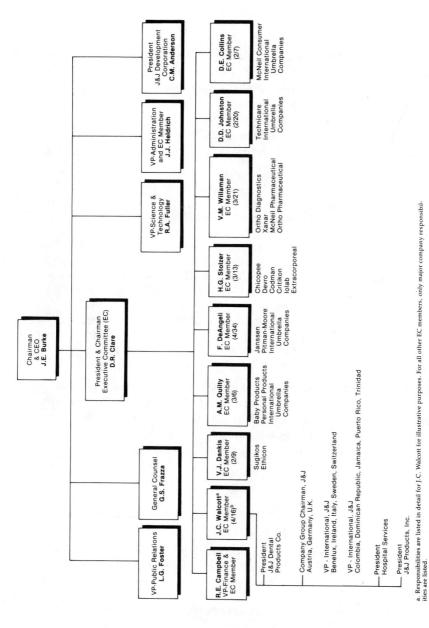

Chairman & CEO
J.E. Burke

VP-Public Relations
L.G. Foster

General Counsel
G.S. Frazza

President & Chairman
Executive Committee (EC)
D.R. Clare

VP-Science &
Technology
R.A. Fuller

VP-Administration
and EC Member
J.J. Heldrich

President
J&J Development
Corporation
C.M. Anderson

R.E. Campbell
VP-Finance &
EC Member

J.C. Walcott[a]
EC Member
(4/16)[b]

V.J. Dankis
EC Member
(2/9)

Sugikos
Ethicon

A.M. Quilty
EC Member
(3/6)

Baby Products
Personal Products
International
Umbrella
Companies

F. DeAngeli
EC Member
(4/34)

Janssen
Pitman-Moore
International
Umbrella
Companies

H.G. Stolzer
EC Member
(3/13)

Chicopee
Devro
Codman
Critikon
Iolab
Extracorporeal

V.M. Willaman
EC Member
(3/21)

Ortho Diagnostics
Xanar
McNeil Pharmaceutical
Ortho Pharmaceutical

D.D. Johnston
EC Member
(2/20)

Technicare
International
Umbrella
Companies

D.E. Collins
EC Member
(2/7)

McNeil Consumer
International
Umbrella
Companies

President
J&J Dental
Products Co.

Company Group Chairman, J&J
Austria, Germany, U.K.

VP - International, J&J
Benelux, Ireland, Italy, Sweden, Switzerland

VP - International, J&J
Colombia, Dominican Republic, Jamaica, Puerto Rico, Trinidad

President
Hospital Services

President
J&J Products, Inc.

a. Responsibilities are listed in detail for J.C. Walcott for illustrative purposes. For all other EC members, only major company responsibilities are listed.

b. Figures indicate the numbers of direct reporting relationships versus the total number of independent units under that particular EC member. Thus, J.C. Walcott has 4 executives reporting directly to him, but is responsible for 16 operating units.

Figure B Organizational structure, 1983.

543

. . . We don't want to lose touch with the operating managers of the businesses. And we don't want to have them feel that they've lost touch with their executive committee or company group chairman member.[1]

Executive Committee

The eleven-member executive committee (EC) was the principal management group responsible for the company's policies and operations. Four of these members (the CEO, the president, and the vice presidents for finance and administration) had corporate general management responsibilities; the other seven were contact executives for specific operating segments.

The EC met almost daily for lunch, usually with a flexible agenda. Quarterly, it would meet for two or three days to discuss major issues. Burke described the role he saw for the EC:

> In my judgment, the executive committee should spend most of its time on two issues: one is resolving conflicts among operating units; and two is selecting the right opportunities to pursue. In this business, there's no longer any problem in finding opportunities. The problem is in sorting them out and taking the ones you can do the best job with.
>
> We don't really want operating companies to worry about these issues. Their primary job is running their businesses. Of course, they are in a good position to identify opportunities or to sense conflicts with other units. When they do, they should bring these issues to the executive committee.
>
> I feel good about the way the executive committee has evolved in recent years. Seven or eight years ago, it was 95 percent involved in operational matters. Today at least 60 percent of its time is devoted to policy issues. It ought to stay that way or even shift further towards policy.

To illustrate the kind of policy issues addressed by the EC, Clare noted: "The major part of an upcoming quarterly meeting will be to review the strategic plans that have been submitted by all our units. Our emphasis is on the five- and ten-year planning horizon and major problems and programs that we see presented by the companies."

Strategic Planning

In the 1970s, J&J institutionalized a bottom-up strategic planning process. Burke described the reasoning behind this action:

> We were growing very fast, but the key decisions were often being made at the operating companies in an opportunistic, ad hoc manner. The operating managers were growing the businesses, but the overall change wasn't planned.
>
> I decided we had to get into strategic planning. But we wanted the planning to come from the bottom. We wanted the managers to understand that every company had the responsibility for its long-term business.

---

1. "World Wide" (J&J company publication), October 1980, p. 6.

The strategic planning approach that was implemented worked on a ten-year cycle. To avoid recasting long-term forecasts each year, the ten-year projections were revised every five years. The emphasis was on qualitative forecasts rather than numbers, as was indicated in Burke's admonition to the company managers.

> If you want numbers, keep them to yourself. We don't want them. What I want as chairman of the operation is a two-page summary for every J&J company in the world. It should be a statement of your strategic mission and should explain the convictions you have about the future of the business and a little bit of how you're going to get there. I'm going to read it, and everybody between you and me is going to read it. I really only want four numbers—sales and profits for the current year, and sales and profits for five years out. Those numbers in aggregate will help us to see whether or not there is enough growth inherent in our current businesses to maintain our historical growth rate. We want you to understand that we're not going to hold you accountable for those numbers. We *are* going to hold you accountable for the strategic mission statement.

In keeping with its decentralization philosophy, senior management eschewed the idea of developing an explicit corporate strategy. In 1980, however, Burke did write "A Statement of Strategic Direction" to serve as a guideline for strategic planning (Figure C).

Operating Plans

In addition to the strategic plan, the operating companies prepared two-year operating plans, which included narrative concerning specific policies, programs, and actions as well as the financial budget for the following year. Financial controls in J&J were characterized by managers as direct and tight.

Operating plans were initiated in the fall as each company president reached agreement on his proposal with an EC member or with his group chairman. Approval had to await an EC meeting in November, where the performance of J&J as a whole was assessed and individual plans adjusted accordingly. In May each budget was subjected to a detailed review, and in August to a less stringent up-date review. Dave Clare pointed out the executive committee's limited role in this process: "As a committee we don't examine in detail the specific short-term plans of an individual company. We rely on the individual executive committee member with his line organization to address these things."

Each operating company was expected to finance its own investments to the extent possible. Investment decisions were based on detailed cash-flow analysis and were normally implemented by granting reductions in a unit's profit-after-tax targets to allow it to retain the needed funds.

Executive Compensation

Historically, senior executives in J&J were well compensated. General Johnson had often said, "Make your top managers rich, and they will make you richer."

We believe the consistency of our overall performance as a corporation is due to our unique form of decentralized management, our adherence to the ethical principles embodied in our Credo, and our emphasis on managing the business for the long term.

There are certain basic principles that we are committed to in this regard:

- The responsibility for our success as a corporation rests in the hands of the presidents and managing directors of our companies. Each must assume leadership in every facet of the business, including the definition of strategic plans and providing for management succession.
- We will attempt to organize our businesses based on the clearly focused needs of the end users of our products and services. In many instances business units will be structured around the worldwide franchise philosophy. We will continue, however, to rely on "umbrella" companies to develop local markets for any of our franchises where this appears to be the best way to initiate cost-effective, long-term growth.
- We will seek, where possible, to achieve or maintain a leadership position in our markets of interest. It is recognized that this can only be accomplished through maintaining, over the long term, end benefits superior to our competition. In this regard, we are committed to improving our internal research and development capability, and to utilizing external sources that provide access to new science and technology.

- We are dedicated to exceptionally high growth. To achieve this we must be well-positioned in growth markets, and each management must be aggressively innovative and strive to grow faster than the markets in which it competes.
- Each management must know how to invest effectively in future earning power while recognizing that it is easier to reduce profits short term than to increase them long term. We further believe that growth should be financed primarily from earnings. This means our companies must generally make above-average profits to support higher rates of growth.
- Acquisitions are viewed as an appropriate way to achieve the strategic goals of a given company or as a way for the corporation to expand the scope of its current business. Such acquisitions - of products, technologies, or businesses - will be evaluated for growth potential, fit with current or future businesses, management capacity, and economic feasibility. There are no other restrictions on the identification of acquisition candidates.

Corporate management is responsible for providing resources, guidance, leadership, and control of the various business entities within the framework of these principles. Management's most important responsibility is the one it shares with presidents and managing directors in attracting the kind of people who can manage our businesses in the future, providing them with the kind of environment that maximizes their potential and with a system that rewards them appropriately for their accomplishments.

Figure C   Statement of strategic direction.

In 1973, J&J's chairman was the highest paid executive in the United States and one of the first to earn more than $1 million a year.

The compensation package for senior executives included a base salary, bonus, stock grants (over a period of three years), stock options, and phantom stock called Certificate of Extra Compensation. These components are shown in Table C.

In an average year, counting only the cash bonus and the current value of the stock grant contract along with its dividend yield, the current incentive compensation typically totaled about 30 percent to 35 percent of base salary. Longer-term compensation, while not readily calculable, added appreciably to that amount.

The compensation awards were the responsibility of the management com-

Table C Compensation package.

Base Salary—company commitment

Bonus—guidelines as a percentage of base salary

Stock Grants—there were no guidelines for annual awards. An executive received the grant over three equal yearly installments. Since there were no restrictions on the sale of these shares, this grant was considered current compensation.

Stock Options—there were guidelines on the maximum awards for different salary categories (e.g., 2× salary for salaries between $50,000 and $70,000). Options were awarded deeper in the organization than for most other companies. Options were not vested for a period of seven years.

Certificate of Extra Compensation (CEC)—no guidelines. CEC was reserved for the top 1% of executives and was not paid out until the executive retired, died, or otherwise left the company. The value of the "units" was determined by a complex formula depending on the overall corporate performance. (A typical operating company president retired with a CEC value in excess of $1 million.)

pensation committee, comprising Jim Burke, Dave Clare, and Bob Campbell (vice president for finance). Its duties were to decide how much in aggregate to award in a given year and how the rewards should be distributed. Its functioning was described as follows by an operating company president: "It's an extremely subjective evaluation but very serious. Burke and Clarke spend two weeks every year on nothing but performance evaluation."

Central Staff Support Functions

J&J had corporate staff groups in human resources and personnel, legal, finance, science and technology, and management information services. Considerable attention was given to defining their roles, so as not to undermine the philosophy of decentralized operations.

Human Resources and Personnel. While the individual operating companies were responsible for all the traditional personnel functions, the corporate staff served to ensure uniformity in such areas as compensation and personnel policies. For this purpose, the corporate HR&P staff conducted yearly organizational planning audits. These audits required each company president to present to top corporate management an overview of the company's human resource situation. This overview was to include projected personnel needs, five-year succession plans, identification of people with advancement potential, and any anticipated changes in organizational structure.

To manage staffing requirements and executive career development, J&J maintained a computerized managerial skills inventory form for each manager. When an open position could not be filled from within an individual company, a comprehensive corporatewide search was conducted for suitable candidates. Conversely, J&J also had a search program to identify opportunities for managers desiring a change in position or in need of developing specific skills.

Legal. Legal support for domestic operating companies was provided through the general counsel's office at headquarters.

Finance. Each operating company had its own chief financial officer reporting to the company president. The corporate financial staff provided budgeting and reporting guidelines and was responsible for overall financial policy. The implementation of financial policies throughout J&J was coordinated by a council of chief financial officers that met quarterly.

Science and Technology. An office of science and technology was created in 1979 to formalize the function of scanning the environment for technological developments. Burke described this new unit as "our radar for new and emerging technology which might have applications to our current businesses or which might suggest a whole new business for J&J."

Management Information Services. This function revealed most clearly the underlying tensions between central staff and the autonomous operating units. When started in 1970, the management information center (MIC) was set up to provide large-scale, efficient computer information handling for J&J as a whole. With advances in computer technology, each company wanted to manage its own information system. An executive described what happened:

> The computer information services was an interesting experience in centralization versus decentralization. And it was not without its conflicts and controversies. During the ten-year period from 1970 to 1980, there was an incredible amount of infighting between the corporate management information center people and the management boards of the individual operating companies. All kinds of white papers were being written about why an operating company should do its own thing, with MIC countering why it would cost more money. Finally, Jim Burke stepped in and said, "Look, if the operating companies can afford to decentralize it, why shouldn't they?"

By 1983 each major operating company had its own computer information system. The corporate MIC primarily served headquarter's needs.

The Challenge to Decentralization

Reflecting on the pressures and changes he saw in J&J, Burke commented:

> There's an increasing merging and interaction between the different segments of our business that runs counter to our decentralized approach. The pharmaceutical business, the hospital and professional business, and the consumer business are merging at a lot of levels that nobody even understands. The public is getting intimately involved in health care. There has been a 1,000 percent increase in health information going to the public through TV in the last seven years. There's a revolution in terms of consumer information and there's a revolution in terms of technology that cuts across our ability to market health care in any of its dimensions.
>
> We've got 150 business units now. We could easily grow to 300 companies over the next 10 to 15 years. If you look at the corporation's central problem, it's how to manage an increasingly larger organization to obtain the same kind of energy that is released from smaller units.

Johnson & Johnson (B): Hospital Services

Decentralization = Creativity = Productivity

J&J's 1981 annual report cover

Immediately after he attended the fall 1982 session of the Harvard Business School Advanced Management Program, Pete Ventrella, vice president corporate staff and general manager of the Hospital Services Group for Johnson & Johnson (J&J), was told of an important change in his responsibilities. The Hospital Services Group, a transitional corporate unit set up to explore a new approach to serving the hospital market, was to become a full-fledged J&J operating company, and Pete was to be its president. Under the new arrangement, J&J's Hospital Services would be responsible for consolidating all order taking, customer invoicing, and distribution of products supplied to hospitals by thirteen other J&J companies that had hitherto performed these functions.

In his new assignment, Ventrella not only faced the normal administrative problems of start-up, he would also have to centralize major operating functions in a company that had made decentralization and managerial autonomy keystones in its corporate philosophy. Describing his new responsibilities, Ventrella said:

> Our customers are changing; the hospital marketplace is changing! We've been asked to develop a corporate capability in the automated order-entry and distribution areas which will lead to the servicing of our customers in a better way than affiliate companies could do on their own. Ultimately the supply companies have the ability to limit where this thing goes. A year from now when Jim Burke and Dave Clare [J&J president] ask the companies "What do you think about Hospital Services?" I want them to say, "It's serving us and the customers better. . . ." Somehow, that has to be the final response.
>
> Each of our companies has a very well-defined mission statement which gives it its own product franchise. The question is, "How can Hospital Services be complementary to this approach without disrupting all the good things you get from decentralization?"

J&J and the Hospital Supplies Business

In 1982, thirteen J&J companies and divisions sold close to $2 billion worth of supplies and equipment to the medical professional markets. Two-thirds of this volume was sold in the United States, and the major part of these sales was to hospitals. As shown in Figure A, these units collectively served all of the twenty-three medical specialties certified by the American Board of Medical Specialties. Each unit operated independently, with its own manufacturing, sales and distribution network, service capability, and research and development.

U.S. health care costs in 1982 were estimated at over $320 billion.[1] Hospital care accounted for almost 40% of this total.[2] The U.S. professional purchases of supplies, pharmaceuticals, and equipment were thought to be around $15 billion in total and around $9 billion for the segments served by J&J.

The hospital system had begun to change dramatically during the 1970s. Rapidly escalating costs, growing government involvement in medical payments (in 1980, about 55 percent of every dollar that went to hospitals was paid by the government), rising consumerism, new and expensive equipment, and increasing competition for the health care dollar were forcing hospitals to seek new ways to provide health care at lower costs. As an indication of these pressures, after 1974 hospitals experienced cost increases at twice the rate of inflation and were able to recover only about 85 percent of these increases.

In response to these pressures, hospitals were adopting strategies to contain costs and to generate revenues. These new efforts in turn were bringing about substantial administrative changes in the industry. While medical professionals continued to have a strong voice in recommending products and services, purchasing decisions were increasingly being shifted from the doctor or nurse to administrators, business managers, and material managers. These business-oriented managers sought cost reductions through more efficient and stringent purchasing practices.

The cost pressures on hospitals also fostered explosive growth of multihospital systems that sought to contain costs through standardization, consolidation of health services, management information services, and group purchasing. As one measure of the change occurring on this front, for-profit hospital chains were reported to have grown even faster than the computer and drug industries in the 1970s, with revenues in excess of $12 billion in 1980.[3] By 1982, multihospital systems represented 30 percent of the total hospital facilities in the United States and were projected to represent 70 percent of all hospital beds by 1990.

The multihospital system had changed the hospital business from a cottage industry to big-league corporate operations. Further, the changes were likely to continue, with an industry forecast indicating that by 1990 as few as 600

1. "Businesses are Forming Coalitions to Curb Rise in Health-Care Costs," *Wall Street Journal*, June 17, 1982, p. 31.
2. *Health Care Financing Review*, Summer 1979, cited in "Health Maintenance Organization Medical Products and Services Markets," Frost & Sullivan, 1980.
3. G. Kinkead, "Humana's Hard-Sell Hospitals," *Fortune*, November 17, 1980, p. 68.

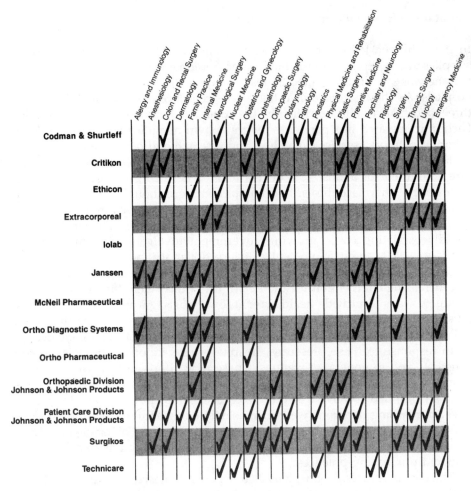

Figure A Companies serving hospitals and medical professionals.

purchasing groups would be making the majority of U.S. hospital purchases. As a result of this trend toward fewer and larger purchasing units, hospitals were gaining leverage vis-à-vis their suppliers.

A firm that had capitalized on these trends was the American Hospital Supply Corporation (AHS). Described as the success story of the 1970s, it had grown from a small distributor to the largest hospital supply manufacturer and distributor in the United States, with $2.5 billion in revenues and 27 percent of the market, by tailoring its strategy to the changes in the hospital industry. This strategy targeted hospital administrators and purchasing managers, rather than medical practitioners, offering volume discounts, guaranteed three-day delivery, and improved information handling. A newspaper article described AHS's success as follows: "American Hospital Supply turned this trend [the emergence of large investor-owned hospital groups] to its advantage by developing computerized inventory control, ordering and distribution systems that could speed its wide range of products across the country more efficiently than its competitors, while cutting hospitals' costs and freeing its salesmen to respond to individual customer needs."[4] The article went on to describe how AHS would do a study of the hospital's paper-flow process before installing, free of charge, a computerized automated ordering system that linked the purchaser with its central computer.

Pete Ventrella commented on how the industry changes evolved:

> It was our distributors which, by the very nature of their business, were adjusting to certain business-oriented changes at the hospitals much more rapidly than were the product-oriented manufacturing concerns. Distributors such as American Hospital Supply began investing heavily in business systems for the marketplace. This approach was in marked contrast to J&J's, which invested primarily in product R&D through its individual companies.
>
> What became increasingly clear over time was that for every dollar hospitals spend on a product, they spend a dollar on administration and logistical support. As manufacturers, we had naturally focused attention on product costs and product value added. We began to appreciate that the opportunity for J&J to add value for the customers was twice as large when distribution logistics were included.

J&J viewed its primary competition as those firms that manufactured goods and equipment for the health care field—corporations such as Baxter Travenol, Procter & Gamble, Bristol-Myers, Warner Lambert, 3M, and Kendall Corporation. Ventrella saw this focus as one reason for J&J's delayed response to the changing environment: "Since we primarily see competitors as manufacturers, we had not thoroughly examined how the distribution companies were responding to new opportunities that resulted from business-centered changes occurring among our hospital customers. And this development is really what triggered our decision to investigate how we could capitalize on these trends."

Hospital Services Group

Genesis

J&J management had been neither unaware of nor unconcerned about the changing nature of the hospital supply and equipment business. Jim Burke explained why the firm had not responded sooner:

> We have looked at this problem of distribution in the hospitals area off and on for fifteen years. Each time we did, we came up against the J&J culture. We would say, "Even though there's a lot of money involved here, the fact is that we seem to be functioning well, and our survival is not at stake. So, let's back off."

4. N. Peagam, "American Hospital's Bays Gets Credit for Turning Distribution into Service," *Wall Street Journal*, September 1, 1981, p. 12.

Dave Clare, who in 1967 had headed up a major study of the hospital supply business, explained how the J&J culture had influenced his committee's
thinking:

> We could see opportunities for economies through centralizing our mar-
> keting services. But we started with a belief that bigness can be bureaucratic
> and ineffective. When we add to that orientation the strong opposition to
> centralized marketing and distribution voiced by a number of company
> presidents, we concluded that the potential benefits were not sufficient at
> the time to make the changes required. We also recommended that the sit-
> uation be reexamined every five years.

The recommendation for a reexamination every five years was not implemented for two reasons. First, Dave Clare, a leading proponent of the change,
had by then been promoted to the executive committee, with responsibility for
companies serving other markets. Second, until 1979 the situation had not been
perceived by top management to have changed sufficiently to trigger any further action. Other problems were seen to have higher priority. For example, in
1976, when Jim Burke was promoted to chief executive officer and Dave Clare
to president, the decision was made to deal with a major reorganization of the
pharmaceutical business before tackling the hospital services problem.

In mid-1979, attention was again turned to the hospital supply question. It
was now apparent that with government action intensifying the cost-containment
pressures on hospitals, change in the medical field would be rapid. J&J was no
longer able to adjust gradually to the shifts occurring with its hospital customers. Toward the end of 1979, Jim Burke and Dave Clare called a meeting of the
hospital and professional company presidents. Top management put the following challenge to the group: "This is a big part of our corporation's business.
Let's talk about how we can grow faster and serve the customer better in the
decade of the 80s!"

Project Chatham

At a meeting in New Brunswick, N.J., home of J&J's corporate headquarters,
a special committee of J&J hospital company presidents was established to examine several marketing strategies and determine how the corporation could
best meet the challenges of the hospital market in the 1980s. The committee
was chaired by Jack Walcott, a member of the executive committee and chairman of J&J Products Inc. Pete Ventrella was one of the members. Thinking
back, Walcott recalled:

> I was well aware of how our strong belief in decentralized operations
> had led us in 1967 to decide against a joint distribution system for hospitals.
> But since then, there were important changes and trends in the hospital
> industry that we could not ignore. Moreover our stake in that business had
> increased through the addition of a broader base of products, including our
> expanded offerings in pharmaceuticals and diagnostic instruments.
>   Clearly, there was a strong impetus from the top for reexamining our

position. Dave Clare, who has considerable experience in operations, was concerned that we were not getting enough leverage out of a billion-dollar business. Jim Burke has a marketing perspective and was concerned about our competitive posture in the field.

The study, code named Project Chatham, gathered momentum over the 1980–81 period. The committee met once or twice a month and added a full-time coordinator. A major consulting firm was commissioned to analyze the hospital business, including regulatory developments. The committee members also sought information directly from medical professionals and hospital administrators.

The committee's deliberations were complicated in two ways. With respect to problem definition, the consultant's market research findings were susceptible to different interpretations about the extent to which buying behavior had really changed or was going to change in the future. This ambiguity left open to debate just when to institute organizational changes.

With respect to possible organizational and procedural changes, the committee had to contend with the problem of finding an approach that was suitable to the different practices and commitments among the participating companies. For example, distribution practices ranged from 100 percent direct sales to 100 percent independent distributor sales among the thirteen companies. Delivery, service, and credit policies also varied widely. Even the importance of the hospital business in comparison with other markets varied from company to company.

Affiliate Company Resistance

During the Project Chatham deliberations, some J&J affiliate companies refuted the suitability of a centralized hospital services concept that would consolidate certain marketing and distribution functions. A senior J&J executive who had been involved with Project Chatham described his impression of the concerns voiced by these companies:

> It came down to some companies not wanting any change that had the potential of usurping the autonomy and control they had in running their respective businesses. Because of our decentralized philosophy that had been ingrained in companies over time, affiliates had the tendency to look parochially rather than broadly at the changes that were taking place in the hospital market. This colored their understanding of how these changes in hospitals could have an effect on the future of their own businesses in the long term.
>
> Ethicon had the strongest reasons for maintaining the status quo. This company held a leading market position in supplying sutures for precise wound closure and had been termed one of the most successful franchises J&J ever had.
>
> On the other side, it was important for HSG to include Ethicon because of the important leverage this well-known company would provide for the whole group. Moreover, Ethicon had become something of a weathervane on the participation issue.

Continuing strong support of the Hospital Services concept by top corporate officers kept a reluctant Ethicon in the project. Burke gave his view of the situation: "Ethicon would say, 'We agree that eventually we're going to have to do this. We also agree that you have to do this now for the other companies, but not for us.' From their point of view they were absolutely correct. They didn't need it now. But they're going to need it someday."

Formation of Hospital Services Group

In April, 1981, the Project Chatham committee recommended that J&J create a unit that would provide a consolidated distribution network, including a common customer-service group and an electronic order entry/customer information system, for those hospitals and hospital distributors ordering from any and all J&J companies. The recommendation included provisions for the development of a corporate (1) purchase agreement program; (2) capital equipment financing program; (3) equipment services program; and (4) identity program.

In making its recommendations, the Project Chatham committee stressed that the plan would allow J&J to position itself better to talk to the hospital as a corporate customer. The committee sought to capitalize more effectively on J&J's highly regarded name and to begin to speak with one voice to the hospital field on a number of business issues.

These recommendations were approved by the executive committee. The Hospital Services Group (HSG) was formed to develop action plans and to implement the approved programs. Ed Hartnett, a former executive vice president of Ethicon and then a group vice president of J&J Products Inc., was appointed general manager of HSG. His support staff soon included one of the company's top distribution experts and a computer specialist.

In March 1982, Hartnett presented to the executive committee a report on HSG that defined its mission and goals and described the status of its programs.

Mission:

Develop and implement programs for J&J as a corporation, on behalf of the professional companies, that respond to the needs of hospitals and distributor customers.

Goals:

1. Improve the corporation's competitive position in the hospital industry through common strategies that can be utilized by its professional companies.
2. Build, with the business leaders in the hospital marketplace, the recognition that Johnson & Johnson as a corporation is responsive to their needs.
3. Develop programs that complement and strengthen the decentralized product franchises each of the companies has established among the medical and nursing professionals.

4. Seek internal economies of scale and productivity gains that result in increased profitability longer term.

The major programs under development were described in detail; these programs included:

1. *Incentive purchase plan (IPP).* A corporate umbrella volume-incentive agreement under which each company would continue to set its individual marketing, pricing, and selling practices.
2. *On-line order entry/customer information system.* A computer system tying all J&J companies into one data base, so as to provide automated order entry, consolidated customer order service, and support for a physical distribution network.
3. *Consolidated physical distribution network.* A network of eleven warehouses for supply items that would provide three-day service for 90 percent of J&J's hospital and distributor customers.
4. *Corporate identity program.* To explain J&J's total role in the hospital supply and equipment business.
5. *Sales cross-training program.* To familiarize J&J sales representatives with the total scope of J&J's hospital business.
6. *Capital equipment leasing program.* To finance the leasing or purchasing of all J&J medical equipment products.
7. *Combined equipment service program.* An intracompany, shared equipment service program to improve overall service capabilities.
8. *Hospital business understanding plan.* Although each J&J company would continue to monitor change in its specific target audience, HSG would be responsible for understanding the administrative and business side of hospital operations and for supplying this information to the appropriate company. Issues would include competition, cost containment, federal and state reimbursement, revenue planning, capital funding, and inventory management.

The committee recommended a three-phase roll-out for involving the J&J companies in the HSG marketing services, starting with supplies, then moving to pharmaceuticals and finally equipment. Table A shows the sequence in which the individual J&J companies would be phased into the program.

Distribution Policies

Under the proposed approach to hospital sales, each J&J product company would continue to be responsible for promoting its products to the appropriate doctors and nurses in the hospitals. HSG would be responsible for distribution. It would play a somewhat different role, however, for direct sales and for sales through distributors (see Figure B).

For direct sales to hospitals, HSG would serve as a direct link between the

Table A   Hospital Services roll-out sequence, 1984–86.

	Supplies	Pharma- ceuticals	Equipment, Instruments, and Other
J&J Products, patient care	✓		
J&J Products, orthopaedic	✓		✓
Surgikos	✓		
Codman	✓		✓
Critikon	✓		✓
Extracorporeal	✓		✓
Ortho Diagnostic Systems	✓		✓
Ethicon	✓		
McNeil Pharmaceutical		✓	
Ortho Pharmaceutical		✓	
Janssen		✓	
Iolab			✓
Technicare			✓
Overall Sales			
Dealer	59%	26%	4%
Direct	41%	74%	96%

supplying company and the customer. Its principal activities would include holding inventories at regional warehouses, processing hospital orders, making deliveries, invoicing hospitals, and handling credit and accounts receivable.

For sales through distributors, HSG would serve as a link between the supplying company and its distributors, performing the same functions for the distributors that it performed for hospitals in direct sales. Should a hospital order distributor-handled goods directly from HSG, the order would be referred to and billed through a distributor, whether the goods were delivered from the J&J warehouses or from the distributor's stock. In such cases, the distributor was urged to service the account directly to earn the 6 percent to 10 percent commission it received.

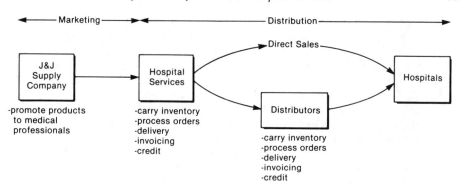

Figure B   Marketing and distribution flows.

Johnson & Johnson Hospital Services

In September 1982, Ed Hartnett was promoted to the position of company group chairman, with responsibility for Ethicon and its related overseas companies. (See the Johnson & Johnson (A) case for a description of the company group chairman's job.) Pete Ventrella took charge of HSG. As 1982 drew to a close, the decision was made to establish HSG as an independent company and to appoint Ventrella as its president.[5] He described some of his concerns as he first took over the new Hospital Services Company:

> There were numerous specific issues to be settled, most of which were important to the companies involved. For example, decisions had to be made as to who should own the inventory in the warehouses, what the credit and payment terms would be, and even whether the supply company field salesmen or Hospital Services people should introduce these programs to the customers. While in no way meaning to lessen the importance of these specific issues, I did come to recognize two broad concerns. One was how to build a company in the J&J environment. The other was how to get this new company accepted inside as well as outside the corporation.
>
> Legal and tax considerations certainly influenced the decision to set up HSG as a separate company. But organizational considerations might have been even more important. We needed experienced people to launch and to run this somewhat delicate operation, and setting it up as a line company made it easier to attract good people in J&J. To give you some idea of the problem, we will soon have over 100 people on board and that number will grow to over 500 in three years' time.
>
> Having a company status helps, but we're not totally out of the woods on how to make Hospital Services an attractive assignment for J&J people. People will want to be able to say, "Look what we've contributed to the corporation." But how do you measure the contribution which results from

5. Ventrella had joined J&J in 1959 after graduating from Colgate University and completing a stint with the Air Force. He had started as a sales representative with the Hospital & Professional Division and rose to vice president and general manager of the Patient Care division by 1979.

our services and distinguish it from the impact which results from the product development and selling efforts performed by the supplying companies?

This difficulty in measuring contribution also affects how we get accepted by the other companies in J&J. It's easy when you have a clear-cut profit to show. And that brings me back to one of the specific issues on my mind. Should Hospital Services charge the companies just for costs or should the charges include a profit margin and return on investment? The participating companies will certainly want to keep their expenses down, and those companies who see this operation as increasing their costs will object strenuously to any increase for the purpose of our showing a profit. But, then again, charging only costs obscures the fact that we might be adding a significant value through our services and trade relationships. Being a break-even cost center in some ways undermines the company concept and deprives me of an important tool for motivating my staff.

In 1983, two new small J&J supply companies were added to the Hospital Services' roster. Xanar, which had been organized in October 1981 to design and manufacture carbon dioxide surgical laser systems, began product sales in January 1983. Irex, acquired in February, 1983, manufactured and distributed ultrasound equipment (nuclear magnetic resonance modality) for cardiovascular applications.

1983 Executive Committee Plan Review

Pete Ventrella was scheduled to report to the executive committee on March 23, 1983, on Hospital Services' status and plans. This would be his first update on the company's activities since becoming president.

The report revealed that the overall net annual operating costs for the Hospital Services activities (total Hospital Services costs less related savings in the supply companies) would be about $26 million (cost and sales figures have been disguised). It went on to point out that this added cost could be covered by an incremental sales increase of roughly 3 percent. The difficulty in making a precise cost-benefit analysis was in ascertaining what the sales performance might have been without the new distribution services.

Among other information, the report delineated the responsibilities to be carried out by Hospital Services and those remaining to the companies (see Table B).

The introduction of a corporate tag-line policy illustrated the kind of details in which Hospital Services was engaged. The following excerpt from a letter Dave Clare wrote to the company presidents emphasized the importance of promoting J&J's corporate identity with the professional market:

> The name Johnson & Johnson is a trademark synonymous with high standards of product performance, bringing instant recognition to the products and companies that carry the name.
>
> In the past we have not used the Johnson & Johnson name with many of our hospital companies. However, the changing nature of the profes-

Table B Division of responsibilities.

Hospital Services Responsibilities	Responsibilities Remaining with Companies
Customer services	Marketing
Order processing	Pricing
Credit	Inventory
Distribution	Recalls
Invoicing	Product
Accounts receivable	performance
Corporate identity	Inquiry
IPP	Nonhospital
Hospital business	business
understanding	Specials
Reimbursement	International
	Internal reporting

sional business has made it important for us to enhance recognition of our corporation as a broad scale supplier of products and services to the professional market. Accordingly, we plan to integrate the corporate tag line, "a Johnson & Johnson company," into our hospital company logotypes as a major step in fostering the recognition.

As a result, ten of the professional companies were to include an identification with J&J as shown below:

ETHICON
a *Johnson-Johnson* company

On March 21, two days before the executive committee review, Pete Ventrella was scheduled to meet with the president and the chairman of Ethicon to try to settle a difference of opinion on inventory placements. Ventrella described the issue for discussion:

Ethicon is willing to stock its most popular items (25 percent of its codes) in all eleven warehouses, but would like to stock its complete line in only three or four locations. Why? Because this step would reduce Ethicon's inventory costs by about $3 million by their estimate. We feel that in order to preserve the original concept of a hospital or distributor customer being able to make one phone call to order any J&J product—and then to have such products shipped on one truck with one bill of lading, one invoice, and one monthly bill to the customer—we cannot make an exception to our plan, at least not initially, until we see what value the customer puts on this capability.

McCaw Cellular Communications, Inc. in 1990

In 1984, it seemed unlikely that a small family-run business could compete successfully with the multibillion-dollar regional Bell operating companies in the emerging cellular phone business. By 1990, however, McCaw Cellular Communications, Inc. was the largest cellular phone service company in the United States. This family-built company, headquartered in Kirkland, Washington, had over 70 million potential customers (or "POPs" in industry parlance) in its service areas, 963,000 current customers, and over $500 million in 1989 revenues. Craig O. McCaw, the company's forty-year-old chairman and CEO, was described by competitors as the "entrepreneur of the eighties." His vision was to build a seamless national cellular phone system, and charge premium rates for top-quality service.

First offered in 1983, cellular phone service had grown to encompass over 4.4 million subscribers in the United States by 1990, penetrating the market faster than televisions, video cassette recorders, or facsimile machines had. Experts predicted there could be 25 million cellular customers in the United States by the year 2000. Cellular phone service revenues had risen from $2 billion in 1989 to $3.2 billion in 1990, with experts predicting an increase to $15 billion by 1995. Observers called cellular service a "victim of its own popularity"; in some urban areas the volume of calls strained capacity.

Industry History

Since the 1927 Radio Act, the U.S. government had regulated use of the radio spectrum to reduce problems of interference. Long before cellular phone service emerged, parts of the radio spectrum were allocated for private radio systems for uses such as police, ambulances, taxis, and industry communications. In 1990, parts of the spectrum had also been allocated to televisions, baby monitors, garage door openers, and remote paging systems.

In 1981, the Federal Communications Commission (FCC) determined that it would award cellular service licenses to two companies in each of 306 Metropolitan Statistical Areas or "MSAs" (which included 75 percent of the United States population) and 428 Rural Statistical Areas or "RSAs" (which included 80 percent of the U.S. land area). According to the FCC rules, one license would be given to the local wireline phone company and the other would be awarded in a lottery; these licenses could be resold, but no entity could control more than one cellular system within a service area. Over 90,000 applicants participated in the lotteries. The first two cellular phone service networks began operation in Chicago and Baltimore in 1983. By 1990, all of the MSAs had cellular service; the last of the RSA lotteries had been completed, and the first twenty-two RSA systems had begun operation.

The process of qualifying to compete in the FCC lottery for cellular service licenses and completing the application was estimated to cost $250,000. Once a company won (or purchased) a license to a service area, it could apply for a construction permit. After the permit was granted, the company had eighteen months in which to begin building a system. If it did not build a system in parts of its service territory within three years, its license for the unbuilt areas reverted back to the FCC. The FCC rarely allowed preconstruction sale of a construction permit, but sale of noncontrolling interests was not regulated, and completed systems also could be sold.

Cellular Communications

To make a call on a cellular phone, the caller had to be within the range of one of the service areas. Then calls could be placed to any location in the world where regular (or cellular) phone service was available. Signal quality was not as good as on regular phones. Voices sometimes faded in and out and cells were occasionally disconnected if the radio signal was blocked by a bridge, building, or forest. Cellular phones could have all of the services regular phones had, such as voice mail, call forwarding, and data transmission. But data transmission such as portable facsimile transmission was slower.

Cellular communication required a cellular phone, battery and antenna, and a subscription with a cellular service company. Manufacturers offered three kinds of cellular phones: mobiles, transportables, and portables. Mobiles were installed in cars or trucks, using power from the vehicle's battery. The phone's own antenna was mounted on the outside of the vehicle. Transportables could be moved from car to car, or could be used in a boat, in the field, or in the house. They drew power from a vehicle's cigarette lighter or from a battery pack. In 1990, a mobile or transportable cellular phone, battery, and antenna cost $100 to $700. A phone that cost $3,500 in 1983 could be purchased for $300 in 1990. Portables were one-piece phones that operated on lower power from a built-in rechargeable battery. The newest portables could be folded to pocket-size and weighed as little as ten ounces. Portable phones cost $400 to $1,500. Portable and transportable phones accounted for about 50 percent of the market in 1990.

For people concerned only about status or appearances, a small California company called Faux Systems sold a $16 ($9.95 on sale) nonworking replica of a car phone and antenna called the Cellular Phoney. By 1990, 40,000 Cellular Phoneys had been sold in California.

Cellular phone transmission service was provided by a network of low-power radio transceivers called cell sites or base stations, each transmitting and receiving signals in a one- to twenty-five-mile radius known as a cell. Smaller cells led to increased system capacity since the same airwave channel could be used simultaneously for different calls in different cells. When a cellular call was made, the voice was transmitted in the form of continuous radio waves to the transceiver at the cell site, and then was transmitted through the regular phone network to the phone number being called. The cell switch periodically monitored the signal strength of calls in progress. If the signal strength fell to a predetermined level, the switch determined if the signal quality was greater at an adjacent cell site, and if so, it passed the call to that cell site. The transfer took a fraction of a second, and was generally not noticeable by the parties on the phone. However, if the switch at the adjacent site was made by a different manufacturer, the handoff would not necessarily work because different manufacturers used different handoff protocols. If the handoff failed, the call abruptly disconnected.

When a cellular phone customer "roamed," or drove into the service area of a different company, the call was passed to an adjacent cellular service with which the subscriber's company had a billing agreement. If there was no cellular service where the customer roamed, or if there was not a billing agreement, the call was disconnected. Cellular phone customers could place calls when they were away from their regular service territory by dialing a ten-digit access code before dialing the call. To receive calls on a cellular phone away from one's service territory, subscribers had to phone the access number and location to the home service company.

Fully digital networks (which were under development) would transmit voices in the form of a series of pulses representing the zeros and ones of computer language. With the digital technology, more calls could be fit on a single channel and the speed of cellular data transmissions for portable fax machines or laptop computers would increase to match the speed of the regular phone system. The possibility of an all-digital network also created the possibility of a standardized network in which phone numbers could be associated with individuals (wherever they traveled) instead of with places. Customers would no longer need access codes for calls when they were out of town. A standardized national digital network would make it possible even for small cellular service companies with few service areas to offer national calling benefits to their customers.

Other portable communication options were increasing in 1990. Remote pagers allowed customers to receive phone messages, but not to make or receive calls. The market for pagers was 7.8 million units in 1988, and was growing at a rate of 30 percent per year. Some customers used both pagers and mobile phones.

Personal communications networks (or PCNs) were under development. PCNs used a type of cellular phone that was pocket-sized and less powerful. Instead of using relatively few cells spread widely (as other cellular systems did), PCNs used thousands of "micro cells" spaced more closely so users would never be far away from one of them. Some telecommunications experts believed that PCNs would become the primary type of wireless phone service in urban areas; others argued that the limited range of the micro cells would make other technologies dominant. In 1990, the FCC had granted experimental licenses to firms to build PCN systems in Washington, D.C., Detroit, Chicago and White Plains, New York.[1]

Satellite phone systems were also under development. For example, Motorola's "Iridium" project was a plan to use seventy-seven low-orbit satellites to bring wireless phone service to every point on earth. Motorola described it as a complement to cellular service. The system, which would cost $2.3 billion, was scheduled to begin service in 1996. Hand-held phones for the Iridium system would cost about $3,000, and calls would cost one to three dollars per minute, plus a $50 monthly service charge. Hugh's Network Systems was also developing a satellite phone system.

Customers

The Cellular Telephone Industry Association and many analysts predicted in 1990 that the number of subscribers would grow at 40 percent to 50 percent per year for the next five years. Revenues from cellular service for the first half of 1990 were $2.13 billion, up 10 percent from six months earlier. A few observers believed that cellular phones would entirely replace wireline phones soon after the turn of the century. In spite of these rosy projections, cellular service company stock prices dropped 50 percent during 1990 amidst fears of recession. Exhibit 1 shows U.S. industry growth statistics from 1984 to 1990.

The average cellular customer in 1990 was college-educated, married, and had a household income of $66,000. Cellular phone use was reported to be 75 percent business calls and 25 percent personal. In 1990, more cellular phones were installed in pickup trucks than in any other type of vehicle. Three years earlier, the average customer was a fifty-five-year-old CEO earning over $90,000, and only 11 percent of cellular phone use was personal. The average monthly bill by a cellular subscriber was about $84 in the first half of 1990, down from about $89 six months earlier and from over $100 in 1987. In general, average monthly bills were higher in rural service areas than in metropolitan areas, although the Los Angeles area had average monthly bills around $140 in 1990.

In high-volume markets such as Los Angeles and New York, callers sometimes had to wait several minutes for a dial tone; about 20 percent of rush-hour callers in these markets were unable to place calls on the first try. Overcrowded systems also had higher numbers of accidentally disconnected calls.

1. Britain had already licensed a PCN company to compete with cellular service.

Exhibit 1 U.S. cellular industry growth.

Date	Subscribers	Revenues	Cell Sites	Employees	Total Capital Investments	Number of Systems Operating	Number of Resellers
Dec. 84	91,600	$ 178,000,000	346	1,404	$ 354,760,500	32	107
June 85	203,600	$ 176,231,000	599	1,697	$ 588,751,000	65	211
Dec. 85	340,213	$ 306,197,000	913	2,727	$ 911,167,000	102	224
June 86	500,000	$ 360,585,000	1,194	3,556	$1,140,163,000	129	213
Dec. 86	681,825	$ 462,467,000	1,531	4,334	$1,436,753,000	166	240
June 87	883,778	$ 479,514,000	1,732	5,656	$1,724,348,000	206	230
Dec. 87	1,230,855	$ 672,000,000	2,305	7,147	$2,234,635,000	312	285
June 88	1,608,697	$ 888,075,000	2,789	9,154	$2,589,588,000	420	247
Dec. 88	2,069,441	$1,073,472,000	3,209	11,400	$3,274,104,000	517	211
June 89	2,691,793	$1,406,463,000	3,577	13,719	$3,675,473,000	559	252
Dec. 89	3,508,944	$1,934,132,198	4,169	15,937	$4,480,141,752	584	303
June 90	4,368,686	$2,126,362,078	4,768	18,973	$5,211,765,025	592	372

Source: Cellular Telephone Industry Association, 1990.

Observers argued that the first company to enhance its capacity in over-crowded systems might win a large share of the market and create loyal customers.

Market research showed that a subscriber's choice of service company was based on the breadth of service coverage and the quality of customer support. Cellular service companies competed fiercely to offer broad service coverage. Participants said that because no firm had dared to experiment with narrow coverage, no one knew if customers would avoid a company that served a small area. Bell operating companies often had marketing advantages based on their reputation as large, stable phone companies.

Marketing and Distribution

The costs of marketing and advertising were $400 to $600 for each new subscriber attracted. Factoring in "churn" (i.e., the fraction of customers who dropped their subscriptions within six months), these costs were $600 to $900 for each new long-term subscriber. Most cellular service companies used a variety of distribution channels to attract and support customers, including dealers, sales agents, direct sales forces, retailers, and resellers.

Dealers and agents were independent companies that contracted to market one cellular service exclusively. They received a commission for each subscription, and an additional commission after the customer had been with the service for six months. Dealers and agents were estimated to account for as much as 60 percent of service companies' sales.

Service companies' direct sales forces called on major corporate accounts, which required a sales process that could last six months. Direct sales forces typically accounted for about 30 percent of cellular service sales. Industry participants explained that marketing to large customers did not yet result in significant marketing economies because of the time and effort required to sign big customers, and because these customers tended to start with relatively small numbers of uses and add volume slowly over time. In the future, cellular service companies hoped that the marketing cost per user might be an order of magnitude lower for major corporate accounts than for sales to individuals.

Retailers such as Sears, Caldor, Highland, Whole Earth Access, and Radio Shack also sold subscriptions to cellular service. Cellular service companies often trained retail sales representatives and paid commissions for each customer signed up. Retailers tended to change service company affiliations if they could get a more favorable commission. Retailers' commissions had risen to $200–$800, up from $50 a few years earlier. One industry report estimated 30 percent of the volume of cellular equipment sales was made at retail stores in 1990, with projected growth of up to 60 percent or 70 percent of the volume of equipment sales by 1995. However, service companies reported that less than 10 percent of their service revenues were from customers who subscribed at retail stores.

Resellers bought cellular airtime in bulk at a discount (usually about 20 percent), and sold it to customers at rates similar to the cellular service company. The cellular service company had no direct link to the customer, who was billed by the reseller. In most areas, resellers accounted for less than 10 percent of cellular service sales. In northern California, however, resellers constituted about 40 percent of sales.

Promotions and Advertising

It was common for dealers and retailers to apply a large fraction of their commissions to customer discounts, reducing equipment prices by up to several hundred dollars; in the late 1980s customers could get a virtually free phone, battery, and antenna when they signed up for service. Other promotions included free long-distance calling on weekends, free voice mail for a month, and free tickets for two to Hawaii when signing up for cellular service for a year.

Cellular service companies' advertising tended to focus on technological capabilities. For example, McCaw advertised its seamless network with smooth handoffs from one cell to the next, preventing customers from being disconnected mid-call. Nynex Mobile Communications promoted 25 percent more calling channels than its competitors.

Pricing and Billing

Rates for cellular phone service were regulated in many states; usually, this simply meant that a public tariff had to be filed before rates could be changed. By 1990, about twenty states including California had stopped rate regulation for cellular service companies, in part because cellular phone service was viewed as a discretionary purchase.

The charge for cellular service was usually a one-time activation fee ($35–$40), a flat rate per month ($19–$45), and an "air charge" for each minute of both incoming and outgoing calls. The rate was forty to sixty cents per minute for "peak" calling times (7 A.M. to 7 P.M. weekdays) and about twenty-five to forty cents per minute for off-peak times. In addition, there were "land charges" for connecting to the local phone company lines unless the cellular service was owned by the local phone company, and applicable long-distance charges.

Most cellular service companies bought long-distance service at a discount and resold it to their customers at retail rates. Wireline phone companies were legally required to offer equal access to all long-distance providers. Some non-wireline companies such as McCaw offered only one long-distance provider in some markets to increase the volume of long-distance purchases from that company. The size of price discounts to cellular service companies was negotiated, and companies involved were unwilling to disclose the terms of deals they struck.

Transmission Licenses

Licenses to provide cellular service (and associated transmission systems if they had been built) were bought and sold among industry participants as each sought to build or consolidate its network. The market value of a license to operate a transmission system in a given area was usually expressed in terms of the price per person in the area, or "POP." In 1990, the value of a POP was hotly debated in the cellular phone industry. Some analysts claimed that a market was worth $200 per POP to a service operator that could sign up 8 percent of the population within ten years. Assuming no new regulation and few competing technologies, Morgan Asset Management Inc. projected that if 15 percent of Americans used cellular phones by the year 2000, and if efficient operations generated sixty-five cents of cash flow for every dollar of revenue, then each POP would be worth $424.

The price per POP in the early eighties was as low as $4 to $6. Prices grew higher in the late 1980s and peaked in 1989 with McCaw's $350 per POP purchase of premium properties in New York and Los Angeles. Three months later, Contel paid $215 per POP for East Coast properties. In July, Pacific Telesis paid $190 per POP in Cleveland and Cincinnati, and in October Crowley Cellular Telecommunications paid $165 per POP for Illinois properties.

Transmission Systems

Cumulative capital invested in U.S. cellular transmission service in 1990 was over $5 billion. Industry participants estimated that building even a small system cost at least $750,000. The capital cost per customer was about $1,500, including equipment, installation, and frequency planning. Since cell size was not fixed, most service areas initially used cells eight miles in radius in more populous areas and twenty-five miles in radius in rural areas. As demand increased, the cell could be split into three to six smaller cells, but beyond this point the cost and complexity of further subdivision became prohibitive. Each time a new cell was added to a network, the frequency use plan for the entire network had to be redesigned so that no two adjoining cells shared the same frequency. If adjoining cells shared a frequency, calls in these cells would interfere with each other. While frequency planning was uncomplicated in flat, open country, it was a time-consuming engineering task when many hills, trees, or buildings required a complicated mosaic of cells.

Industry participants said that an efficient transmission system was one with enough cell sites to cover the marketing and use region and with enough transmission channels to meet demand for cellular phone use in the region. However, in 1990, no one could characterize an efficient system in terms of customers per cell site or customers per transmission channel. Observers watched the workloads of cellular companies' engineers and the service quality to customers to estimate which regions had system capacity well matched with demand.

The operating cellular phone network in 1990 used analog technology. To increase system capacity, cellular service companies were planning to replace analog transmission technology with one of two new digital technologies, Time Division Multiple Access (TDMA) or Code Division Multiple Access (CDMA). New transceivers, amplifiers, and controllers would be required, but the new equipment would fit on the same racks as analog equipment. Although both new technologies were compatible with analog transmission, the two possible digital technologies were incompatible, so if adjacent cells used different digital transmission technologies, callers moving from one cell to the other would have to be switched using the analog setting. If no analog channel was available, or if the caller's phone was digital only, the call would be disconnected. In 1990, cellular phones were analog or analog and digital, but in the future digital-only phones were expected to be smaller, lighter, and less expensive. Some industry participants believed that in the future software would be created to make the two digital technologies compatible.

TDMA was the standard in Japan and in some European countries, and had been backed since February 1989 by the Cellular Telecommunications Industry Association as the U.S. standard for first-generation digital cellular technology. It was expected to be available for installation in the United States in 1991; proponents referred to it as a "proven" technology. TDMA was widely licensed and was being developed by many cellular telephone equipment manufacturers. TDMA offered a threefold increase in capacity, and thus the capital cost per customer was estimated to be about $500 (one-third of the $1,500 per customer analog capital cost). TDMA required channels to be set aside for digital transmission and would therefore reduce the analog capacity in systems in which TDMA was installed. Experts expected TDMA technology to reduce system operating costs by 10 percent to 25 percent. They also expected the first TDMA/analog phones to be bigger and heavier than analog cellular phones, and to cost 10 percent to 15 percent more. Developers said that improvements in TDMA might offer a six-fold or ten-fold increase in capacity by the late 1990s.

CDMA was a proprietary technology of Qualcomm, Inc. that was projected to allow a ten-fold to twenty-fold increase in capacity. Although CDMA technology had been used in some military communications since World War II, CDMA had first been proven technically feasible for use in cellular phones in late 1989. Some participants believed CDMA could be available for use by late 1991 or 1992, but others were skeptical about CDMA being ready before the mid-1990s. CDMA was described as more flexible, because in theory CDMA could be overlaid on cells still serving analog users without disrupting the analog calls, and because CDMA cells all operated on the same frequencies and thus did not require frequency plans. CDMA also was described as leading the industry closer to a generation of technology that enabled individuals to carry hand-held phones with them anywhere. Furthermore, CDMA was predicted to have cost advantages both in installation and operation because it required fewer transmitters and combiners than TDMA. Proponents also argued that because CDMA used the spread spectrum and covered many frequencies, interference would be reduced, sound quality would be enhanced by more robust signals, and privacy would be increased by reduced interception problems, but critics argued that improvements in sound quality and privacy were benefits of any digital technology.

A new analog technology called Narrow Advanced Mobile Phone Services (NAMPS) was announced by Motorola in October 1990. NAMPS broadcast on a smaller band width, enabling triple the current capacity without adding cells. Field tests were scheduled to begin in January 1991, and Motorola said NAMPS would be available in mid-1991 for companies that needed a short-term capacity enhancement before investing in digital technology. The cost of new NAMPS transceivers was projected to be "significantly less" than digital transceivers, but more precise price estimates were not yet available in late 1990. Installation would require redesign of frequency planning since NAMPS tripled the number of frequencies in each cell. Customers in NAMPS systems would need new phones, which Motorola planned to market at a $100 price premium over other cellular phones.

Procurement

Cellular service companies bought transmission equipment in large volume purchases from equipment suppliers. Small rural cellular service companies usually purchased equipment jointly with an adjacent metropolitan service company to get the advantages of volume discounts. The metropolitan companies benefited from this arrangement because they were then assured that the adjacent companies had compatible switches.

Motorola had 32 percent of the $627 million U.S. market for cellular switches and cell site transmission gear. AT&T had 30 percent and Ericsson had 22 percent. Northern Telecom, General Electric, Nippon Electric Company, Astronet, NovAtel, and CTI/E.F.Johnson shared the rest of the market. All of these companies made analog switches, and most were expected to offer TDMA technology in 1991. Ericsson and Motorola were reported to be gearing up to produce large quantities of TDMA equipment. A Motorola spokesperson noted that when cellular service companies upgraded to digital networks, "the deck would be shuffled among suppliers."[2]

Only Qualcomm offered CDMA technology in 1990. Qualcomm had contracts with PacTel, Nynex, and Ameritech Mobile Communications to initiate testing of CDMA transmission, and with AT&T to make CDMA phones. Each of the companies that contracted with Qualcomm stated to the press that they were not abandoning TDMA, and pointed out the importance of technological innovation in this industry and the excitement with which they viewed the potential capabilities of CDMA.

International Markets

Although the concept for cellular phones was first developed in the United States, other countries began cellular phone service earlier. Industry observers

2. Quoted by John J. Keller in the *Wall Street Journal*, March 11, 1990, p. B13.

had attributed the U.S. delay to legislative lags in allocating the radio spectrum and in licensing service companies. Japan began commercial cellular service in 1979, and by 1984 had 20,000 subscribers to networks in Tokyo, Osaka, and five other cities. Norway, Sweden, Denmark, and Finland began commercial service in 1981, and had over 75,000 subscribers by 1984. Cellular systems were also in place in Saudi Arabia, Indonesia, and Spain before the United States.

In 1990, cellular service was available in more than seventy countries with over 6.5 million subscribers (over half of them in the United States). The highest penetration levels were in Norway, Sweden, Iceland, Denmark, and Finland. Most countries had a single cellular service system rather than competing service companies. National standards often differed among countries, resulting in incompatible systems. Europe had eight incompatible regional and national systems, but in 1989 discussions were begun to map plans for a pan-European network based on TDMA technology.

Competitors

By law, each service area in the United States was served by two companies, one of which was the local phone company for that area. To combat the name recognition of the local phone companies, the new operators created a nationwide image with the shared trademark, "Cellular One." The Cellular One service mark was licensed by the Washington/Baltimore Cellular Telephone Company (a consortium of American TeleServices, Graphic Scanning, Metrocall, Metromedia, and Metropolitan Radio TeleSystems) to other companies for a minimal fee. (Wireline service companies could not use the Cellular One brand within their wireline service territories.) The license was perpetual, subject to compliance with service quality standards. Each company using the Cellular One brand, however, remained independent.

By 1990, a number of service companies had built large service networks. Exhibits 2 and 3 show the number of POPs served by the largest companies, and the licensed operators in the largest markets. Exhibit 4 shows financial results for leading competitors. Cash flow margins from cellular service operations were estimated to average just under 50 percent.

Industry observers believed regulators might allow additional competition in each region in the future. In New York, petitions had been filed for a third license. In addition, some firms were lobbying for permission to offer mobile telephone service on frequencies reserved for other uses. This section briefly profiles five selected cellular service companies illustrating different strategies, as well as Fleet Call, a company that had petitioned to create a third cellular system in several major cities.

GTE Mobilnet, Incorporated. GTE Mobilnet, Inc. was a subsidiary of GTE Corporation. GTE was a wireline company in parts of the southwestern and midwestern U.S., but had sold its Sprint long-distance telephone service for $500 million in April 1990. The Mobilnet subsidiary was incorporated in 1981

Exhibit 2   Largest U.S. cellular operators.

Operator	MSA #	Major Markets Served (top 30 only)	Total Population Served (in thousands)
McCaw Cellular Communications, Inc.	1	New York, NY	60,887
(includes LIN Broadcasting)	4	Philadelphia, PA	
	9	Dallas, TX	
	10	Houston, TX	
	12	Miami, FL	
	13	Pittsburgh, PA	
	15	Minneapolis, MN	
	19	Denver, CO	
	20	Seattle-Everett, WA	
	22	Tampa, FL	
	24	Kansas City, MO-KS	
	30	Portland, OR	
GTE Mobilnet, Inc.	7	San Francisco, CA	40,680
(includes Contel and Providence Journal)	10	Houston, TX	
	16	Cleveland, OH	
	22	Tampa, FL	
	27	San Jose, CA	
	28	Indianapolis, IN	
	30	Portland, OR	
BellSouth Mobility, Inc.	2	Los Angeles, CA	30,705
(includes American Cellular Comm)	12	Miami, FL	
	17	Atlanta, GA	
	29	New Orleans, LA	
PacTel Cellular	2	Los Angeles, CA	30,083
	5	Detroit, MI	
	7	San Francisco, CA	
	17	Atlanta, GA	
	18	San Diego, CA	
	27	San Jose, CA	
Southwestern Bell Mobile Systems	3	Chicago, IL	28,545
	6	Boston, MA	
	8	Washington, DC	
	9	Dallas, TX	
	11	St. Louis, MO	
	14	Baltimore, MD	
	24	Kansas City, MO-KS	

Exhibit 2   Largest U.S. cellular operators. (*continued*)

Operator	MSA #	Major Markets Served (top 30 only)	Total Population Served (in thousands)
Nynex Mobile Communications	1	New York, NY	25,076
	6	Boston, MA	
	25	Buffalo, NY	
Ameritech Mobile Communications	3	Chicago, IL	20,271
	5	Detroit, MI	
	21	Milwaukee, WI	
	23	Cincinnati, OH	
Bell Atlantic Mobile Systems, Inc.	4	Philadelphia, PA	16,369
	8	Washington, DC	
	13	Pittsburgh, PA	
	14	Baltimore, MD	
U.S. West Cellular	15	Minneapolis, MN	14,881
	18	San Diego, CA	
	19	Denver, CO	
	20	Seattle-Everett, WA	
	26	Phoenix, AZ	
Centel Cellular Company			12,332
Metro Mobile CTS	26	Phoenix, AZ	9,747
Cellular Communications, Inc.	16	Cleveland, OH	9,519
	23	Cincinnati, OH	

Source: CTIA, *State of the Cellular Industry,* Spring 1990.

to provide cellular phone service and related equipment. In 1984, in a limited partnership with Ameritech, Hancock Rural Telephone, and Monrovia Telephone, GTE launched the second operational cellular system in the United States, serving Indianapolis. Through a series of acquisitions, including the 1990 purchase of the Providence Journal Cellular ($710 million for 3.5 million POPs) and Contel Cellular Communications ($6.2 billion for 22.3 million POPs), GTE Mobilnet became the second largest U.S. cellular service company (measured by POPs). Sales increased 214 percent between 1989 and 1990 to $34 million.

GTE Mobilnet was targeting national business accounts as a way to increase profitability. A spokesperson said GTE planned "to be the first cellular concern to offer business one-stop shopping nationwide for service and equipment."[3]

3. Quoted by Janet Guyon in the *Wall Street Journal,* May 5, 1989.

Exhibit 3 Cellular operators in the largest U.S. cities.

Rank	City	Population	Cellular Service Operators
1	New York, NY	14,696,685	LIN Broadcasting Corp. (McCaw) Nynex Mobile Communications
2	Los Angeles, CA	10,968,394	PacTel Cellular American Cellular Communication Corp.[a,b]
3	Chicago, IL	7,103,624	Southwestern Bell Mobile Systems Ameritech Mobile Communications
4	Philadelphia, PA	4,716,818	LIN Broadcasting Corp. (McCaw) Bell Atlantic Mobile Systems
5	Detroit, MI	4,618,161	PacTel Cellular Ameritech Mobile Communications
6	Boston, MA	3,853,177	Southwestern Bell Mobile Systems Nynex Mobile Communications
7	San Francisco, CA	3,250,630	PacTel Cellular GTE Mobilnet, Inc.
8	Washington, DC	3,060,922	Southwestern Bell Mobile Systems Bell Atlantic Mobile Systems, Inc.
9	Dallas, TX	2,974,805	Southwestern Bell Mobile Systems LIN Broadcasting Corp. (McCaw)
10	Houston, TX	2,905,353	LIN Broadcasting Corp. (McCaw) GTE Mobilnet, Inc.
11	St. Louis, MO	2,356,460	Southwestern Bell Mobile Systems CyberTel Cellular Telephone Co.
12	Miami, FL	2,643,981	BellSouth Mobility, Inc. McCaw Cellular Communications, Inc.

Source: CTIA, *State of the Cellular Industry,* Spring 1990.

a. ACCC is owned by BellSouth Corp.

b. ACCC owns 60% of the L.A. non-wireline license; LIN owns 40%.

Where it could not buy or develop cellular operations, GTE Mobilnet was acquiring resale rights (buying cellular airtime for resale) from the licensed service providers.

In late 1990, GTE Mobilnet announced plans to replace Motorola with AT&T as its major equipment vendor. A spokesperson said the company wanted the future flexibility to put in either TDMA or CDMA switches, and Motorola's digital equipment could support only TDMA.

Exhibit 4 Financial data for selected competitors ($ thousands).

	FYE 12/31/89	FYE 12/31/88	FYE 12/31/87	FYE 12/31/86	FYE 12/31/85
American Information Technologies Corp.					
Net sales	10,211,300	9,903,300	9,547,500	9,384,800	9,021,100
Cost of goods	2,539,800	2,516,000	2,365,000	2,465,500	1,646,900
SG&A expense	3,720,200	3,497,700	3,076,700	2,789,300	3,482,500
Income before tax	1,784,900	1,818,600	1,905,800	2,067,800	1,897,400
Net income	1,238,200	1,237,400	1,188,100	1,138,400	1,077,700
Return on sales (ROS)	12%	12%	12%	12%	12%
Return on assets (ROA)	6%	6%	6%	6%	6%
Return on equity (ROE)	16%	16%	16%	15%	14%
Total debt to equity	73%	63%	64%	62%	64%
% of sales by cellular subsidiary	1.5%	N/A	N/A	N/A	N/A
GTE Corp.					
Net sales	17,424,360	16,459,852	15,421,030	15,111,528	14,371,659
Cost of goods	N/A	N/A	N/A	N/A	N/A
SG&A expense	14,235,130	13,408,299	12,268,365	11,873,480	11,170,925
Income before tax	2,064,062	1,840,962	1,751,950	2,090,611	(162,386)
Net income	1,417,270	1,224,681	1,118,817	1,184,312	(161,091)
Return on sales (ROS)	8%	7%	7%	8%	-1%
Return on assets (ROA)	4%	4%	4%	4%	-1%
Return on equity (ROE)	18%	15%	14%	15%	-2%
Total debt to equity	N/A	N/A	111%	108%	108%
% of sales by cellular subsidiary	0.2%	N/A	N/A	N/A	N/A
Nynex Corp.					
Net sales	13,210,600	12,660,800	12,084,000	11,341,500	10,313,600
Cost of goods	3,375,000	3,303,100	2,268,400	2,185,700	2,119,500
SG&A expense	5,762,000	4,965,400	5,392,700	4,984,800	4,450,800

Income before tax	1,073,500	1,688,200	1,954,700	2,105,000	1,891,100
Net income	807,600	1,315,000	1,276,500	1,215,300	1,095,300
Return on sales (ROS)	6%	10%	11%	11%	11%
Return on assets (ROA)	3%	5%	6%	6%	5%
Return on equity (ROE)	9%	14%	14%	14%	13%
Total debt to equity	69%	66%	68%	62%	65%
% of sales by cellular subsidiary	1.5%	N/A	N/A	N/A	N/A
Pacific Telesis Group					
Net sales	9,593,000	9,483,000	9,156,000	8,977,000	8,498,000
Cost of goods	1,870,000	1,966,000	2,068,000	1,534,000	1,676,000
SG&A expense	3,360,000	3,179,000	3,243,000	3,443,000	3,331,000
Income before tax	2,038,000	1,972,000	1,614,000	1,979,000	1,739,000
Net income	1,242,000	1,188,000	950,000	1,079,000	929,100
Return on sales (ROS)	13%	13%	10%	12%	11%
Return on assets (ROA)	6%	6%	4%	5%	5%
Return on equity (ROE)	16%	15%	12%	14%	13%
Total debt to equity	70%	69%	73%	74%	82%
% of sales by cellular subsidiary	5.21%	N/A	N/A	N/A	N/A
Metro Mobile Cts Inc.					
Net sales	111,295	55,983	19,490	7,856	3,454
Cost of goods	46,705	27,221	9,756	4,853	3,369
SG&A expense	56,091	41,333	19,073	18,518	4,025
Income before tax	(47,276)	(37,108)	(17,791)	(11,487)	(5,198)
Net income	(46,589)	(36,845)	(17,596)	(11,315)	(5,129)
Return on sales (ROS)	-42%	-66%	-90%	-144%	-148%
Return on assets (ROA)	-13%	-15%	-8%	-13%	-8%
Return on equity (ROE)	N/A	N/A	-11%	-110%	-26%
Total debt to equity	-347%	-989%	37%	725%	51%

Source: Lotus OneSource.

PacTel Cellular. PacTel was a subsidiary of Pacific Telesis Group, one of the regional Bell operating companies. In 1990, PacTel was the third largest cellular operator in the United States (measured in POPs), and was estimated to have a 10 percent national subscriber share. Revenues rose 40 percent between 1988 and 1989 to $453 million. Analysts estimated PacTel return on investment at 40 percent.

PacTel was leading a trend toward consolidation and regionalization. It made an agreement with Cellular Communications Incorporated (CCI) to merge the companies' Ohio and Michigan holdings to improve customer support and regional marketing power. The agreement enabled PacTel to buy CCI after five years, which would give PacTel 15 million POPs and a 27,000-square-mile territory in that region. One observer explained, "What we're seeing is basically telephone companies reclaiming an aspect of the industry which had temporarily been claimed by nontelephone interlopers."[4]

Although PacTel's president first urged the Cellular Telephone Industry Association in 1989 to adopt TDMA as an industry standard, PacTel (working with Qualcomm) completed the first successful test of CDMA less than a year later. Following this test, PacTel announced that CDMA was far superior to TDMA, and had potential benefits too great to ignore. Faced with a dire need to increase capacity in its Los Angeles market by late 1991 or early 1992, PacTel announced it would use CDMA switches.

Some observers said PacTel's choice would compel the industry to follow; others said PacTel might lose its leadership in the L.A. market by risking incompatibility with adjacent TDMA systems that might be installed. PacTel's director of advanced technology asserted, "We will stay compatible with the industry, but if we go with CDMA first and the industry goes with TDMA, we would implement both systems in Los Angeles."[5]

In Los Angeles, PacTel's rival was L.A. Cellular, jointly owned by McCaw and BellSouth Corporation. Since L.A. Cellular had taken over the Los Angeles license in 1987, PacTel's market share had fallen from 69 percent to 57 percent. Analysts noted that L.A. Cellular had higher quality ratings than PacTel in nine of twelve quarters. The number of Los Angeles subscribers was growing in both companies.

Nynex Mobile Communications Company Incorporated. Nynex Mobile was a subsidiary of Nynex Corporation and had begun cellular service operation in New York City in early 1984. By 1990, the company had become the fifth largest cellular operator in the United States (measured in POPs) with sales of $200 million. Unlike the other big cellular operators, Nynex had not pursued expansion through acquisition. Instead it had concentrated on expanding usage in its own regions, particularly the New York to Boston region. According to Charles Many, Nynex Mobile's president, "Our fundamental philosophy is to get the

---

4. Herschel Shosteck quoted in *Telephone Engineer & Management*, September 1, 1990, p. 28.
5. *Mobile Phone News*, "Qualcomm, PacTel Complete First CDMA Mobil Call," November 23, 1989.

basic business running and then build off the core. We prefer to stay in the Northeast because we can really make that system hum and make it profitable."[6]

By the end of 1991, Nynex planned to have the first operational CDMA. personal telephone system (PTS) for pedestrians, with 200 microcells covering Manhattan Island. The system would use AT&T equipment and Qualcomm digital phones (both in prototype phase in 1990) and would cost $100 million. Unlike personal communication networks, which required the FCC to reallocate space in the radio frequency, the PTS would use 5 Mhz of Nynex's existing spectrum. Service options would include two-way calling, outgoing calling only, or outgoing calling plus paging service.

Nynex had not decided which digital standard it would support for its cellular phone service. A spokesperson explained: "That is a political decision. We have to consider the rest of the industry as far as roaming is concerned."[7] Nynex had applied to test CDMA and TDMA in areas of New York City, Boston, and White Plains, New York, with equipment from AT&T and Qualcomm.

Ameritech Mobile Communications. One week after the FCC began licensing cellular operators in October 1983, American Information Technologies turned on the United States' first available cellular phone service in Chicago. Later that year, Ameritech Cellular Communications was incorporated. By 1990, it had become the sixth largest cellular operator by acquiring licenses throughout the United States.

In 1990 Ameritech Mobile decided to allocate spectrum for the testing of both CDMA and TDMA mobile transmission, using AT&T and Qualcomm equipment and telephones. By the end of 1991 or early 1992, Ameritech Mobile hoped to introduce a telephone that would transmit over traditional analog channels as well as CDMA. These phones were expected to be priced at a 20 percent premium over all-analog or all-digital phones. The company also planned to continue to support TDMA technology.

Another large-scale project at Ameritech Mobile was the two-year test of a microwave personal communication system (PCS). The test, to be held in Chicago, was scheduled to try out three versions of PCS service: the first version would allow the subscriber to make outgoing calls near any public base station; the second version would include a pager signifying incoming calls; the third version would allow two-way calling, with roaming capability. Ultimately, Ameritech wanted subscribers to be able to change services without owning multiple phones and pagers, and without paying for all three services when only one was being used.

Metro Mobile CTS, Inc. Metro Mobile was a nonwireline cellular service company founded in 1980 by George Lindemann. By 1990, the company owned

6. Maribeth Harper, "Will the RHCs Devour the Cellular Industry?" *Telephony*, July 11, 1988.
7. *Industrial Communications*, August 10, 1990.

and operated cellular telephone systems in seventeen markets located in three regional clusters: Massachusetts/Connecticut/Rhode Island, the Carolinas, and Arizona/New Mexico. It had approximately 140,000 subscribers as of September 1990.

Metro Mobile explained its "three interrelated strategies" as (1) obtaining cellular interests in areas with favorable demographics or population growth indicating substantial potential for cellular phone use; (2) clustering cellular systems in proximate areas for economies of scale and efficient operation and marketing; and (3) controlling (rather than having a minority interest in) all of its systems. Metro Mobile was one of the first companies to institute the concept of "calling party pays" so that the person placing a call to a cellular phone paid rather than the owner of the cellular phone. It used this billing system in parts of its Southwest region, and was discussing implementation in other areas with the local land line telephone companies.

Metro Mobile had no announced plans to expand its capacity with digital technology. Management had indicated that the company was not a going concern for the long term and would consider purchase offers. No transaction was imminent in late 1990.

Fleet Call. Fleet Call was a taxi dispatch service with $30 million in revenue in 1989. In 1990, Fleet Call applied to the FCC for permission to upgrade its taxi dispatch service to include cellular phone service, by dividing its service areas into cells and installing new digital transmission equipment. Cellular service companies described Fleet Call's effort as an attempt to create a third cellular system in the markets it would serve. Fleet Call was seen as a viable alternative for cellular customers who did not need the roaming capability of cellular service.

Fleet Call was founded in 1987 by a former FCC staff lawyer and a former executive of a cellular and paging company. In the ensuing three years, the company spent about $250 million acquiring, 1,600 dispatch channels in New York, Los Angeles, Chicago, San Francisco, Dallas, and Houston. It paid an average of about $5 per megahertz, compared to $166 per megahertz that McCaw had recently paid for a part interest in a Los Angeles cellular system.[8] Fleet Call's president explained that the company already completed mobile calls for some customers at a charge which amounted to $15 for seventy-five minutes, compared to a $100 charge for the same length call on a cellular service. If the FCC approved the application as Fleet Call expected, the firm planned to spend $500 million to construct its system, which would be fully operational by 1995.

Many analysts expected FCC approval for Fleet Call's plans. They argued that regulators were unlikely to object to a third party that would compete on price and lower industry rates. However, several large cellular service compa-

8. There were no dollars per POP comparisons because Fleet Call was buying access to the radio spectrum while cellular companies were buying access to the radio spectrum and a license to provide cellular service in a specified region.

nies were lobbying against Fleet Call. For example, McCaw hired a former FCC chairman as its lawyer to work against the rule change.

McCaw Cellular Communications, Inc.

Craig O. McCaw began his communications career in high school, selling subscriptions for his family's fledgling cable television company. When his father died in 1969, the family business was deep in debt. In 1973, Craig McCaw graduated from Stanford with a degree in history and joined the family business, McCaw Communications, a cable system in Centralia, Washington. In 1978, at the age of twenty-eight, he became the head of the company.

In 1983, when the FCC began issuing licenses for cellular phone operations, McCaw budgeted $3.5 million to enter the business. Shortly thereafter, McCaw began buying franchises for top dollar (then about $5 per POP) in what one competitor described as a "piranha frenzy" of acquisitions. At the same time, McCaw expanded into the paging business. In 1986 McCaw paid $122 million for the cellular and radio paging operations of MCI. McCaw sold the paging business for $75 million and kept the 7 million cellular POPs, which effectively cost just over $6 per POP.

By 1987, McCaw had rights to build cellular systems serving ninety-four markets. To raise cash, the cable television operations were sold for $755 million, and 11 percent of McCaw Cellular Communications was sold to the public. McCaw then put up the cash and junk bond financing for additional cellular operating rights from coast to coast By 1988, McCaw owned more U.S. cellular phone franchises than any other group. McCaw had about 35 million POPs, with 38 percent of them in the thirty biggest markets.

In December 1989, the company won a tough bidding battle with BellSouth Corporation for the acquisition of a majority of LIN Broadcasting company. The LIN acquisition gave McCaw control of an additional 25 million POPs, including controlling interests in licenses in Los Angeles, New York, Philadelphia, Dallas, and Houston, which McCaw referred to as "gateway" cities. For these markets, McCaw paid about $3.4 billion. Analysts calculated a price of $350 per POP. As part of the LIN deal, McCaw had committed itself to buy the remaining LIN shares at "private market value" (the price paid by a buyer seeking control of a company) or to sell its 52 percent stake within five years.

LIN had $226 million in revenues in 1989; over $100 million of its revenues came from its TV stations and publishing operations. Its cellular division was reported to have 50 percent operating profit margins, in spite of a reputation for poor service in its New York City network. McCaw acknowledged that the LIN acquisition could result in losses exceeding $1 billion during the next several years. But, he said to an interviewer, "The key to having dreams is to make sure they come true. Waking up in a cold sweat is not what you want. . . . Debt is clearly not a challenge we want today."[9]

9. *New York Times*, May 6, 1990.

Craig McCaw has been referred to as a "strategic visionary." He explained, "We are certainly aware of changing times. You make decisions on long-term planning, not on short-term changes in the environment."[10] Managers who had worked for him for years said, "He thinks so far down the road that his ideas are out of context for the rest of us."[11] Under his guidance, the company's assets had grown from $27 million in 1980 to $4.6 billion in 1990. In 1989, McCaw, who owned 9.8 percent of the company, earned almost $54 million, including a salary and bonus of $289,000 plus $53.6 million from the exercise of stock options on 1.5 million shares awarded to him in 1983 and 1986.

Marketing

McCaw stated that it aimed to sell high-quality cellular phone service, including add-ons such as voice mail and call waiting, at a premium price. To boost the number of calls on the network, the company also planned to sell information services (which the regional Bell companies were prohibited from selling). Services under consideration included stock quotes and local weather and traffic reports.

Craig McCaw was known as a meticulous manager with a fetish for quality. Industry observers said it was not unusual for McCaw to fly his own Lear jet into a city, rent a car, and test the local cellular system. After one such test (in 1987) he decided that McCaw's marketing was too aggressive, because the company's billing, accounting, and transmission systems were not growing as fast as the subscriber base. Credit policies were tightened, commissions were slashed, advertising was cut, rates were raised, and a number of new managers were hired. As a result of disagreements about these decisions, the executive vice president, western operations vice president, and head of national accounts left the company.

McCaw had a 750-person direct sales force targeting national accounts. The company expected national accounts to contribute more than a third of revenues within ten years. In 1990, major national accounts included IBM with more than 1,000 cellular phones (mostly for sales people) and Consolidated Freightways with 800 phones. McCaw also had a partnership with AT&T to provide national cellular service as part of AT&T's multibillion-dollar contract to rebuild the federal government's telecommunications network. In 1990, 12 percent of McCaw's sales were to companies with more than 1,000 employees, up from 2 percent in 1988.

Transmission Systems

McCaw sought to develop regional clusters of cellular operations, each built around a core metropolitan area. In Florida, McCaw served the contiguous Miami, West Palm Beach, and Fort Pierce markets; in Colorado, it served the

10. *New York Times*, May 6, 1990.
11. Brian J. McCauley, former V.P., quoted in *Business Week*, December 5, 1988, p. 140.

contiguous markets of Denver, Colorado Springs, Fort Collins, Greeley, and Pueblo; in the Pacific Northwest, McCaw served Seattle, Tacoma, and Portland.

One observer claimed McCaw had efficient systems in the Northwest, Florida, and Northern California, based on the activity level of McCaw engineers and the absence of overcapacity problems. The LIN systems were large enough to cover their marketing and use regions, but observers were not sure if these systems were efficient. In other areas McCaw's holdings were dispersed. John E. DeFeo, president of rival U.S. West New Vector Group, explained, "this business is about local traveling areas, and McCaw is spread out all over God's green earth." [12] In 1990, including the LIN systems, 65 percent of McCaw's POPs were in the thirty biggest markets.

Craig McCaw said, "automatic, effortless call delivery anywhere in North America has long been among our most important strategic objectives." [13] To do this, McCaw needed compatible switches throughout the continent. The company pursued control of licenses in many major metropolitan areas throughout the United States, and sought to convince many rural service providers to join the Cellular One network, of which McCaw was a part. To induce rural operators to join, McCaw offered marketing and technical support, and in some cases financial support (or equity investment). In return, McCaw hoped to receive a fee on calls made on those systems, after it helped them to purchase compatible switches.

In 1990 the LIN system in the Northeast used Motorola switches, the Pacific Northwest system used AT&T switches, a joint venture of Ericsson and General Electric supplied McCaw's California and Florida systems, and still other switches were supplied by Northern Telecom Ltd. McCaw estimated that replacing the switches in the company's major markets with new switches would cost about $250 million over a period of five years. This cost would not include modernizing the systems in the central United States; these systems would need to have upgraded software to enable them to communicate with the new switches in other parts of the system. Some industry analysts estimated that capital expenditures would cost closer to $800 million over the next several years.

Extensions of Cellular Service

McCaw applied for FCC authorization in 1990 to test new wireless technologies in Orlando, Florida, and Seattle, Washington. The planned tests included two types of cordless telephone equipment for communications in offices, shopping malls, or other localized areas. McCaw said it would work with vendors to develop prototype equipment that would enable customers to use a single handset to make or receive calls employing one or more technologies, with the goal of potentially linking these localized systems to McCaw's network.

12. *Business Week*, December 5, 1988, p. 151.
13. Quoted by John J. Keller in the *Wall Street Journal*, October 4, 1990, p. B1.

Exhibit 5 McCaw Cellular Communications, Inc. income statement ($ thousands) and financial ratios.

	1989	1988	1987	1986	1985	1984
Income Statement						
Net sales	504,138	310,826	196,420	68,665	7,372	297
Cost of goods	169,290	130,967	111,815	31,818	7,657	254
Gross profit	334,848	179,859	84,605	36,847	−285	43
SG&A	282,709	186,844	145,406	44,525	7,784	229
Income before depreciation	52,139	−6,985	−60,801	−7,678	−8,069	−186
Depreciation and amortization	202,876	156,358	80,804	16,912	749	4
Non-operating income	101,709	53,054	108,874	12,385	−479	241
Interest expense	238,740	199,137	108,055	29,566	3,582	N/A
Income before tax	−287,768	−309,426	−140,786	−41,771	−12,879	51
Provision for income tax	760	−12,431	−52,081	N/A	N/A	N/A
Net income before extraordinary items	−288,528	−296,995	−88,705	−41,771	−32,879	51
Extraordinary items	N/A	N/A	138,383	N/A	N/A	N/A
Net income	−288,528	−296,995	49,678	−41,771	−12,879	51
Financial Ratios						
LT debt to equity	1.75	−164.6	3.55	−8.90	11.16	N/A
Total assets to equity	3.03	−186.6	5.30	−9.91	36.63	N/A
Interest coverage	−0.21	−0.55	−0.30	−0.41	−2.6	N/A
Gross margin %	66.40	57.9	43.1	53.7	−3.9	14.5
Return on sales %	−57.20	−95.6	25.3	−60.8	−174.0	17.2
Return on equity %	−28.70	N/A	16.8	N/A	−525.0	N/A
Return on assets %	−9.50	−14.3	3.2	−6.6	−14.3	N/A

Exhibit 6 McCaw Cellular Communications, Inc. balance sheet ($ thousands).

	1989	1988[a]	1987	1986[a]	1985
Assets					
Cash and marketable securities	897,653	505,917	424,867	42,663	1,625
Other current assets	98,020	55,067	260,010	142,814	4,541
Total current assets	995,673	560,984	684,877	185,477	6,166
Net property plant and equipment	630,264	491,851	292,902	121,765	22,497
Investment and advance payments	358,326	73,344	84,980	35,663	21,297
Intangibles	928,603	920,814	491,682	208,850	37,935
Other noncurrent assets	128,478	28,760	14,228	79,950	1,914
Total assets	3,041,344	2,075,753	1,568,669	631,705	89,809
Liabilities					
Total current liabilities	222,256	193,571	154,353	215,810	59,480
Long-term debt	1,738,896	1,821,663	1,032,760	402,781	27,351
Other long-term liabilities	47,780	32,641	26,000	12,750	N/A
Total liabilities	2,008,632	2,047,875	1,213,113	631,341	86,831
Minority interest	28,743	38,998	59,724	64,123	526
Shareholder's equity	1,003,969	−11,120	295,832	−63,759	2,452
Total liabilities and shareholder's equity	3,041,344	2,075,753	1,568,669	631,705	89,809

a. Restated as required by SEC

Exhibit 7 Projected financial results for McCaw Cellular Communications, Inc. pro forma 1990–2000 ($ thousands).

	1990	1991	1992	1993	1994	1995
Total revenues	555,498	771,972	1,013,874	1,279,156	1,563,293	1,860,108
Net income	(469,783)	(462,307)	(346,731)	(137,365)	66,839	299,373
Available funds	(1,872,972)	(187,909)	(126,705)	23,636	259,930	544,969

	1996	1997	1998	1999	2000
Total revenues	2,164,125	2,470,530	2,775,138	3,074,356	33,366,985
Net income	582,373	569,967	759,766	912,835	1,091,012
Available funds	889,065	915,027	1,121,641	1,290,793	1,482,265

Source: Donaldson, Lufkin & Jenrette, Inc.

Notes: 1. Pro forma performance results are for McCaw Communications on a stand-alone basis. 2. Effects of the LIN acquisition are not shown here. 3. Ceilings for the LIN and warrants purchase obligations are $5 billion in 1995 and $81 million in 1997, repectively.

Also in 1990, McCaw formed a partnership with Hughes Network Systems to construct and operate in-flight cellular phone and data services on commercial airlines. Unlike GTE Airfone, customers would be able to receive calls as well as make them. Alaskan and Northwest Airlines had agreed to carry the service, and agreements with other airlines were under negotiation.

Finance

In 1981, McCaw formed a partnership with the cash-rich publisher of the *Boston Globe,* Affiliated Publications Inc. At the time, McCaw was anxious to expand its cable business, and Affiliated's chairman wanted to diversify into more venturesome businesses. During the 1980s, Affiliated invested almost $1 billion in McCaw, of which it owned 43 percent. While Affiliated had several seats on the board, it did not try to set directions for McCaw. "One of the keys to his success has been our willingness to let him run the show," an Affiliated executive explained.[14] Affiliated's strong balance sheet provided credibility for McCaw with bankers and institutional investors. Affiliated spun off its McCaw holdings to its shareholders in May 1989.

In 1987, McCaw sold its cable business for $755 million to help fund its cellular system acquisitions. The same year, Drexel, Burnham Lambert Inc. helped take McCaw public, offering 13,050,000 Class A common shares (12 percent of outstanding shares) for $21.75 each. The same year, McCaw raised $600 million with triple C-rated bonds. McCaw's monthly closing stock price moved from $16.13 in December 1987 to a high of $43.75 in May 1989. It then dropped to $11.50 by October 1990 and closed the year at $17.25. In 1990, Craig McCaw and his three brothers owned 32 percent of the company (and 88 percent of the voting stock).

As McCaw moved into the 1990s, it faced considerable financial uncertainty. Stock analysts were unwilling to make explicit projections of sources and uses of funds due to the high level of uncertainty surrounding McCaw Communications and the cellular communications industry. Exhibits 5 and 6 give income statements and balance sheets for McCaw for recent years. Exhibit 7 gives projections of revenues, net income, and funding needs from 1900 to 2000.

On the sources side, McCaw had a number of alternatives. The company had a $1.6 billion line of credit, and further bank financing was a possibility. McCaw could elect to sell assets. In 1990, for example, the company raised $1.2 billion on a gain from sale of 6.1 million POPs in Tennessee, Kentucky, and Alabama to Contel Cellular. McCaw could also raise funds through a public offering or private placement. It had raised $1.37 billion in 1990 from the sale of 20 percent of the company to British Telecommunications PLC, which was limited by law to owning not more than 20 percent of any U.S. cellular carrier.

On the uses side, McCaw was committed to acquiring all outstanding LIN stock by 1995 or selling its stake in LIN; one balloon payment in 1995 was

14. Arthur Kingsbury, quoted in the *Wall Street Journal,* July 31, 1987, p. 6.

expected to cost McCaw $5 billion, but the company could begin acquiring additional stock before 1995. Between 1991 and 1997, McCaw also had to either exercise or repurchase warrants it had issued for one of its previous acquisitions. This obligation could cost up to $81 million. McCaw also had debt service projected to total $2.4 billion between 1990 and 1995. In addition, McCaw faced the uncertain expenses of updating its switches and creating a compatible national network.

Monsanto Company: The Queeny Division

"Well, all hell broke loose this morning. What do I have to do this afternoon to pull my group together and get some agreement?" Chris Hubbard asked himself. As General Manager of Monsanto's "Queeny Division" [a fictitious designation], Hubbard had spent the best part of the last day and a half with his immediate subordinates trying to get consensus on next year's operating budget. After a rough morning, he had used lunch as an opportunity to get away and plan how he could resolve the issues that were blocking progress.

In the past, budgeting had been straightforward: The previous year's budget was adjusted according to the changes that Hubbard and his department managers agreed would be necessary. This year, however, the Queeny Division had been asked to employ a new budgeting process, Priority Resources Budgeting (PRB), as part of Monsanto's effort to improve the management of overhead costs. The new process had proved to be far more time-consuming and complicated than the old.

During the past several months, Hubbard's department managers had worked with their subordinates to identify explicitly the tasks for which they were responsible and to attach specific estimates of benefits and costs to each task or activity. Each manager had then met with his key subordinates to rank the tasks ("increments," in PRB terms) from highest priority to lowest. The primary goal of this effort was to give priority to overhead activities that supported the unit's tactical and strategic business plans. A second important goal was to control the level of overhead expenditures.

Based on meetings with each of his department managers to discuss their rankings, Hubbard believed that the process was achieving these two goals. PRB had required reams of paper and a substantial commitment of time, but until today, notwithstanding a certain amount of grumbling and confusion, the effort appeared to have gone smoothly.

Hubbard was now in the middle of his divisional ranking meeting. The goals of the meeting were the same as at the department level, but the task was more complex. While ranking increments within departments had often required that difficult decisions be made, the commonalities among the functional activities facilitated choices and trade-offs. Trying to decide whether the next $300,000 should be spent on sales or R&D was altogether different. This interfunctional ranking seemed to Hubbard to produce an atmosphere of competition. Managers behaved as if they were in a zero-sum game, and Hubbard was worried that the conflict would undermine his efforts over the past two years to develop a spirit of teamwork in his group.

"I've never seen John Coulson so angry," he reflected, "and his commodities group produced three-quarters of last year's cash flow. And sales really has me stumped. What is the right level of support for that function? I guess we are wrestling with some issues we should have confronted before, so things aren't all bad. But I'm sure of one thing—if we can't pull together on this budget, it's going to be a tough year."

Monsanto Company

Monsanto's headquarters were located in a campuslike setting on the outskirts of St. Louis, Missouri, not far from where John F. Queeny founded the company in 1901 to manufacture saccharin. In 1978, Monsanto's sales of $5 billion were fourth largest in the U.S. chemical industry. Net income before taxes was $576 million. Over 62,000 employees staffed its 175 plants and 135 offices around the world. Exhibit 1 shows recent financial results.

Monsanto's widely diversified line of chemical products included agricultural chemicals (herbicides, pesticides, etc.); chemical intermediates (petrochemicals, process chemicals, etc.); industrial chemicals (detergents and phosphates, rubber chemicals, plasticizers, etc.); plastics and resins; textiles (manmade fibers); and industrial process controls. To a large extent, Monsanto sold its products to other industries rather than to end users. A major exception was agricultural chemicals.

Exhibit 1   Financial results ($ million).

	1978	1977	1976	1975	1974	1972	1969
Sales	5,019	4,595	4,270	3,625	3,498	2,225	1,939
Operating income	632	610	668	547	550	216	191
Net income	303	276	366	306	323	122	116
Total assets	5,036	4,350	3,959	3,451	2,938	2,237	2,012
Long-term debt	1,224	1,031	915	845	587	576	454
Shareowners' equity	2,579	2,401	2,253	1,977	1,755	1,294	1,205
Net income as a percentage of							
Net sales	6.0%	6.0%	8.6%	8.4%	9.2%	5.5%	6.0%
Average shareowners' equity	12.2%	11.9%	17.3%	16.4%	20.0%	9.7%	9.8%
Average total assets	6.4%	6.6%	9.9%	9.6%	11.8%	5.6%	5.0%

Sources: Monsanto Company 1978 annual report; and Monsanto Company 1978 corporate data book.

The Management Style

In 1972 John M. Hanley joined Monsanto as president. Aged fifty, Hanley had spent his entire career at Procter and Gamble, and his arrival from the outside broke with a long-standing Monsanto tradition to grow its own leaders. His arrival signaled a new approach to management and, especially, an increased emphasis on marketing.

From the start, Hanley saw a need to develop a new administrative structure with which to formulate and implement changes. By 1974, such a structure began to emerge, and with it a distinctive management style. Later Hanley was to write: "The Monsanto Management Style is the process by which we define what we want to accomplish and the framework in which we pursue our Corporate Objectives."

The process by which the Management Style was implemented is shown in Exhibit 2. Top management set corporate objectives and policies. Given these statements, Monsanto's senior operating managers produced explicit statements of strategy ("Direction Papers"). Operating companies and similar units then produced "Summary Long-Range Plans," followed by more detailed statements of strategies and tactics, called "Operational Plans." Next, individual managers identified the results they must achieve (the "Management by Results" program) to support the Operational Plans. The budgeting process was then supposed to develop explicit statements of organizational goals and resource commitments for a one-year period.

In the late 1970s, Hanley and other senior managers became increasingly concerned with the weakness of the link between business strategies and the budgets for Marketing, Administration, and Technology (MAT) expenses and for Factory Indirect Expense (FIE). Specifically, Hanley said:

> As we continue to extend the entire planning process, it is important for Monsanto to ensure that its total MAT expenses are both optimally allocated to support the various business strategies of the company and held to a level consistent with the planned overall financial results of the corporation.[1]

After investigating a variety of budgeting systems, it was decided that zero-based budgeting (ZBB) offered the most potential. In 1978, Priority Resource Budgeting (PRB),[2] a form of ZBB modified to fit Monsanto's particular needs, was tested in several Monsanto units. PRB was introduced throughout two Monsanto Companies in 1979, including the Monsanto Commodity Chemicals Company.[3]

---

1. In 1978, MAT expenses for Monsanto totaled $643 million. This amount represented almost 14.7 percent of total operating costs for the year.
2. See the Appendix for a description of the Priority Resource Budgeting (PRB) system.
3. The Monsanto Company was organized into major business units, each of which was also called a company. Exhibit 3 shows the corporate organizational structure. The Monsanto Commodity Chemical Company is a fictitious unit.

Exhibit 2 Schematic of Monsanto's management style.

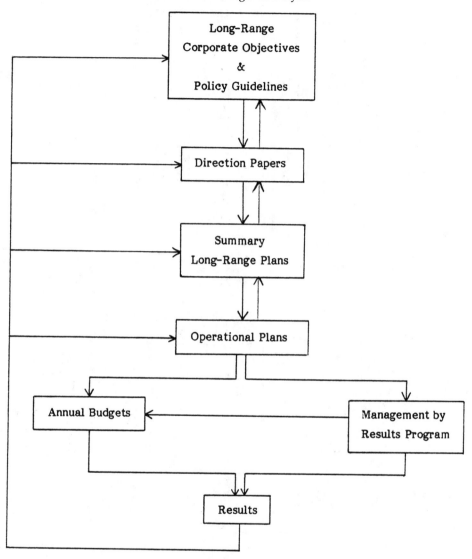

The Queeny Division

The Queeny Division was one of three operating divisions that made up the Monsanto Commodity Chemicals Company. (See Exhibit 4 for an organization chart). For most of its history, the Queeny Division's product line had been dominated by six successful commodity chemicals for the food-processing and related industries. Management of these products had been divided between two departments, each of which had responsibility for three of the major com-

Exhibit 3 Corporate organization structure, 1978.

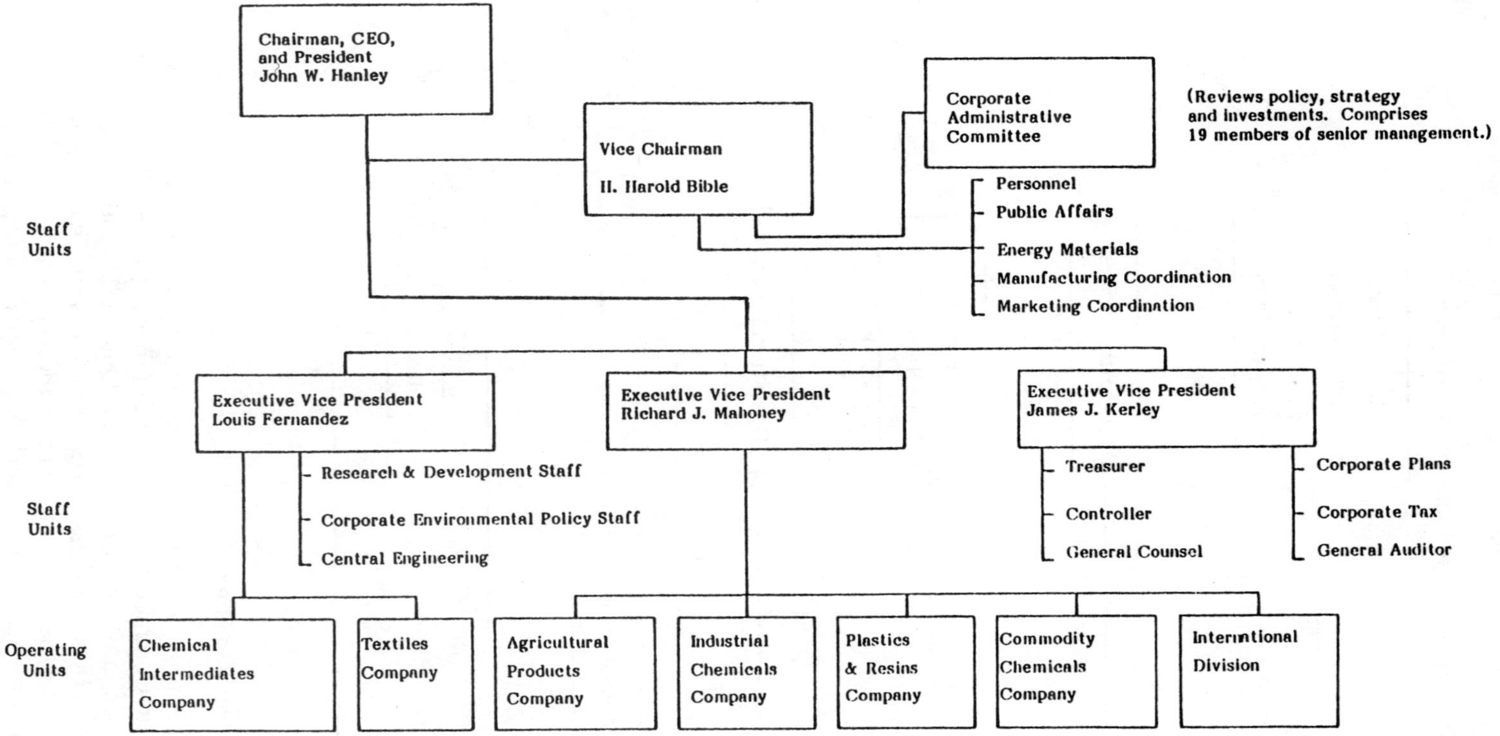

Staff Units

Staff Units

Operating Units

Chairman, CEO, and President John W. Hanley

Vice Chairman H. Harold Bible

Corporate Administrative Committee

Personnel
Public Affairs
Energy Materials
Manufacturing Coordination
Marketing Coordination

(Reviews policy, strategy and investments. Comprises 19 members of senior management.)

Executive Vice President Louis Fernandez

Research & Development Staff
Corporate Environmental Policy Staff
Central Engineering

Executive Vice President Richard J. Mahoney

Executive Vice President James J. Kerley

Treasurer
Controller
(General Counsel

Corporate Plans
Corporate Tax
General Auditor

Chemical Intermediates Company

Textiles Company

Agricultural Products Company

Industrial Chemicals Company

Plastics & Resins Company

Commodity Chemicals Company

International Division

592

Exhibit 4   Monsanto Commodity Chemical Company organization structure.

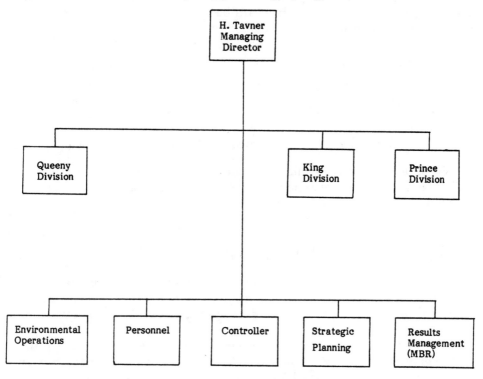

modity items as well as a number of minor related commodity and consumer products. In 1970, Chris Hubbard and Norm Brewster were the department heads of these units.

Market analysis during the early 1970s had shown that four of the six commodity products were in the "mature" stage of their product life cycle and the other two were in "late growth." While the 1972 profit picture was quite good, Queeny management confronted the prospect of little, if any, further growth from its major products.

George Rinder, then the General Manager of Queeny, had responded by increasing the division's support of several of its newer products and by stepping up new product-development efforts. One of his first moves was to place the promising oil additive chemical products into a newly created department. Norm Brewster, who had championed this relatively new line, left his department to head up the new unit. In 1975, Rinder decided to separate the faster growing consumer chemicals from the slower growing commodity chemicals. As a result of the reorganization, Chris Hubbard's department was given responsibility for all commodity chemicals, and Fred Ellis (who stepped in when Brewster moved to oil additives) was given responsibility for all consumer chemicals.

In May 1977, Rinder was promoted to Managing Director of the Commodity Chemicals Company.[4] In turn, Hubbard became General Manager of Queeny, and Coulson took charge of the Commodity Chemicals Department.

In 1979 Queeny's performance was projected to be as follows (dollars in millions):

Department	Sales	Net pretax income	Growth rate
Commodity Chemicals	$600	$90	Slow
Consumer Chemicals	$ 80	$ 9	Rapid
Oil Additive Chemicals	$220	$60	Medium

The structure of the organization managed by Hubbard in 1979 was essentially identical to that which he took over in 1977. (Exhibit 5 contains an organization chart for the Queeny Division.)

The Queeny Division Ranking

"In an hour we begin again," thought Hubbard. "I'd better figure out how to make sense from the confusion we generated this morning. When this is all over, I'm going to have to spend a quiet weekend sorting out all I've seen of PRB."

"The seeds for what has been happening in this ranking meeting were planted in the one-on-one review sessions I held with each of my manager's over a week ago," Hubbard reflected.[5] "Joe Roboh's was the easiest and most informative session. As soon as he knew I was committed to doing some basic research, he loosened up. I like the result of his R&D ranking meeting in that they fit our strategy. But I could see some potential problems coming from the big shift in research effort from Commodity Chemicals to Consumer Chemicals. I expected a backlash on that from John Coulson, and we sure got it."

"John is doing a good job with Commodity Chemicals, and his PRB analysis showed it. Still, I don't think he's fully taken to heart that he is in a mature market. He thinks he can grow and resents all the attention Fred Ellis is getting with Consumer. Competent but defensive is the way I'd characterize his behavior in our one-on-one meeting. He knew he wasn't going to get as much R&D as he wanted."

"Leo Nicholson was disappointing. His analysis was not so hot. He said his salesmen were all busy selling, and there was no time to fill out the forms.

---

4. Rinder was seriously injured several months later as a result of an accident and elected to retire early from Monsanto. He was replaced by Henry Tavner, General Manager of the King Division.
5. The "one-on-one" review meetings were held between a ranking manager and each of his decision unit managers prior to the ranking meeting. According to the Monsanto Company Priority Resource Budgeting Manual (1978): "This meeting is *not* a decision-making meeting but rather an informational meeting." Exhibit 6 contains background information on each of the key managers in the Queeny Division.

Exhibit 5   Queeny division organization structure.

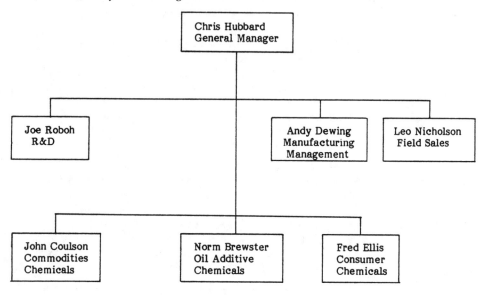

I must admit, though, I have a tough time defining a sales increment myself."

"The other men were about as I expected. Fred Ellis was well prepared and aggressive. He intends to grow, and he can make a good case for it with Consumer. Norm Brewster was confident and protective. Too confident, maybe; Oil Additives has been so successful that they may only have looked at where they needed *more* resources. I'm not sure they checked to see which areas are fat, and some are, for sure. Andy Dewing, on the other hand, was a little discouraged. He didn't see that PRB made any sense for manufacturing, and I think he still feels that way.

"When I think back on it, every one of those guys gave me signals about what was likely to happen during this Division ranking meeting. At least next year I'll try to make better use of that information."

The Division Ranking Meeting: First Day

Hubbard's thoughts turned to the ranking meeting. Yesterday morning the ranking had seemed mechanical, easy—almost trivial. The thresholds reviewed in the one-on-one meetings were accepted without debate, except that Nicholson hadn't studied all the other guys' work and that slowed things down a bit. Andy got a laugh when he said, "Hell, Leo, you're in the big leagues now. You've got to read this stuff *before* you come to meetings."

Ranking the items just after the threshold was no real problem, although during the later afternoon there were a few disagreements. As could be antic-

Exhibit 6 Biographies of participants at Queeny's PRB ranking meeting.

Chris Hubbard, age 41, had worked at Monsanto for 18 years. His first job had been as field salesman, but he was soon transferred into a product department where he worked for George Rinder. He became a department head when Rinder moved up to the Division General Manager's post. In 1977 he replaced Rinder as General Manager of Queeny. Hubbard was an intelligent, reasonable man with a low key management style. He had worked hard to build team spirit among his managers.

Joe Roboh, age 45, had been at Monsanto for over 20 years, the entire time in R&D. His staff now numbered over 60 and along with most of them he shared an enthusiasm for basic research. He believed that most of Monsanto's R&D dollars had to be spent on immediately commercializable research, but as he told his people: "We do the commercial stuff because it pays the bills, but it's basic research that keeps us intellectually alive and secures the future of this company!"

Andy Dewing, age 57, had spent his career in manufacturing at Monsanto. Seven plant managers, and through them several thousand people, reported to him. Only his divisional headquarters staff was being ranked at this meeting; all the others would be ranked within their own plants. Dewing was widely respected as a hard-nosed guy who got things done.

Fred Ellis, age 35, had joined Monsanto in manufacturing in 1967. Four years later he moved to field sales, then to the marketing staff. He became a product department head in 1973. Ellis believed strongly that Queeny's growth would have to come from Consumer Products.

Norm Brewster, age 39, had joined Monsanto in the early sixties as an engineer. After three years in a plant, he had taken a leave of absence to go to a well-known midwestern business school. On his return he had progressed rapidly and was one of the two product department heads when Rinder became Queeny's General Manager. When Rinder created the Oil Additive Chemicals Department, he put Brewster in charge of it.

John Coulson, age 37, had been at Monsanto for thirteen years. When Hubbard was promoted to General Manager, Coulson took over the Commodity Chemicals Department. He was ambitious for his area and hoped that he could appeal for support to Hubbard. He had a somewhat excitable personality but was well liked and respected by his subordinates.

> *Leo Nicholson,*   age 35, was new to his job as Manager of Queeny's field sales. Only two months before he had headed up the Central Region Sales Office, where he had worked for almost thirteen years. He had made his reputation as a salesman, and his skills as an administrator were not yet fully tested.
>
> *Jack Eckert,*   age 29, was a first-level manager in Monsanto Chemical Commodities Company's Controllers Department. This was his first time as a PRB analyst, and he was unsure what to think of it. On the one hand he wanted the exposure; on the other hand he was frightened of making mistakes or antagonizing anyone.

ipated, most differences of opinion centered on the question of relative priorities of untried growth products versus proven and profitable mature products. Agreement was reached amicably in each case. Exhibit 7 contains the final page of the Queeny Division's PRB ranking table as it appeared at the end of the first day. It shows that eighty-two increments had been ranked with cumulative expenses at 88 percent of the current level and headcount at 85 percent of the current level.

When the meeting broke up at around four in the afternoon, Hubbard was confident that, while the next day would bring some difficult issues, the group would continue to work well together to resolve them. "In retrospect," he mused, "I can see why those disagreements yesterday afternoon were so easily resolved. We were still well below what everyone figured to be the minimum funding level."

The Division Ranking Meeting: Second Day

Trouble had started early in the morning. Hubbard remembered one exchange almost word for word. John Coulson, defending his interest, had thrown up his hand like a traffic cop to confront Joe Roboh on the ranking of the R&D increments.

"Wait a minute Joe, your next four increments all involve basic research aimed at Consumer products."[6]

"Well, that's where the future is, John."

"But we're in the present and won't ever reach the future unless we pay our bills," Coulson said adamantly. "There's no support for my stuff!"

"Calm down. If we want to get to the future, we have to start now. Besides,

6. Exhibit 8 shows the R&D ranking table.

Exhibit 7 Queeny division ranking table after the first day of the ranking meeting.

PRIORITY RESOURCE BUDGETING RANKING TABLE

Ranking level: Queeny Division

Rank	Increment Number	Decision Unit Name	Incremental		Cumulative		1979		% of 1979		Notes
			Expense($K)	Headcount	Expense ($K)	Headcount	Expense ($K)	Headcount	Expense	Headcount	
77	2 of 4	Manufacturing mngt	98	2	9,793	95			82	77	Better liaison with plants. Faster A.R. analysis.
78	1 of 1	A2-42 Cost reduction (R&D)	385	3.5	10,178	98.5			82	80	Attempt 2¢/1b cost reduction
79	5 of 10	East region (field sales)	85	1.5	10,263	100			86	81	Open office in No. Carolina (includes p/t secy.)
80	2 of 5	R&D mngt	49	1	10,312	101			86	82	Assistant to the Director
81	2 of 4	Consumer products	150	2	10,462	103			87	84	Develop new markets for A2 products
82	3 of 4	Consumer products	112	1	10,574	104			88	85	Full development of all identified market areas. Advertising research.

(Current commitments to decision increments were to be indicated in these columns. Since decision increments were being used for the first time, these data were not available for inclusion).

Exhibit 8   R & D ranking table showing increments at point of debate between Coulson and Ellis.

PRIORITY RESOURCE BUDGETING RANKING TABLE

Ranking level: R&D Director

Rank	Increment Number	Decision Unit Name	Incremental		Cumulative		1979		% of 1979		Notes
			Expense ($K)	Headcount	Expense ($K)	Headcount	Expense ($K)	Headcount	Expense	Headcount	
54	3 of 5	R&D mngt	22	1	4,162	52			78	75	Statistical typist
55	2 of 5	AZ-42 liquid (Chemical Commodities)	115	2.5	4,277	54.5			80	79	Liquid applications research (high temperature)
56	3 of 4	S.P.P.-29 (Consumer)	195	1.5	4,472	56			84	81	Process development
57	4 of 4	S.P.P.-29 (Consumer)	85	.5	4,557	56.5			85	82	Process development
58	3 of 5	Food Products Preservatives (Consumer)	115	2	4,672	58.5			87	85	New process research
59	1 of 3	NH-42 High Density (Consumer)	120	1.5	4,792	60			90	87	Manufacturing yield improvement
60	1 of 2	ALPHA-12 (Commodities)	180	2	4,972	62			93	90	Basic research on use as paint base

(See explanation on Exhibit 7.)

we have applications research and production service for Commodity Chemicals in the threshold."

"But that's just a tiny bit. Hell, my products pay the salaries around here, and we deserve a fair shake. I want those increments that have my stuff in them ranked now, before we spend all we've got on a future we're not sure exists."

At that point, Fred Ellis broke in. "John, demand in your markets isn't growing, and competition may soon start to drive your margins down. I know you're producing most of the cash generated by Queeny, but we ought to use that cash to support the best opportunities we've got, and right now those opportunities are in Consumer. Besides, when you consider . . ."

Coulson interrupted, "That's bull! Our demand continues to grow and our competition won't change all that much. The fact of the matter is, Commodity Chemicals continues to be the mainstay of this division, and we would be crazy to weaken it. Process improvements, and that means R&D, and hard-driving marketing are what it will take to keep this cash cow producing."

Hubbard recalled that he had interrupted at that point to get the facts straight. He had asked Joe Roboh exactly how much applications research and production support for Commodities was in the budget so far. Joe confirmed that production support was equal to 100 percent of the level expended during the past year. "I don't think we can change that, since all our production is sold in advance and we have to be able to deliver," he said. But applications research had been cut to 30 percent of the current level for Commodities. For Oil Additive Chemicals, production support was at 120 percent and applications research at 140 percent. Consumer was at 140 percent and 100 percent, respectively for the two same areas. Roboh thought that more should be spent for Consumer applications research.

Hubbard wondered whether getting the facts helped, though. Coulson had just sat there without saying a word. Looking for a way to calm the situation down, Hubbard had turned—mistakenly as it turned out—to Andy Dewing.

"Tell me, Andy, what about you? What kind of manufacturing support do you have in the budget for John? Is it enough to see that all of his stuff is out the door on time?"

"Sure, just as long as I have my eight people.[7] Frankly, Chris, I think this whole thing is dumb. We know how to run our business. I sure as hell know how I run my end of it. This is just another system trying to tell us what to do, and you know, I told that guy, that PRB, ABC, alphabet-soup guy that was supposed to help me with this, 'I only have one increment, eight people, and ten years on the job has taught me that eight is the right number.' But no, he made me play games, and now I have four levels or increments[8] or whatever they're called, and who knows or cares what's in them? You want the plants to produce on time and at spec? I need eight guys, no more, no less. And no

7. Dewing's staff at headquarters consisted of eight people. The manufacturing line personnel in the plants were not included in these deliberations.
8. Exhibit 9 shows Dewing's PRB analysis.

matter how many increments or whatever you cut that into, it adds up the same. I can't guarantee anything until I get *all* my men."

Hubbard was flustered a bit by that, he remembered. "You mean you can't operate with less than eight?"

"I mean I can't say what will happen with less than eight. It all depends on the risk you want to take. Four may be enough, or two, or none if you're lucky."

That was the first time I got angry, Hubbard reflected. "Well, why *isn't* your threshold eight people? What are we fooling around with less for?"

"Don't ask me. I tried to do the right thing and make it eight. Ask him," Andy said, and pointed at Jack Eckert, the PRB coordinator. "It was my PRB analyst who said I couldn't have eight in my threshold."

"Wait a minute, Andy," replied a very much on-the-spot Eckert. "I wasn't at your sessions when you did your original analysis, but I suspect that the guy who worked with you said that the threshold could not be *equal* to the current level. That's a basic assumption in PRB. You have just told us how to view your department: The major issue is *risk*. How willing is Queeny to risk a production delay or quality-control problem? For which products? Which customers? What are the costs of a delay?"

"We can't take those risks and keep our customers. How much risk do you say we should take, Jack?" countered Andy.

"You have to make that decision," Jack replied. "My job here is to facilitate the process, not to make operating or budgeting decisions. You have to make that decision, and you have made it, year after year. All the system does is help you attach different prices to different levels of risk. The choice is yours."

Andy smiled ironically. "You say that like it's easy."

"I don't mean it to sound easy," Eckert said, looking around the room.

Coulson spoke up, "I think we should give Andy all of his men right now. All these management systems sound fine, but we know what's going to happen if the plants back up. We need the same amount of production as last year, and his staff worked full time then."

Nodding his head, Brewster called out, "I agree with John; let Andy have his people next."

Hubbard moved to get closure. "I think that's right. Anyone disagree? . . . No? Then Andy, we'll accept all your other increments now."

Relaxing, Andy responded, "Good! That finishes my part. Can I get back to work now, Chris?"

"No, I want you involved in the rest of the ranking. A lot of the decisions we still have to make could indirectly affect your department."

Hubbard wondered whether he had moved for closure too soon. Andy's impassioned complaint had interrupted the flow of the meeting, and Hubbard had wanted to return to the question of how much research support to devote to Commodity Chemicals.

Coulson raised the point immediately. "We still haven't answered the question we began with. I still think I should get more support from R&D."

Exhibit 9 Summary of Dewings's analysis.

PRIORITY RESOURCE BUDGETING DECISION UNIT SUMMARY

1) Decision Unit Name: Cost Cent. # Manufacturing Management #0100	2) Division/Department Queen/MCCC	3) Decision Unit Mgr. Andy Dewing	4)Date 8/1/79

7) Decision Unit Results to be Worked Towards in 1979

A. Improve production yields 10% in S.P.P. –29.

B. Improve COGS in ALPHA-12 by 5%.

C. Implement $1.5 million of cost reduction programs.

D. Implement rehabilitation of existing facilities to meet safety and environmental needs.

Unit Res. Sup.	People	Incremental		
		% 1979	Expense	% 1979
	3	38%	225	50

5) Purpose of Decision Unit

Manage the utility and service functions of the Queeny Division plants and manage the manufacture of Queeny's commodities, oil additive, and consumer products to meet the agreed to unit costs and volumes.

6) What Does Your Unit Do and What Resources Are Used to Do It?

8 people. *Director of Manufacturing* is department manager. He supervises those below him and is responsible for overall planning; 4 *Managers, Manufacturing* each assigned to one or more products, follows up on all manufacturing problems, coordinates capital appropriation requests, provides technical assistance and expertise when required and coordinates with division R&D. 2 *Manufacturing Services Managers* for Utilities and Service at plant locations and coordination of Division function; and one *secretary.*

8) What Will Be Done at the Threshold Level?

Maintain major administrative activities for plants.

– Manage only most profitable products in division
– Minimal planning and control of all other products
– Generally treat plants as a "wasting asset"

Requires:
    1 Director Manufacturing,
    1 Manager Manufacturing,
    1 Secretary

9) Why Are These Activities Essential

• Need to keep plants operating at economic production levels.

• This level of effort would result in problems in production scheduling, lower yields, and higher COGS.

12) Incr. No.	13) What will be done at this Increment and what Resources are needed?	14) Why should this increment be funded?	15) Unit Res. Sup.	16) What Incremental Resources are needed?		17) What Cumulative Resources are needed?			
				People	Expense	People	% 1978	Expense	% 1978
2 of 4	Reallocation plant management to pick up limited planning and control for all products. Begin low level of cost reduction programs (.5 million) Requires: 2 Managers	Ensure that all product areas are "covered" from manufacturing planning/control. Bring yield and COGS down to planned levels.		2	98	5	63	323	72
3 of 4	Cover all plants and product areas. Allow for coordination of capital projects, full cost reduction program, and limited implementation of rehabilitation program. Requires: 2 Managers	Achieve planned increases in yield, improvements in COGS, and cost reduction programs.	A B C	2	108	7	88	431	96
4 of 4	Full implementation of rehabilitation program. Additional cost reduction opportunities (.5 million) Requires: 1 Manager	Meet government imposed deadlines on plant rehabilitation.	D	1	49	8	100	480	106
		ESTIMATED EXPENSE 1979 (Basis: Six-month Act.)				8	100	450	100

Hubbard nodded, he recalled. "Joe, where is the rest of John's support?"

"Spread across my last eight increments, numbers 67 to 74."[9]

"OK, John," Hubbard said as he turned to examine the display that explained what was in each of those increments, "if you could have two of those, which would they be?"

"I'll need three. Number 67 is the area where we have the best opportunity, but 67 alone doesn't do much for us. Increments 68 and 71 will give that project the punch it needs to produce some applications we can take to the market."

Brewster broke in, "Remember, Chris, we haven't yet funded any of those new Oil Additives projects I spoke to you about, and . . ."

Coulson interrupted. "We have already ranked three of your exploratory research projects, Norm. The increments you have left look like long shots to me, and my projects have pretty clear near-term benefits."

"These new projects have a lot of potential," Brewster countered, "and I think the results we've gotten in my group over the last five years show that investments in R&D for our business pay off."

Dewing spoke up, "Look, why don't we give John one of his increments, then Norm one of his, then John, and so on?"

Coulson responded before anyone could reply. "But aren't we supposed to rank each increment with the idea that it really is the most important thing available, and not simply trade around? My projects are critical and should go in the budget now!"

Everyone started speaking at once. After some fifteen minutes of spirited argument, Hubbard intervened. "Look, we're getting nowhere on this one. Let's move on to something else for awhile and come back to this later."

The group made good progress on several items until Norm Brewster got upset. At the time, the group was discussing advertising, and the debate was whether Oil Additive Chemicals' increment should come before Consumer Chemicals.

"Right now I've got 90 percent of current advertising expense in the budget," Brewster said. "Rates will go up at least 15 percent, and if we take my next increment I'll be just short of my current level in advertising purchase power. If we take Consumer's increment, Fred will be at 160 percent of current. I don't even understand why we're wasting time talking about it."

"Maybe it's time to start cutting your advertising," Chris explained. "You've been spending at high levels, but you dominate the market now, and you keep telling me you get terrific word-of-mouth. You haven't convinced me that this advertising increment will have much effect on either your share or profitability."

"I'm the one who needs the advertising," Fred Ellis interrupted. "Consumer is right where you were a few years ago. We are at 'take-off.' We have terrific products in a growth market, and we have to get out there and establish a dominant position. Right now, getting more awareness and supporting our distributors is critical."

9. Exhibit 10 shows the R&D ranking.

Exhibit 10 Last page of Joe Roboh's R & D ranking table, expressing the priorities of Queeny's R & D department.

PRIORITY RESOURCE BUDGETING RANKING TABLE

Ranking level: R&D director

Rank	Increment Number	Decision Unit Name	Incremental Expense ($K)	Incremental Headcount	Cumulative Expense ($K)	Cumulative Headcount	1979 Expense ($K)	1979 Headcount	% of 1979 Expense	% of 1979 Headcount	Notes
65	4 of 5	R&D mngt	39	1	5,325	67.5			99	98	Budgeting and financial assistant
66	5 of 5	R&D mngt	22	1	5,347	68.5			100	99	Second statistical typist
67	3 of 5	AZ-42 liquid	115	2.5	5,462	71	(See explanation on Exhibit 7.)		102	103	Liquid applications research
68	4 of 5	AZ-42 liquid	230	2.5	5,692	73.5			105	107	High altitude applications
69	3 of 3	SUR food preservative	85	1	5,777	74.5			108	108	New freezing applications
70	1 of 2	SUR cost reduction	185	1.5	5,962	76			111	110	Achieve 1¢/100 lb by 1982
71	5 of 5	AZ-42 liquid	98	1.5	6,060	77.5			113	112	Low temperature applications
72	2 of 2	SUR cost reduction	75	.5	6,135	78			114	113	Achieve 1¢/100 lb by 1981
73	5 of 5	PV-12	105	1	6,240	79			116	114	Continue environmental hazard tests to fail safe level
74	3 of 3	IAPA	300	2	6,540	81			122	117	New fertilizer applications

Brewster looked straight at Chris. "If our ad budget gets cut, I can't promise the profits we've delivered in the past. We've been damn successful, and our advertising has been an important part of our marketing program. It doesn't make sense to change a successful strategy."

Hubbard wasn't sure whether he was grateful that Nicholson interrupted at this point, or whether it would have been better if they had resolved the ad question.

"Here we are talking about advertising, and we don't even have enough people in the field to take orders. Right now the budget only gives me skeleton crews in three sales offices. We don't have anyone out traveling around."

"You mean we haven't ranked your whole staff yet?" Coulson asked in amazement.

"No."

Coulson sat up straight, exasperated. "That means the whole ranking is screwed up! What are we supposed to do now?"

Hubbard broke in, "Leo, if you were going to add one person to those ranked so far, what office would you do it in?"

"There's no way to answer that Chris, We may sell in the East, but then again the East could be slow and all our sales come from the West or Central. There's no way to tell."

Coulson chimed in, "We've just never gotten a handle on how to judge the marginal utility of a salesperson. There's no useful information."

"What you mean," said Ellis, "is that we don't know what information is useful."

Leo replied, with a look that said he had been through all this before, "Whichever, we don't have it. We know we need to add salespeople, and that means we need to add them everywhere."

That comment led to an extended discussion about how many salespersons were needed. The discussion produced lots of ideas but no resolution. Eventually everyone agreed that the Queeny sales force could not be cut, and that probably Nicholson should be given budget for two new people to be added where necessary.

Then came the issue of where the sales force should fit in the ranking. Should it simply be added now, or should it be inserted among increments ranked earlier in the meeting? The group decided to put it in earlier, but after twenty minutes of discussion still had not decided where.

"This is a mess," Coulson protested. "There's no way to compare Leo's need for salesmen with my need for more R&D and for more guys on my commercial staff. How are we supposed to compare one against the other? They're apples and oranges."

"I don't think there's an easy way," Hubbard replied.

"I don't want an easy way . . . just a way!" Coulson was pushing.

"But you know, John," said Ellis, "this is the first time we've sat down together and really talked about all our departments in this much detail."

"How is the talk helping?" asked Coulson.

"That's a good question, John," Chris said. "Why don't you guys try to answer it over lunch, and let's meet again at 1:30."

As Hubbard finished his own lunch he began to formulate a plan for resolving the issues that remained open.

Appendix: The Priority Resource Budgeting (PRB) Concept*

How do you plan your vacation? Do you say: "Last year, we went to Florida and spent $1,000. Let's add 10 percent for inflation, and go!" Or do you think: "Should we go on vacation, or use the money and time for something else? What other expenditures do we have coming up? How much money do we have to spend for a vacation? Where should we go? Should we fly or drive? Should we camp or stay at a motel?"

The second approach, of course, makes more sense. Priority Resource Budgeting (PRB) encourages the same kind of approach. PRB asks us to question the costs themselves. Why are we spending the money? What are we getting in return? How can we better spend the money? PRB involves cost/benefit trade-offs throughout the organization.

How PRB Works

1. Identify "Decision Units." A Decision Unit is the smallest meaningful group of people and/or other resource devoted to achieving a common significant business purpose. It can be a traditional cost center, a program, or a group of activities. Typical Decision Units include between five and fifteen people and a dollar budget of about $150,000 to $400,000.
2. Analyze each Decision Unit. Each manager is asked to analyze the Decision Unit(s) for which he or she is responsible. Answers to the following seven specific questions guide this analysis.
   - What is the purpose (goal) of the Decision Unit?
   - What Decision Unit results (special accomplishments) are to be worked toward next year?
   - What does the Unit do (activities), and what resources are used to do it?
   - What alternative methods for achieving the purpose are feasible?
   - What is the minimal level of service the Unit could provide and still remain viable? Why are those services essential? In PRB language, this is defined as the "threshold level."
   - What additional increments of service can be provided?[1]
   - Why should these additional increments be funded?

1. Think of increments as the building blocks of resources (either money or people) that are added to achieve more completely the Unit's purpose and results. Each increment you add should be able to stand alone. Increment Two (for example) could be the addition of two people. The activities and services they provide will be above and beyond the first threshold limit. And if the two people were not added, the services and activities of the threshold limit would still be performed. Continue the same logic with Increment Three, Four, etc.
*Source: Monsanto Company PRB Manual.

Exhibit 11 Decision unit analysis.

You as Manager A have developed your increments. Managers B and C have done the same.

You all have established threshold and current levels, and additional increments.

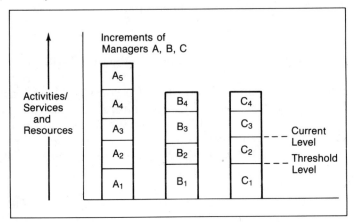

3. Rank in order of priority the Decision Unit increments obtained from the analysis in Step 2. The first ranking actually occurs at the Decision Unit level when the manager arranges his or her increments in order of their importance (Exhibit 11). The next ranking occurs at the organizational level immediately above. The ranking involves the manager, peers, and their immediate supervisor. Together, these people rank all their increments—based on the objectives of the group and the organization (Exhibit 12). That ranking is based on the written analyses and

Exhibit 12 Decision unit ranking.

The next step is "ranking." This is where your increments (after the threshold level) are compared with others — in terms of payout on the investment of resources. At ranking sessions with your peers and supervisors, you will rank all your increments.

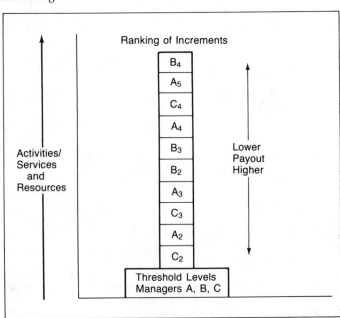

Exhibit 13   Ranking process summary.

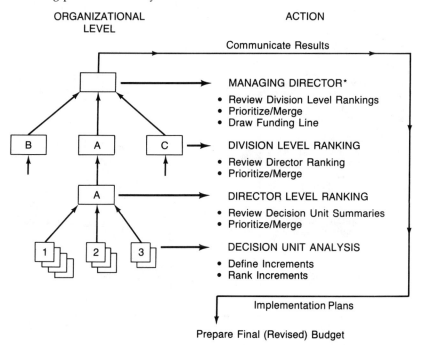

ORGANIZATIONAL LEVEL

ACTION

Communicate Results

MANAGING DIRECTOR*
• Review Division Level Rankings
• Prioritize/Merge
• Draw Funding Line

DIVISION LEVEL RANKING
• Review Director Ranking
• Prioritize/Merge

DIRECTOR LEVEL RANKING
• Review Decision Unit Summaries
• Prioritize/Merge

DECISION UNIT ANALYSIS
• Define Increments
• Rank Increments

Implementation Plans

Prepare Final (Revised) Budget

* Corporate management reviews the budget.

discussions between the Decision Unit managers and the ranking manager. The give and take of those meetings is vital in determining the priorities that are ultimately published. Exhibit 13 portrays an overview of the ranking process.

4. Prepare the organization's formal budget, based on the decisions made in Step 3. The final product of the preceding meetings and analyses is a ranking table for the entire organization. Subsequent to the final ranking meeting, that ranking manager studies the resulting ranking table, makes any required adjustments, decides which increments should and which should not be funded, and draws a "funding line" on the table that indicates the increments that have been approved, those that have not, and costs of each.[2] The ranking table thus is a record of all the decisions that have been made in the Priority Resource Budgeting process (Exhibit 14). Not only does it show what will and will not be funded in the upcoming year, it also ranks activities in priority so that adjustments during the year can be made more easily.

2. While the funding was "drawn" or set by the Managing Director of each Monsanto Company, each divisional general manager would indicate a recommended funding level for his unit at the conclusion of the divisional ranking.

Exhibit 14 Funding the increments.

As the supervisor looks at the ranking of increments, the "normal" breakout would look something like the diagram. Beyond the threshold limits, there are some areas where the payout is high. At the top of the tower there might be some increments which are not likely to merit serious consideration. In between, lies the "grey area" where the desirability of the increment is arguable. The funding line typically falls somewhere in the grey area.

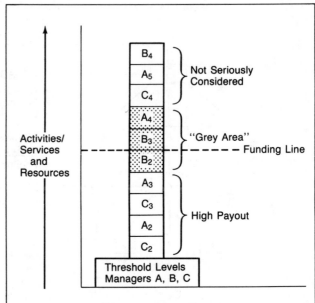

5. The final budget, although prepared in a vastly different fashion from traditional budgets, is similar in format to the end product of the traditional approach. The cost breakdowns (e.g., salaries, bonuses, travel) feed directly into the company's existing budgeting and control system.

National Medical Enterprises

> This company will be fulfilled when we encompass all aspects of health care in a totally coordinated system. We are in the total health care market; an individual product is irrelevant. Right now the situation is like a jigsaw puzzle: We have 1,000 pieces and no picture to go by.

Richard K. Eamer (age fifty-six), chairman and chief executive officer of National Medical Enterprises (NME), was discussing his vision for the company he had founded with two colleagues in 1969, fifteen years earlier. In 1984, the company reported sales in excess of $2.5 billion and a net income of $121 million. (Both sales and net income had experienced an annual growth rate of more than 40 percent over the preceding ten-year period.) Among proprietary (for-profit) hospital management companies, NME had singled itself out with respect to its diversification, participating in nearly all major areas of health care including acute, long-term psychiatric and home care, as well as the supply of health products. "We could be as big as GE by the turn of the century . . . or bigger," continued Eamer, leaning forward to emphasize his point. "We're not limited."

Chairman Eamer's optimism about the business prospects in health care was not shared by everyone in the industry. Articles expressing doubts and warnings about the future health of the industry appeared in the national press. According to Forbes (June 4, 1984); "American hospitals are in more trouble than even pessimists may suspect. . . . Depending on whose estimates you use, hundreds of the nation's 7,088 hospitals may become insolvent over the next four years."

In another article on June 18, Forbes commented, "Anyone who thought the health care business could only go in one direction—up—is now in for . . . disillusionment."

Certainly, the 1980s marked a time of discontinuity for the U.S. health care industry as pressure mounted to contain ballooning costs. A major change to the basis for Medicare payments, the rapid growth of health maintenance organizations (HMOs),[1] and the introduction of other payment schemes had encouraged the emergence of new approaches to health care delivery. The industry was in visible ferment, and the general or acute care hospitals—which were

1. See glossary at the end of the case.

the traditional providers of surgical, diagnostic, therapeutic, and related ancillary (clinical laboratory testing, ambulance, emergency) services—were the most seriously threatened by the new competition for each health care dollar.

To deal with these pressures, NME reorganized its core acute-care hospital service to encourage experimentation and adaptation. In 1984, a new division, the Health Care Systems and Services Group, was created to develop new approaches for feeding patients to NME's hospital facilities. As part of this move, two experienced young men, Scott Gross and Bill Piche, both age thirty-eight, were put in charge of the Hospital Group (acute care hospitals) and the newly created Health Care Systems and Services Group respectively. It would be their task to work out new health care approaches and the relationships of their units with each other as well as with the other units in the new organizational structure. The outcome of their efforts would undoubtedly affect the future of NME.

As noted by John C. Bedrosian (age 49), senior executive vice president and one of the three NME founders:

> It is hard to predict where the health care industry is going. Up to now, a company should have done well competitively with any sense at all. Now there will be winners and losers for the first time in the industry. The question is: who wins? who loses? who suffers? in the coming shake-out.

The U.S. Health Care Industry

Health care had come under public and legislative scrutiny in the 1980s as a result of skyrocketing costs. By 1984, various proposals to limit health care spending coupled with new approaches for delivering health care promised to increase competitive pressures and to disrupt further what had been a safe and profitable business.

The traditional health care field had been modest in size and fairly simple in structure. In 1950, total national health care expenditures were $12.7 billion, or 4.9 percent of the gross national product (GNP). In 1960, these figures were $26.9 billion and 5.3 percent. The industry was made up primarily of nonprofit general-purpose facilities and private physicians who provided services paid for by private insurance programs such as Blue Cross/Blue Shield or by the patient directly. By 1983, total expenditures had risen to $355 billion, or 10.8 percent of the GNP, making health care the second largest industry in the U.S., following food and agriculture.

The health care industry had become a complex structure of nonprofit and for-profit business facilities offering many products and services paid for by a multitude of public and private programs. The impetus for this change had its roots in one piece of legislation under the Johnson administration: the federally funded Medicare and Medicaid national health care insurance programs that assured treatment for the elderly and the poor. With the availability of public money, the health care industry entered a phase of explosive growth.

Table A Selected health care cost increases, 1980–82.

	Inflation Rate (CPI)	*Medical Care*	*Hospital Room*	*Physicians' Services*
1980	13.5%	10.9%	13.1%	10.6%
1981	10.4%	10.8%	14.9%	11.0%
1982	6.1%	11.6%	15.7%	9.4%

Source: U.S. Bureau of Labor Statistics, Consumer Price Indexes, Annual Averages.

The reimbursement scheme allowed hospitals to charge whatever they needed to cover their costs. These guaranteed payments prompted established hospitals to initiate programs of capital expansion. The legislation also included provisions allowing investor-owned hospitals a reasonable return on equity (about 11 percent pretax at that time) on government reimbursed services. This lured new for-profit organizations into the field. Expenditures for hospital services soared from $9 billion per year in the early 1950s to close to $150 billion in 1983, representing 41.4 percent of total health-care spending for that year.

Accompanying the national debate that had led to the federal health programs was a growing public expectation of entitlement with respect to health care. Pressure mounted for more company-sponsored group employee health care plans. The resulting shift from individual to company-supported payments in turn encouraged further expansion and upgrading of medical facilities, since many of the programs followed the government's lead in calculating reimbursements based on a hospital's most recent entitled costs.

By the 1980s, spokesmen for both public and private insurers were becoming increasingly vociferous in their criticism of health care costs as out of control. They pointed to data, such as shown in Table A, to make their case.

The culprit was clearly identified. As reported in *Business Week* (October 15, 1984), "There were no real controls within the system," says Donald R. Melville, President and Chief Executive of Norton Co. in Worcester, Mass. "We wrote a ticket to provide free health care without limits."

Added J. Alexander McMahon, president of the American Hospital Association, "The whole message was to expand." And *Forbes* (September 10, 1984), described how the "message to expand" worked:

> Third party insurance is perfectly engineered to remove incentives to keep costs down. Businesses pay premiums for employees, and insurance companies pay the bills. Employees have no reason to shop for cheaper care; so providers have no reason to be cost-effective.
>
> A system of blank checks is bad. Worse, since doctors charge on a fee-for-service basis, they have strong incentives to sell as much as they can. Because the doctors dominate the demand for services, they have the power to do so.
>
> Doctors decide whether hospitalization is necessary (and for how long),

what tests to perform and what medicine to give. Doctors' fees might be a small portion of the bill, but "they control 80 percent to 85 percent of costs," says Glenn Witt of the Iowa Health Policy Group. "We found that doctors put patients in hospitals too often, asked for too many tests and kept them there too long."

The bubble of expanding costs was burst by Congress in 1983 when it changed the basis for hospital reimbursement. Under the new law, Medicare set flat-fee rates for 467 categories of treatment, called "diagnostic-related groups" (DRGs). These payments were to cover all hospital costs except those for physician services, the cost of capital, outpatient services, and services associated with psychiatric or rehabilitation units.

While the full force of the new law was not expected to take effect until 1987, there was an immediate twofold response to DRG legislation by the health care industry: hospitals reduced patients' average stay to reduce costs; and specialized health care facilities, not covered by DRG fee limitations, sprouted to siphon off patients requiring minor treatment. The net impact of these two developments was to reduce markedly hospital utilization (census).

New DRG legislation was not the only threat to hospital revenues. Hospital utilization was further reduced by a rapid growth of hospital maintenance organizations. HMOs were organized health clinics operated to provide comprehensive treatment for a flat fee. Kaiser-Permanente, the first HMO, was set up in the 1940s, but the concept did not flourish until 1973, when Congress passed the Health Maintenance Act providing federal funds to aid in the establishment of such preventative health units. By 1984, approximately 15 million Americans (6 percent of the population) belonged to some 300 HMOs in the United States, making it a $7.5 billion industry growing at a 20–25 percent annual rate.

Much of the impetus for the expansion of HMO membership came from U.S. corporations and insurance companies as a way to contain health costs. Industrial companies like Ford, GM, and IBM initiated HMO programs for their employees. (Ford reported a savings of $12 million over two years as a result of its employee-based HMO.) Prudential, Blue Cross/Blue Shield, and CIGNA were among the insurance companies operating HMOs with large enrollments.

To protect their position, hospitals too began to adopt more aggressive approaches. Their response to HMOs was the preferred provider organization (PPO), a hybrid between HMOs and the traditional fee-for-service. Under this arrangement, treatment continued to be offered on the basis of fee-for-service. The fee schedule, however, was reduced when member physicians and hospitals were used. An important distinction between HMOs and PPOs was the party at risk. With PPOs, the losses and gains associated with heavier and lighter than normal health care usage were borne by the paying party (i.e., insurance company, corporation, or individual). With HMOs they were born by the health care provider.

Notwithstanding these attempts by hospitals to stem the tide of change, industry observers were predicting a further erosion of their heretofore preeminent position in the health care field. According to *Forbes* (June 4, 1984):

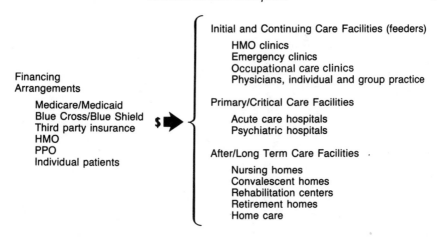

Figure A Overview of the U.S. health care system.

Even such for-profit hospital operations as Humana and Hospital Corporation of America are not immune to the onslaught of HMOs and other new competition. According to a study by the California Hospital Association, 64 percent of the for-profit hospitals will experience revenue shortfalls in the first year that DRG-based Medicare payments go into effect.

Emerging Industry Structure. A net effect of the changes to health care was to lessen the overwhelmingly dominant role that hospitals and private practice physicians once played. Figure A depicts a simplified view of the health care industry in 1984. The typical interrelationships between patients, the financing arrangements, and the health care delivery systems are described in Exhibit 1.

As indicated in Exhibit 1, for-profit organizations had become a major force in the various health care delivery systems. Ownership of clinics and nursing homes was highly fragmented in 1984, but five companies dominated the acute-care segment, owning over 40 percent of the approximately 1,100 for-profit hospitals in the U.S. Exhibit 2 provides comparative information on the size and activities of these five companies.

The Growth of NME

National Medical Enterprises could trace its roots to Richard Eamer's professional background. On graduating from law school in 1960, he began specializing in health care and hospital law. His earlier training as a CPA gave him a special interest in the economics of hospital operations. During the next eight years his clients included over eighty hospitals, both voluntary nonprofit and proprietary, and hundreds of physicians.

By 1968, a number of his clients were urging him to form a proprietary company in order to facilitate the raising of capital and to assure more effective organizational growth for their hospitals. Joined by colleagues Leonard Cohen,

Exhibit 1 Typical health care provider and financing relationships.

	Acute-Care Hospitals	HMO Centers	Emergency Care (Free standing)	Nursing Homes/Rehab. Centers	Psychiatric Hospitals
Purpose	Emergency and general patient care / Surgery / Medicine / Out-patient services	Preventative, on-going health care	Emergency care for minor injuries and major problems	Long-term and on-going convalescent and rehabilitative care	Care for acute and chronic psychiatric patients
Primary Source of Funds	Blue Cross/Blue Shield / Medicare/Medicaid / Private insurers	Employees / Individuals	Privately insured individuals	Medicare/Medicaid / Private Insurance	Medicare / Private Insurance / Blue Cross (extended benefits only)
For-Profit Share of Total Market, (1983)	12% of beds / 17% of hospitals (Source: Federation of American Hospitals)	28% of all plans (Source: Interstudy, Inc. HMO Status Report, 6/83)	98% (30% chain owned) (Source: SMG Marketing Group)	Nursing homes only: 81% (15% chain owned) (Source: American Health-care Association)	17% of hospitals (Source: National Assn. of Private Psychiatric Hospitals)

Health Care Reimbursement and Insurance Organizations

	Medicare/Medicaid	Third Party	HMO	PPO
Health Care Delivery				
Physicians	Selected by patient	Selected by patient	Contracted by HMO	Selected by patient from employer approved list
Hospitals	Selected by physician or patient	Selected by physician or patient	Owned or on contract / Emphasis on out-patient clinics or doctors' offices	Selected by physician or patient
Reimbursement				
Physicians	Payment on rigid schedule	Paid based on standard fees / Fee-for-service / Rigid schedule for Blue Shield	Standard rate schedule for salaried basis	On contract: Fee-for-service / Not on contract: Based on standard rates, but patient pays larger amt.
Hospitals	Standard rate schedule / DRGs	Reimbursed for standard charges / Fee-for-service	Standard rate schedule	Fee-for-service

Exhibit 2 Comparative data for the five largest hospital management companies (1984).

	Total acute and psychiatric hospitals (owned, managed and under construction)		Gross Revenues ($ million)	Percentage of revenue by sector			
	Beds	Facilities		Hospitals	Psychiatric and Substance Abuse	Nursing	Other
Hospital Corporation of America	59,946	417	4,178.2	89.6	5.5	—	4.9
American Medical International	19,673	142	2,422.7	92.0	8.0	—	—
Humana	18,311	92	2,606.4	100.0	—	—	—
National Medical Enterprises	16,311	142	2,524.0	53.8	8.1	25.8	12.3
Charter Medical Corporation	5,798	56	493.3	49.3	41.7	—	9.0

Sources: 1985 Directory of Investor-Owned Hospitals; and company annual reports.

also an attorney and CPA, and John Bedrosian, an attorney, Eamer launched NME in 1969 with an initial public offering. With the proceeds of $23 million, the new company purchased four general (acute-care) hospitals, three convalescent (nursing) homes, and two office buildings. By the end of its first year, NME had acquired an additional general hospital, an additional convalescent home, and three building sites for new acute-care hospitals. At the same time, it had entered the health care equipment and supply business with the acquisition of one company and the start-up of a second.

Eamer had a definite vision for NME, which he articulated in the company's first report:

> We think it important that you who share in the ownership of NME have some insight into the motivation of its management as well as our views on the problems that confront the industry, because these views—which we hold very strongly—will have a continuing effect on our policies and operations.
>
> The health care field has become the sick man of the American economy, and no token action is going to make it well. Nothing less than a massive coordinated effort by the government, the existing voluntary hospital system, the medical and the paramedical profession and private enterprise can solve the problem.
>
> [The traditional] hospital typically lacks any of the basic advantages enjoyed by any modern, sophisticated business organization—mass purchasing, statistical comparisons and evaluation, competent business development and financial management.
>
> The hospital industry is essentially where the grocery industry was at the advent of the supermarket chain. Although it deals with life and death and not food supply, our industry can still learn the lessons that other industries have already absorbed.

While NME's initial principal focus had been on expanding its acute-care hospital network, it also made major inroads in the convalescent home field with the purchase of an 84.5 percent stake in Hillhaven Nursing Homes in 1979 for $38.7 million and in the psychiatric care field with the acquisition of Psychiatric Institute of America (PIA) in July 1982 for $150 million. Hillhaven was second in the industry in the number of nursing home beds; PIA was the largest in its field. By 1984, NME owned, operated or managed a total of 553 health care facilities in the U.S. and abroad. The geographical location of these facilities is shown in Exhibit 3.

By design, acquisitions had accounted for the preponderance of NME's growth. Leonard Cohen, president and chief operating officer, explained the company's policy, "Time and experience were the reasons for our emphasis on acquisitions. The field was fast moving, and we wanted to strike while the iron was hot. We were able to get an established position and experienced managers. And by keeping the acquired management on board, we also got new blood in the company."

To support the rapid pace of expansion and the many acquisitions, NME was involved in a continuous stream of financing. Over the 1975–84 ten-year

Exhibit 3 Facilities owned, operated or managed by National Medical Enterprises in 1984. *Source:* 1984 Annual Report.

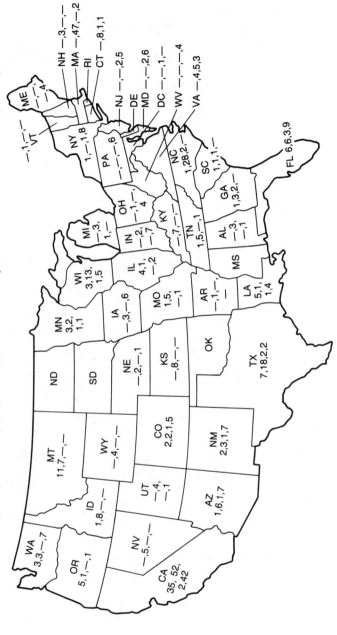

Key: Acute and Primary Care, Long Term Care, Psychiatric and Substance Abuse, Home Care

	Acute and Primary Care	Long Term Care	Psychiatric and Substance Abuse	Home Care
Total facilities	98*	271	31	153
Total beds	12,595	34,980	2,220	N.A.

*Includes 1 in Puerto Rico and 3 in Saudi Arabia

619

Exhibit 4 National Medical Enterprises' financial data. *Source: Value Line.*

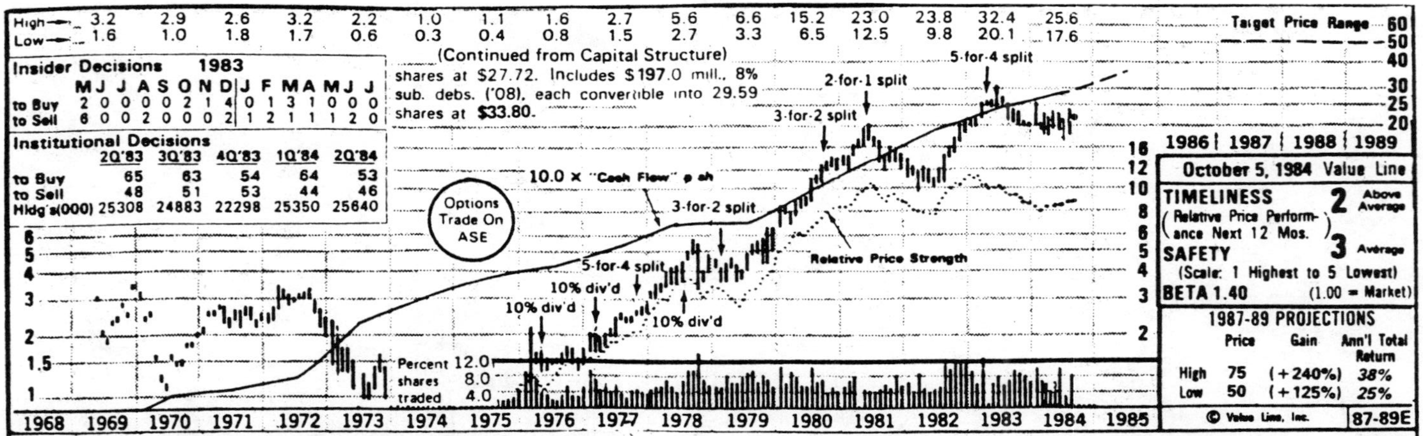

1968	1969	1970	1971	1972	1973	1974	1975	1976	1977	1978	1979	1980	1981	1982	1983	1984	1985	© Value Line, Inc.	87-89E
--	.76	.99	1.22	1.50	2.64	3.69	4.69	5.26	7.11	8.23	7.80	13.37	15.93	19.89	27.11	29.73	**33.50**	Revenues per sh (A)	**50.00**
--	.06	.10	.12	.15	.23	.30	.37	.42	.54	.68	.60	.97	1.36	1.92	2.45	2.94	**3.55**	"Cash Flow" per sh	**6.00**
--	.06	.09	.10	.11	.16	.17	.20	.25	.30	.40	.47	.73	.99	1.28	1.47	1.74	**2.10**	Earnings per sh (B)	**3.35**
--	--	--	--	--	.01	.01	.01	.03	.05	.08	.13	.16	.24	.31	.38	.43	**.50**	Div'd Decl'd per sh ■ (C)	**.80**
--	--	--	.42	1.20	1.01	.62	1.01	1.24	.82	.77	2.02	1.01	2.30	3.46	5.79	5.59	**6.70**	Cap'l Spending per sh	**9.00**
--	1.26	1.27	1.33	1.44	1.60	1.82	2.01	2.11	2.36	2.60	3.05	4.38	6.72	7.70	9.95	11.03	**17.60**	Book Value per sh (D)	**19.50**
--	19.66	20.75	21.32	21.73	21.48	20.34	20.29	22.09	22.41	25.60	35.84	45.70	56.02	58.67	65.10	69.46	**12.60**	Common Shs Outst'g (E)	**90.00**
--	33.9	24.3	18.0	22.0	13.3	5.2	3.0	4.1	5.0	6.6	8.8	8.6	14.1	11.5	13.6	13.7		Avg Ann'l P/E Ratio	**18.0**
--	2.06	1.74	1.15	1.51	1.31	.73	.40	.52	.65	.90	1.27	1.14	1.71	1.27	1.15	1.21		Relative P/E Ratio	**1.50**
--	--	--	--	--	.5%	1.3%	1.8%	2.6%	3.1%	3.0%	3.1%	2.6%	1.7%	2.1%	1.9%	1.8%		Avg Ann'l Div'd Yield	**1.3%**

CAPITAL STRUCTURE as of 5/31/84

Total Debt $976.5 mill.   Due in 5 Yrs $80.0 mill.
LT Debt $946.5 mill.   LT Interest $97.0 mill.

(LT interest earned: 3.8x; total interest coverage: 3.7x)

Incl. $84.0 mill. 9% sub. debs. ('06), each cv. into 40.32 shares at $24.80; $103.0 mill., 12¾% sub. debs. ('01), each cv. into 36.08
(Continued on Chart)   (55% of Cap'l)

Leases, Uncapitalized Annual rentals $31.0 mill.
Pension Liability None vs. None in '83

Pfd Stock None

Common Stock 69,464,901 shs.   (45% of Cap'l)

													(A)
Revenues ($mill)	75.0	95.2	116.1	159.3	210.8	279.5	610.8	892.4	1167.1	1764.7	2065.0	2450	**4500**
Operating Margin	19.2%	17.3%	16.2%	16.0%	16.3%	16.0%	15.7%	17.3%	17.9%	17.5%	17.8%	19.0%	**20.0%**
Depreciation ($mill)	2.6	3.4	3.8	5.3	7.7	7.7	15.5	25.0	38.0	66.3	83.6	110	**225**
Net Profit ($mill)	3.5	4.1	5.4	6.9	9.8	13.8	29.5	51.8	75.2	92.9	121.3	150	**300**
Income Tax Rate	48.3%	48.3%	41.3%	42.1%	43.6%	46.9%	45.7%	46.2%	43.5%	44.2%	43.8%	44.0%	**44.0%**
Net Profit Margin	4.7%	4.3%	4.7%	4.3%	4.7%	5.0%	4.8%	5.8%	6.5%	5.3%	5.9%	6.1%	**6.7%**
Working Cap'l ($mill)	7.2	9.2	13.4	18.1	24.0	27.9	74.8	156.0	214.6	359.9	202.0	200	**350**
Long-Term Debt ($mill)	66.9	79.3	98.5	110.6	109.7	131.7	258.5	282.6	475.2	849.0	946.5	1200	**2000**
Net Worth ($mill)	37.0	40.8	46.7	52.9	66.6	114.2	205.3	381.3	457.0	648.0	766.2	920	**1750**
% Earned Total Cap'l	5.8%	6.3%	6.5%	7.2%	8.5%	7.8%	9.2%	10.3%	10.7%	9.0%	9.7%	10.0%	**10.5%**
% Earned Net Worth	9.4%	10.0%	11.6%	13.0%	14.7%	12.1%	14.4%	13.6%	16.5%	14.3%	15.8%	16.5%	**17.0%**
% Retained to Comm Eq	8.9%	9.5%	10.4%	11.1%	11.9%	9.0%	11.3%	10.2%	12.6%	10.6%	12.0%	12.5%	**13.0%**
% All Div'ds to Net Prof	6%	5%	10%	15%	19%	24%	24%	26%	25%	26%	24%	24%	**24%**

CURRENT POSITION ($mill.)	5/31/82	5/31/83	5/31/84
Cash Assets	151.0	282.1	95.0
Receivables	219.0	279.8	378.0
Inventory (FIFO)	44.4	50.6	60.0
Other	8.5	14.4	21.0
Current Assets	422.9	626.9	554.0
Accts Payable	66.3	90.8	128.0
Debt Due	20.7	28.4	30.0
Other	121.3	147.8	194.0
Current Liab.	208.3	267.0	352.0

(A) Fiscal year ends May 31 of cal. yr. Primary earnings. Next earn'gs rep't due mid-Oct. Includes a nonoperating gain: 12¢ in '82. Est'd current cost egs./sh.: '84. | (B) $1.35. (C) Next div'd meet'g about Oct. 26. Goes ex about Nov. 18. Div'd paym't dates: 15th of Mar., June, Sept. & Dec. ■ Div'd reinvestment plan av'ble. (D) Incl. in- | tangibles. In '84: $213.0 mill., $3.07/sh. (E) In millions, adjusted for stock splits and dividends.

Factual material is obtained from sources believed to be reliable but cannot be guaranteed.

Company's Financial Strength	B
Stock's Price Stability	35
Price Growth Persistence	100
Earnings Predictability	90

period, long-term debt increased twelve times (from $79 to $947 million) and net worth almost nineteen times (from $41 to $766 million). See Exhibit 4 for a summary of financial data and a 1984 assessment of NME for investment purposes. Exhibit 5 gives a breakdown of revenues and operating profits by lines of business.

1984 Organizational Restructuring

During 1983 and early 1984, NME's operations were organized into four major business units. The Hospital Group comprised acute-care hospitals (inpatient) and alternative care (outpatient) clinics. The Long-Term Health Care Group included convalescent care, rehabilitative services, and medically supported retirement housing. Psychiatric and Substance Abuse Services included psychiatric hospitals and chemical dependency centers (to deal with drug and alcohol dependency problems). And the Health Products and Services Group comprised home-care products, equipment, and services; respiratory, anesthesia, and cardiopulmonary equipment and supplies; and general contracting services.

In June 1984, NME reorganized its operations, creating three new groups. The Health Care Systems and Services Group was assigned rsponsibility for managing NME's growing involvement with HMOs, PPOs, and freestanding clinics—activities theretofore under the aegis of the Hospital Group. This move reflected management's desires to give these businesses more visibility and freedom of action than they might receive as part of the established hospital operations. For similar reasons, home-care services were spun off from the Health Products and Services Group. See Exhibit 6 for the company's organizational structure as of September 1984.

Leonard Cohen (age fifty-nine), to whom the seven operating units reported in his capacity as president and chief operating officer, saw his role as an adviser. He explained, "I don't want to interfere with the business operations. If the group presidents need help framing an acquisitions deal or with public relations, fine. Otherwise I'll be looking to them for exciting ideas and sound operations."

The reorganization came at a time when NME's hospital census (capacity utilization) was declining. It was also a time when competition for investment funds was increasing in the hospital care field in general as well as among NME's business groups.

Hospital Group

"The centerpiece of our company is the acute-care hospital operation. But despite its past accomplishments, or maybe because of them, this division had begun to lose some of its zip." Scott Gross well understood the nature of the critical job he had been given in taking over NME's largest and most profitable group in July 1984. He went on to describe the task as follows: "One of my

Exhibit 5 Revenues and operating profits by lines of business ($ millions).

Years Ended May 31	1980	1981	1982	1983	1984
Operating Revenues					
Acute and primary care	$ 465.3	$ 710.6	$ 927.4	$1,208.8	$1,357.1
Long term care	205.7	252.4	318.0	507.3	651.9
Psychiatric and substance abuse services	—	—	—	182.4	205.7
Health products and services	70.5	96.2	144.8	249.2	309.3
	$ 741.5	$1,059.2	$1,390.2	$2,147.7	$2,524.0
Operating Revenues % of Total					
Acute and primary care	62.8%	67.1%	66.7%	56.3%	53.8%
Long term care	27.7	23.8	22.9	23.6	25.8
Psychiatric and substance abuse services	—	—	—	8.5	8.1
Health products and services	9.5	9.1	10.4	11.6	12.3
	100.0%	100.0%	100.0%	100.0%	100.0%
Operating Profits					
Acute and primary care	$ 58.0	$ 89.4	$ 101.7	$ 134.0	$ 151.8
Long term care	14.9	21.5	27.2	45.2	67.3
Psychiatric and substance abuse services	—	—	—	30.1	37.5
Health products and services	6.5	7.6	17.8	18.4	28.8
	$ 79.4	$ 118.5	$ 146.7	$ 227.7	$ 285.4
Operating Profits % of Total					
Acute and primary care	73.1%	75.4%	69.3%	58.8%	53.2%
Long term care	18.8	18.1	18.6	19.9	23.6
Psychiatric and substance abuse services	—	—	—	13.2	13.1
Health products and services	8.1	6.5	12.1	8.1	10.1
	100.0%	100.0%	100.0%	100.0%	100.0%

Three psychiatric hospitals, owned before the acquisition of Psychiatric Institutes of America, are included in acute and primary care for 1982 and earlier years.

Exhibit 6 Company organizational chart, September 1984.

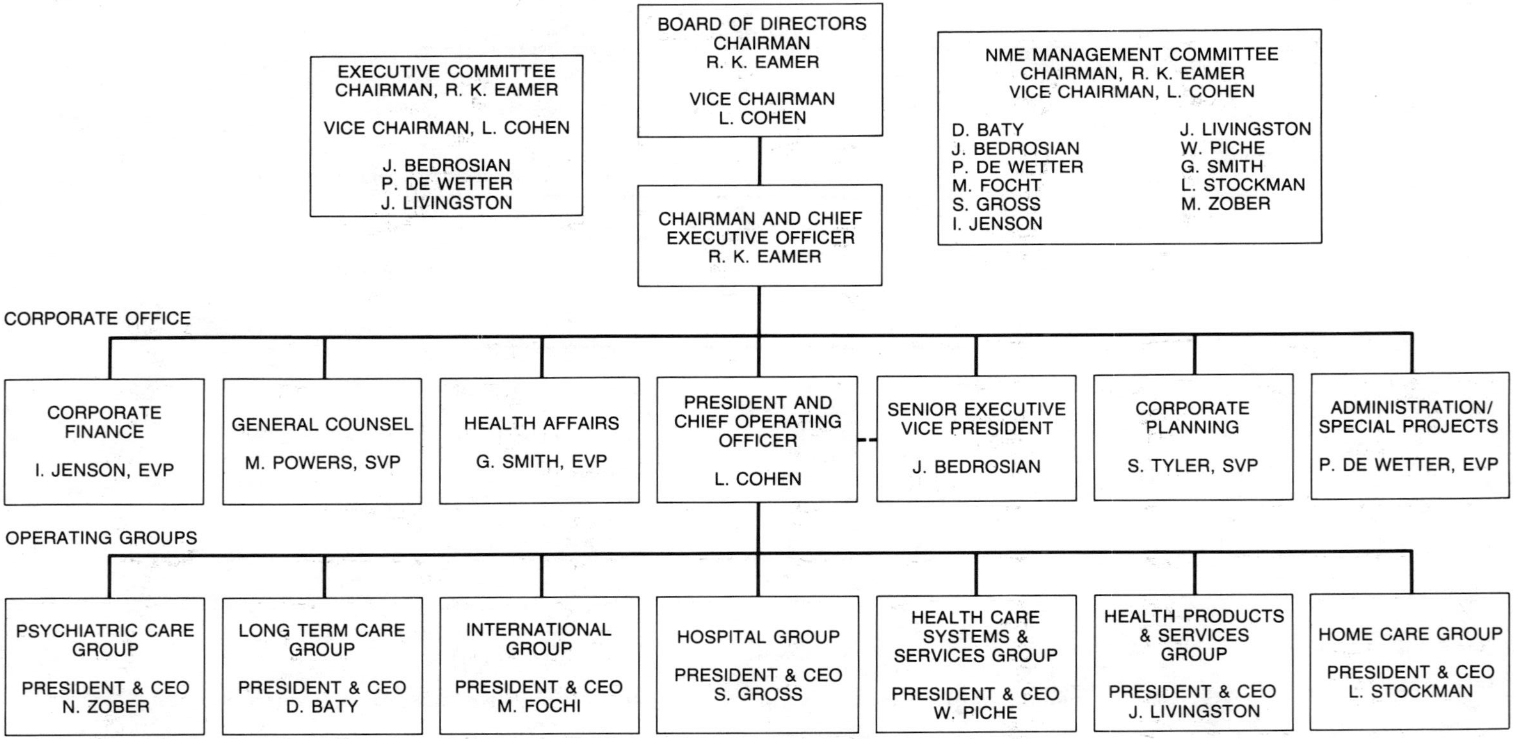

CORPORATE OFFICE

OPERATING GROUPS

BOARD OF DIRECTORS
CHAIRMAN
R. K. EAMER

VICE CHAIRMAN
L. COHEN

EXECUTIVE COMMITTEE
CHAIRMAN, R. K. EAMER
VICE CHAIRMAN, L. COHEN

J. BEDROSIAN
P. DE WETTER
J. LIVINGSTON

NME MANAGEMENT COMMITTEE
CHAIRMAN, R. K. EAMER
VICE CHAIRMAN, L. COHEN

D. BATY   J. LIVINGSTON
J. BEDROSIAN   W. PICHE
P. DE WETTER   G. SMITH
M. FOCHT   L. STOCKMAN
S. GROSS   M. ZOBER
I. JENSON

CHAIRMAN AND CHIEF
EXECUTIVE OFFICER
R. K. EAMER

PRESIDENT AND
CHIEF OPERATING
OFFICER
L. COHEN

SENIOR EXECUTIVE
VICE PRESIDENT
J. BEDROSIAN

CORPORATE
FINANCE
I. JENSON, EVP

GENERAL COUNSEL
M. POWERS, SVP

HEALTH AFFAIRS
G. SMITH, EVP

CORPORATE
PLANNING
S. TYLER, SVP

ADMINISTRATION/
SPECIAL PROJECTS
P. DE WETTER, EVP

PSYCHIATRIC CARE
GROUP
PRESIDENT & CEO
N. ZOBER

LONG TERM CARE
GROUP
PRESIDENT & CEO
D. BATY

INTERNATIONAL
GROUP
PRESIDENT & CEO
M. FOCHI

HOSPITAL GROUP
PRESIDENT & CEO
S. GROSS

HEALTH CARE
SYSTEMS &
SERVICES GROUP
PRESIDENT & CEO
W. PICHE

HEALTH PRODUCTS
& SERVICES
GROUP
PRESIDENT & CEO
J. LIVINGSTON

HOME CARE GROUP
PRESIDENT & CEO
L. STOCKMAN

624

biggest challenges is to change the group culture. That requires changing the structure as well as the way decisions are made."

On September 5, he announced major changes to the group's organizational structure and operating philosophy. Key elements of the new approach included a restructuring of the hospital groupings and the way the units would be managed, continued support for the cost-control information system under development, and increased emphasis on both business development and marketing.

Hospital Operations

In Scott Gross's judgment, the Hospital Group's earlier regional organization failed to recognize the different managerial challenges and opportunities connected with large versus small hospital units. To provide the special management attention called for by NME's eight largest hospitals (over 200 beds), he grouped them in a new Medical Center Division. The smaller, acute-care hospitals (eighty-seven in all), continued to be grouped and run on a regional basis.

Accompanying the organizational restructuring, Gross introduced the concept of "guided autonomy." He explained the new approach in reporting relationships and the reasons for it:

> Our major competitors are the free-standing, not-for-profit hospitals serving the communities in which our units are located. Years ago, these hospitals were not very competitive, but as pressures on them have mounted, they have become increasingly aggressive and innovative. As new opportunities arose in the community, by the time an NME hospital manager was able to get regional and group headquarters' approval, the local competition had already made the decision and moved on it. We were becoming a lumbering giant.
>
> To my mind, the local unit has to have more say in deciding competitive moves. I want us to realize that the role of group headquarters is to give guidance, to make funds available, and to provide technical assistance to the local level with respect to negotiations, advertising, management systems, and the like.
>
> The guidance part of the formula has to do with limits. Controls have to be in place so that a St. Mary's hospital, on its own, cannot just go out and buy an expensive piece of equipment.

Some colleagues saw limits on Gross's freedom to employ the concept of guided autonomy. As one executive noted, "Delegation requires subordinates capable of handling it. The hospital CEOs are not used to such independence, and some of the people Scott inherited may not be up to much responsibilities."

In Scott Gross's view, an essential element for the success of guided autonomy was providing managers, at all levels, with timely information. He noted, "We need good information, so that we can spend less time reacting and improvising and more time managing ahead." A major new effort to develop a computerized management information system for hospitals gave testimony to this view.

Hospital MIS

Early in 1984, the Hospital Group data processing staff was given the assignment to improve hospital and financial data reporting. According to Don Amaral, chief financial officer for the Hospital Group, "Not long ago, hospital information systems were in the dark ages. Tying clinical information with financial data was considered impossible, or at least impractical. DRG's discipline on fees has changed all that. Now a hospital has to integrate treatment and costs in its management of operations."

Soon after Scott Gross took charge, the MIS assignment was broadened to include clinical, as well as financial, data. By October, a proposal to develop a system capable of providing the following information was being prepared.

1. Hospital financial data
2. Admittance, discharge, and outpatient registration
3. Pharmacy information (make medical checks with respect to possible adverse side effects for each individual patient; generate labels and medication ministration schedule; record charges)
4. Medical records information (trace a patient's chart and abstract a patient's experience for quality control)
5. Order-entry information (order and schedule initial clinical tests for incoming patients; record charges)

The proposed system, which envisaged locating eight IBM System 38 minicomputers in larger NME hospitals across the country to serve as hubs for collecting data daily from forty-five facilities, would require an investment of $25 to $30 million over three years. (The normal data-processing annual budget was about $12 million.) The most important benefit expected from such a system was that patients would be moved in and out of a hospital faster. As one executive explained, "With a DRG fixed-price arrangement, hospitals can no longer afford to have patients sitting around waiting for tests and diagnosis. There is pressure to compress the patient's stay as much as possible within the bounds of good medical treatment."

Another benefit of the system would be in selecting the optimal DRG for each patient. A particular set of patient symptoms quite often could be associated with more than one DRG. Since each DRG had its own reimbursement ceiling, the selection could affect hospital revenues.

Business Development

Henry Mordoh, a senior vice president who had headed the Hospital Group's Northwest Region, returned to headquarters to take over the newly created job of business development. He explained the significance of this move. "In the past we had a strong operational bias. We basically focused on adding and running acute-care hospitals. My new assignment reflects on important changes in management's thinking." As of late 1984, Mordoh had initiated four primary efforts. The first of these was the development of rehabilitation facilities. The kinds of services under study included simple rehabilitation for postoperative patients, stroke-patient rehabilitation, chemical imbalance (drug and alcohol) rehabilitation, major trauma (e.g., spinal-cord injury) rehabilitation, and surgical trauma rehabilitation. Mordoh explained his views on the project: "These rehabilitation patients are now dispersed in hospitals in an indiscriminate manner. We are looking at developing rehabilitation as a special new line of business for the Hospital Group."

The second effort involved joint ventures with doctors to offer out-patient services. Mordoh explained:

> As fees have been reduced, doctors, in looking for other means of earning an income, have increasingly become involved in setting up independent out-patient facilities to provide health care treatment formerly handled in hospitals. Surgicenters, for minor surgery, are a good example. By collaborating with the doctors, we see a way of averting this threat with an opportunity for growth. NME can provide legal, management, and financial expertise in return for a share of the profits and access to the patient. By working with doctors not connected with our hospital network, we can broaden our patient base. These activities also provide us with a way to enter new areas of health care.

An organized system for assimilating new acquisitions into NME was the third of Mordoh's developments. The task of assimilating each new hospital into the NME system had been the responsibility of regional managers. Mordoh planned to have headquarters' management team take over this function. He explained the reasons for the move:

> By their very nature, the pressing requirements connected with assimilating a new hospital acquisition distracted the regional executive from managing ongoing operations. Moreover, since it was a job they didn't do every day, they tended to handle these situations in a disorganized fashion . . . and the results were sloppy at times, despite our efforts and good intentions. By dealing with new acquisitions on a systemwide basis, we can professionalize the job and at the same time reduce the disruption to our important ongoing operations.

The final of the four efforts was a model hospital project. This undertaking represented a systematic effort to define effective and efficient hospital procedures and policies. It was intended to cover all aspects of hospital operations. As an illustration of its scope, Mordoh noted:

> We are trying to lay out ideal approaches to each and every aspect of hospital operations. Attention must obviously be given to such important considerations as patient care, pharmaceutical operations, laboratory operations, and the like, but small things are also important. For example, a

patient's impression of his or her hospital experience tends to be strongly affected by the last person with whom he or she deals. If the discharge staff person is not attuned to the patient's needs, you miss out on an opportunity for good public relations. And so we are focusing attention on this typically overlooked administrative duty.

University Medical Center

In 1984, negotiations were under way with the University of Southern California to develop a major medical complex to serve as the medical school's primary teaching facility. This venture—to include an acute-care hospital, an ambulatory care center, a research building, and a hotel for visitors—would require an investment of about $100 million for which NME would be responsible.

NME would operate the facility and would bear the full financial risk of the venture. Dallas Riddle, a principal negotiator for NME, noted, "The venture, if concluded, will add significantly to NME's prestige in the medical community. It also could serve as a prototype for similar future undertakings with other universities. What's more, we expect it to make a profit."

Marketing

Increasing hospital utilization (census) was the primary task for the newly created marketing function. Nathan Kaufman explained how he viewed his new job, "As you might expect, we are developing TV and print ad campaigns to promote our facilities with the public. Our principal focus, however, is directed at the physicians. They are really our primary customers because they are the ones who refer most patients to the hospital. So an important part of my job is to make NME increasingly attractive to the physician."

Pressures to cut health care costs both aided and complicated Kaufman's job. He saw opportunities for NME to enter into new arrangements with physicians that could strengthen the bonds between these two parties. The joint ventures being developed by Mordoh were cited as a case in point. On the negative side, NME's entry into HMO and PPO arrangements were viewed with disfavor by many physicians who saw them as potential threats to their practices. Since the Hospital Group operations were affected in one way or another by activities in other NME units, Kaufman, and Scott Gross on a broader scale, had to work across divisional lines to deal with these developments.

Relations with Other NME Units

In early years, acute-care hospital operations not only dominated NME's activities, they were also largely independent of the company's other ventures. The increase in the size and diversity of NME's other health care operations, the general emergence of new approaches to health care, and the recent declines in acute-care census all served to increase the Hospital Group's dependency on other NME units. The need for interaction occurred in two principal ways.

The more straightforward form of collaboration had to do with the use of related health care services to support and enhance the hospitals' operations. For example, an empty hospital wing might be devoted to substance-abuse treatment for people suffering from alcohol and drug dependencies. This health care activity would be handled by the Psychiatric Group. Convalescent facilities represented another area involving divisional interaction. As cost-cutting pressures required early discharge from hospitals, the need for available convalescent facilities increased. Since there was a general shortage of such facilities, especially in California, the Hospital Group sought to have the Long Term Care Group locate convalescent facilities near NME hospitals.

More complex was the problem of coordinating the Hospital Group's needs with the new developments taking place in the Health Care Systems and Services Group. The HMO, PPO, and free-standing clinic programs all held great potential for affecting Hospital Group results. Kaufman gave one indication of the impending impact, "Traditionally, patient flow in hospitals has been physician directed. Third party payors, industry HMOs and PPOs, will increasingly control this vital element." Since these health care arrangements were all still relatively new developments for NME, the Hospital Group management had little experience to fall back on as it tried to influence the evolution of these new activities.

Reflecting on the diverse activities of his group, and its relationship to other groups, Scott Gross saw all efforts as directed toward one shared goal: "Anything that we do is ultimately designed to get more utilization of our facilities." Though acute-care hospitals were critical to NME's continued success, Gross realized that from 1979 to 1984 they had contributed a decreasing share to overall earnings. Vital new businesses were growing rapidly within NME, and the need for intragroup cooperation and coordination became imperative. Gross was particularly attuned to those currents of change within the company.

Health Care Systems and Services Group

As the new general manager of a newly created division, Bill Piche soon found himself confronting a variety of knotty issues. The more salient of these included decisions on how to develop the new health care activities he had inherited, managing the independent-minded physicians who headed several of the ventures, working out a proper relationship with the Hospital Group, and defining the role HCSSG was to play within NME. While Piche had already been involved with the group's ventures before his move from the Hospital Group, his expanded duties as group president left him with little time to reflect with leisure on these matters.

The HCSS Group was responsible for four principal business operations. The largest and most complex of these was the insurance-related subgroup of activities, including both PPO and HMO ventures. Piche explained how NME had first entered this field, "In 1983, as cost-cutting pressures mounted in California, it soon became obvious to us that negotiations between hospitals and private insurance companies would become a one-way street. The insurance companies were playing off the hospitals one against the other to push down rates. The providing organizations also had to be organized."

In March 1984, NME introduced Health Pace, a fully underwritten "preferred provider organization" health care plan (PPO), in Southern California, with intentions to move subsequently to selected markets throughout the United States. NME was responsible for establishing and administering the preferred-provider network. A national insurance brokerage firm, Corroon & Black, had been engaged to market and service Health Pace through independent brokers and agents, and New York Life Insurance Company was the underwriter for the plan.

While moving ahead in the development of the PPO program, NME management was also interested in gaining experience with health maintenance organizations (HMOs). In June 1984, the company acquired Av-Med, Inc., a Florida-based corporation operating federally qualified prepaid health plans with 75,000 subscribers and a provider network of more than 1,100 physicians and thirty-five hospitals in the Miami and Tampa regions. NME took over 80 percent of the ownership; the founding physician retained a 20 percent ownership share.

Three independent clinic groups constituted HCSSG's other businesses. In October 1983, NME acquired an 80 percent share of Instant Care Centers of America, an owner and operator of fourteen free-standing urgent-care centers in Louisiana, California, Texas, and Florida. The purpose of the acquisition, as reported in the annual report, was to facilitate establishing a national network of such ambulatory-care centers. The founding physician retained 20 percent ownership.

In March 1984, NME acquired the Stein Women's Center, a small clinic in St. Petersburg, Florida. The unit was viewed as a possible base for creating a chain of gynecological clinics throughout the U.S. The remaining HCSSG business operation was to manage six occupational health care clinics in California. This activity had been organized in 1980.

In describing the Health Care Systems and Services Group's operations, the 1984 annual report concluded, "These highly competitive health care distribution alternatives, consolidated into a national program under a new operating group, will reinforce utilization of NME hospitals while creating a new product to market to employers and health care insurers." A careful reading of this statement revealed some of the ambiguities Piche faced in defining the role his unit was to play. The group had been formed with several goals in mind: to conduct experimentation and program development for NME; to feed patients to existing hospital units; and to create profitable new growth businesses. Deciding on the right balance among these somewhat conflicting aims was viewed by Piche as one of the most pressing strategic issues he faced. Several operational problems were certain to influence the outcome of his consideration.

One problem concerned the mixed feelings of hospital administrators and physicians about the impact such programs would have on the hospitals' financial performance. While these parties welcomed the additional patients HMOs and PPOs might provide, they were less favorably disposed to the reduced-fee features of these programs. The resulting trade-off between additional patients versus any loss of revenue associated with full-paying patients transferring to the contract service was difficult to predict.

The net effect of the free-standing clinics on hospital patient loading was also difficult to predict. These clinics potentially could enlarge the patient base available to feed the acute-care hospitals, but they also promised to compete with these hospitals for outpatient and emergency care. One executive noted wryly, "The introduction of PPOs, HMOs, and alternative health care facilities is like a bad-tasting medicine for the physicians. They know that they need to take it, but they want to put it off as long as possible."

For Piche, physician resistance to the introduction of alternative health care arrangements touched on a broader strategic issue. He remarked:

> Why should I have to force a PPO on to an NME hospital that doesn't want it when there are plenty of other hospitals eager for it? Beyond ease of entry, there is also a question of profitability. Should the group establish an HMO or PPO in support of NME hospitals in an area with profit potential limited by demographics versus moving into more attractive locales? And even in areas where NME hospitals are located, an HMO or PPO will probably have to include competing hospitals in the plan in order to create a sufficiently large provider network to secure a viable membership base. For example, were we to set up an HMO in the Boston area, it would be necessary to include hospitals in the city and the suburbs to provide an effective health care network. Selecting our initial PPO and HMO targets is going to require some careful thinking and probably some hard negotiating with the Hospital Group and top management.

Such negotiations were complicated by the ownership structures for the new health-care ventures. Av-Med (HMO), Instant Care Centers of America (urgent care centers), and Stein Women's Center (gynecological clinics) were each owned 20 percent by the founding physician. Each of these entrepreneurs had joined NME with the expectation of achieving rapid profitable growth, and consequently they held aggressive priorities for their particular units. Piche faced a problem in getting these key people to back a strategy aimed primarily in support of NME hospitals. As one executive pointed out, "We are already encountering internal strife between the venture leaders and the hospital-related advisory board of physicians." According to Piche, a related problem was whether NME would approve the business-development expenditures that each of the entrepreneurial physicians wanted and expected.

Entrepreneurship and Synergy

One outcome of the reorganization was the installation of a new generation of group presidents. These men were young, energetic, and eager to prove themselves. Just as Scott Gross had set out to expand and improve hospital operations, and Bill Piche to introduce and develop new approaches to health care, the other group executives were actively implementing promising growth opportunities for NME.

As an indication of these opportunities, the 1984 annual report stated in connection with the Long Term Care Group:

> The accelerating growth of a longer-living elderly population, coupled with a new emphasis on cost-effective alternative care settings for all age groups, has made long-term care the fastest growing segment of the U.S. health care industry. . . .
>
> In addition to expansion of its network of skilled nursing facilities, development of retirement complexes and rehabilitation centers was accelerated, and special care units for the treatment of Alzheimer's Disease were established.
>
> Of particular significance to the emerging market for long-term care services are the economic incentives to reduce lengths of stay at acute-care hospitals. . . . Another factor fueling the growth of the long-term care market is the increasing economic independence of the emerging elderly population.

Along with the acquisition in 1984 of forty-nine additional long-term care facilities with a total of 5,366 beds, the Long Term Care Group had also opened four special care units for the treatment of Alzheimer's Disease and were developing seven more. In addition, a new subsidiary—Cadem Corporation—had been formed to develop retirement complexes, rehabilitation centers, long-term care hospitals, and other health facilities. The group's president, Don Baty (age forty), had a reputation as a hard-driving and profit-oriented executive.

Psychiatric care also offered NME major growth opportunities. Under the new leadership of Norman Zober (age forty-one), the Psychiatric Group planned to accelerate its expansion of diagnostic and treatment facilities. With more than ten out of every 100 employees and more than 3 million teenagers dependent on alcohol or drugs, a special emphasis was to be placed on chemical-abuse treatment, with an expansion of both free-standing and in-hospital facilities. And with the statement, "The home health market is at the threshold of a new era of growth," NME's annual report also recognized the Home Care Group as another contender for investment funds.

With opportunities beckoning in every direction and with the size of meaningful NME ventures becoming ever larger, the future availability of funds was of growing concern to a number of group executives. As one observed, "Given its size and ambitions, the company is beginning to encounter capital constraints. The problem of who gets money is beginning to surface. Since NME has not had any problem raising funds, we don't really have a system for allocating capital, nor do we have any experience along these lines. In the old days, if you wanted something, you got it. Now you have to justify it."

A competition for funds among groups promised to unsettle the traditional laissez-faire character of divisional relationships. Sidney Tyler, senior vice president for corporate planning, described the company's dilemma, "We expect the future of health care to involve long-term mental, home, and primary treatments in some integrated fashion. Putting them all together under a health care plan and learning how to get the different lines of business to talk to each other and to feed each other will present a major challenge to our management. This is one of the downsides in having an entrepreneurial setup. You're not rewarded for building bridges to each other."

Other senior officers echoed concern with the organizational dilemma described by Tyler. Peter de Wetter, executive vice president and member of the board, referred to the compensation system to illustrate the problem: "A group CEO can earn up to $250,000 with a 40 percent annual incentive bonus opportunity. This incentive is based on group and personal performance. If we want these executives to increase focus on total corporate performance, we will obviously have to strengthen our long-term incentive program, but this has to be balanced with our corporate culture, which stresses entrepreneurial autonomy."

John Bedrosian, senior executive vice president and member of the board, emphasized the importance of individuals and was inclined to prefer people selection over organizational restructuring as a response. He argued, "People are very important around here. You need structure, but more importantly, you need people who will work well together." Leonard Cohen, NME president, made clear the full force of the dilemma as the need for restructuring argued by some clashed with the entrepreneurial climate prized by others: "In the past we have been able to fit the pieces together on an informal basis. It would be foolish for me to say that this approach will necessarily continue to work in the future."

Management's concerns with synergy were clearly connected to another concern as to just how many ventures NME should pursue. Bedrosian explained the pressure to diversify: "The reason that NME is involved in so many aspects of health care is that there is uncertainty as to where the industry is going. We want to be sure that we are in position when the market changes."

As chief operating officer with responsibility for operational performance, Cohen advanced a note of caution to this strategy: "We are moving into a lot of businesses we know little about. Sometimes I worry that we are trying to juggle too many balls at one time and that bothers me. Obviously, the company needs to keep its options open. Sometimes we're afraid that we might be missing something. But there's an important distinction between doing a million things and doing them well."

Serving as a reference point to management in its analysis of these issues was Richard Eamer's overarching vision of health care:

> There are things we should keep in mind. First, we are in a simple business. Basically, we are in the business of delivering patient care. Acute, long-term psychiatric and home care are all part of this business. People will want an integrated package of total health care from birth to death.
>
> Second, very little really changes in our business. Ninety percent of what you do this year, you will do next year. People focus too much on the 10 percent change. Changing this business is like turning the S.S. *Queen Elizabeth*. . . . It takes a lot of time.

Glossary

Acute-care facilities. Traditionally referred to as hospitals.

Average Length of Stay. Average period that inpatients spend during a reporting period. Derived by dividing the number of inpatient days by the number of admissions.

Blue Cross/Blue Shield. A not-for-profit third-party insurer.

Capitation. A payment plan based on the number of patients seen over a specified time.

Census. Occupancy rate in an acute-care hospital.

Diagnostic Related Groups (DRGs). Federally defined categories of medical services and procedures that apply to the fixed amount a hospital will receive as reimbursement for services rendered to Medicare patients.

Fee-for-Service. The traditional system of payment in specified amounts for services rendered by physicians.

Health Maintenance Organizations (HMOs). Organized system of health care that assure the delivery of comprehensive, continuous preventative and treatment services to members. Subscribers pay a predetermined flat fee and are entitled to specified health care services as needed.

Medicaid. Federally supported health insurance for the indigent.

Medicare. Federally supported health insurance for the elderly.

Preferred Provider Organization (PPO). A group of health care providers—including hospitals, physicians, dentists, optometrists and so on—who agree to provide medical services to members on a discount fee-for-service schedule.

Third-party insurers. Insurance companies who provide health care insurance. (e.g., Blue Cross/Blue Shield, Traveler's Insurance Company).

The Philips Group: 1987

In his first videotaped message to the worldwide Philips organization since becoming president in April 1986, Cor van der Klugt opened with the following admonition: "Philips must be profit-oriented. The top priority for Philips, and hence our main objective for the coming years, is profit."

He went on to enumerate four other major policy statements that were to provide the driving forces for achieving this objective:

> Philips must be globally oriented! Philips with its structure of product divisions and national organizations is ideally positioned to combine "a global presence with local faces."
>
> Philips must be a quality-driven, customer-oriented organization. . . . There is a growing percentage of our people who never see or "smell" a customer in the marketplace. . . . A strong commitment in serving the customer must be cultivated at every level.
>
> Philips must be faster and even more innovation-oriented. Fifty percent of the products marketed in the next five years do not exist today. Moreover, changes in the market succeed one another at ever shorter intervals. We must work faster.
>
> The Philips organization has to adapt itself. Which means we have to organize our internal activities on the basis of what I like to describe as contractual relationships. Product divisions have the ultimate responsibility for products and profits.

In this last point, van der Klugt was signaling the coming change to organizational structure and to the managerial mindset that would be necessary for implementing Philips' new strategic thrust. By June 1987, van der Klugt had made or announced a number of sweeping changes that affect almost every aspect of how Philips would be managed. This proud company had turned down a new road as it approached its centennial milestone, making changes that would not be easily, if ever, reversed.

The History of Philips

Philips was founded in 1891 by Gerard Philips, a Dutch engineer who had developed an inexpensive process to manufacture incandescent lamps. In 1987,

N.V. Philips' Gloeilampenfabrieken was the fourth largest industrial company outside the United States and was reputedly the world's most widely known manufacturer of household appliances, television and radio sets, professional electronic equipment, lighting, and related products. Exhibit 1 shows the company's product deliveries, geographic sales, and value added for 1986. Exhibit 2 presents group financial data for 1977–1986.

The company had several hundred subsidiaries in sixty countries and operated plants in more than forty countries (more than 380 plants in the world) manufacturing thousands of different products. It employed approximately 344,000 persons at the end of 1986.

Organization. Until 1940, Philips had been managed from Eindhoven, the Netherlands, where R&D and financial control were centered. During World War II, the Philips' subsidiaries, which were cut off from the Netherlands, began to operate independently. Following the war, Philips' management decided that the company could be rebuilt most successfully through its national organizations for several reasons, the most compelling of which was the severe trade restrictions imposed by European nations during the reconstruction period. Aside from tariff walls, the self-contained networks of plants in individual countries serving only local markets minimized Philips' identity as a foreign company and enabled it to respond more effectively to local preferences. The war-weakened condition of the headquarters organization also facilitated decentralization.

Over the years, Philips had developed a matrix management structure to relate its many products with its broad geographical interests. Product policy throughout the world was the responsibility of fourteen product divisions (PDS). This responsibility was to be exercised in consultation with the general managements of the national organizations (NOs).

The general management boards of more than sixty national organizations were responsible for operations and overall Philips' policies (in consultation with the product divisions) in each country. Most national organizations comprised a group of subsidiary companies ranging from pure marketing organizations to complete industrial enterprises.

A ten-man board of management was the top policy- and decision-making organ in the company. While the board members shared general management responsibility for the whole concern, each typically maintained special interest in one of the functional areas (e.g., R&D, sales, finance). Members of this board were selected by a twelve-member supervisory board, which in turn was responsible to shareholders.

The board of management, the product divisions, and the national organizations were supported by a number of staff departments and the research laboratories in Eindhoven and elsewhere. Exhibit 3 shows the broad structure of Philips' operating management organization for 1972.

Decision Making. The management of Philips during the early 1970s was based on coordination and consultation among these major units. The compli-

Exhibit 1 The Philips Group: commercial activities for 1986. *Source:* Philips 1986 Annual Report

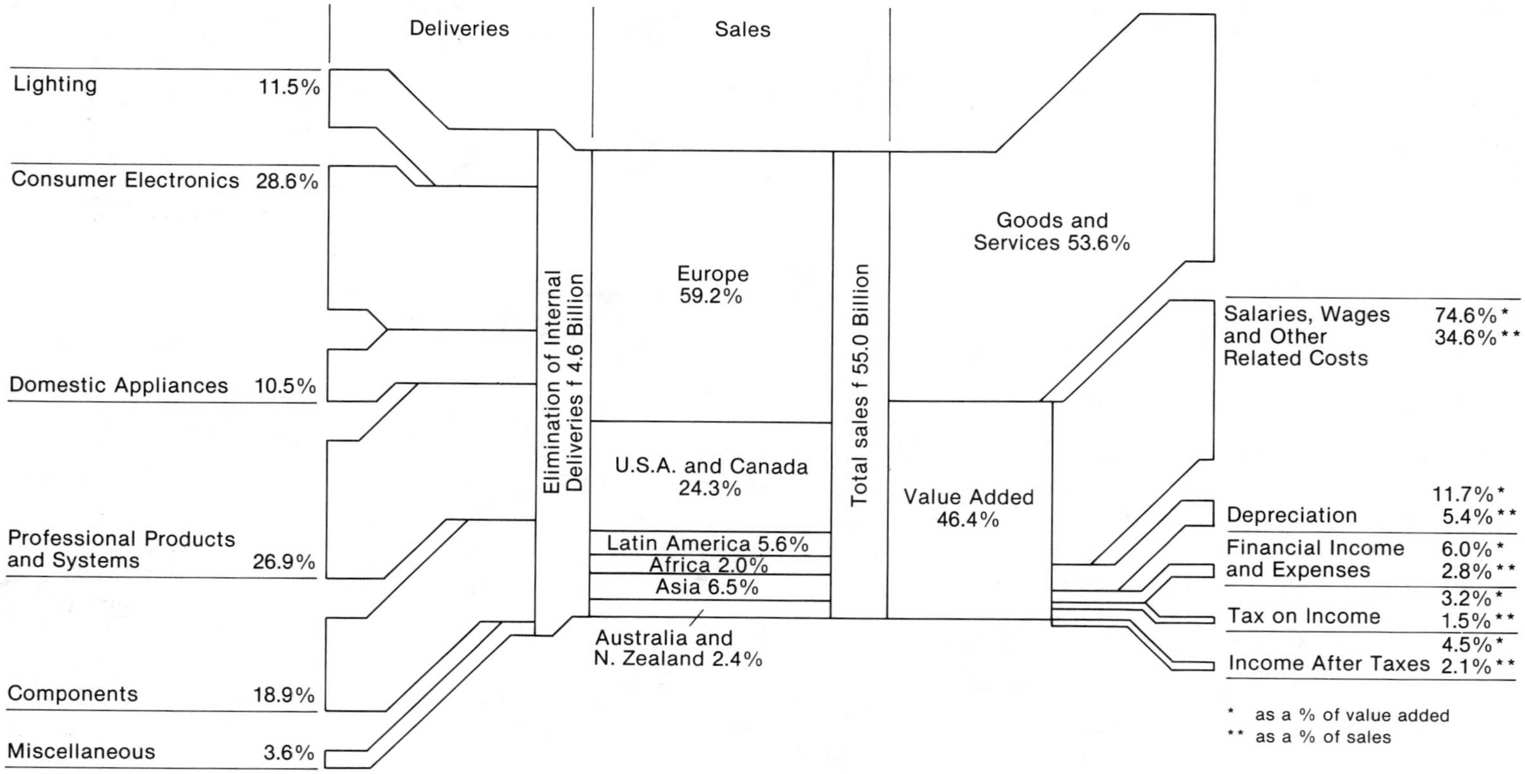

Lighting 11.5%

Consumer Electronics 28.6%

Domestic Appliances 10.5%

Professional Products and Systems 26.9%

Components 18.9%

Miscellaneous 3.6%

Deliveries

Sales

Elimination of Internal Deliveries ƒ 4.6 Billion

Total sales ƒ 55.0 Billion

Europe 59.2%

U.S.A. and Canada 24.3%

Latin America 5.6%

Africa 2.0%

Asia 6.5%

Australia and N. Zealand 2.4%

Goods and Services 53.6%

Value Added 46.4%

Salaries, Wages and Other Related Costs 74.6% * 34.6% **

Depreciation 11.7% * 5.4% **

Financial Income and Expenses 6.0% * 2.8% **

Tax on Income 3.2% * 1.5% **

Income After Taxes 4.5% * 2.1% **

* as a % of value added
** as a % of sales

637

Exhibit 2 The Philips Group: Financial* and related information, 1977–1986.

	1986	1985	1984	1983	1982	1981	1980	1979	1978	1977
Net sales	55,037	60,045	53,804	46,183	42,991	42,411	36,536	33,238	32,658	31,164
Income from operations	3,194	3,075	3,473	2,755	2,130	2,193	1,577	1,796	2,210	2,162
Net income	1,015	919	1,113	647	433	357	328	564	651	583
as percentage of stockholders' equity	6.3	5.6	6.9	4.9	3.4	3.0	2.7	5.0	6.0	5.6
Inventories	12,851	13,942	15,547	13,615	12,199	12,374	11,974	10,468	9,362	9,226
Accounts receivable	13,992	15,094	14,825	12,963	11,258	11,081	10,370	9,636	9,370	8,465
Current assets	28,167	30,770	31,964	28,266	24,879	24,748	23,687	21,417	20,009	19,155
Total assets	50,630	52,883	54,535	47,758	43,295	42,730	39,647	35,150	31,967	31,108
Current liabilities	18,453	19,693	19,781	17,601	15,747	15,198	14,204	12,121	11,229	10,397
Long-term liabilities	13,840	14,609	15,108	12,503	11,395	11,755	11,028	10,192	8,719	8,851
Equity	18,337	18,581	19,646	17,654	16,153	15,777	14,415	12,837	12,019	11,860
Employees (thousands)	344	346	344	343	336	348	373	379	388	384
Wages, salaries	19,755	21,491	20,240	18,364	17,488	17,369	15,399	14,159	13,471	12,816

1986 Percentage of Total

Product Sector	Sales	Operating Income
Lighting	12	17
Consumer electronics	31	23
Domestic appliances	11	7
Professional products	29	36
Components	13	8
Miscellaneous	4	9

Area	Sales	Operating Income
Netherlands	7	17
Europe (rest of)	52	59
USA/Canada	24	2
Latin America	6	13
Africa	2	1
Asia	7	7
Australia/N.Z.	2	—

Source: Philips Financial Statements, 1986.

*All amounts are expressed in millions of guilders unless otherwise stated. (The exchange rate on October 1, 1987, was 2.07 guilders per U.S. dollar.) Due to factors such as consolidations and divestments, the stated amounts are not directly comparable over time.

Exhibit 3 The Philips Group: Company organization chart, 1972. *Source:* Philips Charts and Tables, November 15, 1972

BOARD OF MANAGEMENT

Organization

Internal Audit

Technical Services	General Services	Commercial Services
Industrial Coordination Technical Efficiency and Organization Building Design and Plant Engineering Central Development Bureau	Financial Affairs Accounting Legal Affairs Fiscal Affairs Personnel Affairs Press Affairs Management Development	Commercial Prognosis and Planning Concern Marketing Services Forwarding Advertising

National Organizations

Country A	Country B	Country C	Direct Export
Country D	– –	– –	– –
– –	– –	– –	– –

Regional Bureaus

Research Lab

Product Divisions

Lighting	Electronic Components and Materials (Elcoma)	Radio, Television and Record-Players*	Major Domestic Appliances	Small Domestic Appliances
Tele-communications and Defense Systems	Medical Systems	Industrial Equipment	Electroacoustics	Data Systems
Allied Industries	Glass	Pharmaceutical Chemical Products		Music (Polygram)

639

cated relations were described in the following account in the January 12, 1972, issue of *Business Week:*

> . . . As Philips views its management process, Eindhoven's role is just to coordinate activities of the highly autonomous national organizations. Says one executive: "Coordination does not mean giving orders. It means negotiation."
>
> Much of the negotiating goes on between the product groups and the national companies, with the management board acting as referee and final arbiter, and even the management board operates by mutual agreement.
> . . . Even the simple matter of setting a sales target is negotiated, with the national company often setting a higher target than the product groups.

Coordination was also the practice within organizational units in Philips, where typically a manager in charge of commercial affairs and a manager in charge of technical activities shared responsibility for general leadership of the unit. This duumvirate form of management, found at all levels in the Philips organizations, had its origins when Anton Philips joined the firm as a salesman to complement his brother Gerard's talents as an engineer. Anton noted at a later date:

> From the moment I joined the company, the technical management and the sales management competed to outperform each other. Production tried to produce so much that sales would not be able to get rid of it; sales tried to sell so much that the factory would not be able to keep up. And this competition has always continued; sometimes the one is ahead, sometimes the other seems to be winning.

In many national organizations, a third person—the financial manager, who was responsible for accounting and cost reporting activities—joined the commercial and technical managers to form a three-man Committee of Coordination and Direction.

The need to coordinate both within and among organizational units in making plans and deciding issues placed its own special demands on the Philips manager. As one executive explained in 1972:

> There is always a great deal of discussion and pressure from different directions working on the individual manager with respect to any major decision. I suppose one reason the system works is that when a man comes to work for Philips, more often than not, it is for life. I cannot think of an executive in our upper management levels who has not been with Philips since his twenties. During his time with the company, he will occupy a number of different positions in different divisions (A Dutchman will normally undertake at least one extended tour of foreign duty). This experience tends to foster a set of informal relationships among managers throughout the organization and an intuitive understanding as to what can be done and what cannot be done.
>
> Another integrating device is the common working language. A man cannot reach a top position without being fluent in English and all key documents are prepared in English. This practice permits an easier coordination and communication of ideas and problems between our national groups than is possible in many multinational companies.

In addition to these unifying practices, there were several headquarters staff departments responsible for coordination within the concern. These included Industrial Coordination, Technical Efficiency and Organization, Commercial Prognoses and Planning, Accounting, Financial Affairs, and External Relations.

Forces for Change

During the 1960s, the emphasis on national autonomy came into increasing question as the firm's environment changed in several important respects. The creation and development of the European Common Market was to remove the trade barriers between many of Philips' most important production centers. This period also witnessed the advent of such items as the transistor and printed circuits, which called for large production runs to obtain efficient operations. Moreover, an increasing amount of electronic equipment was being produced by U.S. (and later Japanese) competitors in the low-wage areas of the Far East and elsewhere.

In the early 1970s, Hendrik van Reimsdijk, the president at the time, created an Organization Committee to examine and redefine managerial relationships between product divisions and national organizations. International Production Centers (IPCs) were organized to supply products to more than one national organization and thereby gain production economies of scale. With this change, PD managers began to control manufacturing operations for the first time.

Despite these moves, Philips' financial performance continued to be disappointing through the 1970s. This could be attributed largely to Europe's troubled economy, where Philips conducted the major part of its business. Already saddled with a high wage structure and an outdated production infrastructure, Europe was particularly hard hit by the oil crises of 1973 and 1978. The rate of unemployment rose calamitously and with it the burden of welfare support.

Added to the sickly condition of its home territory, Philips found itself facing another challenge. As the 1970s wore on, the electronics field continued to change in character, driven in part by the nature of the technology and in part by the aggressive competitive drive of Japanese firms. By the early 1980s, Philips' management had come to the following general understanding of the role, nature, and direction of the electronics business.

Role of Electronics. Electronics and information technology had become the driving force of the post-industrial age. By 1990, the electronics industry would employ between 4 and 5 million people to produce some $850 billion in products and software.

Nature of Electronics. A salient characteristic of the electronics field was a trend toward integration. A clear-cut movement from components to ever more encompassing systems dominated the technology proper. The rapid succession from semiconductors to integrated circuits, large-scale ICs (integrated circuits), very large-scale ICs, and so on, since the early 1950s, provided a dramatic example of this evolution. At the same time, developments in electronics were affecting the development and use of optics, magnetics, and other technologies. The net impact of these parallel developments for firms in the field was to increase greatly the scope and complexity of the required technological capabilities and the cost of new product innovations.

Another consequence of the increasing interplay of various technologies with electronics was the speedup of product innovation. No longer could firms count on years of undisturbed profit-making for a successful product.

Evolving Competitive Situation. For Philips, with 63.3 percent of its 1980 sales and 73.5 percent of its assets in Europe, one of the more alarming developments was the gradual shift of the world's economic concentration from the Atlantic to the Pacific Basin, and with it the electronics business. This shift was pronounced for consumer electronics, a core business for Philips.

The competitive structure in consumer electronics was also experiencing strong integrating forces. No longer could individual firms act as independently of others in the field as had been true in earlier times. The following account about Philips' experience with the compact-disc concept gives an indication of this development. According to R. H. van Meurs, senior director in charge of Consumer Electronics Compact Discs:

> One of the first things Philips wanted to do was to reach an agreement with competitors selling technical specification standards for the world. It was then necessary to get enough participants into the business to be able to give the market some assurance of the product's future viability. Philips also had to negotiate with the software suppliers—in this case, the record industry—to ensure that everyone received attractive future returns. In effect, a large collaborative effort had to be organized prior to launching this new product.
>
> Once launched, we could expect many new entrants, since innovations now can be copied in three to four months instead of the one to two years that had been true in former years. As a result, Philips could now hope for a maximum market share of 10 percent to 15 percent versus the 45 percent to 50 percent it had enjoyed in earlier times.

Laying the Groundwork

By the time he had been appointed president of the company and chairman of the board of management on January 1, 1982, Wisse Dekker was convinced of the need to accelerate and extend the changes his predecessors, Hendrik van Reimsdijk (1971–1979) and Dr. N. Rodenburg (1979–1982), had begun. His sense of urgency was understandable: in 1981, the company's margin had fallen to less than 1 percent. He later noted how he had gone about launching a program of change:

> When I took over the company, the world saw us as a sleeping giant. The company had a great technological heritage, but it lacked aggressiveness and a marketing orientation, nor was it cost competitive. I knew that

the firm would have to be changed in ways that would be difficult for most of our management to accept.

My first priority was to communicate a sense of urgency to our employees. I had to make clear to our generally comfortable staff that Philips could not continue to survive without dramatic changes.

As part of his communication campaign, Dekker began to speak out in public, an unprecedented move for this traditionally secretive company. He explained: "I sought public visibility basically to send the message to my own employees. It's one thing to receive a message from management through company channels and quite something else to read it in the newspapers or hear it on television."

The message that Dekker sent was that Philips' resources were limited and that the company would have to increase its profitability. He announced the objectives for 1984: sales of 50 billion guilders; net profit of 1 billion guilders; and an inventory ratio decline of 10 percent. He then began to redefine the Philips strategy and structure to achieve these goals.

Strategy. Dekker was the first to express explicitly Philips' commitment to a global strategy. He noted:

The Japanese taught us the value of pursuing a global strategy with standard products. They had a tremendous cost advantage in being able to supply the world market from their factories at home. We were trying to compete on a country-by-country basis with all the additional costs associated with a fragmented operation.

In line with this new thinking, he pushed for manufacturing rationalization, creating more International Production Centers, and closing many small, inefficient plants, particularly in Europe. The company's earlier efforts to divest businesses that were seen as falling outside its areas of primary interest were continued with the sale of such businesses as welding, energy cables, and furniture. At the same time, Philips continued acquiring ownership of businesses that fit the firm's new direction. These acquired interests included 35 percent of Grundig (audio and video equipment) and Westinghouse Electric's lamp activities in the United States and Canada.

Somewhat of a departure from earlier practices was Dekker's recognition of the need for Philips to expand significantly its collaborative arrangements with other leading firms in the professional electronics sector. His reasoning, as stated by a senior executive, reflected the evolving nature of electronics technology:

The functional expansion of electronic products also means that an ever increasing level of knowledge and skill are required to put one product or system on the market. . . . Even the largest industrial research centers no longer have all the knowledge available in-house to be able to guarantee sufficient progress in every sector.

He also pointed to an important change in Philips' approach to such collaborations:

. . . Probably with Japanese examples in mind, Philips clearly shifted the emphasis when looking for cooperation arrangements. These are now sought with companies which have something to offer that Philips cannot develop itself, or cannot develop in time.

For 1982, the company reported a contract with Control Data Corporation for the joint development of an optical storage system and an agreement with RCA and Intel for cooperation with respect to certain types of integrated circuits. The 1983 annual report announced an agreement with AT&T to cooperate in the field of public telephony and transmission, explaining:

The high development costs in the field of digital telephone exchanges and the need to acquire a greater supporting structure were the reasons for embarking on a cooperative activity. The strong technological position of AT&T in the field of public telephony, together with Philips' competence in developing systems based on the [European] specifications, our transmission technology, and our international marketing experience, constitutes a good basis for the future.

In 1984, the arrangement with CDC was extended to include the manufacture and sale of optical discs and readout equipment. In 1985, the CDC collaborative effort was folded into a fifty–fifty joint venture in optical media for consumer and professional applications with DuPont. Philips also established two joint ventures with Kyocera Corporation—one for developing and manufacturing new interactive systems for use in the home and for its sale in Japan and another for introducing the Philips communication network system into the Japanese market—and a fifty–fifty joint venture with the Beijing Radio Factory to build an audio factory. In 1986, joint ventures were entered into with R. R. Donnelley & Sons (United States) and Toppan Printing Company (Japan) to promote the development of software for interactive compact discs and with Willi Studer (Switzerland) for research and development relating to professional CD systems for radio and television studios.

Organization. Dekker acted to revitalize Philips' ponderous management structure. At the operating level, he continued Dr. Rodenburg's initiative to replace the dual leadership arrangement (commercial and technical co-directors) that had been in place since the firm's founding with a single general manager. To energize a management board that he had characterized as "too large, too distant, and too uninvolved, where each person was almost a baron protective of his particular territory," Dekker reduced the number of members, brought in people with strong operating experiences, and created subcommittees to deal with difficult issues.

In line with the new emphasis on global involvement, Dekker continued to "tilt the matrix" away from national organizations by creating a Corporate Council on which the heads of product divisions would join the heads of the national organizations to discuss issues of importance to both. At the same time, product divisions were to play an increasingly important role in the firm's decision making with respect to product design, manufacturing, and research.

To facilitate change, a management-by-objectives system was introduced and emphasis on incentive compensation increased. In an attempt to improve costs, plants were closed and staff reduced through early retirement.

In April 1986, van Riemsdijk reached the mandatory retirement age for chairman of the supervisory board and Dekker moved up to that position. His efforts to redefine the Philips' strategy and structure would now be in the hands of Cor van der Klugt, his selected successor as president and chairman of the board of management.

In his farewell speech, Dekker reminded Philips' 300 senior managers that the firm's performance in recent years had been less than satisfactory. He pointed to its slow growth and low profitability when compared to leading U.S. and Japanese competitors, concluding with the admonition: "We are still far from being where we want and would like to be. In just over four years, we shall be on the eve of our centennial anniversary. Shall we be able in 1991 to celebrate the achievement of our objectives?"

Cor van der Klugt

More than one executive noted how the change in leadership seemed well-suited to Philips' evolving needs. The following comment typified senior management's thinking:

> Dekker was conceptual and a statesman. He sensed danger, sounded the alarm bell, and pointed the organization in a new direction for survival and success. Van der Klugt is an organization builder and a fighter. He likes to convince people and has the emotional force to bring about the needed changes.

Van der Klugt spoke of the change in leadership as one involving continuity with change:

> A new CEO steps into an ongoing process, inheriting many things that were started by his predecessor. He must build on the past, but needs to go beyond the past. In a way, each CEO is a new light in the firm's sky who must set the stage for the next decades.

The objectives set forth in van der Klugt's first message to the Philips organization was in large part a reaffirmation of earlier policies. But in specifying profits as the central measure and the product divisions as having the ultimate responsibility for achieving profits, the new president was beginning to impose his own imprint on developments. In his second videotaped message to the Philips organization, given in November 1986, he further defined his agenda and priorities by spotlighting the management of human resources, stating, "People are our most important resource. The unavoidable conclusion is that human resources management is a strategic activity which demands top priority." The speech went on to describe responsibilities and policies, and included among the firm's objectives: improving identification and guidance of young talent; improving management education, job rotation, and international exchange; and creating challenging career prospects and an attractive organizational climate.

Major actions accompanied the words. In late 1986, van der Klugt terminated the U.S. Philips trust that had been given control of North American Philips during World War II. He explained:

> The United States is the largest and most sophisticated arena for a number of important electronics products. To compete, Philips needs to have a direct and clear-cut presence there. The termination of the trust accords with our global strategy, which for the future requires a more integrated international organization capable of facing the challenge of worldwide competition.

No longer would North American Philips operate as a quasi-independent corporation.

At the same time, the management board had begun to refine corporate strategy. Henceforth, Philips would focus on selected sectors of electronics along with its large and profitable lighting business. Consumer electronics would continue as one area for emphasis because of the firm's strong market position in Europe. The increasing global character of consumer electronics products also offered Philips an opportunity to expand in other major markets through its already established worldwide organization.

Professional electronics would also remain an area of focus because of its importance as a place where "technological push" was strongest. The professional user's willingness to experiment with new concepts and products made this sector a natural staging ground for new consumer electronics products.

A continued presence in components was also seen as critical since it was in this sector that the foundations were laid for new generations of systems and products. The rationale for this commitment was later described by a senior director:

> The American consumer electronics industry . . . lost out completely because . . . the production of essential components was left to the Far East. . . . It is easy to guess what happened: the Far East, partly helped by high volume production for American customers, entered the American market with its own labels. The American industry was left standing. . . . The essential fact is that components development is creating new possibilities and that, if at all possible, we must endeavor to keep these new possibilities in our own hands.

In May 1987, van der Klugt announced a major restructuring of the Philips concern: the Consumer Electronics, Components, and Telecommunications and Data Systems product divisions were designated core-interlinked units; the lighting division was to become a core, stand-alone unit; and all other operating units were noncore. At the same time, the top management structure was to be reconstituted so as "to enhance efficiency and flexibility . . . reducing the number of levels of management in the organization." Specifically, the board of management would be reduced in size and its policy-making responsibility would devolve to a newly created group management committee comprising the remaining board members, the heads of the three core-linked product divisions, and the directors of key functional staffs. Exhibit 4 shows the new top management organizational structure.

In placing the core-linked unit managers on the group's policy-making body, the new structure completed the tilting of Philips' matrix in favor of the product divisions. So as to avoid any misunderstanding, the announcement went on to spell out this point: "In the proposed organizational structure, the Philips Group will be directed primarily via the product divisions."

Van der Klugt was later to comment on the dilemma that Philips faced in tilting the matrix:

> Competitive forces in electronics call for a global approach and that means that we must now emphasize product divisions with a global perspective. But we cannot afford to forget that national organizations are still very important, especially the large units such as those in Germany, France, and the United Kingdom. The head of a national organization has an important presence in his community, enjoying considerable prestige and power. Our challenge is to combine the strengths of national organizations and product divisions. In my view, the answer is to let national organizations govern, but to let product divisions fight it out in the battlefield.

The policy of joining forces with other firms for noncore businesses was put into practice almost simultaneously with its announcement. In May 1987, Philips reached agreement with General Electric Company of Britain to combine their medical electronics businesses in a fifty–fifty joint venture. Negotiations were also underway with Whirlpool to combine their major appliance businesses.

To strengthen the firm's capital structure, Philips issued 20.75 million common shares in April 1987 to raise $480.6 million. According to Dick Snijders, director of corporate finance, this had been the first time since 1962 that the Group had offered shares on a global basis. (In 1985, the Philips Group had offered 10 million shares in the U.S. market.) He thought that the firm would continue to raise its equity base through small additional offerings every two or three years.

On August 18, 1987, Philips offered $50 a share, or $610 million, for the 42 percent of North American Philips that it did not already own. According to the press release, the company hoped to bring its U.S. sales—already more than a quarter of its 55 billion guilder ($26 billion) total revenues—into line with the United States' share of the world market. A Philips spokesman in Eindhoven said that the acquisition was not related to the recent capital increase and that existing lines of credit would be used to finance the transaction.

If there had been any doubts in the Philips organization as to top management's commitment to a new strategy and structure, van der Klugt's bold moves were calculated to put them to rest. He recognized, however, the formidable task before him to realign his people's attitudes and abilities in accordance with the new Philips:

> Categorizing businesses was a cultural shock. Everyone had always felt that they were part of the family. There was a strong sense that we had betrayed a number of our managers.

Exhibit 4 The Philips Group: Group management committee, September 1, 1987

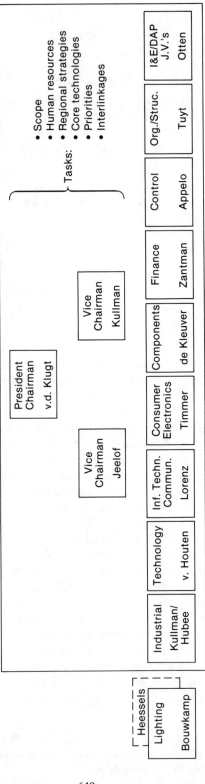

The emphasis on profits is also foreign to our thinking. Sales volume had always been the measure of success. The difficulty in changing this thinking can perhaps be seen in the following experience. Soon after taking over, I began a campaign to cut our enormous overhead costs. Among other things, we discussed eliminating such things as 38 million guilders for corporate aircraft, 1.5 million guilders for cigarettes, and 4 million guilders for alcohol. Admittedly, these are small things, but they have a tremendous symbolic value. The reaction of many of my colleagues was that we were sacrificing the quality of life. What they failed to realize was that no quality of life can exist when there are no profits.

The importance van der Klugt attached to his people's attitudes and abilities was clearly indicated in his remark, "A president can redirect a corporation only with the support of many senior managers and corporate staff." The remainder of this case describes how the Philips situation in 1987 appeared to various managers in the organization.

Lighting Division

Philips was the largest producer of lighting in the world, with 1986 sales of about 7 billion guilders. The business was divided between consumer lamps, accounting for 45 percent of this total, and professional lamps and fixtures, accounting for the rest. The industry was characterized as a profitable, low-growth business that was becoming increasingly global in nature. Technical content was changing: in the 1990s, about 20 percent of lighting was expected to be connected with electronics (e.g., an electronic ballast to permit changing the intensity of fluorescent lamps).

In May 1987, the lighting division was instructed to submit concrete proposals to the board of management regarding just how it would be organized as an autonomous business enterprise. Y. G. Bouwkamp, the newly appointed senior managing director who had had a distinguished career in various national organizations, described how he viewed the challenge before him:

> The lighting division has been the most profitable operating unit in Philips and over the years has generated cash flow to fund other units. We have to find a way to operate as a separate business while taking advantage of the Group's strengths and also contributing to its other initiatives. We have engaged McKinsey to help us figure out how to deal with the various problems associated with such a change.
>
> Our objective is to maintain product leadership. We need to create a culture which would make people proud to work for lighting. Otherwise we run a risk of losing our best people to the core, interlinked electronics business units with their appeal as the Philips heartland.

Bouwkamp saw the present relationship between the lighting division and the national organizations as unsatisfactory. He explained:

> Lighting is a protected business in many countries and can be very profitable. Because of this, lighting is often used to make up for any profit short-

falls a national organization might encounter. For example, it might choose to sacrifice market share for additional income, even though that might weaken us against an aggressive competitor. Or, if the lighting division is trying to build its forces, a national organization might veto adding people because it has a personnel hiring stop policy or has other priorities.

In my view, we shall probably have to set up autonomous lighting organizations in the major countries. For the rest of the world, we would continue to use Philips' national organizations as agents, provided they fulfill certain conditions and agree to specific turnover and profit goals. To be sure, such changes will not occur without controversy.

According to Bouwkamp, many of the existing Philips management information systems were designed to serve several purposes and as a result, were complicated and often inappropriate for lighting's specific needs. He saw a need to introduce new systems suitable for a global lighting organization. He also questioned the future role of Philips' Elcoma Division as a supplier of electronic components, noting that, "Elcoma has more expertise with respect to ICs and electronics circuitry than with the power ICs suitable for high temperatures and the voltages associated with lighting. We might need to seek another source of components."

Bouwkamp held no illusions about the difficulties he would encounter in proposing the kind of changes he had in mind:

A lot of people in Eindhoven are not ready to change. We are talking about the possibility of altering important responsibilities and power. One of the biggest battles will be to change the cash-generating role that lighting has played in the past. Its not that I oppose funding other businesses. It's just that I would like to see lighting get full credit for its profits and an end to saddling it with charges of other operations.

Only partly in jest, Bouwkamp pointed out that it was lighting, the original Philips business, that was entitled to celebrate the centennial anniversary, adding, "I like to think that under the new government, it is really lighting that is divesting itself of all the other products that Philips had accumulated over the years."

Medical Systems Division

In June 1987, W. Stoorvogel, senior managing director of the Medical Systems Division, was engrossed in the job of extricating his operation from Philips and merging it with Picker International, a month after an agreement had been reached with General Electric Company (United Kingdom) to set up a fifty–fifty joint venture. The two businesses—making a wide range of medical diagnostic equipment, including X-ray machines, computerized axial tomography (CAT) scanners, and magnetic resonance scanners—would have combined sales of $1.9 billion, giving the new entity world market share leadership. (In July 1987, General Electric (United States) recaptured the lead with its acquisition of Thomson's [France] medical electronics business.)

According to Stoorvogel, the new venture would benefit the Medical Systems Division in three ways. First, added resources would be available to compete in a business with high fixed costs. For example, the division's R&D costs ran about 10 percent compared with Philips' average of 7 percent. The large service organization required in this business was also costly. Second was the geographical complementarity of the two units. The Medical Systems Division's sales of about $1.3 billion were primarily in Europe; most of Picker International's revenues came from the United States. The U.S. presence also put the division in closer touch with the major center of medical electronics technological innovation. Third was a healthier management arrangement. Stoorvogel explained:

> It was difficult for a high-tech, professional business like ours to survive in the Philips matrix. We had to deal with noses pointed in too many different directions. A lot of energy was lost in the friction of making joint decisions. A rapidly developing business calling for large investment decisions really needs a single worldwide management.

The new ownership arrangement also posed several serious future problems for the Medical Systems Division. The difficulty the division had experienced in its relationships with the national organizations—whereby some NOs were not willing to invest in developing their markets and would handle only its most profitable products—was likely to be exacerbated by the organizational decoupling. The national organizations with their political clout played a critical role in selling the expensive equipment to the government-supported health programs in Europe and elsewhere.

Another major problem facing Stoorvogel was to disentangle the medical products activities from the Philips operations. Many of its manufacturing, selling, technical, and administrative functions had been interconnected in various ways with other Group activities to lessen costs. He expected that the new unit would continue to depend on Philips for legal and financing relationships and to tap into corporate research.

Stoorvogel also faced a morale problem. Many of the division's 11,000 people were upset by the termination of their direct relationship with Philips. There was also the threat of employee redundancy in the United States that would require some cutbacks in administration and sales. The new company, which still had no name, would require approval of the parents for major restructuring and for the selection of its CEO.

He agreed with the conclusion that the medical products business was not interlinked with other businesses in the Philips Group. What he did not understand was how top management had decided that it was not a core business in view of its high electronics technology and future growth potential.

Headquarters

While support for the changes underway had gained widespread support, no one expected them to be easily carried out. The company had a long and proven tradition, and the new approach laid out by Dekker and van der Klugt had to contend with the entrenched Philips way of doing business. As one senior official observed:

> One of the new objectives is to focus on profits, but we are trained to think about turnover and market share. We are now supposed to think in global terms, but we have a strong country orientation. We are supposed to engage in strategic alliances, but we are conditioned to having 100 percent control over our operations and to being boss. After four years, the mentality has not really changed.

A senior staff manager identified two other transitional problems:

> Headquarters has a staff of some 3,000 people, the product divisions have about 2,500. Many of the headquarters staff will have to be reallocated to the PDs. This move will be most painful for the staff associated with the board of management. This group of 1,200 will be considerably reduced. They will be transferred with the same pay but will suffer a loss in status.
>
> Reassigning key people in line with the shift in power from national organizations to PDs and maintaining morale while making all the necessary job changes will also be a very difficult task. There has been a tradition at this company that the strongest people went to NOs. Indeed, most of senior group management has come up through the NOs. Take van der Klugt as an example. He spent nineteen years in Chile, Uruguay, and Brazil before returning to Eindhoven to join the board of management in 1978. So, whether true or not, there is a widely shared perception that the quality of the managers in the NOs is higher than at the PDs. What this means, of course, is that the national organizations will not simply defer to the product divisions. Product division management must win the right to direct strategy on a worldwide basis.

Changing the relationship between product divisions and national organizations without unduly hampering Philips' ability to function smoothly during the next several years was clearly uppermost in everyone's mind. The nature of the difficulty was revealed in the following observation:

> Philips' management is based on intricate webs of relationships. These strong networks have been the glue that has provided cohesion for almost 100 years. Personal relationships involving power and status will not change easily or quickly. They are deeply rooted and entrenched.

Whether or not van der Klugt would succeed in transforming Philips to carry out its new global and focused strategy and whether or not Philips would achieve its profit margin of 4 percent by 1991 remained to be seen. Failure, however, would not be for lack of trying, as a senior executive noted: "Van der Klugt will move with bold strokes. He knows that it would be a mistake to try to deal with nuances in communicating to the organization. Besides, he has four years to complete his program before he reaches his retirement age."

Richardson Hindustan Limited

Two projects of major potential interest to the Richardson-Vicks Inc. (RVI) Indian subsidiary were very much on the mind of Gurcharan Das, president of Richardson Hindustan Limited (RHL), as he reviewed his company's strategic plan in early 1984. The first would take the Indian firm into products not included among the parent company's worldwide offerings. The second would set up RHL as a supplier of a key raw material for RVI's global operations. Both propositions went counter to existing corporate policies and practices, which stressed products capable of being transferred to markets around the world and which favored investments in marketing over manufacturing. A recent forced reduction of RVI's ownership from 55 percent to 40 percent was sure to affect corporate management's thinking about these two ventures, as well as about a host of other activities and expectations that defined the relationship between parent and its distant subsidiary.

"Balancing the requirements of headquarters and those of the local organization in a way which serves the long-term interests of both is clearly one of the most critical parts of my job," noted Das. "RHL is a loyal subsidiary, yet it has a kindred spirit of its own. As a result, I have to promote RHL's interests at headquarters and then turn around to promote RVI's interests in Bombay. Luckily, I am dealing with excellent people at both ends, or the job would not be much fun."

RVI and RHL

Richardson-Vicks, Inc., was a leading worldwide marketer of branded consumer products for health care, personal care, home care, and nutritional care. The company's product line could be traced to 1905, when Lunsford Richardson, a North Carolina pharmacist, formed a company to sell Vicks VapoRub, which he had developed "especially for children's croup or colds." The company experienced rapid growth following World War II with the addition of new products and the expansion of overseas operations.

In management's view, marketing had been the key to RVI's success. The 1982 annual report described RVI's corporate strategy as follows:

> The company seeks leadership positions for each of its brands by developing products that meet distinct consumer needs. It then produces them

under high manufacturing standards to ensure high performance and consumer acceptance. Finally it supports them with outstanding advertising, promotion and distribution.

In 1983, RVI had revenues of $1.1 billion based on the sales of such products as Vicks VapoRub (cold product), Oil of Olay (skin care), Clearasil (acne medication), Vidal Sassoon (hair care), Vicks Throat Drops (cough drops), Sinex (nasal spray), NyQuil (nighttime cold medication), and Homer Formby (home-care products). According to company records, one out of every four dollars spent in the U.S. on cold remedies went to purchase a Vicks product. Overseas sales had grown even faster than domestic and in 1983 accounted for more than half the company's total sales and profits. Exhibit 1 shows financial information for RVI.

RHL was one of more than thirty subsidiaries in the Richardson-Vicks worldwide network. The Indian company was founded in 1964 to oversee the construction of a pharmaceutical plant and to take over the marketing efforts then being handled by a small RVI branch operation. Upon completion of the plant in 1966, 45 percent of RHL's equity was sold to the Indian populace through a public stock offering. RVI retained 55 percent ownership.

Starting from annual sales of $2.5 million in its first year of operation (1966–67 fiscal year), RHL posted a record sales volume of $23 million in 1983 and had become an important unit to the parent company. Its facilities in 1984 included headquarters in Bombay, a modern 160,000-square-foot factory on a sixteen-acre site at Kalwa (twenty miles north of Bombay), and a menthol-distillation center at Bilaspur (150 miles north of Delhi).

Gurcharan Das at Richardson Hindustan Limited

When Das returned to his native India in January 1981 to head RHL after working in different parts of the world for thirteen years (see Exhibit 2 for details of his career), he found a company in trouble. He recounted his initial impressions:

> I was very excited to go back home as head of the company where I had started as a trainee eighteen years earlier. But what I found when I got there was a real mess. The company was cash poor, morale was low, labor was hostile, labor-management relations were adversarial, and turnover in the management ranks was very high. Because of governmental price controls, management for years had stressed volume, selling at any price and producing at any cost. I can tell you, it was a difficult homecoming for me.

Das, together with RVI management, quickly mapped out a strategy to turn around the situation. He explained the resulting priorities and actions:

> The top priority was to increase profitability. We raised prices wherever we could, reduced inventories and accounts receivable, cut low-yielding sales and distribution activities, and got the sales force to push the more profitable lines. RHL suffered some decline in volume, but not as much as the marketing people had predicted in resisting these moves. The cash flow improved dramatically.

Exhibit 1   Richardson-Vicks Inc. financial summary, 1979–83 ($ millions).

	Year Ended June 30				
Summary of Operations	*1983*	*1982*	*1981*	*1980*	*1979*
Sales	$1,116	$1,116	$1,088	$929	$829
Investment, royalty, and other income	9	17	16	14	8
Total Income	1,125	1,133	1,104	943	837
Cost of products	444	433	428	360	329
Selling, advertising, and administrative	517	502	485	408	362
Research	35	32	29	22	19
Interest	21	23	14	11	9
Other	10	29	13	11	20
Total costs and expenses	1,027	1,019	969	812	739
Earnings before taxes	98	114	135	131	98
Income taxes	46	47	52	56	50
	$52	$67	$83	$75	$48
Discontinued operations	—	—	(4)	9	15
Earnings for the year	$52	$67	$79	$84	$63
Earnings per common and common equivalent share	$2.10	$2.74	$3.31	$3.56	$2.66
Key Statistical Data					
Cash	$119	$91	$106	$109	$142
Tangible net assets	265	395	361	461	373
Working capital	245	225	198	290	268
Current ratio	2.0	2.1	1.8	2.0	2.2
Long-term debt	168	41	13	18	19
Stockholders' equity	471	486	452	550	498
Property, plant, and equipment (net)	242	247	209	184	209
Expenditures for property, plant, and equipment	34	58	49	53	48
Depreciation	21	19	16	13	12
Advertising and promotional expenditures	278	276	268	230	206
Average common and common equivalent shares (in thousands)	24,511	24,448	23,982	23,678	23,706
Cash dividends paid per-share common	$1.48	$1.48	$1.32	$1.20	$1.06
Number of employees	10,700	11,000	10,800	15,000	15,000
Stock price					
High	32.5	30.9	42.5	27.0	31.0
Low	22.4	20.5	22.3	17.5	19.8

Source: Annual reports.

Exhibit 2 Gurcharan Das' career.

June 1963	Graduated from Harvard University, A.B. cum laude
July 1963	Joined Richardson-Merrell Inc., as a management trainee in New York
December 1963	Marketing Trainee—Vicks, Bombay
January 1966	Product Manager—Richardson Hindustan Ltd., Bombay
December 1968	Group Product Manager—Vicks, Latin America/Far East, New York
January 1971	Marketing Manager—Mexico
July 1971	Marketing Manager—Richardson Hindustan Ltd.
April 1972	Marketing Controller—Richardson Hindustan Ltd.
February 1974	Marketing Director—Richardson Hindustan Ltd.
February 1976	General Manager, Nutritional Division, Richardson-Merrell S.A. de C.V. Mexico
January 1980	Assistant General Manager, General Foods, Spain
January 1981	President, Richardson Hindustan Ltd.
May–June 1982–83	91st Advanced Management Program, Harvard Business School

Gurcharan Das, born in Punjab, India, in 1943, was the author of several plays which were successfully produced and published. *Larins Sahib,* a prize-winning play about the British in India, was produced in Bombay and by the BBC in London, and published by Oxford University Press in England. *Mira* was staged in New York to critical acclaim and had long and successful runs in many cities in India. A Spanish version was performed in Mexico City and Madrid. In 1984 Das was completing a novel about an Indian family. He is married and has two sons.

Next, I dealt with the labor situation. Labor relations could be characterized as bitterly adversarial. Management advocated the approach of "stick it to the workers," and the workers, I am sure, would have happily done the same back.

I set out to convince the workforce that we had a problem which could only be worked out together. To help change the prevailing hostile attitudes, we mounted an attitude-change program—first for managers, then for supervisors, and finally for workers. In October, 1981, the old personnel manager was replaced by someone who shared my views on how to work with labor instead of against it. A year later we succeeded in signing a three-year contract that made sense to both sides.

The final step was to identify and commit to new opportunities for future growth. I tend to favor participative management and have found the strategic-planning process to be a splendid vehicle for involving and motivating young managers throughout the organization.

As a result of the turnaround, profits had almost doubled, return on equity employed had increased from 22.6 percent to 30.5 percent, accounts receivable had been reduced from seventy days outstanding to thirty, and headcount had been reduced from 750 to 675 with a sales-volume increase of close to 50 percent. In tune with these results, RHL stock prices had more than doubled. (See Exhibit 3 for the RHL financial results.)

Das summed up his assessment of RHL's situation as of mid-1984: "Given the results for 1983 and the situation today, the company has more than met the objectives I had set in 1981. Profits are good, relations with the government have improved greatly, labor is happy, and management is enthusiastic—not one key manager has left the company in the past eighteen months. The central challenge for us now is profitable growth."

Strategy for Profitable Growth

RHL's five-year growth objectives were to double sales revenues and to triple profits by 1988. (See Exhibit 4 for the company's key financial projections.)

An expansion and extension of RHL's core product lines was to serve as the basis for this sales growth. The company planned to launch twelve new products and relaunch one other product during this period. Entry into two new businesses had also been proposed to serve as a base for future growth.

Expansion and Extension of Core Product Lines

RHL prided itself on its marketing skills; its advertising programs and extensive distribution system were the primary engines for sales growth. Arun Bewoor, General Sales Manager, explained the company's approach:

> About 75 percent of the Indian population live in some 526,000 rural communities. That's a potential market of almost one-half billion people. And RHL has built the largest rural distribution structure in our field. We do grass-roots marketing and draw upon Indian culture for unique campaign ideas. India is a country with many people outside the monied economy, so we sell small tins of Vicks for fifteen cents. Television is still in its infancy, so we advertise through the movie halls. Our market research showed that people had colds in the rainy season as well as winter, so we started to do intensive market promotion during the monsoons. The land and people are heterogeneous, so we segment our advertising based on language, economic development, and market development.

Colds Care and Casual Therapeutics

Colds care and casual therapeutics products accounted for about 80 percent of RHL's 1983 total sales, and Vicks VapoRub for the greater part of these. The strategic plan aimed to continue the company's dominance in these market segments in order to generate funds for new-product expansion.

VapoRub was the single largest product in its category and its dominance was expected to continue. However, competition was intensifying from lower-

Exhibit 3 RHL financial highlights (table in lakhs: units of 100,000 rupees)[a] (1983 financial details in $ millions).

					Years Ending June 30					
Summary of Operations	1983	1982	1981	1980	1979	1978	1977	1976	1975	1974
Sales	2,330	2,000	1,919	1,656	1,335	1,389	1,247	1,086	889	738
Earnings before taxes	390	229	159	174	96	201	185	125	124	57
Income taxes	297	155	103	123	71	156	132	85	92	36
Earnings after taxes	92	74	56	51	25	45	53	40	32	21
Dividends	54	36	36	30	18	36	26	26	26	11
Retained profits	39	38	20	21	7	9	27	14	6	10

Profit and Loss Account for Year Ended June 30, 1983

Sales	$23.3
Expenses	19.7
Raw and packaging materials	8.0
Wages	2.7
Operations	5.5
Sales and excise taxes	3.3
Other	0.2
Profit before taxes	3.9
Profit after taxes	0.9

Balance Sheet as of June 30, 1983

Inventories	$5.3
Current assets	7.2
Fixed assets	3.0
Total assets	$10.2
Current liabilities	5.6
Long-term debt	1.0
Deferred payment credits	0.2
Equity	3.4
Total liabilities	$10.2

a. The exchange rate as of late 1983 was approximately 10 rupees to one U.S. dollar.

Source: Richardson Hindustan Limited annual report.

Exhibit 4   Key financial objectives (comparison to industry average).

	Industry Average[a] (1982)	Our Company	
		Actual 1982–83	Objective 1987–88
Sales growth (5-year compound)	15.2	10.7	20.0
Operating profit (% sales)	NA	[b]	[b]
Earnings before tax (% sales)	9.8	19.1	22.3
Earnings growth (5-year compound)	9.2	14.2	23.9
Earnings after tax (% sales)	3.9	4.6	7.5
ROI (%)	19.0	19.6	29.2
Debt/Equity	0.43	0.33	0.30
Net working capital (% sales)	20.0	7.7	7.0
Return on shareholders equity (%)	21.8	27.1	36.0
Price earnings multiple	8.1	9.6	10.0

Our financial performance for 1982–83 compares favorably with industry average on all financial indicators. Our financial ratios are expected to further improve by 1987–88. The most dramatic improvement is expected in the PAT ratio, which will rise as a result of our plan to invest in tax-designated areas. Our tax rate would come down to 48 percent as a result and PAT ratio go up to 11.6 percent. In the interest of producing a conservative plan, we have not projected the full benefit of tax incentives and have shown tax rate at 66.4 percent (v. 76 percent today).

a. Industry average is based on the performance of the following companies. Industries sales figures include excise tax (10–15%) which ours do not. (1) Warner Hindustan, (2) Pfizer, (3) Abbott Laboratories, (4) Parke-Davis, (5) Colgate-Palmolive, (6) Beechams (HMM), (7) Cadbury, (8) Ponds, (9) Nicholas, (10) Nestle (FS), (11) Brooke Bond, (12) German Remedies, (13) May & Baker, (14) Cyanamid.
b. Deleted.

Source: RHL Strategic Plan, August 1983.

priced regional "look-alike" brands. According to Arun Bewoor, "We have a lot of problems with mushroom competitors. These are small, fly-by-night manufacturers who make copies of VapoRub, sell them for a month or two, and then disappear, only to reappear somewhere else later. When RHL raised its price on the popular five-gram tin from one rupee to two rupees, we brought these hit-and-run outfits out in droves."

The colds-care line also included the following products: Formula 44 cough liquid; Formula 44 Disc cough lozenges; and Action-500 cold tablets, which was scheduled to be relaunched with an aromatic formulation, new packaging, and premium pricing, and eventually extended with an antihistamine formula (Action-500 Plus). Vicks Sinex Nasal Spray was also scheduled to be introduced as a new product.

Dominant in the casual-therapeutics line of products was Vicks Cough Drops, which accounted for about 20 percent of RHL's total sales. It held a 40 percent national market share, followed by Boots' Strepsils (23 percent) and Halls (17 percent). Arun Bewoor noted, "Cough drops has big growth potential, and Halls is a big threat as it moves more aggressively in the north and south of

India from its strong base in Bombay. It was Hall's successful growth which prompted us to launch a single-portion twist-wrapped candy throat drop to combat their successful offering of this product type."

The first results of RHL's test marketing of the Vicks Herbal twist-wrapped throat drop were considered very positive. As a result, the company planned to launch this product nationally in July 1984.

Vicks Inhalers, which dominated its small but growing market, were also included in the casual therapeutic line.

Personal Care

In management's judgment, Clearasil was synonymous with pimple care in India and overwhelmingly dominated the acne-remedy market. According to market studies, although only about 24 percent of young urban pimple sufferers used acne medication, increasing urbanization, literacy, social interaction, and spending power would make young people more and more conscious of their skin problems. For this reason, management considered the young people's skin-care market segment as ready for a major takeoff. The strength of the Clearasil franchise was reflected in its ability to hold sales volume while its price tripled to almost $1 per tube. To capitalize on this potential, the company planned to introduce related Clearasil products (soap, medicated cleanser, and super-strength lotion).

Future Business Climate

RHL's plans were to unfold in an expected climate of steady business growth. The strategic plan reported that the economy and consumer spending would continue to grow at 3–4 percent; the country would become increasingly self-reliant in petroleum; the rupee would gently weaken (5–8 percent per annum versus the U.S. dollar) as the trade gap widened; and per capita income for the top 20 percent of the population would continue a modest growth. Population was projected to grow at a 2.2 percent rate; as a result, 16 million people (the equivalent of the population of Australia) would be added to India's population each year.

Entry into New Business Areas

Clearly labeled in the RHL strategic plan as a hedge against the possible underachievement of the projected sales growth for core products were two new business ventures. Each in its own way was considered by Gurcharan Das as important to his goal of rapid profitable growth.

Ayurvedics

Das and Dr. Victor Moreno, vice president of research and development for Vick Americas/Far East division, had been intrigued for some time with the possible opportunity to commercialize the supply of herbal medicines that had been widely popular in India for some 2,000 years. Das characterized ayurvedic, or natural (herbal) medicines as safe, slow, and long acting, and therefore ideally suited for chronic diseases. Dr. T. G. Rajagopalan was hired in 1982 to develop an ayurvedic line of products. Rajagopalan had received an M.S. in biochemistry from the University of Madras and a Ph.D. in the same field from Duke University and had worked in Ciba Geigy's laboratories as a biochemist for fifteen years.

Rajagopalan described his approach to this challenge:

> To decide on the best initial target areas, we began with a broad study of twelve areas of medicine, such as skin, liver, hair/teeth, respiratory, etc. With the help of a consultant and several university students, we collected over 7,000 ayurvedic recipes and had them translated from Sanskrit. These recipes included anywhere from one to ninety plants. Since the plant names were only in Sanskrit, it was a task to find the equivalent botanical names.
>
> We next developed a computer program to categorize the pharmacological properties of the plants, as well as the vehicles for administering the medication. Since we wanted to meet Western pharmacological and toxicity standards, we screened the products to show toxicity based on reports in Western literature published from 1905 to 1982. The data bank we have on herbal plants is unique. Nobody has done this before.

Opinions about RHL's entry into ayurvedic products differed widely. Das saw great commercial possibilities in India and eventually abroad from ayurvedic medications and personal-care products. Bharat V. Patel, vice president of marketing for RHL, was much less enthusiastic about its market potential, viewing the effort as more of a move to gain favor with the Indian government by promoting indigenous medicinal practices. Lou Mattis, with line responsibility for RHL as general manager for Vick Americas/Far East, was undecided as to the project's profit potential, but willing to give it a try.

Patel questioned RHL's ability to devise an ayurvedic product that could compete with the efficacy of a Western drug:

> I am opposed to the idea of our introducing a serious drug for several reasons. First, such a drug would take us into a domain where doctors hold sway. RHL does not have expertise in this arena; our strength is in over-the-counter products. Second, ayurvedics will never be able to provide the quick relief that people want in this day and age. Finally, such a product does not fit into our specialty of casual therapeutics for minor ailments.
>
> If we do come out with such a product, the company should not project it as an ayurvedic drug. It should be offered with modern packaging emphasizing its attributes rather than its natural herbal content.

Somewhat in line with Patel's thinking, RHL management had as its objective to offer proprietary medicinal products that could be advertised and sold over the counter. Furthermore, introducing ayurvedic toiletries was seen as easier than introducing herbal medicinal products, because of the latter's more stringent requirements for quality consistency (difficult to achieve with natural plants).

In 1984, RHL was committed to constructing an R&D facility for developing ayurvedic products. Construction was estimated at $275,000, and initial equipment orders would run about $330,000. Das estimated these investments would increase to a total of $1 million in two years and to $2 million in five years. (Figures disguised.)

Dextromethorphan-Hydrobromide

As a way of increasing exports and of making a high-technology basic drug to comply with government pressures, RHL management began looking into the possibility of producing dextromethorphan-hydrobromide, an antitussive ingredient used in products to counter cough symptoms. RVI was reportedly the world's largest consumer of dextro with its annual purchases of almost $9 million (figure disguised), at the 1983 price of $285 per kilogram, from two established suppliers. RHL proposed to become a global source of dextro for RVI, producing the same quality product at a lower price with the aim of making a profit and of gaining important goodwill with the government.

The person pushing the dextro-manufacturing venture was B. K. Patney, RHL's vice president of manufacturing. His plan was to import the intermediate materials and produce the dextromethorphan at a cost 20 percent below RVI's current price. Although he preferred to license the process in Italy or even to develop his own version, Patney proposed to license from one of the current suppliers, despite the higher cost, so as more readily to gain headquarters' approval.

Tax savings were also an important element in the dextro proposal. In this case, the company would qualify for a duty draw-back and cash incentive if the intermediate chemicals were imported into a duty-free site and at least 30 percent value added. Moreover, by being based in a trade-free zone, RHL would have its profits from this operation tax free for seven years. Overall, the investment in dextro facilities would total about $2.2 million (figure disguised); the payback for this investment was calculated to be less than two years.

Notwithstanding RHL's enthusiasm for the dextro project, RVI's response was seen by Das as unenthusiastic. He recognized several reasons for headquarters' reluctance. Perhaps most important was RVI's general policy of focusing its resources on marketing investments and keeping down its investments in manufacturing plant. Moreover, dextromethorphan-hydrobromide was a complicated chemical compound requiring special processes with which RVI had had no direct experience.

RHL's failure to deliver on an earlier promise to produce low-cost menthol exports possibly provided some people with further grounds for opposing the project. In the 1960s, RHL management had proposed to grow the mentha arvensis plant in India, both as a means of import substitution and as a source of low-cost menthol for the parent company. For a variety of agricultural reasons, the costs of producing menthol in India turned out to be much higher than had been anticipated when compared to production in Brazil.

On the positive side, Das felt that RHL's strong financial performance over the past two years had done much to improve its credibility at headquarters. Patney's successful track record in manufacturing also went a long way in having headquarters take the dextro project seriously. He had developed a reputation as a person who submitted carefully prepared capital-investment proposals and who had successfully implemented each approved project within a typically tight budget limit.

Despite these strong pluses for the dextro project, Das recognized their limits, "RHL is 10,000 miles from the home office in Wilton, Connecticut. And so there is still a healthy dose of skepticism there as to what RHL can do."

Building and Balancing Constituency Relationships

Notwithstanding his deep interest and involvement in products and markets, Das saw as a special part of his job that of serving several important RHL constituencies. The most important of these constituencies were the parent company, the RHL employees, the Indian government, and the Indian shareholders. For the most part, the requirements and expectations among these parties were different and often in direct conflict. Not only was it important for Das to figure out what balance to strike with respect to specific decisions; it was also vital to convince each party to accept the concessions it might perceive itself making. His ability to argue each case on its own merits was limited where RHL was viewed as only a small element in a total picture, such as might be the case for an RVI headquarters executive or even more so for an Indian government official.

RVI Headquarters

As a worldwide marketer of branded consumer products, RVI followed a strategy of developing or acquiring a brand leader in one market and then transferring its experience to other markets around the world. Each of the operating divisions was relatively autonomous and had complete responsibility for its product line. The corporate level organization structure is shown in Exhibit 5.

Louis Mattis, president and general manager of the Vick Americas/Far East division since 1982, was responsible for thirteen country managers and twenty-six countries with sales of $232 million in 1983. He had joined the company in 1979 from Warner-Lambert Co. At the age of forty-two, he had established a reputation as a hard-driving and successful consumer-product manager who encouraged and expected high-level performance from his people. Lou Mattis was to become an executive vice president of RVI and a member of a newly formed corporate strategic-planning committee, along with the company's other two executive vice presidents, as of January 1, 1985. With this promotion, he would also gain responsibility for RVI's nutritional care products in the United States.

Mattis described the evolution of corporate/divisional relations as follows:

Exhibit 5 Richardson-Vicks, Inc., corporate and divisional organization structure, February 1983.

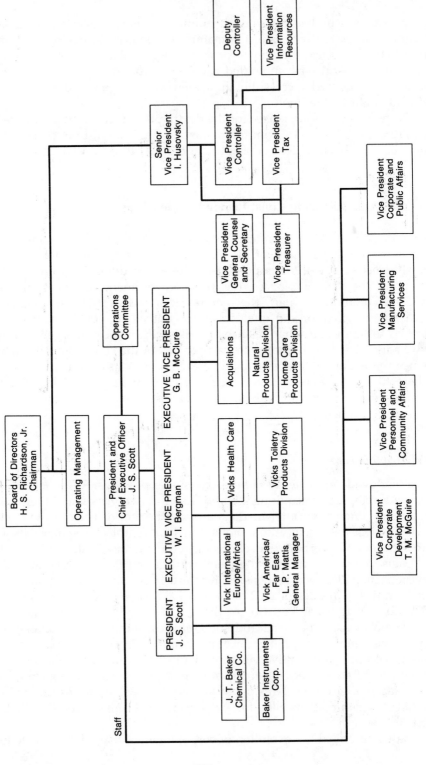

We've gone through several stages of evolution in dealing with our multicountry operation. In the 1960s we said, "Young man, go do your thing." We had a very small home-office staff and exercised loose control. In the 1970s, the pendulum swung to the other end, and the division was centralized very tightly in terms of home-office control. Staff was set up in every function—manufacturing, personnel, finance, policy. The staff became decision makers, and the field were implementers.

My predecessor made some really good decisions and business did very well in the 1970s. . . . But the control system had an impact on the country managers. They became upward looking, bureaucratic and procedural oriented.

In the last four years, we have given country managers independence with financial controls. We still use a continuous planning and review system, but staff executives don't have to concur on the line manager's decisions before they can be implemented, as was true earlier.

To achieve decentralization, four areas had been created (namely, Mexico, Japan, Canada and South America, and Australia and the Far East) with an area director in charge of each. As Mattis described it:

We've put line responsibility and authority with the area directors. The staff is a resource to the countries and to me. The way our process works, the country managers first discuss their ideas and then budget with their area director and then with the home-office staff. Only then do the country managers come with their area director to me for approval. My review is for each country, not for an areawide budget.

Capital expenditures require corporate approval, and so I get involved. I also get into plans for products that are new to the entire division. If a product is new to a country but is already in the division, it is the area director's concern.

Area Director. Don Glover was area director for Australia and the Far East, an area that covered eleven countries and some miscellaneous South Pacific islands. Eight of these countries had independent companies. The area director's staff consisted of a marketing research director, a personnel director, and a finance director.

He described his role as follows, "The work of the area director is not to be a policeman. It's a link between the country manager and the home office and between countries. We look for similarities and common problems, so that we can avoid reinventing the wheel."

Country Manager. Under Mattis, the country manager played a pivotal role with full responsibility for the bottom line of the subsidiary company. RVI's manager's guide defined the main role of the country manager as follows: "To ensure that the market strategic and operational objective and standards set and implemented are the most advantageous for the market environment and are consistent with area and division plans and policies."

With this purpose in mind, the manager's guide defined a set of nine key result areas by which country managers were to be evaluated:

- Market strategic plans
- Profitability
- Today's products and markets
- Tomorrow's products and markets
- Organizational effectiveness
- Corporate responsibilities
- Social responsibilities
- Supply of product
- Asset protection and utilization

A typical career path for a country manager was to start in marketing, move on to marketing director, next to general manager in a small country with no manufacturing operations, then to a small country with integrated operations (marketing and manufacturing), and finally to head up a major national organization.

As for RHL, Das had been rerecruited from General Foods to take on the job of country manager and subsequently worked closely with Mattis and Glover in his efforts to turn around this troubled subsidiary. Both men were generally pleased with RHL's progress and performance and had a high regard for Das' abilities and accomplishments.

RHL Organization

Gurcharan Das' philosophy and style of management set the tone for the RHL organization. His stress on people was clearly signaled in a letter accompanying the first annual report, "Our success over the years is a result of the development of our people. . . . We seek the best qualified individuals we can find for every job. Employment, training, advancement, and compensation are on the basis of merit."

The following year, the introductory letter was devoted exclusively to the subject of "people excellence." In it, Das stated:

> My main job today is to create an environment where new ideas thrive and people develop their full potential. Otherwise good people do not stay. At RHL, we are working hard to create a climate which fosters innovativeness and encourages risk taking.
>
> Our philosophy of growth through people excellence is based on the following tenets:
> 1. A basic belief that people can grow.
> 2. To help people grow, we need to invest in them.
> 3. We believe that a consultative and participative management style is more effective than an authoritarian or paternalistic one.
> 4. We believe the best form of motivation is through achievement.

In practice, Das spoke softly, listened well, smiled often, and had an air of enjoying his work. He interacted frequently with his managers individually and in groups, encouraging debate and seeking new ideas. Clearly, he was respected and well liked by his subordinates. Exhibit 6 contains an organizational chart for RHL.

Exhibit 6 Richardson Hindustan Limited organizational structure, 1983.

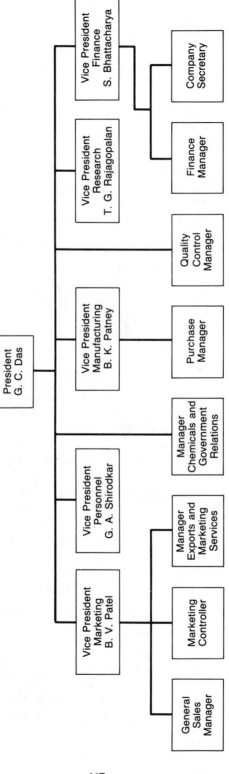

Ginil Shirodkar, vice president-personnel, saw RHL as being in transition from a task-oriented organization to one concerned with task *and* people. In an organizational development plan, the earlier managerial atmosphere was described as one characterized by "jockeying for power, functional empires, interfunctional conflicts, low morale, legalistic management style, low mutual trust, and high management turnover." Faced with this company culture, he set out to replace it with one reflecting the philosophy Das had articulated.

To help change attitudes, Shirodkar developed a training and development program for people at all levels of the organization. One of the most important elements in this program, in his view, was a series of top management workshops in team building and sensitivity training held in March and September, 1982, and February, 1983. The objectives for these sessions were to build management teamwork, to set new goals, and to instill the new RHL values. Other elements in the overall program included a ten-day residential workshop for field sales supervisors and managers focused on people-management and selling skills; a one-week residential program for senior middle managers with emphasis on developing general management skills; a personal growth laboratory for union leaders, workers, supervisory staff, and executives; and a team-building workshop for manufacturing managers.

The training program was connected with a formal appraisal system. Shirodkar described the procedure: "At the start of each year, every manager and his or her immediate superior agree on several major objectives for the junior manager. At the end of the year, both of them rate the assessee's performance. It is mandatory for the appraisal interview to last for at least two hours. It may go on for six hours. The discussion of the junior manager's strengths and weaknesses forms the basis on which the senior manager prepares a report identifying the training needs of the assessee."

Subsequently, the assessee and the appraiser individually charted a career path for the assessee. These were compared and the objectives for the next year set by agreement. To ensure objectivity, a second appraiser then made an independent assessment of the appraisee's performance potential and charted a career path. For the "high fliers" in each division, Shirodkar would meet with Das and the relevant functional director to chart a separate five-year career path.

A growing concern for Shirodkar had to do with the second-class status nonmarketing managers perceived themselves to have in RHL. In an in-house management seminar held in January, 1984, several middle-level managers in manufacturing and finance voiced unhappiness with the limitations of their careers, because of the importance Das attached to the marketing function. This strong focus on marketing was evident in a remark made on another occasion by Patney: "This is a consumer marketing-oriented company. Everything else must fall in line. It's very difficult to talk to top management about manufacturing or the need to invest there. They will spend $5 million on advertising at the drop of a hat, but will study to death a $50,000 capital investment for plant."

Das acknowledged this bias and was puzzled as to how he might deal with it: "This company will live or die on its marketing. I would like all of our managers to gain first-hand experience in marketing, but so far I have not had much success in getting my managers in finance or manufacturing to transfer to a marketing position."

Indian Government

Taxes, price controls and licenses made the government a significant factor in the business planning for any company operating in India. As a low-technology, high-return, foreign-owned consumer-product company, RHL was particularly vulnerable to governmental restrictions and penalties.

Most of the company's decisions with respect to products, markets and investments attempted to reduce this vulnerability and to build good will by being a "good citizen." This approach reflected the parent company's deep-seated commitment to conducting a sound business in an ethical manner. In management's thinking, everyone involved—the consumer, the host country, and RVI—had to benefit for the business to be sound.

Patel, summed up the company's situation, saying, "Selling our kind of products in India is not difficult. The real problem is to get the government's permission to sell it and to do so profitably, given the complex and tough tax structure."

Taxes. Faced with an effective tax rate of 76 percent, management viewed the reduction of taxes as the most important element in its plan to improve RHL's profitability. The target was to reduce the tax rate to 48 percent by 1987–88.

RHL paid high taxes because of its low capital base, high advertising expenditure, and high profitability. These taxes included a basic corporate income tax of 55 percent; a surcharge levied on the resulting profit after taxes exceeding 15 percent of net worth (bringing taxes up to 70 percent); a disallowance of 20 percent of advertising expenditures as a deduction for tax purposes; a federal excise tax of 105 percent of sales price for toiletry items; and various state and city taxes (e.g., 4 percent for Bombay and 15 percent sales tax for Maharashtra, the state in which Bombay is located).

Basically, RHL's approach to reducing taxes was to utilize in a responsible manner the variety of tax incentives offered by the Indian government as a means of directing business investments for purposes of social and economic improvement. For example, the company planned to introduce toiletries based on natural herbs in line with India's policy of favoring the sale of such products by excusing them from excise tax. To reduce corporate taxes, RHL planned to construct a satellite plant in an industrially backward area. The tax incentive for a new manufacturing unit was an eight- to ten-year tax holiday on 25 percent of the profits; locating in a backward area qualified an additional 20 percent for the tax holiday. In addition, Das was also actively engaged in working with industry associations to convince the government to eliminate the advertising disallowance.

The tax consequences at times played an important role in RHL's efforts to obtain headquarters' approval for new investments. Sumit Bhattacharya, vice president-finance, noted, "Last year the government imposed a heavy tax on advertising [the 20 percent disallowance]. Investments in R&D, however, could serve as a tax set-off. This certainly helped RHL to get approval for additional R&D expenditures."

Along these same lines, Patney remarked:

> Over the years, I've learned the need to justify my requisitions for plant and equipment investments for other than manufacturing reasons. Let me give you an example. With the introduction of the new herbal drops, the plant needed additional capacity. Any request for added capacity based on a straightforward manufacturing rationale would have been hard to sell. Headquarters would probably have urged me to squeeze more production out of my existing plant. My approach, therefore, was to emphasize the tax advantages we could obtain from setting up new equipment. The tax savings alone would pay for the equipment in eight to nine months. Since the equipment has to be installed within a year from the time the product is introduced, I received approval in record time.

Das noted in connection with this new capacity investment, "Here's a good case in point where a tax incentive benefited everyone involved. RHL got needed additional capacity; RVI got an attractive investment; and India got new, efficient facilities for a new product."

Overview. In light of the importance of governmental actions to business, RHL's strategic plan contained an analysis of the political and regulatory outlook. The report predicted political stability: Democracy would continue; Mrs. Gandhi would return to power in 1985; and regional problems (e.g., Punjab and the Sikhs) would be contained, but with a greater devolution of power and funds to the states. It also predicted that "pragmatic socialism" would continue to be the ideology of the government, with a high degree of bureaucratic control. With respect to regulation and taxes, the report predicted the continuing decontrol of prices, except for essential and life-saving drugs, and the unlikelihood of dramatic change in indirect and direct taxes, except for an expected discontinuation of the advertising disallowance in 1985.

Taking into account business-government relations in India as a whole, Das noted:

> The environment in India is generally not supportive of business and certainly not of multinational corporations operating in India. The private sector and the market mechanism are constantly questioned. The government evaluates business with respect to the extent to which it can help the country to achieve national social objectives. As a result of this situation, RHL's credentials are constantly challenged, making it important for us to prove that we are contributing to Indian society. The proposals to increase exports and to develop products with a social benefit, such as an ayurvedic remedy for chronic pain, are good examples of how RHL is attempting to strengthen its national franchise by helping to solve Indian problems.

Shareholders

The Indian government's regulations also led to a change in RHL's shareholders structure in 1983.

Recent expansion had been impossible because as a company with greater than 40 percent foreign equity, RHL came under the Foreign Exchange Regulation Act (FERA). Manufacture and sale by all industrial companies in India had to be carried out in accordance with an industrial license issued by the Indian government. Since many companies, including RHL, were outgrowing their industrial license, the Indian government had been obliged from time to time to grant both general increases in production in excess of licensed capacity, as well as specific requests for such increases. As had been the case with all FERA companies, however, RHL's request for grants of specific increased production had been rejected. For Das, this situation presented serious limits to growth.

Then in the late 1970s, the Indian government began to push for reducing foreign ownership to no more than 40 percent in all companies except those involved in high technology or those primarily in export. Das described his experience in dealing with this challenge to RVI, with its 55 percent equity share of RHL:

> A number of the corporate executives were strongly opposed to any dilution of RVI's holdings in RHL. For one thing, RVI has 100 percent ownership of most of its subsidiaries and does not hold a minority position in any. For another, the sale of shares would incur a book loss. Major devaluations in the rupee resulted in RVI's investment being overvalued on the balance sheet.
>
> Whatever the merits of individual cases, the Indian government was committed to the electorate for reducing foreign ownership in Indian companies. RHL's management tried to get an exception on the grounds that its pioneering work in developing a strain of mentha arvensis sufficiently drought and disease resistant to be grown in India qualified the company as involved in high technology. The Indian government rejected this claim on the basis of the low manufacturing technology involved in producing RHL's products.

While battling the Indian government for an exception to the new requirement for foreign ownership, Das was at the same time trying to convince headquarters of the advantages attached to reducing its ownership to 40 percent. This reduction in foreign ownership would remove the company from the severe FERA restrictions to growth. Das explained:

> I tried to make clear that RVI would do better owning a smaller share of a larger operation than a larger share of a smaller one. In any event, the company might have been able to delay the equity restructuring for another year or two by dragging out the dispute in the courts, but eventually it would have been compelled to reduce its ownership. By agreeing to reduce the foreign ownership when we did, we were able to gain some recognition as a high-tech company for our agricultural research. This recognition enabled

us to avoid being placed in the same category as Colgate and Ponds, who are viewed as manufacturers of nonessential items.

A senior executive at RVI headquarters provided further perspective to management's thinking:

> To start with, there was a major split in headquarters on whether or not to reduce RVI's ownership to a minority position. It was not a matter of being unwilling to share the profits or to open our affairs to scrutiny. After all, Indian investors already owned 45 percent of RHL. Rather it was a reluctance to lose positive control of a business with our good name on it. RVI holds its managers to high standards of behavior as well as of performance. And there were those of us who opposed any possible impairment of our ability to ensure that these standards be met. After all, our name and reputation mean a lot to us.

Following RVI's decision to reduce its ownership to 40 percent, Das made every effort to reassure headquarters of his intentions to continue his dedication to RVI. The strategic plan stated:

> Our objective will be to continue to get full and continuing access to RVI products, technology, and ways of working. In turn we will manage the Indian business in order to maximize RVI's interest and continue to add value to RVI through transfer of management people to RVI subsidiaries.

With the reduction in ownership to 40 percent, RVI was obliged by U.S. accounting regulations to remove RHL's figures from its consolidation and to carry it as an "investment in an affiliate." Since the 40 percent ownership could be presumed to control the financial results of RHL, RVI would have to employ "equity accounting," which required it to adjust its investment each year to show any gain or loss in RHL's new worth. To reflect these accounting changes, the RHL plan indicated a change in strategy: "After deconsolidation focus should shift from Operating Profit to Profit after Tax. Strategy is to maximize PAT even at expense of O.P."

Notwithstanding these efforts to maintain former allegiances, there were signs of some change in the parent-subsidiary relationship. Glover, the area director, described his views about the change: "With the equity divestment, my role will change to balancing RVI's interests with those of local shareholders. And my responsibilities will change. I won't have the same kinds of controls to play with. It'll be a more entrepreneurial role, and I'll act as a conduit through which new market ideas and opportunities are communicated."

Das also recognized that the new shareholder structure might put RHL at some disadvantage as compared to before: "If I was at headquarters, I probably wouldn't invest as much in India as before. If I had to make a choice between solving a serious manufacturing problem in Japan or in India, I would probably go to the subsidiary where I had the greatest ownership. In other words, the reduced equity might give us reduced leverage for attention."

As of late 1984, the make-up of the Indian share ownership was as follows:

Total Indian ownership	1,485,000 shares
	(60 percent of total)
Number of Indian shareholders	approximately 8,750
Average holding of individual Indian	
shareholders	approximately 100 shares
Largest shareholders:	
Government-owned financial	
institutions	264,600 shares
Mr. S. C. Banta, RHL chairman	147,700 shares

The 1984 shareholders' annual meeting, held in a theater, was attended by some 1,200 shareowners.

*   *   *   *   *   *

It was in this new context that Gurcharan Das had to try to move ahead with his proposals to introduce thirteen new products, to develop an ayurvedics business, and to gain RVI support for the dextro manufacturing and export project.

T Cell Sciences, Inc.

On October 22, 1986, T Cell Sciences, Inc., published the following excerpted news release for immediate dissemination:

T CELL SCIENCES NAMES JAMES D. GRANT CHAIRMAN
AND CHIEF EXECUTIVE OFFICER

Cambridge, Mass. (Oct. 22)—T Cell Sciences, Inc. (NASDAQ: TCEL) announced today the election of James D. Grant as chairman and chief executive officer, effective November 1.

Grant, 54, is currently vice-president of scientific development for CPC International, Inc., Englewood Cliffs, N.J., a Fortune 100 food products corporation. He also served as deputy commissioner of the U.S. Food and Drug Administration in Washington, D.C. from 1969 to 1972. In addition, he has held public policy, research and development, and commercial technology management positions with branches of the Federal government.

Headquartered in Cambridge, Mass., T Cell Sciences is an emerging health-care products company focusing on white blood cells called T cells. Using the latest biotechnology techniques, T Cell Sciences is developing diagnostic and therapeutic products to detect, monitor, and treat immune-system disorders.

"Jim's broad experience in government and industry significantly enriches the scientific and management resources we've assembled to achieve our business objectives," said Patrick C. Kung, Ph.D., founder and scientific director of T Cell Sciences, Inc. "His leadership will solidify and accelerate our growth into a successful medical diagnostics and pharmaceutical company."

Grant holds an MBA from the Wharton School of the University of Pennsylvania and a B.S. in chemistry from the College of William and Mary, and did postgraduate study at Stanford University on a Ford Foundation fellowship. He is listed in *Who's Who in America*.

Pursuant to his employee agreement, Grant was to receive an annual base salary of $115,000 plus certain merit and cost of living increases. He was also granted options to purchase an aggregate of 200,000 shares of the company's common stock at an exercise price of $2.81 per share.

This case describes Grant's views and experiences as a new chief executive officer of T Cell Sciences during his initial months on the job.

The Company at the Time of Grant's Decision to Join

Incorporated in Delaware on December 9, 1983, T Cell Sciences was organized for the purpose of engaging in the development of diagnostic and therapeutic products for the detection, monitoring, and treatment of immune disorders and autoimmune diseases. Based on scientific observations about the properties of T cell antigen receptors[1] and the genes that encode them, the company intended to develop products capable of detecting, monitoring, and activating T cell functions. The company believed that this approach would lead to highly specific, less costly diagnostic and therapeutic products to treat diseases for which current therapy was deficient or nonexistent.

The firm's technological capabilities were grounded in two major interacting groups: an in-house scientific staff of thirty under the leadership of Patrick Kung; and a group of leading scientists in the field who served as consultants and advisers under exclusive arrangements. T Cell Sciences also had licensing agreements with Ontario Cancer Institute, California Institute of Technology, Dana-Farber Cancer Institute, Stanford University, and National Technical Information Service for rights to employ certain patents germane to T cell antigen receptor technology.

An important element in the company's strategy was to perform research and development work under contract to well-established pharmaceutical firms. According to management's reasoning, such arrangements would help T Cell Sciences to focus on products with commercial value, would make strong marketing capabilities available when needed, and would provide needed research funds. In October 1986, the company had two R&D contracts and was negotiating a third. An agreement with Syntex U.S.A. aimed to develop diagnostic tests for breast cancer and cytomegalovirus. An agreement with Pfizer aimed to develop therapeutic products for treating rheumatoid arthritis and type-1 diabetes.

T Cell Sciences had introduced two product lines to the preclinical (scientific) test market in 1986. The first, called ACT-T-SET, provided information about an immune system's stage of stimulation (acute or chronic). A related test kit, called CELLFREE, was then developed to provide greater user convenience for measuring the amount of released interleukin-2 (a protein produced

---

1. Glossary: *T cell*—A white blood cell that specializes in distinguishing host cells from foreign cells; *receptor*—A protein structure on the surface of a cell that serves as a receiver of chemical messages; *T cell antigen receptor*—a T cell receptor that specializes in reacting with foreign bodies (antigens) to activate the T cell. T cells can be activated to enhance an immune response, to suppress an immune response, or to kill target cells (e.g., tumor cells) by rupturing their membranes. For additional information about T cell technology, see Exhibit A.

Exhibit A   T Cell Technology.

Immunology is the branch of medical science devoted to the study of the human body's response to foreign substances, such as bacteria, viruses, parasites, and cancers. The immunological response of the human body to these foreign substances (or antigens) is critical to human survival. Proper immunological function recognizes and effectively combats infection and disease, while inadequate function allows infection or disease to spread within the human body or, in the case of autoimmunity, can, in fact, cause disease.

The human immune system is made up of two separate, yet complementary, white blood cell response systems: the B cell complex, which is more widely understood, and the T cell complex.

B cells are derived from the bone marrow and circulate in the body's fluid (i.e., blood and the lymph). Ordinarily, B cells remain in a passive state concentrated in the major lymphatic organs (e.g., the lymph nodes and spleen). In response to an antigen, however, after instruction from certain T cells, B cells divide and set in motion a process that is designed to eliminate the invading antigen.

The initial response of the B cell to an antigen is to bind to such antigen. The binding function is carried out by an antigen receptor protein located on the B cell's membrane. The antigen and the receptor bind together and, as a result, the B cell divides and secretes a specific antibody that has the same antigen-binding chracteristics as the original B cell receptor molecule. These antibodies then flow through the blood and lymph and bind to the antigens, marking them for destruction by other components of the immune system.

Seemingly, the T cell response to invading antigens is similar to that of the B cell. T cells, also derived from bone marrow, undergo maturation in the thymus gland. Like B cells, T cells circulate in the blood and lymph and are concentrated in the lymphatic organs. In addition, T cells are able to detect the presence of invading antigens through T cell antigen receptors, the function of which is analogous to the B cell antigen receptor protein. T cells, however, are able to determine if another cell or cell component is "self" (i.e., host) or "non-self" (i.e., foreign). It is this ability that distinguishes T cells from all other cells.

T cells, unlike B cells, do not secrete antibodies. Instead, having determined that the antigen is a foreign subtance, T cells undergo a clonal expansion, and certain of these T cell clones release hormonelike molecules called lymphokines which, in turn, trigger B cell division and antibody secretion. Thus, the production of antibodies by B cells is a two-step process: (1) T cell recognition of an antigen and the resulting release of lymphokines by T cell clones; and (2) after instruction by such lymphokines, B cell division and secretion of antibodies. T cells also exhibit a capacity to recognize a much broader range of antigens than do B cells. This capacity is the result of the versatile encoding capabilities of the T cell antigen receptor's DNA.

Another distinguishing characteristic of T cells is the variety of functions they play in the immunological response. There are three types of T cells: (1) killer T cells; (2)

helper T cells; and (3) suppressor T cells. Each of these T cell types binds to antigens through its antigen receptor and then proceeds with the clonal expansion process; however, following such clonal expansion, the continuing function of T cells depends on the type of T cell involved. Killer T cells directly destroy antigens and host cells that have been infected by the antigen. Helper T cells release lymphokines that direct B cells to make antibodies and augment killer T cell function. Suppressor T cells release lymphokines notifying other T cells to suppress the further release of lymphokines and, accordingly, to slow down the immunological response, thereby avoiding autoimmune disorders.

Source: T Cell Sciences, Inc., prospectus dated May 15, 1986.

by T cells, essential for the growth of certain white blood cells) receptors in a patient's blood. Depending on FDA approval, management expected the company to market its first clinical diagnostic product by early 1988. Clinical trials for its first therapeutic products would not begin for several years because of the complexity of the scientific research and the FDA approval process.

Equity investment from December 9, 1983 (date of inception), through January 31, 1986, totaled approximately $5.5 million from the sale of common shares, convertible preferred shares, and warrants to venture capital investors and to officers, employees, and consultants. In May 1986, a public offering resulted in proceeds of $11.1 million. Exhibit 1 shows equity ownership; Exhibit 2 shows the company's financial results as of October 31, 1986. Appendix A provides additional information about the company.

Grant's First Six Months as CEO

The remainder of this case follows events in T Cell Sciences during James Grant's first six months as CEO, largely as he viewed them.

Interview with James Grant, November 10, 1986

When the board asked you to become CEO of T Cell Sciences, what were some of the goals and responsibilities that defined this new challenge for you?

The board wanted a CEO who could accomplish several things. First, it was looking for a person with broad experience to put an organization together. The company had recently grown from ten people to forty-five people, and from a small group in the laboratory to a publicly held company. In addition to building a management team, this person would also have to develop a board that would have breadth and could call attention to the company. The board now has only three initial investors and one insider on it. We also need an organization that can relate to university-based scientific people in immunology, especially those working on T cell receptors. We want to establish an

Exhibit 1   T Cell Sciences, Inc.: Equity ownership as of October 31, 1986.

Common shares outstanding   8,224,474
Voting Class B Preferred Stock   1,233,102

| | *Percentage of* | | |
Beneficial Ownership	Common Stock	Preferred Stock	Voting Capital Stock**
Dr. Patrick Kung	11.8	—	9.6
Peterson, Jacobs & Co.	2.5	38.5	6.7
Aetna Life and Casualty Company	—	28.8	5.0
Gary Takata	5.8	—	4.7
Ronald Urvater	4.6	—	3.7
CW Ventures	—	22.2	2.7
F. Daniel Frost [et al]	—	7.7	1.3
All other directors and officers	*	—	*
Total of beneficial ownership by major shareowners, officers, and directors	24.7	97.2	33.7
All other shareholders	75.3	2.8	66.3

*Less than 1 percent.

**Voting capital stock includes all outstanding common and preferred stock, plus currently exercisable warrants.

interest group broad enough so that the company gets identified with any breakthroughs in immunology relating to T cells. Building an organization, in effect, encompasses not only building an in-house team, but also a board, a group of scientific advisors, and alliances with a number of pharmaceutical firms.

Second, while the company was on the forefront of immunology, it needed a long-range strategy that could convert its science and medicine into a business. To my mind, it's important that we involve the research people in developing a business definition and strategy. For this kind of venture, a business plan with just numbers really has no meaning. The key is in getting the medical research people to articulate what they are doing in such a way that we can then identify potential new products.

As the potential applications are identified, the company then can build relationships with the pharmaceutical firms who are major players in the particular medical areas that we target. For example, we are looking to Pfizer for applications in rheumatoid arthritis and diabetes. Pfizer is big in these medical applications and even though it has no product of the kind that we might develop—in fact, we might replace some existing Pfizer products—it is the best organization for marketing anything we come up with dealing with these medical segments. The same is true for our relationship with Syntex, which specializes in diagnostics for cancer. The challenge is to develop an effective alli-

Exhibit 2   T Cell Sciences, Inc.: Financial record as of October 31, 1986 ($ thousands).

	Year ended April 30			Six months, ended
Statement of Operations	*1984*	*1985*	*1986*	*October 31, 1986*
Revenues				
Product sales	—	—	—	122
Contract revenues	—	—	13	659
Interest income	2	40	130	374
Total revenues	2	40	143	1,155
Expenses				
Research and development	30	760	1,248	895
All other operating expenses	91	335	619	670
Total expenses	121	1,095	1,867	1,565
Net income (loss)	(119)	(1,055)	(1,724)	(410)

Condensed balance sheet (as of October 31, 1986)

Cash and short-term investments	$13,098	Current liabilities	$ 316
Other current assets	186	Deferred income	160
Property and equipment	498	Convertible preferred stock	2,466
Other assets	24	Shareholders' equity	10,865
Total assets	$13,806	Total liability and equity	$13,806

ance strategy with Pfizer, Syntex, or whomever. The more we can get them involved, the better will be our chances of success.

In order to build a business plan, we are going to need to articulate these ideas in ways that all agree and understand—the managers, the board, the corporate partners, and the scientific advisors.

I don't know of any start-up companies that have tried this approach. Most of them have a particular product or technology that they try to develop. None have followed our broad strategy with the aim of a major breakthrough. You might ask how we can compete with NIH [National Institutes of Health]? As a matter of fact, we have more flexibility than NIH. We have money, and we have an equity position that can be attractive to a university-based research group. It has been a rage for these people to leave the university so as to start their own companies. What we offer is a mechanism that provides the benefits of starting up a new company and still allows them to do what they really want to do—which is to continue research at the university.

As CEO, what freedom of action do you have? What constraints were imposed on you? What is your time horizon, and what are the investors' expectations?

Surprisingly, there are no constraints. Our investors, both private and public, recognize that long lead times are involved in developing biotechnology products. They do not really expect any significant products to be on the market for at least five to ten years. In my view, we could have something within two to three years in the diagnostic area and that would be quite a plus for us. A further help is the general expectation in the financial community of a very big future return from biotech. The best proof of this is Genentech. For 1986, it reported an operating profit of $16 million and a market value of about $3 billion. This boggles the mind. Right now, we are greatly undervalued at $3 a share. With 8 million common shares outstanding, we have cash and assets of roughly $3 a share, and this does not take into account the value of our proprietary information.

The medical technology we are working on will be done. The question is whether it will be us or someone else. What our backers really want is for me to build a company and to articulate a strategic plan so that if the research and medicine work, it all comes together as a successful business.

As you decided on whether or not to take on this job, what were the most important considerations? What was most attractive to you? What features might have been cause for concern?

I felt there were three critical issues. First was the state of the science and technology. I wanted to know what the long-range potential would be. I was also concerned with how good the people were. I know medical people all over the country, and one of the first things I did was to spend a week to ten days visiting all these people to learn what I could about the medical research. By the end of that trip I was ready to take a board exam on immunology.

Second, I wanted to know if there was a focus on and a commitment to a particular medical therapy. Let me explain that. Many of the biotech firms are really only good at producing proteins. They are good at recombinant DNA and fermentation techniques, and after that it is pretty much an open question as to whether they will come up with new products to deal with any particular disease. Most of their so-called discoveries replicate products that were already available. We already had insulin, we already had growth hormones, we already had hepatitis-B vaccine.

The next generation of biotech companies will be more like T Cell Sciences. Indeed, the Genentechs and Cetuses are going to have to focus and commit to a real medical niche in order to survive. We are focusing on immunology and organ transplantation, on diseases that relate to immunology.

The third question I had concerned the funding situation. Unless there are adequate funds, this job would be no fun.

Those were the three major considerations: the medical technology, the market segment, and the funding. I felt that if we had those three in place, everything else could be taken care of. We could hire people; we could build relationships; we could build facilities. It was clear that we had good financial connections in New York. We had Peat Marwick Main to handle the books and Pryor, Cashman, Sherman, and Flynn of New York to serve as our general legal counsel. I have recently engaged the Washington, D.C., law firm Covington and Burling for FDA representation. We are now looking for good firms for patent law and public relations.

Another important consideration is that I had been a deputy commissioner in the Food and Drug Administration. In getting an FDA application through, it is not only important to get the application right the first time, it's also helpful to talk at the higher levels in the FDA. Such talks are not going to substitute for good medicine, but you have to understand that the commissioner and deputy commissioner have a sense of history. If they have a choice between something that is mundane and something that represents a new generation of medicine, they are going to want to be associated with something that will have counted.

You started on the job last Monday. What did you do the first day? The first week? And what did you learn and discover since you have been on the job?

The first thing I wanted to do was to get to know the people. Success in this business is not going to depend so much on strategy as it will on personal relationships. So I set out to get to know the people, not only the research people in Cambridge, but the outside people, including some of the board members whom I had not met, the law firm representatives, and so on. I also set out to get to know the outside scientific advisors. I have met about half of them and will meet the rest over the next few weeks. Then there is also a need to meet with Pfizer and Syntex. The Pfizer people are coming in this week to see what has happened with their multimillion dollar investment. I can't blame them for that.

So the most important thing was to get to know the people. The second thing was to take a look at the financial controls and the financial state of the company. I have a young chief financial officer from Dartmouth who is very competent, so I am relaxed about this dimension.

Looking ahead, I am starting to prepare for a shareholders' meeting in eight weeks. We have 400 to 500 shareholders and no experience as a public company, so it will take some time. Over the next few weeks I also want to start conversations with my people over the questions of business definition and strategy.

Finally, there are so many things we need that we don't have, such as health and safety procedures. I did check to see that we were in compliance with the various FDA, EPA, and City of Cambridge regulations and requirements. We don't have a compensation system, it is kind of random. Then we have to think about the organization. This is a first job for about thirty out of the forty-five people now on board. They are mostly out of university research laboratories. They have no idea about how to handle themselves in a commercial enterprise.

You had mentioned the young CFO. Who else do you have to help you manage the company? What plans do you have in this regard?

The other day, one of the investors asked me what I thought about the administrative team in the company. I told him, "You are looking at it." While we do have one fellow who handles the marketing and sales—and I know Dave will grow into the job—we have to add many key players. Clearly we are going to need someone in the patent area, probably a Ph.D. scientist who can be trained as a paralegal person. The company's greatest need is to protect its proprietary rights. Second, we very quickly have to bring someone on who can serve as a regulatory affairs officer. This person will be responsible for getting approvals through the FDA.

Right now we are strong in the controllership function. Over the next year, once we have articulated the company's strategy, we are going to have to be increasingly good with respect to financial planning and capital budgeting. We are probably going to have to add someone in that area even though we have good advice from our investment bankers. We are going to be marketing the diagnostics ourselves so we will also need an operations manager. We are also going to have to add a human resources person. We have a health plan, but we are going to need a pension plan. We are going to need policies with respect to educational leaves, especially for the kind of people we have. In effect, we are going to have to articulate a whole host of policies and plans as the company grows.

Basically, I am going to try to keep the management side lean. We want to concentrate the money on the research staff even at the risk of some management chaos to do that. By keeping the management lean, I am trying to force the research people to be more concerned about business issues. This way they can't look to some manager to take care of these things; they have to get involved themselves. Overall I don't see us adding even ten people on the non-research side over the next two years.

Interview with James Grant, November 17, 1986

What happened during your second week as CEO of T Cell Sciences?

Basically, I refined my priorities as to what needs to be done. There were four items having to do with outside considerations and three items having to do with inside considerations.

My first outside priority was to strengthen the board. This I have accomplished with the addition of two experienced businessmen as new outside directors. Our first meeting is to take place in early December, and the annual meeting will be held in February. The second outside priority was in getting the scientific advisory board to develop a sense of mission. I have met with three or four more members of this group during last week and intend to meet with the others during the next few weeks. The third outside priority was to get the patent situation in shape. This was a good week for patents in that I have been able to consolidate the various patent proceedings with Pennie and Edmonds, a prestigious New York patent law firm. The fourth outside priority was to get going on FDA approvals.

There are several important milestones that security analysts look at when assessing a new high-technology venture. These include: the breadth and status of its outside scientific advisory board; how many patents the firm has submitted; and whether or not it has filed anything with the FDA. Only when a firm has jumped these particular hurdles will it qualify for their attention.

Getting the attention of security analysts is important to a firm such as ours. At the current rate of R&D activity, we could probably run for the next ten years with our present funding. But to do what we ought to do in R&D, we will at least have to quadruple the investment in this firm, and more than that will be required for clinical trials. To raise the money, we will have to get the stock price up for another round of equity financing. The timing of such a public offering would, of course, depend on a window of opportunity in the stock market as well as on our plans to use the funds. A sizable offering would probably result in a significant dilution in shareholders' value. But this should be acceptable to the investors if it were preceded by a, let's say, four-fold increase in share price.

Turning to the inside priorities, the first will be to develop a strategy, and more importantly a strategic planning process. The company now has good cost-control procedures. But good cost control is not why the investors have committed their money to the firm. We are going to have to increase our commitment rate in order to increase the results and payoffs. My target, admittedly ambitious, is to have a strategic planning process in place by year end. This schedule may realistically slip a bit, but it is better to have an aggressive target and slip a little than to have a slack target and slip a little.

The second inside priority is to deal with the company's needs for people. This challenge is a more time-consuming process than I had thought likely. It's not that we are having trouble attracting good people, but it takes time to evaluate them and to get them on board. We have to bring people here so that they can see our operation and for us to see how the personal chemistry evolves.

The third area of internal priority has to do with developing the necessary human resource policies. The company needs a personnel manual, it needs a tuition reimbursement plan, it needs a maternity plan, and so forth.

There are not many things to keep T Cell Sciences from being a viable company. The three major potential show-stoppers, in my opinion, would be inadequate funding for whatever reason (for example, were there to be a severe recession), failure to obtain product liability insurance coverage, and the emergence of harsh regulatory policies. As an example of the product liability problem, we are negotiating new contracts with Dana-Farber and Harvard University involving some $300,000 to $500,000. Harvard wants T Cell Sciences to indemnify the university and to provide product liability insurance in the event of product liability damages. Harvard understandably doesn't want to put its name and reputation on the line with exposure to product liability. But T Cell Sciences is unable to obtain such insurance coverage. It is a dilemma for Harvard and for us.[2]

Basically, I am trying to organize the company so that many of the important processes can run themselves to the extent possible. This has now been accomplished with respect to patents. The FDA submissions process should be in place by the end of this week. In contrast, board relationships is something that I'll have to do personally on a continuing basis.

Because of its small size, anything this company does can have a major

---

2. Harvard University subsequently dropped the requirement for product liability insurance, relying on T Cell Science's agreement to indemnify it for damages.

impact on its share price. If it submits a new patent, or enters into a new contract with some pharmaceutical company, the price could go up appreciably. Anything I say or do could conceivably come back to haunt me as somehow being connected with providing inside information to someone. For example, if a pharmaceutical company inquires into acquiring a small biotech firm, and the target company begins due diligence investigations, people will soon know something is up and that could affect the stock price. Another risk the biotech's CEO runs has to do with assessing the company's value for such a sale. If the CEO thinks the company is worth more than the offering bid, he could be sued by shareholders who object to its rejection. Conversely, if he recommends the board accept the offer, he could be sued by shareholders for not holding out for a higher price. The rules and guidelines for insider trading and takeover activities are unclear and leave a person in my position seriously exposed.

Interview with James Grant, January 6, 1987

Grant greeted the interviewer with a copy of the following news release:

T CELL SCIENCES, YAMANOUCHI PHARMACEUTICAL SIGN MULTI-MILLION DOLLAR PRODUCT DEVELOPMENT AGREEMENT

Cambridge, Mass., January 5, 1987—T Cell Sciences, Inc. (NASDAQ: TCEL) today announced that it has signed a $3.7 million, three-year product development agreement with Yamanouchi Pharmaceutical Co. Ltd. (YPC), Tokyo, Japan, an international manufacturer and marketer of ethical and over-the-counter drugs and diagnostic products. This agreement will fund the development of autoimmune disease and cancer diagnostic products based on T Cell Sciences' proprietary technology of using T cell antigen receptor proteins as direct detection elements.

Under the terms of the agreement, YPC will provide funding to support the development of products which directly use genetically engineered elements of the human immune system, specifically T cell antigen receptors, to diagnose rheumatoid arthritis and lung cancer. YPC will receive rights to market the resulting products in Japan. In addition to receiving compensation on all Japanese sales of test kits based on this technology, T Cell Sciences will retain the rights to market these products in the rest of the world.

Yamanouchi Pharmaceuticals Co., Ltd., headquartered in Tokyo, Japan, is a leading pharmaceutical company in the Far East. The company estimated annual revenues of $850 million (yen equivalent) for the year ended December 31, 1986.

Grant went on to explain:

This arrangement puts T Cell Sciences in the attractive Japanese market with a good partner. It involves about a $1 million up-front payment. However, this deal involves a high R&D risk. Yamanouchi can lose money. The major cost for us is in committing scarce research resources to a project that loesn't work. We cannot afford to do that too often.

I see this arrangement and the ones with Syntex and Pfizer as alliances in which we do research on behalf of a partner. T Cell Sciences provides access to the technology; the partner provides access to the market.

The need to keep these alliance research projects independent from each other is an issue for the company. I made sure to contact both Syntex and Pfizer before the public announcement on Yamanouchi so as to avert any surprises on their part. It was interesting; both asked, "How does the Yamanouchi agreement differ from our contract with you?" I had no problem satisfying them in this regard, but their query points out a problem. If these people are unable to see the demarcation between the work we do for them and that for Yamanouchi, just think how confusing these arrangements must be for people with less information and expertise.

With the addition of the Yamanouchi research contract, T Cell Sciences has achieved a favorable cash flow situation. The company's cash receipts over the next three years of some $15 to $16 million will slightly exceed its cash outflow based on its current R&D program. The annual income includes roughly $1 million interest from $13 million in the bank, $3.5 million from research grants, and income from the sale of products growing from the current one-half million dollar base.

Of course, as important as a healthy cash flow is to a new venture like T Cell Sciences, the ultimate success of this company will rest on the success of its research. If our research fails, we fail. We have to be careful to keep from overspending just because we have money. The critical investment has to be in the quality of our research.

At present, T Cell Sciences has about one-third of its business connected with basic research, divided evenly between in-house work and work funded in the laboratories of its scientific advisors. Another one-third is devoted to diagnostics, primarily in connection with Syntex and Yamanouchi. The remaining one-third is devoted to therapeutic work in connection with Pfizer. [Grant described the company's diagnostic business as producing products that block or otherwise affect T cell receptors for curing or preventing particular diseases.]

As for staffing, we are currently looking for a regulatory affairs officer. Since we cannot afford to have an experienced person at $50 to $75 thousand per year, we decided to search for a young person who could grow into the position. Ideally, this person should have a scientific degree and some experience in regulatory work for a drug company. More importantly, he or she has to be detail oriented and able to deal nondefensively with comments from FDA examiners. Accurate detail work is very important in filing FDA applications. And an effective intermediary between examiners and researchers can make the difference between getting approval in two years and having to wait five years.

One important advantage to the Boston area is that it is one of only three locations in the United States—along with San Francisco and the Los Angeles/San Diego area—where you can find a pool of talented people for biotech work. For the regulatory affairs position, almost fifty people responded to an advertisement we had placed in the *Globe*. Ten to twelve of these applicants fit the company's specifications. Now I have the time-consuming job of picking the one.

Interview with James Grant, January 19, 1987

With the first shareholders' meeting coming soon, what issues are foremost in your mind?

One of the key issues for me is to decide on the company's rate of research activity. At present, the company is operating close to break-even in terms of cash flow. With some $13 to $14 million in the bank, the question is whether to increase the investments in research and go further into the red, or to keep at the present rate.

As I see it, the investors did not invest in the company to earn interest. On the other hand, they want a sound company. The board reflects these two points of view. The venture capitalists on the board are looking for a big play and would probably favor increased spending on research. The board members who have come from large companies are probably more interested in having the company get into the black. I am somewhere in the middle with an open mind.

The biotech field is in a ferment today, and there is considerable pressure for a firm like ours to grab hold of a market segment before someone else does. But cranking up the R&D pace, and the attending losses, accelerates the investors' expectations for results. In effect, the stakes go up.

Assessing the technological probabilities for success is difficult, to say the least. Some of our researchers are convinced that we could double our research pace with little added risk. Others think that we are moving as fast as we can, given the state of present know-how. As for Patrick [Kung], one day he is on one side of the debate, and the next day he is on the other side. It's not a simple question of money. If we succeed in the research, we'll have no trouble raising the funds needed. But if the research doesn't bear fruit, the game could be up before we are ready to quit.

A second broad strategic issue for me has to do with the direction of the company. To what extent should it focus on diagnostic work versus a full-scale operation including therapeutic products. The therapeutic area promises the big payoff in the future. Moreover, companies like Abbott Laboratories and Becton, Dickinson & Company are too strong in diagnostics for a company like T Cell Sciences to compete over the long term in that arena.

One possible move for a company like ours would be to sell off the diagnostic business after establishing itself in the therapeutics area. If the divested business were earning $5 million and could be sold for twenty-five times earnings, it could be worth something in excess of $100 million. That money could then be plowed into therapeutics or clinical trials.

A third issue is to consider the nature of our business. Some people would argue that the company should focus on the generation of scientific ideas and rely on other companies to manufacture and sell the resulting products under license. In my view, selling technology is not enough. The company should try to hold on to as much of the process as possible. It might produce some of the simpler materials and enter into a joint venture with a partner to produce the finished products. Any arrangement should ensure that T Cell Sciences receives more than just royalty payments. Maybe our policy should be to integrate forward so long as the margin increases.

For now, the principal things to watch are cash flow and head count. Our future growth will depend on finding good people, our ability to integrate these people into an effective team, and building systems and processes to manage the company's operations.

In terms of attracting people, our salaries are competitive, but the real incentives are in the options. For example, for a senior person, the company might offer 20,000 shares at market price, let's say $4. If the company were to grow in value from $30 million to $600 million, the shares could increase by twenty times from $4 to $80. This would translate roughly into $1.5 million for this individual.

We have a rather unusual potential problem with respect to teamwork. Several of our scientific advisors are contenders for the Nobel Prize. Dr. Mark Davis of Stanford University and Dr. Stephen Hendrick of the University of California at San Diego are credited with discovering the genes related to T cell antigen receptors in mouse cells. Dr. Tak Mak of the Ontario Cancer Institute is credited with a similar discovery as it relates to human cells. Dr. Leroy Hood could get a Nobel Prize for his gene sequencing work. The worst thing that could happen is for only one of them to get recognized. You just can't imagine the fierce rivalry the Nobel brings out in the scientific community.

Interview with James Grant, April 14, 1987

What have you done since January as CEO of T Cell Sciences?

Shareholder relations have become a major task for me. We retained Kekst & Company, a first-class public relations firm in New York, to help us tell the company's story to the financial community. We have developed a pretty good road show, and I am now doing an average of one presentation per week. While it is difficult to assess the impact of this effort, share price has done well. It increased to over $5 and then held up as some of the original investors sold off a large number of shares. Incidentally, this sell-off is good for the company long-term in broadening the shareholder base. The number of shareholders has increased to over 2,000, and institutional holders are growing in importance.

I also chaired our first shareholders' meeting in February. One of the things we did was to change the company's bylaws so as to limit the personal liability of company directors to the full extent permitted by the recent amendment to Delaware corporate law.

Internally, we have put in place several important planning tools. First, we now have a clearly articulated corporate mission statement and strategy. Our mission is to become a leader in the field of immunology, producing distinctive

Exhibit 3 T Cell Sciences, Inc.: Product–market analysis for company's technology.

1986 Worldwide sales for existing products (1992 worldwide markets for TCS technology)

Technology Slice	Disease	In Vitro Diagnostic			In Vitro Diagnostic		Therapeutics		Therapeutics		Therapy			Therapy
		A	B	C	D	E	F	G	H	I	J	K	L	M
Autoimmune ⎰	Rheumatoid arthritis	$ 50MM			Not currrently available		Not currently available		Not currently in use	$1600MM Immuno-therapy drugs	Not currently available ($800MM)			Not currently available
	Type-1 diabetes	(Does not include glucose monitoring)								$1000MM Nonsteroidal antiinflam-matory				
	Multiple sclerosis	Autoimmune total ($188MM)					←($ 220MM)→							
Cancer ⎰	Lung cancer	$ 39MM ($104MM)			Not currently in use ($ 50MM)		Not currently in use ($800MM)		$ 22MM ($2546MM)	$2000MM Chemo-therapy ($4625MM)	Not currently available ($560MM)			Not currently available
	Breast cancer	$ 35MM ($ 93MM)												
	Colorectal cancer	$ 37MM ($ 99MM)												

688

Stomach cancer	$ 8MM ($ 22MM)						$ 250MM ($1000MM)
Total cancer	$204MM ($550MM)					Not currently available	
Infectious Disease — AIDS	$108MM ($356MM)	Not applicable	Not currently available			Not currently available	
Cytomegalovirus and other sexually transmitted diseases	$ 86MM ($199MM)				Not currently available		
Hepatitis	$234MM ($313MM)	←($1000MM)→					
Organ transplantation	$ 1MM ($ 10MM)	Not applicable	$ 5MM ←($ 92MM)→	Not currently available	$ 120MM ($ 184MM)	Not currently available	Not applicable
Allergy/hypersensitivity	$ 25MM ($ 60MM)	Not applicable	Not currently available			Not currently available	Not applicable

diagnostic and therapeutic products for autoimmune diseases and cancers. Our strategy is to rely on proprietary technology, to add value to research, to have a product orientation, and to move in stages from diagnostic to therapeutic products. This product evolution is a reflection of the technology. In stage one, most of our technical effort is devoted to improving our understanding of the T cell antigen receptor function. Our findings will provide the basis for new diagnostic products. In stage two, our effort will focus increasingly on how to manipulate the T cell receptor function, and that work will lead to therapeutic products.

In conjunction with strategy, we have developed a marketing plan. [See Exhibit 3 for an example of the company's analysis of its markets.] We have also developed a management control system, specifying quarterly objectives over a three-year period for the company's twenty major research programs. Interestingly, after some ten years of operations, Biogen's management has just announced in its annual report the introduction of a research cost control system.

On the people side, we hired a young woman with a Ph.D. in toxicology to be our regulatory affairs officer. I have also been able to track down a first-year Harvard MBA who could do an excellent job studying the market for AIDS-related products as a guide for our technical commitments in this arena. He has expressed his interest, but I have a problem. I would like the summer job to lead to long-term employment after graduation assuming things work out well, but we cannot come close to matching the high salaries offered by the investment banking and consulting firms. For such a person, we would probably include a significant stock option. While this form of compensation in time could more than offset the salary differential, it does not provide the same immediate cash inflow. In a way, our difficulty reflects a more serious problem for our nation where so many talented young people are being diverted from value-creating industries to what are essentially ancillary, and to some extent parasitic, service activities.

All in all, the company is progressing nicely. Sales are up to an annual rate of $600,000. Our R&D contract work is expanding, and we now have sixteen patents on file. We are also beginning to set up manufacturing operations.

What, if anything, would you have done differently since you first decided to accept the offer to become CEO of T Cell Sciences some six months ago?

Not enough time has elapsed to know where big mistakes might have been made, but at this point, I am not sure that I would have done anything differently.

Sure, I wish we had a director of operations on board now so that we could move faster on that front. But it was a question of priorities. We have been running full out, and other issues had greater priority. As I look back, I feel pretty good about the first six months. [Exhibit 4 contains financial results as of April 30, 1987.]

What are some of the major challenges you see before you?

One of the major challenges is to raise enough capital to do what we want

Exhibit 4   T Cell Sciences, Inc.: Financial results, April 30, 1987, and share price record ($ thousands, except share price).

Statement of Operations (ending April 30, 1987)

Revenues	
Product sales	$ 378
Contract revenues	1,798
Interest income	852
Total revenues	3,027
Expenses	
Research and development	2,251
All other operating expenses	1,601
Total expenses	3,852
Net income (loss)	($ 825)

Condensed Balance Sheet (as of April 30, 1987)

Cash and short-term investments	$13,469	Current liabilities	$ 600
Other current assets	515	Deferred income	1,076
Property and equipment	602	Convertible preferred stock	2,466
Other assets	22	Shareholders' equity	10,466
Total assets	$14,608	Total liability and equity	$14,608

Common Share Price Record

Date, 1987–1988	10/31	12/1	12/31	2/2	3/2	3/31	4/30
Price($)*	2⅞	3⅝	3⅜	4⅛	4¼	5	4½
Biotech shares index**	125	117	108	119	148	150	186
Dow Jones Industrial Average	1878	1913	1896	2179	2220	2305	2283

*Average of closing bid and asked prices. Highest at $6⅛ on March 16, 1988.

**Source: TracKing. January 1, 1986 = 100, for twenty-eight biotechnology companies.

to do. We could probably triple our size in short order if we were willing to expand our contract R&D work, but that would go against our objective of developing T Cell Sciences into a full-fledged pharmaceutical company. With equity funding, we own the technology; with contract funding, our sponsors own exclusive rights to it, and we become a technical arm to them.

To raise equity on favorable terms, we are going to have to distinguish T Cell Sciences from the other biotech players. The problem we face in growing our share price is in dealing with the financial community's limited understanding of this new and rapidly changing industry. The investment mentality of today could be characterized: so goes Genentech, so goes the industry.

We have to distinguish ourselves from Genentech. We have to show how we are different from other biotech firms and why we can succeed where others might not. What this all means for me is doubling the time I devote to making presentations to investors and analysts.

Another major challenge is to develop our people. We now have fifty-five employees and are adding roughly one person every two weeks. Our target is to have eighty people a year from now and 110 the year after.

Integrating the new people into the organization continues to be a problem for us, especially for research. We have to find a way to get people with a university postdoctoral research experience to learn how to work in groups. Among our six technical managers under Patrick, only two have some commercial experience. The other four are new to this. One step we have taken to deal with this problem has been to have a Harvard Business School professor who has had considerable experience working with research organizations meet with our people. We might develop some kind of training program.

Last week, another challenge landed on my desk—that of finding new quarters. As you can see, we have doubled our space since January, but the building rental management has just informed me that the added space we were hoping to take next year would not be available. So now I have to find a suitable location in the vicinity for occupation within the next eighteen months or so. This is a good example of the kind of nitty-gritty issues that compete with the big-picture stuff for my time and attention.

Many of the major issues have immediate implications as well. In our last meeting I spoke about the need to decide on the company's rate of research activity. That decision is not postponable. It is made every day, since inaction is a de facto decision to move at our present measured pace.

The strategic direction issue I mentioned then also has current action implications. I see diagnostics and therapeutics as two separate and separable businesses. Others might argue that it makes more sense to organize around specific diseases, coupling the diagnostic and therapeutic work for each disease focus. The fact of the matter is that we have to make organizational moves now that commit us to one of these directions. The marketing organization has to be aligned one way or the other. Pretty soon we'll face the same decision in the way we set up our manufacturing operations. And within twelve months our research organizational structure has to be decided.

Possibly less pressing, but not less important, is the challenge I face in figuring out how to maintain the entrepreneurial spirit that has characterized T Cell Sciences to date as the company grows in size and complexity. Everything we do or don't do can have an important impact on this critical issue.

How we move on all these issues really depends on our basic decision to develop T Cell Sciences as an independent company. If we are taking the route of preparing a property for acquisition, we might do things very differently with respect to planning and organization building.

Appendix A: Information about the Company
Up to the Time of Grant's Arrival

T Cell Sciences was conceived in early 1983 when venture capitalists Ron Urvater and Gary Takata approached Patrick Kung with the idea of setting up his own company.

Kung, a recognized pioneer in immunological research, had begun his career in Johnson & Johnson's Orthopharmaceutical Company, where he worked on T cell receptor research from 1978 to 1981. He was credited with developing methods and technologies for the identification of T cells and T cell antigen receptors and their response to disease in the human body. Looking forward to starting his own company, Kung left Johnson & Johnson in 1981 to join a small biomedical company where he could get experience relevant to his purpose. The recent success Urvater and Takata had in launching another venture in the T cell business gave him confidence in their proposal.

T Cell Sciences was incorporated in Delaware on December 9th, 1983. Kung received 1 million shares for $1,000 and the two venture capitalists each received 500,000 shares for $500. The fledgling company raised $300,000 seed money in March 1984 and another $700,000 in July, a time period when biotech stock prices were depressed.

The company had been organized for the purpose of developing diagnostic and therapeutic products for detecting and treating immune disorders and autoimmune diseases, utilizing the special properties of T cell antigen receptors. See Exhibit A for a description of T cell technology.

The company quickly set out to establish close ties with leading scientists in the field of T cell immunology. By 1986, about twenty people were engaged in such arrangements. The principal research advisory group comprised five eminent researchers: Dr. Leroy Hood, professor at California Institute of Technology; Dr. Mark Davis and Dr. Irving Weissman, professors at Stanford University; Dr. Tak Mak of the Ontario Cancer Institute; and Dr. Jack Stominger, professor at Harvard University and associated with the Dana-Farber Cancer Institute. T Cell Sciences provided funds to their laboratories for work under their direction on the company's behalf.

The company also had contracted with a number of institutions to perform clinical work of a diagnostic nature. These institutions included: Massachusetts General Hospital; Scripps Clinic and Research Foundation; Dana-Farber Cancer Institute; Joselin Diabetes Center; and Deaconess and Childrens Hospital.

In April 1985, T Cell Sciences entered into an agreement with Syntex U.S.A., a major supplier of pharmaceutical products, for research and development contract funding. In March 1986, Syntex agreed to fund, over four years, $4.7 million for research in the general areas of cancer and infectious diseases, and in particular to try to develop *in vitro* diagnostic tests using monoclonal antibodies against T cell antigen receptors for breast cancer and cytomegalovirus. T Cell Sciences was expected to contribute as much as $1.8 million for the project. Syntex U.S.A. would pay T Cell Sciences a 5 percent royalty on net sales of any products resulting from the funded research.

In August 1986, T Cell Sciences entered into an agreement with Pfizer to develop therapeutic products for treating rheumatoid arthritis and type-1 diabetes. Funding for the initial three-year term was to total between $4.5 and $7.0 million. Pfizer would receive worldwide exclusive rights to therapeutic products resulting from the work. T Cell Sciences would receive royalties on any sales of these therapeutic products and retained exclusive rights to all diagnostic applications.

At the end of July 1986, T Cell Sciences signed a domestic product distribution agreement with Boehringer Mannheim Biochemicals (BMB), a leading U.S. manufacturer and distributor of biochemicals and biomedical products. While BMB would be sold distributor using its direct sales force, T Cell Sciences would continue its own telemarketing and mail-order sales programs.

Other Information

The company's April 30, 1986, 10-K report provided the following information concerning competition, government regulation, property. legal proceedings, and dividend policy.

Competition

The company is engaged in a rapidly expanding area of biotechnology in which research is being conducted in universities, public and private foundations and major pharmaceutical companies throughout the U.S. and in foreign countries. . . . [A]dditionally, a number of companies with a focus on immunology have been formed recently. Several of these companies are involved in research and product development of monoclonal antibodies and T cells.

The company believes that it is one of the few organizations engaged in research specifically targeted towards the use of T cell antigen receptor structure as the key to new diagnostic and therapeutic products.

Government Regulation

Present and proposed products of the company are included in a field in which regulation by federal and other governmental authorities is a significant factor. . . . [A]t present, the company is subject to and in compliance with regulations of the City of Cambridge, Massachusetts, with respect to control of recombinant DNA activities. The company is not aware of any proposed actions by any governmental authorities which might materially impair its ability to continue its research or conduct its proposed business.

Property

In March 1986, the company entered into a new lease for its corporate offices and research facilities at 840 Memorial Drive in Cambridge, Massachusetts. The company leases approximately 8,800 square feet of this building, all of which is currently utilized for its offices and laboratories. The lease agreement expires in February 1989 and is renewable at the company's option for an additional two years. Rent through 1988 will be approximately $16,500 per month.

As of April 30, 1986, approximately $537,000 had been invested by the company in leasehold improvements, office furniture and laboratory equipment. Leasehold improvements have consisted primarily of the cost necessary to convert the rented space to a laboratory and office configuration. The company owns all of its laboratory equipment, which includes some of the most technologically advanced equipment available.

Legal Proceedings
None.

Dividends.
The company has never paid a cash dividend. The company intends to retain all of its earnings, if any, for use in its business and does not intend to pay cash dividends in the foreseeable future.

Appendix B: Comments by Company Officers

Dr. Patrick Kung, executive vice president and scientific director, Geoffrey Clear, chief financial officer, and David Corbet, director of commercial development were asked to describe their duties in T Cell Sciences and to comment on their perceptions of James Grant's strengths and weaknesses as CEO. The interviews were held on January 12, 1987.

Dr. Patrick C. Kung

[Born in Nanjing, China, Kung, age thirty-nine, received a B.S. degree in 1968 from Fu Jen Catholic University, Taiwan, and a Ph.D. in 1974 from the University of California, Berkeley.]

My job is to make sure that the company's product strategy works. In my view, the distinctive strength T Cell Sciences should have is to introduce practical applications from basic research faster and better than do others in the field. The normal time for new scientific ideas to get translated into clinical results is about five years. T Cell Sciences' challenge is to shorten this cycle. To illustrate what can be done in this regard, the company came out with its first product in the summer of 1986 based on some scientific findings that were reported in December of 1985. In this effort, not only do we have to identify product possibilities from the basic research findings, we then have to design and prepare user-friendly kits for clinician use.

One of my principal duties is to develop appropriate in-house technological capabilities. The current technical staff of thirty people is divided into two groups. One group of twenty-five is dedicated to determining the feasibility of converting new scientific discoveries into products. These people interact closely with our scientific advisors. The second group of five is responsible for reducing the first group's ideas into something marketable.

Both groups are expected to expand rapidly in 1987. Recruiting research scientists for the first group poses no serious problem for us. Hiring scientists for product development is another matter. The field is very new, and the pool of talent is small. It's taken me six months to find one person to meet this need.

Some of my other responsibilities include: seeing that technical milestones are met; advising Grant and the board concerning the company's technological strategy; and managing the company's technological licensing arrangements.

My relationship with Grant is excellent. He is particularly strong with respect to strategic thinking, financial controls, motivating scientists, understanding the product development process, investor relationships, and managing the board of directors.

Grant also has some potential shortcomings for his position. One is his limited understanding of the company's specific technology and of how to market its products. We plan to immerse him in a series of technology briefings to bolster his capabilities in this regard.

Grant also needs to redefine his time frame. At CPC International, it was common for people to spend six months on a decision. At T Cell Sciences, decisions have to be made in one-fifth the time. One has to move fast here, and Grant is not used to this. Along these same lines, he probably also has to adjust to the limited staff support we have and the need for each person to wear many hats.

Geoffrey P. Clear

[Clear, age thirty-seven, received his MBA in 1974 from the Amos Tuck School at Dartmouth College, concentrating in accounting and finance. Because of his lack of practical experience, he decided to join Arthur Andersen & Company in the auditing function and spent three years in that job. In August 1977, he joined W.R. Grace, where he held a series of jobs relating to control and finance. In April 1986, he joined T Cell Sciences.]

My responsibilities as chief financial officer include: investor relations, which take about 20 percent of my time; managing reports and budgets for the contract work with Syntex, Pfizer, and Yamanouchi; decentralizing the budgeting process to increase department manager involvement; overseeing the accounting for government grants; and the treasury function—managing the firm's investment of $13 million. The primary financial goals for these investments are security, availability, and reasonable yields. The one thing I can blow is in not having money available when it is needed. So, half the money is managed by Merrill Lynch with a medium-term perspective and the other half by U.S. Trust investing in short-term obligations.

My job has changed with the change of CEOs. [Smith (fictitious name)] had an accounting and finance background and had done my job before I was hired. So we tended to work as collaborators. In contrast, Grant's background in R&D and government has him delegating more to me. There are two things Grant wants to see: actual results compared to budget, and cash flow.

The change in relationships that I mentioned also reflects other differences between the two men. Smith was very much involved in internal operations; Grant is more involved with external considerations. Smith was fairly relaxed about management; Grant places more emphasis on formal systems and procedures.

With the changes, I have now also taken on the duties of an administrative officer. In effect, Patrick is responsible for R&D, Dave Corbet for sales and marketing, and I am responsible for all the other functions—insurance, payroll, personnel, facilities, EDP [electronic data processing], you name it. I hope to hire a controller this year to share the burden.

David L. Corbet

[Corbet, age thirty-three, received a B.S. degree from the University of Rhode Island before joining American Hospital Supplies in 1976 as a salesman for diagnostic test kits. In 1980, he joined Baxter Travenol's marketing staff as a new product development manager, moving to Cooper Laboratories in 1982 as his division changed parent companies. In July 1985, he joined T Cell Sciences, having worked for Grant's predecessor at Baxter Travenol.]

When I first joined the company, I spent most of my time working on financing and company planning, as well as learning the nature of T cell product possibilities and the related potential markets. In time, I began to focus more on developing a marketing strategy for scientific [preclinical] applications of diagnostic products, and now I am spending most of my time implementing this plan. Over the next six months, over half of my time will probably be devoted to planning our entry into the clinical market for diagnostic products. As you can see, my position is still evolving.

The change in CEOs obviously has colored the nature of my job. For one thing, the company will grow faster under Grant. He is more readily willing to invest money in hiring people and building an organization. For another, Grant is away from the office much more, building the company's image in the investing community and working other external relationships. And their professional strengths also differ. [The previous CEO] had considerable experience in this industry and in small ventures; Grant comes with more broad executive experience. I find that I have learned different skills from each.

As I look ahead, I have begun to wonder about how my role with T Cell Sciences will evolve. Grant has come to see the company as being involved in two businesses—diagnostics and therapeutics. In my view, there are important business synergies between the two, particularly for our firm. If the company were to decide to separate these operations, I would be faced with a dilemma. On the one hand, diagnostics is where the company's marketing action is now. Moreover, all of my prior experience has been in marketing to the diagnostic market. On the other hand, the company's greatest potential lies in therapeutics, and this area represents a greater personal challenge to me.

Grant's real interest over the long term is in pushing therapeutic products. As R&D shifts in its emphasis from diagnostics to therapeutics, one of two things could happen. If the company has developed a line of successful diagnostic products, it might sell off this business to fund the move into therapeutics. If the diagnostic product offerings fall short, this line of business could be left to wither away.

Right now, it is very difficult to predict just where T Cell Sciences will end up. The company is R&D-driven. We do not have any important products in a box or in a vial. When we finally hit on that something, it will undoubtedly shape our activities and direction in ways we probably cannot foresee.

BIBLIOGRAPHY

Abegglan, James, and George Stalk, Jr. *Kaisha, The Japanese Corporation*. New York, 1985.

Aguilar, Francis J. *Scanning the Business Environment*. New York, 1967.

Andrews, Kenneth R. *The Concept of Corporate Strategy*. Rev. ed. Homewood, IL, 1980.

———. "Directors' Responsibility for Corporate Strategy." *Harvard Business Review*, 58, no. 6 (Nov.–Dec. 1980), 30–42.

———. "Replaying the Board's Role in Formulating Strategy." *Harvard Business Review*, 59, no. 3 (May–June 1981), 18–26.

———. "Corporate Strategy as a Vital Function of the Board." *Harvard Business Review*, 59, no. 6 (Nov.–Dec. 1981), 174–84.

Armour, H. O., and D. J. Teece. "Organizational Structure and Economic Performance: A Test of the Multidivisional Hypothesis." *Bell Journal of Economics*, 9 (Spring 1978), 106–22.

Auletta, Ken. "A Certain Poetry," *The New Yorker*, June 6 and 13, 1983, pp. 46–109 and 50–91, respectively.

Barnard, Chester I. *The Functions of the Executive*. Cambridge, MA, 1960.

Barnes, Louis B., and Mark P. Kriger, "The Hidden Side of Organizational Leadership," *Sloan Management Review*, 28 no. 1 (Fall 1986), 15–25.

Bartlett, Christopher A., and Sumantra Ghoshal. *Managing Across Borders*. Boston, 1989.

Bartlett, Christopher A., Yves Doz, and G. Hedlund, eds. *Managing the Global Firm*. London, 1990.

Beckhard, Richard, and Reuben T. Harris. *Organizational Transitions: Managing Complex Change*. Reading, MA, 1977.

Beer, Michael, Russell A. Eisenstat, and Bert Spector, *The Critical Path to Corporate Renewal*. Boston, 1990.

Beer, Michael, et al. *Managing Human Assets*. New York, 1984.

Berle, Adolf A., Jr. *Power Without Property*. New York, 1959.

Bierman, Harold, Jr., and Seymour Smidt. *The Capital Budgeting Decision*. 2nd ed. New York, 1966.

Black, Stanley B., and Timothy J. Gallagher. "The Use of Interest Rate Futures and Options by Corporate Financial Managers." *Financial Management*, 15 (Autumn 1986), 73–78.

Blake, Robert, and Jane S. Mouton. *Productivity: The Human Side*. New York, 1982.

Brealey, Richard A. and Stewart C. Myers. *Principles of Corporate Finance*. 3rd ed. New York, 1988.

Burgelman, Robert A. "A Process Model of Internal Corporate Venturing in the Diversified Major Firm." *Administrative Science Quarterly*, 28, no. 2 (June 1983), 223–44.

Burrough, Bryan, and John Helgar. *Barbarians at the Gate: The Fall of RJR Nabisco*. New York, 1990.

Chandler, Alfred D. "The Enduring Logic of Industrial Success." *Harvard Business Review*, 68, no. 2 (March–April 1990), 130–40.

Choi, Frederick D.S., and Richard M. Levich. *The Capital Market Effects of International Accounting Diversity*. Homewood, IL, 1990.

Contractor, Farok J., and Peter Lorange, eds. *Cooperative Strategies in International Business*. Lexington, MA, 1988.

Cooper, Ian, and Julian Frank. "Treasury Performance Measurement." *Midland Corporate Finance Journal*, 4, no. 4 (Winter 1987), 29–43.

Deal, Terrence E., and Allan A. Kennedy. *Corporate Cultures*. Reading, MA, 1982.

Donaldson, Gordon. *Managing Corporate Wealth*. New York, 1984.

Donaldson, Gordon, and Jay W. Lorsch. *Decision Making at the Top*. New York, 1983.

Drucker, Peter F. *Management*. New York, 1972.

———. *The Practice of Management*. New York, 1954.

Durfee, Edmund H., Victor R. Lesser, and Daniel Corkill. "Cooperation Through Communication in a Distributed Problem Solving Network." *Distributed Artificial Intelligence*, ed. M. N. Huhns. Los Altos, CA, 1987, pp. 29–58.

Elofson, Gregg, and Benn Konsynski. "Delegation Technologies: Environmental Scanning with Intelligent Agents." *Journal of Management Information Systems*, 8, no. 1 (Summer 1991), 37–62.

Encarnation, Dennis J. *Beyond Trade: Foreign Investment in the U.S./Japan Rivalry*. Ithaca, NY, 1992. In press.

Etzioni, Amitai. *The Moral Dimension: Toward a New Economics*. New York, 1988.

Fabozzi, Frank J., and T. Dessa Fabozzi. *Bond Markets, Analysis and Strategies*. Englewood Cliffs, NJ, 1989.

Fayol, Henri. *Administration Industrielle et Générale*. Paris, 1916.

Finnerty, John D. "Financial Engineering in Corporate Finance: An Overview." *Financial Management* 17 (Winter 1988), 14–33.

Friedman, Milton. *Capitalism and Freedom*. Chicago, 1962.

———. "The Social Responsibility of Business Is to Increase Its Profits." *The New York Times Magazine*, Sept. 13, 1970, pp. 32–33, 122–26.

Froot, Kenneth A., Andre F. Perold, and Jeremy C. Stein. "Shareholder Trading Practices and Corporate Investment Horizons." National Bureau of Economic Research, Inc., working paper no. 3638, March 1991.

Ghoshal, Sumantra, and Seok Ki Kim. "Building Effective Intelligence Systems for Competitive Advantage." *Sloan Management Review*, 28, no. 1 (Fall 1986), 49–58.

Goodman, Laurie S. "The Use of Interest Rate Swaps in Managing Corporate Liabilities." *Journal of Applied Corporate Finance*, 2, no. 4 (Winter 1990), 35–47.

Granger, Charles H. "The Hierarchy of Objectives." *Harvard Business Review*, 42, no. 3, (May–June 1964), 63–74.

Greiner, Larry E. "Evolution and Revolution as Organizations Grow." *Harvard Business Review*, 50, no. 4 (July–August 1972), 37–46.

Gulick, L. H., and L. F. Urwick, eds. *Papers on the Science of Administration*. New York, 1937.

Hambrick, Donald C. "Specialization of Environmental Scanning Activities Among Upper Level Executives." *Journal of Management Studies*, 28, no. 3 (1981), 299–320.

———. "The Top Management Team: Key to Strategic Success." *California Management Review*, 30, no. 1 (Fall 1987), 88–108.

Hamel, Gary, and C. K. Prahalad. "Strategic Intent." *Harvard Business Review*, 67, no. 3 (May–June 1989), 63–76.

Hamel, Gary, Yves L. Doz, and C. K. Prahalad. "Collaborate with Your Competitors—and Win." *Harvard Business Review*, 67, no. 1 (Jan.–Feb. 1989), 133–39.

Haugen, Robert A., *Modern Investment Theory*. Englewood Cliffs, N.J., 1988.

Hayes, Robert H., and William J. Abernathy. "Managing Our Way to Economic Decline." *Harvard Business Review*, 58, no. 3 (July–August 1980), 67–77.

Hedlund, G. "Autonomy of Subsidiaries and Formalization of Headquarters—Subsidiary Relations in Swedish MNCs." *The Management of Headquarters—Subsidiary Relationships in Multinational Corporations*. Ed. Lars Otterbeck. Aldershot, UK, 1981, pp. 25–78.

Henderson, Bruce D. "The Experience Curve—Reviewed; I. The Concept." Boston: The Boston Consulting Group, 1974.

———, "The Experience Curve—Reviewed; IV. The Growth Share Matrix or The Product Portfolio." Boston: The Boston Consulting Group, 1973.

Hergert, Michael, and Deigan Morris. "Trends in International Collaborative Agreements." In Farok J. Contractor and Peter Lorange, eds., *Cooperative Strategies in International Business*. Lexington, MA, 1988, pp. 99–109.

Higgins, Robert C. *Analysis for Financial Management*, 2nd ed. Homewood, IL, 1989.

Hull, John. *Options, Futures, and Other Derivative Securities*. Englewood Cliffs, NJ, 1989.

Jensen, Michael C. "Eclipse of the Public Corporation," *Harvard Business Review*, 67, no. 5, (Sept.–Oct. 1989), 61–74.

Jensen, Michael C., and William H. Meckling. "Theory of the Firm: Managerial Behavior, Agency Costs and Ownership Structure." *Journal of Financial Economics*, 3, no. 4 (Oct. 1976), 305–60.

Karpoff, Jonathan. "The Relation Between Price Changes and Trading Volume: A Survey." *Journal of Financial and Quantitative Analysis*, 22 (1987), 109–26.

Kogut, Bruce. "Designing Global Strategies: Comparative and Competitive Value-Added Chains." *Sloan Management Review*, 26, no. 4 (Summer 1985), 15–28.

———. "Designing Global Strategies: Profiting From Operational Flexibility." *Sloan Management Review*, 27, no. 1 (Fall 1985), 27–38.

Kotter, John P. *A Force for Change: How Leadership Differs From Management*. New York, 1990.

———. *The General Managers*. New York: 1982.

Lawrence, Paul R. "The History of Human Resource Management in American Industry." In Richard E. Walton and Paul R. Lawrence, eds. *HRM Trends & Challenges*. Boston, 1985, pp. 15–34.

Lazonick, William. "Controlling the Market for Corporate Control." Paper presented at the Third International Joseph A. Schumpeter Society Conference, Airlie, VA, June 3–5, 1990.

Lessard, Donald R., and Nitin Nohria. "Rediscovering Functions in the MNC: The Role of Expertise in Firms' Responses to Shifting Exchange Rates." In Christopher A. Bartlett, Yves Doz, and Gunnar Hedlund, eds., *Managing the Global Firm*. London, 1990, pp. 186–212.

Lewin, Kurt. *Field Theory in Social Sciences*. New York, 1951.

Lewis, Jordan D. *Partnership for Profit*. New York, 1990.

Lorsch, Jay W. *Pawns or Potentates*. Boston, 1989.

March, James, and Herbert Simon. *Organizations*. New York, 1958.

Marr, Wayne, and John Trimble. "The Persistent Borrowing Advantage in Eurodollar Bonds: A Plausible Explanation." *Journal of Applied Corporate Finance*, 1, no. 2 (Summer 1988), 65–70.

Merchant, Kenneth A. *Rewarding Results*. Boston, 1989.

Miles, Raymond E., and Charles C. Snow. "Fit, Failure and the Hall of Fame." *California Management Review*, 26, no. 3 (Spring 1984), 10–28.

———. *Organizational Strategy, Structure, and Process*. New York, 1978.

Mintzberg, Henry. "The Design School: Reconsidering the Basic Premises of Strategic Management." *Strategic Management Journal*, 11, no. 3 (March–April 1990), 171–95.

———. *The Nature of Managerial Work*. New York, 1973.

Mishkin, Frederic S. "Financial Innovations and Current Trends in U.S. Financial Markets." *National Bureau of Economic Research, Inc. Working Paper No. 3323*, April 1990.

Mullins, David W., Jr., "Does the Capital Asset Pricing Model Work," *Harvard Business Review*, 60, no. 1, (Jan.-Feb. 1982), 105–13.

Murray, Michael J., and Frank C. Reid. "Financial Style and Corporate Control." *Journal of Applied Corporate Finance*, 1, no. 1 (Spring 1988), 77–84.

Nader, Ralph. *Unsafe at Any Speed: Design and Dangers of the American Automobile*. New York: 1965.

Nadler, David A. "Managing Organizational Change: An Integrative Perspective." *The Journal of Applied Behavioral Science*, 17, no. 2 (1981), 191–211.

Nadler, David A., and Michael Tushman. "Beyond the Charismatic Leader: Leadership and Organizational Change." *California Management Review*, 32, no. 2 (Winter 1990), 82–85.

Nash, Ogden. *The Private Dining Room and Other Verses*. Boston, 1953.

Ohmae, Kenichi. *Triad Power*. New York, 1985.

O'Reilly, Charles. "Corporations, Culture, and Commitment: Motivation and Social Control in Organization." *California Management Review*, 31, no. 4 (Summer 1989), 9–25.

O'Reilly, Charles, and Jennifer Chatman. "Organizational Commitment and Psychological Attachment: The Effects of Compliance, Identification and Internalization on Prosocial Behavior." *Journal of Applied Psychology*, 71 (1986), 492–99.

Pascale, Richard T. "Perspectives on Strategy: The Real Story Behind Honda's Success." *California Management Review*. 26, no. 3 (Spring 1984).

Pascale, Richard T., and Anthony G. Athos. *The Art of Japanese Management*. New York, 1981.

Perlmutter, H. V. "The Tortuous Evolution of the Multinational Corporation." *Columbia Journal of World Business*, 4, no. 1 (Jan.–Feb. 1969), 9–19.

Peters, Tom. "Get Innovative or Get Dead." *California Management Review*, 33, no. 1 (Fall 1990), 9–26.

Pierce, John A., II, and Shaker A. Zahra. "The Relative Power of CEOs and Boards of Directors: Associations with Corporate Performance." *Strategic Management Journal*, 12, no. 2 (Feb. 1991), 135–54.

Porter, Michael E. *Competitive Advantage of Nations*. New York, 1990.

———. *Competition in Global Industries*. Boston, 1986.

———. *Competitive Advantage*. New York, 1985.

———. *Competitive Strategy*. New York, 1980.

Prahalad, C. K., and Gary Hamel. "The Core Competence of the Corporation." *Harvard Business Review*, 68, no. 3 (May–June 1990), 79–91.

Prahalad, C. K., and Yves L. Doz, *The Multinational Mission: Balancing Local Demands and Global Vision*. New York, 1987.

Quinn, James Brian. *Strategies for Change: Logical Incrementalism*. Homewood, IL, 1980.

Reinhardt, A. W. "An Early Warning System of Strategic Planning." *Long Range Planning*, 17, no. 5 (1984), 25–34.

Ring, Peter Smith, Stefanie Ann Lenway, and Michele Govekar. "Management of the Political Imperative in International Business." *Strategic Management Journal*, 11, no. 2 (Feb. 1990), 141–51.

Ross, Stephen A., "The Arbitrage Theory of Capital Asset Pricing," *Journal of Economic Theory*, 13 (Dec. 1976), 341–60.

Rumelt, Richard P. *Strategy, Structure and Economic Performance*. Boston, 1974.

Salter, M. S., and W. S. Weinhold. *Diversification Through Acquisition*. New York, 1979.

Sayles, Leonard R. *Leadership*. 2nd ed. New York, 1989.

Schaller, L. E. *The Change Agent*. Nashville, TN, 1978.

Schein, Edgar H. *Organizational Culture and Leadership*. San Francisco, 1985.

Schwartz, Howard, and Stanley M. Davis. "Matching Corporate Culture and Business Strategy." *Organization Dynamics*, 1 (Summer 1981), 30–48.

Simons, Robert. "Strategic Orientation and Top Management Attention to Control Systems." *Strategic Management Journal*, 12, no. 1 (Jan. 1991), 49–62.

Smith, Clifford W., Jr., Charles W. Smithson, and D. Sykes Wilford. *Managing Financial Risk*. New York, 1990.

Sousa de Vasconcellos e Sá, Jorge Alberto, and Donald C. Hambrick. "Key Success Factors: Test of a General Theory in the Mature Industrial-Product Sector." *Strategic Management Journal*, 10, no. 4 (July–August 1989), 367–82.

Stein, Jeremy C. "Efficient Capital Markets, Inefficient Firms: A Model of Myopic Corporate Behavior." *Quarterly Journal of Economics*, 104 (Nov. 1989), 655–69.

Taylor, William. "The Logic of Global Business." *Harvard Business Review*, 69, no. 2 (March–April 1991), 90–105.

Van Horne, James C. *Financial Management and Policy*. 8th ed. Englewood Cliffs, NJ, 1989.

Vatter, Paul A., et al. *Quantitative Methods in Management*, Homewood, IL, 1978.

Walmsley, Julian. *The New Financial Instruments*. New York, 1988.

Walton, Richard E. "Toward a Strategy of Eliciting Employee Commitment Based on Policies of Mutuality." In Richard E. Walton and Paul R. Lawrence, eds. *HRM Trends & Challenges*. Boston, 1985, pp. 35–65.

Watson, Maxwell, Donald Mathieson, Russell Kincaid, David Folkerts-Landau, Klaus Regling, and Caroline Atkinson. "Innovations and Institutional Changes in Major Financial Markets—A Ten-Year Perspective." *International Capital Markets—Developments and Prospects*. Washington, D.C., 1988.

Watson, Thomas J., Jr. *A Business and Its Beliefs*. New York, 1963.

Welch, John F., Jr. "Competitiveness from Within—Beyond Incrementalism." Hatfield Fellow Lecture, Cornell University, April 12, 1984.

White, Roderick F., and Thomas A. Paynter. "Organizing for Worldwide Advantage." In Christopher A. Bartlett, Yves Doz, and Gunnar Hedlund, eds. *Managing the Global Firm*. London: 1990, pp. 95–113.

Zaleznik, Abraham. *The Managerial Mystique*. New York: 1989.

———. "Managers and Leaders: Are They Different?" *Harvard Business Review*, 55, no. 3 (May–June 1977), 67–78.

INDEX

Since this comprehensive overview of general managment was published, the business world has witnessed major changes: an accelerated drive toward global business operations among leading North American, Western European, and Pacific Rim firms, a proliferation of new strategic alliances, the continuing revolution in information and communications technologies, the diminished role of junk bonds, and a newfound emphasis on business ethics and corporate governance have all meant dramatic readjustment in the corporate world. The second edition of *General Managers in Action* addresses these changes and offers a wealth of new materials and choice case studies developed at the Harvard Business School focusing on industry and competitive analysis and the job of the general manager. Three new chapters discuss the growing need for general managers to strive for world-class competitive advantage in global business activities, the major concerns general managers face in deciding how to ensure sound financial policies and structure in the context of the firm's overall corporate strategy, and the often conflicting interests and responsibilities of general managers and boards of directors for U.S. publicly-owned corporations as they face large and sometimes unexpected changes in public expectations. Other chapters have been expanded to provide more extensive coverage of ethics, strategic alliances, Europe 1992, company capabilities and value chain analysis, and the management of change. An ideal text for management seminars and MBA courses, the second edition of *General Managers in Action* is also an invaluable reference for executives and for anyone who needs to understand general management and the challenges that top executives face.